ASTRA
LOST IN SPACE

5

[FRIEND-SHIP]

KENTA SHINOHARA

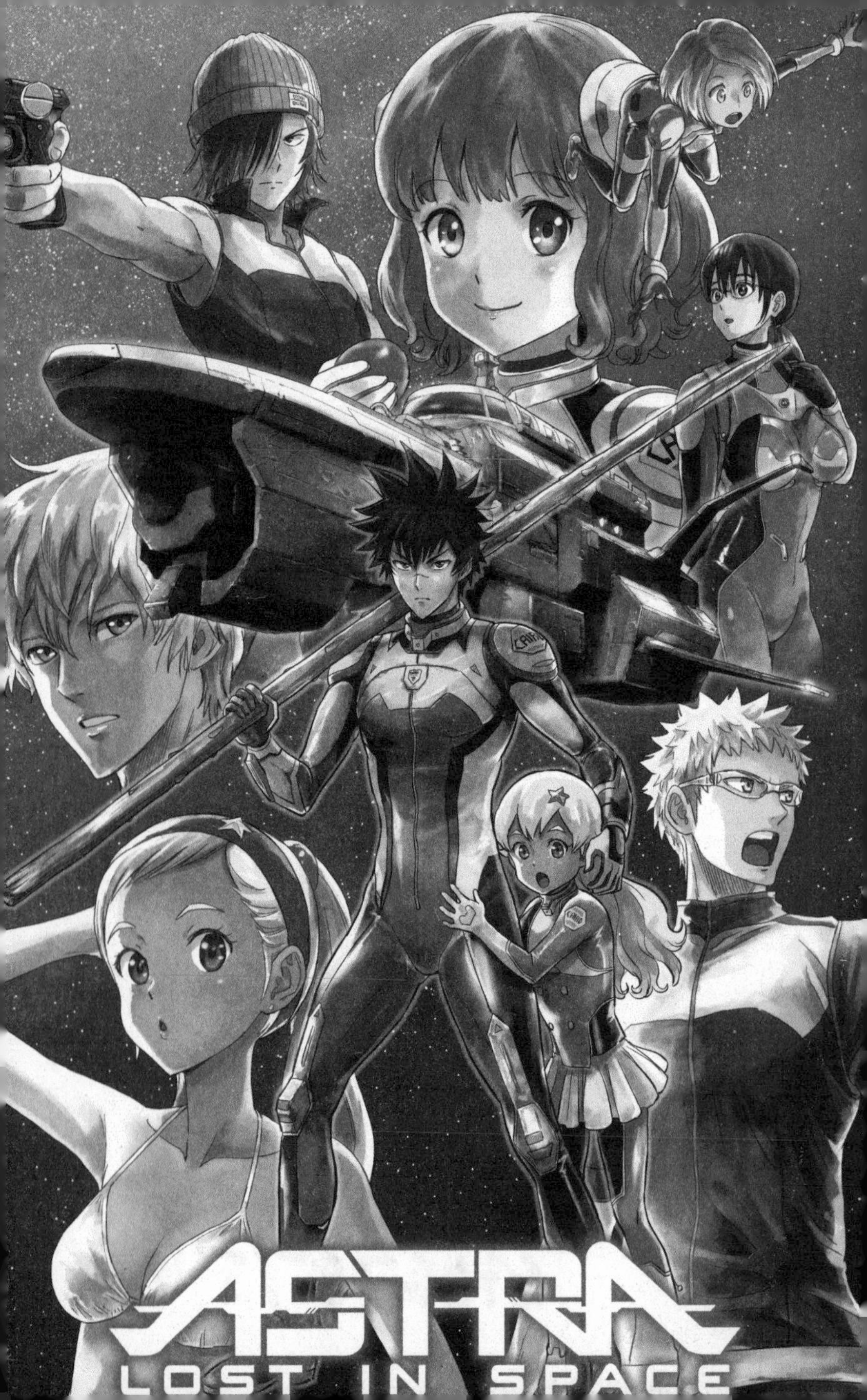
ASTRA
LOST IN SPACE

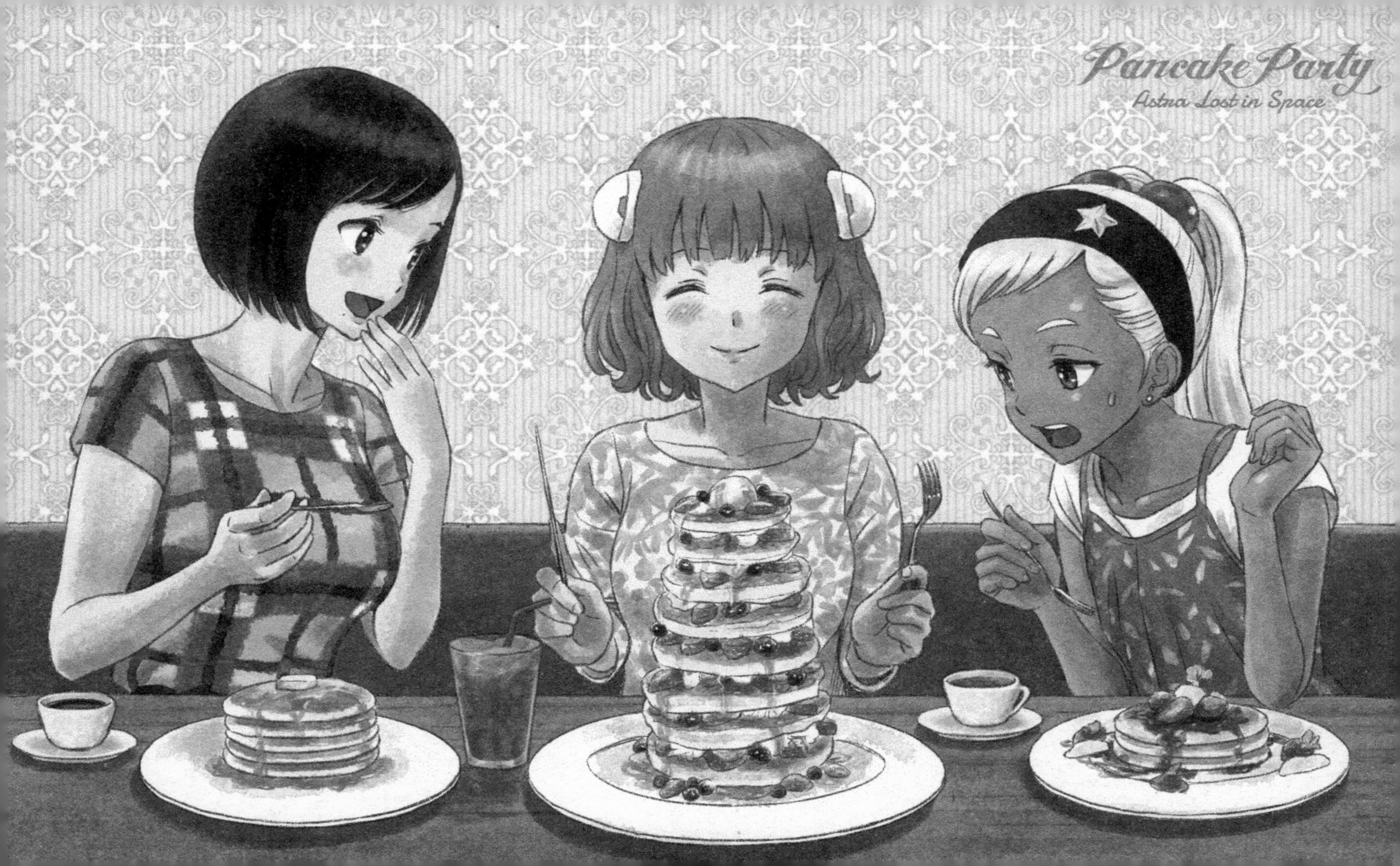
Pancake Party
Astra Lost in Space

CHARACTERS&STORY

Polina
Livinskaya

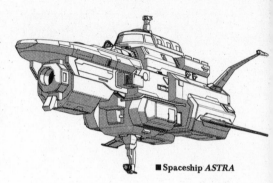

■ Spaceship *ASTRA*

STORY

It's the year 2063, and interstellar space travel has become the norm. A group of students from Caird High School are set to take off for a five-day camp on Planet McPa at the Mousanish Spaceport. However, shortly after arriving, the group encounters a mysterious glowing orb that swallows them up and spits them out into the depths of space. By a stroke of good luck, they find an abandoned spaceship where they can take shelter, but its long-range communications system is offline. Not only that, they quickly discover they weren't spat out above McPa as they initially thought, but were instead transported 5,000 light-years away! Critically short on both food and water, the group manages to piece together a string of five planets where they can forage for supplies while making their way home one planet at a time. But just as things barely get under way, they find out one of the crew may be a killer sent on a suicide mission to murder all of them!

On Planet Icriss, the fourth stop on the crew's journey home, they discover the *Ark VI*, a spaceship identical to the *Astra*. Aboard it is a lone survivor–Polina. The crew warmly welcomes her aboard and begins preparations for the next leg of their trip. Along the way they make a shocking discovery of something they all have in common–they are all clones. Their stranding was part of a plot by their originals to cover up a secret illegal rejuvenation project. Determined to forge their own futures, the crew sets out on the next leg of their journey home. On the way, they finally catch a glimpse of their home planet in the ship's long-range telescope. The crew rejoices, but Polina is in shock! The planet displayed on the bridge monitor isn't her beloved Earth!

ASTRA
LOST IN SPACE

CHARACTERS

Zack Walker

Aries Spring

Kanata Hoshijima

Luca Esposito

Funicia Raffaeli

Quitterie Raffaeli

Charce Lacroix

Yun-hua Lu

Ulgar Zweig

ASTRA
LOST IN SPACE
CONTENTS

5

[FRIEND-SHIP]

ASTRA
LOST IN
SPACE

#38

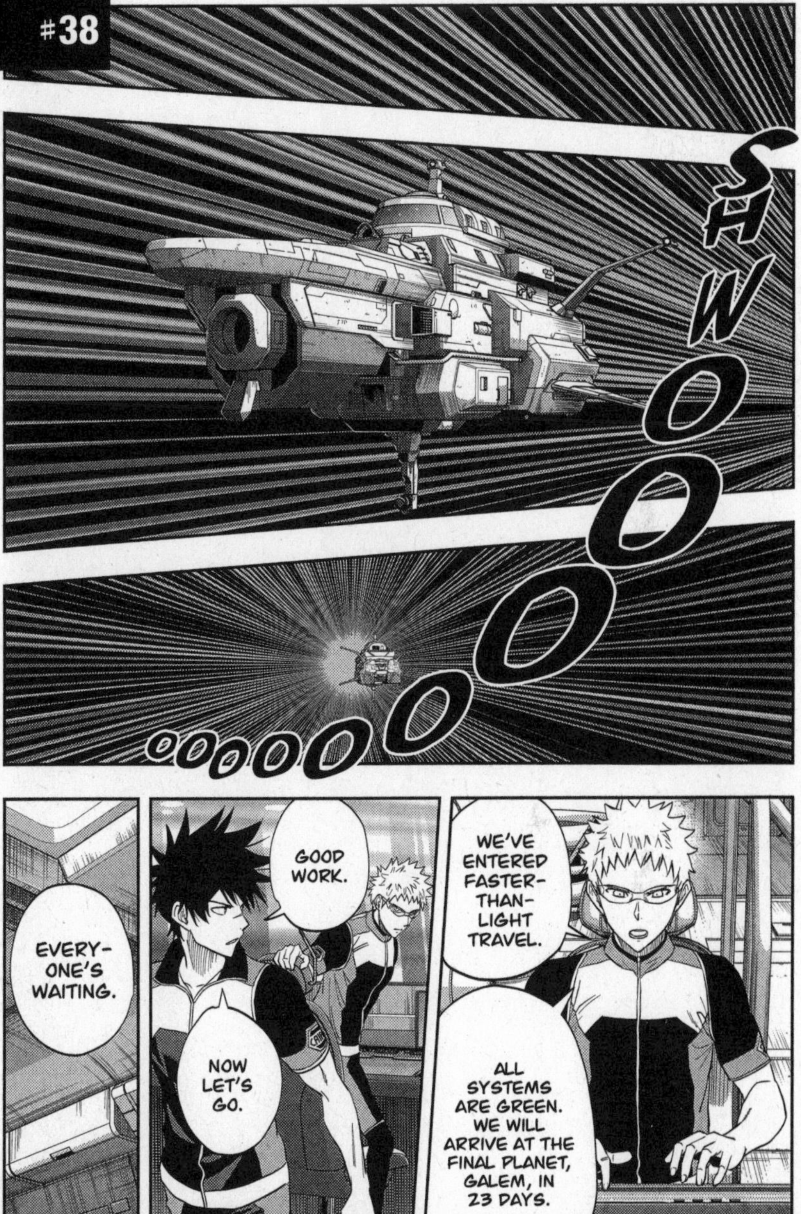
SHWOOOOOOOOOOOO
WE'VE ENTERED FASTER-THAN-LIGHT TRAVEL.
ALL SYSTEMS ARE GREEN. WE WILL ARRIVE AT THE FINAL PLANET, GALEM, IN 23 DAYS.
GOOD WORK.
NOW LET'S GO.
EVERY-ONE'S WAITING.

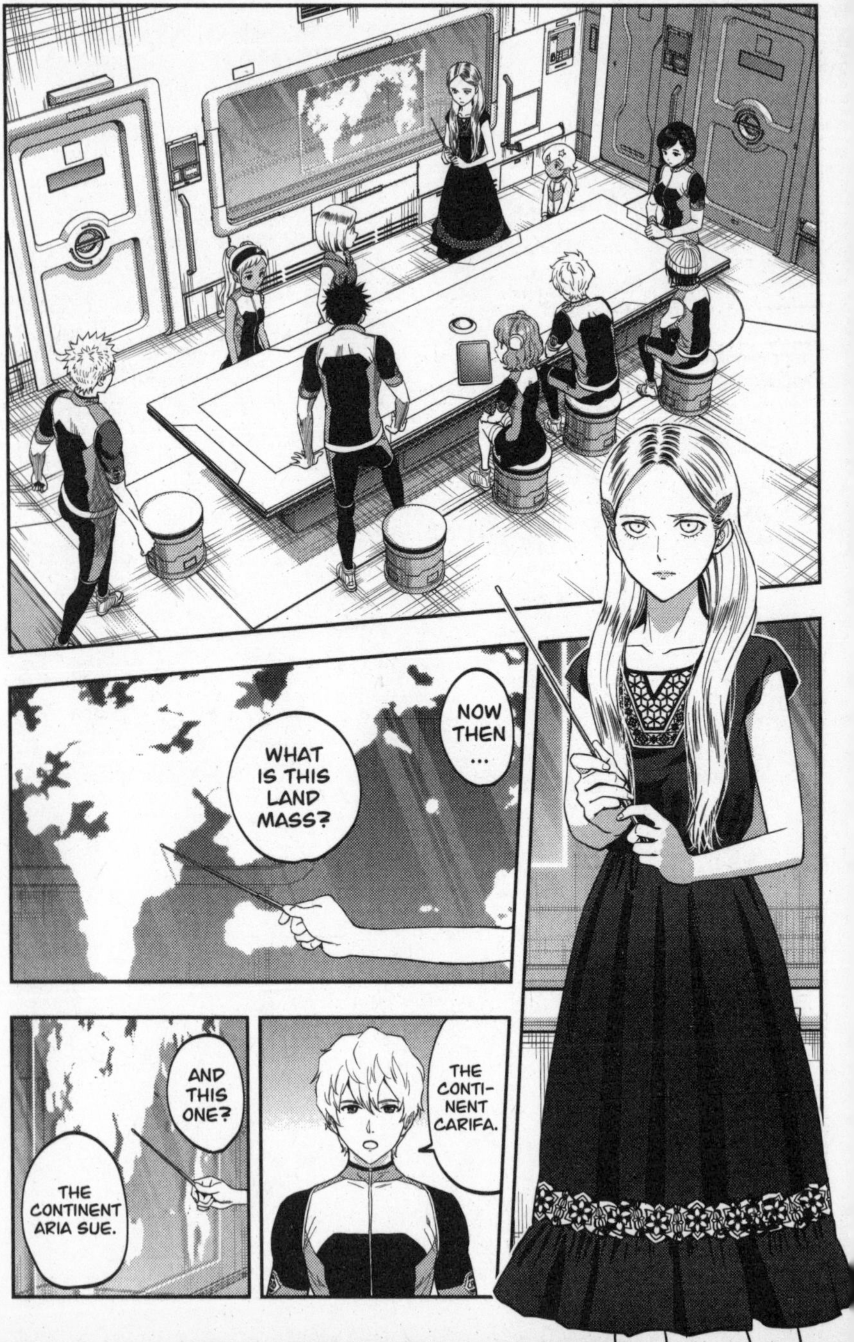
NOW THEN ...
WHAT IS THIS LAND MASS?
THE CONTINENT CARIFA.
AND THIS ONE?
THE CONTINENT ARIA SUE.

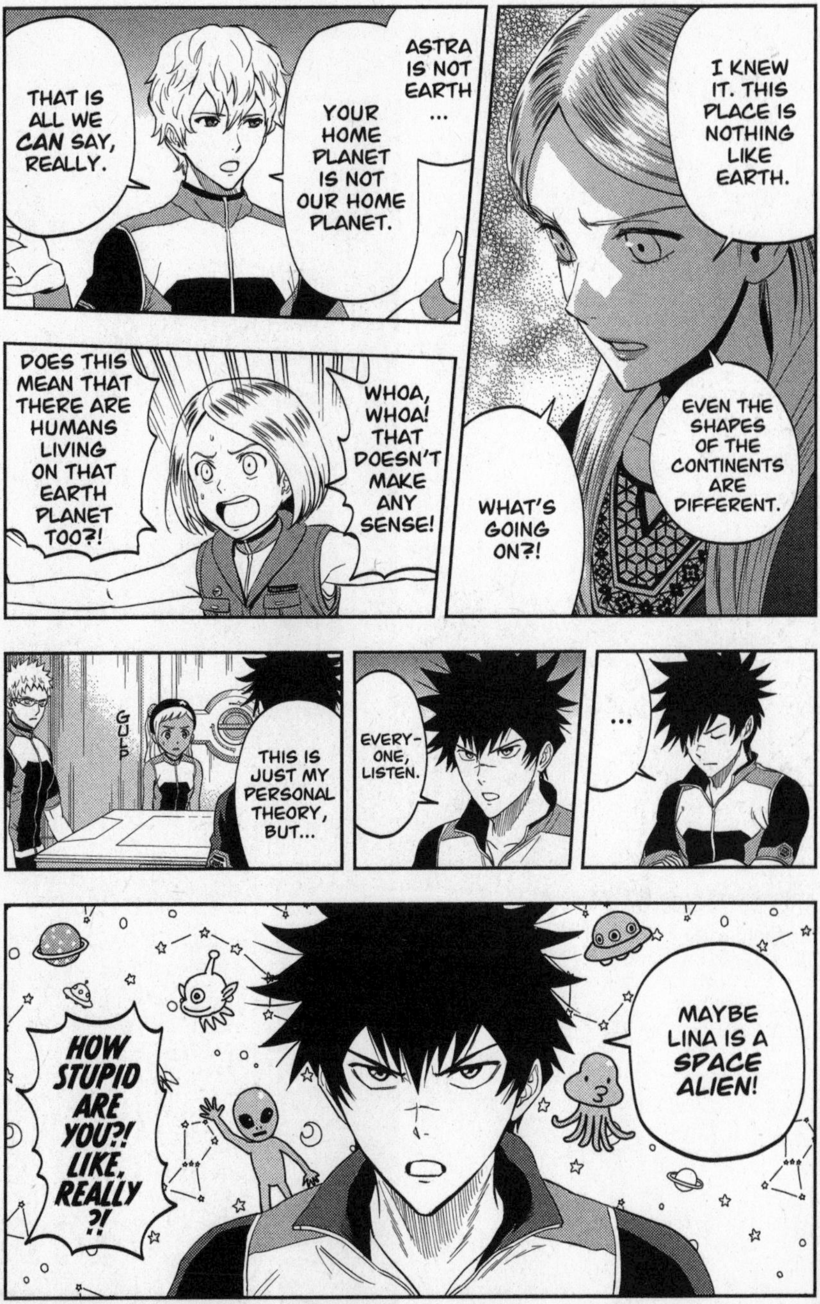
I KNEW IT. THIS PLACE IS NOTHING LIKE EARTH.
EVEN THE SHAPES OF THE CONTINENTS ARE DIFFERENT.
WHAT'S GOING ON?!
ASTRA IS NOT EARTH ...
YOUR HOME PLANET IS NOT OUR HOME PLANET.
THAT IS ALL WE CAN SAY, REALLY.
WHOA, WHOA! THAT DOESN'T MAKE ANY SENSE!
DOES THIS MEAN THAT THERE ARE HUMANS LIVING ON THAT EARTH PLANET TOO?!
...
EVERY-ONE, LISTEN.
THIS IS JUST MY PERSONAL THEORY, BUT...
GULP
MAYBE LINA IS A SPACE ALIEN!
HOW STUPID ARE YOU?! LIKE, REALLY?!

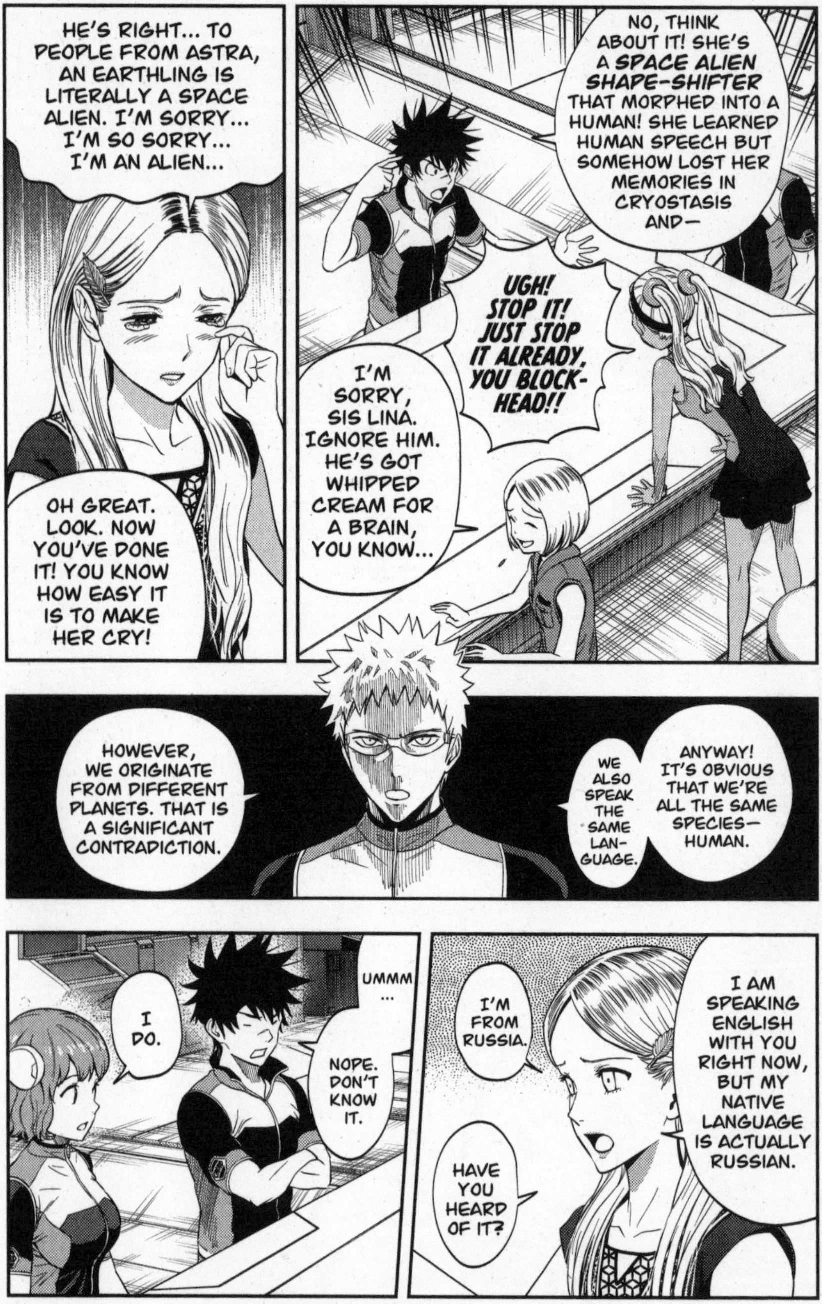
NO, THINK ABOUT IT! SHE'S A **SPACE ALIEN SHAPE-SHIFTER** THAT MORPHED INTO A HUMAN! SHE LEARNED HUMAN SPEECH BUT SOMEHOW LOST HER MEMORIES IN CRYOSTASIS AND—
UGH! STOP IT! JUST STOP IT ALREADY, YOU BLOCKHEAD!!
I'M SORRY, SIS LINA. IGNORE HIM. HE'S GOT WHIPPED CREAM FOR A BRAIN, YOU KNOW...
HE'S RIGHT... TO PEOPLE FROM ASTRA, AN EARTHLING IS LITERALLY A SPACE ALIEN. I'M SORRY... I'M SO SORRY... I'M AN ALIEN...
OH GREAT. LOOK. NOW YOU'VE DONE IT! YOU KNOW HOW EASY IT IS TO MAKE HER CRY!
ANYWAY! IT'S OBVIOUS THAT WE'RE ALL THE SAME SPECIES—HUMAN.
WE ALSO SPEAK THE SAME LANGUAGE.
HOWEVER, WE ORIGINATE FROM DIFFERENT PLANETS. THAT IS A SIGNIFICANT CONTRADICTION.
I AM SPEAKING ENGLISH WITH YOU RIGHT NOW, BUT MY NATIVE LANGUAGE IS ACTUALLY RUSSIAN.
I'M FROM RUSSIA.
HAVE YOU HEARD OF IT?
UMMM...
NOPE. DON'T KNOW IT.
I DO.

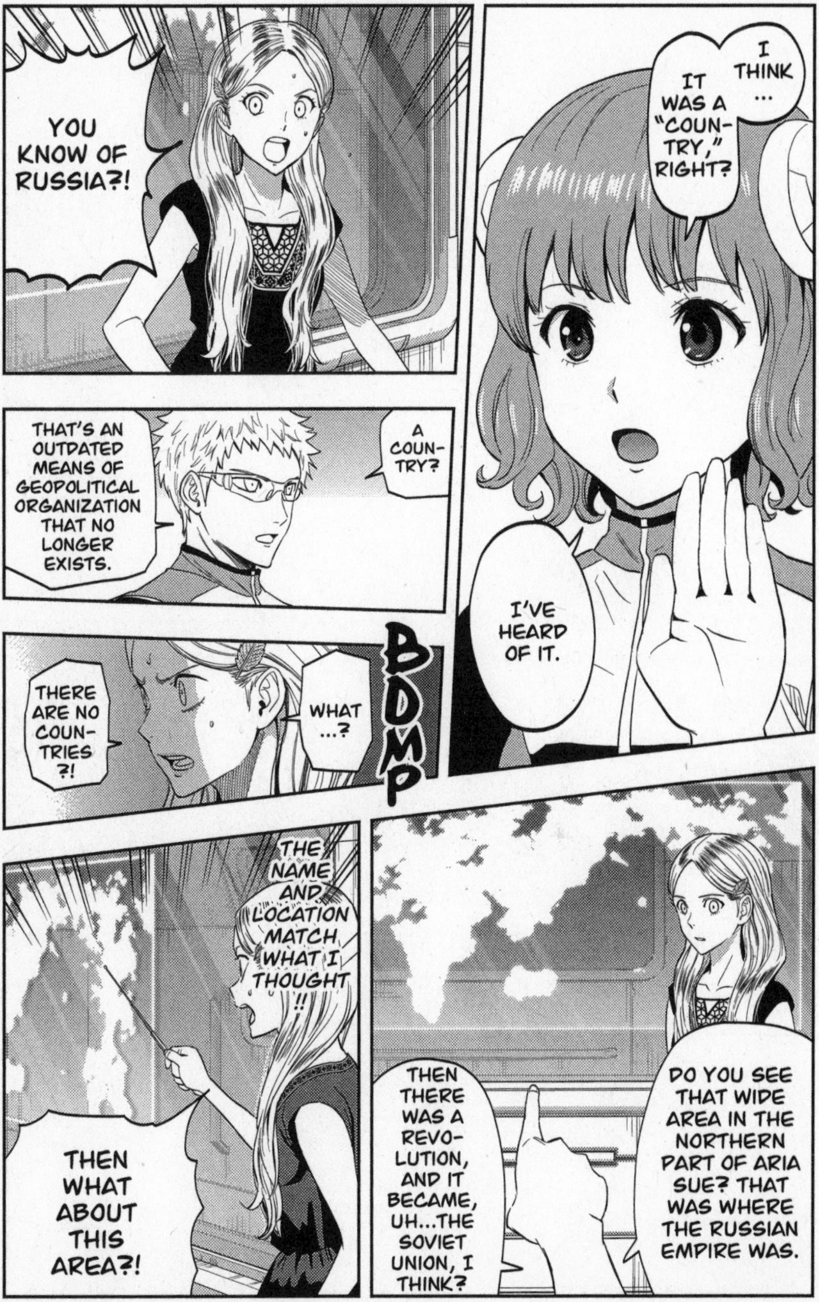
I THINK ... IT WAS A "COUNTRY," RIGHT?
I'VE HEARD OF IT.
YOU KNOW OF RUSSIA?!
A COUNTRY?
THAT'S AN OUTDATED MEANS OF GEOPOLITICAL ORGANIZATION THAT NO LONGER EXISTS.
WHAT ...?
BDMP
THERE ARE NO COUNTRIES ?!
DO YOU SEE THAT WIDE AREA IN THE NORTHERN PART OF ARIA SUE? THAT WAS WHERE THE RUSSIAN EMPIRE WAS.
THEN THERE WAS A REVOLUTION, AND IT BECAME, UH...THE SOVIET UNION, I THINK?
THE NAME AND LOCATION MATCH WHAT I THOUGHT !!
THEN WHAT ABOUT THIS AREA?!

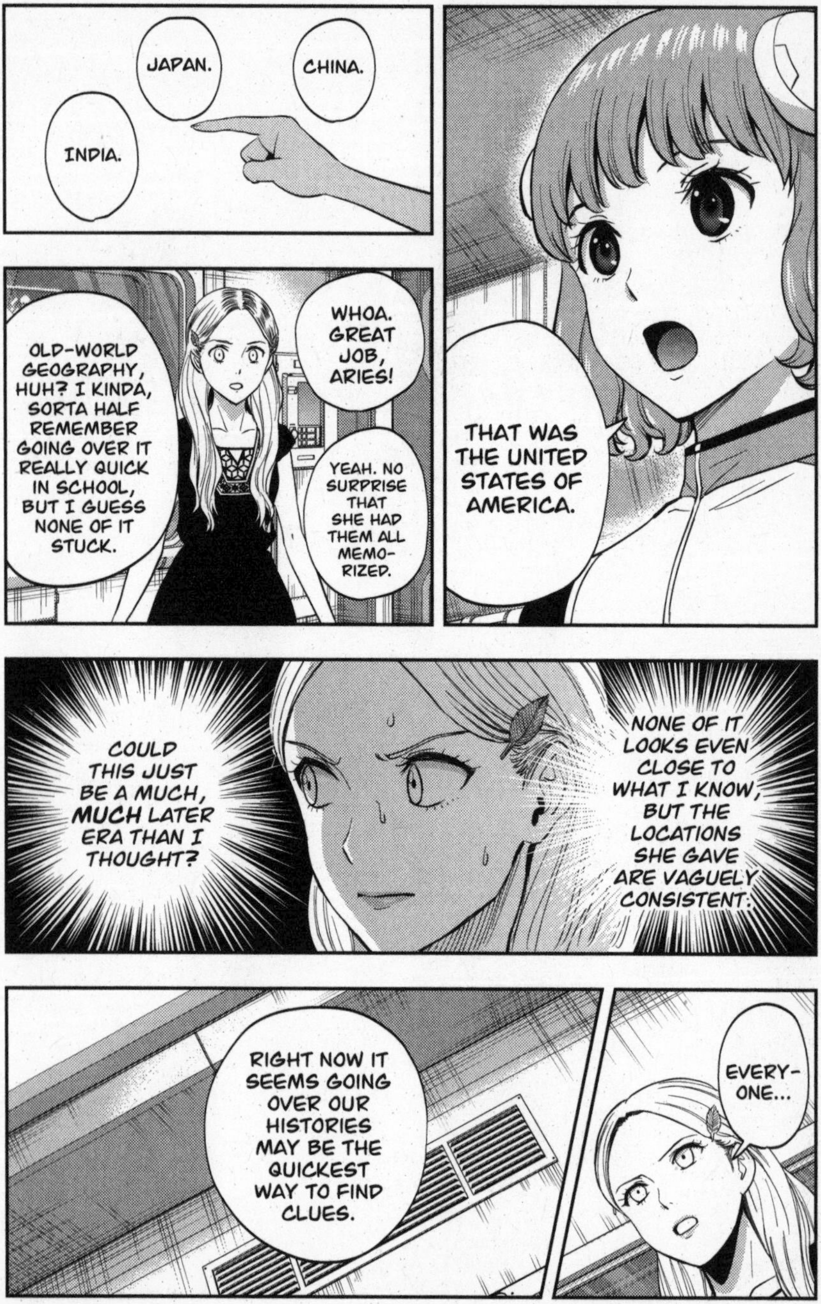
THAT WAS THE UNITED STATES OF AMERICA.
CHINA.
JAPAN.
INDIA.
WHOA. GREAT JOB, ARIES!
YEAH. NO SURPRISE THAT SHE HAD THEM ALL MEMO-RIZED.
OLD-WORLD GEOGRAPHY, HUH? I KINDA, SORTA HALF REMEMBER GOING OVER IT REALLY QUICK IN SCHOOL, BUT I GUESS NONE OF IT STUCK.
NONE OF IT LOOKS EVEN CLOSE TO WHAT I KNOW, BUT THE LOCATIONS SHE GAVE ARE VAGUELY CONSISTENT.
COULD THIS JUST BE A MUCH, MUCH LATER ERA THAN I THOUGHT?
EVERY-ONE...
RIGHT NOW IT SEEMS GOING OVER OUR HISTORIES MAY BE THE QUICKEST WAY TO FIND CLUES.

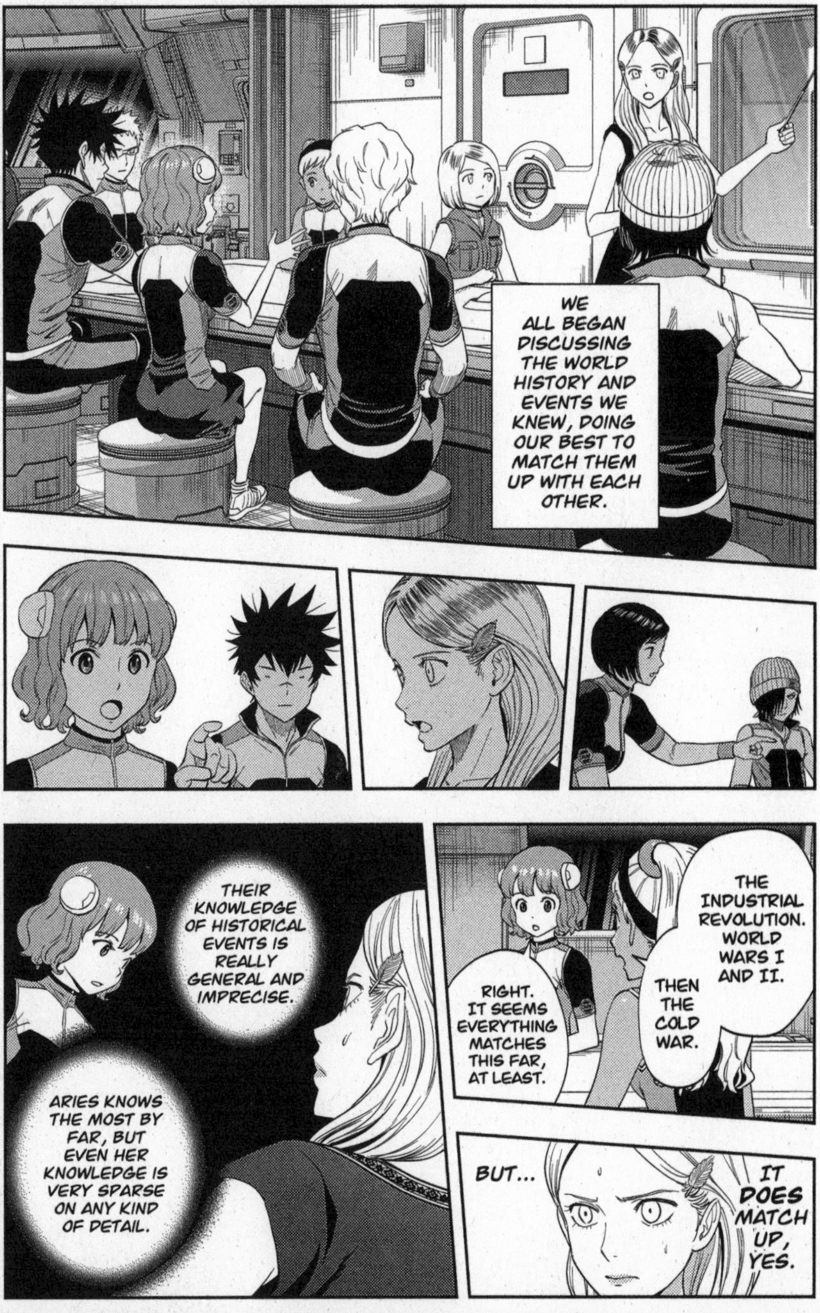
WE ALL BEGAN DISCUSSING THE WORLD HISTORY AND EVENTS WE KNEW, DOING OUR BEST TO MATCH THEM UP WITH EACH OTHER.
THE INDUSTRIAL REVOLUTION. WORLD WARS I AND II.
THEN THE COLD WAR.
RIGHT. IT SEEMS EVERYTHING MATCHES THIS FAR, AT LEAST.
IT DOES MATCH UP, YES.
BUT...
THEIR KNOWLEDGE OF HISTORICAL EVENTS IS REALLY GENERAL AND IMPRECISE.
ARIES KNOWS THE MOST BY FAR, BUT EVEN HER KNOWLEDGE IS VERY SPARSE ON ANY KIND OF DETAIL.

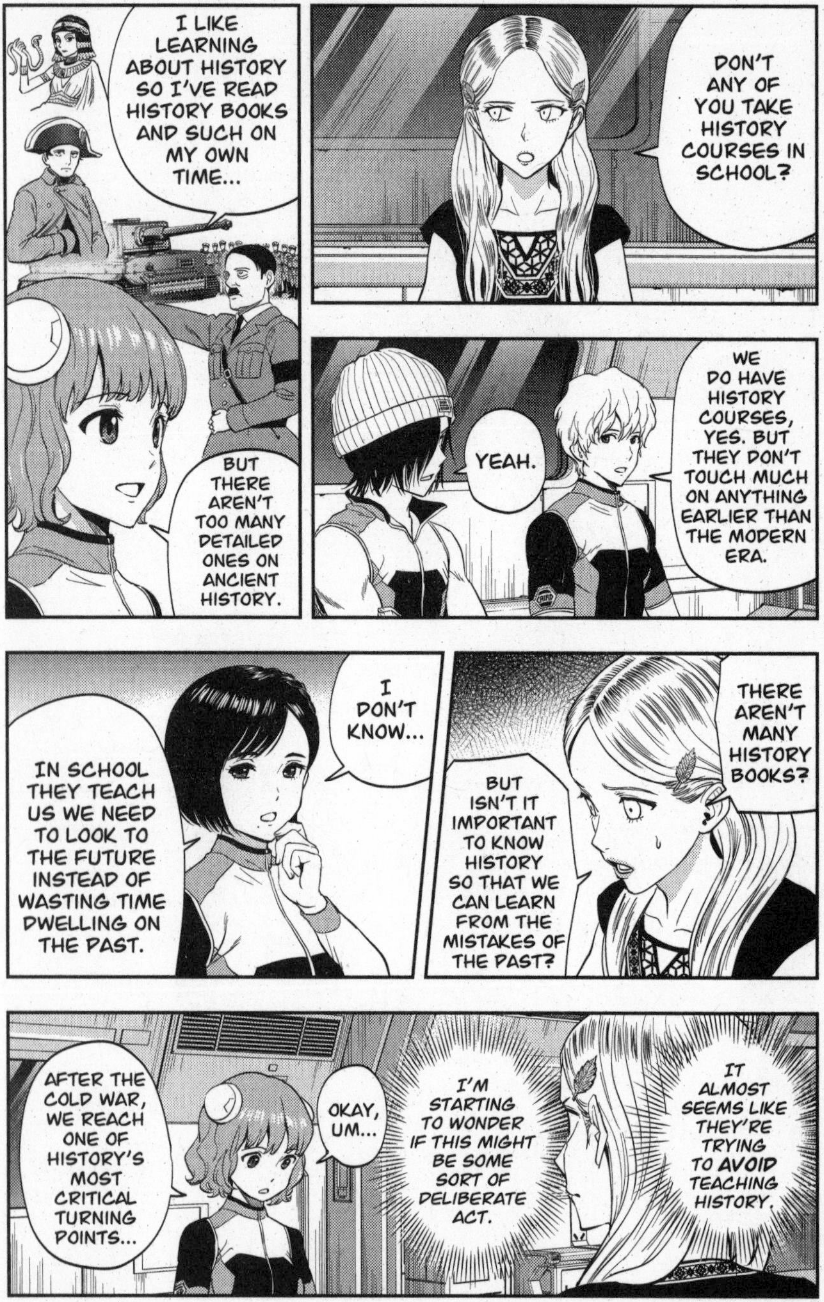

DON'T ANY OF YOU TAKE HISTORY COURSES IN SCHOOL?
WE DO HAVE HISTORY COURSES, YES. BUT THEY DON'T TOUCH MUCH ON ANYTHING EARLIER THAN THE MODERN ERA.
YEAH.
I LIKE LEARNING ABOUT HISTORY SO I'VE READ HISTORY BOOKS AND SUCH ON MY OWN TIME...
BUT THERE AREN'T TOO MANY DETAILED ONES ON ANCIENT HISTORY.
THERE AREN'T MANY HISTORY BOOKS?
BUT ISN'T IT IMPORTANT TO KNOW HISTORY SO THAT WE CAN LEARN FROM THE MISTAKES OF THE PAST?
I DON'T KNOW...
IN SCHOOL THEY TEACH US WE NEED TO LOOK TO THE FUTURE INSTEAD OF WASTING TIME DWELLING ON THE PAST.
IT ALMOST SEEMS LIKE THEY'RE TRYING TO AVOID TEACHING HISTORY.
I'M STARTING TO WONDER IF THIS MIGHT BE SOME SORT OF DELIBERATE ACT.
OKAY, UM...
AFTER THE COLD WAR, WE REACH ONE OF HISTORY'S MOST CRITICAL TURNING POINTS...

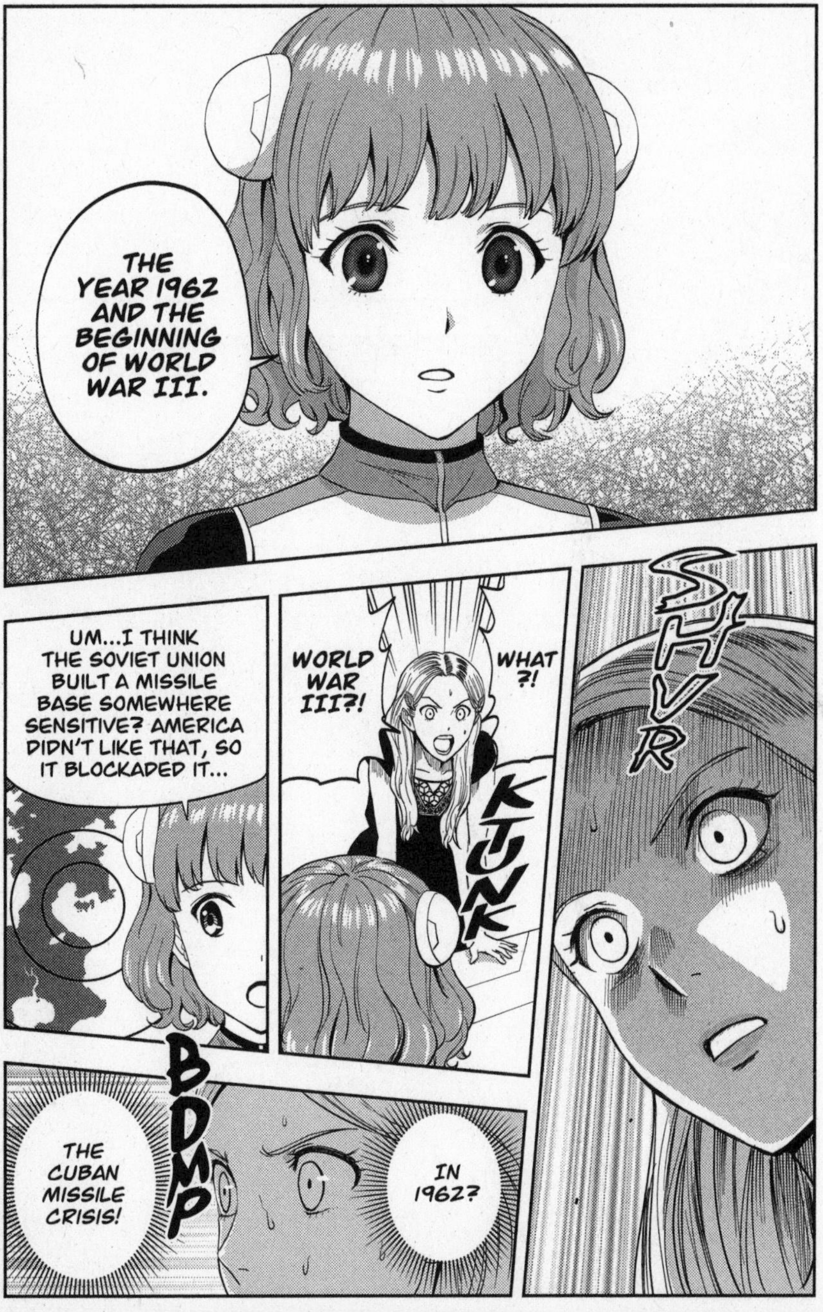
THE YEAR 1962 AND THE BEGINNING OF WORLD WAR III.
SHVR
WHAT?!
WORLD WAR III?!
KTUNK
UM...I THINK THE SOVIET UNION BUILT A MISSILE BASE SOMEWHERE SENSITIVE? AMERICA DIDN'T LIKE THAT, SO IT BLOCKADED IT...
IN 1962?
BDMP
THE CUBAN MISSILE CRISIS!

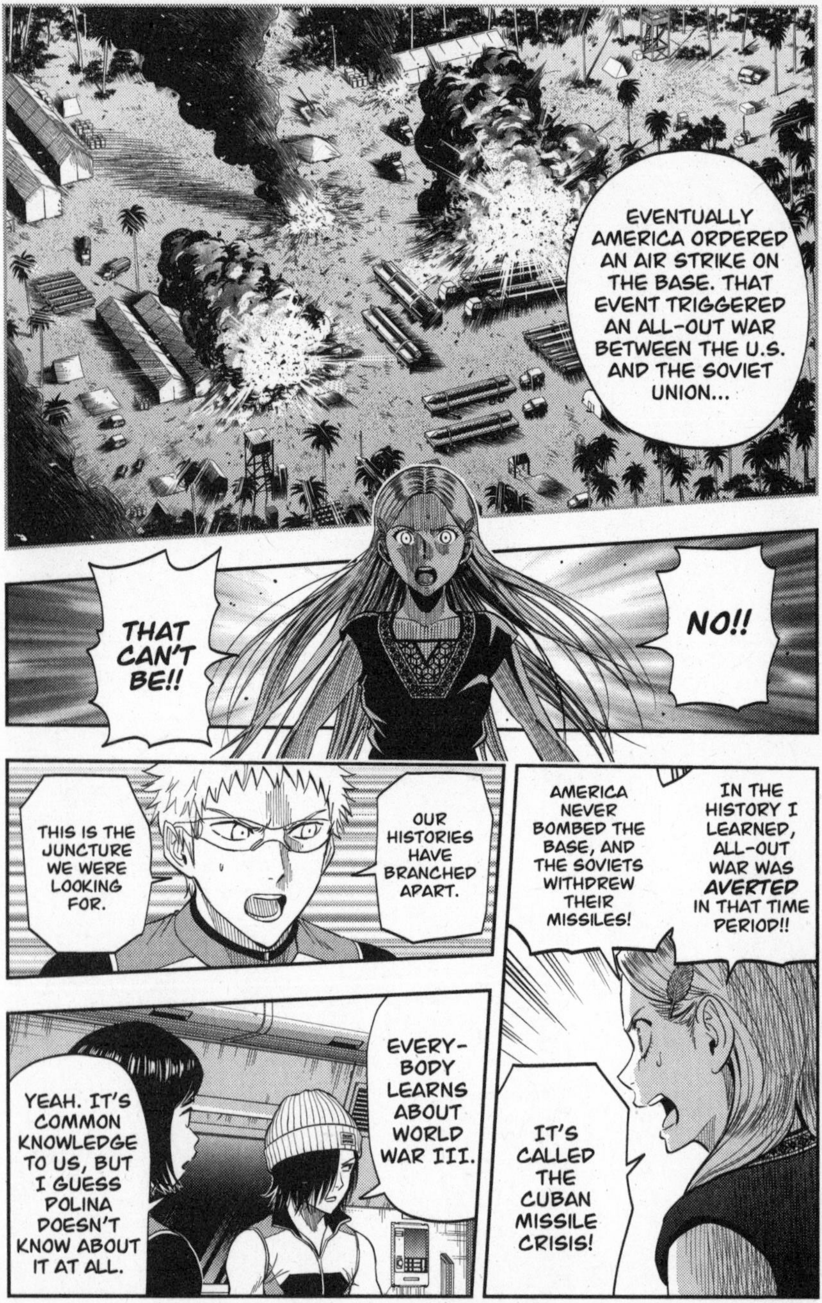
EVENTUALLY AMERICA ORDERED AN AIR STRIKE ON THE BASE. THAT EVENT TRIGGERED AN ALL-OUT WAR BETWEEN THE U.S. AND THE SOVIET UNION...
NO!!
THAT CAN'T BE!!
IN THE HISTORY I LEARNED, ALL-OUT WAR WAS AVERTED IN THAT TIME PERIOD!!
AMERICA NEVER BOMBED THE BASE, AND THE SOVIETS WITHDREW THEIR MISSILES!
IT'S CALLED THE CUBAN MISSILE CRISIS!
OUR HISTORIES HAVE BRANCHED APART.
THIS IS THE JUNCTURE WE WERE LOOKING FOR.
EVERY-BODY LEARNS ABOUT WORLD WAR III.
YEAH. IT'S COMMON KNOWLEDGE TO US, BUT I GUESS POLINA DOESN'T KNOW ABOUT IT AT ALL.

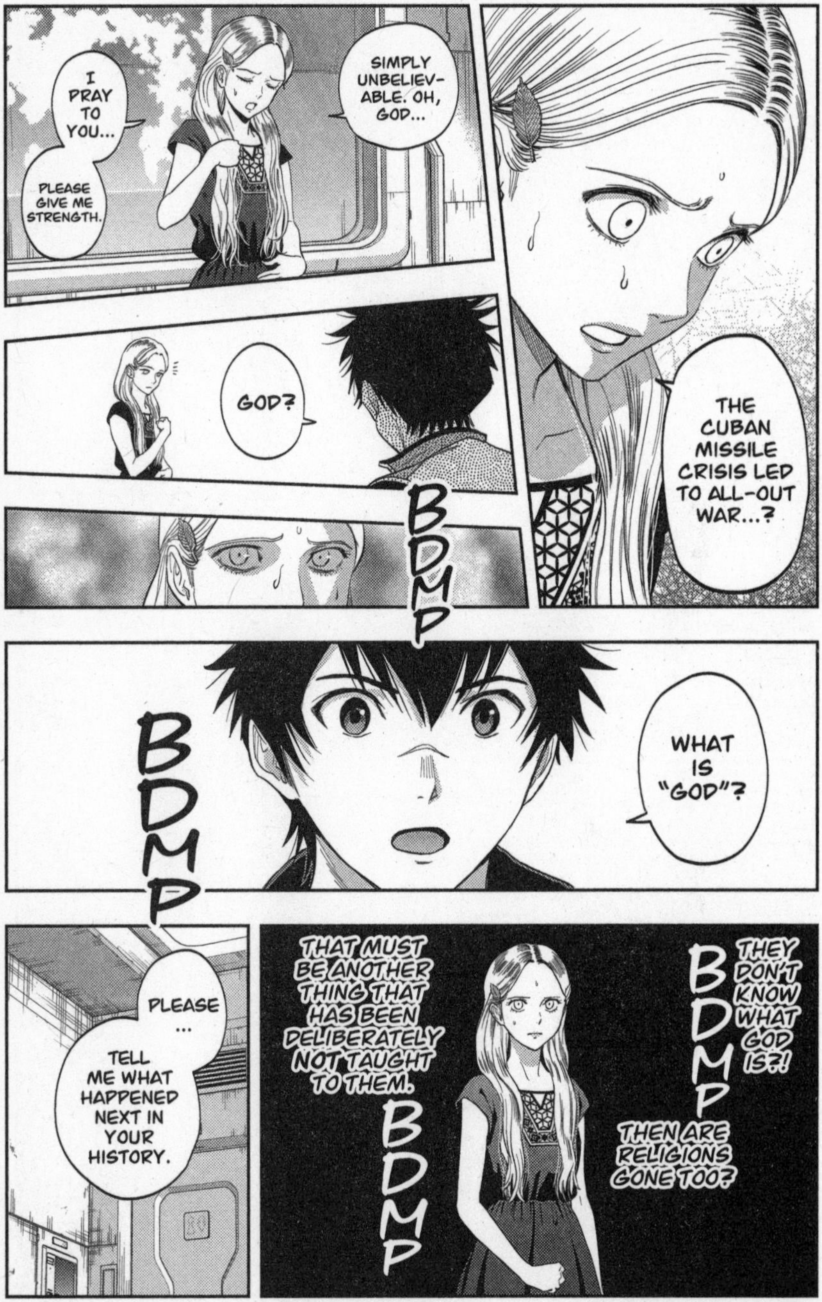
THE CUBAN MISSILE CRISIS LED TO ALL-OUT WAR...?
SIMPLY UNBELIEVABLE. OH, GOD...
I PRAY TO YOU...
PLEASE GIVE ME STRENGTH.
GOD?
BDMP
WHAT IS "GOD"?
BDMP
THEY DON'T KNOW WHAT GOD IS?!
BDMP
THEN ARE RELIGIONS GONE TOO?
THAT MUST BE ANOTHER THING THAT HAS BEEN DELIBERATELY NOT TAUGHT TO THEM.
BDMP
PLEASE...
TELL ME WHAT HAPPENED NEXT IN YOUR HISTORY.

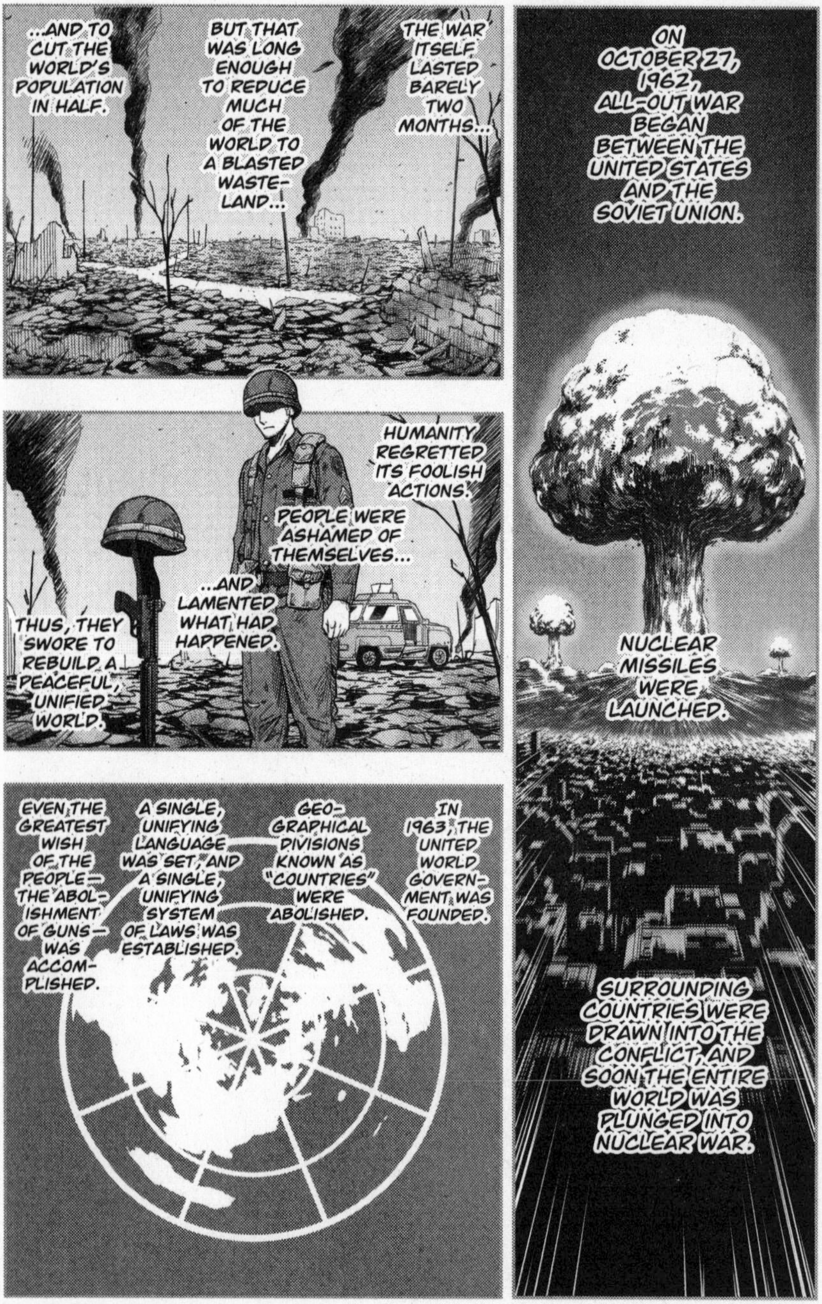
ON OCTOBER 27, 1962, ALL-OUT WAR BEGAN BETWEEN THE UNITED STATES AND THE SOVIET UNION.
NUCLEAR MISSILES WERE LAUNCHED.
SURROUNDING COUNTRIES WERE DRAWN INTO THE CONFLICT, AND SOON THE ENTIRE WORLD WAS PLUNGED INTO NUCLEAR WAR.
THE WAR ITSELF LASTED BARELY TWO MONTHS...
BUT THAT WAS LONG ENOUGH TO REDUCE MUCH OF THE WORLD TO A BLASTED WASTE-LAND...
...AND TO CUT THE WORLD'S POPULATION IN HALF.
HUMANITY REGRETTED ITS FOOLISH ACTIONS.
PEOPLE WERE ASHAMED OF THEMSELVES...
...AND LAMENTED WHAT HAD HAPPENED.
THUS, THEY SWORE TO REBUILD A PEACEFUL, UNIFIED WORLD.
IN 1963, THE UNITED WORLD GOVERN-MENT WAS FOUNDED.
GEO-GRAPHICAL DIVISIONS KNOWN AS "COUNTRIES" WERE ABOLISHED.
A SINGLE, UNIFYING LANGUAGE WAS SET, AND A SINGLE, UNIFYING SYSTEM OF LAWS WAS ESTABLISHED.
EVEN THE GREATEST WISH OF THE PEOPLE—THE ABOL-ISHMENT OF GUNS—WAS ACCOM-PLISHED.

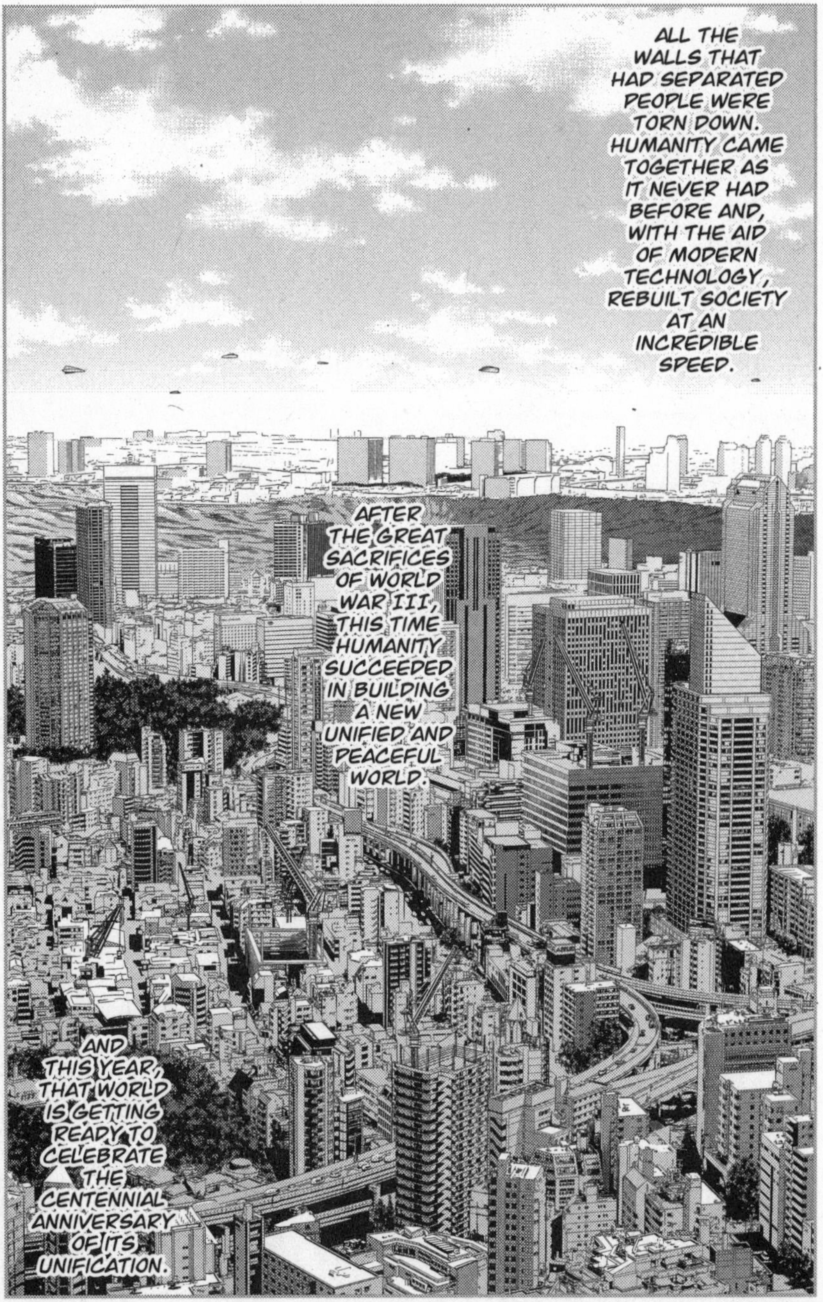
ALL THE WALLS THAT HAD SEPARATED PEOPLE WERE TORN DOWN. HUMANITY CAME TOGETHER AS IT NEVER HAD BEFORE AND, WITH THE AID OF MODERN TECHNOLOGY, REBUILT SOCIETY AT AN INCREDIBLE SPEED.
AFTER THE GREAT SACRIFICES OF WORLD WAR III, THIS TIME HUMANITY SUCCEEDED IN BUILDING A NEW UNIFIED AND PEACEFUL WORLD.
AND THIS YEAR, THAT WORLD IS GETTING READY TO CELEBRATE THE CENTENNIAL ANNIVERSARY OF ITS UNIFICATION.

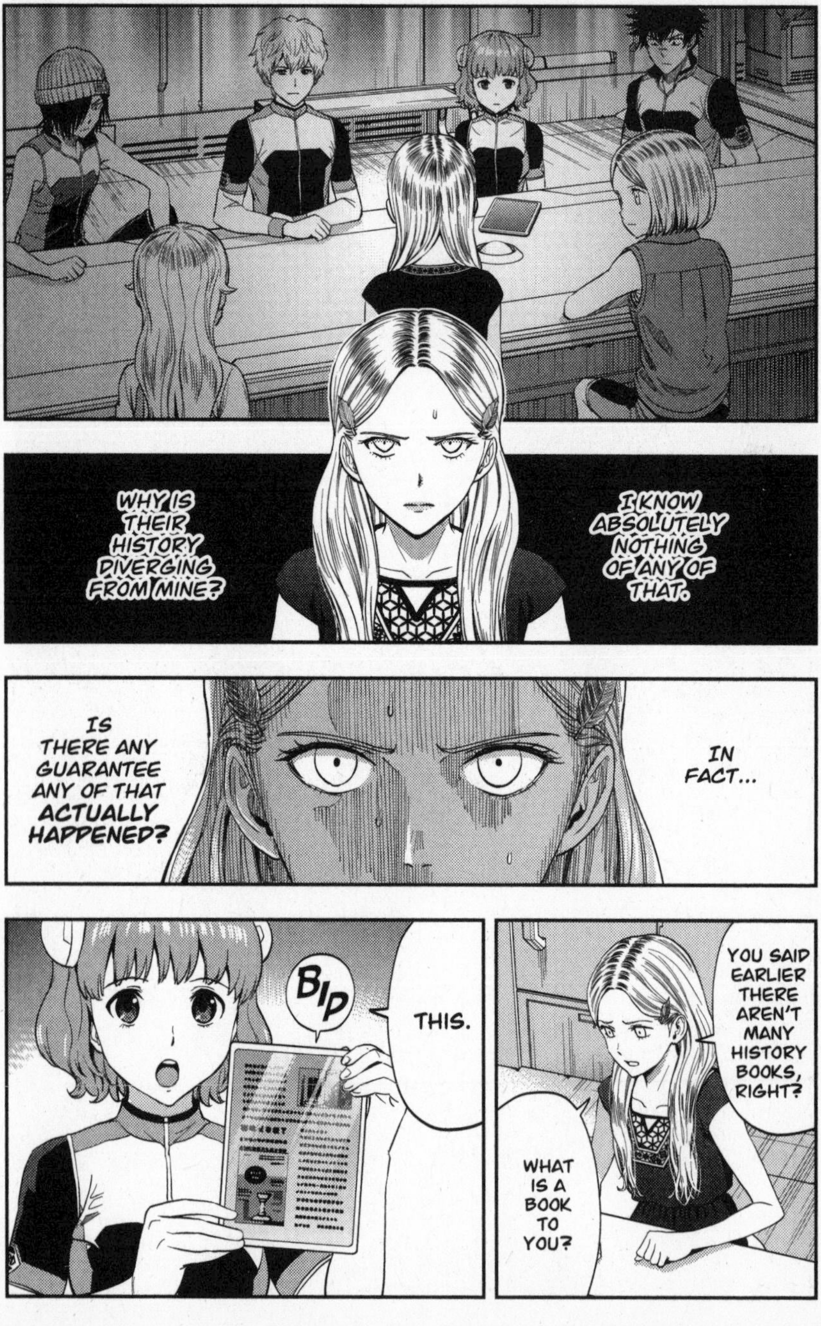
I KNOW ABSOLUTELY NOTHING OF ANY OF THAT.
WHY IS THEIR HISTORY DIVERGING FROM MINE?
IN FACT...
IS THERE ANY GUARANTEE ANY OF THAT **ACTUALLY HAPPENED?**
YOU SAID EARLIER THERE AREN'T MANY HISTORY BOOKS, RIGHT?
WHAT IS A BOOK TO YOU?
BIP
THIS.

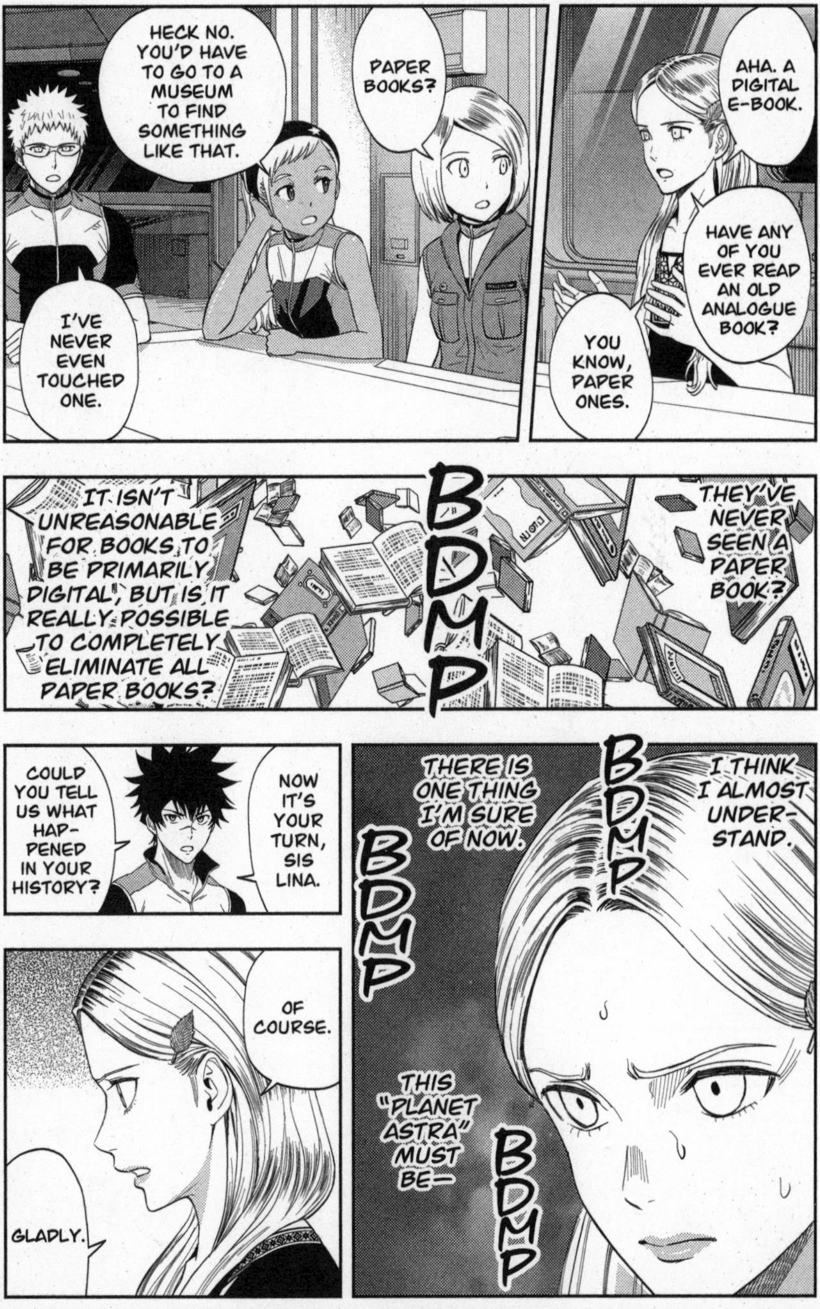
AHA. A DIGITAL E-BOOK.
HAVE ANY OF YOU EVER READ AN OLD ANALOGUE BOOK?
YOU KNOW, PAPER ONES.
PAPER BOOKS?
HECK NO. YOU'D HAVE TO GO TO A MUSEUM TO FIND SOMETHING LIKE THAT.
I'VE NEVER EVEN TOUCHED ONE.
THEY'VE NEVER SEEN A PAPER BOOK?
BDMP
IT ISN'T UNREASONABLE FOR BOOKS TO BE PRIMARILY DIGITAL, BUT IS IT REALLY POSSIBLE TO COMPLETELY ELIMINATE ALL PAPER BOOKS?
I THINK I ALMOST UNDER-STAND.
BDMP
THERE IS ONE THING I'M SURE OF NOW.
BDMP
THIS "PLANET ASTRA" MUST BE—
BDMP
NOW IT'S YOUR TURN, SIS LINA.
COULD YOU TELL US WHAT HAP-PENED IN YOUR HISTORY?
OF COURSE.
GLADLY.

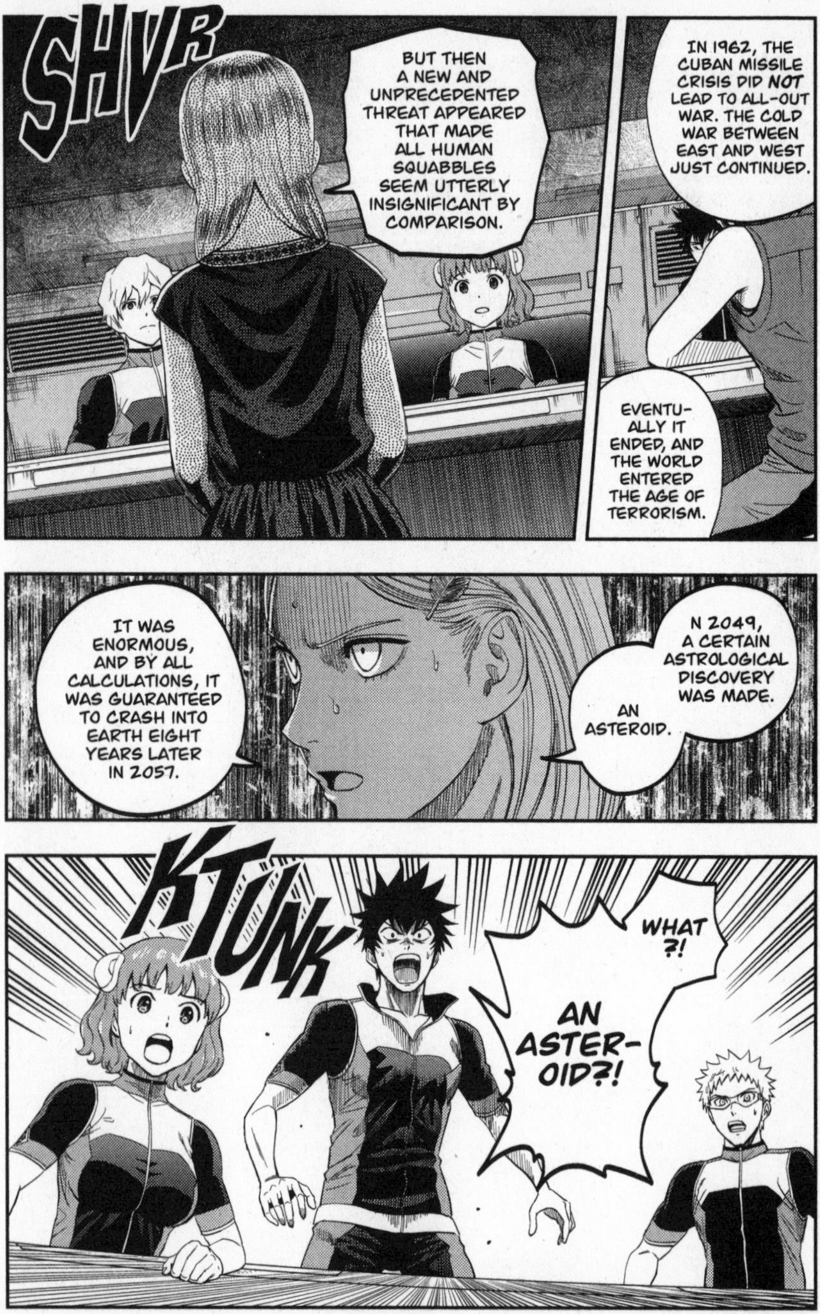
IN 1962, THE CUBAN MISSILE CRISIS DID **NOT** LEAD TO ALL-OUT WAR. THE COLD WAR BETWEEN EAST AND WEST JUST CONTINUED.
EVENTU-ALLY IT ENDED, AND THE WORLD ENTERED THE AGE OF TERRORISM.
SHVR
BUT THEN A NEW AND UNPRECEDENTED THREAT APPEARED THAT MADE ALL HUMAN SQUABBLES SEEM UTTERLY INSIGNIFICANT BY COMPARISON.
N 2049, A CERTAIN ASTROLOGICAL DISCOVERY WAS MADE.
AN ASTEROID.
IT WAS ENORMOUS, AND BY ALL CALCULATIONS, IT WAS GUARANTEED TO CRASH INTO EARTH EIGHT YEARS LATER IN 2057.
WHAT?!
AN ASTER-OID?!
KTUNK

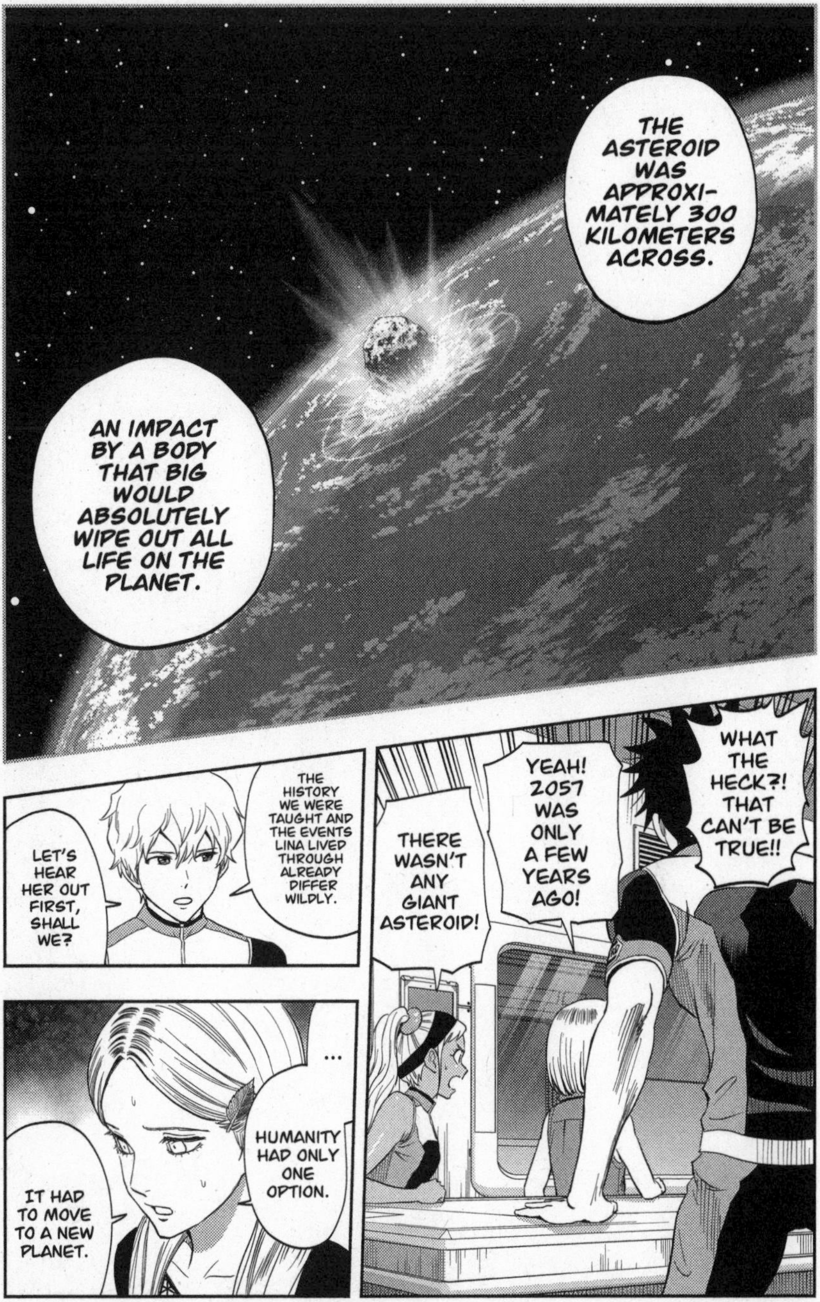
THE ASTEROID WAS APPROXIMATELY 300 KILOMETERS ACROSS.
AN IMPACT BY A BODY THAT BIG WOULD ABSOLUTELY WIPE OUT ALL LIFE ON THE PLANET.
WHAT THE HECK?! THAT CAN'T BE TRUE!!
YEAH! 2057 WAS ONLY A FEW YEARS AGO!
THERE WASN'T ANY GIANT ASTEROID!
THE HISTORY WE WERE TAUGHT AND THE EVENTS LINA LIVED THROUGH ALREADY DIFFER WILDLY.
LET'S HEAR HER OUT FIRST, SHALL WE?
...
HUMANITY HAD ONLY ONE OPTION.
IT HAD TO MOVE TO A NEW PLANET.

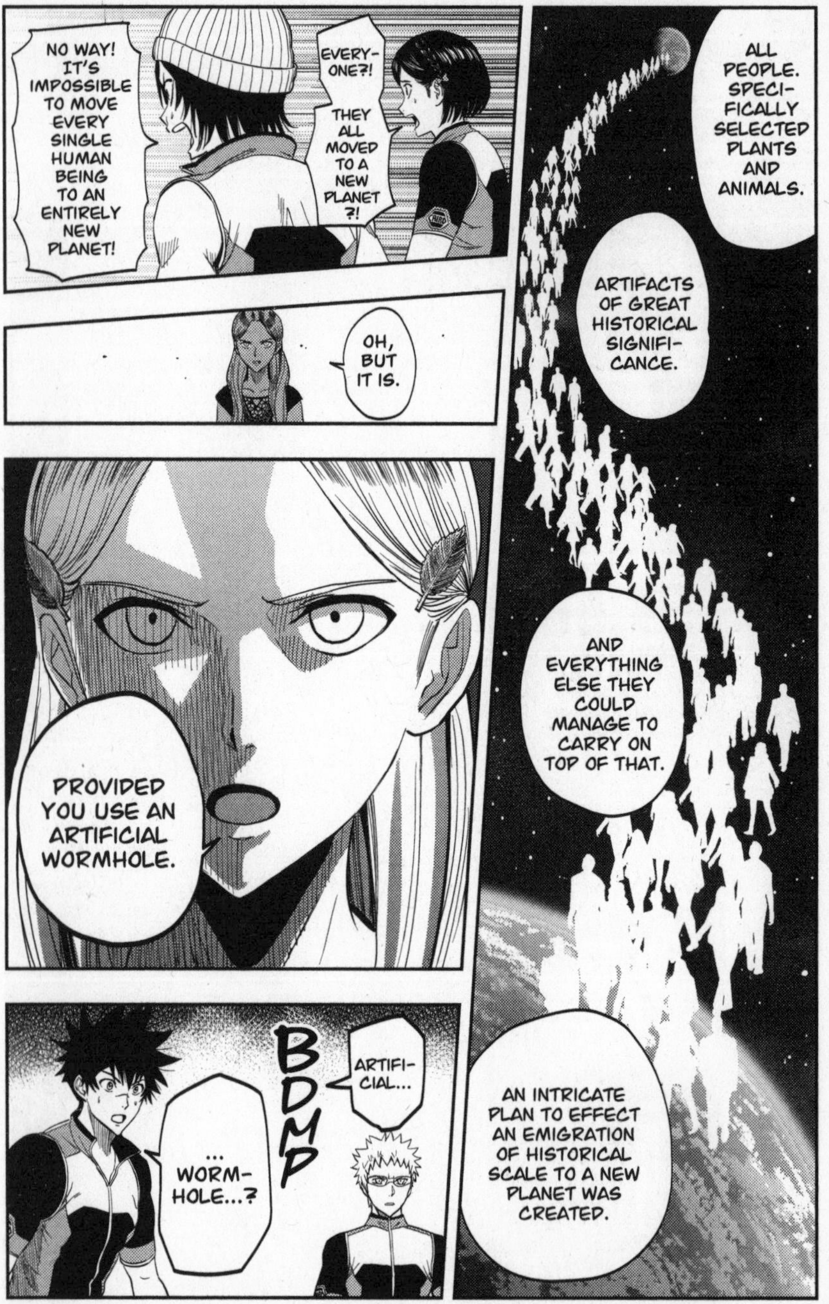
ALL PEOPLE. SPECIFICALLY SELECTED PLANTS AND ANIMALS.
ARTIFACTS OF GREAT HISTORICAL SIGNIFICANCE.
AND EVERYTHING ELSE THEY COULD MANAGE TO CARRY ON TOP OF THAT.
AN INTRICATE PLAN TO EFFECT AN EMIGRATION OF HISTORICAL SCALE TO A NEW PLANET WAS CREATED.
EVERYONE?!
THEY ALL MOVED TO A NEW PLANET?!
NO WAY! IT'S IMPOSSIBLE TO MOVE EVERY SINGLE HUMAN BEING TO AN ENTIRELY NEW PLANET!
OH, BUT IT IS.
PROVIDED YOU USE AN ARTIFICIAL WORMHOLE.
ARTIFICIAL...
BDMP
... WORMHOLE...?

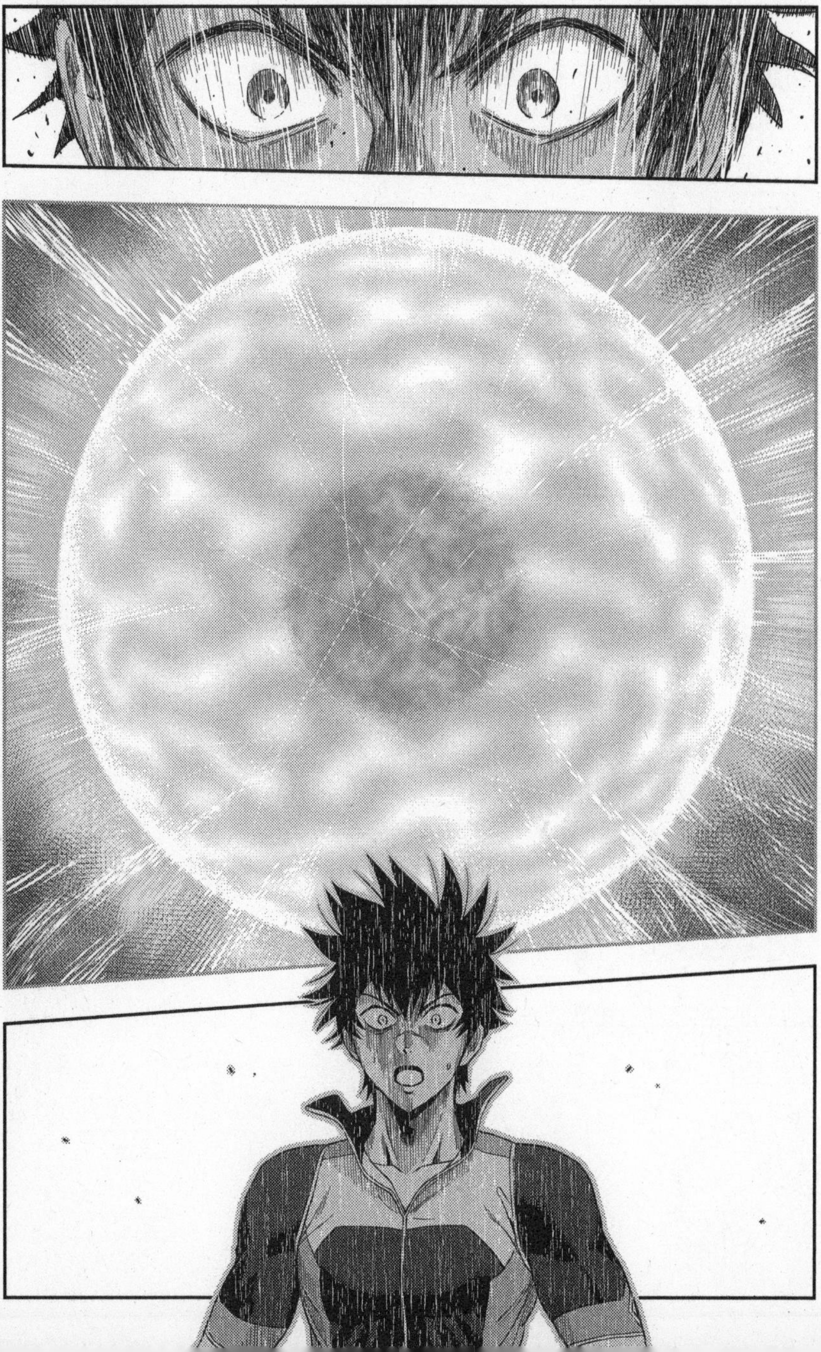

Material Collection

The Making of Spaceship *ASTRA*

1:80 Scale Model: Part 1

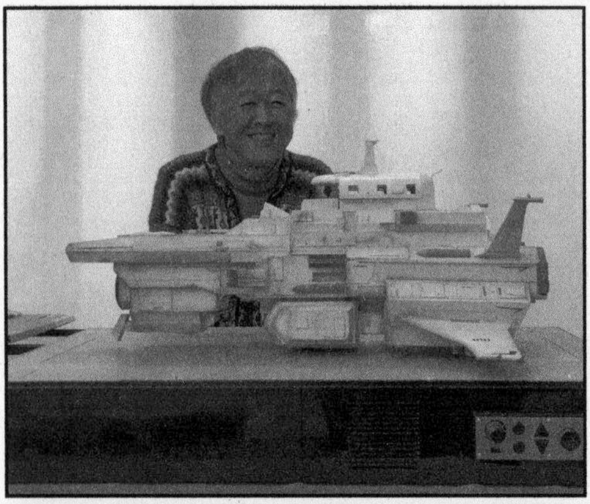

This model was built by one Mr. Wataru Kubo, a longtime plastic model hobbyist and an employee of a certain toy company.

I was honored when he sent me a request saying he would like to try his hand at building the *Astra*. So I took the liberty of sending him a few diagrams.

It took about six months to complete. Here are some photos of the completed model. I'll have some work-in-progress shots later.

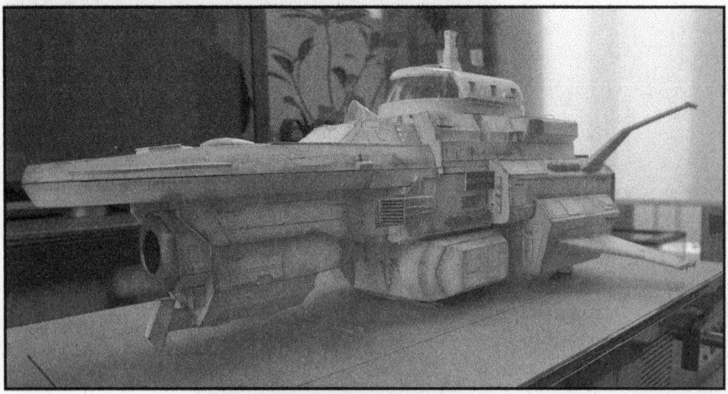

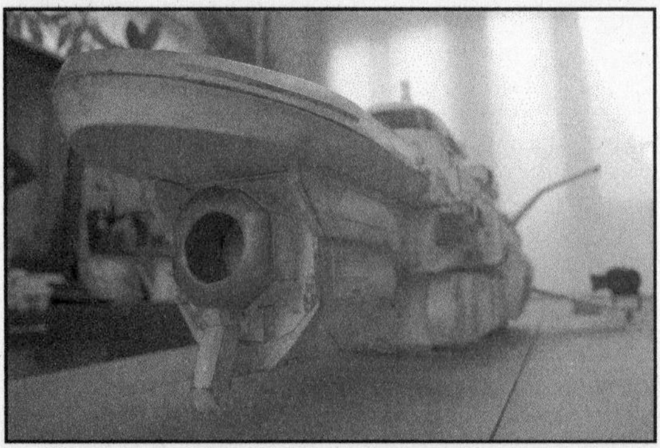

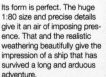

Its form is perfect. The huge 1:80 size and precise details give it an air of imposing presence. That and the realistic weathering beautifully give the impression of a ship that has survived a long and arduous adventure.

ASTRA
LOST IN SPACE
#39

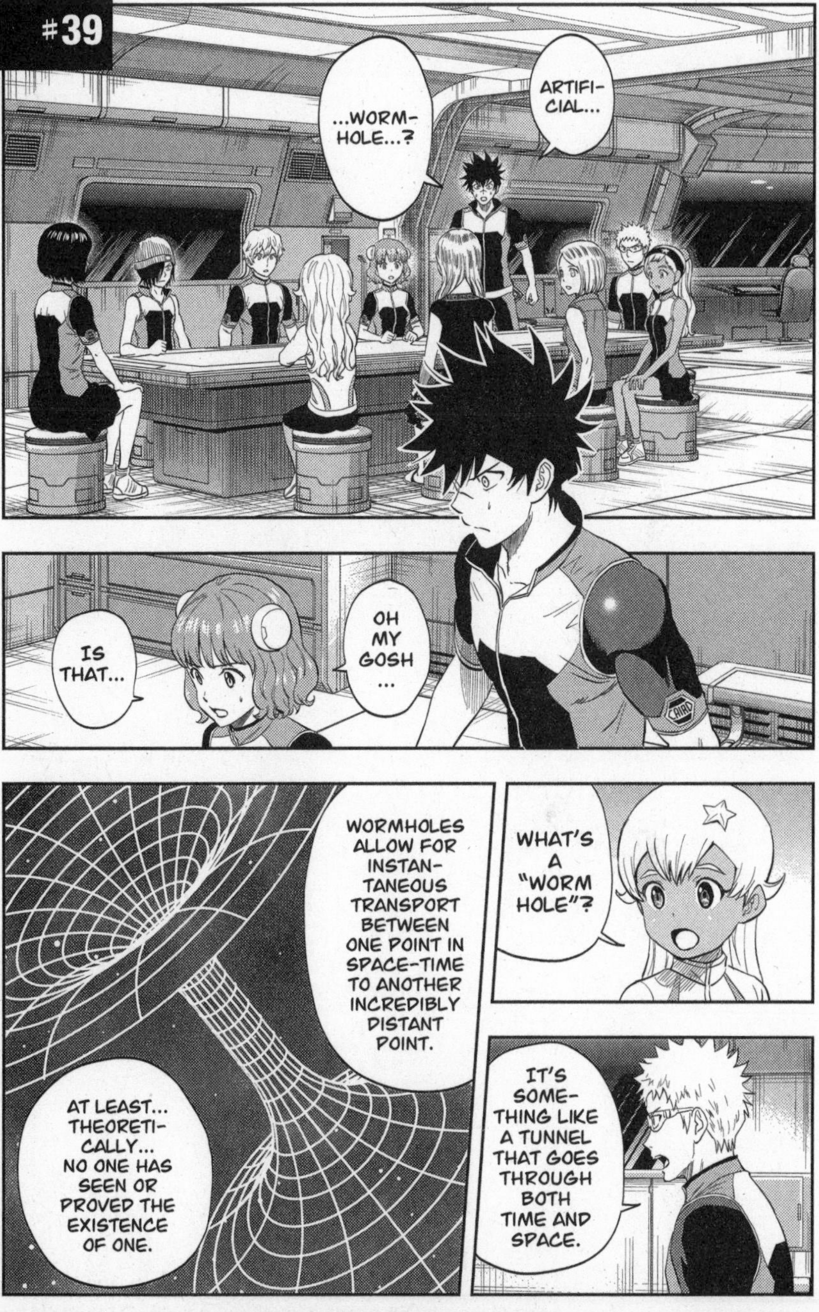
ARTIFI-CIAL...
...WORM-HOLE...?
OH MY GOSH ...
IS THAT...
WHAT'S A "WORM HOLE"?
IT'S SOME-THING LIKE A TUNNEL THAT GOES THROUGH BOTH TIME AND SPACE.
WORMHOLES ALLOW FOR INSTAN-TANEOUS TRANSPORT BETWEEN ONE POINT IN SPACE-TIME TO ANOTHER INCREDIBLY DISTANT POINT.
AT LEAST... THEORETI-CALLY... NO ONE HAS SEEN OR PROVED THE EXISTENCE OF ONE.

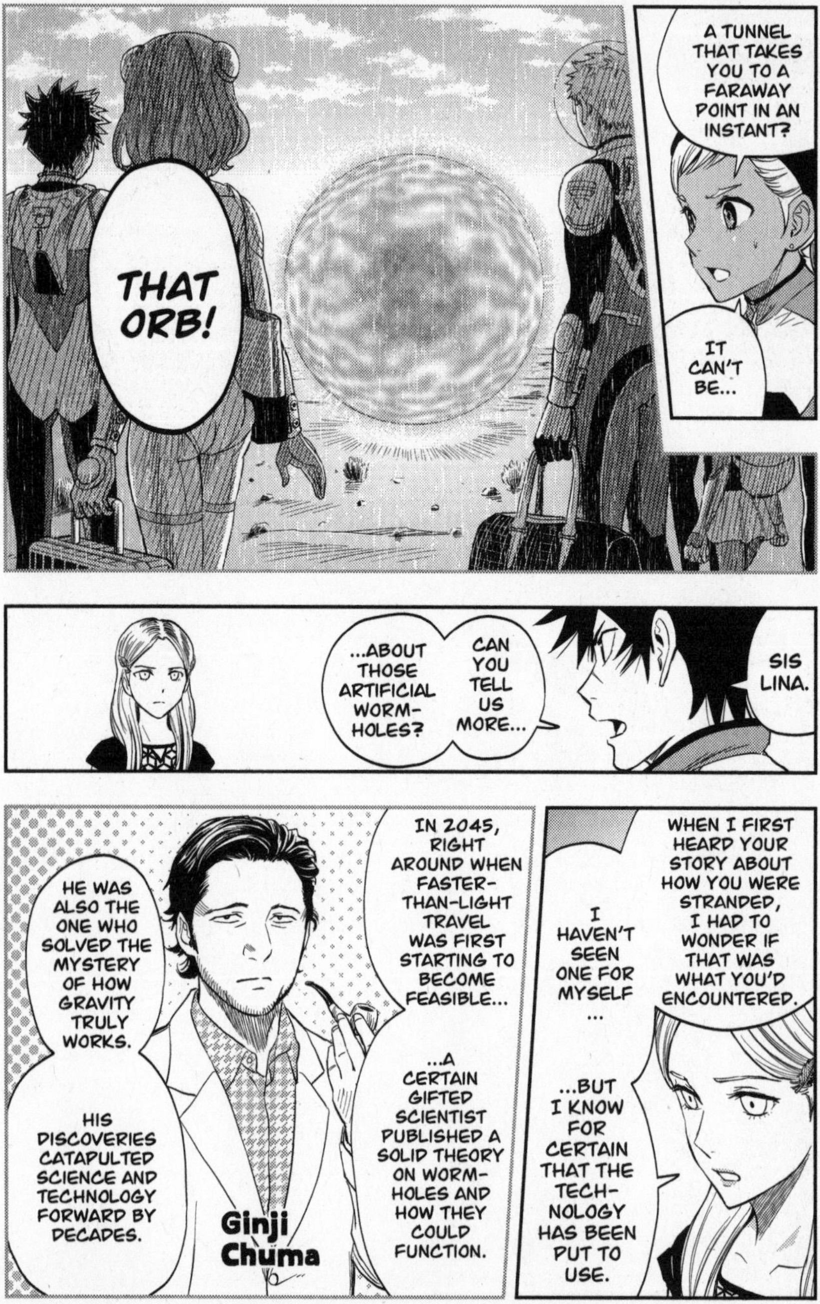
A TUNNEL THAT TAKES YOU TO A FARAWAY POINT IN AN INSTANT?
IT CAN'T BE...
THAT ORB!
SIS LINA.
CAN YOU TELL US MORE...
...ABOUT THOSE ARTIFICIAL WORMHOLES?
WHEN I FIRST HEARD YOUR STORY ABOUT HOW YOU WERE STRANDED, I HAD TO WONDER IF THAT WAS WHAT YOU'D ENCOUNTERED.
I HAVEN'T SEEN ONE FOR MYSELF...
...BUT I KNOW FOR CERTAIN THAT THE TECHNOLOGY HAS BEEN PUT TO USE.
IN 2045, RIGHT AROUND WHEN FASTER-THAN-LIGHT TRAVEL WAS FIRST STARTING TO BECOME FEASIBLE...
...A CERTAIN GIFTED SCIENTIST PUBLISHED A SOLID THEORY ON WORMHOLES AND HOW THEY COULD FUNCTION.
Ginji Chuma
HE WAS ALSO THE ONE WHO SOLVED THE MYSTERY OF HOW GRAVITY TRULY WORKS.
HIS DISCOVERIES CATAPULTED SCIENCE AND TECHNOLOGY FORWARD BY DECADES.

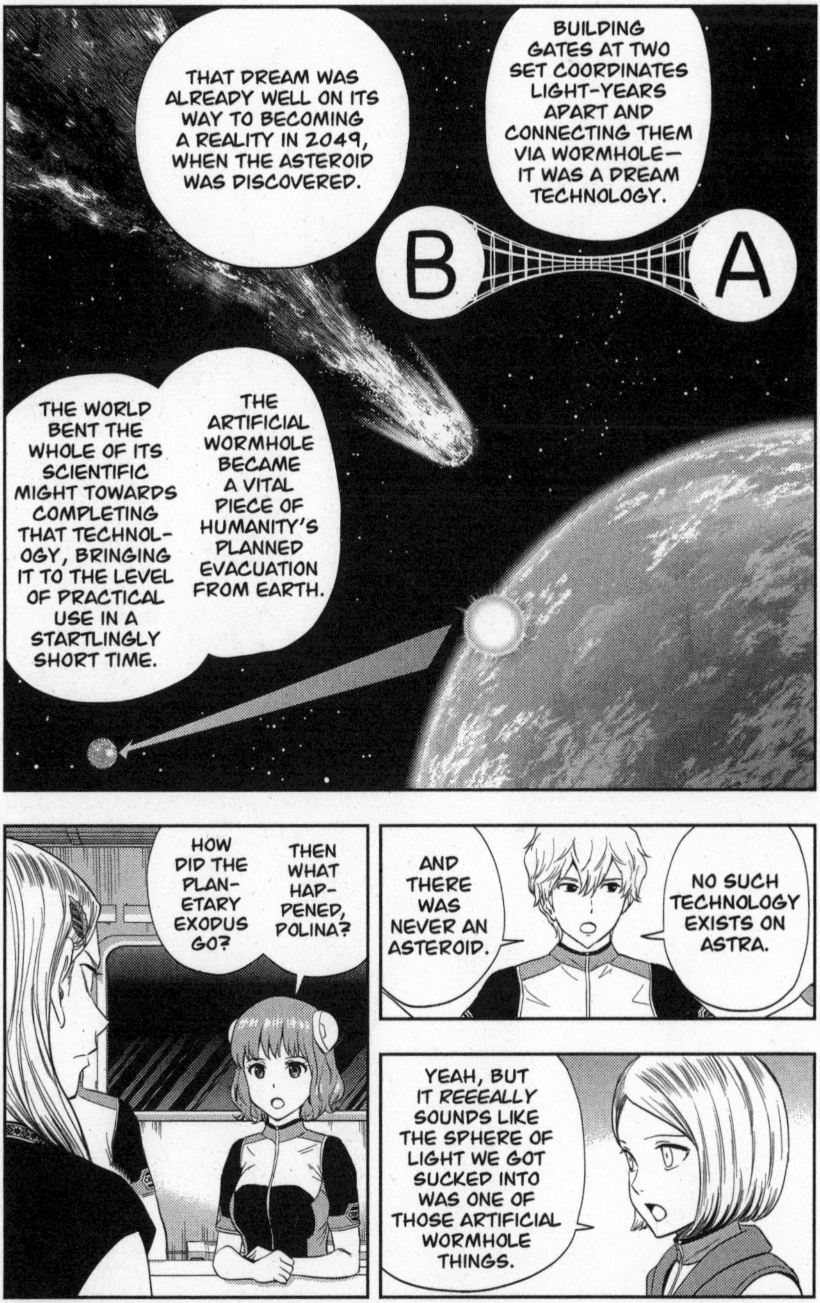
BUILDING GATES AT TWO SET COORDINATES LIGHT-YEARS APART AND CONNECTING THEM VIA WORMHOLE—IT WAS A DREAM TECHNOLOGY.
THAT DREAM WAS ALREADY WELL ON ITS WAY TO BECOMING A REALITY IN 2049, WHEN THE ASTEROID WAS DISCOVERED.
B
A
THE ARTIFICIAL WORMHOLE BECAME A VITAL PIECE OF HUMANITY'S PLANNED EVACUATION FROM EARTH.
THE WORLD BENT THE WHOLE OF ITS SCIENTIFIC MIGHT TOWARDS COMPLETING THAT TECHNOLOGY, BRINGING IT TO THE LEVEL OF PRACTICAL USE IN A STARTLINGLY SHORT TIME.
NO SUCH TECHNOLOGY EXISTS ON ASTRA.
AND THERE WAS NEVER AN ASTEROID.
YEAH, BUT IT REEEALLY SOUNDS LIKE THE SPHERE OF LIGHT WE GOT SUCKED INTO WAS ONE OF THOSE ARTIFICIAL WORMHOLE THINGS.
THEN WHAT HAPPENED, POLINA?
HOW DID THE PLANETARY EXODUS GO?

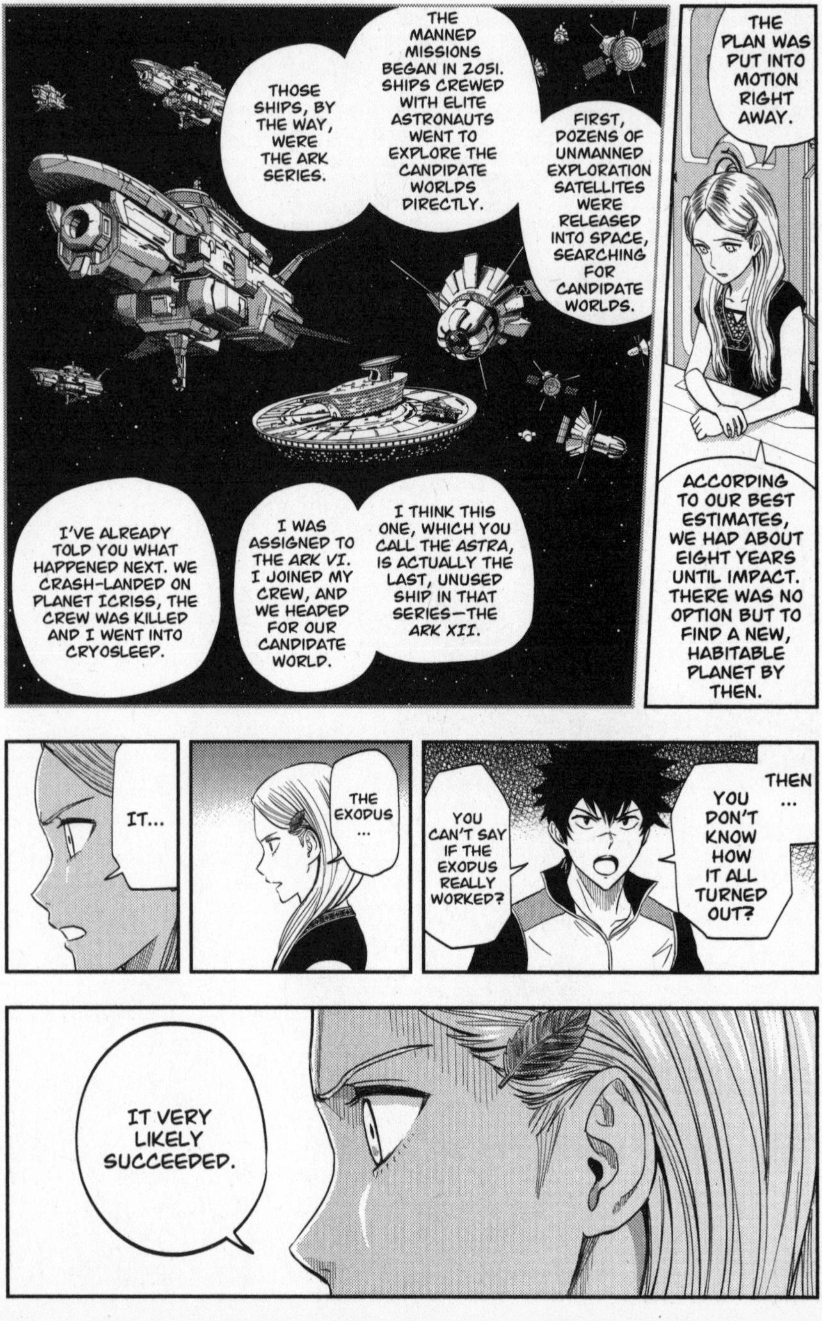
THE PLAN WAS PUT INTO MOTION RIGHT AWAY.
ACCORDING TO OUR BEST ESTIMATES, WE HAD ABOUT EIGHT YEARS UNTIL IMPACT. THERE WAS NO OPTION BUT TO FIND A NEW, HABITABLE PLANET BY THEN.
FIRST, DOZENS OF UNMANNED EXPLORATION SATELLITES WERE RELEASED INTO SPACE, SEARCHING FOR CANDIDATE WORLDS.
THE MANNED MISSIONS BEGAN IN 2051. SHIPS CREWED WITH ELITE ASTRONAUTS WENT TO EXPLORE THE CANDIDATE WORLDS DIRECTLY.
THOSE SHIPS, BY THE WAY, WERE THE ARK SERIES.
I THINK THIS ONE, WHICH YOU CALL THE ASTRA, IS ACTUALLY THE LAST, UNUSED SHIP IN THAT SERIES—THE ARK XII.
I WAS ASSIGNED TO THE ARK VI. I JOINED MY CREW, AND WE HEADED FOR OUR CANDIDATE WORLD.
I'VE ALREADY TOLD YOU WHAT HAPPENED NEXT. WE CRASH-LANDED ON PLANET ICRISS, THE CREW WAS KILLED AND I WENT INTO CRYOSLEEP.
THEN...
YOU DON'T KNOW HOW IT ALL TURNED OUT?
YOU CAN'T SAY IF THE EXODUS REALLY WORKED?
THE EXODUS...
IT...
IT VERY LIKELY SUCCEEDED.

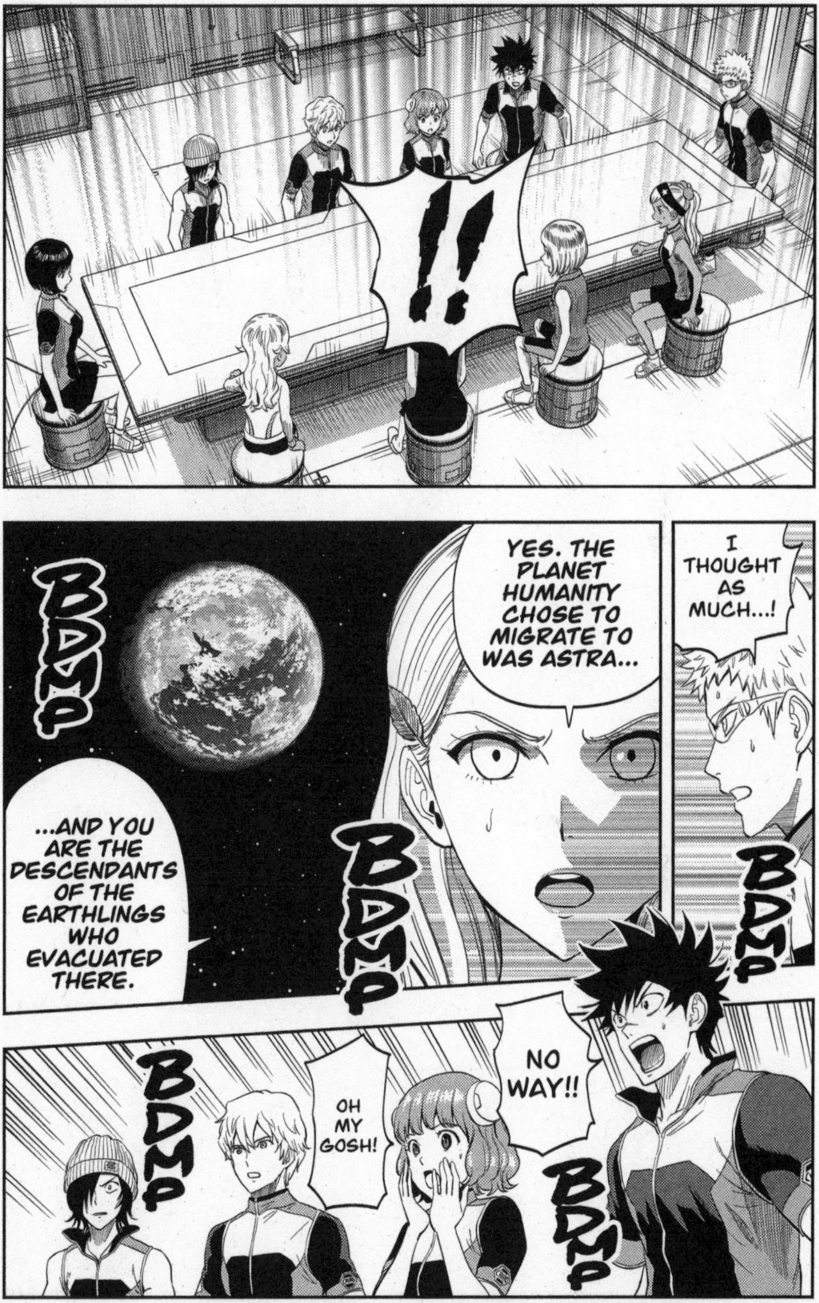
!!
I THOUGHT AS MUCH...!
BDMP
YES. THE PLANET HUMANITY CHOSE TO MIGRATE TO WAS ASTRA...
BDMP
...AND YOU ARE THE DESCENDANTS OF THE EARTHLINGS WHO EVACUATED THERE.
BDMP
NO WAY!!
BDMP
OH MY GOSH!
BDMP

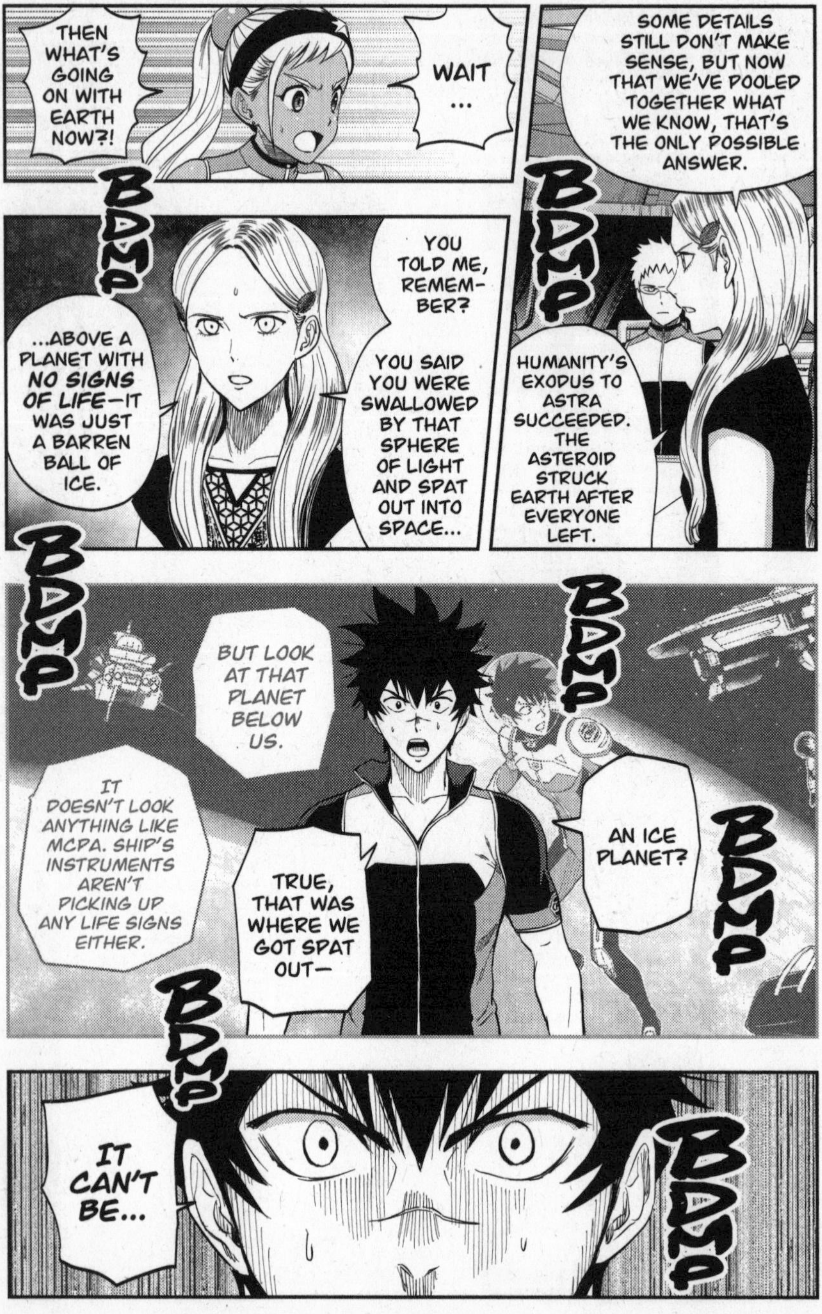
SOME DETAILS STILL DON'T MAKE SENSE, BUT NOW THAT WE'VE POOLED TOGETHER WHAT WE KNOW, THAT'S THE ONLY POSSIBLE ANSWER.
BDMP
HUMANITY'S EXODUS TO ASTRA SUCCEEDED. THE ASTEROID STRUCK EARTH AFTER EVERYONE LEFT.
WAIT ...
THEN WHAT'S GOING ON WITH EARTH NOW?!
BDMP
YOU TOLD ME, REMEMBER?
YOU SAID YOU WERE SWALLOWED BY THAT SPHERE OF LIGHT AND SPAT OUT INTO SPACE...
...ABOVE A PLANET WITH NO SIGNS OF LIFE—IT WAS JUST A BARREN BALL OF ICE.
BDMP
BDMP
AN ICE PLANET?
BDMP
TRUE, THAT WAS WHERE WE GOT SPAT OUT—
BUT LOOK AT THAT PLANET BELOW US.
IT DOESN'T LOOK ANYTHING LIKE MCPA. SHIP'S INSTRUMENTS AREN'T PICKING UP ANY LIFE SIGNS EITHER.
BDMP
BDMP
IT CAN'T BE...
BDMP

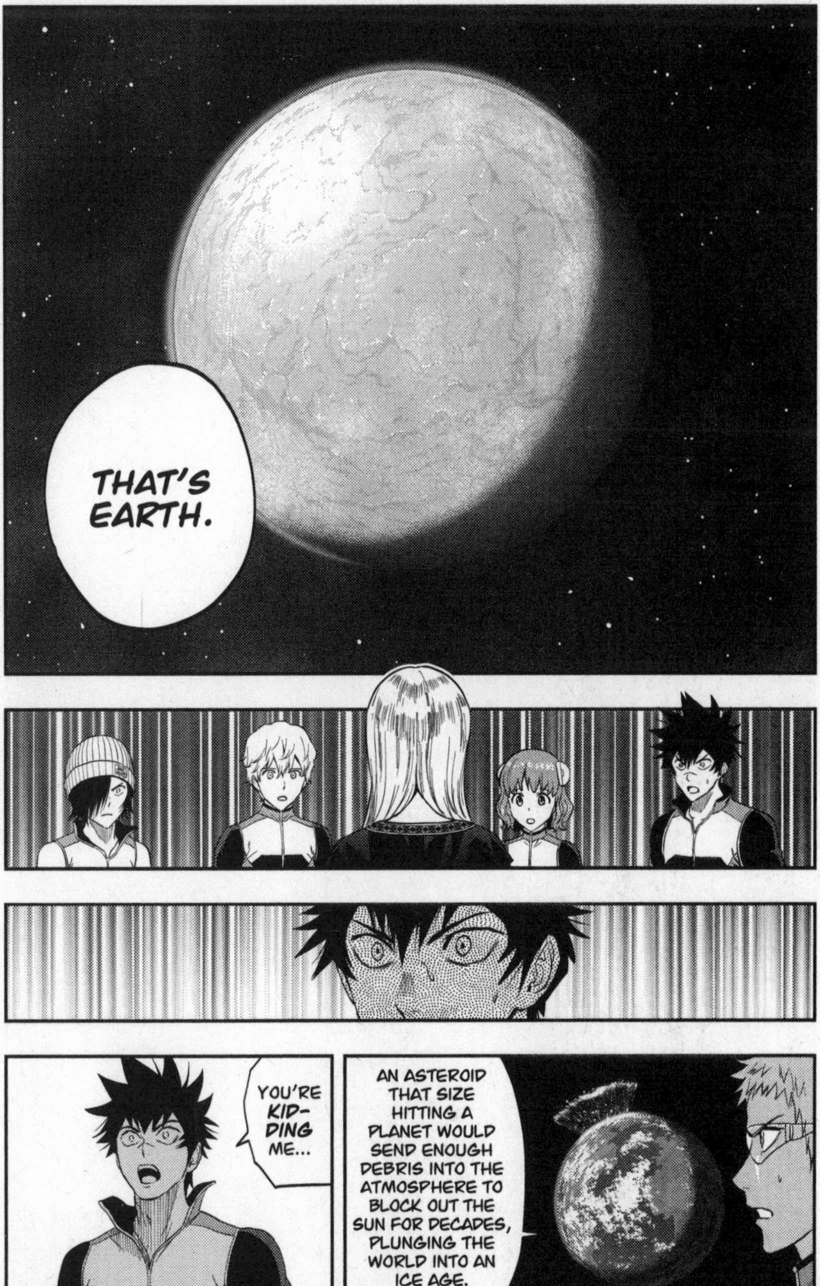
THAT'S EARTH.
AN ASTEROID THAT SIZE HITTING A PLANET WOULD SEND ENOUGH DEBRIS INTO THE ATMOSPHERE TO BLOCK OUT THE SUN FOR DECADES, PLUNGING THE WORLD INTO AN ICE AGE.
YOU'RE KID-DING ME...

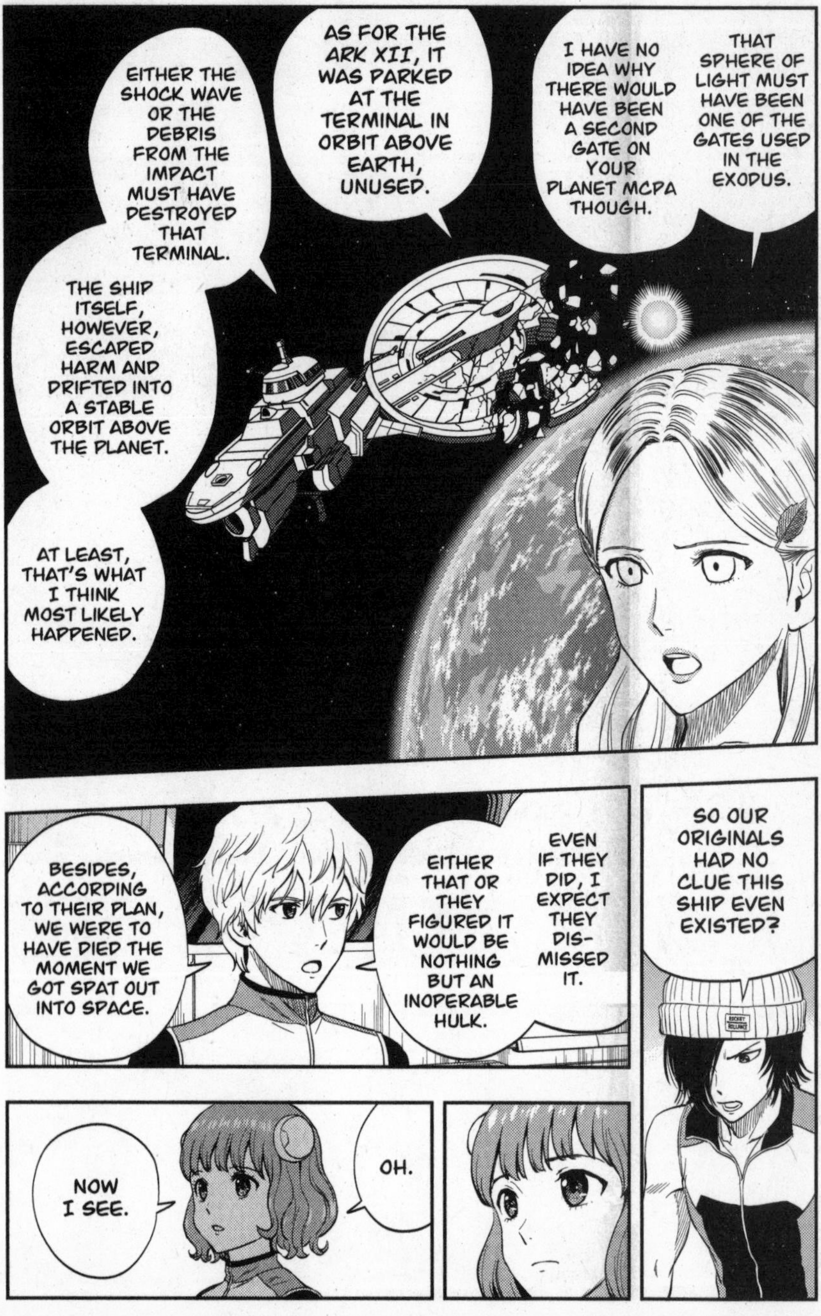
THAT SPHERE OF LIGHT MUST HAVE BEEN ONE OF THE GATES USED IN THE EXODUS.
I HAVE NO IDEA WHY THERE WOULD HAVE BEEN A SECOND GATE ON YOUR PLANET MCPA THOUGH.
AS FOR THE ARK XII, IT WAS PARKED AT THE TERMINAL IN ORBIT ABOVE EARTH, UNUSED.
EITHER THE SHOCK WAVE OR THE DEBRIS FROM THE IMPACT MUST HAVE DESTROYED THAT TERMINAL.
THE SHIP ITSELF, HOWEVER, ESCAPED HARM AND DRIFTED INTO A STABLE ORBIT ABOVE THE PLANET.
AT LEAST, THAT'S WHAT I THINK MOST LIKELY HAPPENED.
SO OUR ORIGINALS HAD NO CLUE THIS SHIP EVEN EXISTED?
EVEN IF THEY DID, I EXPECT THEY DIS-MISSED IT.
EITHER THAT OR THEY FIGURED IT WOULD BE NOTHING BUT AN INOPERABLE HULK.
BESIDES, ACCORDING TO THEIR PLAN, WE WERE TO HAVE DIED THE MOMENT WE GOT SPAT OUT INTO SPACE.
OH.
NOW I SEE.

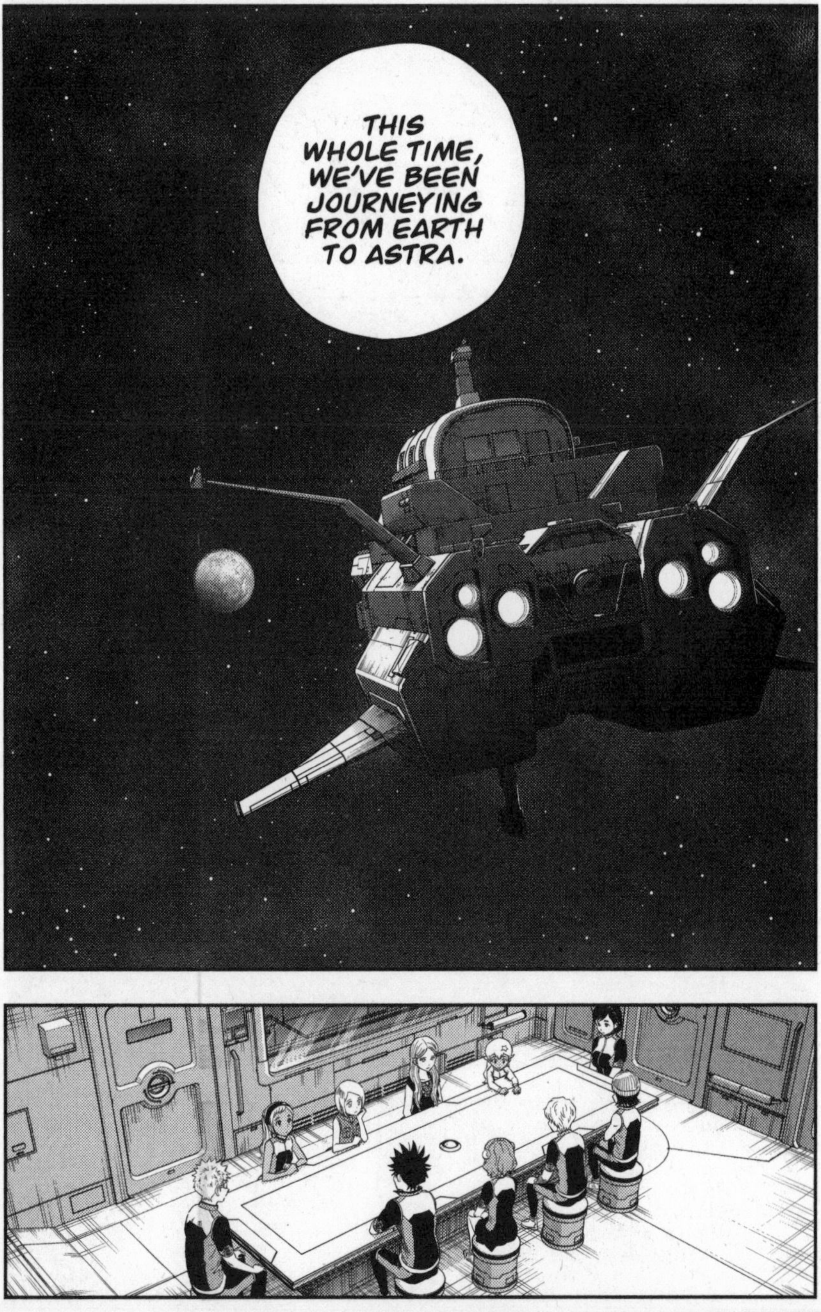
THIS WHOLE TIME, WE'VE BEEN JOURNEYING FROM EARTH TO ASTRA.

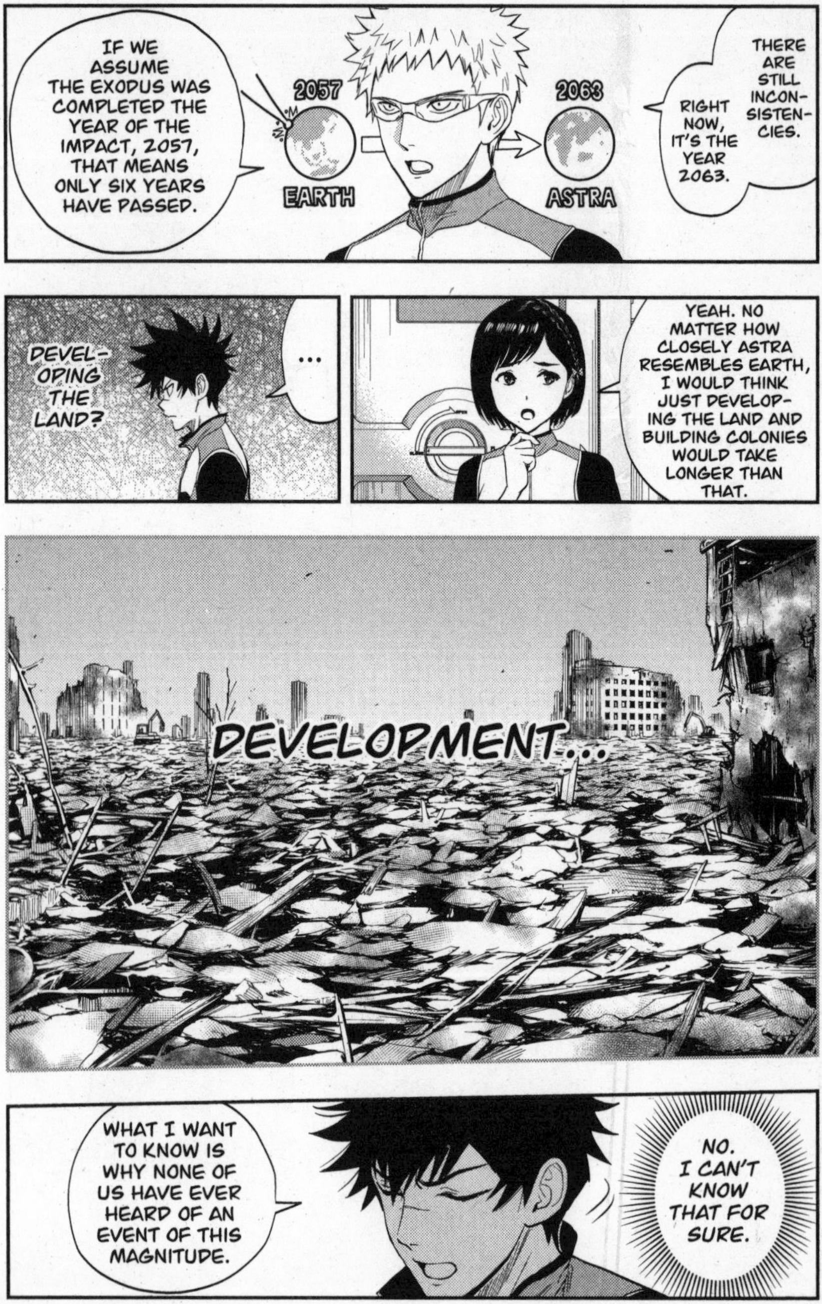
THERE ARE STILL INCONSISTENCIES.
RIGHT NOW, IT'S THE YEAR 2063.
2063
ASTRA
2057
EARTH
IF WE ASSUME THE EXODUS WAS COMPLETED THE YEAR OF THE IMPACT, 2057, THAT MEANS ONLY SIX YEARS HAVE PASSED.
YEAH. NO MATTER HOW CLOSELY ASTRA RESEMBLES EARTH, I WOULD THINK JUST DEVELOPING THE LAND AND BUILDING COLONIES WOULD TAKE LONGER THAN THAT.
...
DEVELOPING THE LAND?
DEVELOPMENT...
NO. I CAN'T KNOW THAT FOR SURE.
WHAT I WANT TO KNOW IS WHY NONE OF US HAVE EVER HEARD OF AN EVENT OF THIS MAGNITUDE.

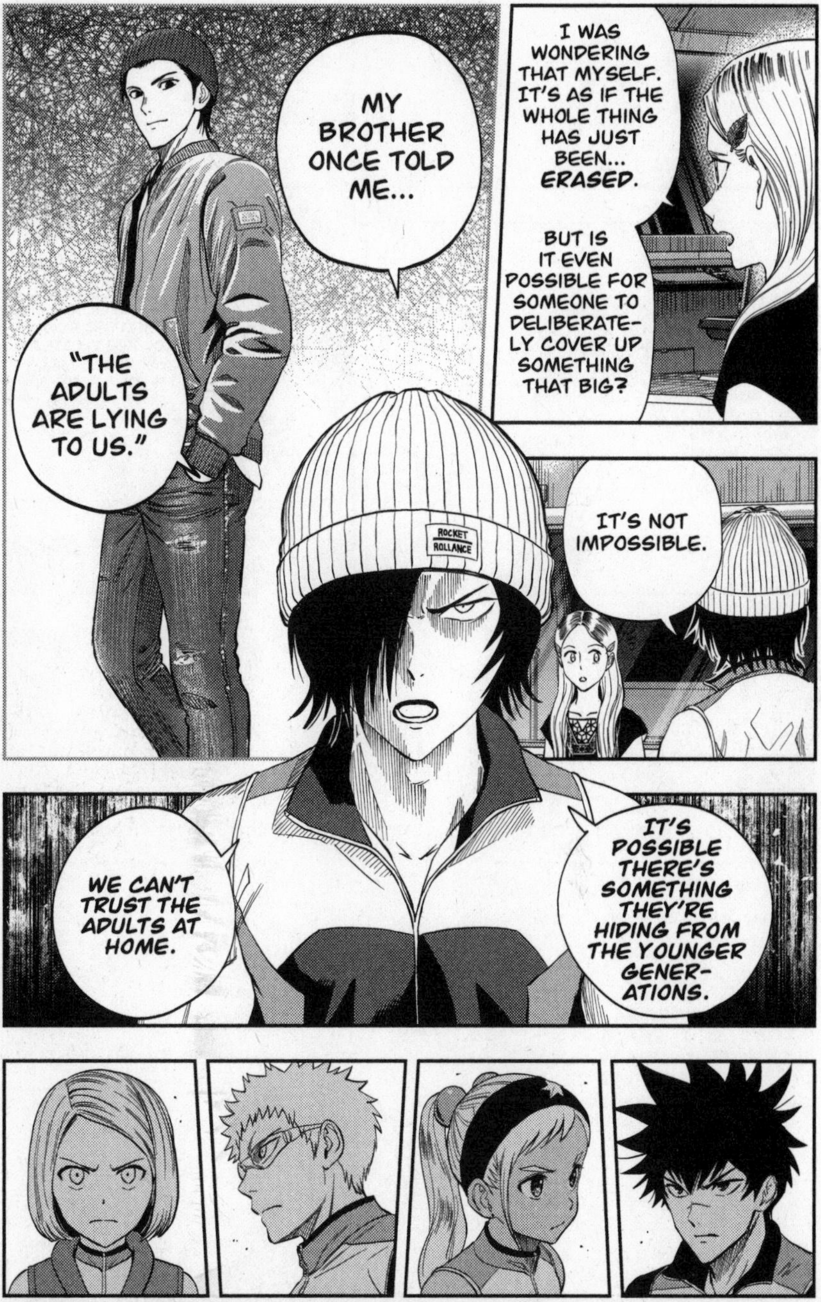
I WAS WONDERING THAT MYSELF. IT'S AS IF THE WHOLE THING HAS JUST BEEN... ERASED.
BUT IS IT EVEN POSSIBLE FOR SOMEONE TO DELIBERATE-LY COVER UP SOMETHING THAT BIG?
IT'S NOT IMPOSSIBLE.
MY BROTHER ONCE TOLD ME...
"THE ADULTS ARE LYING TO US."
ROCKET ROLLANCE
IT'S POSSIBLE THERE'S SOMETHING THEY'RE HIDING FROM THE YOUNGER GENER-ATIONS.
WE CAN'T TRUST THE ADULTS AT HOME.

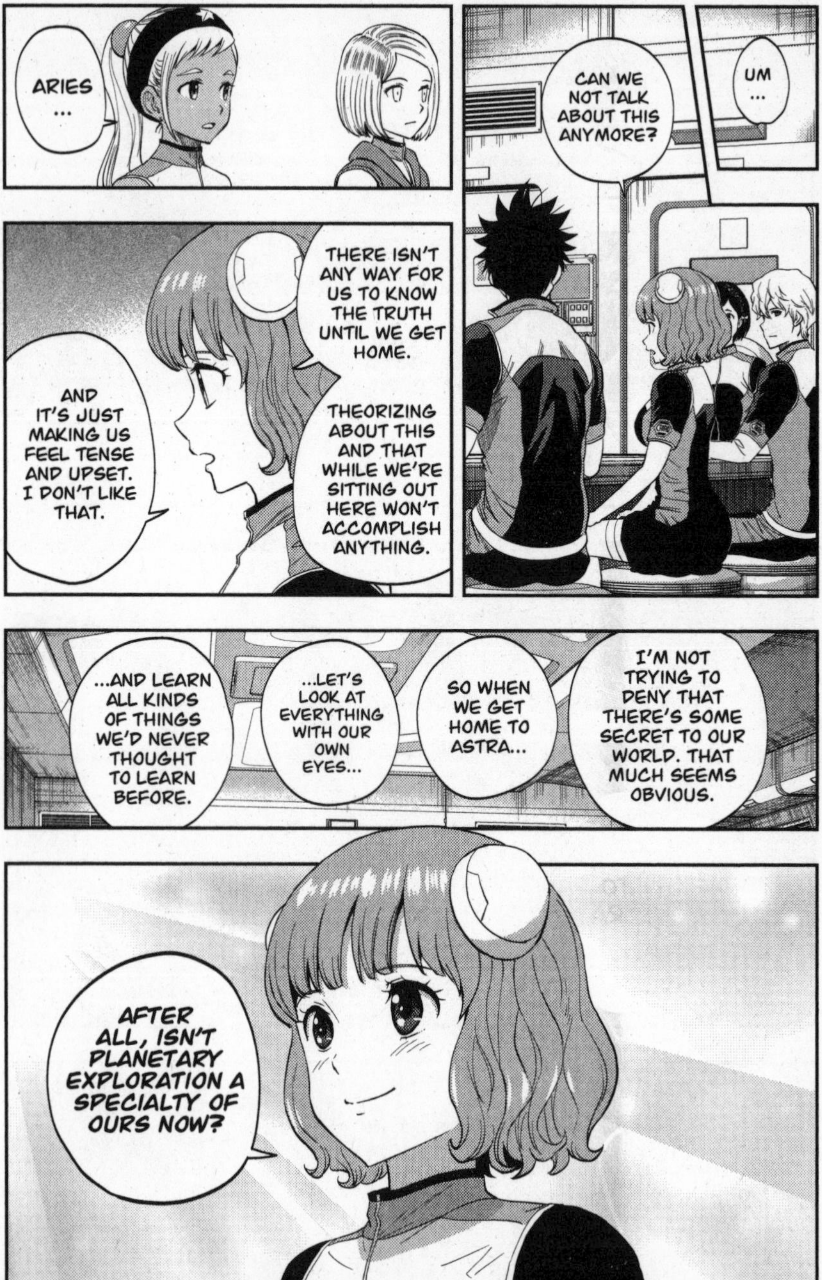
UM ...
CAN WE NOT TALK ABOUT THIS ANYMORE?
ARIES ...
THERE ISN'T ANY WAY FOR US TO KNOW THE TRUTH UNTIL WE GET HOME.
THEORIZING ABOUT THIS AND THAT WHILE WE'RE SITTING OUT HERE WON'T ACCOMPLISH ANYTHING.
AND IT'S JUST MAKING US FEEL TENSE AND UPSET. I DON'T LIKE THAT.
I'M NOT TRYING TO DENY THAT THERE'S SOME SECRET TO OUR WORLD. THAT MUCH SEEMS OBVIOUS.
SO WHEN WE GET HOME TO ASTRA...
...LET'S LOOK AT EVERYTHING WITH OUR OWN EYES...
...AND LEARN ALL KINDS OF THINGS WE'D NEVER THOUGHT TO LEARN BEFORE.
AFTER ALL, ISN'T PLANETARY EXPLORATION A SPECIALTY OF OURS NOW?

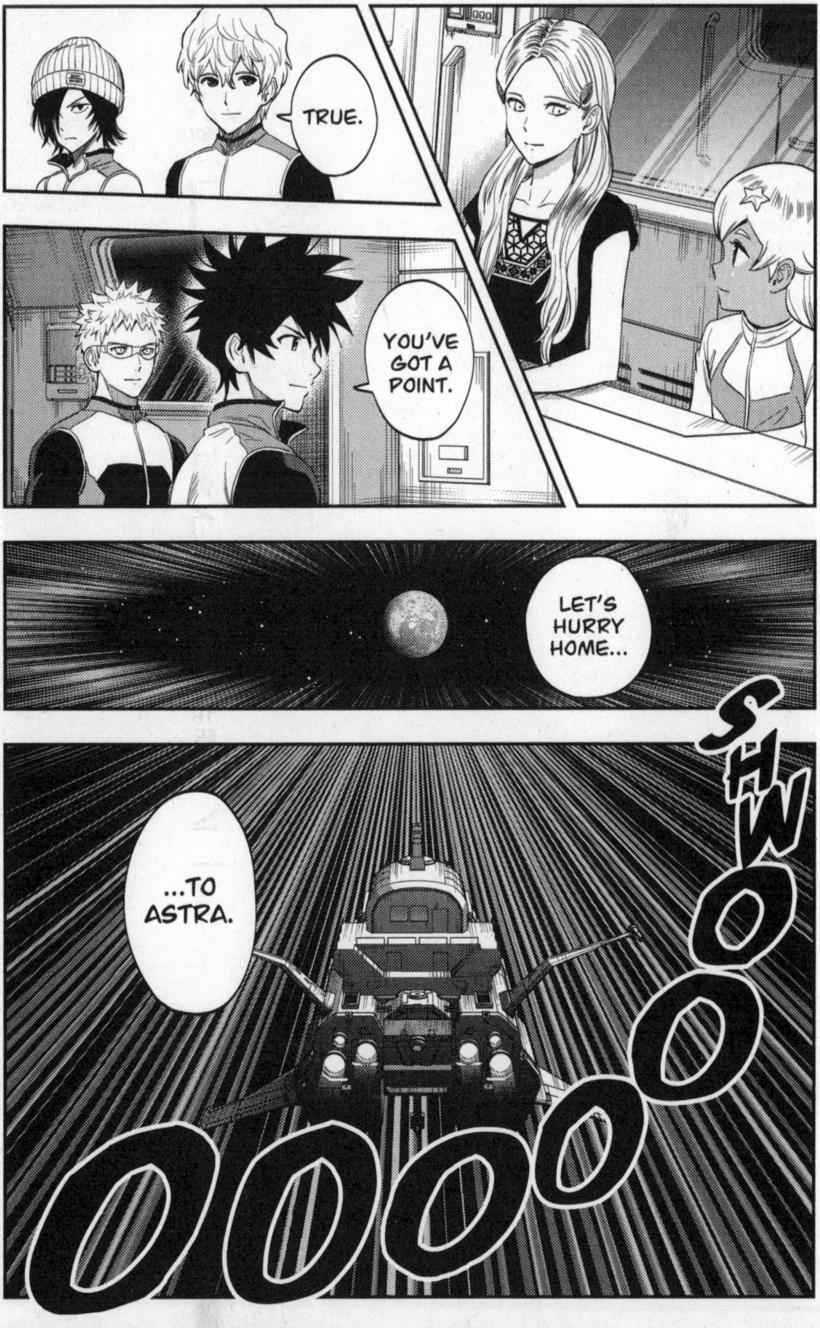
TRUE.
YOU'VE GOT A POINT.
LET'S HURRY HOME...
...TO ASTRA.
SHWOOOOOO

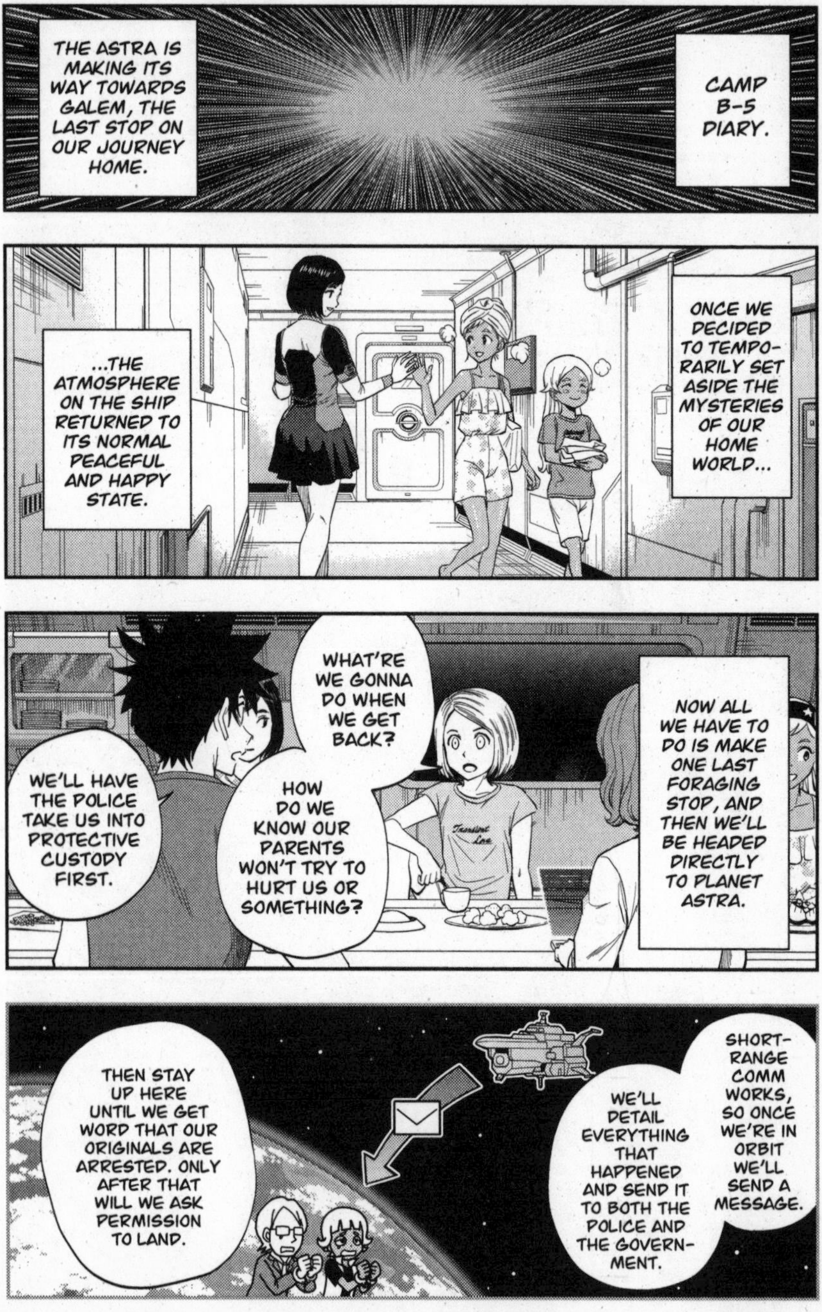
CAMP B-5 DIARY.
THE ASTRA IS MAKING ITS WAY TOWARDS GALEM, THE LAST STOP ON OUR JOURNEY HOME.
ONCE WE DECIDED TO TEMPORARILY SET ASIDE THE MYSTERIES OF OUR HOME WORLD...
...THE ATMOSPHERE ON THE SHIP RETURNED TO ITS NORMAL PEACEFUL AND HAPPY STATE.
NOW ALL WE HAVE TO DO IS MAKE ONE LAST FORAGING STOP, AND THEN WE'LL BE HEADED DIRECTLY TO PLANET ASTRA.
WHAT'RE WE GONNA DO WHEN WE GET BACK?
HOW DO WE KNOW OUR PARENTS WON'T TRY TO HURT US OR SOMETHING?
WE'LL HAVE THE POLICE TAKE US INTO PROTECTIVE CUSTODY FIRST.
SHORT-RANGE COMM WORKS, SO ONCE WE'RE IN ORBIT WE'LL SEND A MESSAGE.
WE'LL DETAIL EVERYTHING THAT HAPPENED AND SEND IT TO BOTH THE POLICE AND THE GOVERNMENT.
THEN STAY UP HERE UNTIL WE GET WORD THAT OUR ORIGINALS ARE ARRESTED. ONLY AFTER THAT WILL WE ASK PERMISSION TO LAND.

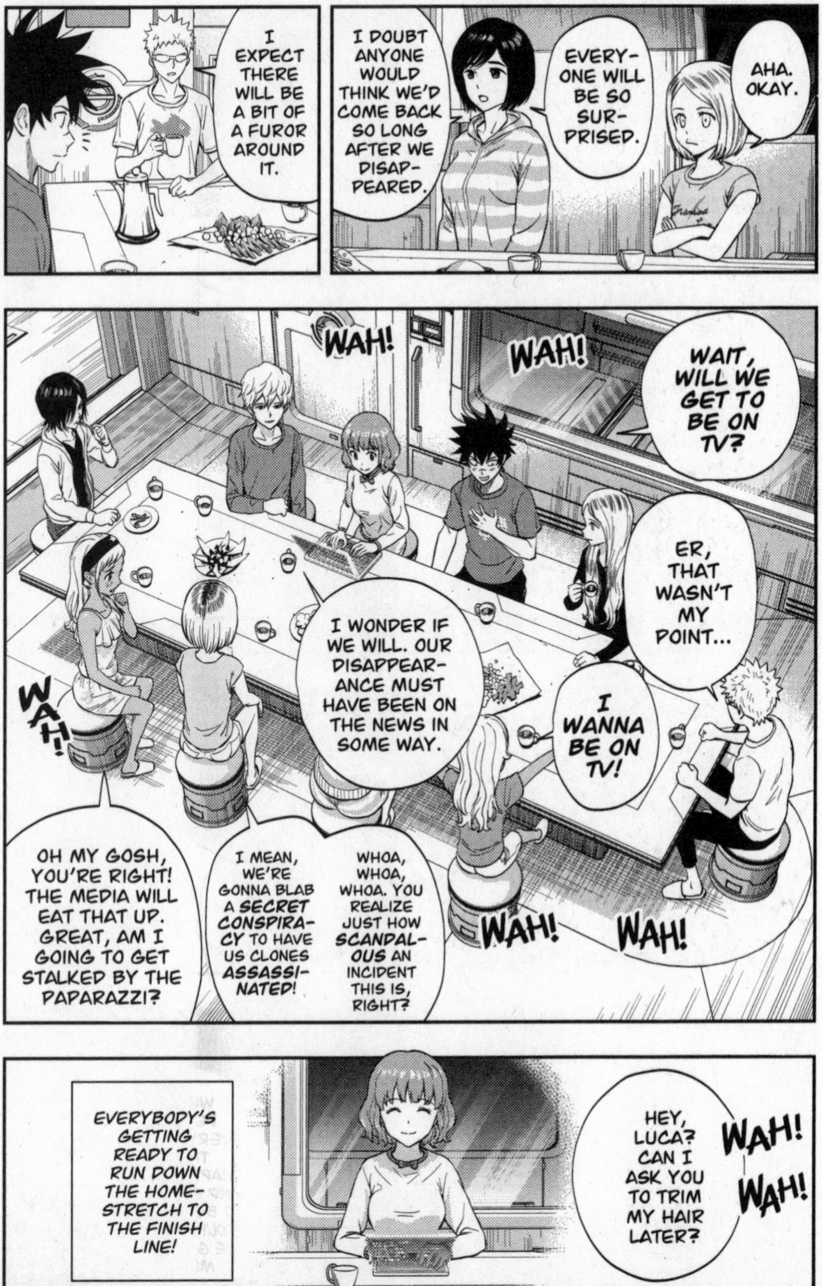
AHA. OKAY.
EVERY-ONE WILL BE SO SUR-PRISED.
I DOUBT ANYONE WOULD THINK WE'D COME BACK SO LONG AFTER WE DISAP-PEARED.
I EXPECT THERE WILL BE A BIT OF A FUROR AROUND IT.
WAH!
WAIT, WILL WE GET TO BE ON TV?
WAH!
ER, THAT WASN'T MY POINT...
I WONDER IF WE WILL. OUR DISAPPEAR-ANCE MUST HAVE BEEN ON THE NEWS IN SOME WAY.
I WANNA BE ON TV!
WAH!
WAH!
WAH!
WHOA, WHOA, WHOA. YOU REALIZE JUST HOW SCANDAL-OUS AN INCIDENT THIS IS, RIGHT?
I MEAN, WE'RE GONNA BLAB A SECRET CONSPIRA-CY TO HAVE US CLONES ASSASSI-NATED!
OH MY GOSH, YOU'RE RIGHT! THE MEDIA WILL EAT THAT UP. GREAT, AM I GOING TO GET STALKED BY THE PAPARAZZI?
WAH!
WAH!
HEY, LUCA? CAN I ASK YOU TO TRIM MY HAIR LATER?
EVERYBODY'S GETTING READY TO RUN DOWN THE HOME-STRETCH TO THE FINISH LINE!

"NO WANDER-ING OFF ON YOUR OWN NOW."
"HEY. WHAT'S THAT?"

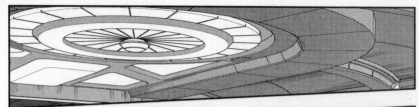

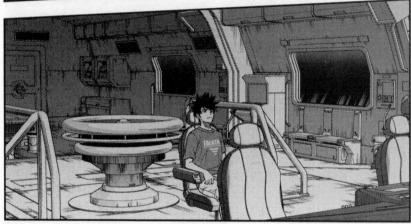

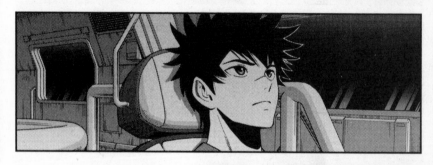

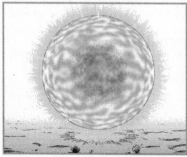

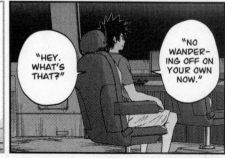

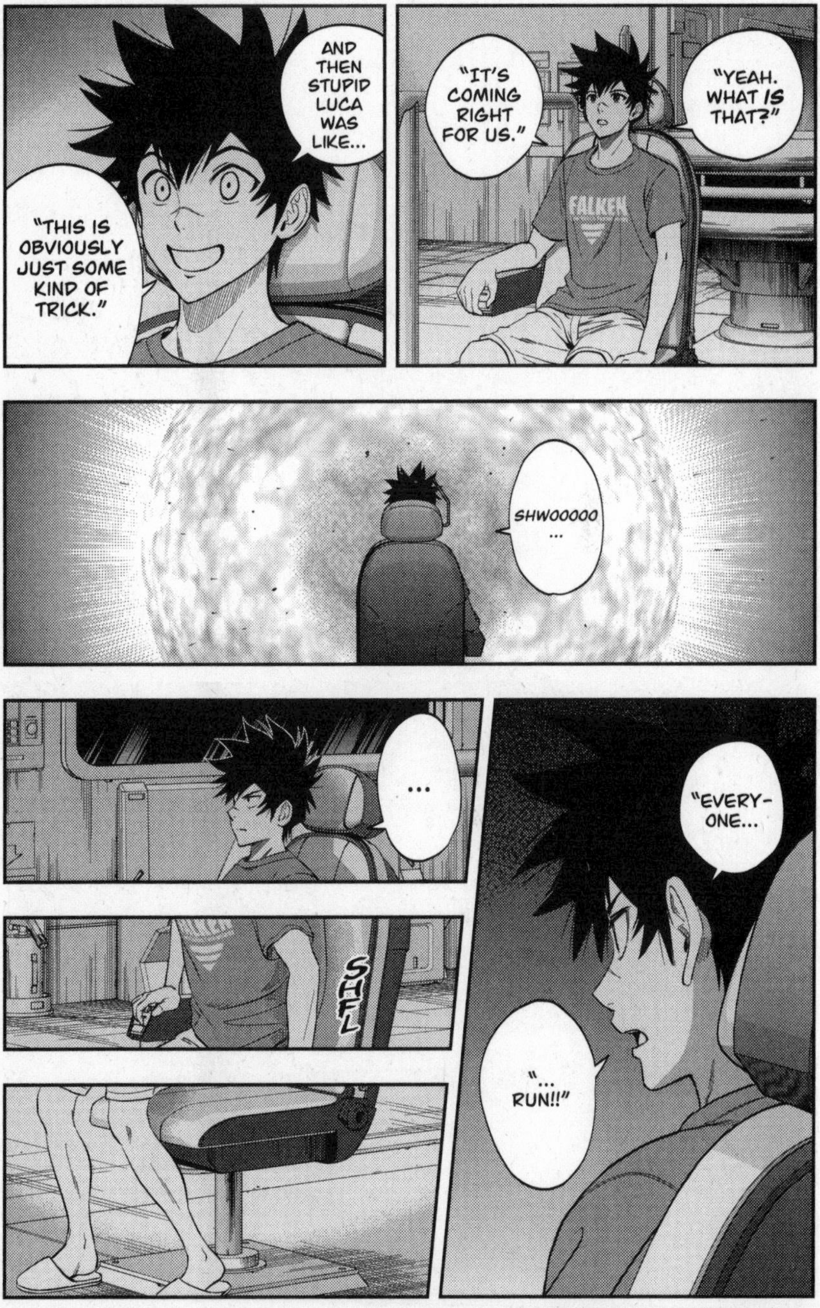
"YEAH. WHAT IS THAT?"
"IT'S COMING RIGHT FOR US."
FALKEN
AND THEN STUPID LUCA WAS LIKE...
"THIS IS OBVIOUSLY JUST SOME KIND OF TRICK."
SHWOOOOO ...
"EVERY-ONE...
"... RUN!!"
...
SHFL

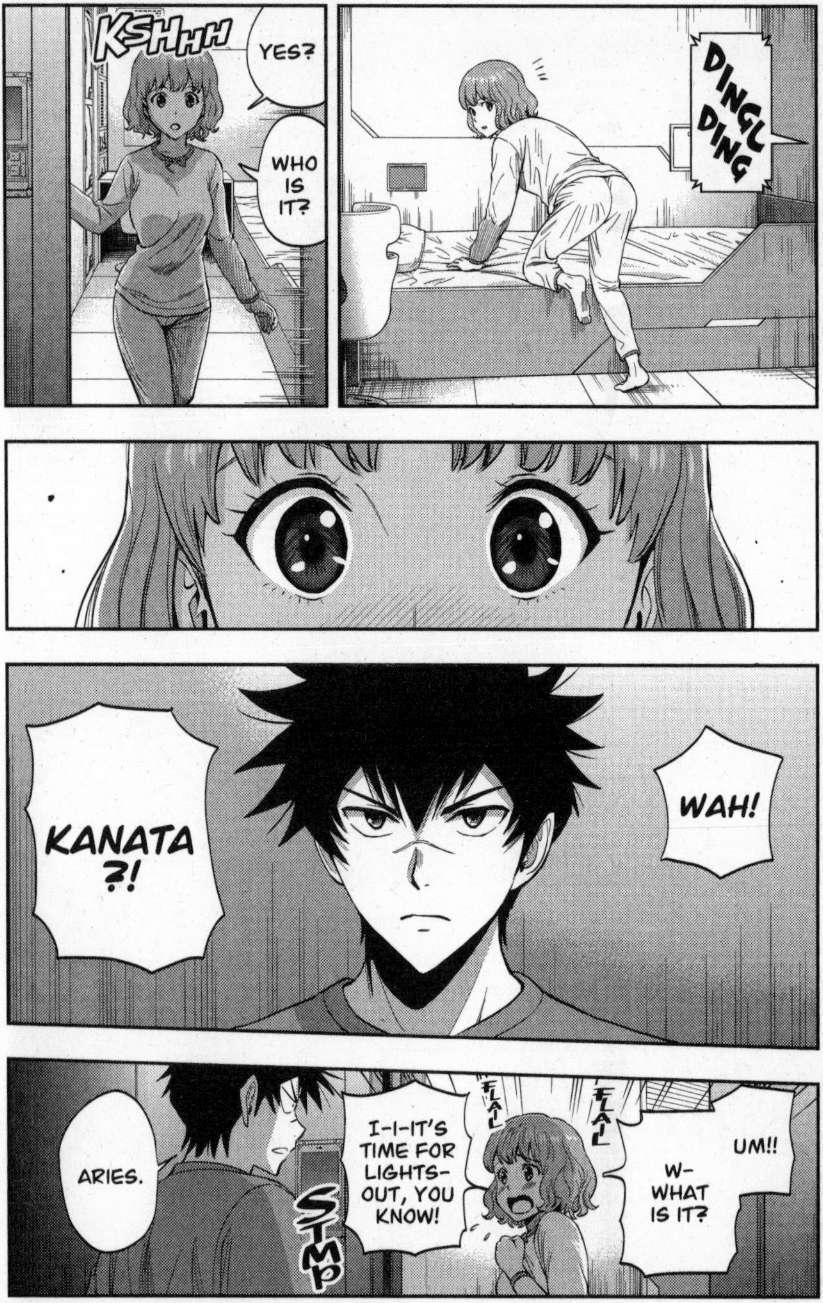
DINGL DING
KSHHH
YES?
WHO IS IT?
WAH!
KANATA ?!
UM!!
W-WHAT IS IT?
FLAIL
FLAIL
I-I-IT'S TIME FOR LIGHTS-OUT, YOU KNOW!
STMP
ARIES.

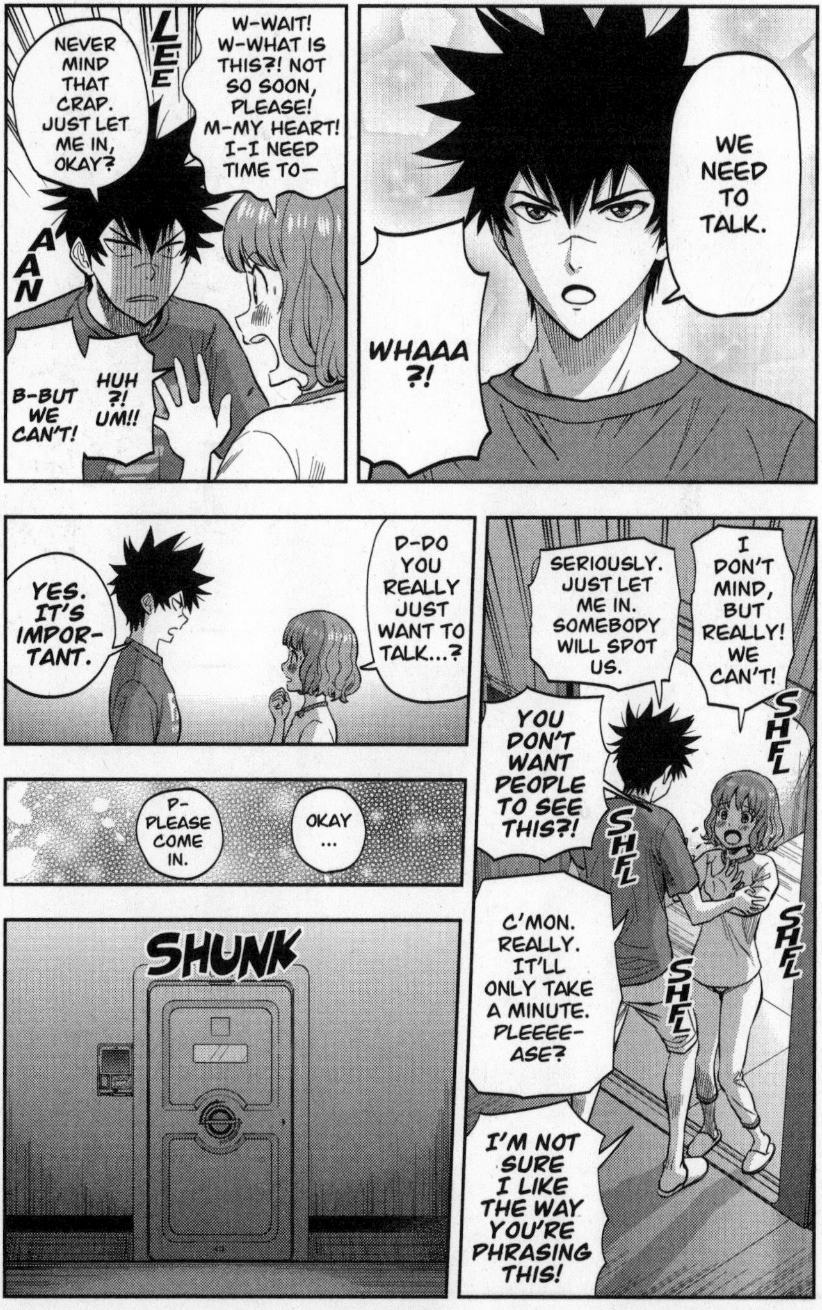

WE NEED TO TALK.
WHAAA?!
W-WAIT! W-WHAT IS THIS?! NOT SO SOON, PLEASE! M-MY HEART! I-I NEED TIME TO—
LEE
NEVER MIND THAT CRAP. JUST LET ME IN, OKAY?
AAN
HUH?! UM!!
B-BUT WE CAN'T!
I DON'T MIND, BUT REALLY! WE CAN'T!
SERIOUSLY. JUST LET ME IN. SOMEBODY WILL SPOT US.
SHFL
YOU DON'T WANT PEOPLE TO SEE THIS?!
SHFL
SHFL
C'MON. REALLY. IT'LL ONLY TAKE A MINUTE. PLEEEE-ASE?
SHFL
I'M NOT SURE I LIKE THE WAY YOU'RE PHRASING THIS!
D-DO YOU REALLY JUST WANT TO TALK...?
YES. IT'S IMPOR-TANT.
OKAY ...
P-PLEASE COME IN.
SHUNK

Material Collection

The Making of Spaceship ASTRA

1:80 Scale Model: Part 2

Tiny LED light bulbs were added. It's so cool when they light up!

Mr. Kubo told me how much work it was to analyze my diagrams and map out a workable blueprint. Apparently the curvature of the bridge and the smaller details on the wings were especially difficult to build.

■ Construction Period: Jun. 26, 2017–Dec. 23, 2017

■ Work Hours Required: Approx. 222

■ Material Costs: Approx. 10,000 yen

■ Materials Used: Paulownia wood, white styrene sheets, clear styrene sheets, poster board, brass wire, styrene rods, fiber optics, guitar strings, LED lights, battery case, slide switch, PVC pipe, plastic model junk parts, plastic model decals, plastic model glue, instant-set glue, epoxy glue, G17 glue, surfacer, enamel paint, acrylic paint, pastels, energy, time, love

Thank you so much, Mr. Kubo, for building this amazing model!

ASTRA
LOST IN SPACE
#40

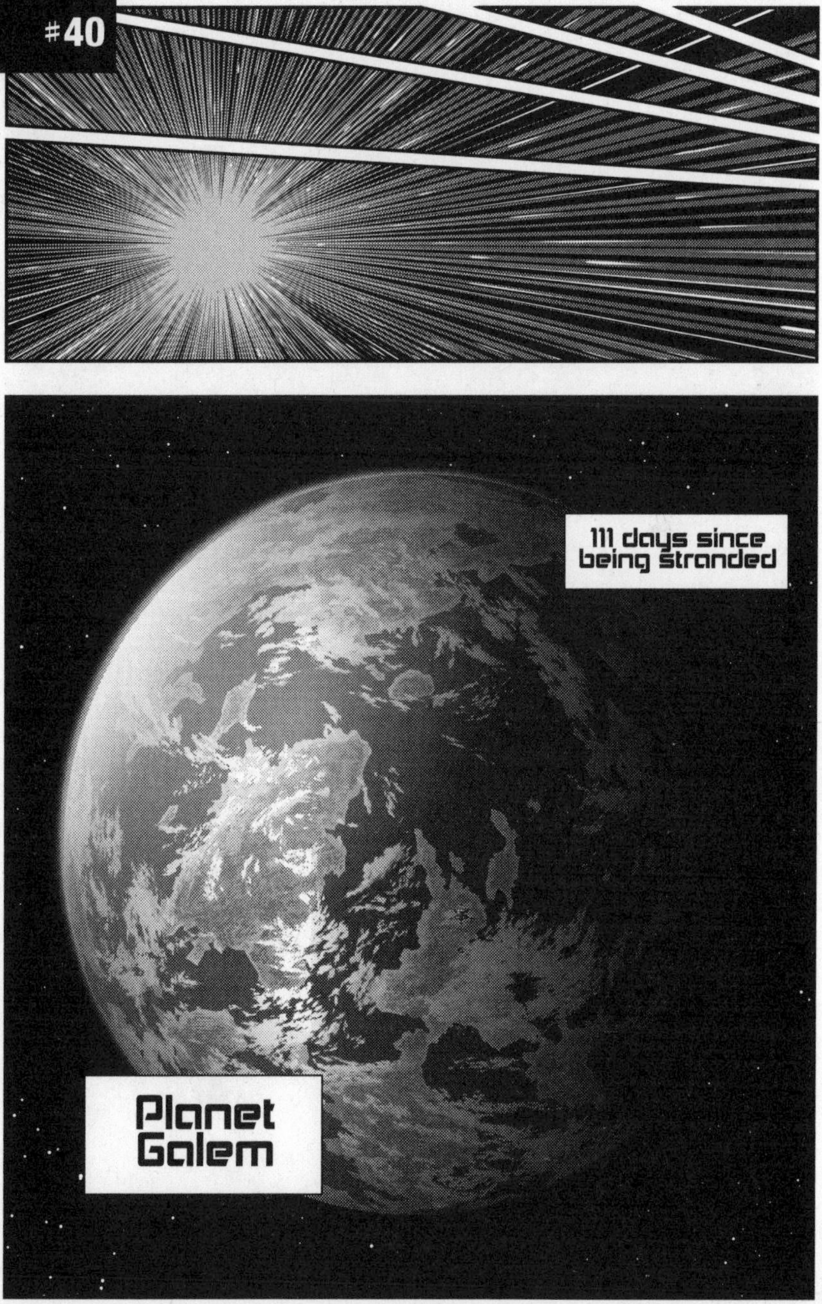
111 days since being stranded
Planet Galem

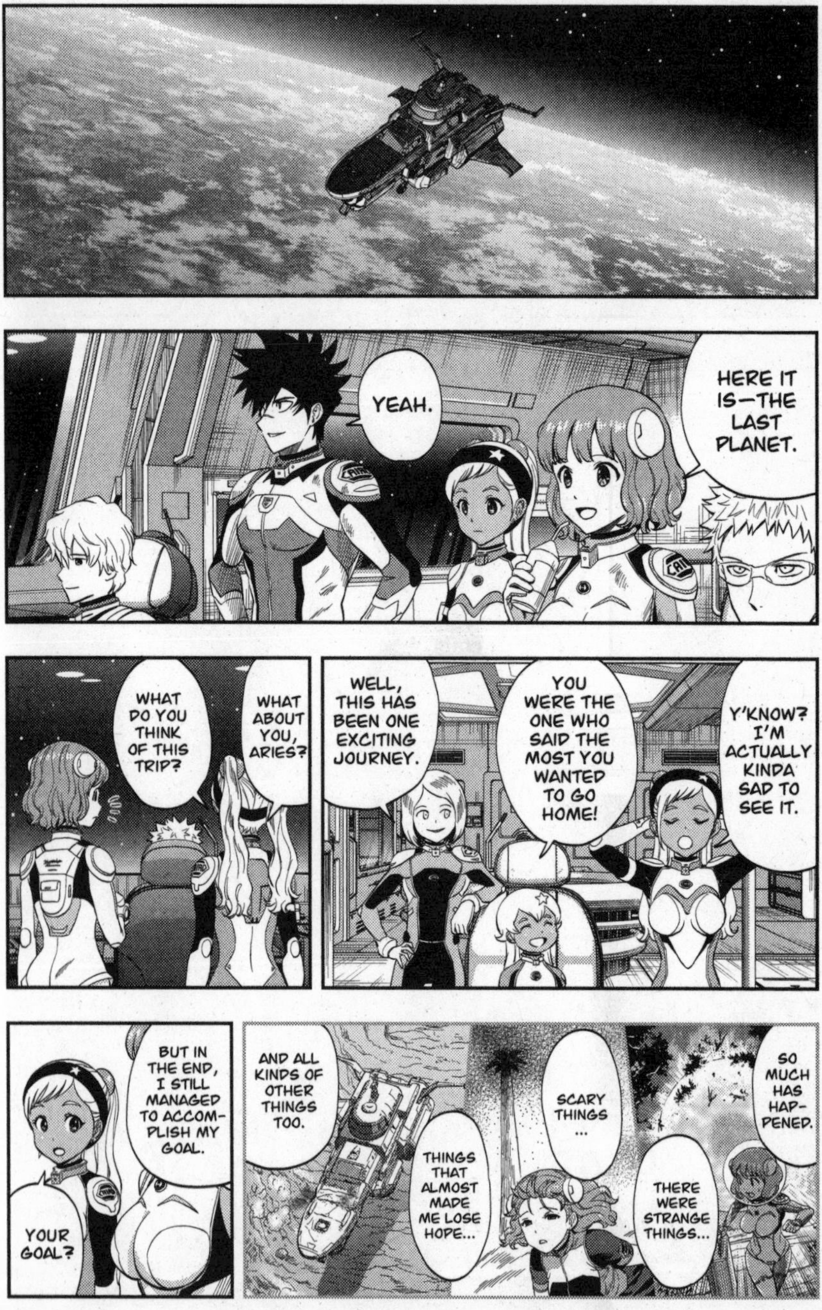
HERE IT IS—THE LAST PLANET.
YEAH.
Y'KNOW? I'M ACTUALLY KINDA SAD TO SEE IT.
YOU WERE THE ONE WHO SAID THE MOST YOU WANTED TO GO HOME!
WELL, THIS HAS BEEN ONE EXCITING JOURNEY.
WHAT ABOUT YOU, ARIES?
WHAT DO YOU THINK OF THIS TRIP?
SO MUCH HAS HAP-PENED.
THERE WERE STRANGE THINGS...
SCARY THINGS...
THINGS THAT ALMOST MADE ME LOSE HOPE...
AND ALL KINDS OF OTHER THINGS TOO.
BUT IN THE END, I STILL MANAGED TO ACCOM-PLISH MY GOAL.
YOUR GOAL?

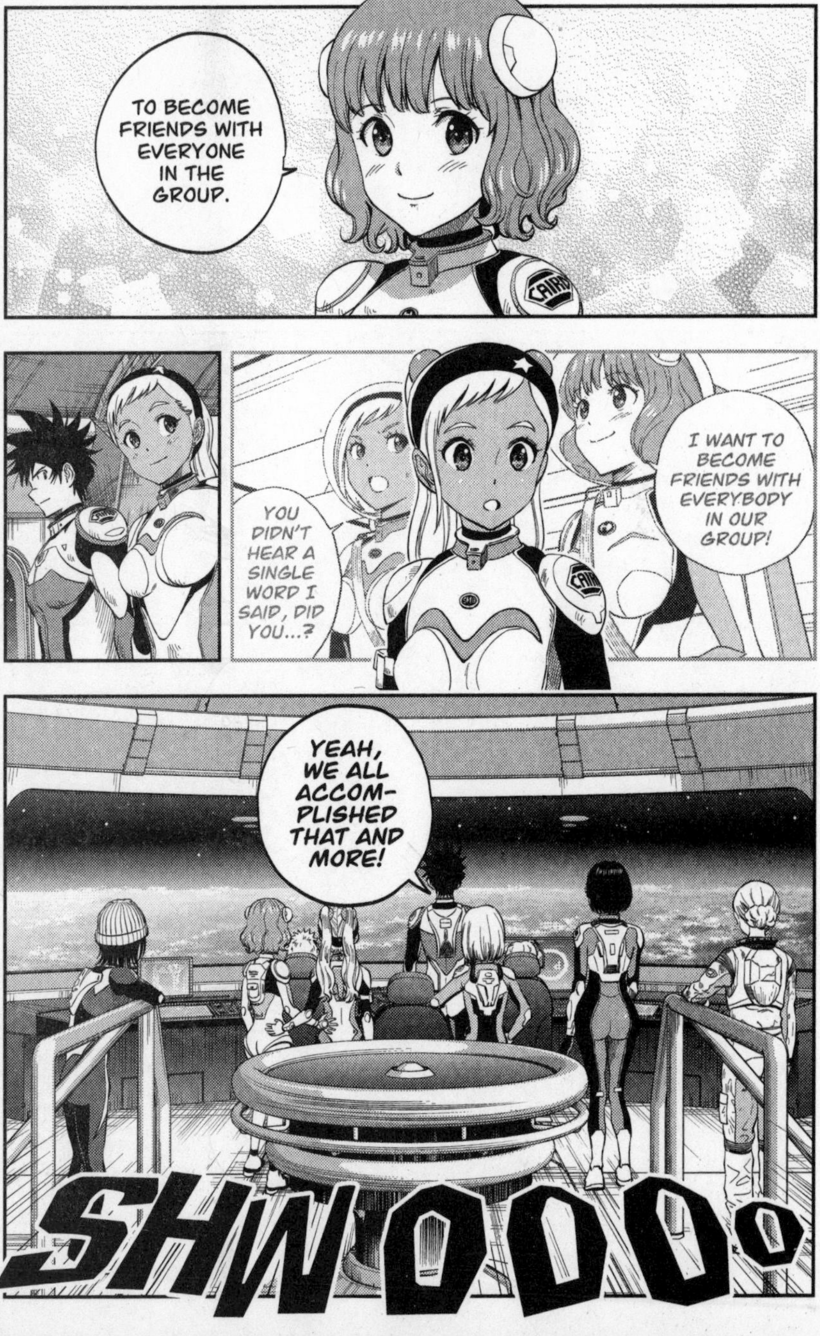
TO BECOME FRIENDS WITH EVERYONE IN THE GROUP.
I WANT TO BECOME FRIENDS WITH EVERYBODY IN OUR GROUP!
YOU DIDN'T HEAR A SINGLE WORD I SAID, DID YOU...?
YEAH, WE ALL ACCOM-PLISHED THAT AND MORE!
SHWOOOO

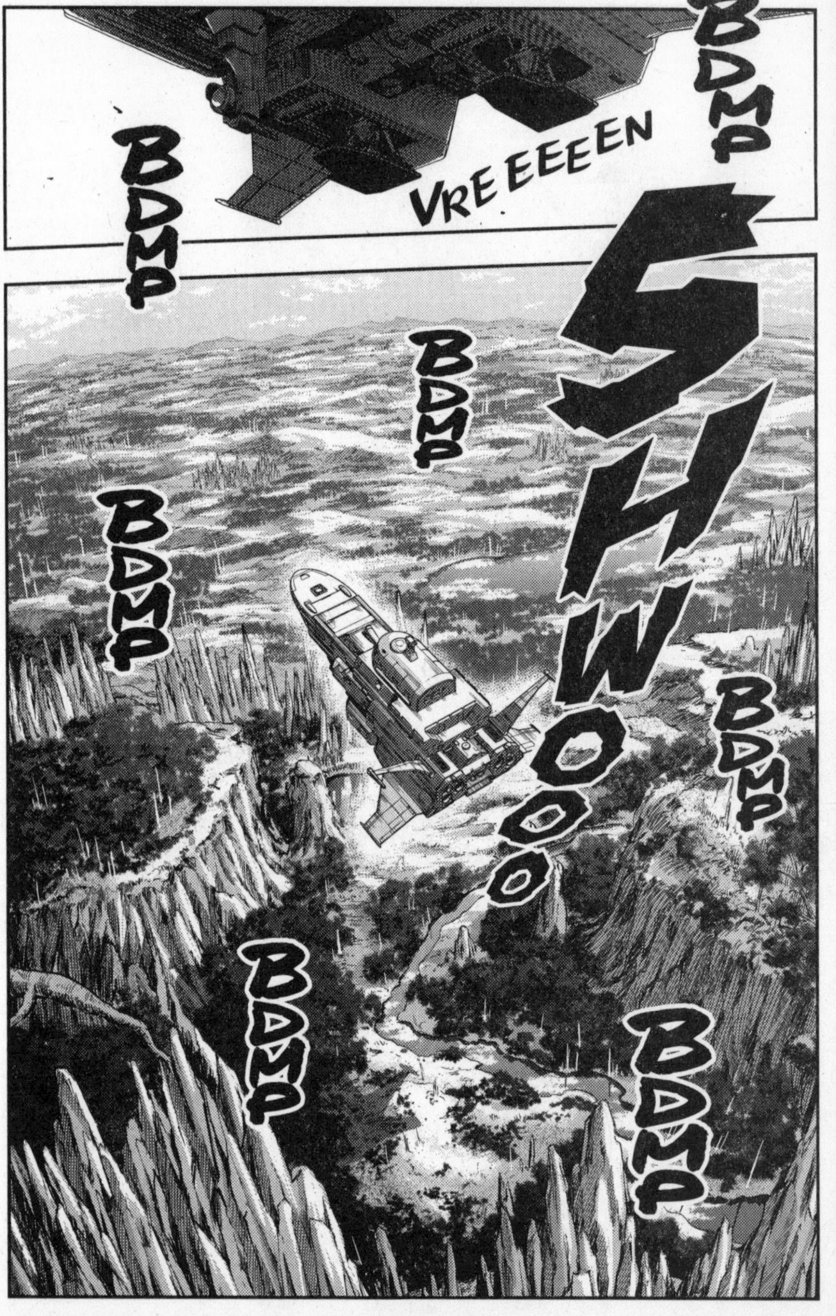
BDMP
VREEEEEN
BDMP
SHWOOOO
BDMP
BDMP
BDMP
BDMP
BDMP

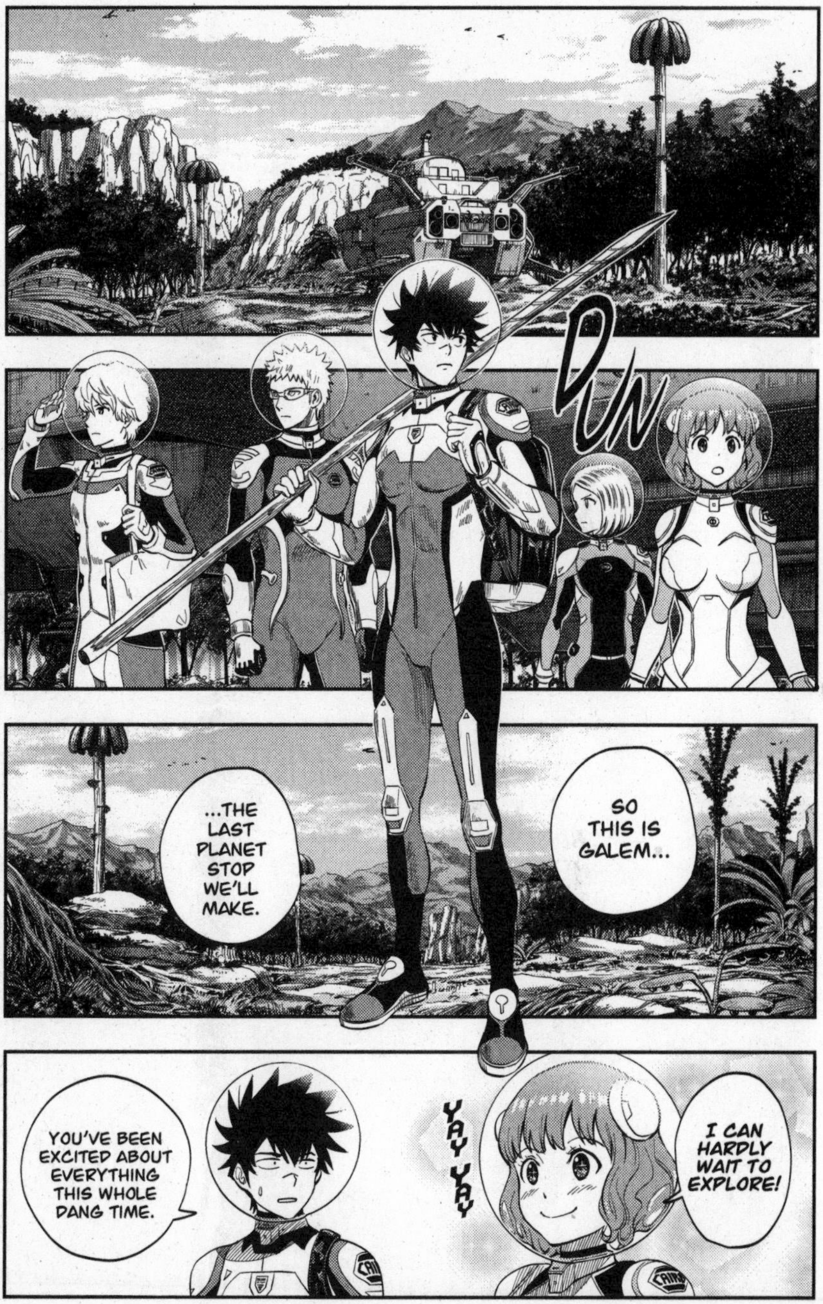
DUN
SO THIS IS GALEM...
...THE LAST PLANET STOP WE'LL MAKE.
I CAN HARDLY WAIT TO EXPLORE!
YAY YAY
YOU'VE BEEN EXCITED ABOUT EVERYTHING THIS WHOLE DANG TIME.

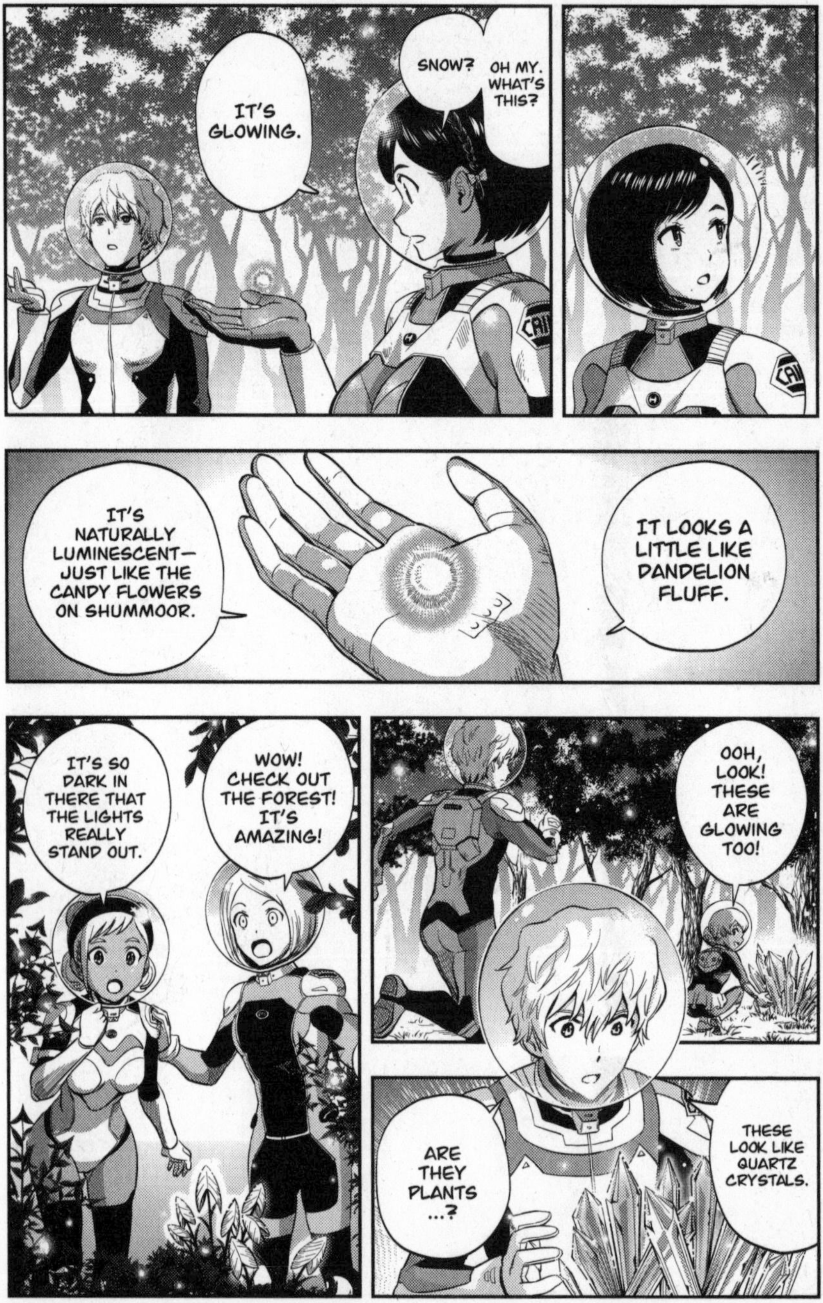
OH MY. WHAT'S THIS?
SNOW?
IT'S GLOWING.
IT LOOKS A LITTLE LIKE DANDELION FLUFF.
IT'S NATURALLY LUMINESCENT—JUST LIKE THE CANDY FLOWERS ON SHUMMOOR.
OOH, LOOK! THESE ARE GLOWING TOO!
THESE LOOK LIKE QUARTZ CRYSTALS.
ARE THEY PLANTS ...?
WOW! CHECK OUT THE FOREST! IT'S AMAZING!
IT'S SO DARK IN THERE THAT THE LIGHTS REALLY STAND OUT.

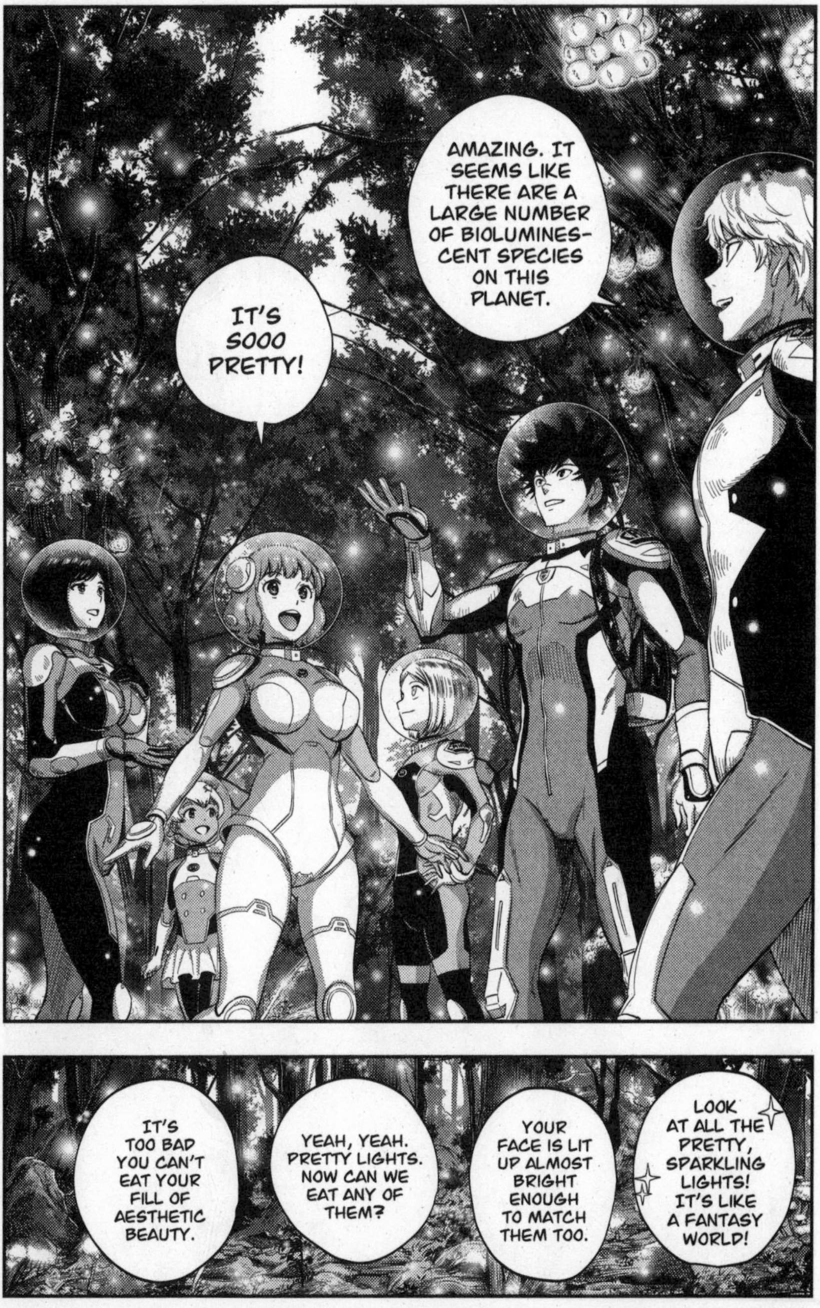
AMAZING. IT SEEMS LIKE THERE ARE A LARGE NUMBER OF BIOLUMINES-CENT SPECIES ON THIS PLANET.
IT'S SOOO PRETTY!
LOOK AT ALL THE PRETTY, SPARKLING LIGHTS! IT'S LIKE A FANTASY WORLD!
YOUR FACE IS LIT UP ALMOST BRIGHT ENOUGH TO MATCH THEM TOO.
YEAH, YEAH. PRETTY LIGHTS. NOW CAN WE EAT ANY OF THEM?
IT'S TOO BAD YOU CAN'T EAT YOUR FILL OF AESTHETIC BEAUTY.

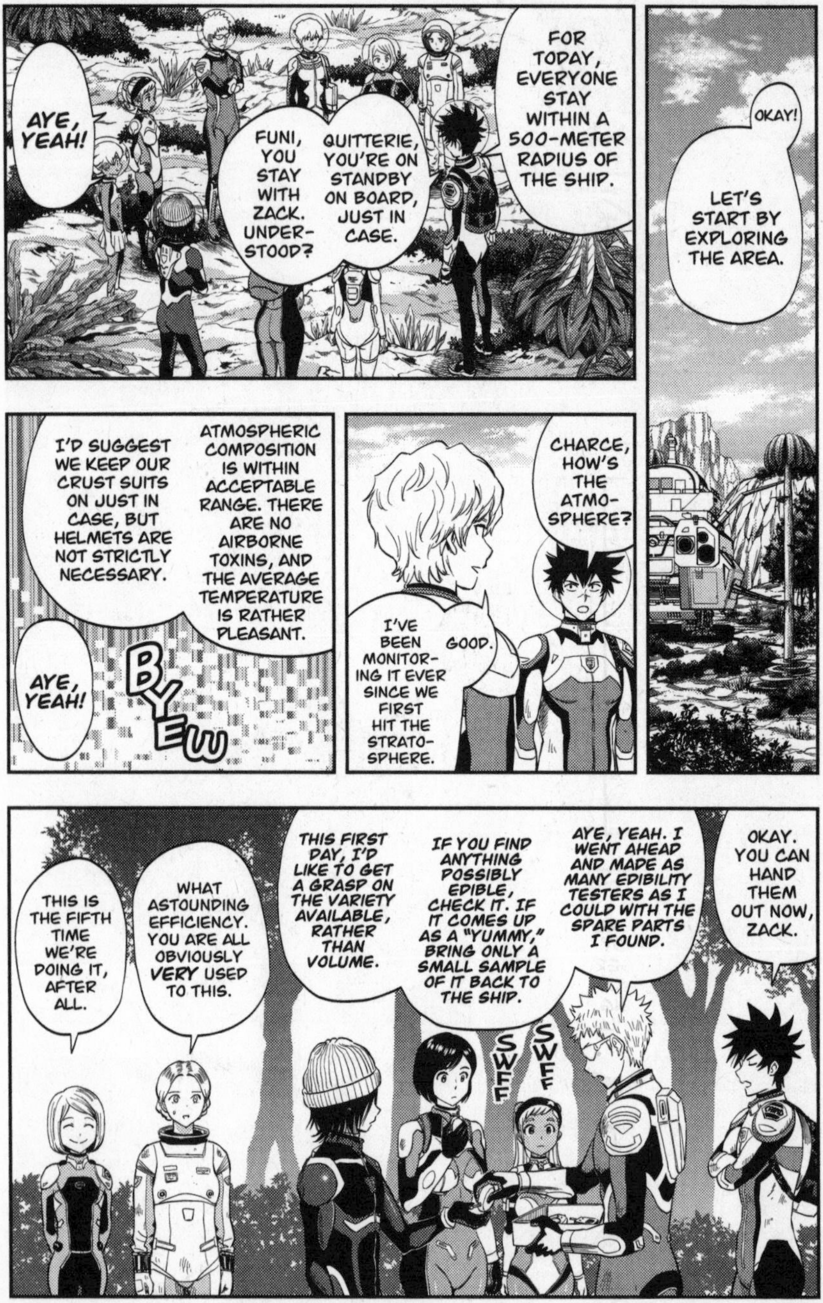
OKAY!
LET'S START BY EXPLORING THE AREA.
FOR TODAY, EVERYONE STAY WITHIN A 500-METER RADIUS OF THE SHIP.
QUITTERIE, YOU'RE ON STANDBY ON BOARD, JUST IN CASE.
FUNI, YOU STAY WITH ZACK. UNDER-STOOD?
AYE, YEAH!
CHARCE, HOW'S THE ATMO-SPHERE?
GOOD.
I'VE BEEN MONITOR-ING IT EVER SINCE WE FIRST HIT THE STRATO-SPHERE.
ATMOSPHERIC COMPOSITION IS WITHIN ACCEPTABLE RANGE. THERE ARE NO AIRBORNE TOXINS, AND THE AVERAGE TEMPERATURE IS RATHER PLEASANT.
I'D SUGGEST WE KEEP OUR CRUST SUITS ON JUST IN CASE, BUT HELMETS ARE NOT STRICTLY NECESSARY.
BYEW
AYE, YEAH!
OKAY. YOU CAN HAND THEM OUT NOW, ZACK.
AYE, YEAH. I WENT AHEAD AND MADE AS MANY EDIBILITY TESTERS AS I COULD WITH THE SPARE PARTS I FOUND.
IF YOU FIND ANYTHING POSSIBLY EDIBLE, CHECK IT. IF IT COMES UP AS A "YUMMY," BRING ONLY A SMALL SAMPLE OF IT BACK TO THE SHIP.
THIS FIRST DAY, I'D LIKE TO GET A GRASP ON THE VARIETY AVAILABLE, RATHER THAN VOLUME.
SWFF
SWFF
WHAT ASTOUNDING EFFICIENCY. YOU ARE ALL OBVIOUSLY VERY USED TO THIS.
THIS IS THE FIFTH TIME WE'RE DOING IT, AFTER ALL.

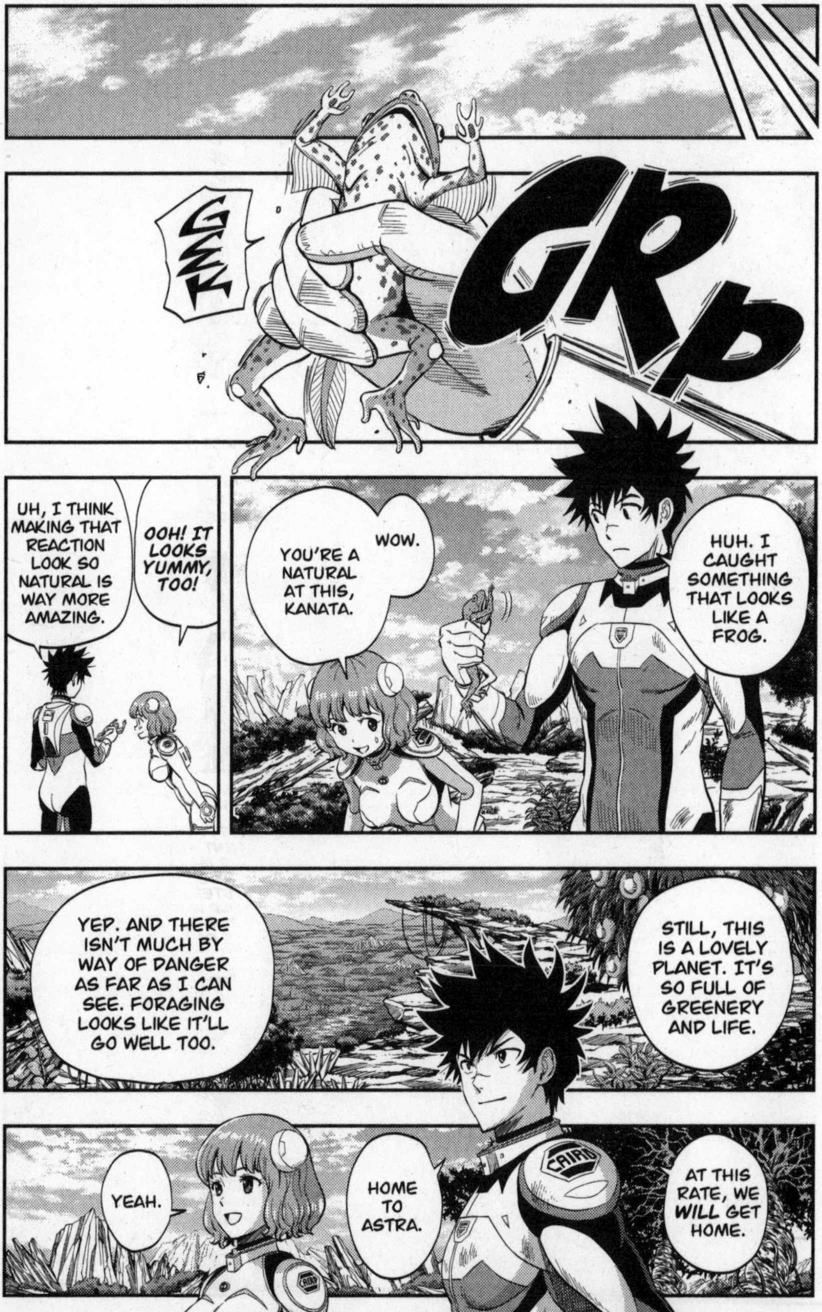
GRIP
GEKK
HUH. I CAUGHT SOMETHING THAT LOOKS LIKE A FROG.
WOW.
YOU'RE A NATURAL AT THIS, KANATA.
OOH! IT LOOKS YUMMY, TOO!
UH, I THINK MAKING THAT REACTION LOOK SO NATURAL IS WAY MORE AMAZING.
STILL, THIS IS A LOVELY PLANET. IT'S SO FULL OF GREENERY AND LIFE.
YEP. AND THERE ISN'T MUCH BY WAY OF DANGER AS FAR AS I CAN SEE. FORAGING LOOKS LIKE IT'LL GO WELL TOO.
AT THIS RATE, WE ***WILL*** GET HOME.
HOME TO ASTRA.
YEAH.

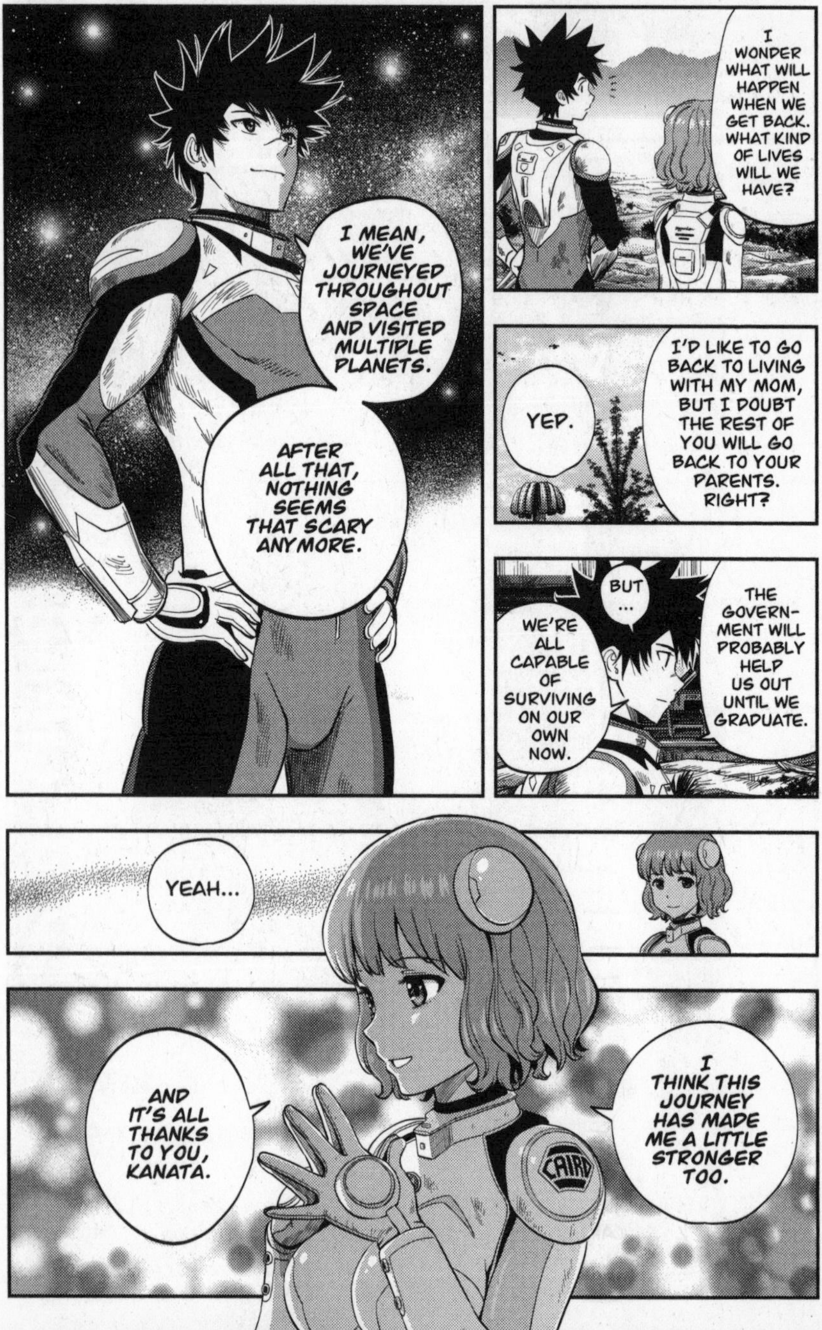
I WONDER WHAT WILL HAPPEN WHEN WE GET BACK. WHAT KIND OF LIVES WILL WE HAVE?
I'D LIKE TO GO BACK TO LIVING WITH MY MOM, BUT I DOUBT THE REST OF YOU WILL GO BACK TO YOUR PARENTS. RIGHT?
YEP.
THE GOVERNMENT WILL PROBABLY HELP US OUT UNTIL WE GRADUATE.
BUT ...
WE'RE ALL CAPABLE OF SURVIVING ON OUR OWN NOW.
I MEAN, WE'VE JOURNEYED THROUGHOUT SPACE AND VISITED MULTIPLE PLANETS.
AFTER ALL THAT, NOTHING SEEMS THAT SCARY ANYMORE.
YEAH...
I THINK THIS JOURNEY HAS MADE ME A LITTLE STRONGER TOO.
CAIRD
AND IT'S ALL THANKS TO YOU, KANATA.

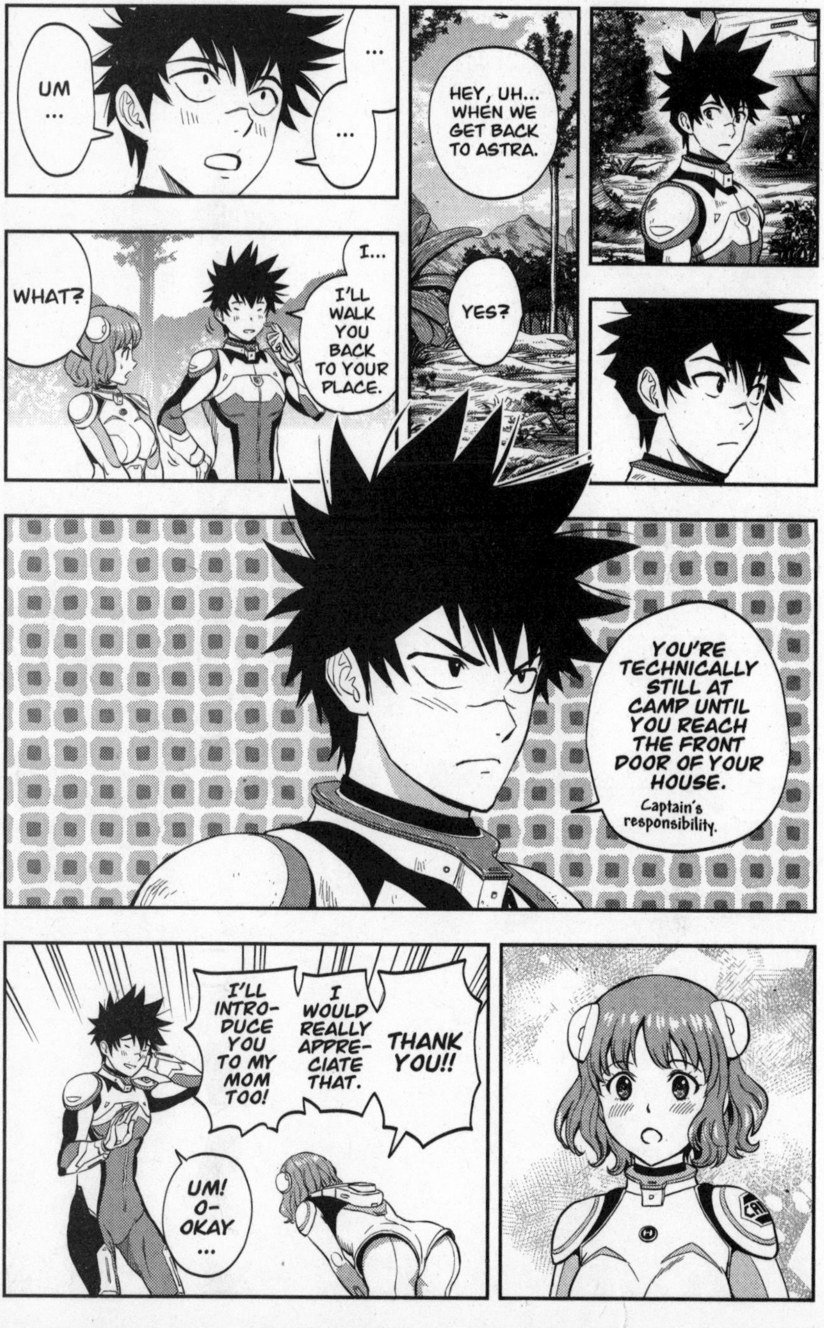
HEY, UH... WHEN WE GET BACK TO ASTRA.
YES?
...
...
UM ...
I...
I'LL WALK YOU BACK TO YOUR PLACE.
WHAT?
YOU'RE TECHNICALLY STILL AT CAMP UNTIL YOU REACH THE FRONT DOOR OF YOUR HOUSE.
Captain's responsibility.
THANK YOU!!
I WOULD REALLY APPRE-CIATE THAT.
I'LL INTRO-DUCE YOU TO MY MOM TOO!
UM! O-OKAY ...

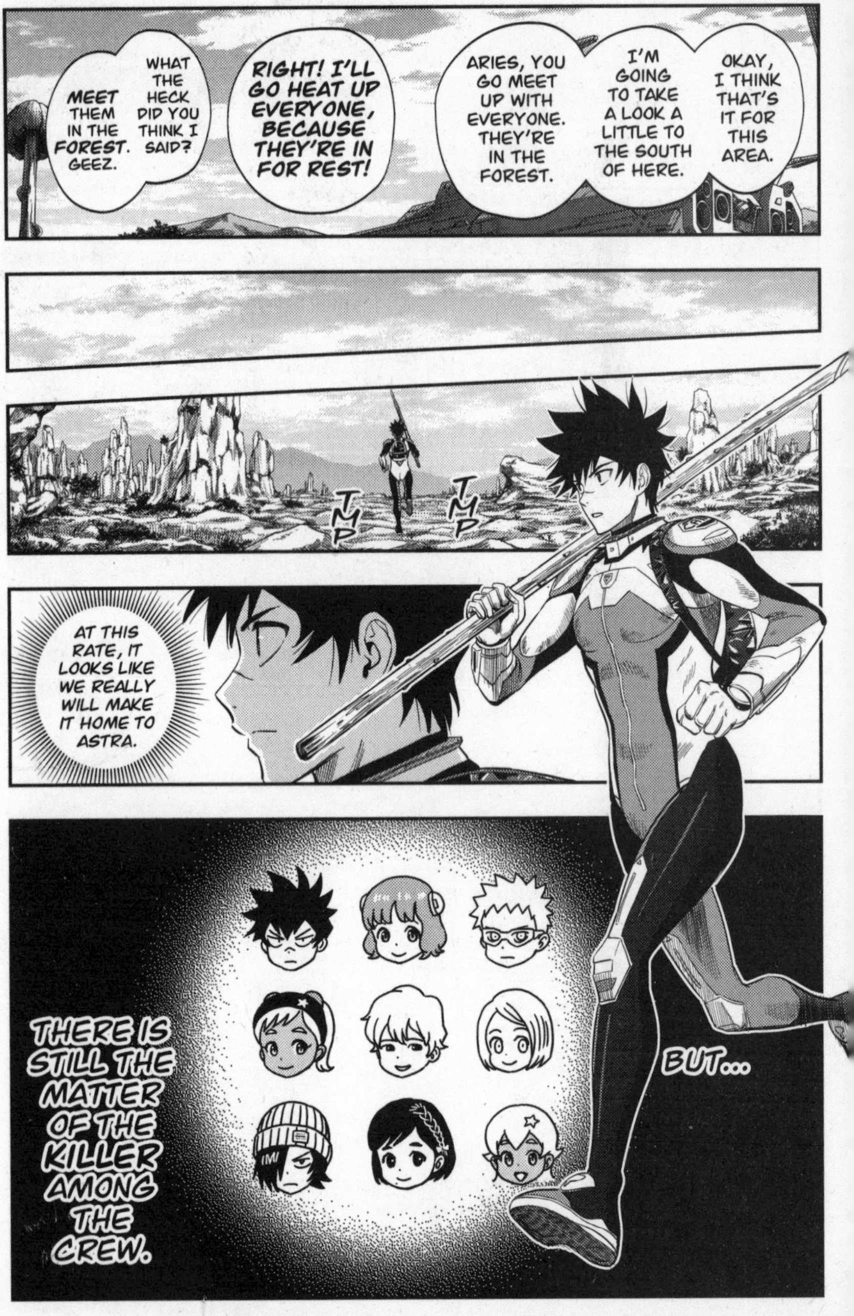
OKAY, I THINK THAT'S IT FOR THIS AREA.
I'M GOING TO TAKE A LOOK A LITTLE TO THE SOUTH OF HERE.
ARIES, YOU GO MEET UP WITH EVERYONE. THEY'RE IN THE FOREST.
RIGHT! I'LL GO HEAT UP EVERYONE, BECAUSE THEY'RE IN FOR REST!
WHAT THE HECK DID YOU THINK I SAID?
MEET THEM IN THE FOREST. GEEZ.
TMP
TMP
AT THIS RATE, IT LOOKS LIKE WE REALLY WILL MAKE IT HOME TO ASTRA.
BUT...
THERE IS STILL THE MATTER OF THE KILLER AMONG THE CREW.

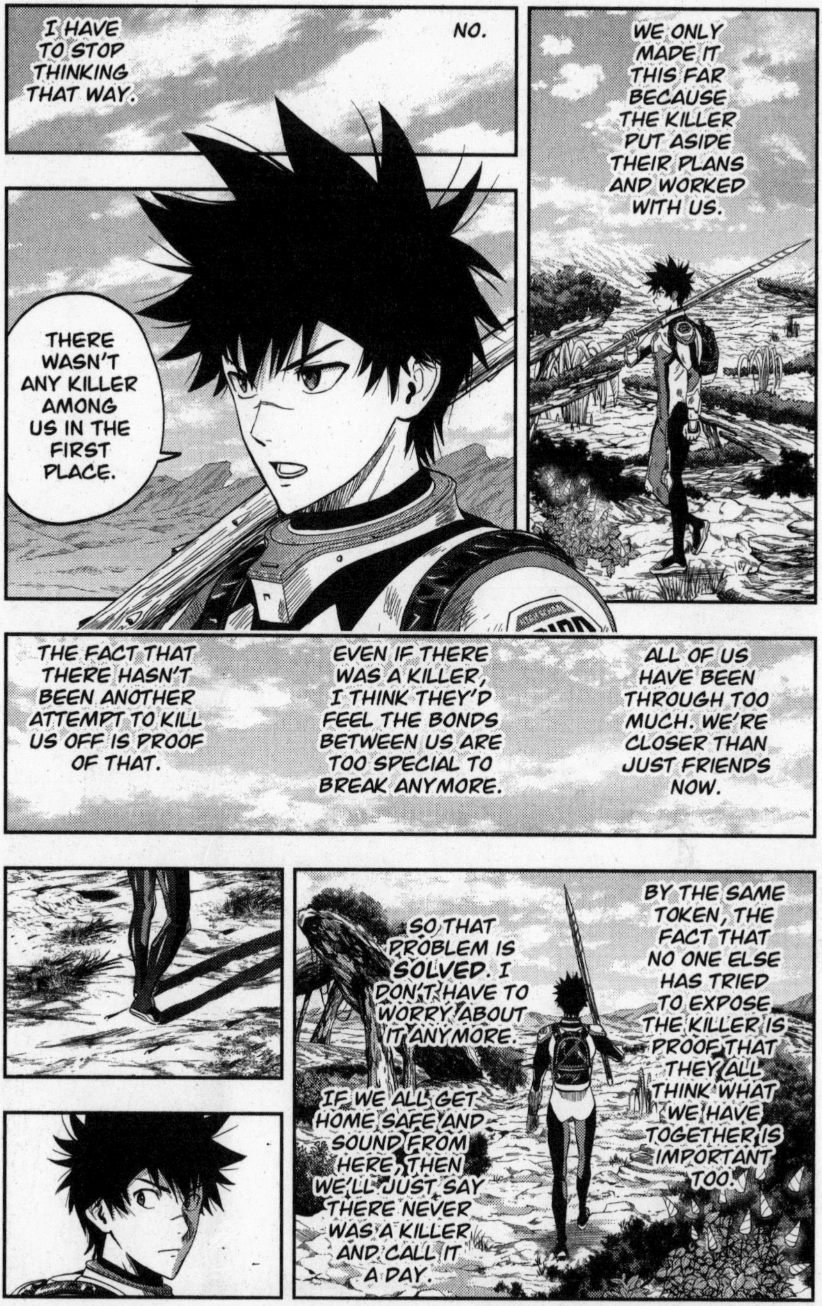
WE ONLY MADE IT THIS FAR BECAUSE THE KILLER PUT ASIDE THEIR PLANS AND WORKED WITH US.
NO.
I HAVE TO STOP THINKING THAT WAY.
THERE WASN'T ANY KILLER AMONG US IN THE FIRST PLACE.
ALL OF US HAVE BEEN THROUGH TOO MUCH. WE'RE CLOSER THAN JUST FRIENDS NOW.
EVEN IF THERE WAS A KILLER, I THINK THEY'D FEEL THE BONDS BETWEEN US ARE TOO SPECIAL TO BREAK ANYMORE.
THE FACT THAT THERE HASN'T BEEN ANOTHER ATTEMPT TO KILL US OFF IS PROOF OF THAT.
BY THE SAME TOKEN, THE FACT THAT NO ONE ELSE HAS TRIED TO EXPOSE THE KILLER IS PROOF THAT THEY ALL THINK WHAT WE HAVE TOGETHER IS IMPORTANT TOO.
SO THAT PROBLEM IS **SOLVED**. I DON'T HAVE TO WORRY ABOUT IT ANYMORE.
IF WE ALL GET HOME SAFE AND SOUND FROM HERE, THEN WE'LL JUST SAY THERE NEVER WAS A KILLER AND CALL IT A DAY.

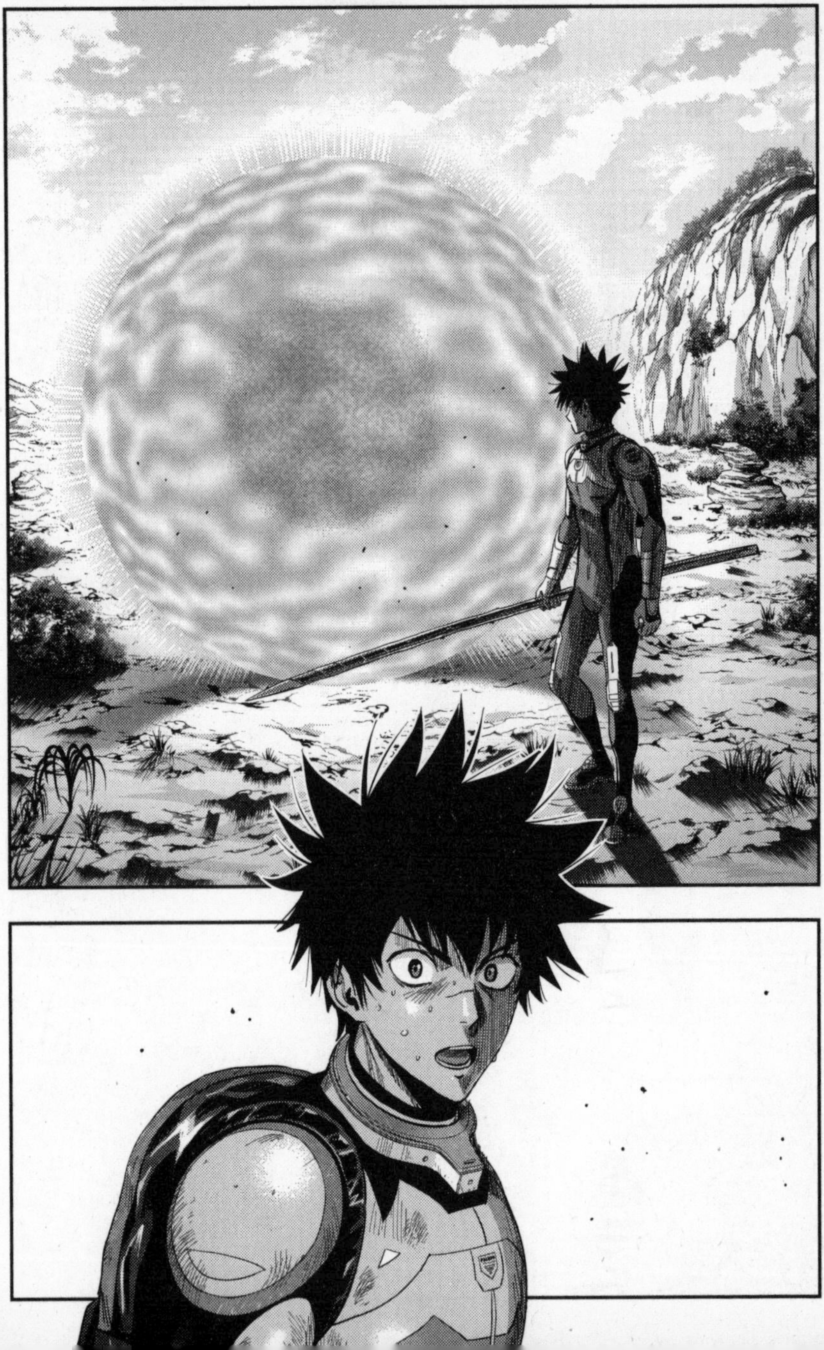

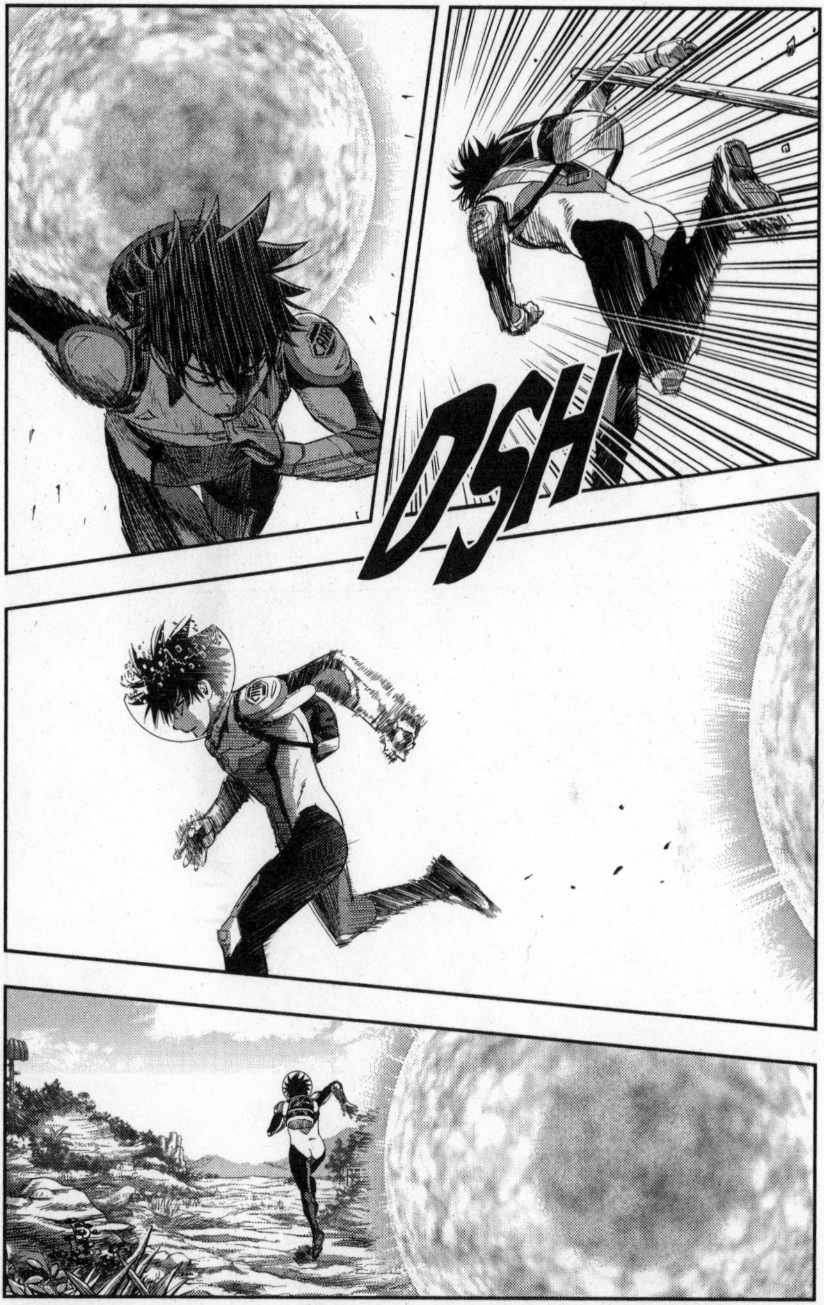
DSH

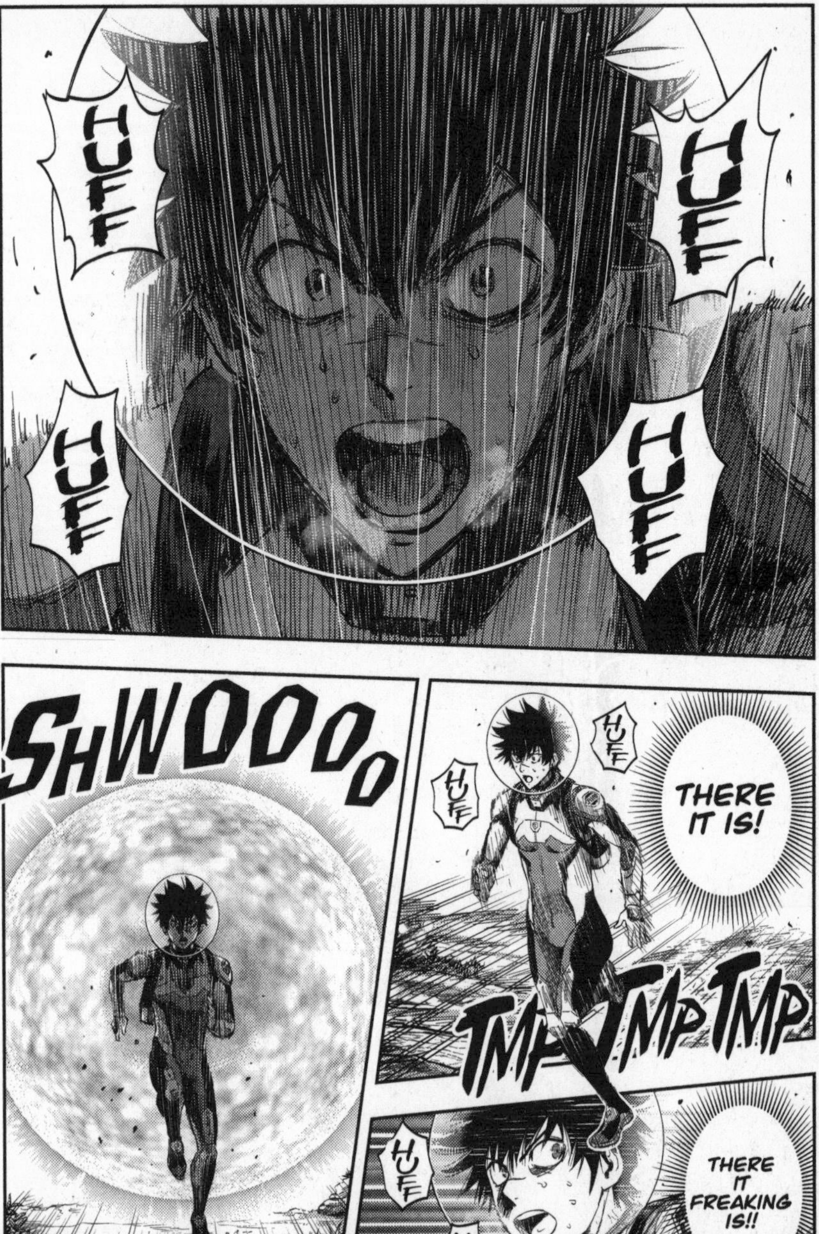
HUFF
HUFF
HUFF
HUFF
HUFF
HUFF
THERE IT IS!
TMP TMP TMP
HUFF
HUFF
THERE IT FREAKING IS!!
SHWOOOO

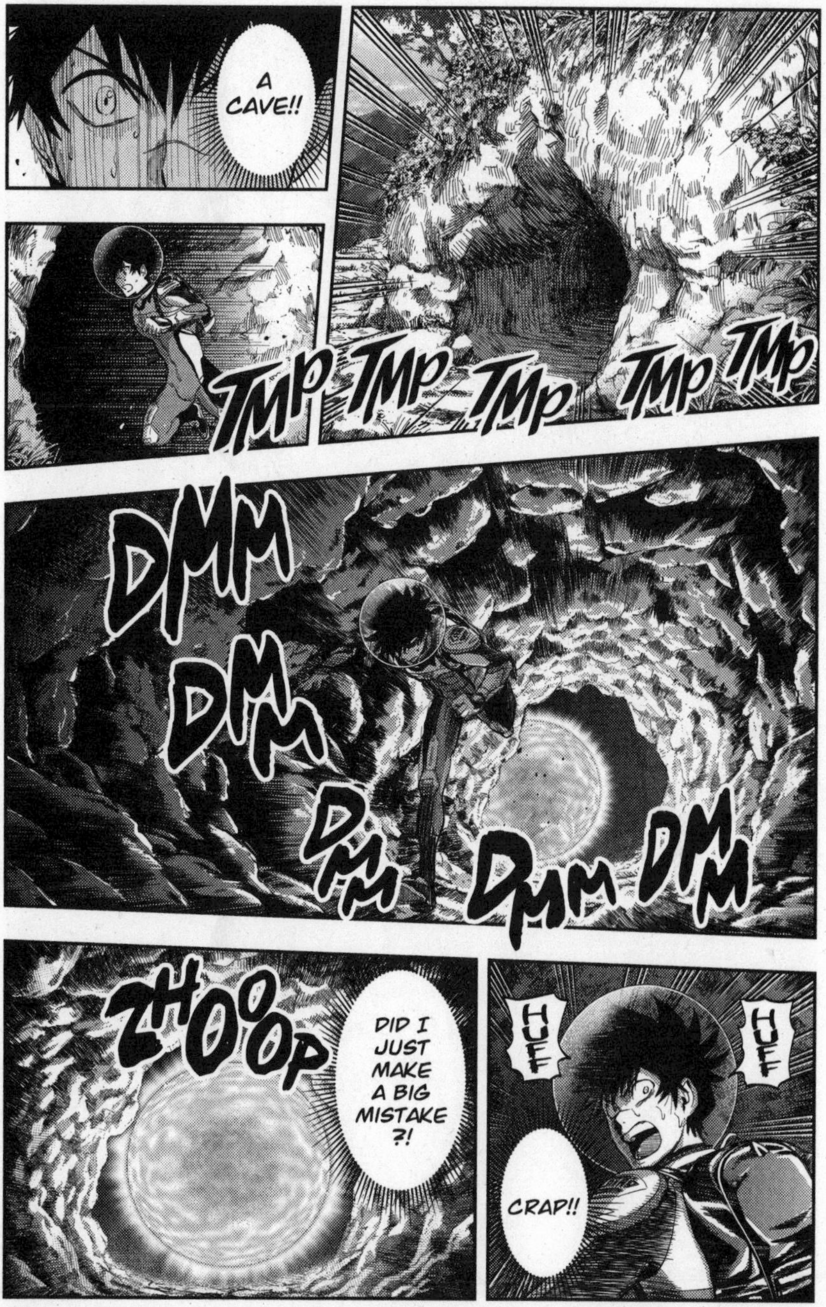
A CAVE!!
TMP TMP TMP TMP TMP
DMM DMM DMM DMM DMM
HUFF HUFF
CRAP!!
ZHOOOP
DID I JUST MAKE A BIG MISTAKE?!

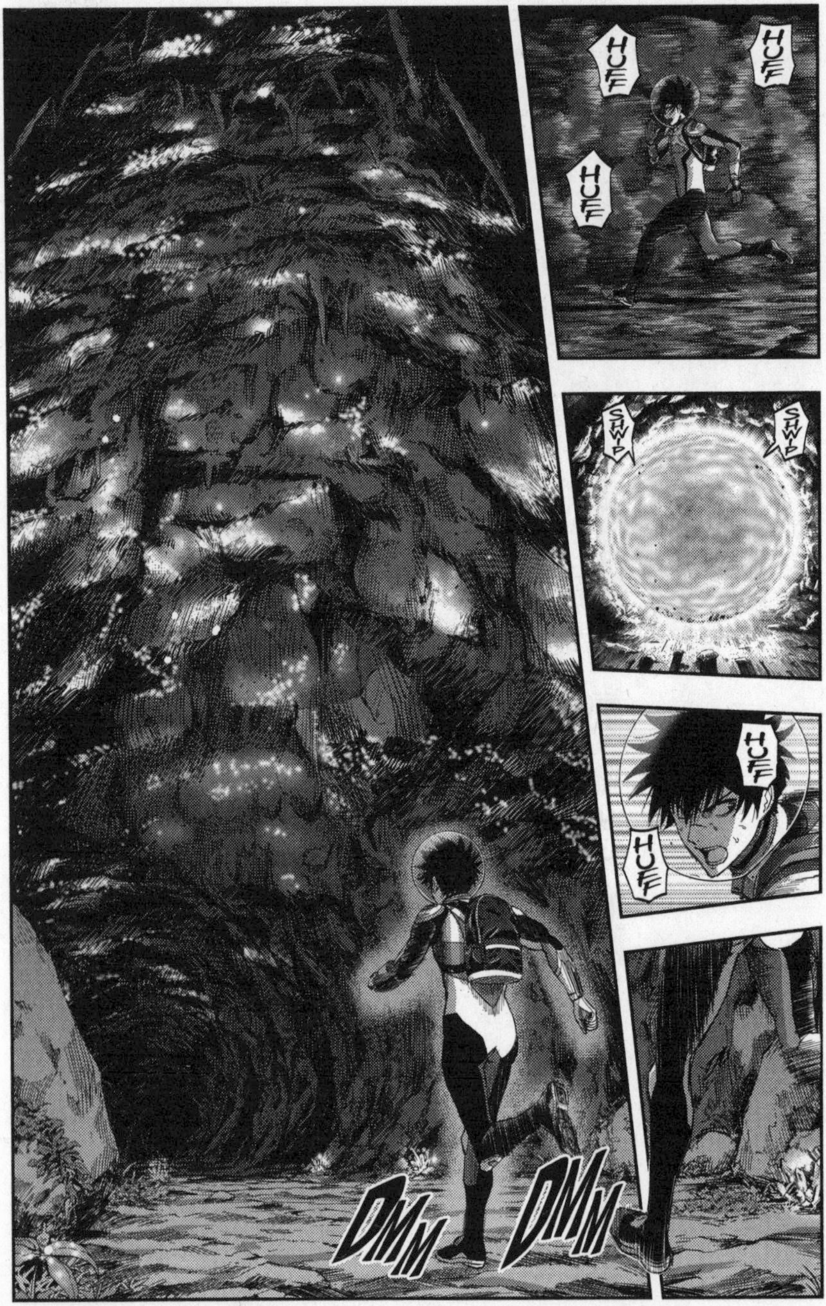
HUFF
HUFF
HUFF
SHWIP
SHWIP
HUFF
HUFF
DMM
DMM

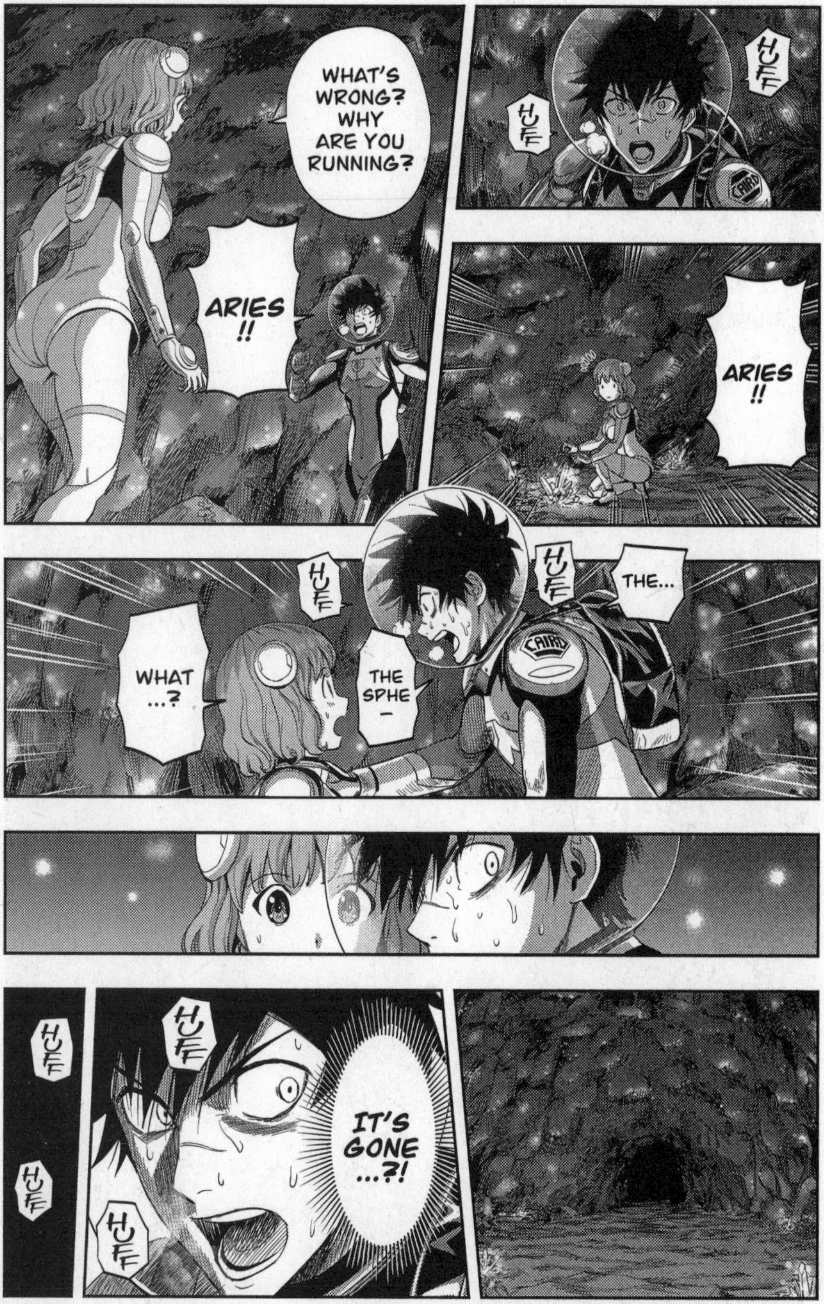
HUFF
HUFF
ARIES!!
WHAT'S WRONG? WHY ARE YOU RUNNING?
ARIES!!
HUFF
THE...
HUFF
THE SPHE—
WHAT...?
HUFF
IT'S GONE...?!
HUFF
HUFF
HUFF

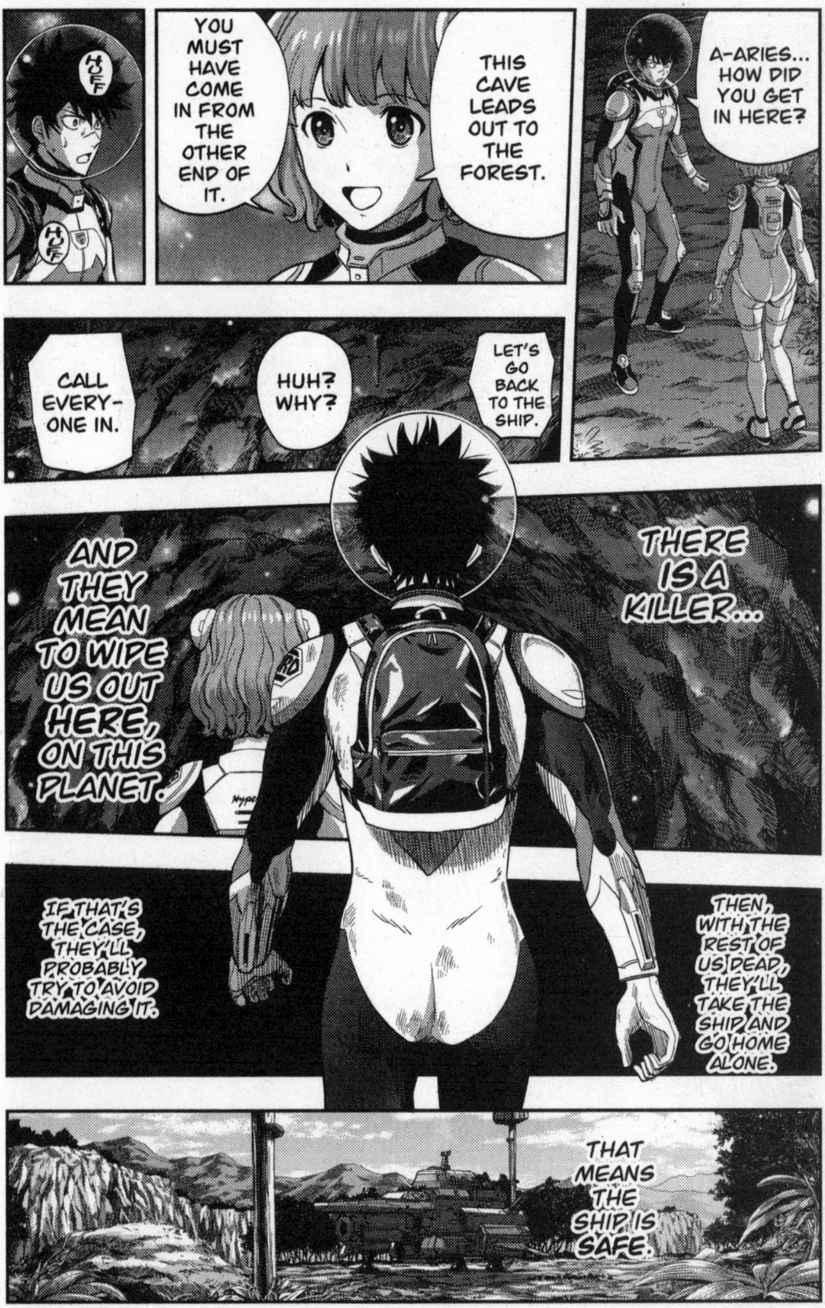
A-ARIES... HOW DID YOU GET IN HERE?
THIS CAVE LEADS OUT TO THE FOREST.
YOU MUST HAVE COME IN FROM THE OTHER END OF IT.
HUFF
HUFF
LET'S GO BACK TO THE SHIP.
HUH? WHY?
CALL EVERY-ONE IN.
THERE IS A KILLER...
AND THEY MEAN TO WIPE US OUT HERE, ON THIS PLANET.
THEN, WITH THE REST OF US DEAD, THEY'LL TAKE THE SHIP AND GO HOME ALONE.
IF THAT'S THE CASE, THEY'LL PROBABLY TRY TO AVOID DAMAGING IT.
THAT MEANS THE SHIP IS SAFE.

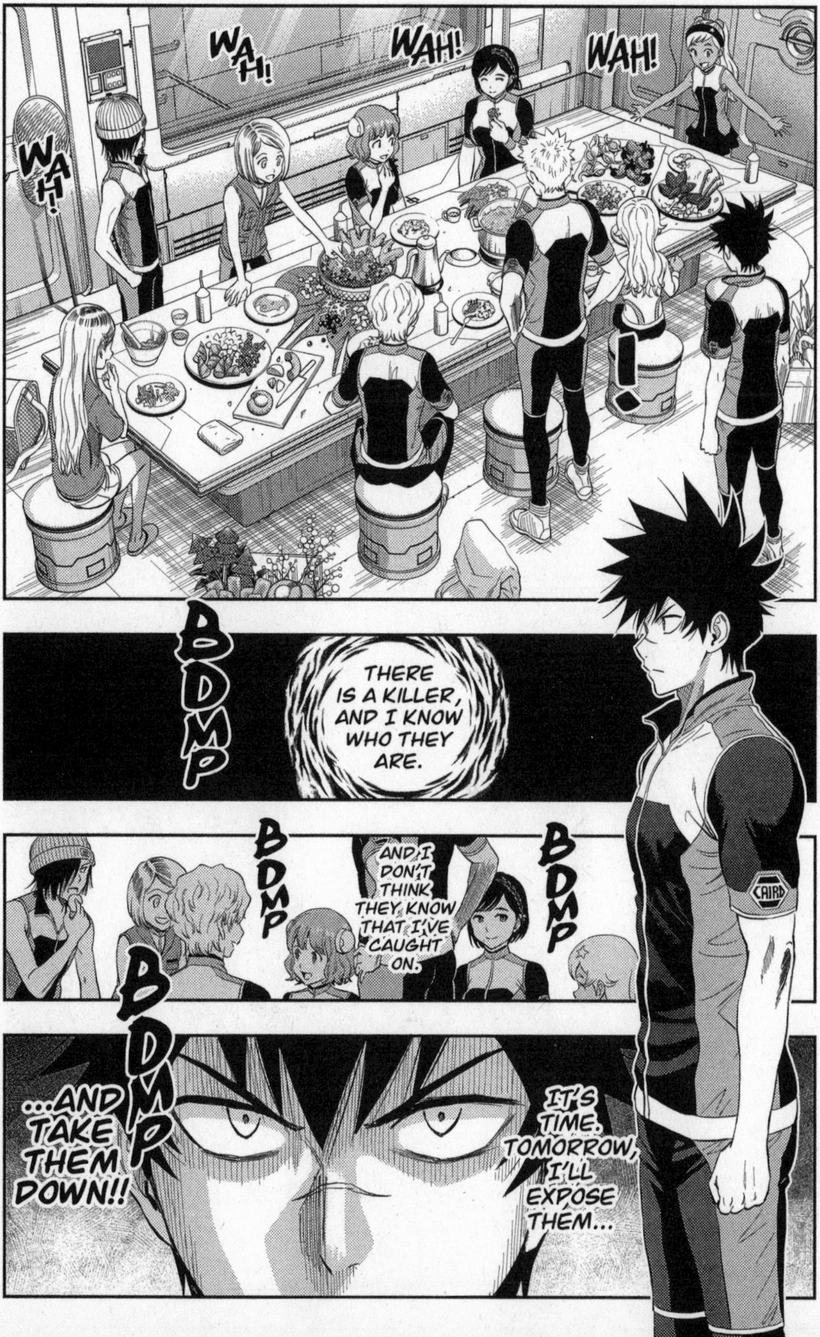
WAH!
WAH!
WAH!
WAH!
THERE IS A KILLER, AND I KNOW WHO THEY ARE.
BDMP
BDMP
AND I DON'T THINK THEY KNOW THAT I'VE CAUGHT ON.
BDMP
IT'S TIME. TOMORROW, I'LL EXPOSE THEM...
BDMP
...AND TAKE THEM DOWN!!

KANATA

The original concept for this manga was based heavily on Jules Verne's *Two Years' Vacation*. I planned to have 15 characters, just like in that story. However, once it was decided this would only be a short-term serialization, the cast was pared down to nine. Some characters were merged together, while others underwent major changes. Here are some rough sketches of those original characters and how they became who they are.

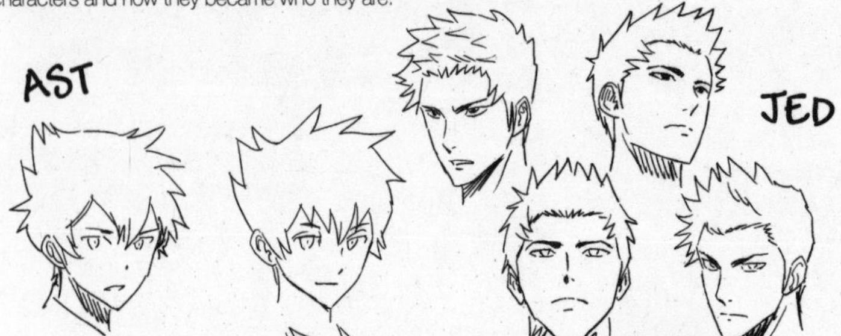
AST
JED

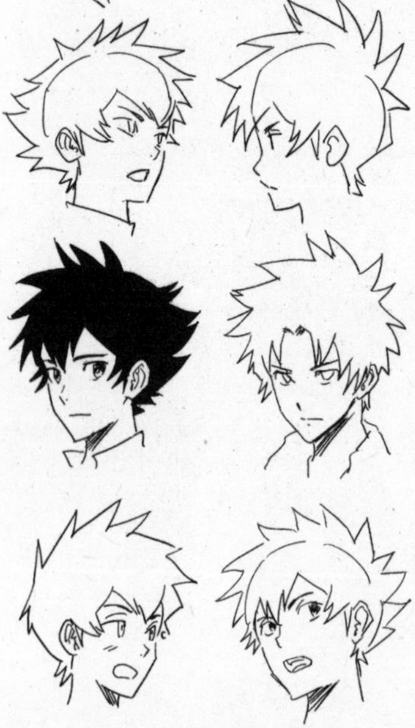

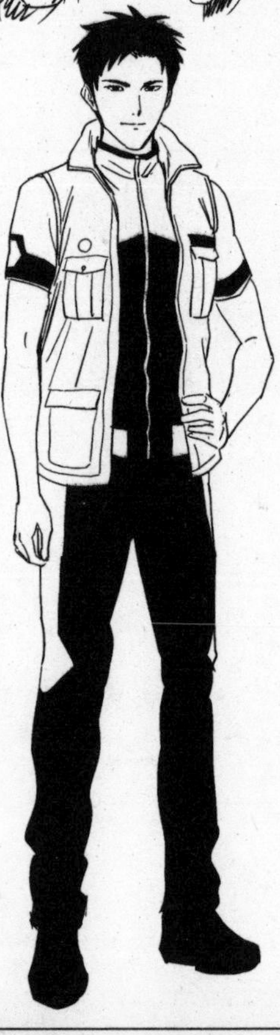

When there were still going to be 15 characters, I decided to challenge myself by making the main character an introverted boy who was very un-main-character-like. The captain was going to be a serious and dependable older boy named Jed. The plan was for him to fall from grace at the story's midpoint, with the main character, who had grown across their journey, rising to take his place. But we eventually decided that having the main character make a bad impression at the start of the story would be too big of a risk and that the captain should be the main character from the get-go. So, in a way, Kanata was the last member of the crew we finalized.

ASTRA LOST IN SPACE

#41

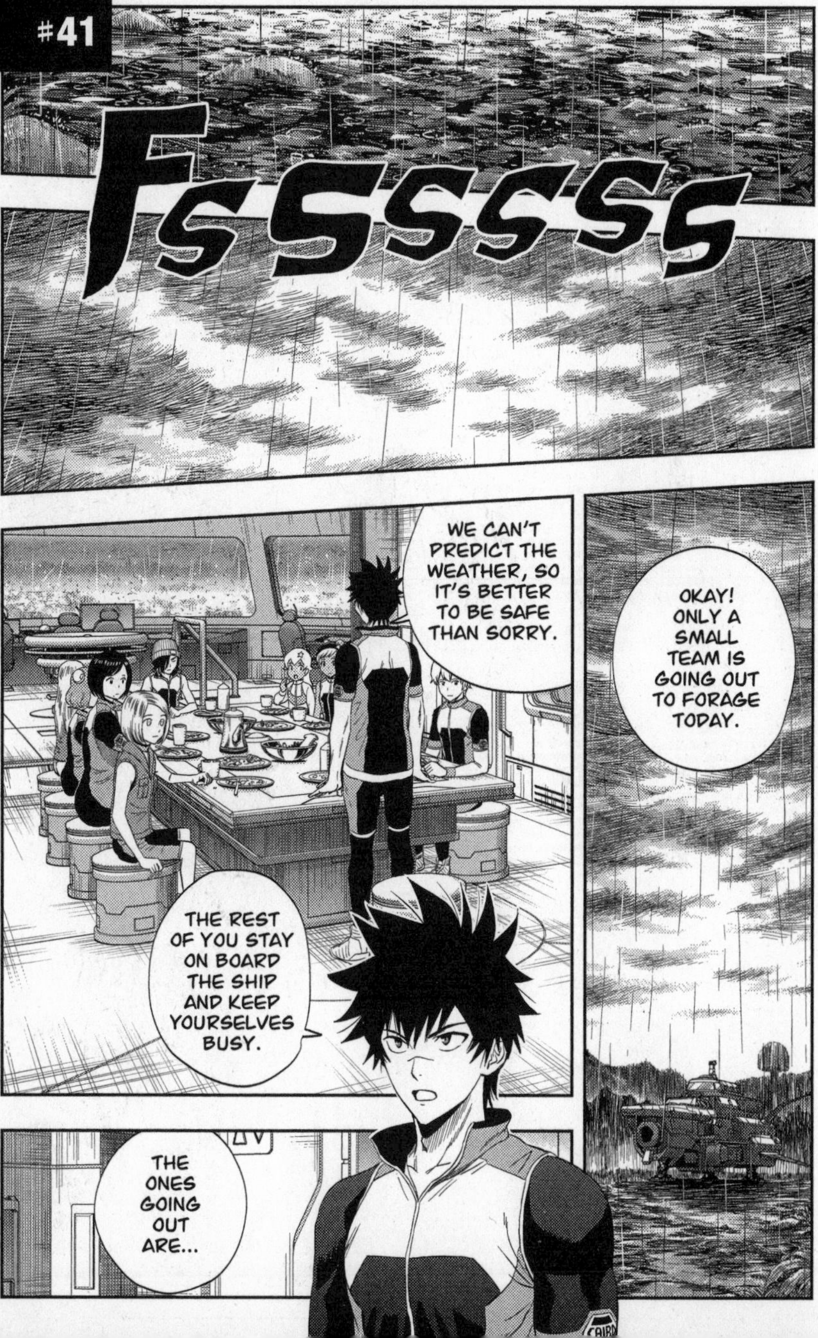
FSSSSSS
OKAY! ONLY A SMALL TEAM IS GOING OUT TO FORAGE TODAY.
WE CAN'T PREDICT THE WEATHER, SO IT'S BETTER TO BE SAFE THAN SORRY.
THE REST OF YOU STAY ON BOARD THE SHIP AND KEEP YOURSELVES BUSY.
THE ONES GOING OUT ARE...

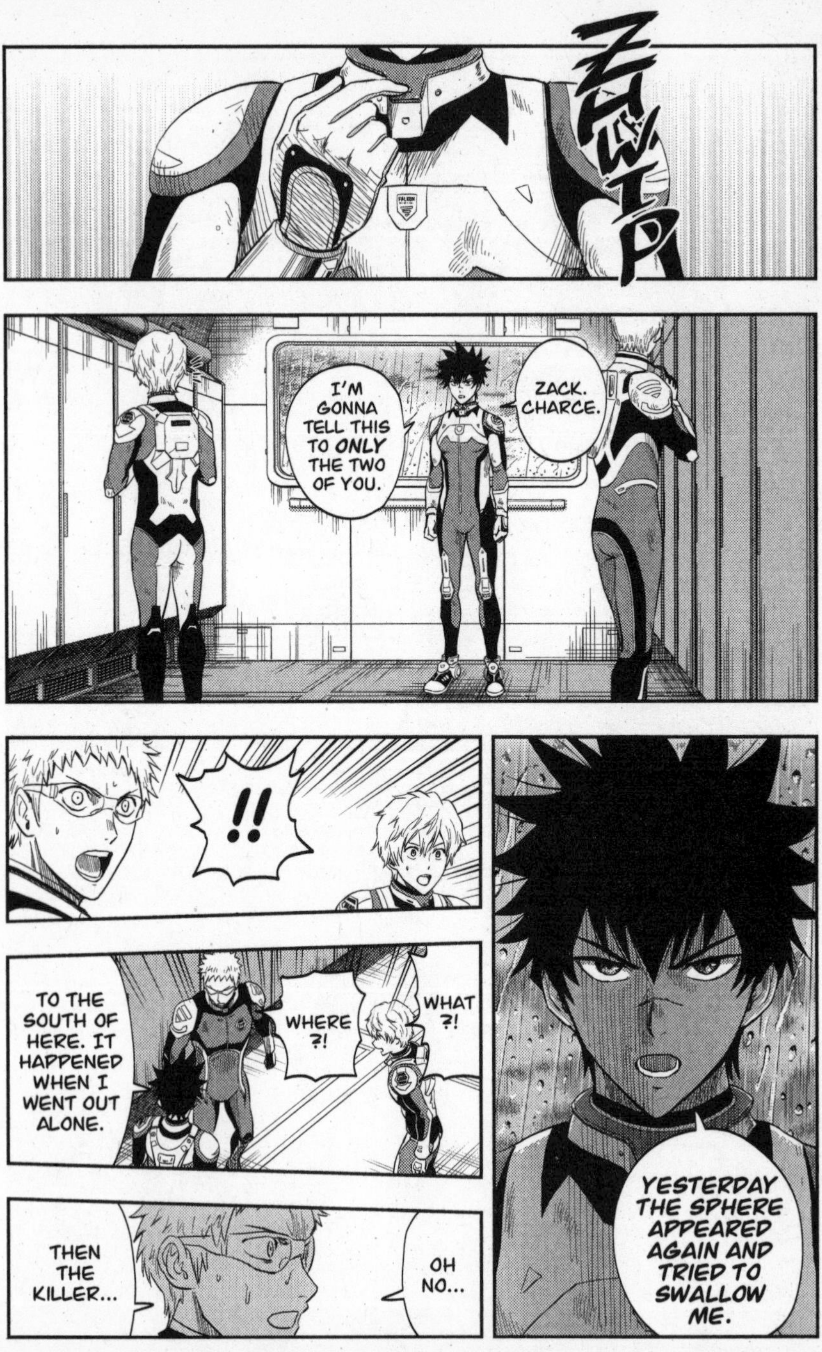
ZWIP
ZACK. CHARCE.
I'M GONNA TELL THIS TO ONLY THE TWO OF YOU.
YESTERDAY THE SPHERE APPEARED AGAIN AND TRIED TO SWALLOW ME.
!!
WHAT ?!
WHERE ?!
TO THE SOUTH OF HERE. IT HAPPENED WHEN I WENT OUT ALONE.
OH NO...
THEN THE KILLER...

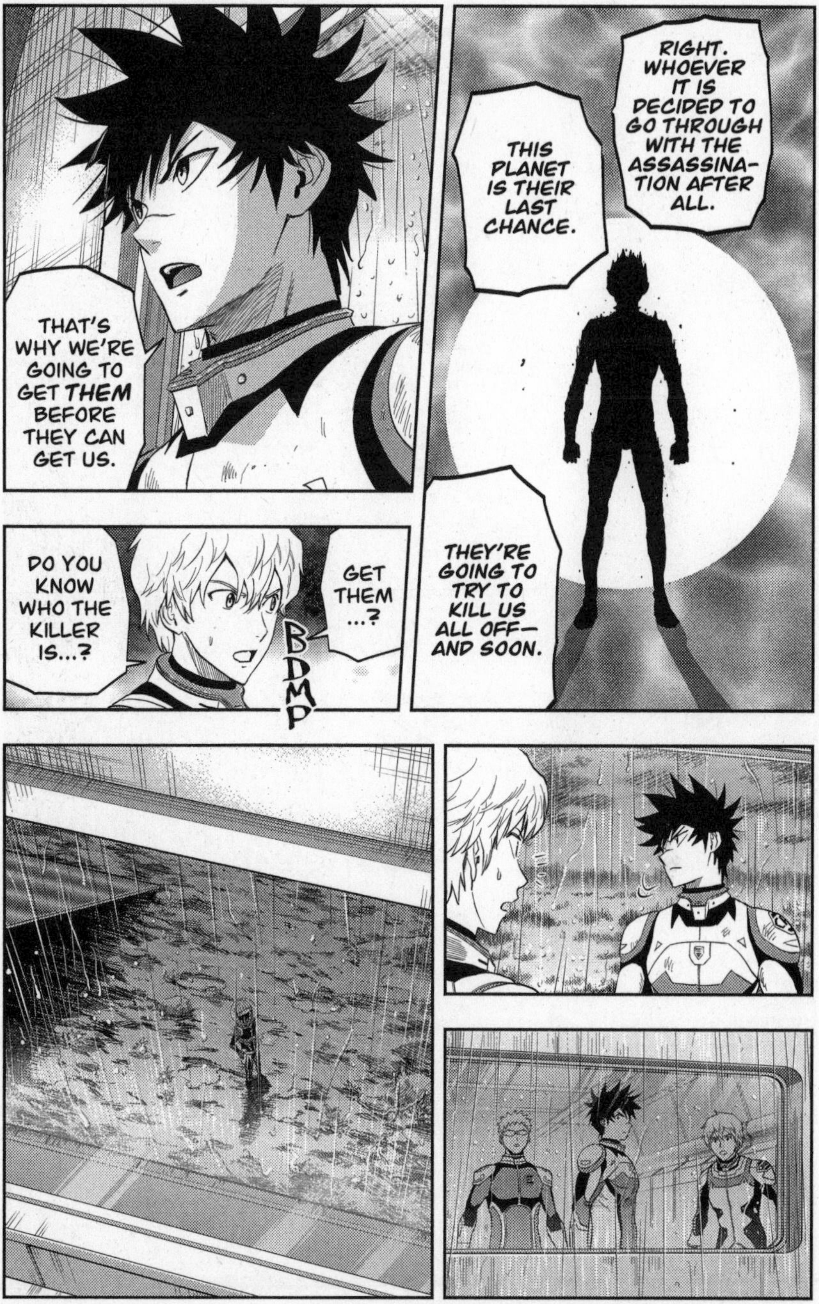
RIGHT. WHOEVER IT IS DECIDED TO GO THROUGH WITH THE ASSASSINATION AFTER ALL.
THIS PLANET IS THEIR LAST CHANCE.
THEY'RE GOING TO TRY TO KILL US ALL OFF— AND SOON.
THAT'S WHY WE'RE GOING TO GET THEM BEFORE THEY CAN GET US.
GET THEM ...?
BDMP
DO YOU KNOW WHO THE KILLER IS...?

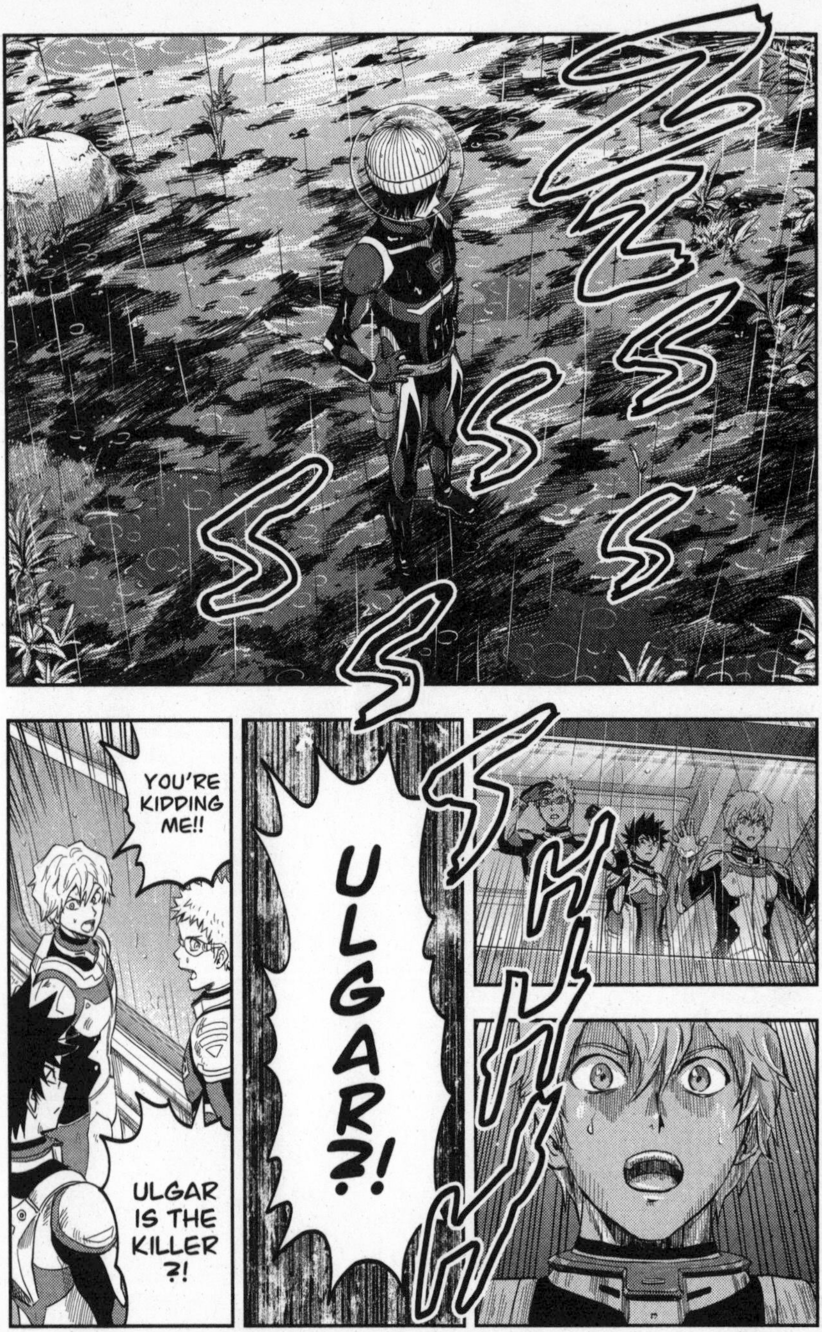
ULGAR?!
YOU'RE KIDDING ME!!
ULGAR IS THE KILLER?!

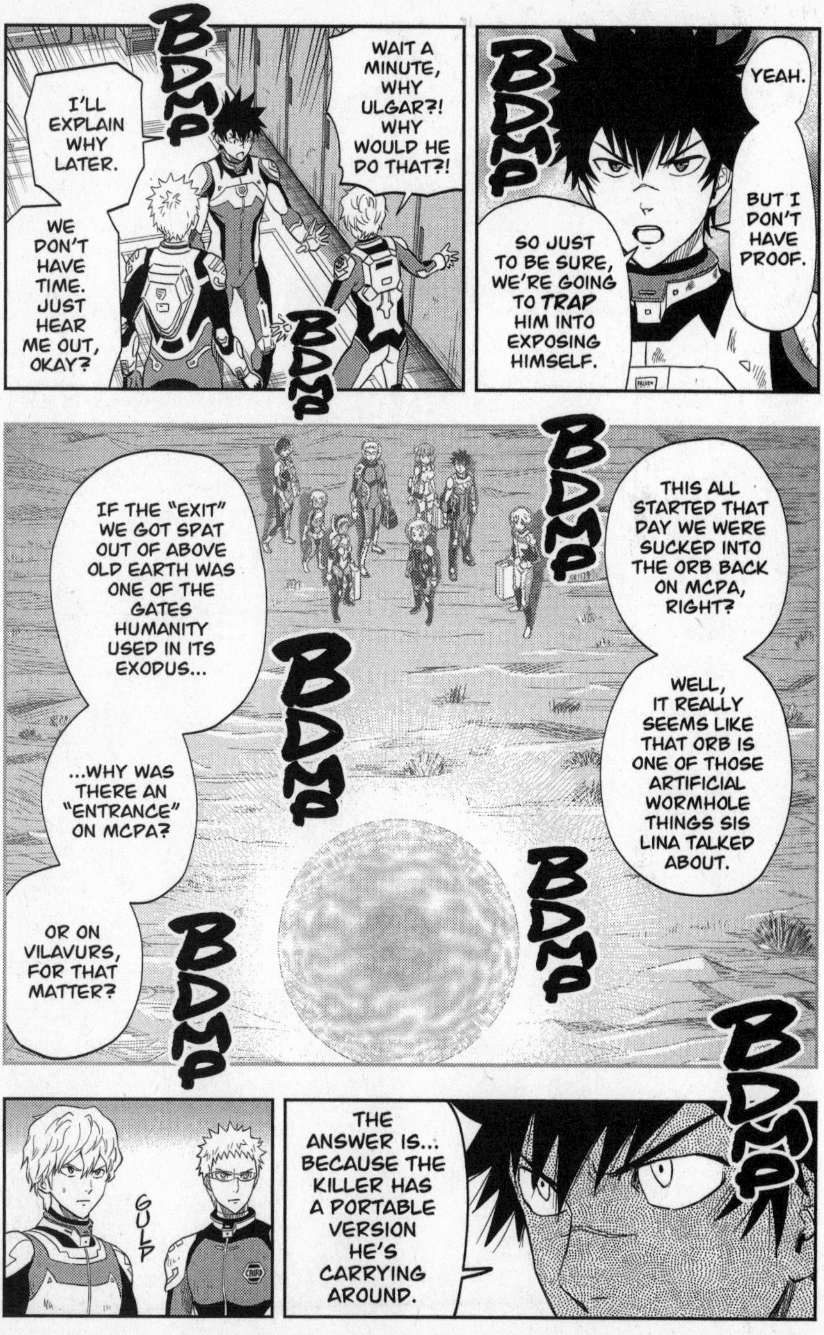
BDMP
YEAH.
BUT I DON'T HAVE PROOF.
SO JUST TO BE SURE, WE'RE GOING TO TRAP HIM INTO EXPOSING HIMSELF.
BDMP
WAIT A MINUTE, WHY ULGAR?! WHY WOULD HE DO THAT?!
I'LL EXPLAIN WHY LATER.
WE DON'T HAVE TIME. JUST HEAR ME OUT, OKAY?
BDMP
BDMP
THIS ALL STARTED THAT DAY WE WERE SUCKED INTO THE ORB BACK ON MCPA, RIGHT?
WELL, IT REALLY SEEMS LIKE THAT ORB IS ONE OF THOSE ARTIFICIAL WORMHOLE THINGS SIS LINA TALKED ABOUT.
BDMP
BDMP
IF THE "EXIT" WE GOT SPAT OUT OF ABOVE OLD EARTH WAS ONE OF THE GATES HUMANITY USED IN ITS EXODUS...
...WHY WAS THERE AN "ENTRANCE" ON MCPA?
OR ON VILAVURS, FOR THAT MATTER?
BDMP
BDMP
THE ANSWER IS... BECAUSE THE KILLER HAS A PORTABLE VERSION HE'S CARRYING AROUND.
GULP

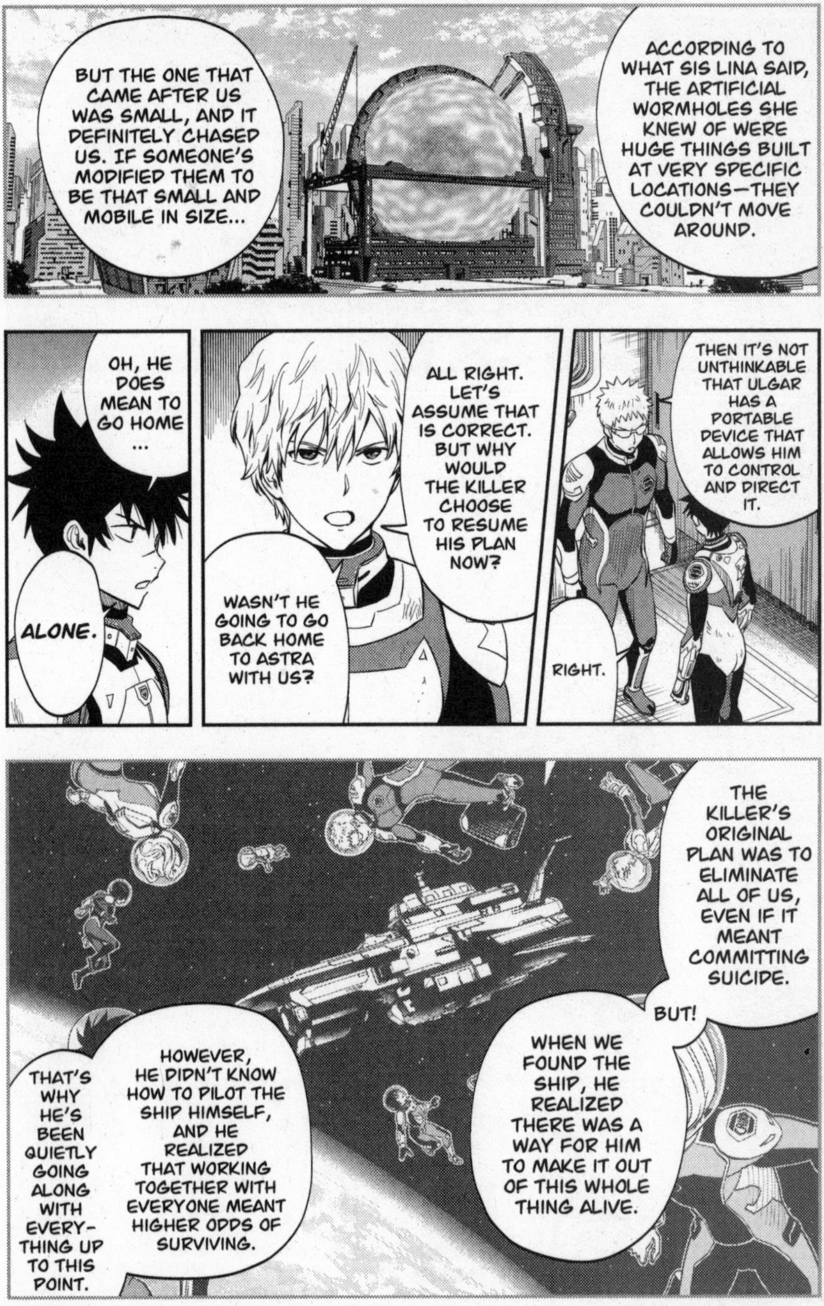
ACCORDING TO WHAT SIS LINA SAID, THE ARTIFICIAL WORMHOLES SHE KNEW OF WERE HUGE THINGS BUILT AT VERY SPECIFIC LOCATIONS—THEY COULDN'T MOVE AROUND.
BUT THE ONE THAT CAME AFTER US WAS SMALL, AND IT DEFINITELY CHASED US. IF SOMEONE'S MODIFIED THEM TO BE THAT SMALL AND MOBILE IN SIZE...
THEN IT'S NOT UNTHINKABLE THAT ULGAR HAS A PORTABLE DEVICE THAT ALLOWS HIM TO CONTROL AND DIRECT IT.
RIGHT.
ALL RIGHT. LET'S ASSUME THAT IS CORRECT. BUT WHY WOULD THE KILLER CHOOSE TO RESUME HIS PLAN NOW?
WASN'T HE GOING TO GO BACK HOME TO ASTRA WITH US?
OH, HE DOES MEAN TO GO HOME ...
ALONE.
THE KILLER'S ORIGINAL PLAN WAS TO ELIMINATE ALL OF US, EVEN IF IT MEANT COMMITTING SUICIDE.
BUT!
WHEN WE FOUND THE SHIP, HE REALIZED THERE WAS A WAY FOR HIM TO MAKE IT OUT OF THIS WHOLE THING ALIVE.
HOWEVER, HE DIDN'T KNOW HOW TO PILOT THE SHIP HIMSELF, AND HE REALIZED THAT WORKING TOGETHER WITH EVERYONE MEANT HIGHER ODDS OF SURVIVING.
THAT'S WHY HE'S BEEN QUIETLY GOING ALONG WITH EVERY-THING UP TO THIS POINT.

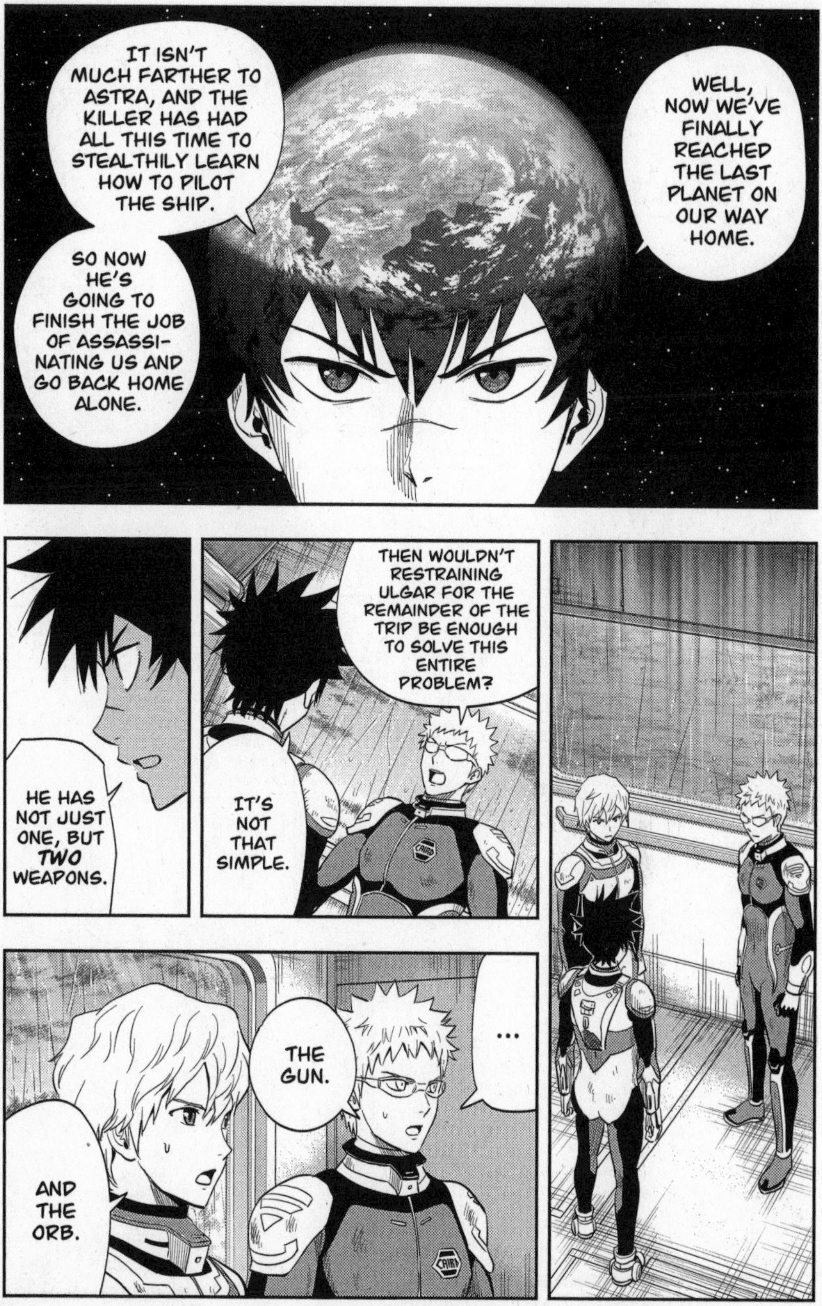
WELL, NOW WE'VE FINALLY REACHED THE LAST PLANET ON OUR WAY HOME.
IT ISN'T MUCH FARTHER TO ASTRA, AND THE KILLER HAS HAD ALL THIS TIME TO STEALTHILY LEARN HOW TO PILOT THE SHIP.
SO NOW HE'S GOING TO FINISH THE JOB OF ASSASSI-NATING US AND GO BACK HOME ALONE.
THEN WOULDN'T RESTRAINING ULGAR FOR THE REMAINDER OF THE TRIP BE ENOUGH TO SOLVE THIS ENTIRE PROBLEM?
IT'S NOT THAT SIMPLE.
HE HAS NOT JUST ONE, BUT *TWO* WEAPONS.
...
THE GUN.
AND THE ORB.

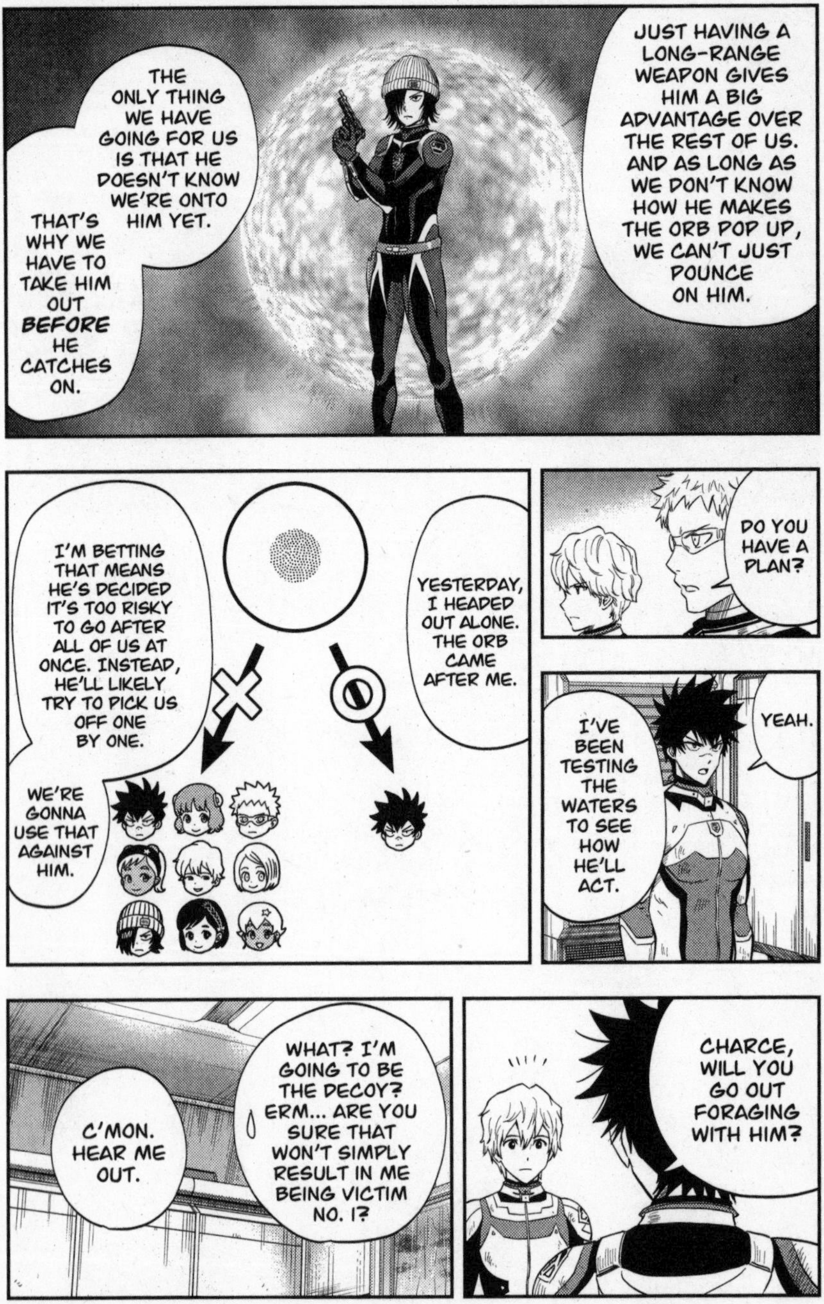
JUST HAVING A LONG-RANGE WEAPON GIVES HIM A BIG ADVANTAGE OVER THE REST OF US. AND AS LONG AS WE DON'T KNOW HOW HE MAKES THE ORB POP UP, WE CAN'T JUST POUNCE ON HIM.
THE ONLY THING WE HAVE GOING FOR US IS THAT HE DOESN'T KNOW WE'RE ONTO HIM YET.
THAT'S WHY WE HAVE TO TAKE HIM OUT BEFORE HE CATCHES ON.
DO YOU HAVE A PLAN?
YEAH.
I'VE BEEN TESTING THE WATERS TO SEE HOW HE'LL ACT.
YESTERDAY, I HEADED OUT ALONE. THE ORB CAME AFTER ME.
I'M BETTING THAT MEANS HE'S DECIDED IT'S TOO RISKY TO GO AFTER ALL OF US AT ONCE. INSTEAD, HE'LL LIKELY TRY TO PICK US OFF ONE BY ONE.
WE'RE GONNA USE THAT AGAINST HIM.
CHARCE, WILL YOU GO OUT FORAGING WITH HIM?
WHAT? I'M GOING TO BE THE DECOY? ERM... ARE YOU SURE THAT WON'T SIMPLY RESULT IN ME BEING VICTIM NO. 1?
C'MON. HEAR ME OUT.

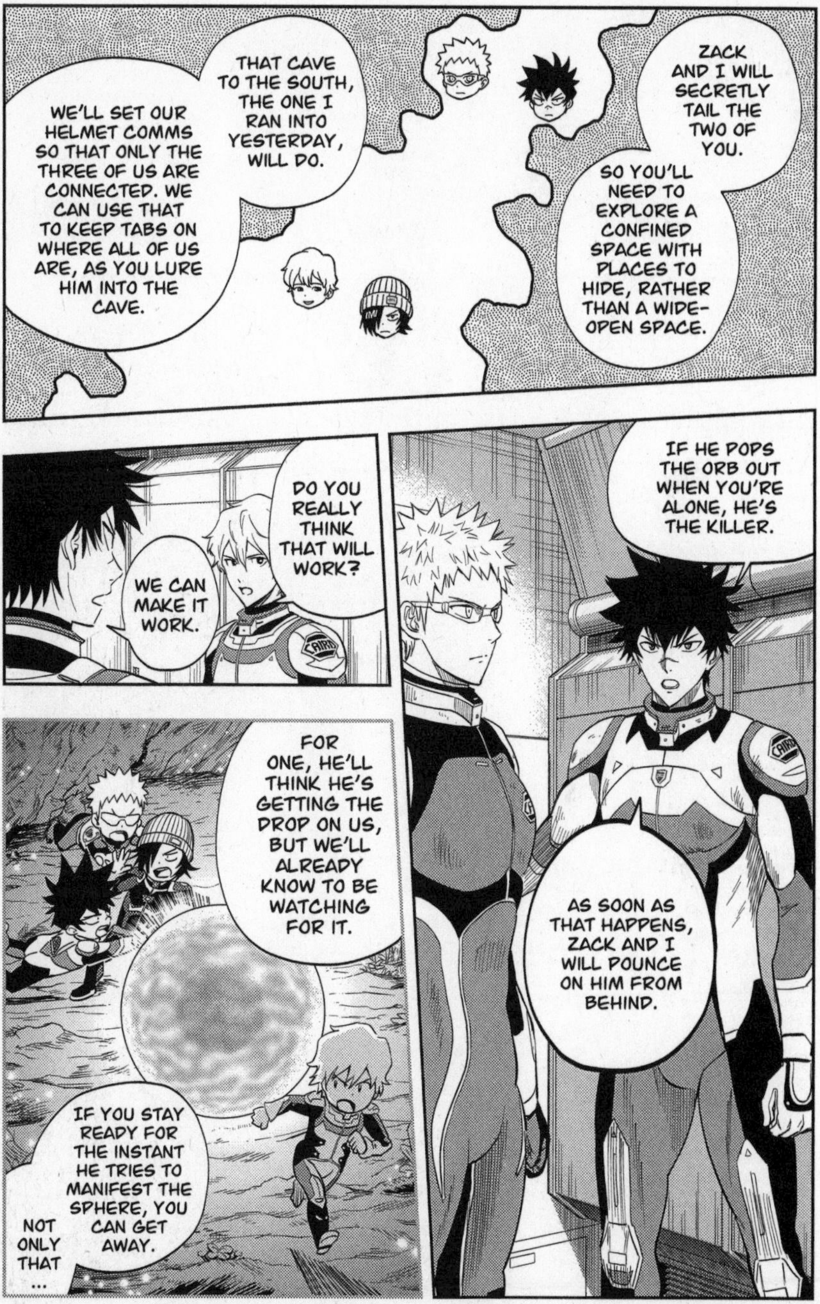
ZACK AND I WILL SECRETLY TAIL THE TWO OF YOU.
SO YOU'LL NEED TO EXPLORE A CONFINED SPACE WITH PLACES TO HIDE, RATHER THAN A WIDE-OPEN SPACE.
THAT CAVE TO THE SOUTH, THE ONE I RAN INTO YESTERDAY, WILL DO.
WE'LL SET OUR HELMET COMMS SO THAT ONLY THE THREE OF US ARE CONNECTED. WE CAN USE THAT TO KEEP TABS ON WHERE ALL OF US ARE, AS YOU LURE HIM INTO THE CAVE.
IF HE POPS THE ORB OUT WHEN YOU'RE ALONE, HE'S THE KILLER.
AS SOON AS THAT HAPPENS, ZACK AND I WILL POUNCE ON HIM FROM BEHIND.
DO YOU REALLY THINK THAT WILL WORK?
WE CAN MAKE IT WORK.
FOR ONE, HE'LL THINK HE'S GETTING THE DROP ON US, BUT WE'LL ALREADY KNOW TO BE WATCHING FOR IT.
IF YOU STAY READY FOR THE INSTANT HE TRIES TO MANIFEST THE SPHERE, YOU CAN GET AWAY.
NOT ONLY THAT ...

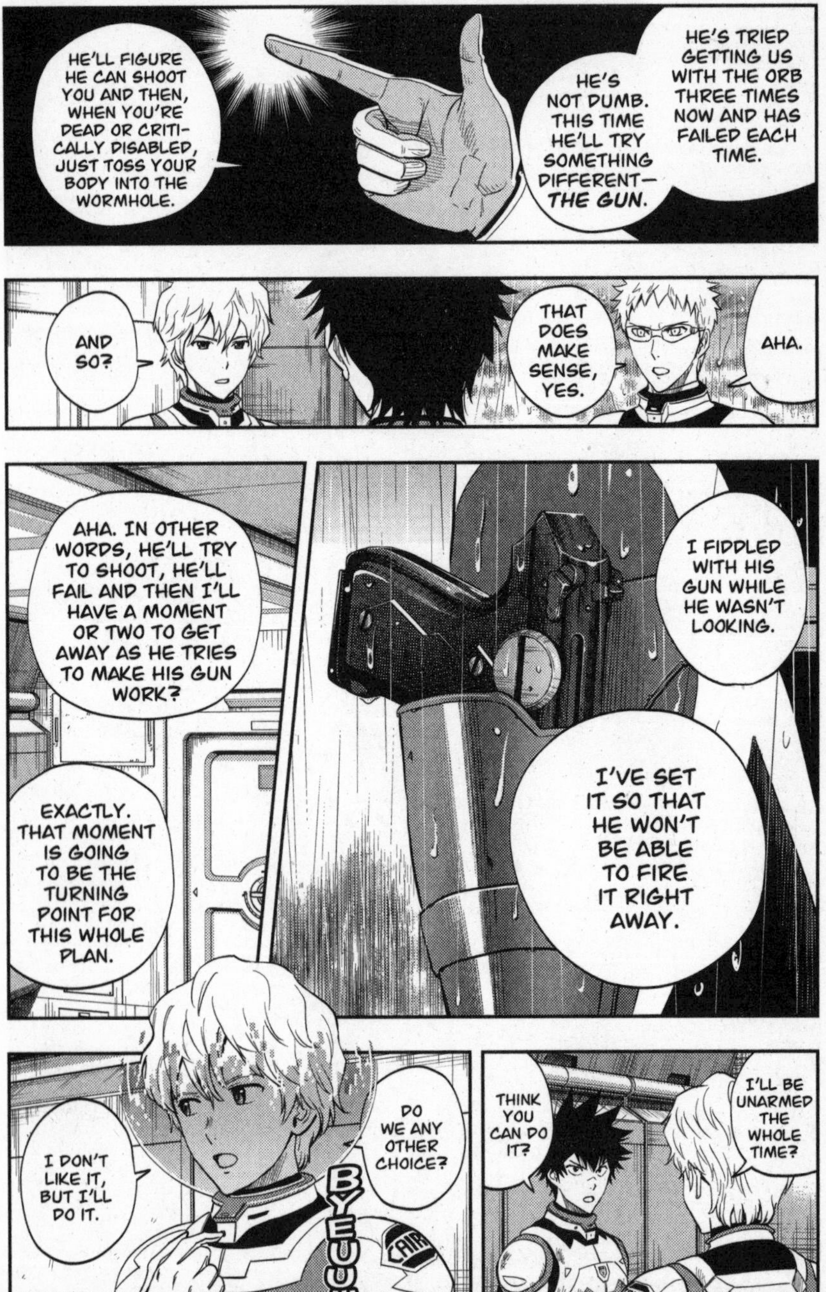
HE'S TRIED GETTING US WITH THE ORB THREE TIMES NOW AND HAS FAILED EACH TIME.
HE'S NOT DUMB. THIS TIME HE'LL TRY SOMETHING DIFFERENT— **THE GUN**.
HE'LL FIGURE HE CAN SHOOT YOU AND THEN, WHEN YOU'RE DEAD OR CRITI-CALLY DISABLED, JUST TOSS YOUR BODY INTO THE WORMHOLE.
AHA.
THAT DOES MAKE SENSE, YES.
AND SO?
I FIDDLED WITH HIS GUN WHILE HE WASN'T LOOKING.
I'VE SET IT SO THAT HE WON'T BE ABLE TO FIRE IT RIGHT AWAY.
AHA. IN OTHER WORDS, HE'LL TRY TO SHOOT, HE'LL FAIL AND THEN I'LL HAVE A MOMENT OR TWO TO GET AWAY AS HE TRIES TO MAKE HIS GUN WORK?
EXACTLY. THAT MOMENT IS GOING TO BE THE TURNING POINT FOR THIS WHOLE PLAN.
I'LL BE UNARMED THE WHOLE TIME?
THINK YOU CAN DO IT?
DO WE ANY OTHER CHOICE?
BYEUUU
I DON'T LIKE IT, BUT I'LL DO IT.

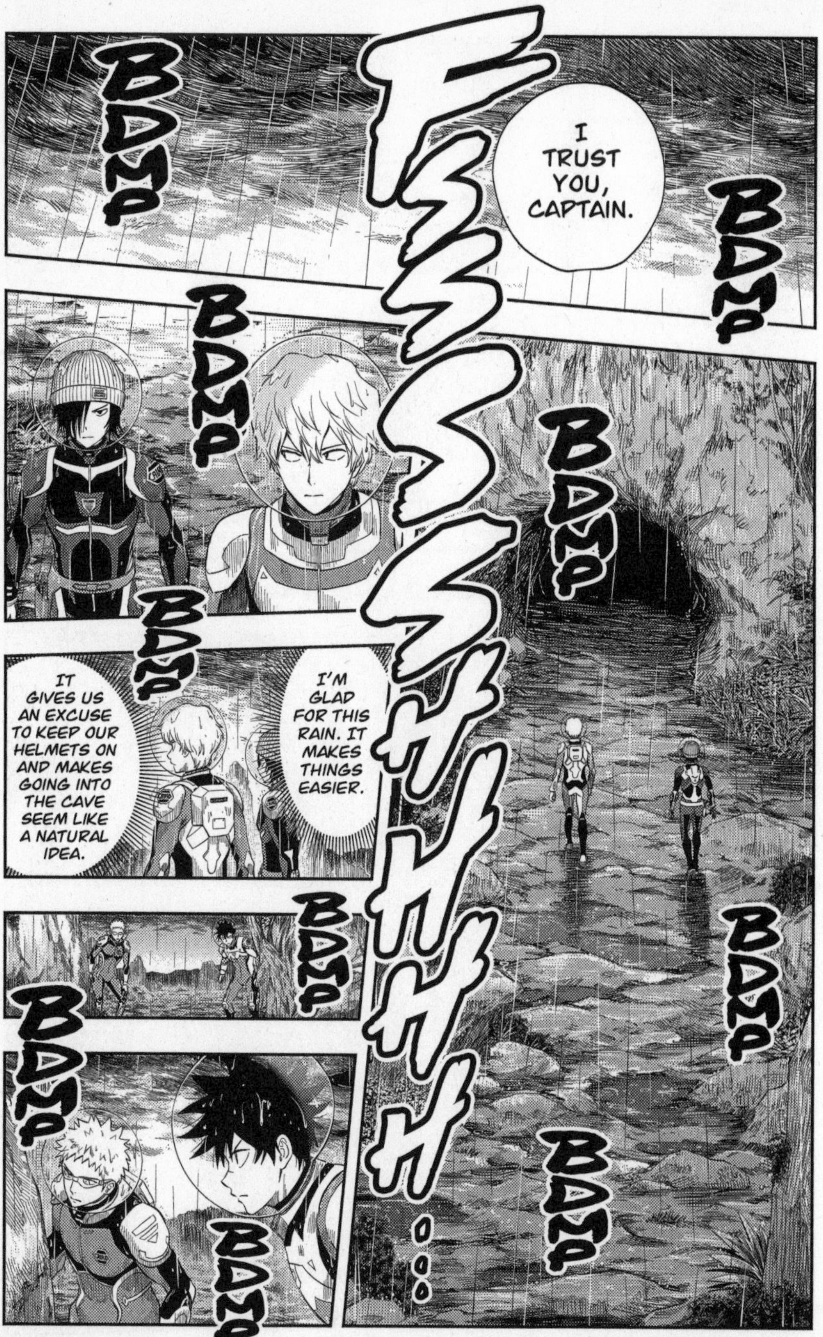
BDMP
I TRUST YOU, CAPTAIN.
BDMP
FSSSSHHHHH...
BDMP
BDMP
BDMP
I'M GLAD FOR THIS RAIN. IT MAKES THINGS EASIER.
IT GIVES US AN EXCUSE TO KEEP OUR HELMETS ON AND MAKES GOING INTO THE CAVE SEEM LIKE A NATURAL IDEA.
BDMP
BDMP
BDMP
BDMP
BDMP

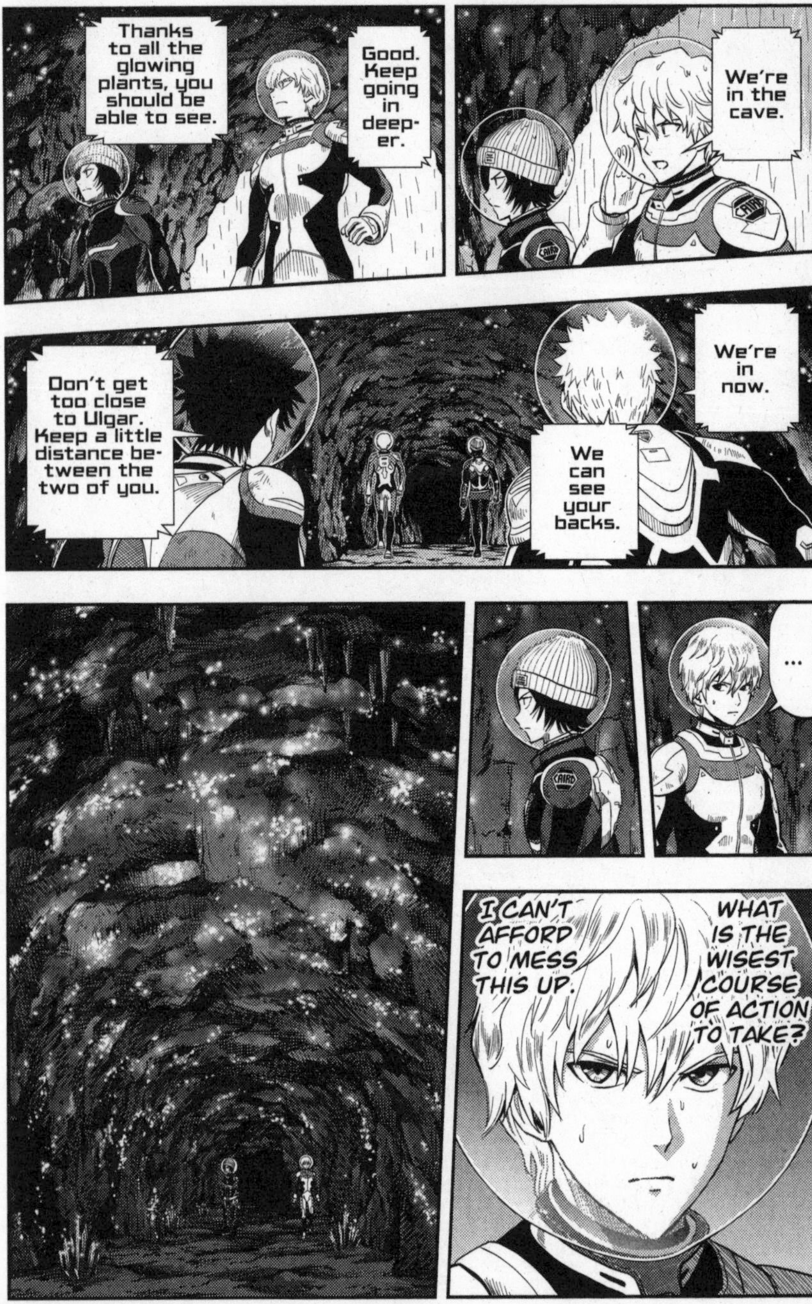
We're in the cave.
Good. Keep going in deeper.
Thanks to all the glowing plants, you should be able to see.
We're in now.
We can see your backs.
Don't get too close to Ulgar. Keep a little distance between the two of you.
...
WHAT IS THE WISEST COURSE OF ACTION TO TAKE?
I CAN'T AFFORD TO MESS THIS UP.

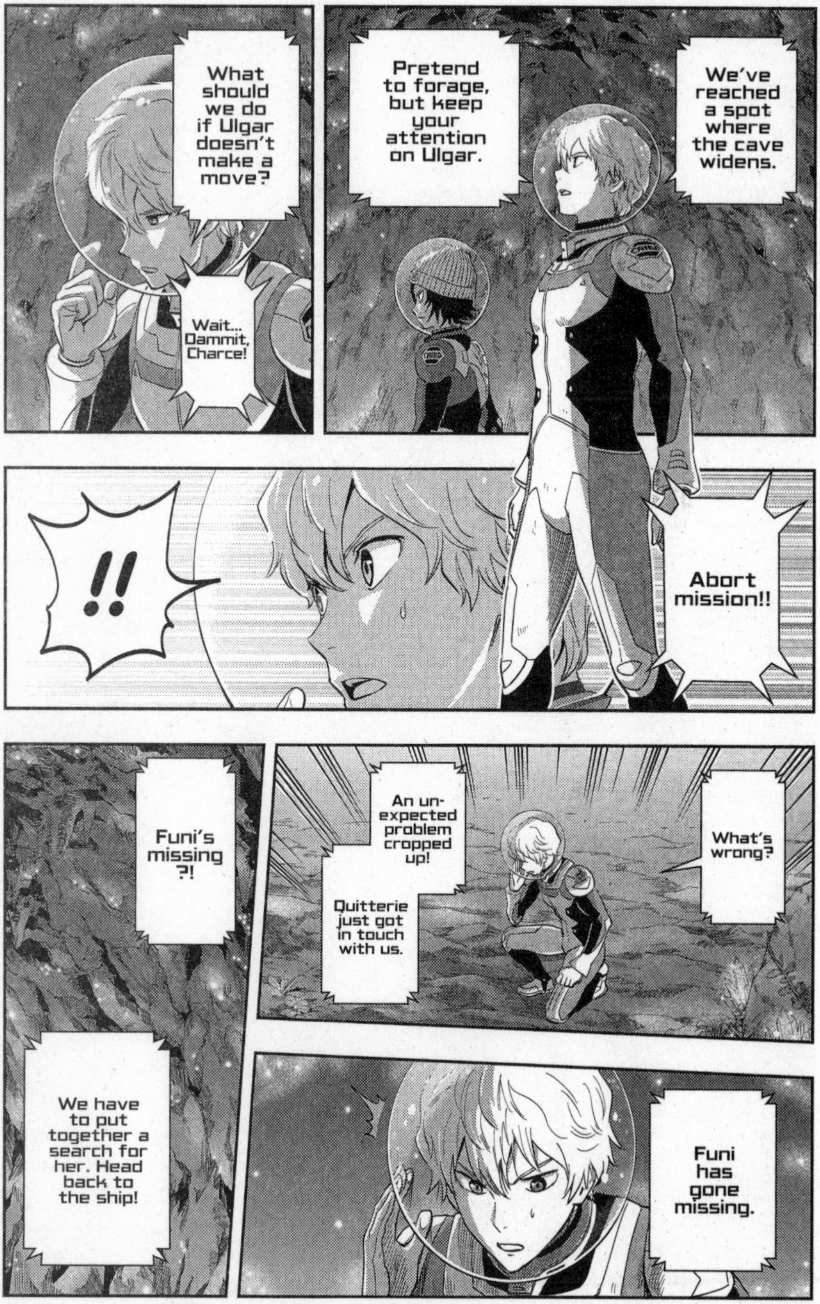
We've reached a spot where the cave widens.
Pretend to forage, but keep your attention on Ulgar.
What should we do if Ulgar doesn't make a move?
Wait... Dammit, Charce!
Abort mission!!
!!
What's wrong?
An un-expected problem cropped up!
Quitterie just got in touch with us.
Funi has gone missing.
Funi's missing?!
We have to put together a search for her. Head back to the ship!

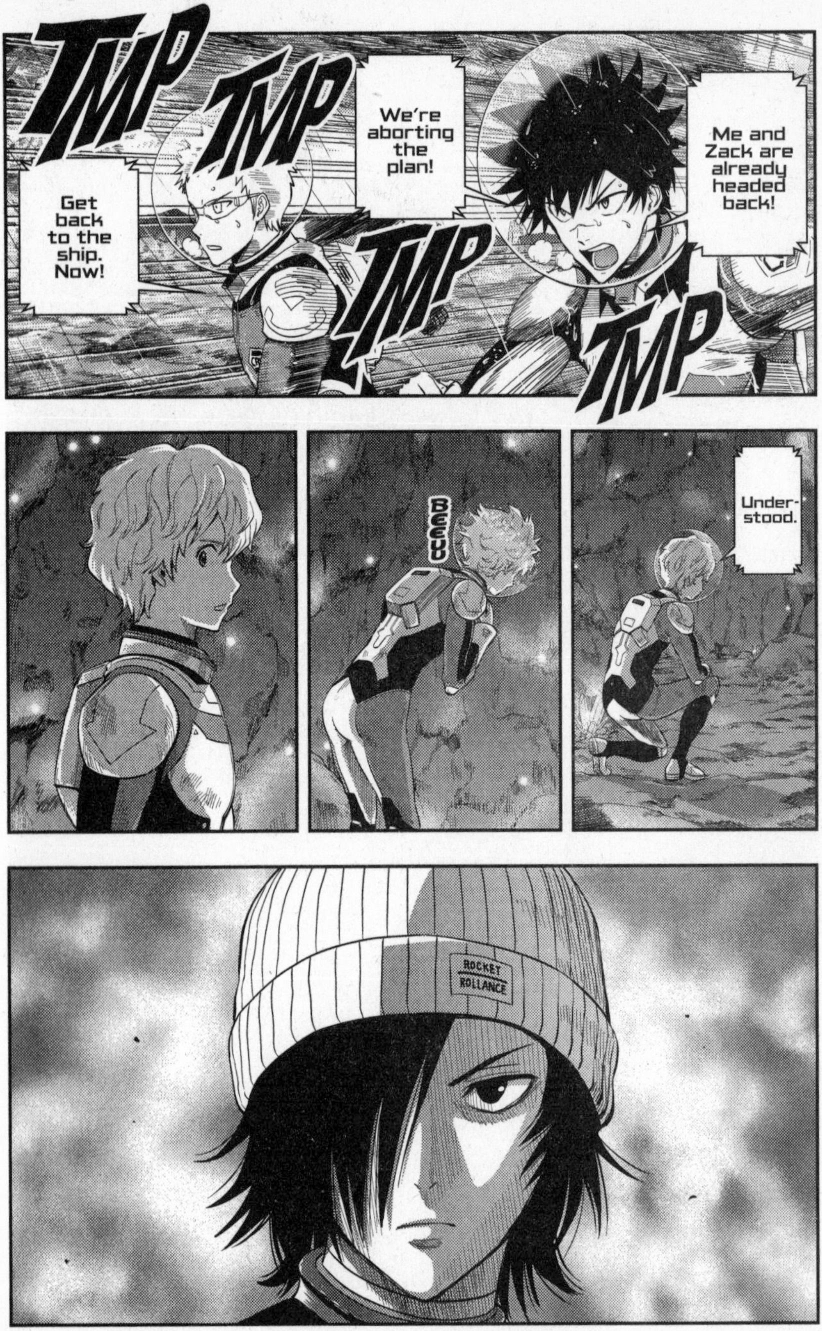
Me and Zack are already headed back!
TMP
We're aborting the plan!
TMP
TMP
Get back to the ship. Now!
TMP
Under-stood.
BEEUU
ROCKET ROLLANCE

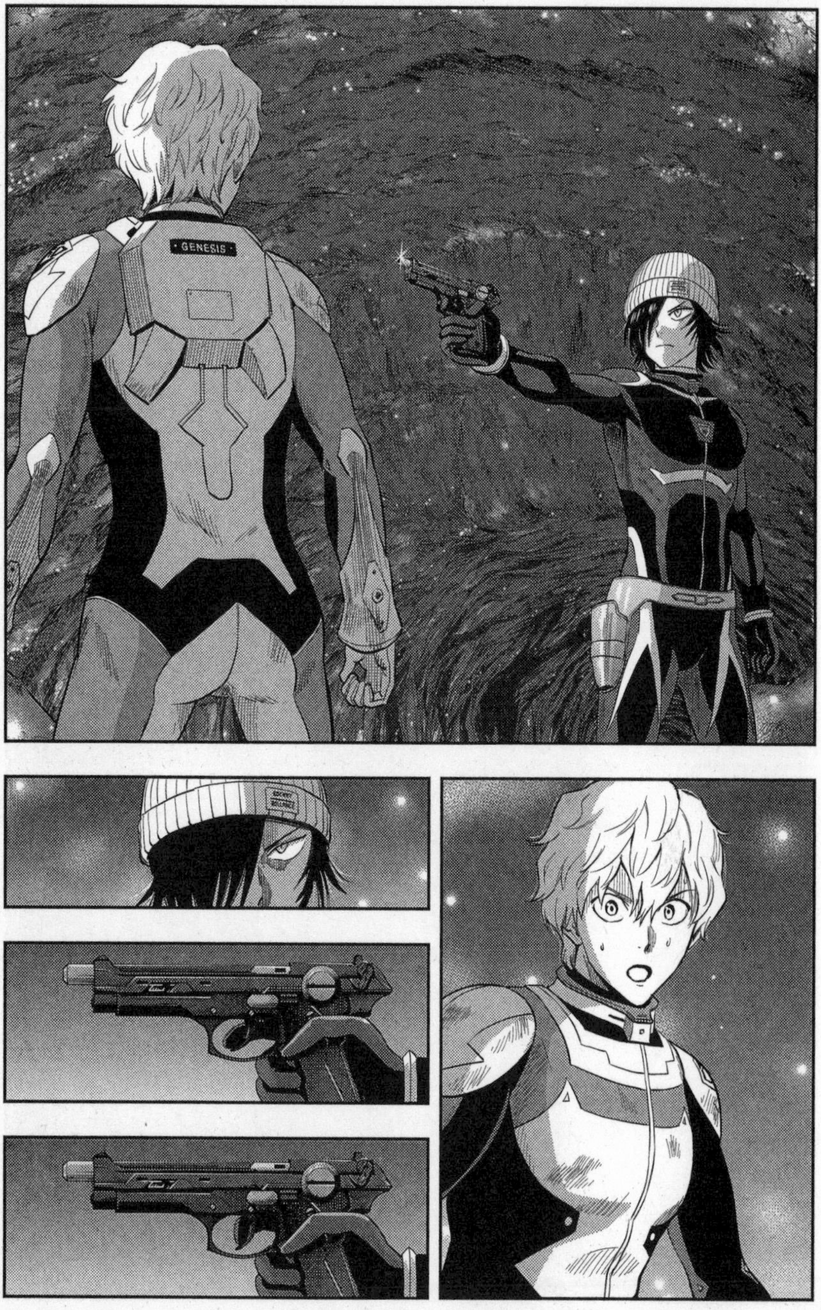
GENESIS

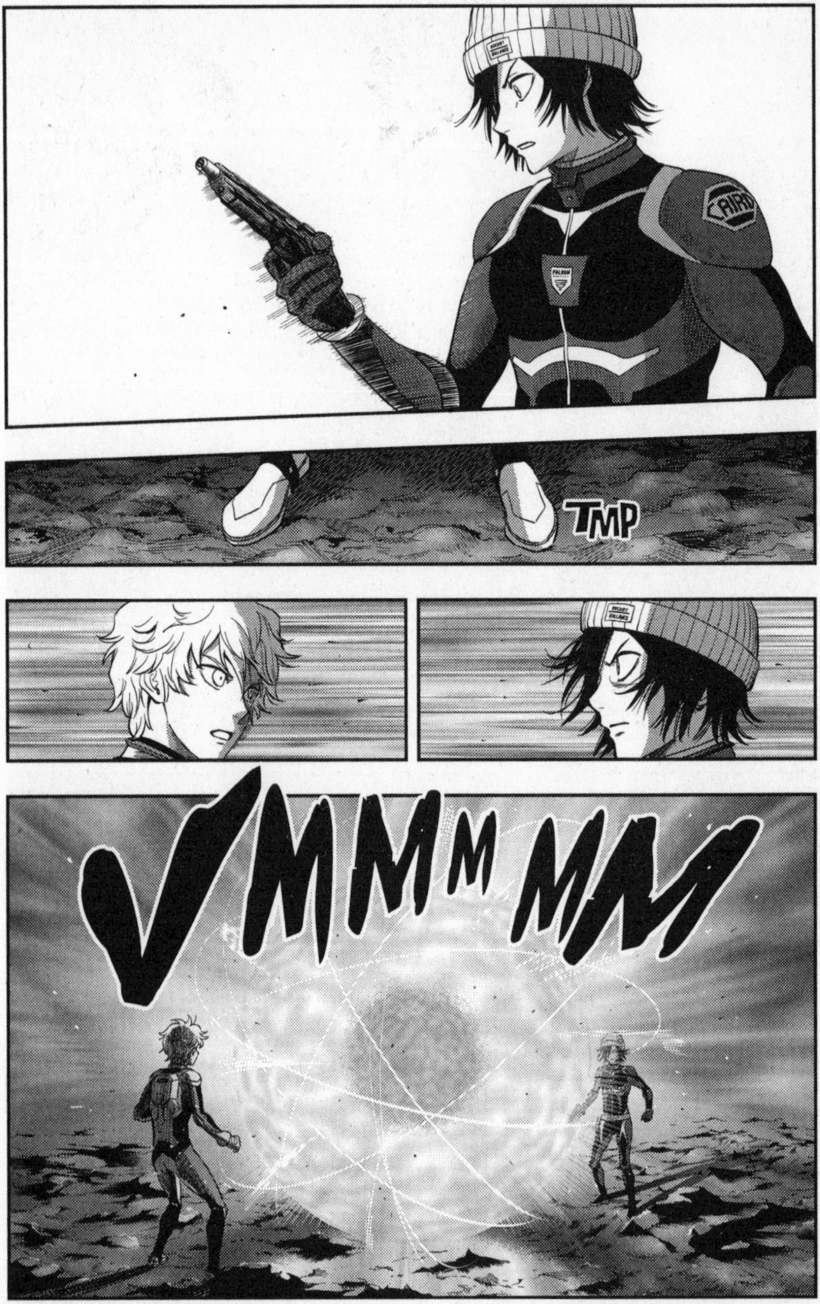
TMP
VMMMMMM

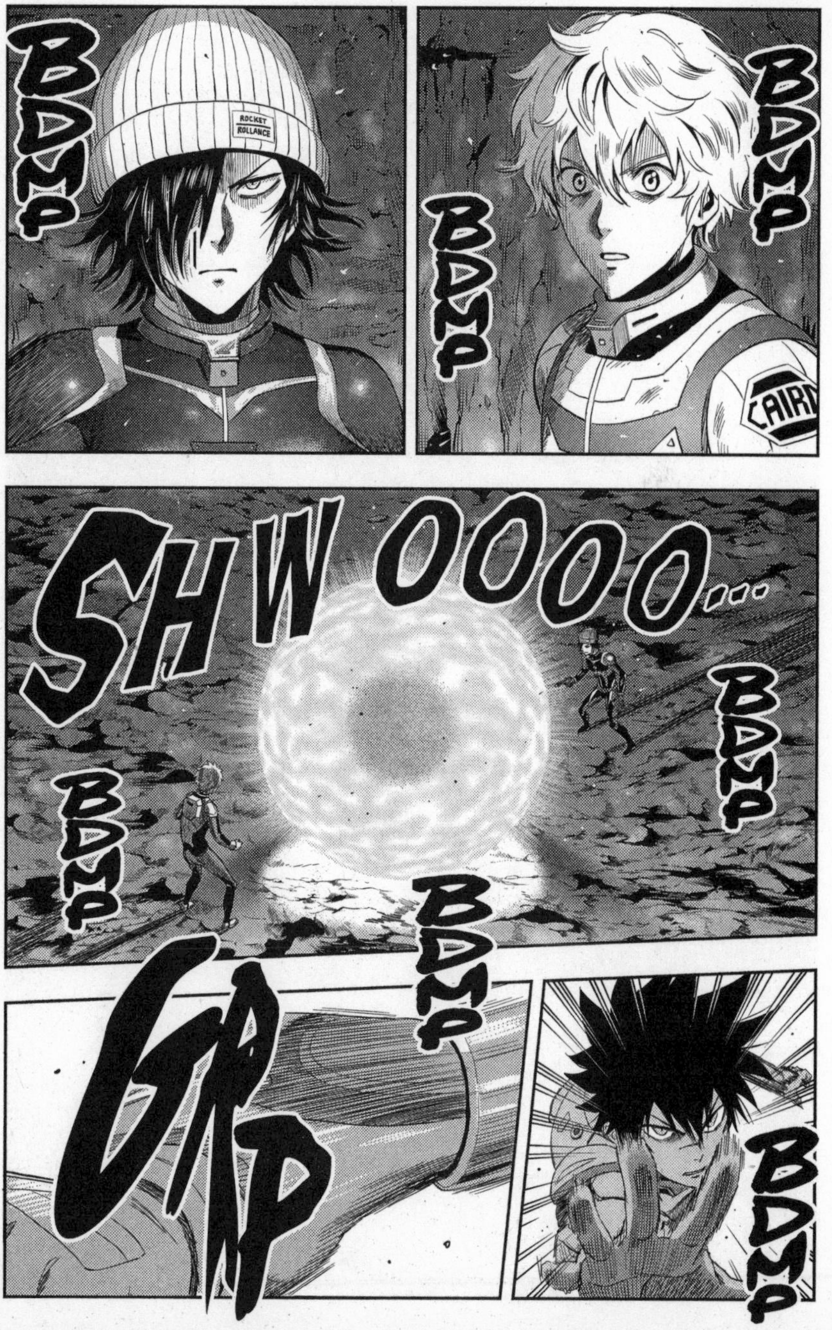
BDMP
BDMP
CAIRD
ROCKET
ROLLANCE
BDMP
SHWOOOO...
BDMP
BDMP
BDMP
BDMP
GRIP

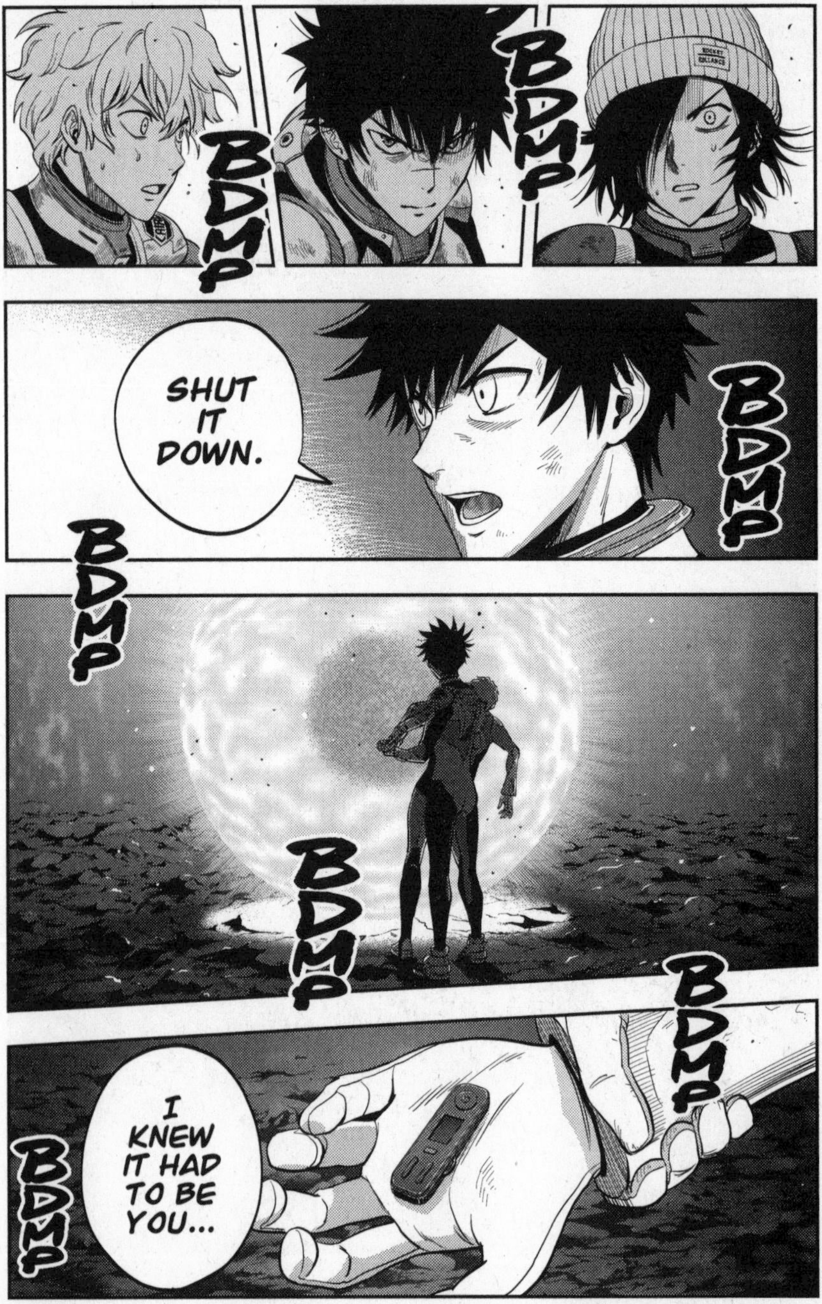
BDMP
BDMP
BDMP
BDMP
SHUT IT DOWN.
BDMP
BDMP
BDMP
I KNEW IT HAD TO BE YOU...
BDMP

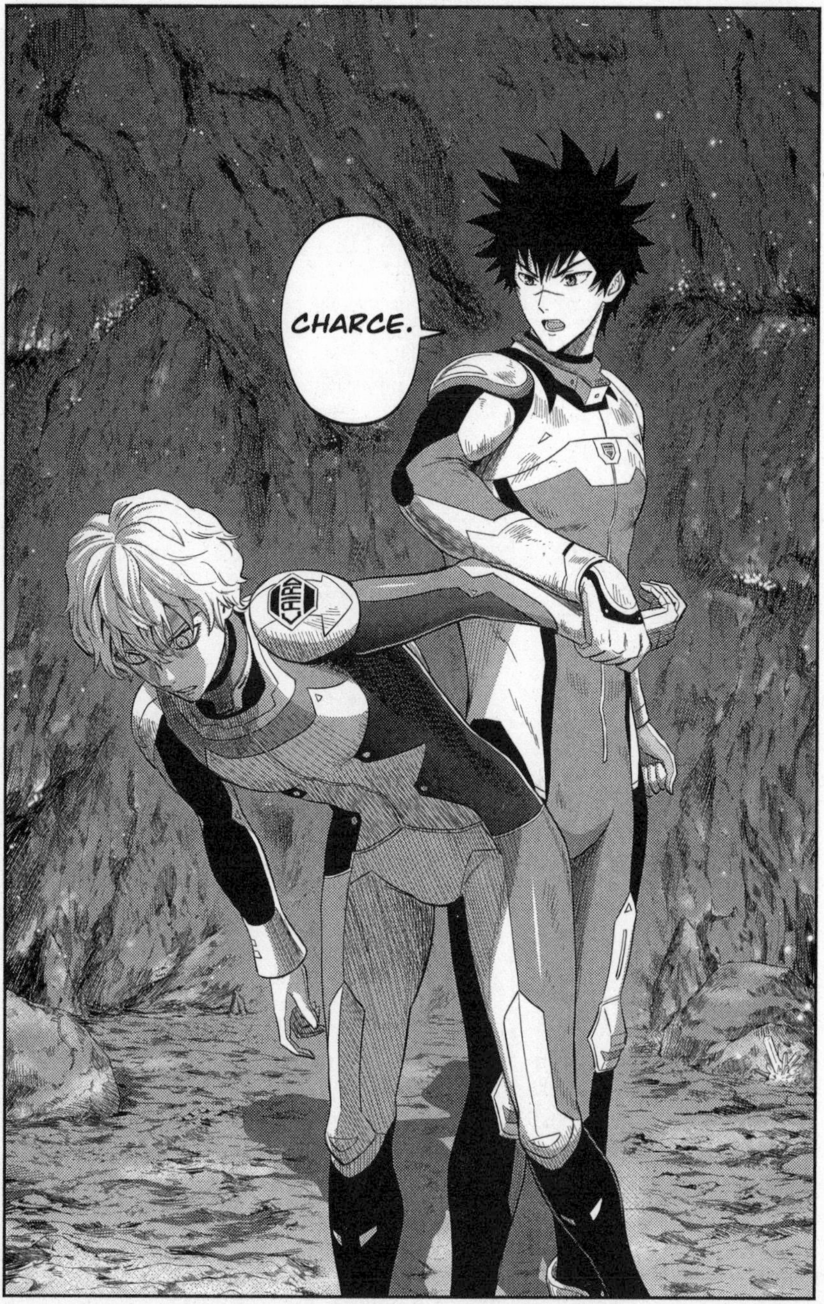
CHARCE.

Material Collection Character Prototype Design

QUITTERIE and ZACK

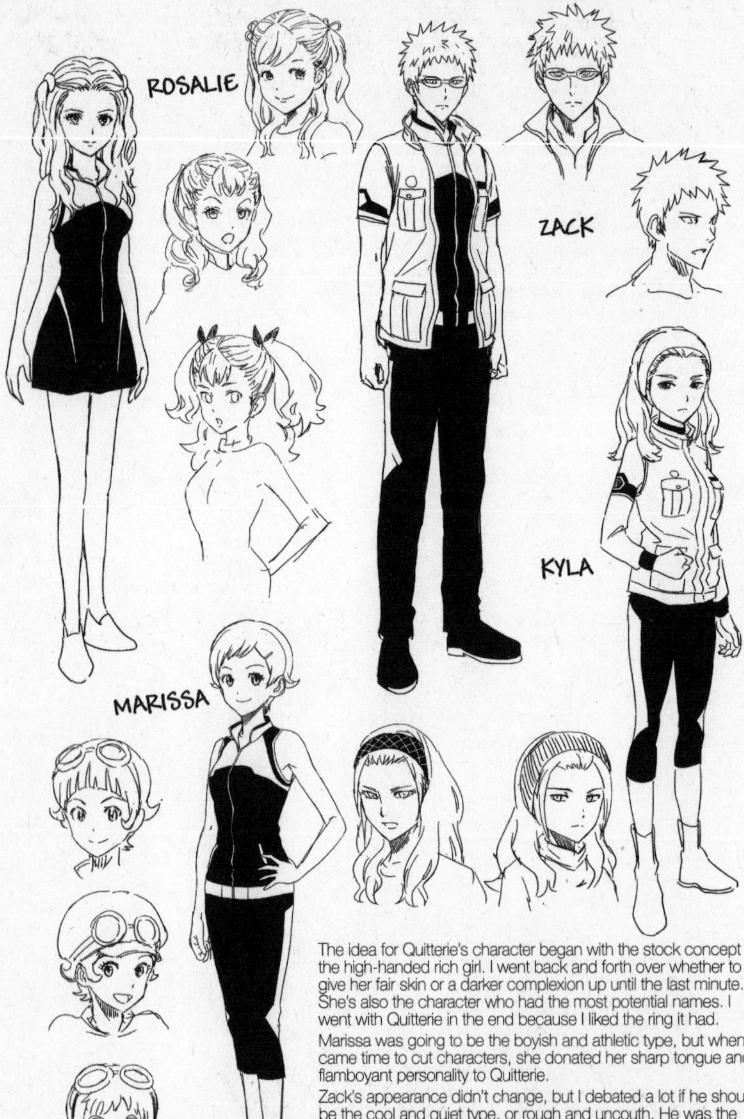
ROSALIE
ZACK
KYLA
MARISSA

The idea for Quitterie's character began with the stock concept of the high-handed rich girl. I went back and forth over whether to give her fair skin or a darker complexion up until the last minute. She's also the character who had the most potential names. I went with Quitterie in the end because I liked the ring it had.

Marissa was going to be the boyish and athletic type, but when it came time to cut characters, she donated her sharp tongue and flamboyant personality to Quitterie.

Zack's appearance didn't change, but I debated a lot if he should be the cool and quiet type, or rough and uncouth. He was the one with the hardest personality to balance so that he didn't overlap too much with any of the other characters.

Kyla was going to be the logical and intelligent one, but when her character was cut, she gave that personality to Zack, while Quitterie took on her darker complexion.

ASTRA LOST IN SPACE

#42

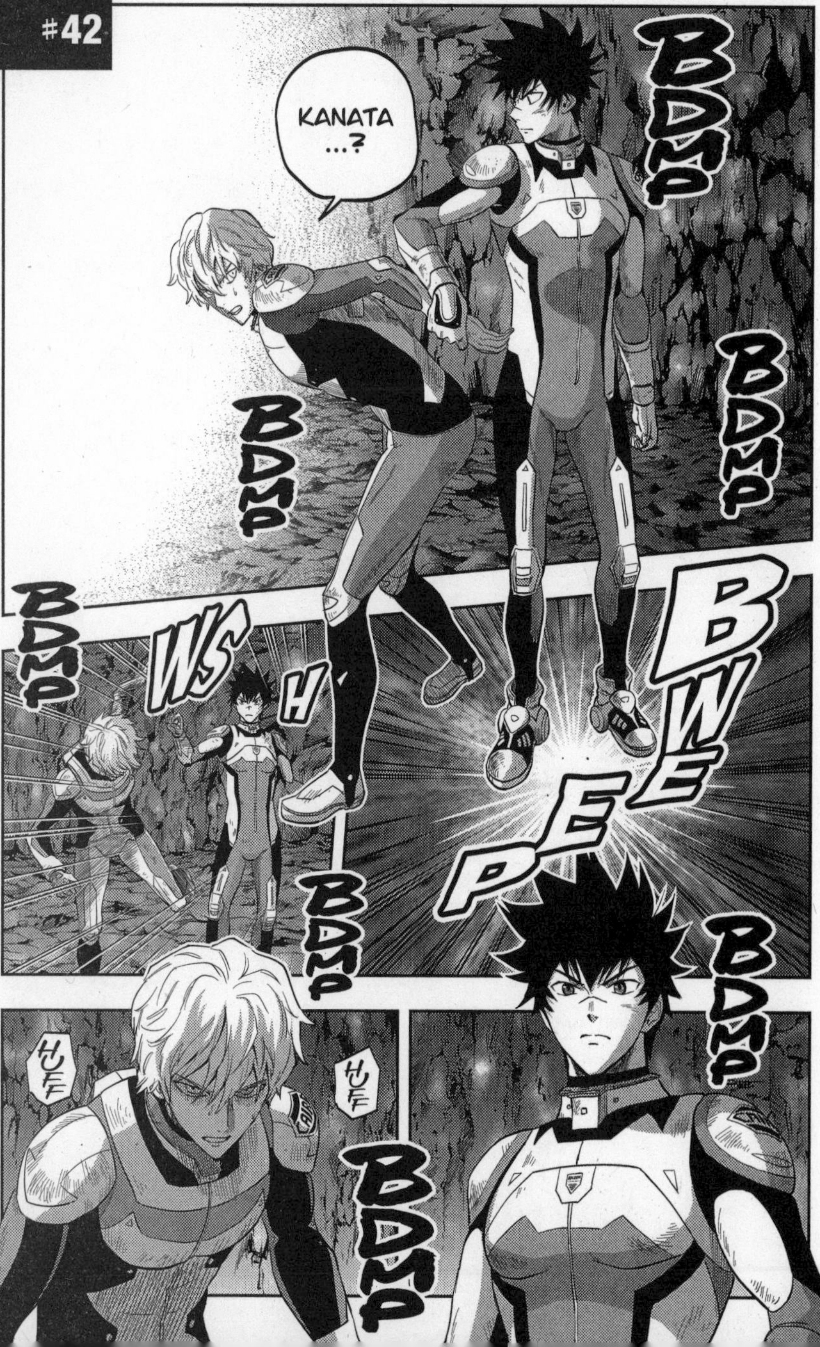
BDMP
KANATA ...?
BDMP
BDMP
BWEEP
BDMP
WSH
BDMP
BDMP
HUFF
HUFF
BDMP

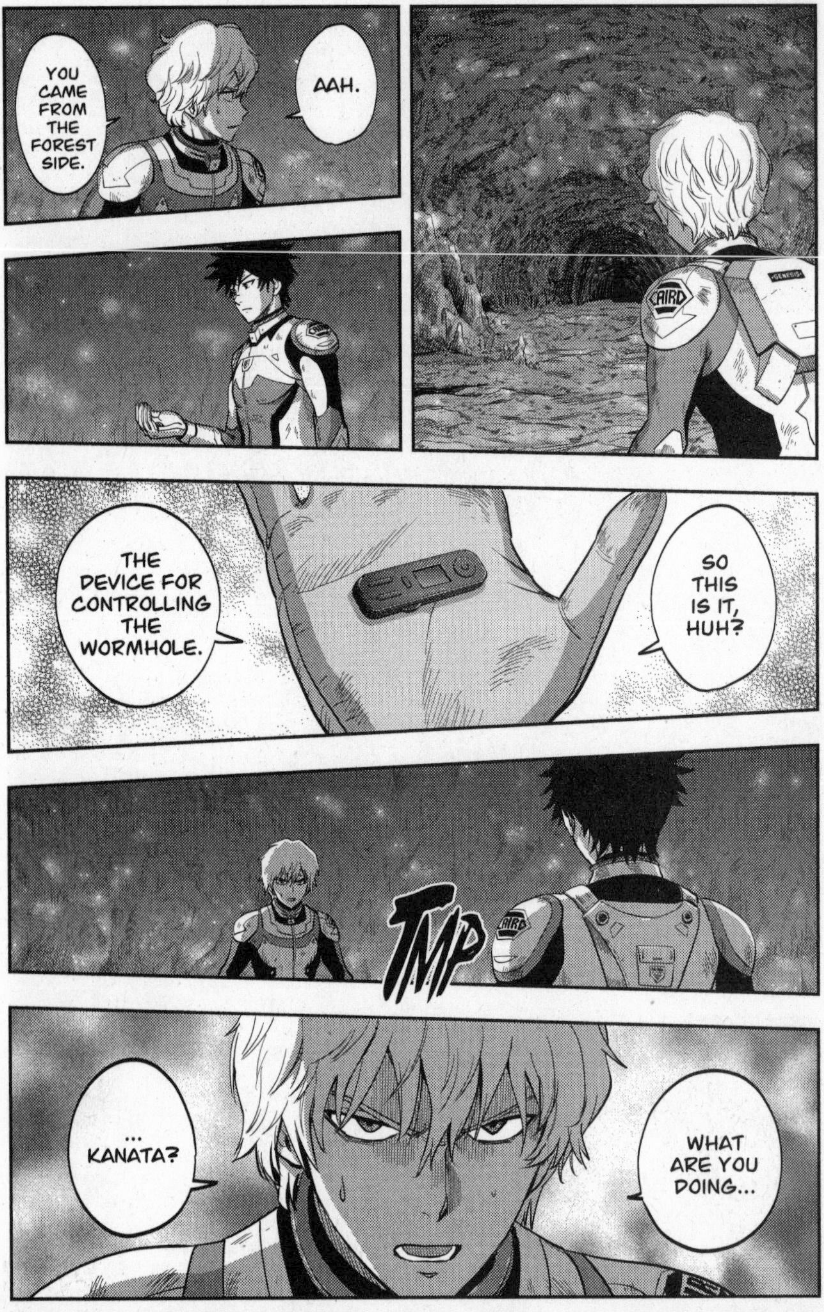
AAH.
YOU CAME FROM THE FOREST SIDE.
SO THIS IS IT, HUH?
THE DEVICE FOR CONTROLLING THE WORMHOLE.
TMP
WHAT ARE YOU DOING...
... KANATA?

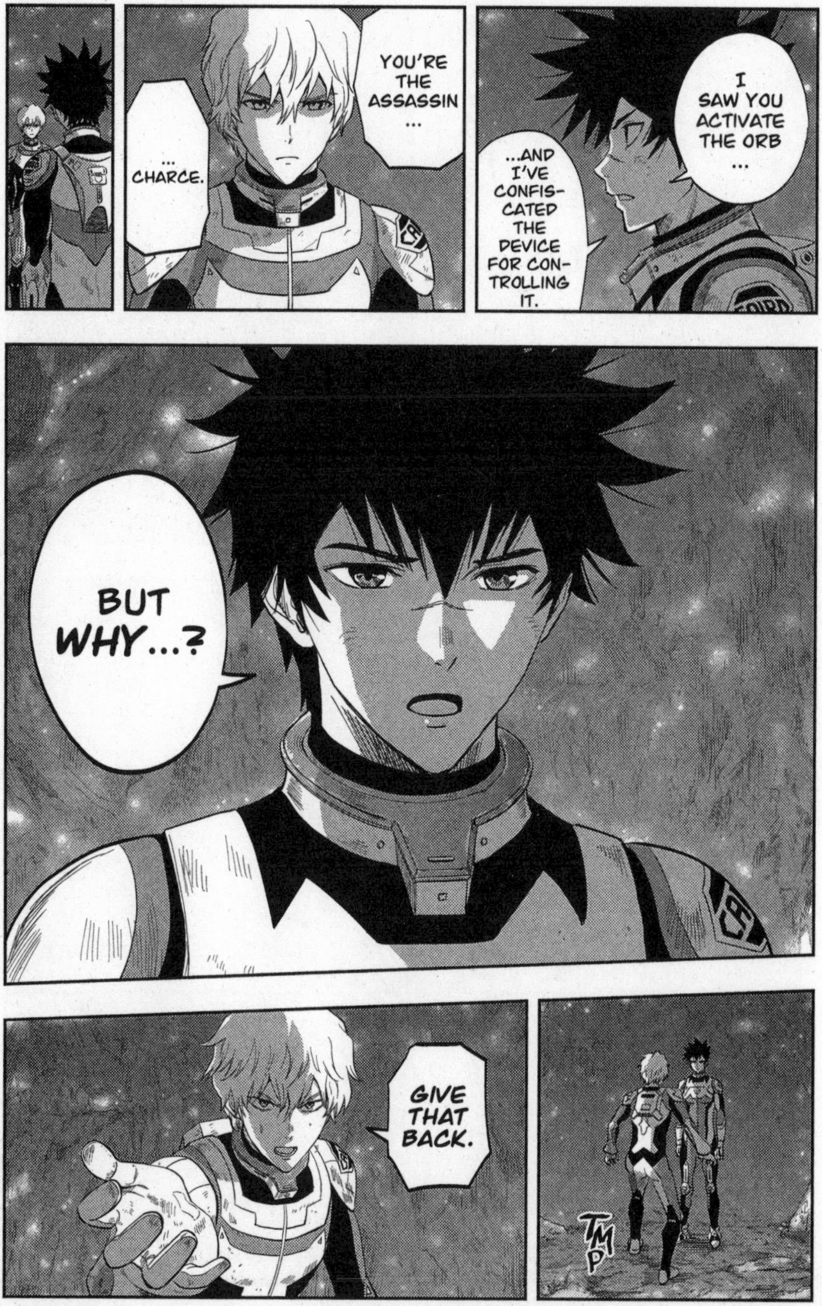
I SAW YOU ACTIVATE THE ORB ...
...AND I'VE CONFISCATED THE DEVICE FOR CONTROLLING IT.
YOU'RE THE ASSASSIN ...
... CHARCE.
BUT WHY...?
TMP
GIVE THAT BACK.

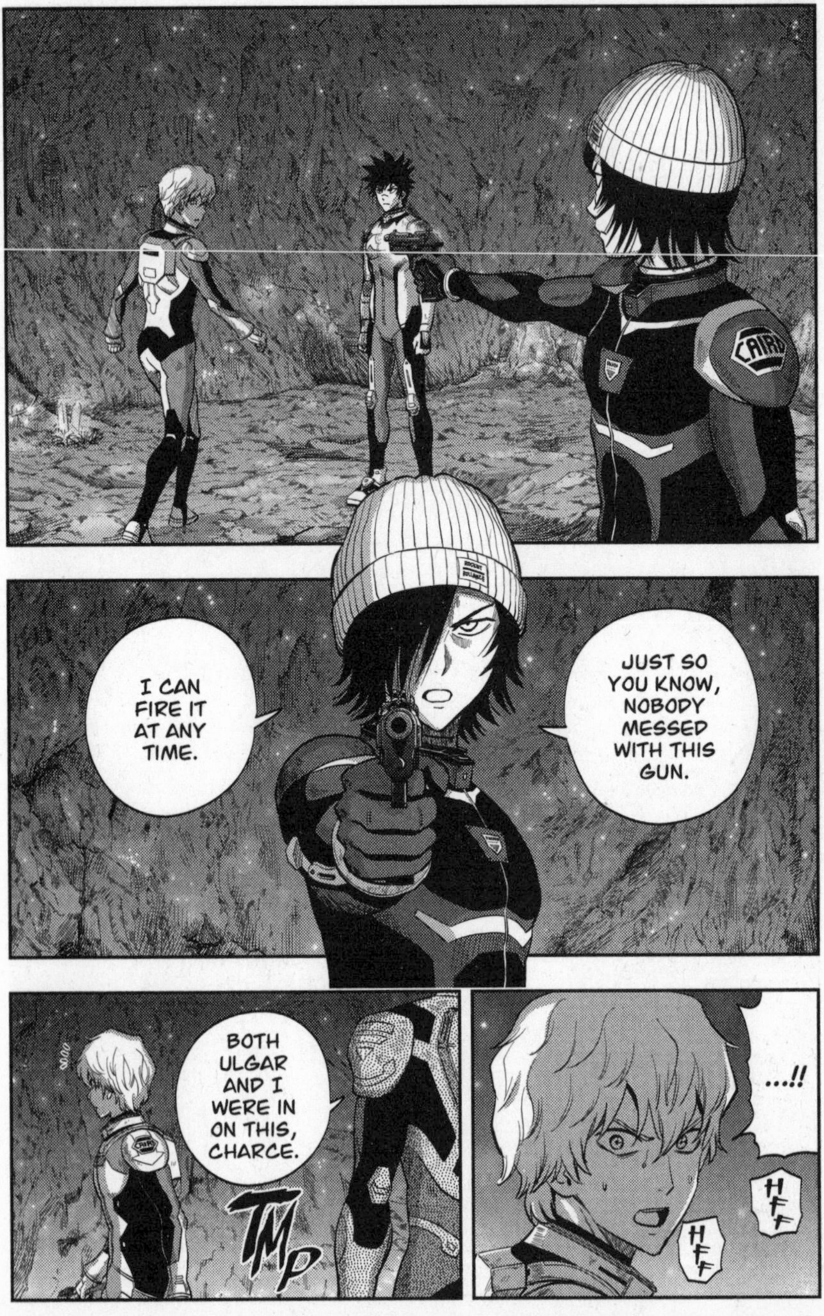
JUST SO YOU KNOW, NOBODY MESSED WITH THIS GUN.
I CAN FIRE IT AT ANY TIME.
...!!
HFF
HFF
BOTH ULGAR AND I WERE IN ON THIS, CHARCE.
TMP

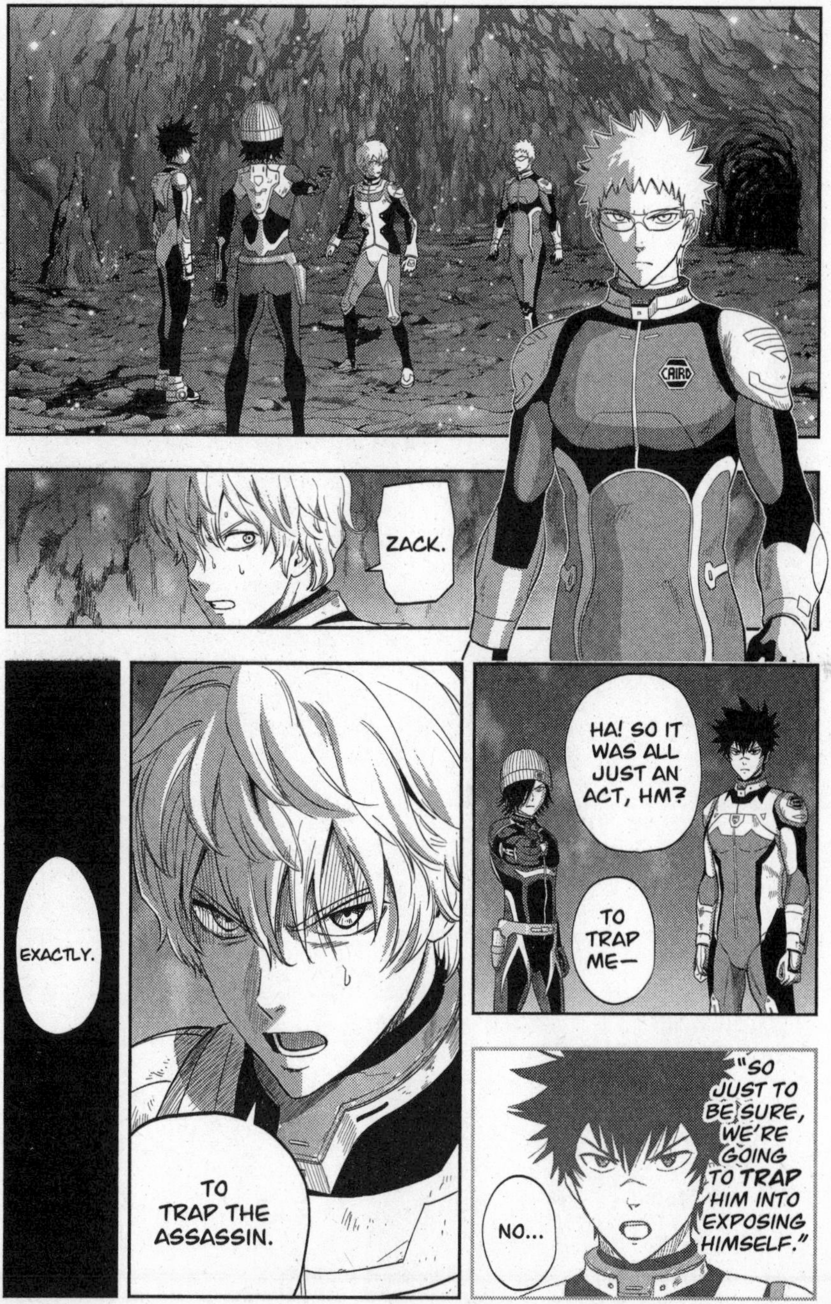
ZACK.
HA! SO IT WAS ALL JUST AN ACT, HM?
TO TRAP ME—
"SO JUST TO BE SURE, WE'RE GOING TO TRAP HIM INTO EXPOSING HIMSELF."
NO...
TO TRAP THE ASSASSIN.
EXACTLY.

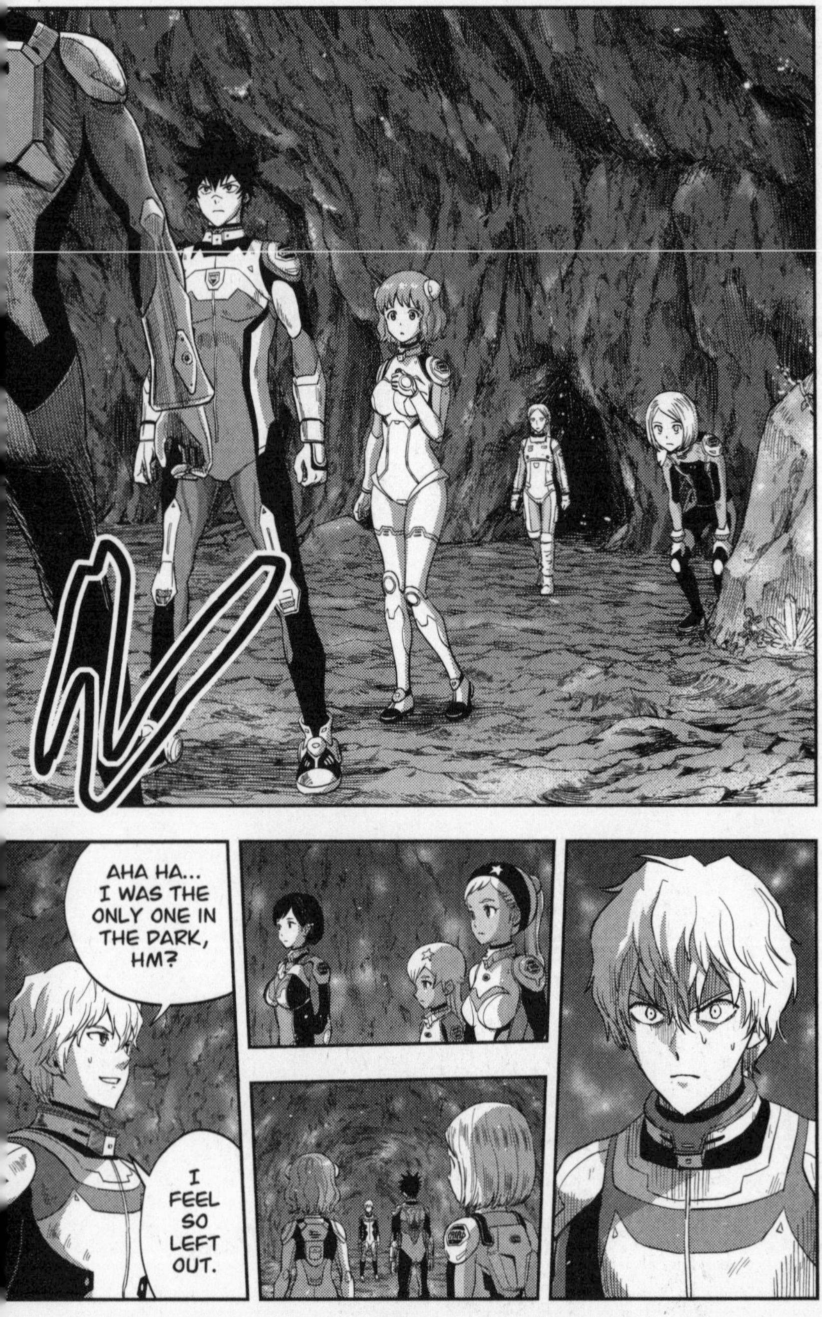
AHA HA... I WAS THE ONLY ONE IN THE DARK, HM?
I FEEL SO LEFT OUT.

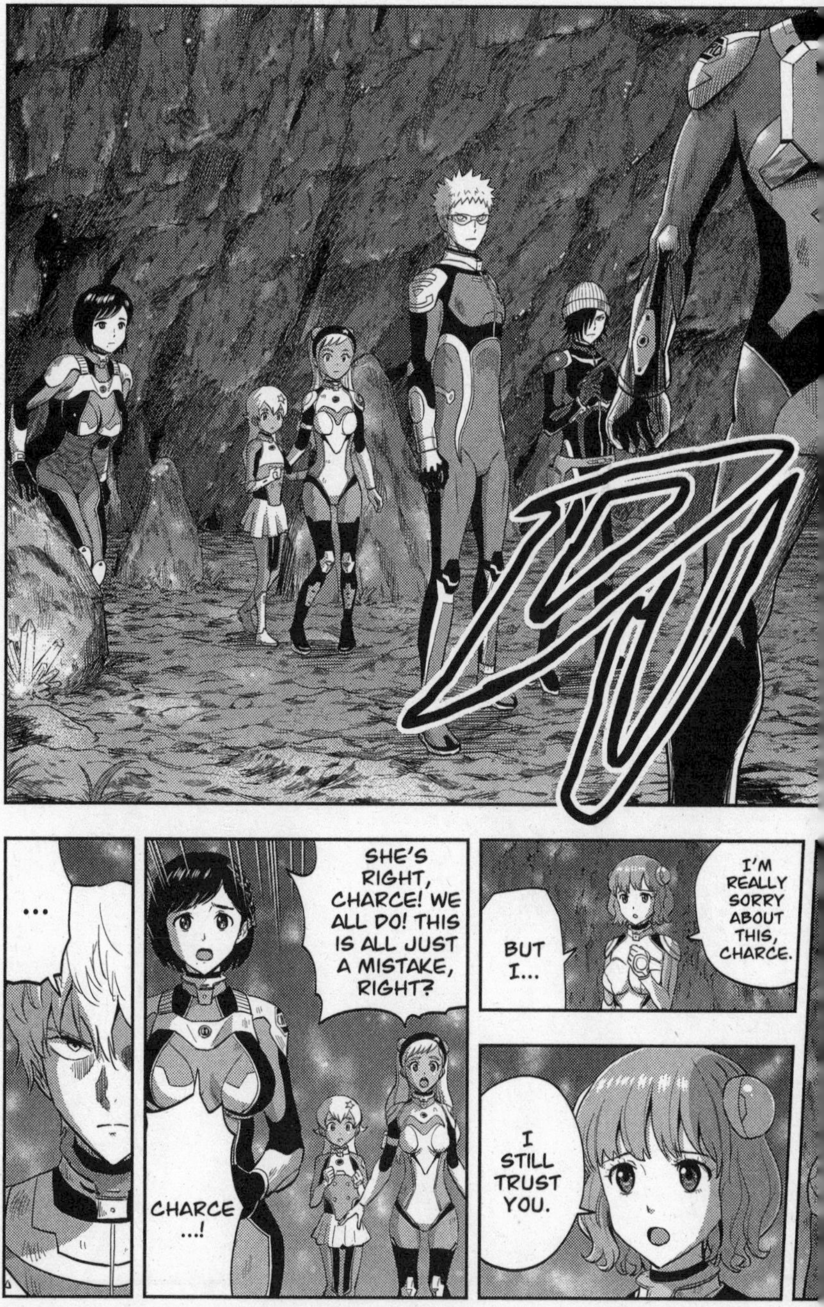
I'M REALLY SORRY ABOUT THIS, CHARCE.
BUT I...
I STILL TRUST YOU.
SHE'S RIGHT, CHARCE! WE ALL DO! THIS IS ALL JUST A MISTAKE, RIGHT?
CHARCE ...!
...

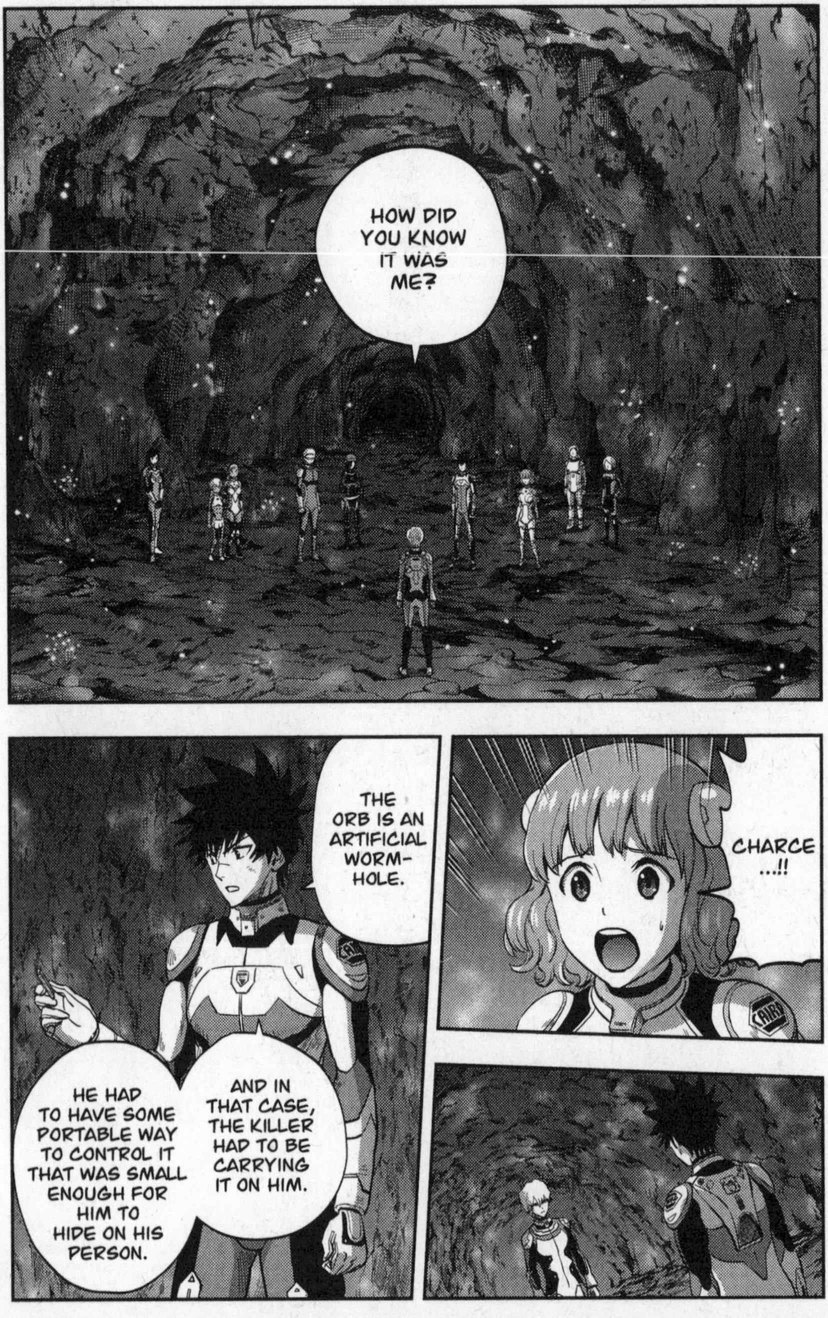
HOW DID YOU KNOW IT WAS ME?
CHARCE ...!!
THE ORB IS AN ARTIFICIAL WORM-HOLE.
AND IN THAT CASE, THE KILLER HAD TO BE CARRYING IT ON HIM.
HE HAD TO HAVE SOME PORTABLE WAY TO CONTROL IT THAT WAS SMALL ENOUGH FOR HIM TO HIDE ON HIS PERSON.

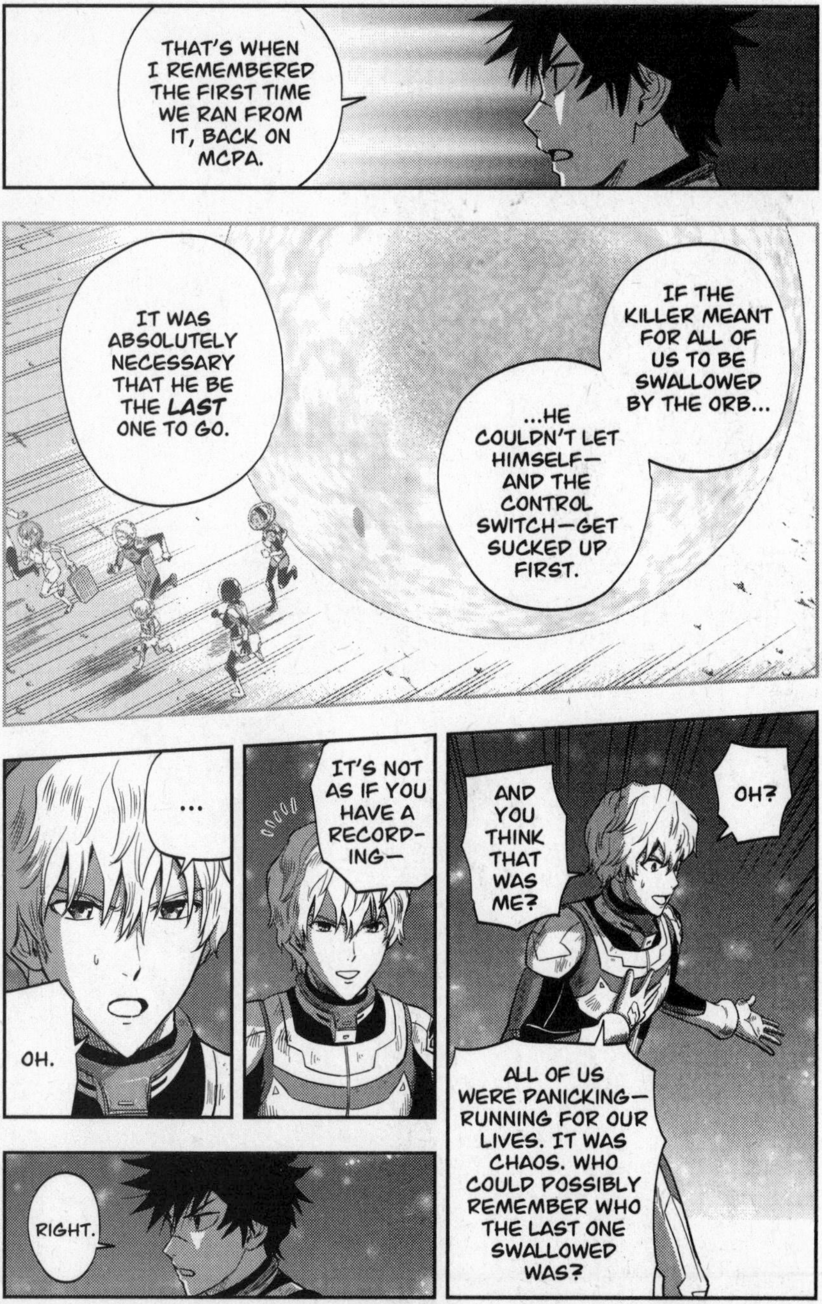
THAT'S WHEN I REMEMBERED THE FIRST TIME WE RAN FROM IT, BACK ON MCPA.
IF THE KILLER MEANT FOR ALL OF US TO BE SWALLOWED BY THE ORB...
...HE COULDN'T LET HIMSELF—AND THE CONTROL SWITCH—GET SUCKED UP FIRST.
IT WAS ABSOLUTELY NECESSARY THAT HE BE THE *LAST* ONE TO GO.
OH?
AND YOU THINK THAT WAS ME?
ALL OF US WERE PANICKING—RUNNING FOR OUR LIVES. IT WAS CHAOS. WHO COULD POSSIBLY REMEMBER WHO THE LAST ONE SWALLOWED WAS?
IT'S NOT AS IF YOU HAVE A RECORDING—
...
OH.
RIGHT.

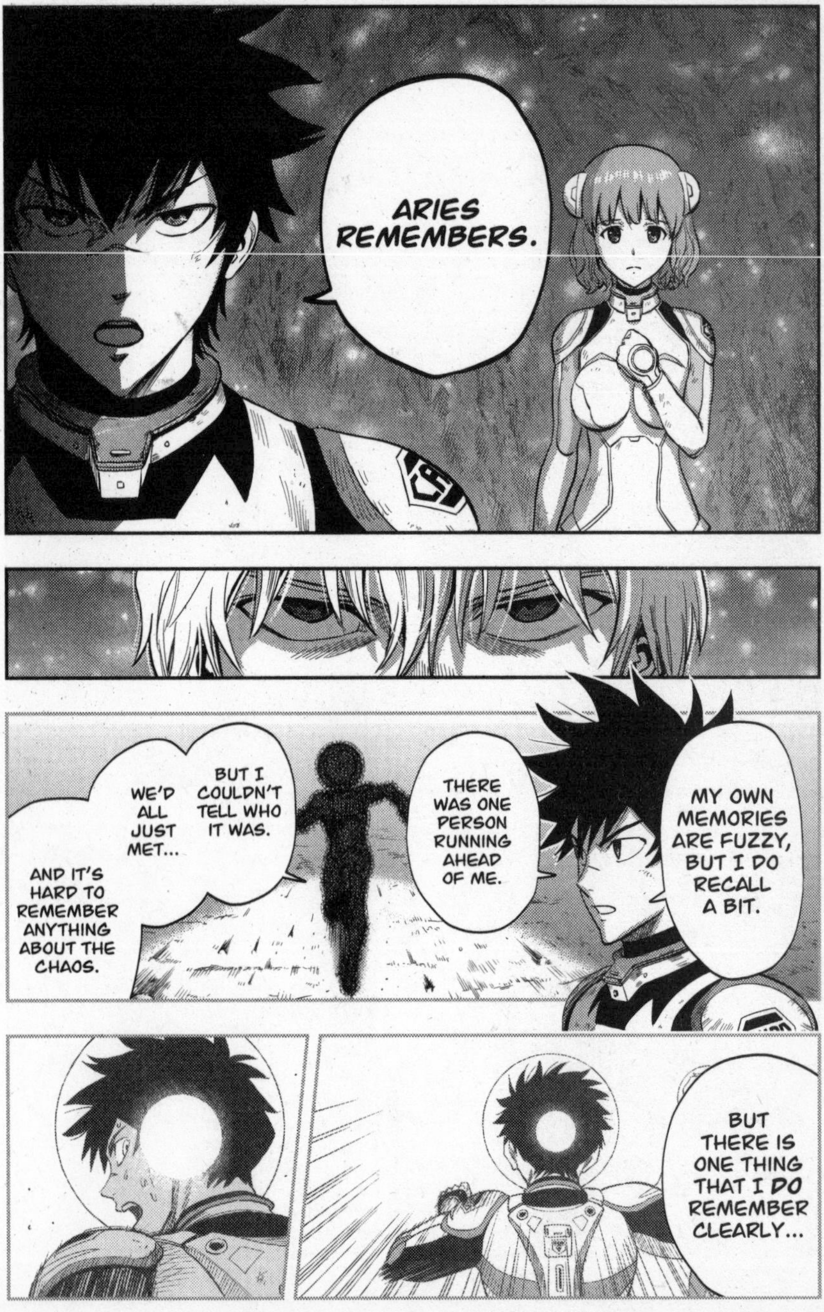
ARIES REMEMBERS.
MY OWN MEMORIES ARE FUZZY, BUT I DO RECALL A BIT.
THERE WAS ONE PERSON RUNNING AHEAD OF ME.
BUT I COULDN'T TELL WHO IT WAS.
WE'D ALL JUST MET...
AND IT'S HARD TO REMEMBER ANYTHING ABOUT THE CHAOS.
BUT THERE IS ONE THING THAT I *DO* REMEMBER CLEARLY...

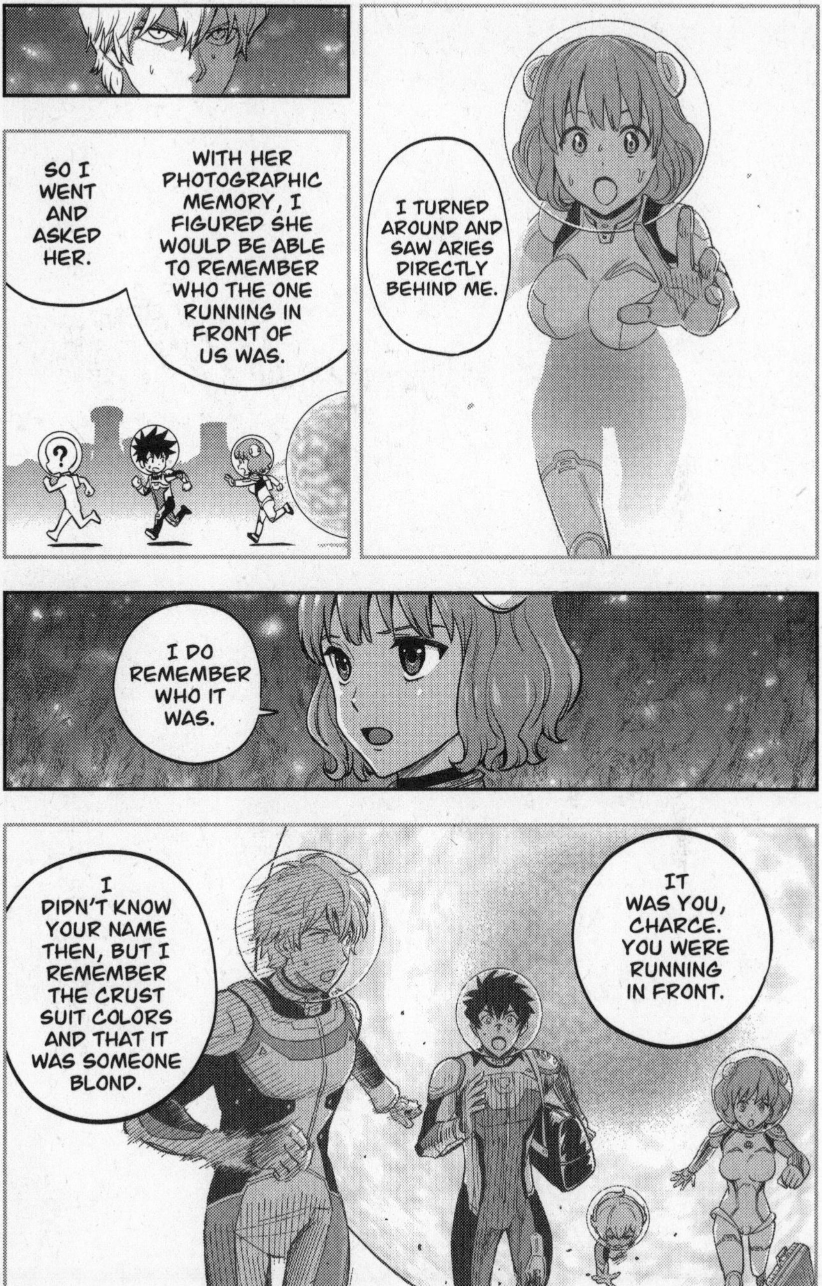
I TURNED AROUND AND SAW ARIES DIRECTLY BEHIND ME.
WITH HER PHOTOGRAPHIC MEMORY, I FIGURED SHE WOULD BE ABLE TO REMEMBER WHO THE ONE RUNNING IN FRONT OF US WAS.
SO I WENT AND ASKED HER.
?
I DO REMEMBER WHO IT WAS.
IT WAS YOU, CHARCE. YOU WERE RUNNING IN FRONT.
I DIDN'T KNOW YOUR NAME THEN, BUT I REMEMBER THE CRUST SUIT COLORS AND THAT IT WAS SOMEONE BLOND.

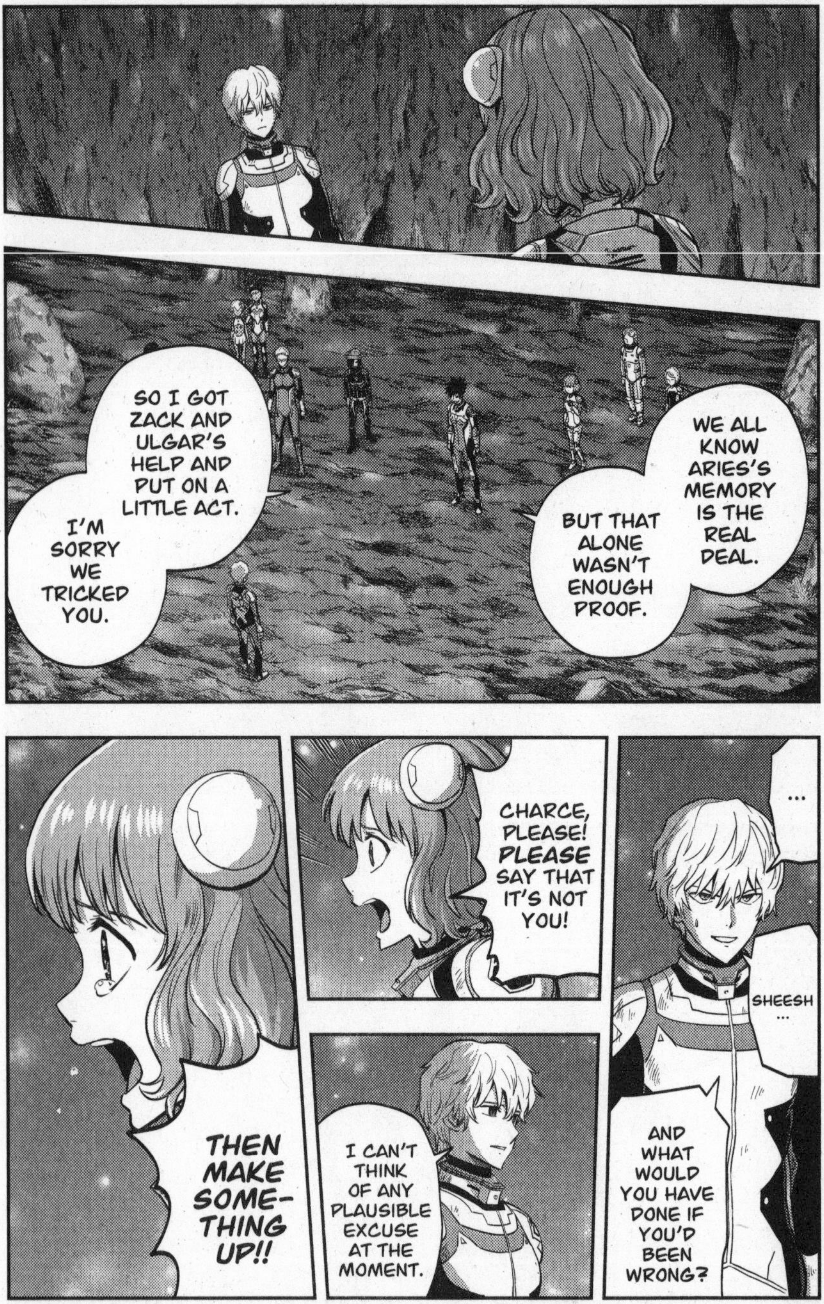
WE ALL KNOW ARIES'S MEMORY IS THE REAL DEAL.
BUT THAT ALONE WASN'T ENOUGH PROOF.
SO I GOT ZACK AND ULGAR'S HELP AND PUT ON A LITTLE ACT.
I'M SORRY WE TRICKED YOU.
...
SHEESH...
AND WHAT WOULD YOU HAVE DONE IF YOU'D BEEN WRONG?
CHARCE, PLEASE! **PLEASE** SAY THAT IT'S NOT YOU!
I CAN'T THINK OF ANY PLAUSIBLE EXCUSE AT THE MOMENT.
THEN MAKE SOME-THING UP!!

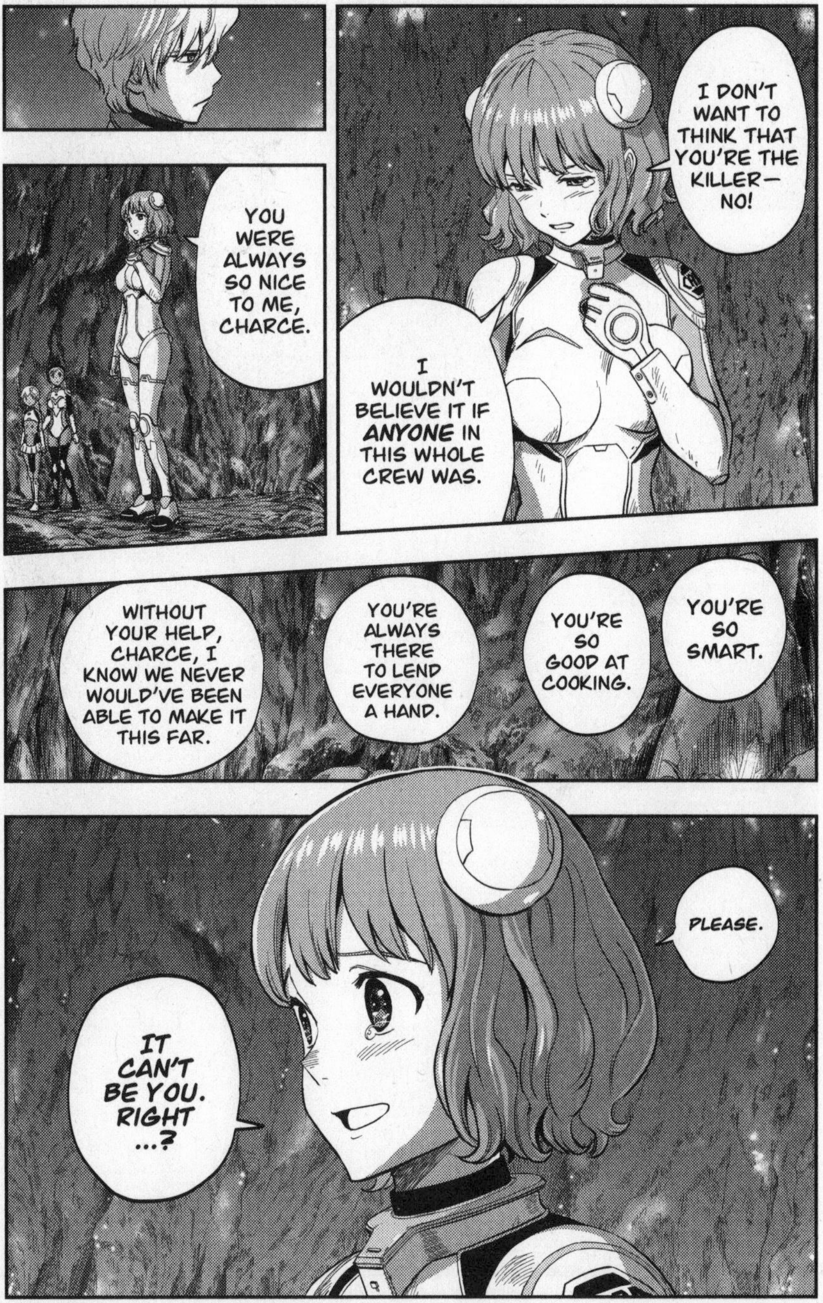
I DON'T WANT TO THINK THAT YOU'RE THE KILLER— NO!
I WOULDN'T BELIEVE IT IF ANYONE IN THIS WHOLE CREW WAS.
YOU WERE ALWAYS SO NICE TO ME, CHARCE.
YOU'RE SO SMART.
YOU'RE SO GOOD AT COOKING.
YOU'RE ALWAYS THERE TO LEND EVERYONE A HAND.
WITHOUT YOUR HELP, CHARCE, I KNOW WE NEVER WOULD'VE BEEN ABLE TO MAKE IT THIS FAR.
PLEASE.
IT CAN'T BE YOU. RIGHT ...?

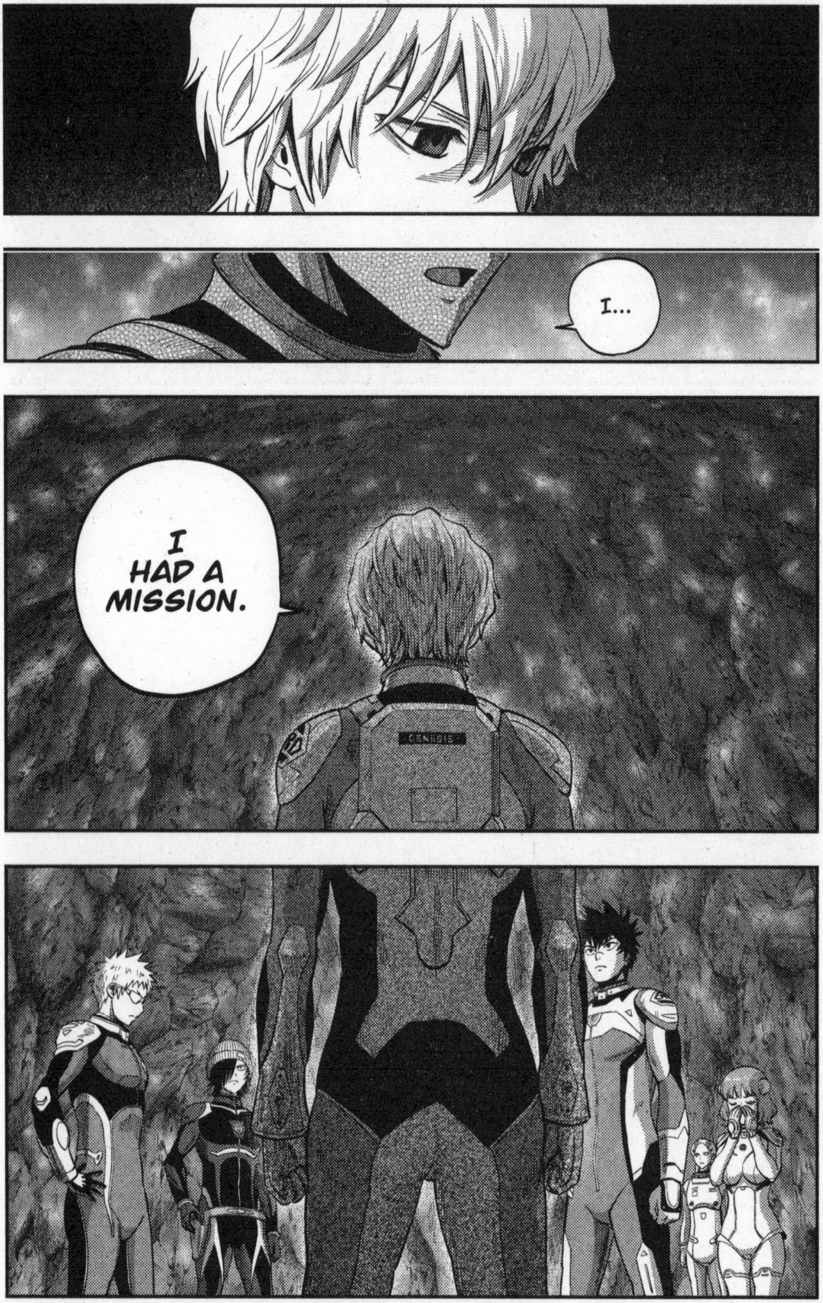
I...
I HAD A MISSION.

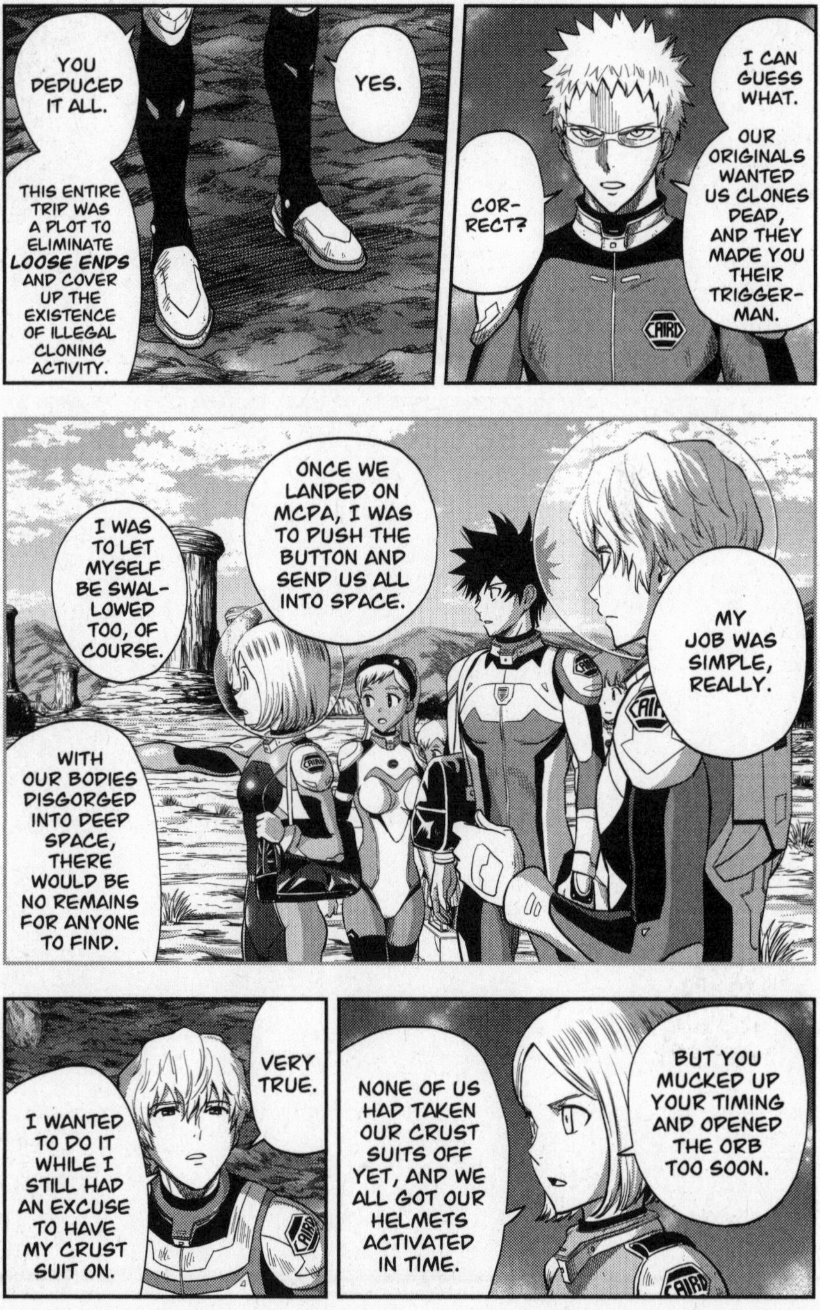
I CAN GUESS WHAT.
OUR ORIGINALS WANTED US CLONES DEAD, AND THEY MADE YOU THEIR TRIGGER-MAN.
COR-RECT?
YES.
YOU DEDUCED IT ALL.
THIS ENTIRE TRIP WAS A PLOT TO ELIMINATE **LOOSE ENDS** AND COVER UP THE EXISTENCE OF ILLEGAL CLONING ACTIVITY.
MY JOB WAS SIMPLE, REALLY.
ONCE WE LANDED ON MCPA, I WAS TO PUSH THE BUTTON AND SEND US ALL INTO SPACE.
I WAS TO LET MYSELF BE SWAL-LOWED TOO, OF COURSE.
WITH OUR BODIES DISGORGED INTO DEEP SPACE, THERE WOULD BE NO REMAINS FOR ANYONE TO FIND.
BUT YOU MUCKED UP YOUR TIMING AND OPENED THE ORB TOO SOON.
NONE OF US HAD TAKEN OUR CRUST SUITS OFF YET, AND WE ALL GOT OUR HELMETS ACTIVATED IN TIME.
VERY TRUE.
I WANTED TO DO IT WHILE I STILL HAD AN EXCUSE TO HAVE MY CRUST SUIT ON.

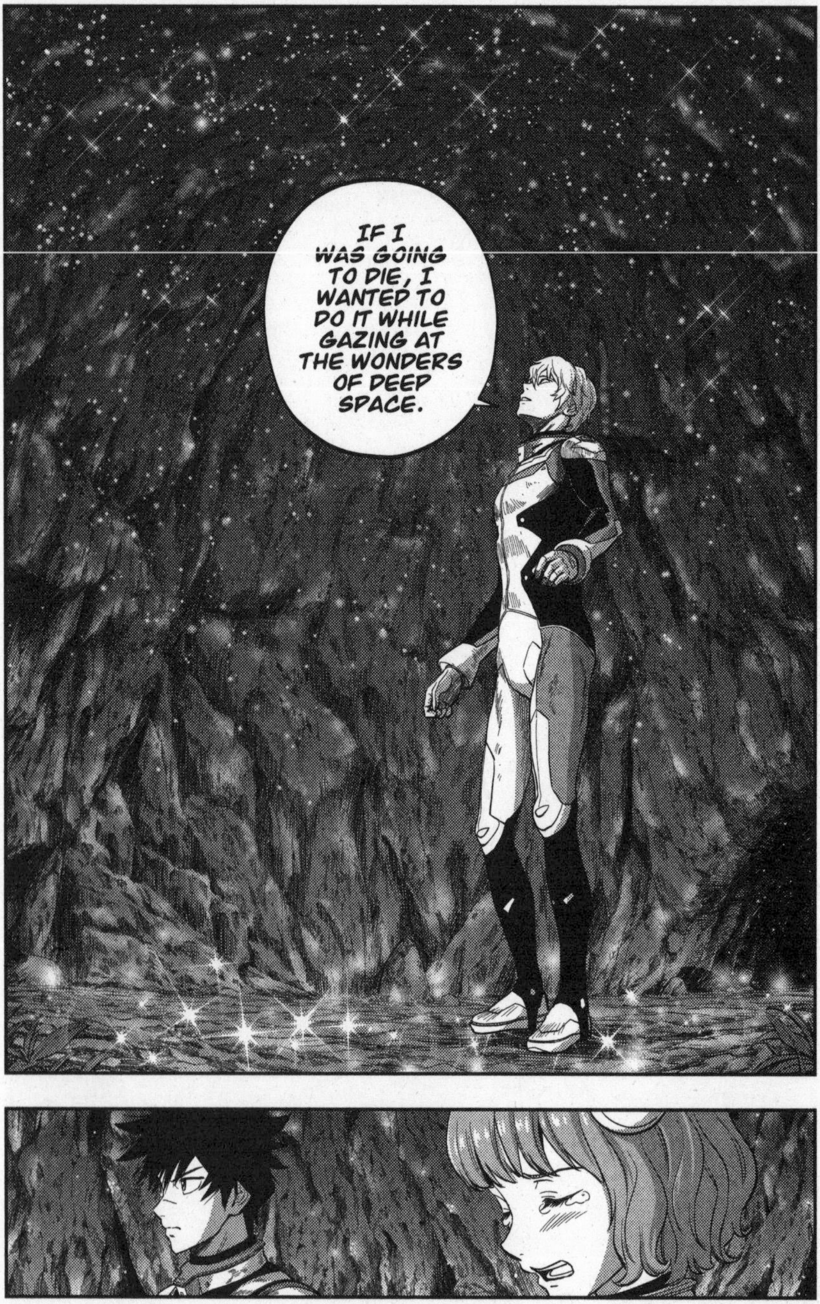
IF I WAS GOING TO DIE, I WANTED TO DO IT WHILE GAZING AT THE WONDERS OF DEEP SPACE.

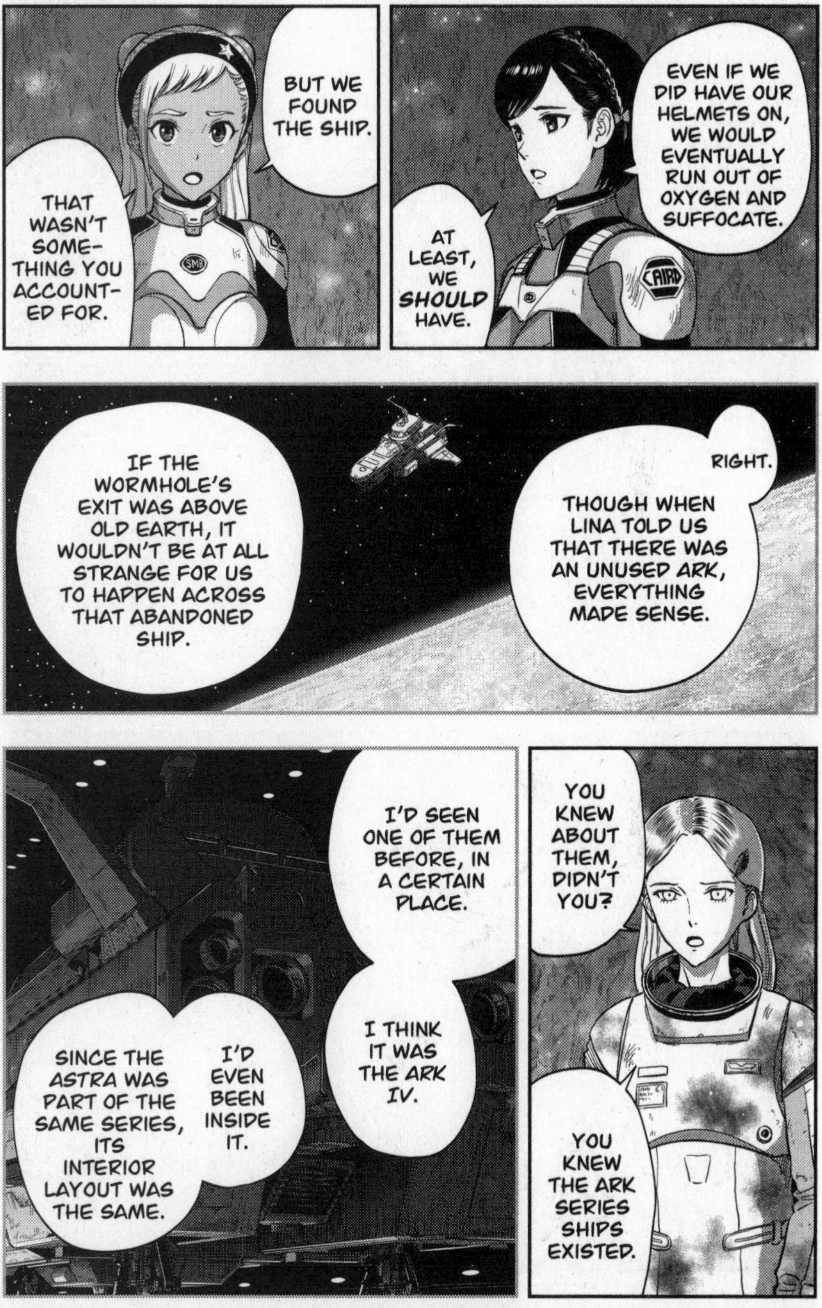
EVEN IF WE DID HAVE OUR HELMETS ON, WE WOULD EVENTUALLY RUN OUT OF OXYGEN AND SUFFOCATE.
AT LEAST, WE SHOULD HAVE.
BUT WE FOUND THE SHIP.
THAT WASN'T SOME-THING YOU ACCOUNT-ED FOR.
RIGHT.
THOUGH WHEN LINA TOLD US THAT THERE WAS AN UNUSED ARK, EVERYTHING MADE SENSE.
IF THE WORMHOLE'S EXIT WAS ABOVE OLD EARTH, IT WOULDN'T BE AT ALL STRANGE FOR US TO HAPPEN ACROSS THAT ABANDONED SHIP.
YOU KNEW ABOUT THEM, DIDN'T YOU?
YOU KNEW THE ARK SERIES SHIPS EXISTED.
I'D SEEN ONE OF THEM BEFORE, IN A CERTAIN PLACE.
I THINK IT WAS THE ARK IV.
I'D EVEN BEEN INSIDE IT.
SINCE THE ASTRA WAS PART OF THE SAME SERIES, ITS INTERIOR LAYOUT WAS THE SAME.

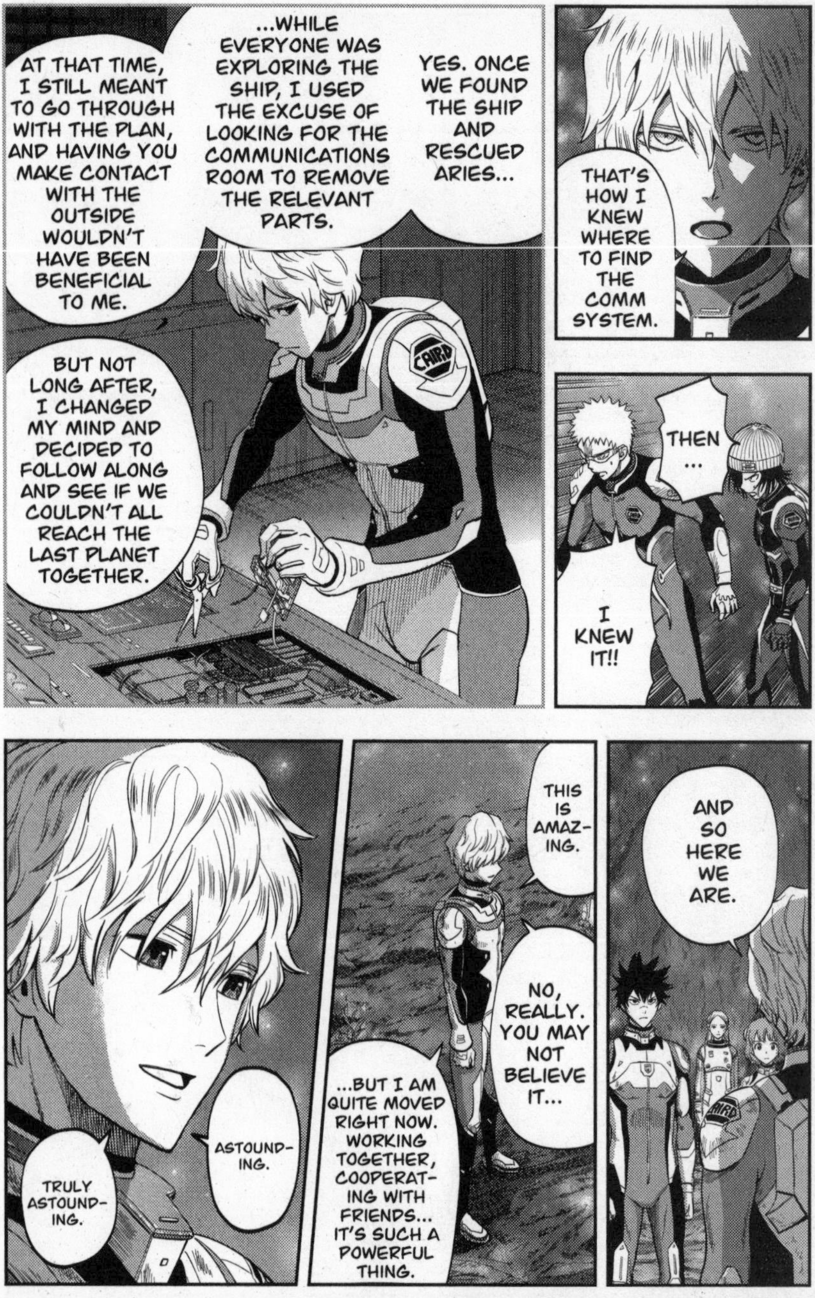
THAT'S HOW I KNEW WHERE TO FIND THE COMM SYSTEM.
THEN...
I KNEW IT!!
YES. ONCE WE FOUND THE SHIP AND RESCUED ARIES...
...WHILE EVERYONE WAS EXPLORING THE SHIP, I USED THE EXCUSE OF LOOKING FOR THE COMMUNICATIONS ROOM TO REMOVE THE RELEVANT PARTS.
AT THAT TIME, I STILL MEANT TO GO THROUGH WITH THE PLAN, AND HAVING YOU MAKE CONTACT WITH THE OUTSIDE WOULDN'T HAVE BEEN BENEFICIAL TO ME.
BUT NOT LONG AFTER, I CHANGED MY MIND AND DECIDED TO FOLLOW ALONG AND SEE IF WE COULDN'T ALL REACH THE LAST PLANET TOGETHER.
AND SO HERE WE ARE.
THIS IS AMAZ-ING.
NO, REALLY. YOU MAY NOT BELIEVE IT...
...BUT I AM QUITE MOVED RIGHT NOW. WORKING TOGETHER, COOPERAT-ING WITH FRIENDS... IT'S SUCH A POWERFUL THING.
ASTOUND-ING.
TRULY ASTOUND-ING.

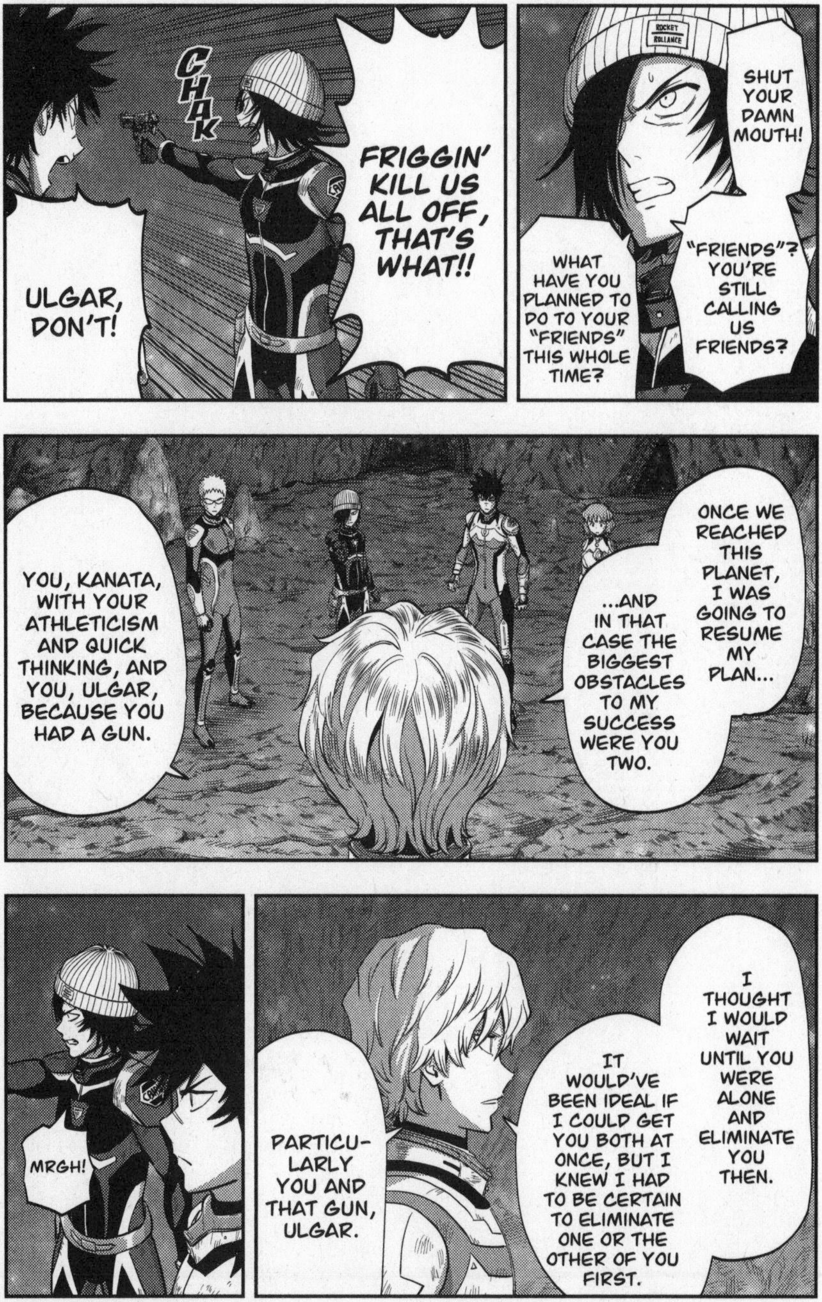
SHUT YOUR DAMN MOUTH!
"FRIENDS"? YOU'RE STILL CALLING US FRIENDS?
WHAT HAVE YOU PLANNED TO DO TO YOUR "FRIENDS" THIS WHOLE TIME?
FRIGGIN' KILL US ALL OFF, THAT'S WHAT!!
CHAK
ULGAR, DON'T!
ONCE WE REACHED THIS PLANET, I WAS GOING TO RESUME MY PLAN...
...AND IN THAT CASE THE BIGGEST OBSTACLES TO MY SUCCESS WERE YOU TWO.
YOU, KANATA, WITH YOUR ATHLETICISM AND QUICK THINKING, AND YOU, ULGAR, BECAUSE YOU HAD A GUN.
I THOUGHT I WOULD WAIT UNTIL YOU WERE ALONE AND ELIMINATE YOU THEN.
IT WOULD'VE BEEN IDEAL IF I COULD GET YOU BOTH AT ONCE, BUT I KNEW I HAD TO BE CERTAIN TO ELIMINATE ONE OR THE OTHER OF YOU FIRST.
PARTICU-LARLY YOU AND THAT GUN, ULGAR.
MRGH!

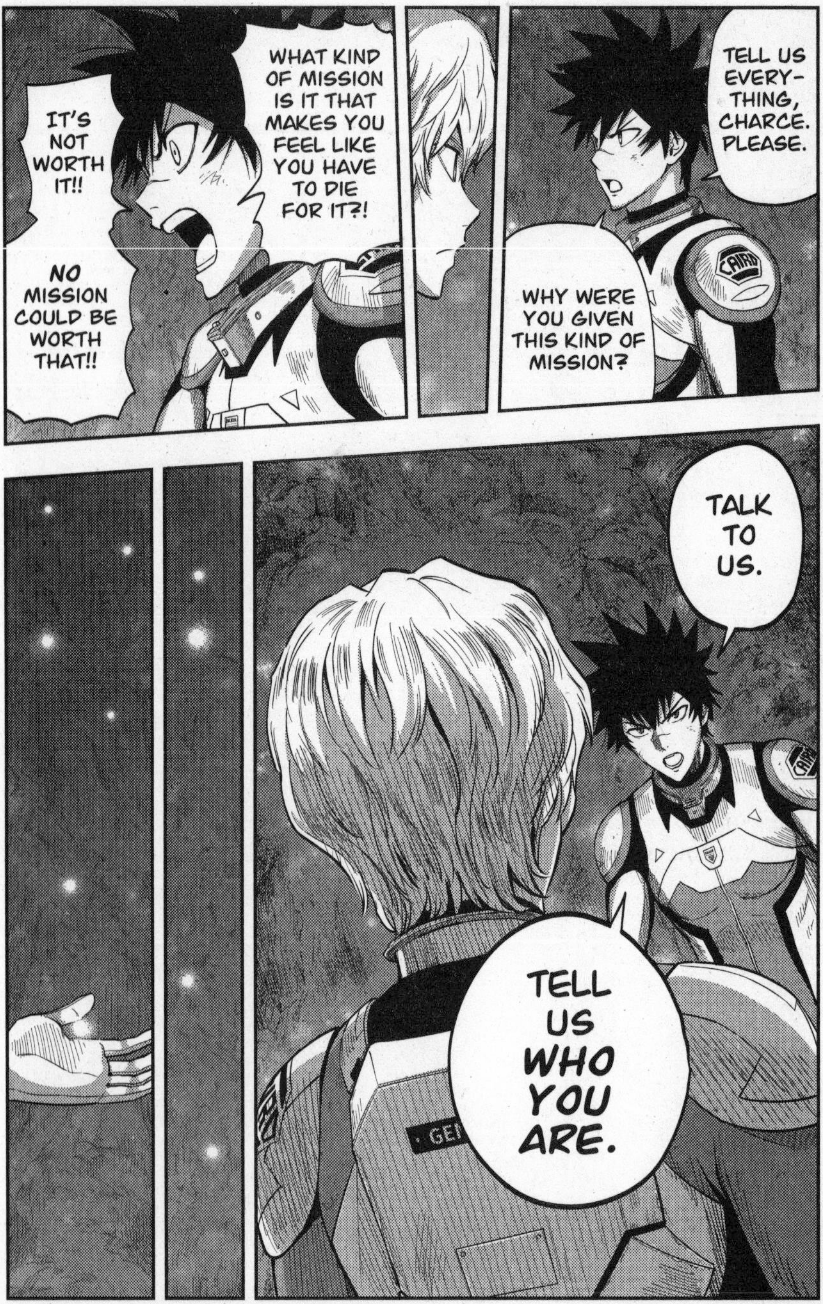
TELL US EVERY-THING, CHARCE. PLEASE.
WHY WERE YOU GIVEN THIS KIND OF MISSION?
WHAT KIND OF MISSION IS IT THAT MAKES YOU FEEL LIKE YOU HAVE TO DIE FOR IT?!
IT'S NOT WORTH IT!!
NO MISSION COULD BE WORTH THAT!!
TALK TO US.
TELL US WHO YOU ARE.

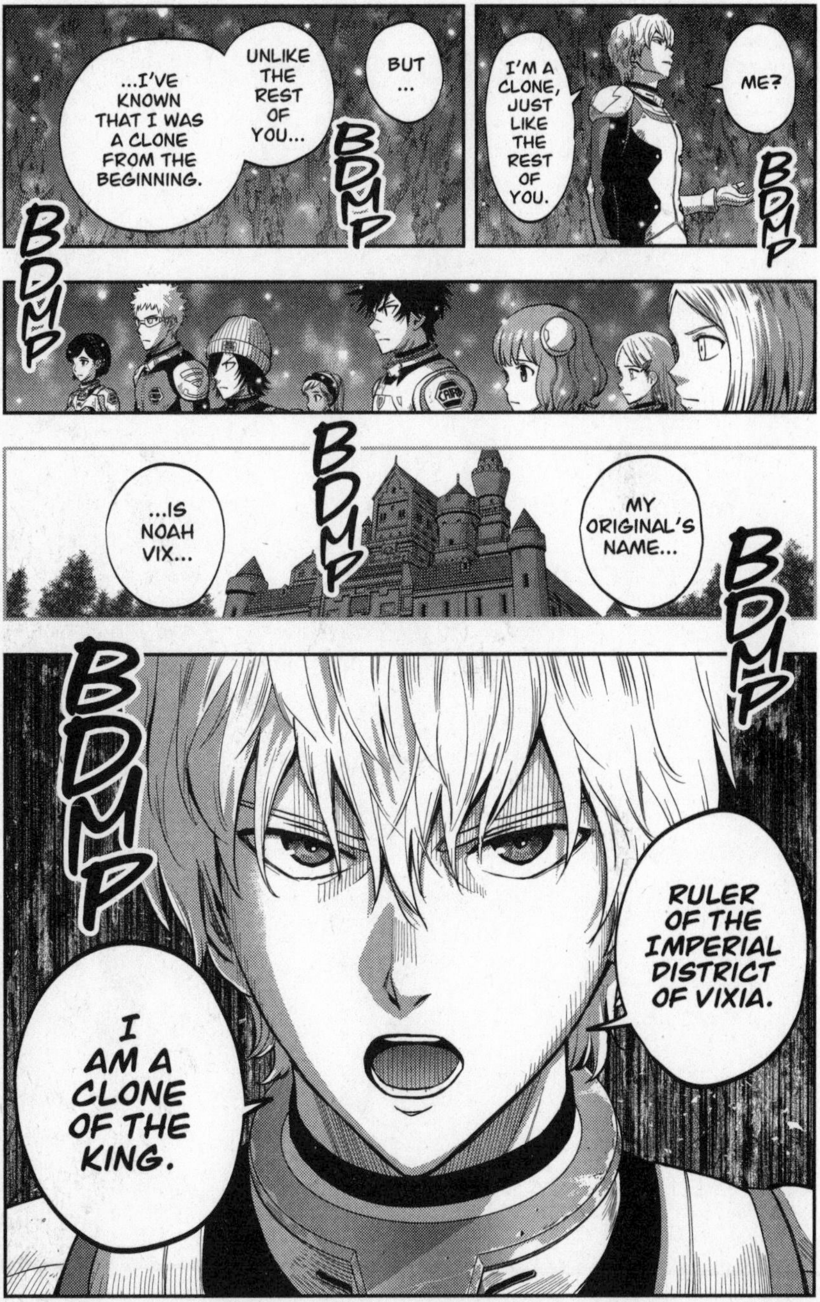
ME?
I'M A CLONE, JUST LIKE THE REST OF YOU.
BDMP
BUT ...
UNLIKE THE REST OF YOU...
...I'VE KNOWN THAT I WAS A CLONE FROM THE BEGINNING.
BDMP
BDMP
BDMP
MY ORIGINAL'S NAME...
...IS NOAH VIX...
BDMP
BDMP
RULER OF THE IMPERIAL DISTRICT OF VIXIA.
I AM A CLONE OF THE KING.

Material Collection | Character Prototype Design

ARIES, CHARCE and YUN-HUA

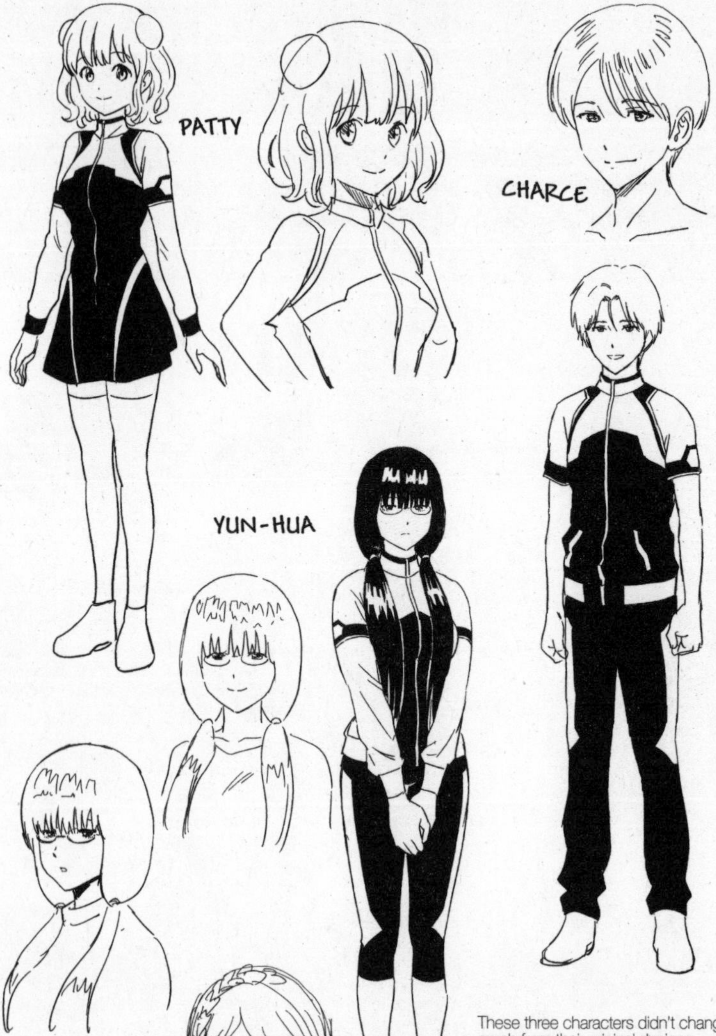
PATTY
CHARCE
YUN-HUA

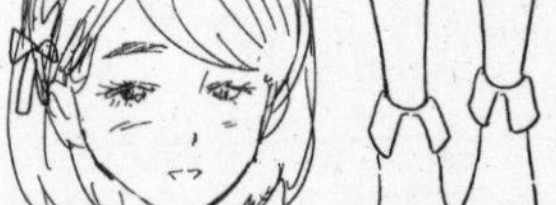

These three characters didn't change much from their original designs. Aries was going to be named Patty at first. Charce's hairstyle was going to be smoother to make him look younger. Everything about Yun-hua, from her personality to her role in the crew to her character arc has stayed the same from the very beginning.

ASTRA
LOST IN SPACE

#43

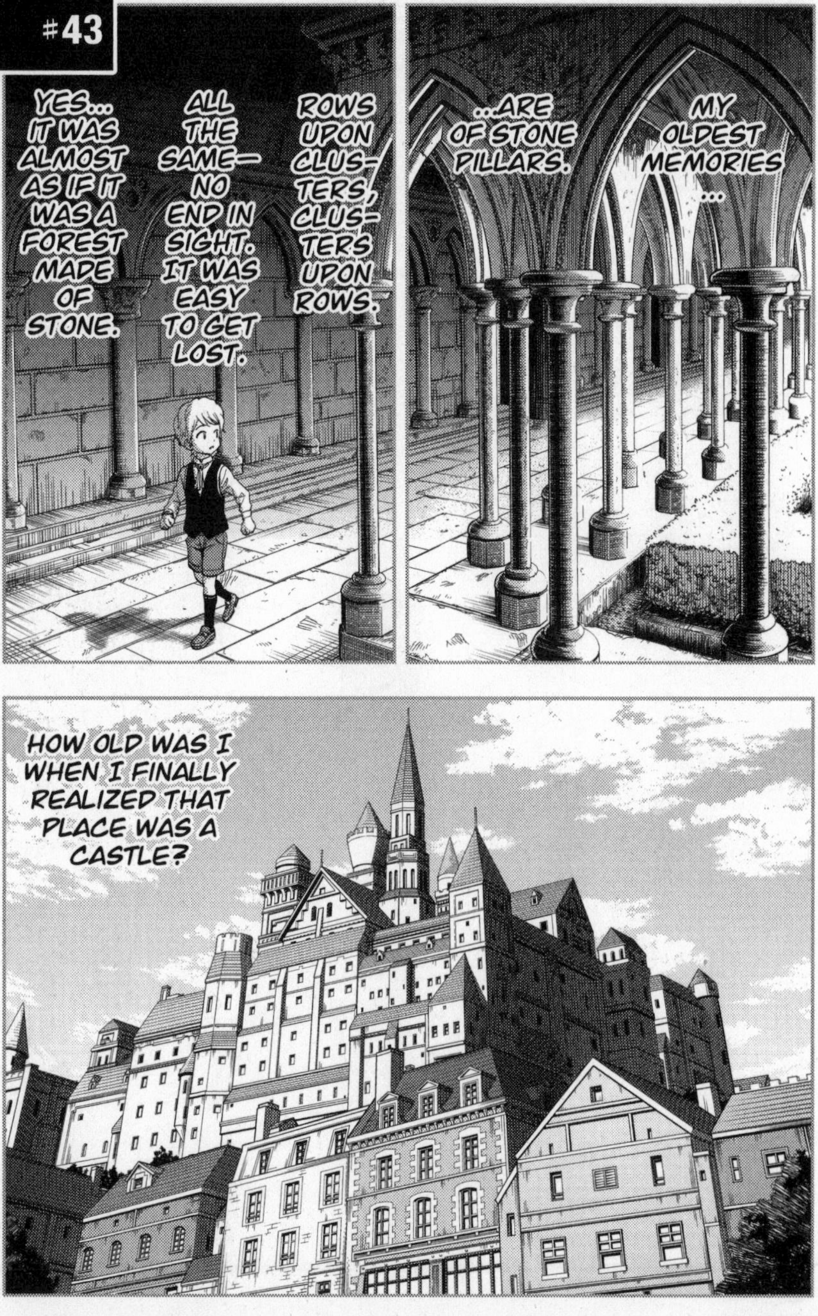
MY OLDEST MEMORIES...
...ARE OF STONE PILLARS.
ROWS UPON CLUSTERS, CLUSTERS UPON ROWS.
ALL THE SAME—NO END IN SIGHT. IT WAS EASY TO GET LOST.
YES... IT WAS ALMOST AS IF IT WAS A FOREST MADE OF STONE.
HOW OLD WAS I WHEN I FINALLY REALIZED THAT PLACE WAS A CASTLE?

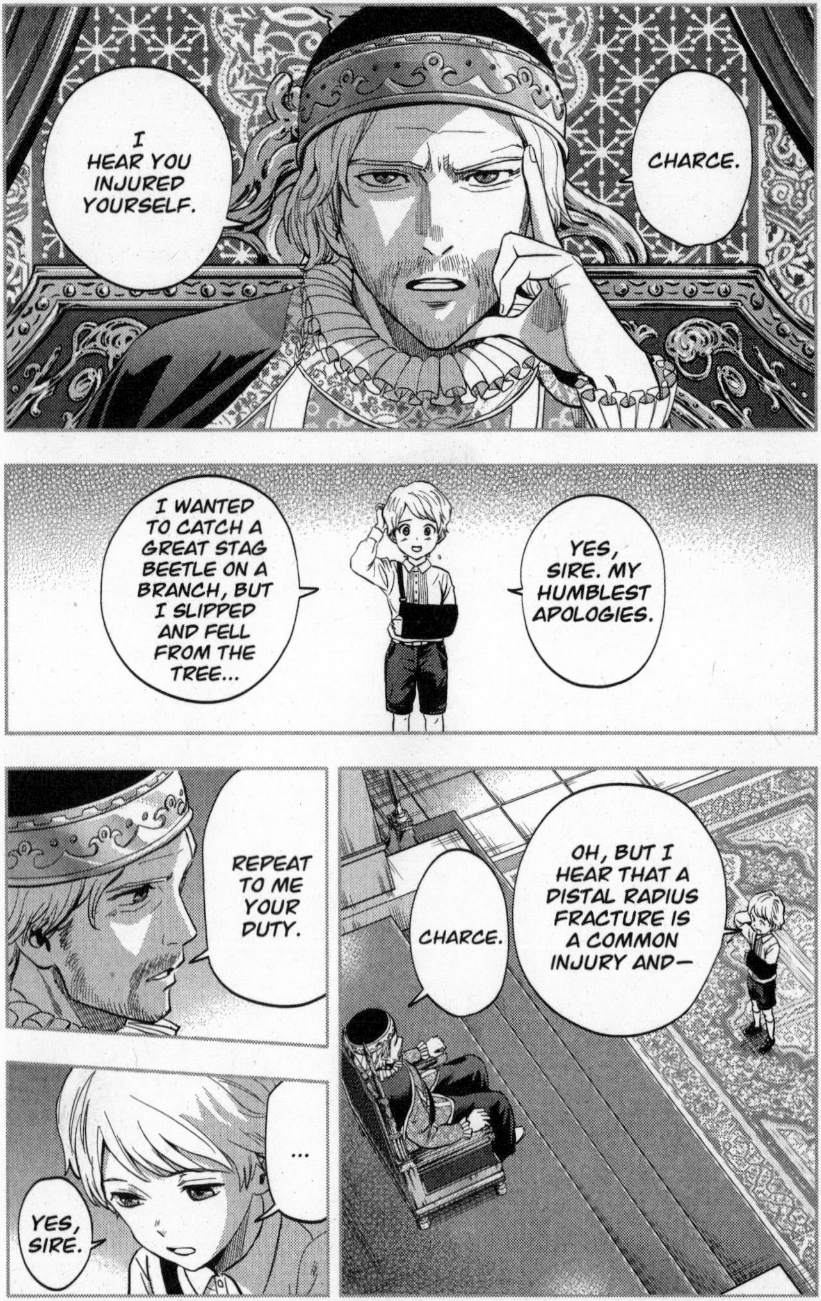
CHARCE.
I HEAR YOU INJURED YOURSELF.
YES, SIRE. MY HUMBLEST APOLOGIES.
I WANTED TO CATCH A GREAT STAG BEETLE ON A BRANCH, BUT I SLIPPED AND FELL FROM THE TREE...
OH, BUT I HEAR THAT A DISTAL RADIUS FRACTURE IS A COMMON INJURY AND—
CHARCE.
REPEAT TO ME YOUR DUTY.
...
YES, SIRE.

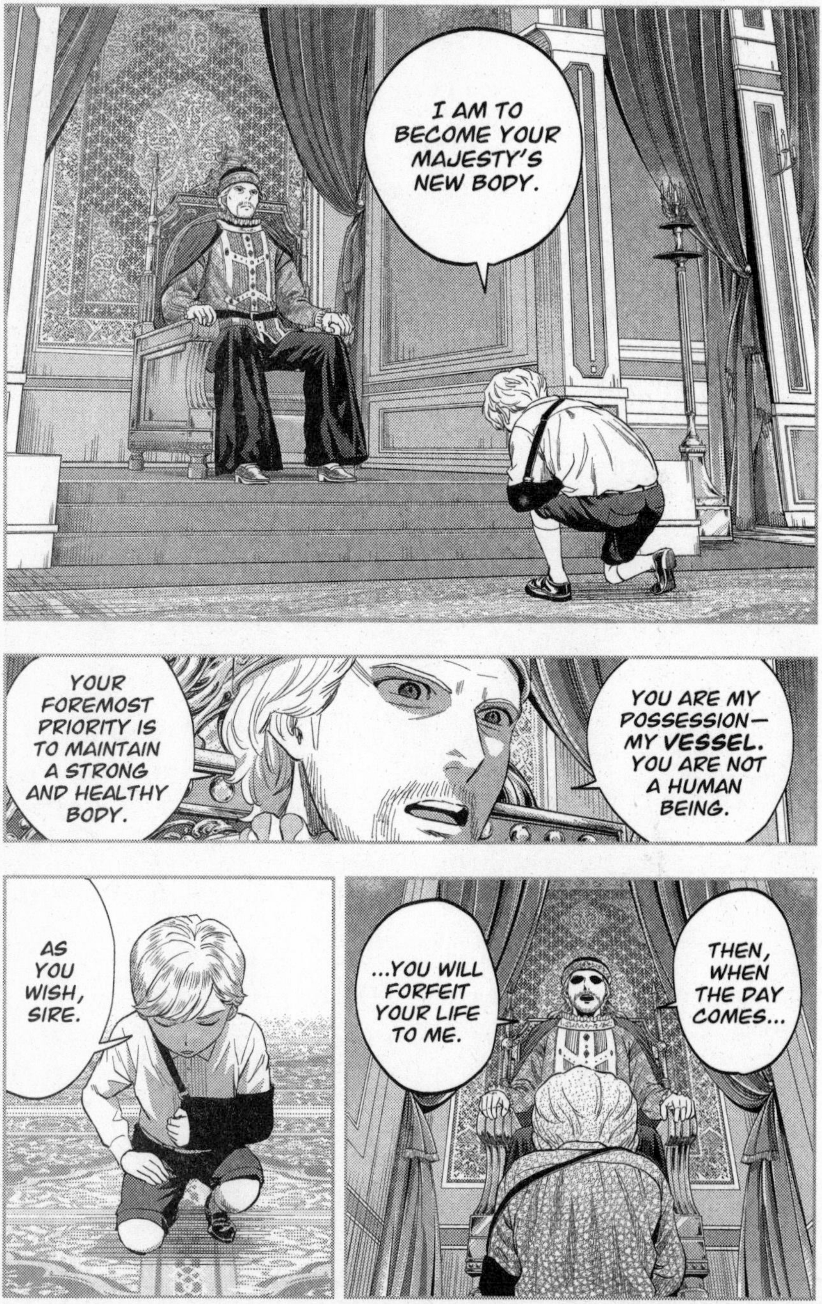
I AM TO BECOME YOUR MAJESTY'S NEW BODY.
YOU ARE MY POSSESSION— MY **VESSEL**. YOU ARE NOT A HUMAN BEING.
YOUR FOREMOST PRIORITY IS TO MAINTAIN A STRONG AND HEALTHY BODY.
THEN, WHEN THE DAY COMES...
...YOU WILL FORFEIT YOUR LIFE TO ME.
AS YOU WISH, SIRE.

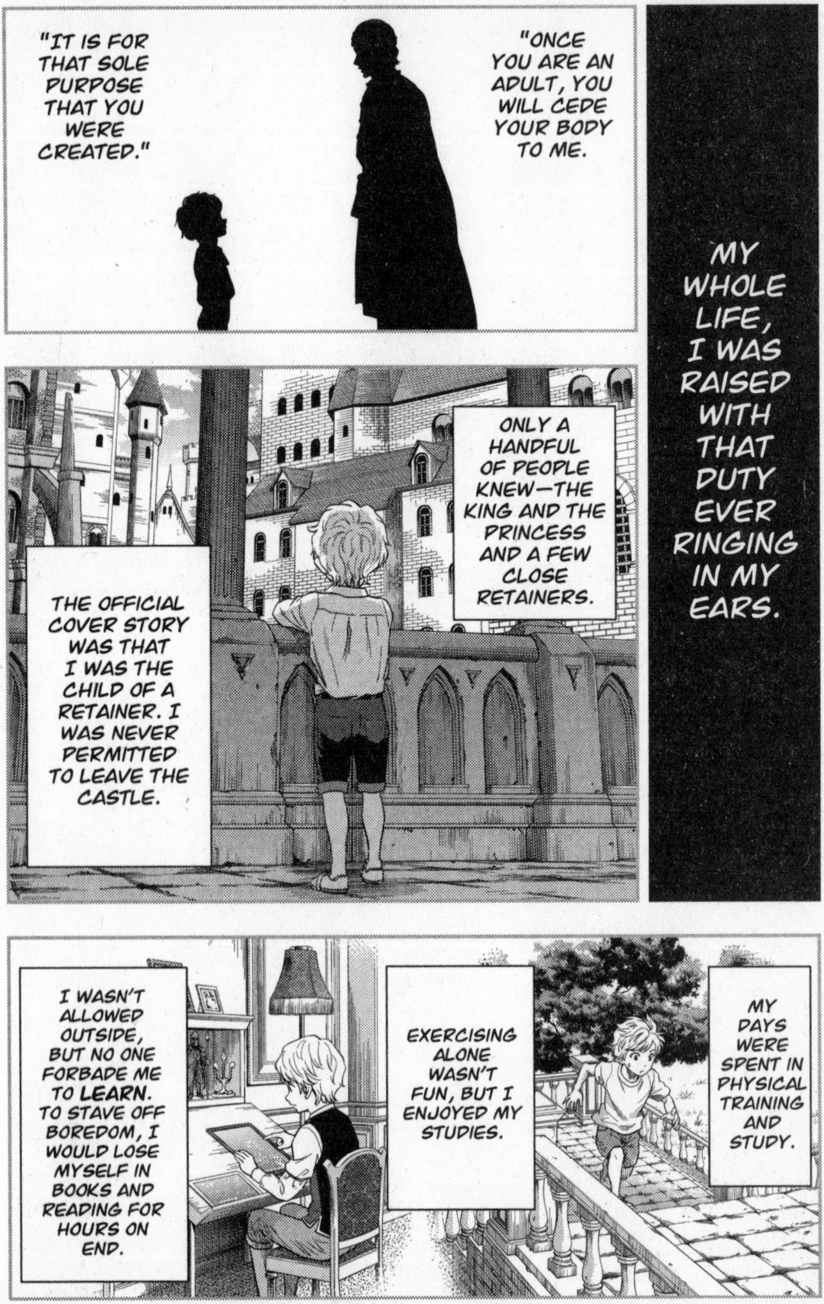
MY WHOLE LIFE, I WAS RAISED WITH THAT DUTY EVER RINGING IN MY EARS.
"ONCE YOU ARE AN ADULT, YOU WILL CEDE YOUR BODY TO ME.
"IT IS FOR THAT SOLE PURPOSE THAT YOU WERE CREATED."
ONLY A HANDFUL OF PEOPLE KNEW—THE KING AND THE PRINCESS AND A FEW CLOSE RETAINERS.
THE OFFICIAL COVER STORY WAS THAT I WAS THE CHILD OF A RETAINER. I WAS NEVER PERMITTED TO LEAVE THE CASTLE.
MY DAYS WERE SPENT IN PHYSICAL TRAINING AND STUDY.
EXERCISING ALONE WASN'T FUN, BUT I ENJOYED MY STUDIES.
I WASN'T ALLOWED OUTSIDE, BUT NO ONE FORBADE ME TO **LEARN**. TO STAVE OFF BOREDOM, I WOULD LOSE MYSELF IN BOOKS AND READING FOR HOURS ON END.

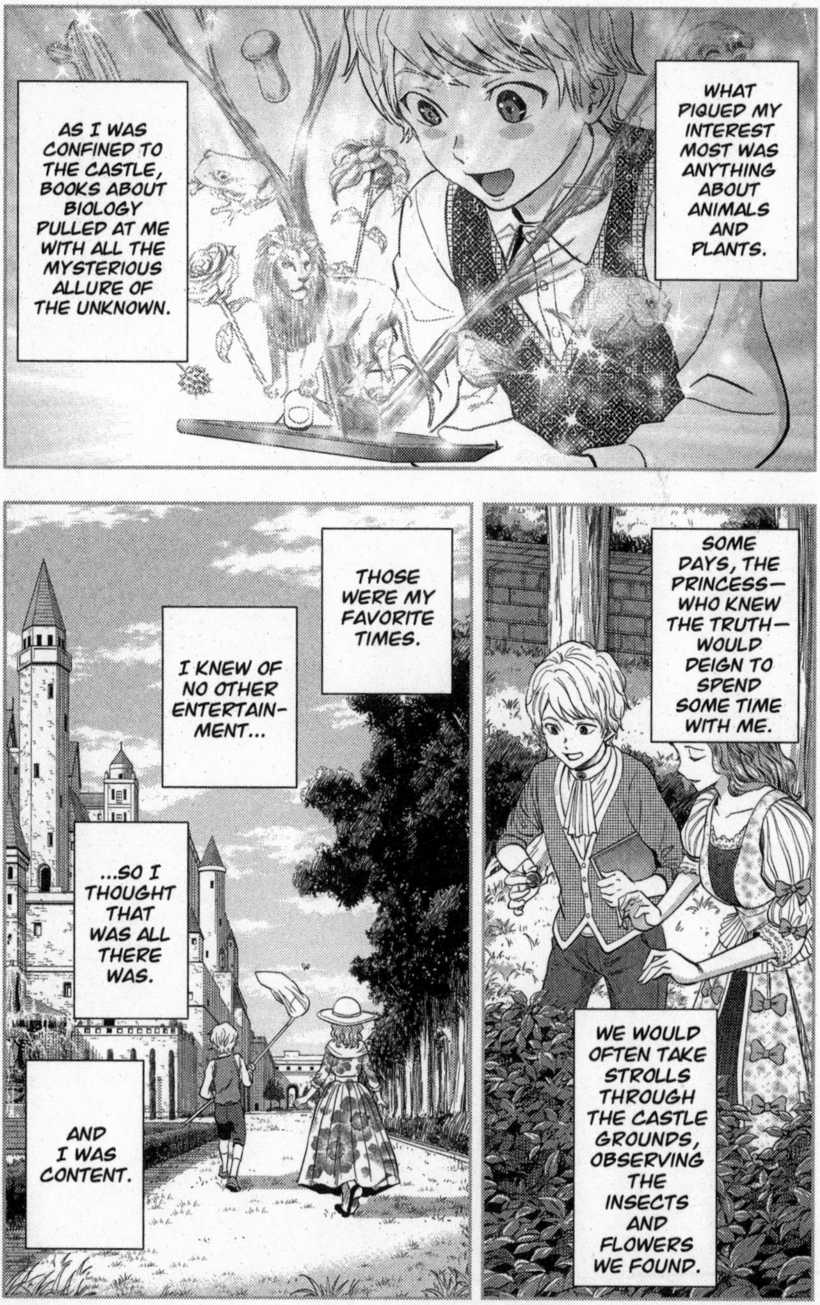
WHAT PIQUED MY INTEREST MOST WAS ANYTHING ABOUT ANIMALS AND PLANTS.
AS I WAS CONFINED TO THE CASTLE, BOOKS ABOUT BIOLOGY PULLED AT ME WITH ALL THE MYSTERIOUS ALLURE OF THE UNKNOWN.
SOME DAYS, THE PRINCESS—WHO KNEW THE TRUTH—WOULD DEIGN TO SPEND SOME TIME WITH ME.
WE WOULD OFTEN TAKE STROLLS THROUGH THE CASTLE GROUNDS, OBSERVING THE INSECTS AND FLOWERS WE FOUND.
THOSE WERE MY FAVORITE TIMES.
I KNEW OF NO OTHER ENTERTAIN-MENT...
...SO I THOUGHT THAT WAS ALL THERE WAS.
AND I WAS CONTENT.

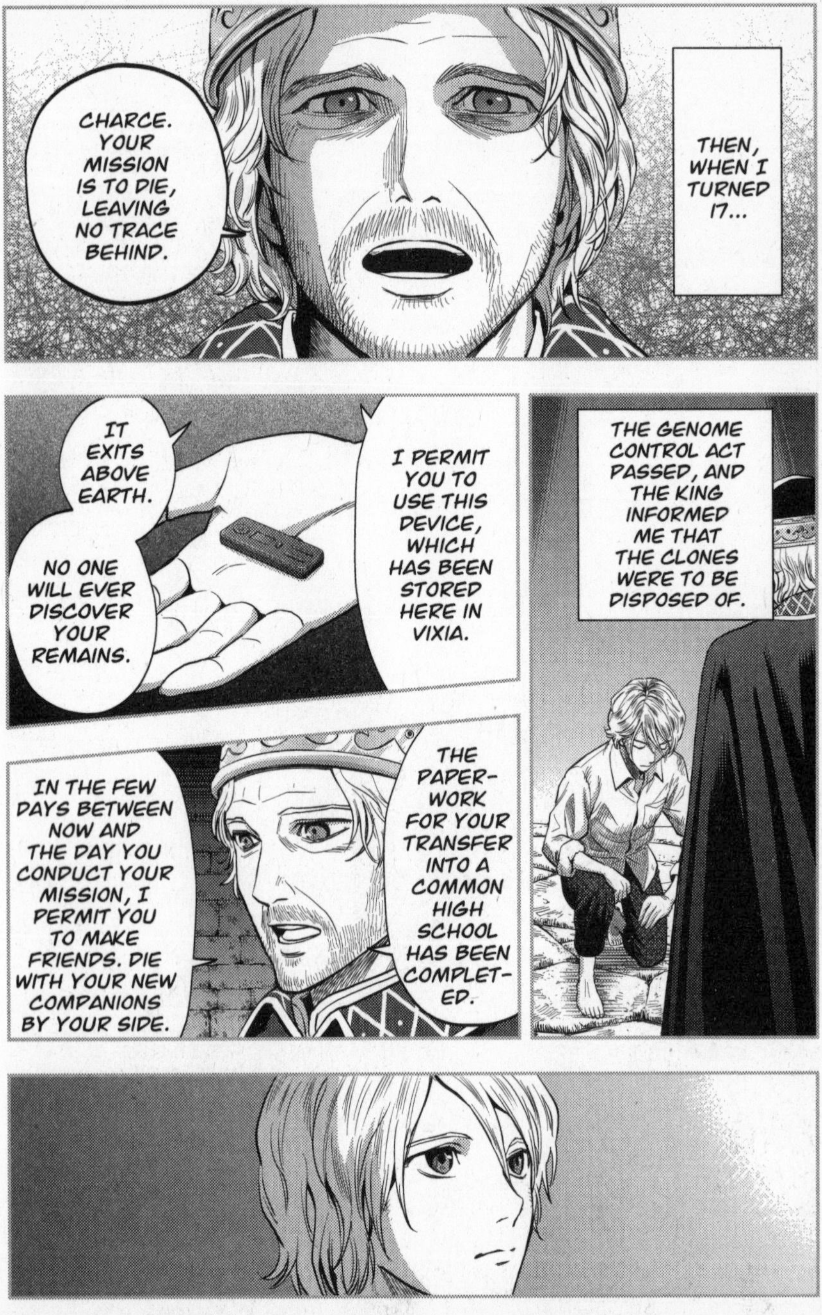
THEN, WHEN I TURNED 17...
CHARCE. YOUR MISSION IS TO DIE, LEAVING NO TRACE BEHIND.
THE GENOME CONTROL ACT PASSED, AND THE KING INFORMED ME THAT THE CLONES WERE TO BE DISPOSED OF.
I PERMIT YOU TO USE THIS DEVICE, WHICH HAS BEEN STORED HERE IN VIXIA.
IT EXITS ABOVE EARTH.
NO ONE WILL EVER DISCOVER YOUR REMAINS.
THE PAPER-WORK FOR YOUR TRANSFER INTO A COMMON HIGH SCHOOL HAS BEEN COMPLET-ED.
IN THE FEW DAYS BETWEEN NOW AND THE DAY YOU CONDUCT YOUR MISSION, I PERMIT YOU TO MAKE FRIENDS. DIE WITH YOUR NEW COMPANIONS BY YOUR SIDE.

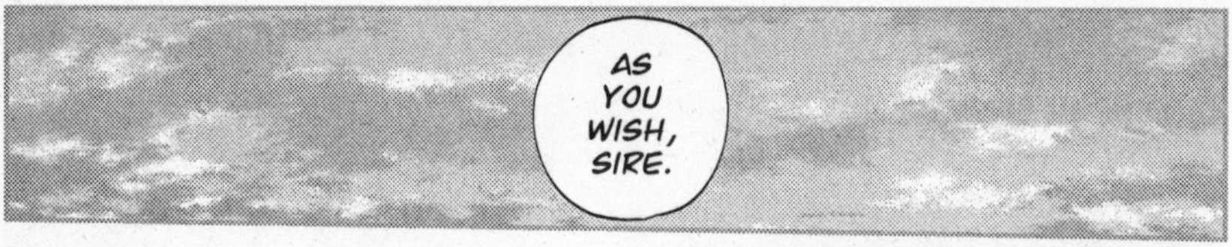
AS YOU WISH, SIRE.

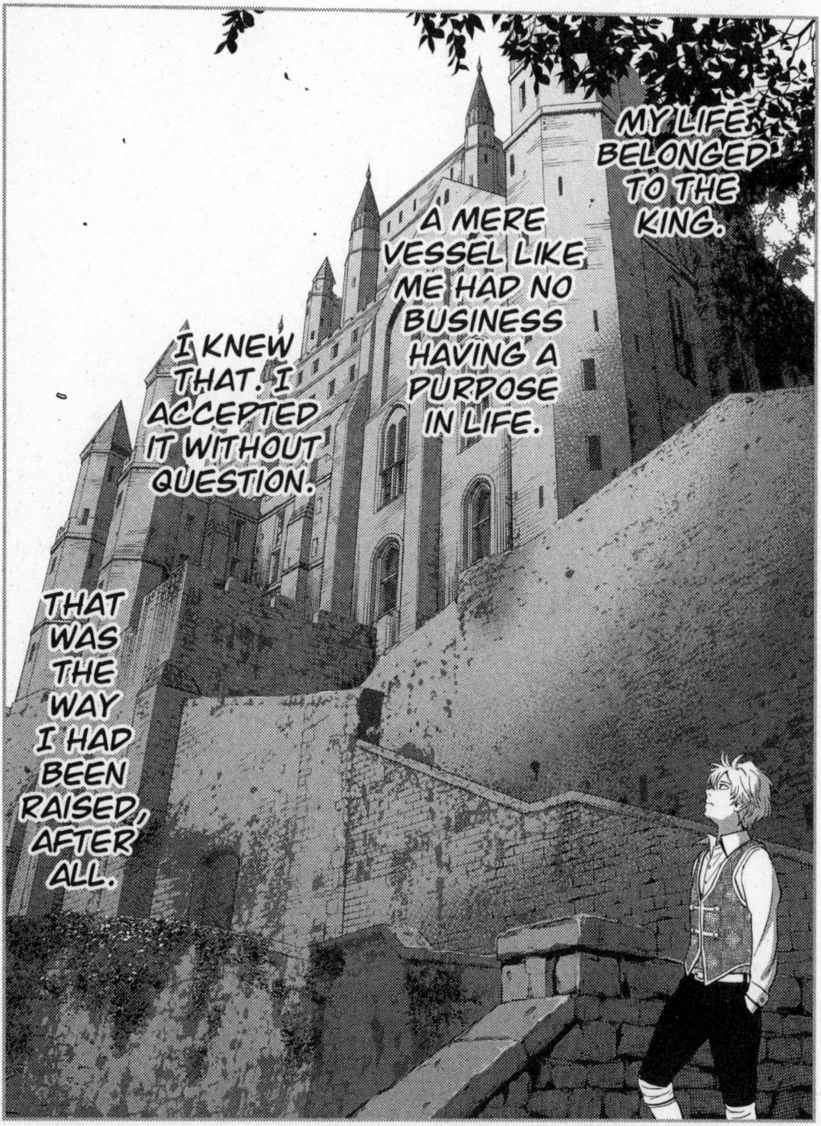
MY LIFE BELONGED TO THE KING.
A MERE VESSEL LIKE ME HAD NO BUSINESS HAVING A PURPOSE IN LIFE.
I KNEW THAT. I ACCEPTED IT WITHOUT QUESTION.
THAT WAS THE WAY I HAD BEEN RAISED, AFTER ALL.

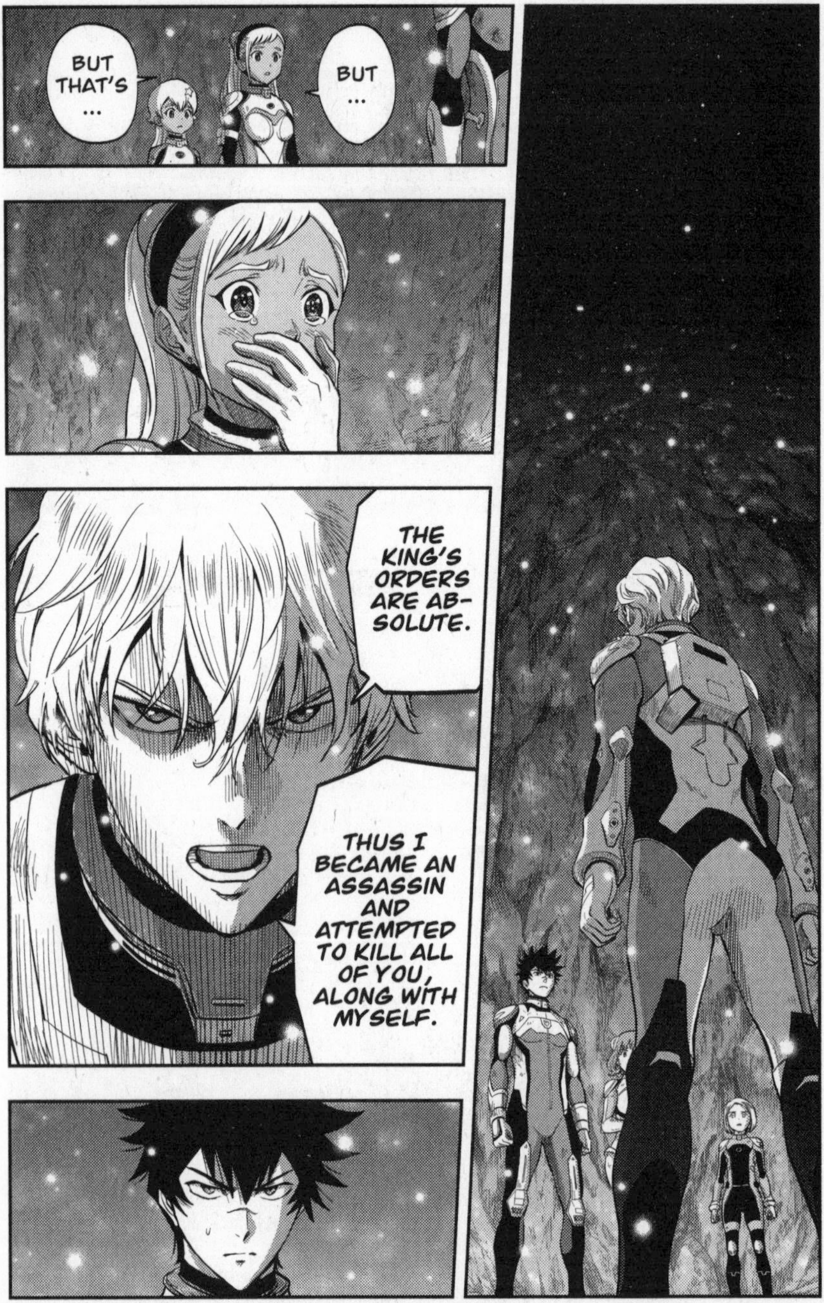
BUT ...
BUT THAT'S ...
THE KING'S ORDERS ARE ABSOLUTE.
THUS I BECAME AN ASSASSIN AND ATTEMPTED TO KILL ALL OF YOU, ALONG WITH MYSELF.

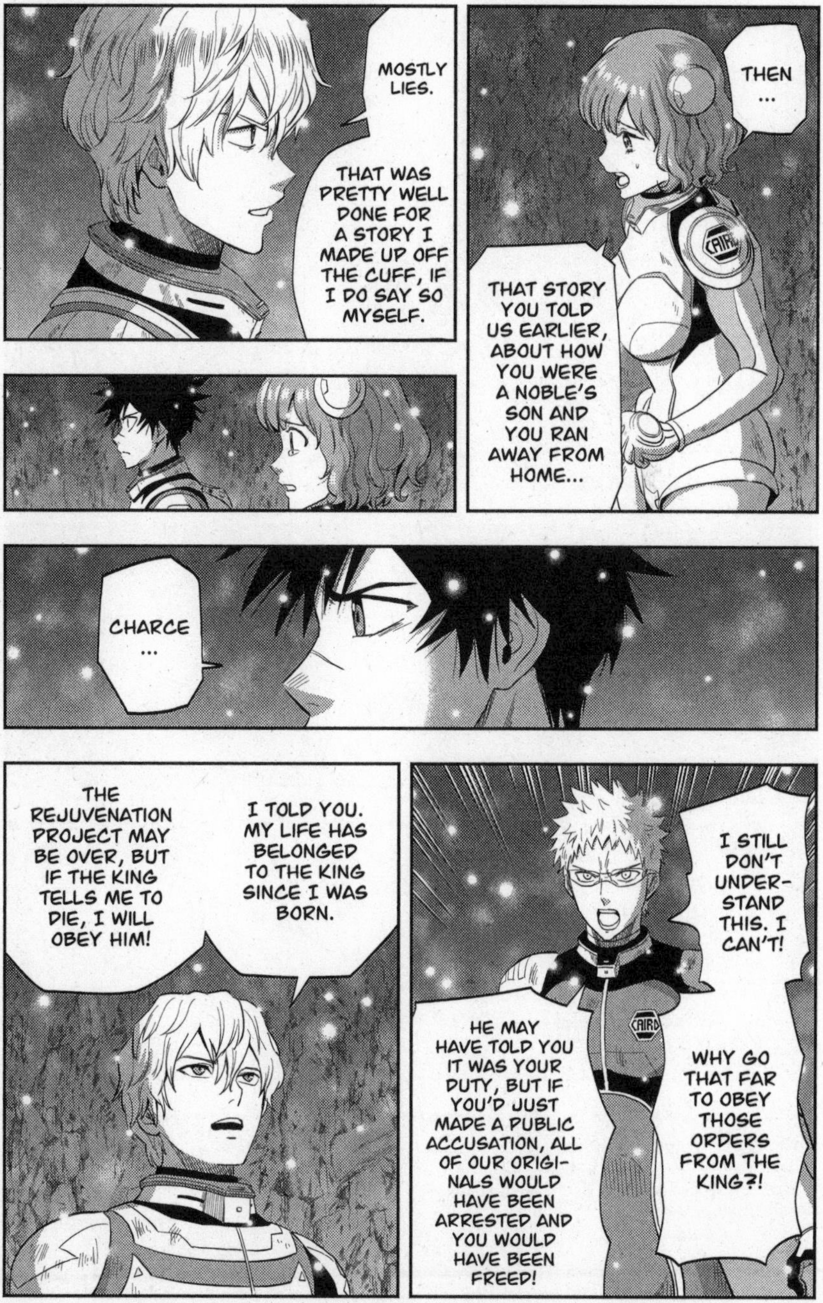
THEN ...
THAT STORY YOU TOLD US EARLIER, ABOUT HOW YOU WERE A NOBLE'S SON AND YOU RAN AWAY FROM HOME...
MOSTLY LIES.
THAT WAS PRETTY WELL DONE FOR A STORY I MADE UP OFF THE CUFF, IF I DO SAY SO MYSELF.
CHARCE ...
I STILL DON'T UNDER-STAND THIS. I CAN'T!
WHY GO THAT FAR TO OBEY THOSE ORDERS FROM THE KING?!
HE MAY HAVE TOLD YOU IT WAS YOUR DUTY, BUT IF YOU'D JUST MADE A PUBLIC ACCUSATION, ALL OF OUR ORIGI-NALS WOULD HAVE BEEN ARRESTED AND YOU WOULD HAVE BEEN FREED!
I TOLD YOU. MY LIFE HAS BELONGED TO THE KING SINCE I WAS BORN.
THE REJUVENATION PROJECT MAY BE OVER, BUT IF THE KING TELLS ME TO DIE, I WILL OBEY HIM!

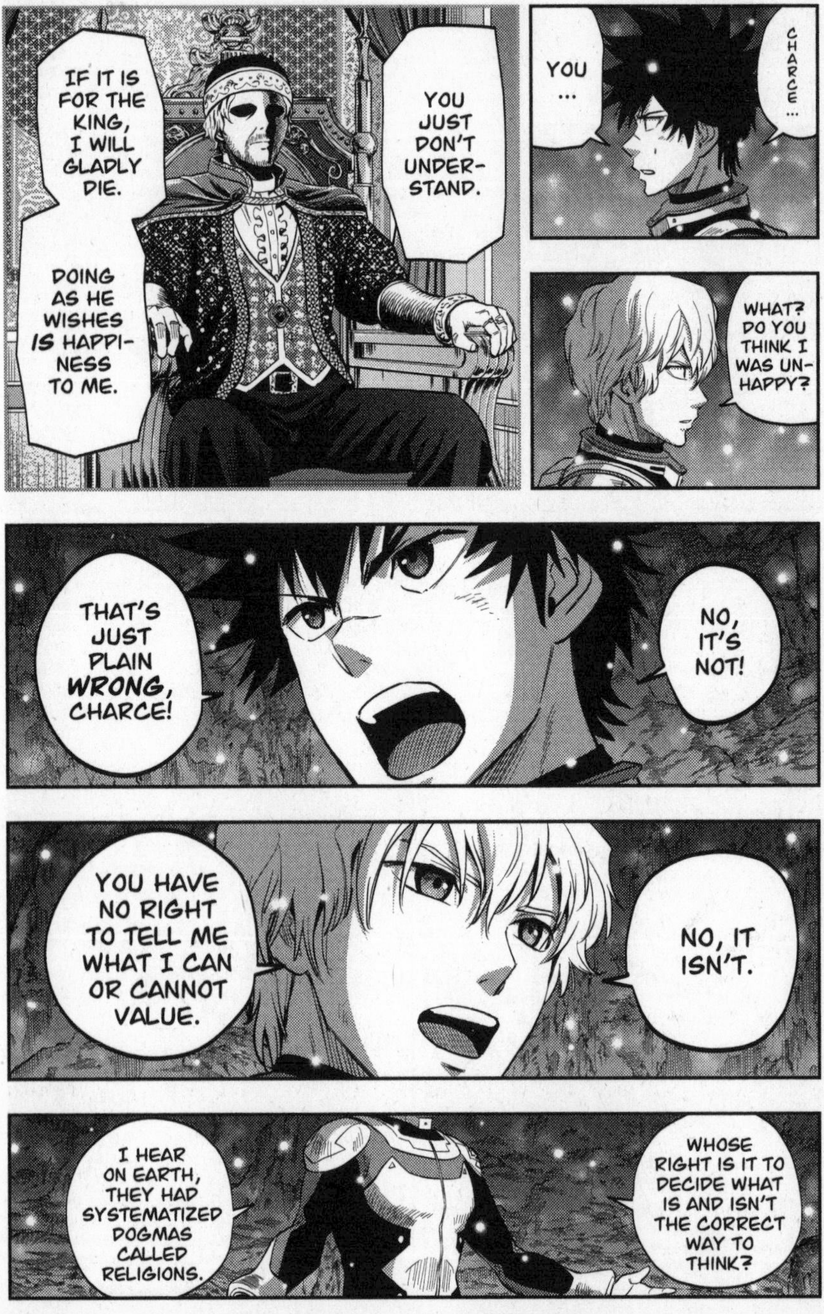

CHARCE...
YOU...
WHAT? DO YOU THINK I WAS UNHAPPY?
YOU JUST DON'T UNDERSTAND.
IF IT IS FOR THE KING, I WILL GLADLY DIE.
DOING AS HE WISHES *IS* HAPPINESS TO ME.
NO, IT'S NOT!
THAT'S JUST PLAIN **WRONG**, CHARCE!
NO, IT ISN'T.
YOU HAVE NO RIGHT TO TELL ME WHAT I CAN OR CANNOT VALUE.
WHOSE RIGHT IS IT TO DECIDE WHAT IS AND ISN'T THE CORRECT WAY TO THINK?
I HEAR ON EARTH, THEY HAD SYSTEMATIZED DOGMAS CALLED RELIGIONS.

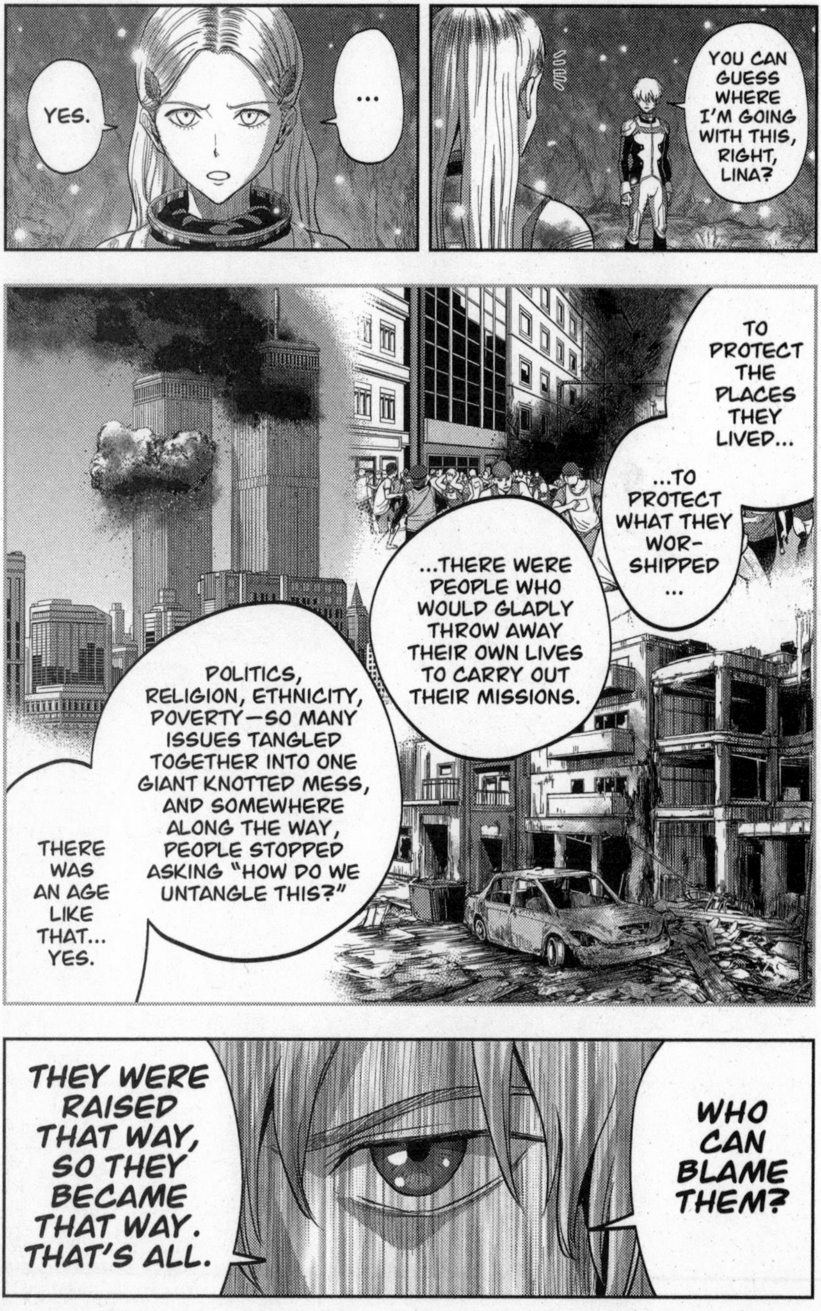
YOU CAN GUESS WHERE I'M GOING WITH THIS, RIGHT, LINA?
...
YES.
TO PROTECT THE PLACES THEY LIVED...
...TO PROTECT WHAT THEY WOR-SHIPPED...
...THERE WERE PEOPLE WHO WOULD GLADLY THROW AWAY THEIR OWN LIVES TO CARRY OUT THEIR MISSIONS.
POLITICS, RELIGION, ETHNICITY, POVERTY—SO MANY ISSUES TANGLED TOGETHER INTO ONE GIANT KNOTTED MESS, AND SOMEWHERE ALONG THE WAY, PEOPLE STOPPED ASKING "HOW DO WE UNTANGLE THIS?"
THERE WAS AN AGE LIKE THAT... YES.
WHO CAN BLAME THEM?
THEY WERE RAISED THAT WAY, SO THEY BECAME THAT WAY. THAT'S ALL.

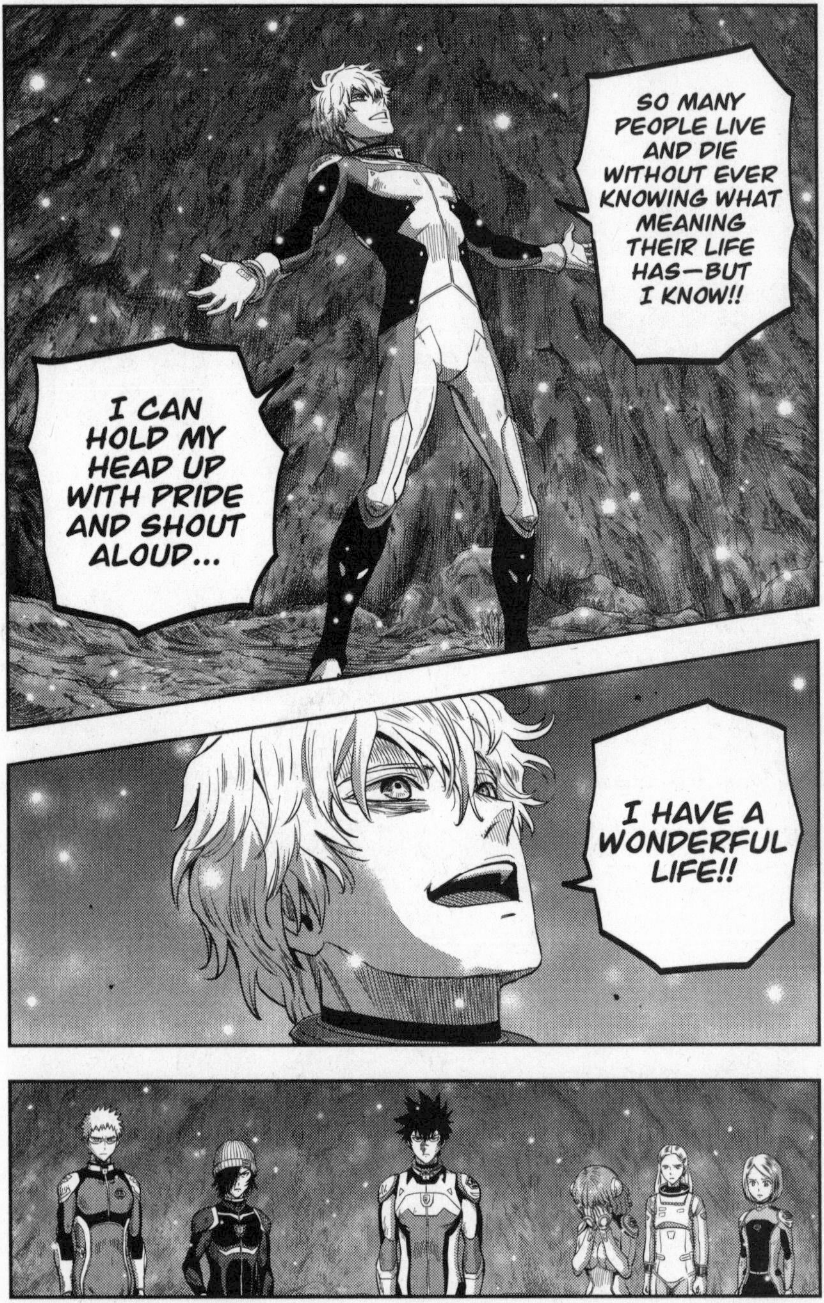
SO MANY PEOPLE LIVE AND DIE WITHOUT EVER KNOWING WHAT MEANING THEIR LIFE HAS—BUT I KNOW!!
I CAN HOLD MY HEAD UP WITH PRIDE AND SHOUT ALOUD...
I HAVE A WONDERFUL LIFE!!

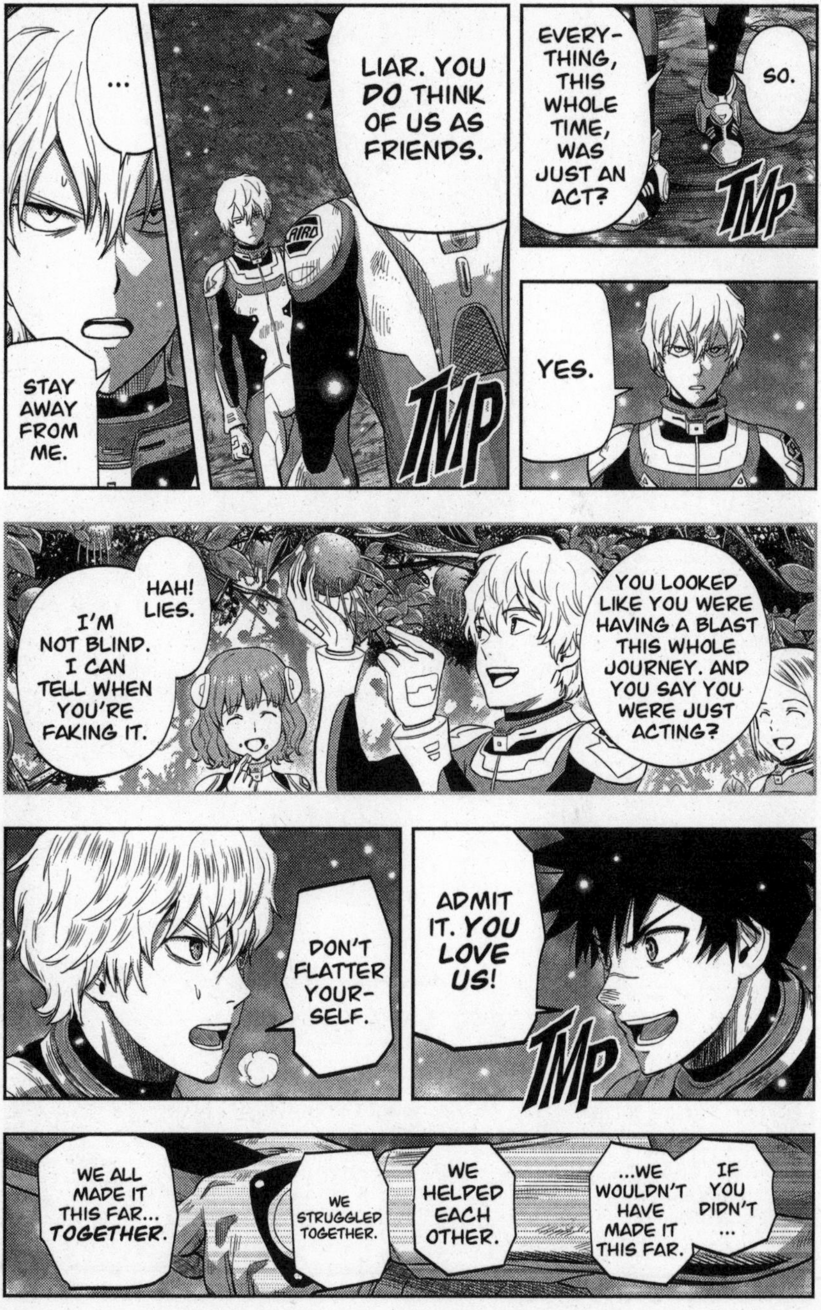
SO.
EVERY-THING, THIS WHOLE TIME, WAS JUST AN ACT?
TMP
YES.
LIAR. YOU DO THINK OF US AS FRIENDS.
TMP
...
STAY AWAY FROM ME.
YOU LOOKED LIKE YOU WERE HAVING A BLAST THIS WHOLE JOURNEY. AND YOU SAY YOU WERE JUST ACTING?
HAH! LIES.
I'M NOT BLIND. I CAN TELL WHEN YOU'RE FAKING IT.
ADMIT IT. YOU LOVE US!
TMP
DON'T FLATTER YOUR-SELF.
IF YOU DIDN'T ...
...WE WOULDN'T HAVE MADE IT THIS FAR.
WE HELPED EACH OTHER.
WE STRUGGLED TOGETHER.
WE ALL MADE IT THIS FAR... TOGETHER.

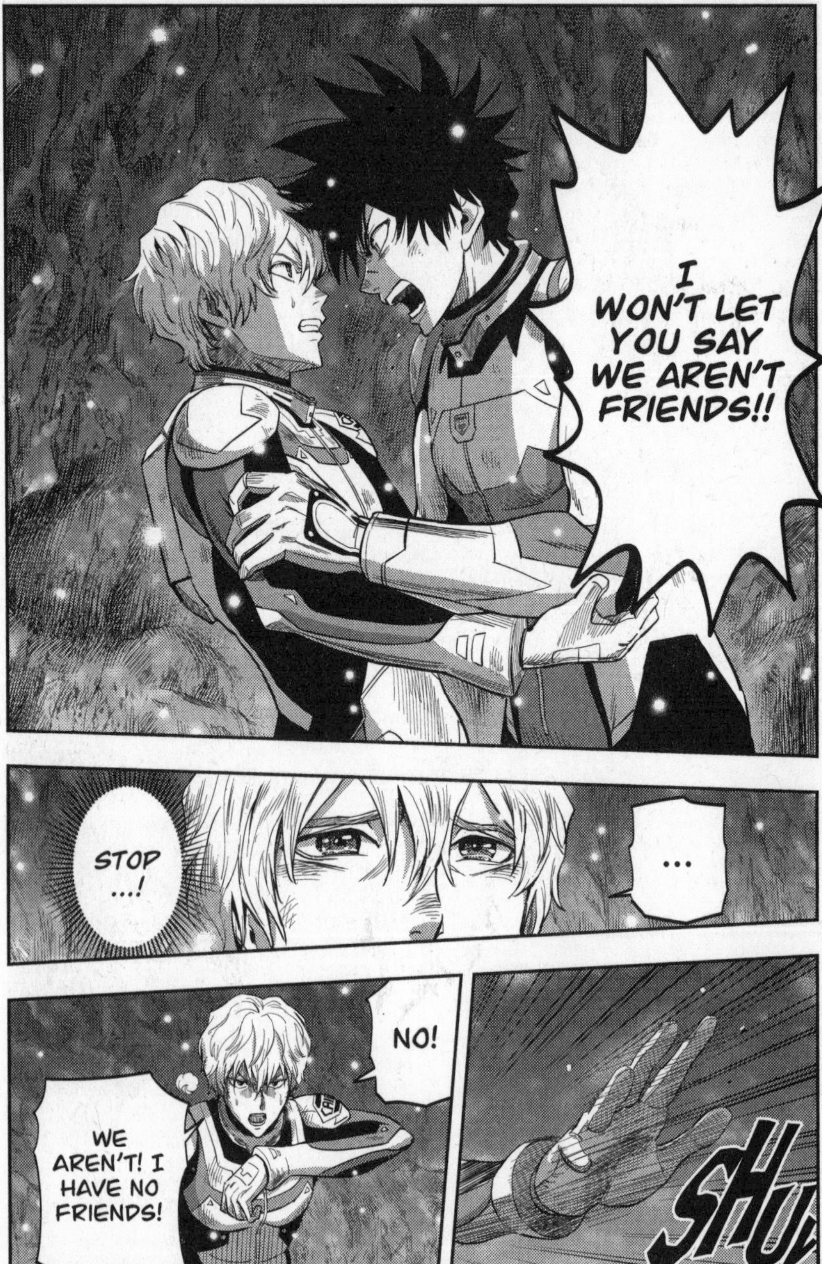
I WON'T LET YOU SAY WE AREN'T FRIENDS!!
...
STOP ...!
SHU
NO!
WE AREN'T! I HAVE NO FRIENDS!

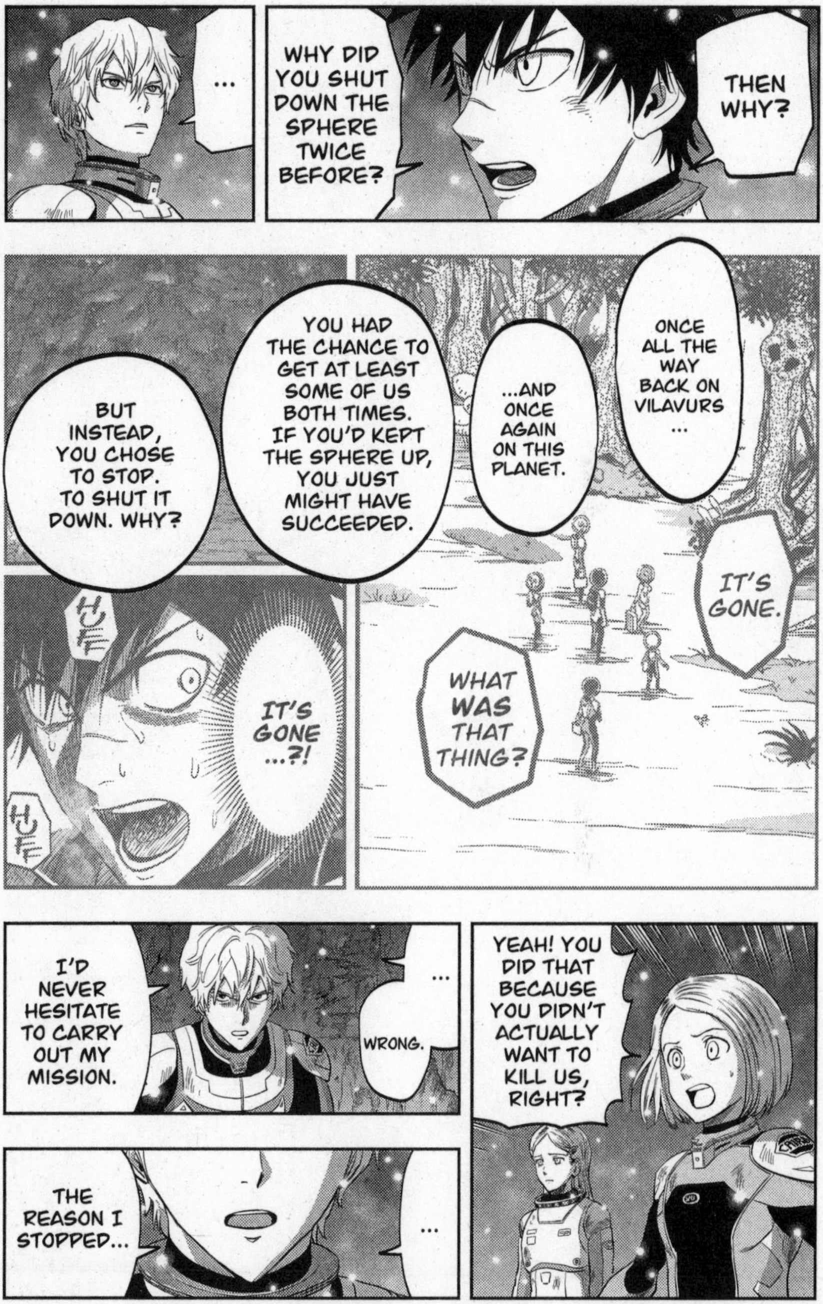
THEN WHY?
WHY DID YOU SHUT DOWN THE SPHERE TWICE BEFORE?
...
ONCE ALL THE WAY BACK ON VILAVURS ...
...AND ONCE AGAIN ON THIS PLANET.
IT'S GONE.
WHAT WAS THAT THING?
YOU HAD THE CHANCE TO GET AT LEAST SOME OF US BOTH TIMES. IF YOU'D KEPT THE SPHERE UP, YOU JUST MIGHT HAVE SUCCEEDED.
BUT INSTEAD, YOU CHOSE TO STOP. TO SHUT IT DOWN. WHY?
HUFF
IT'S GONE ...?!
HUFF
YEAH! YOU DID THAT BECAUSE YOU DIDN'T ACTUALLY WANT TO KILL US, RIGHT?
...
WRONG.
I'D NEVER HESITATE TO CARRY OUT MY MISSION.
...
THE REASON I STOPPED...

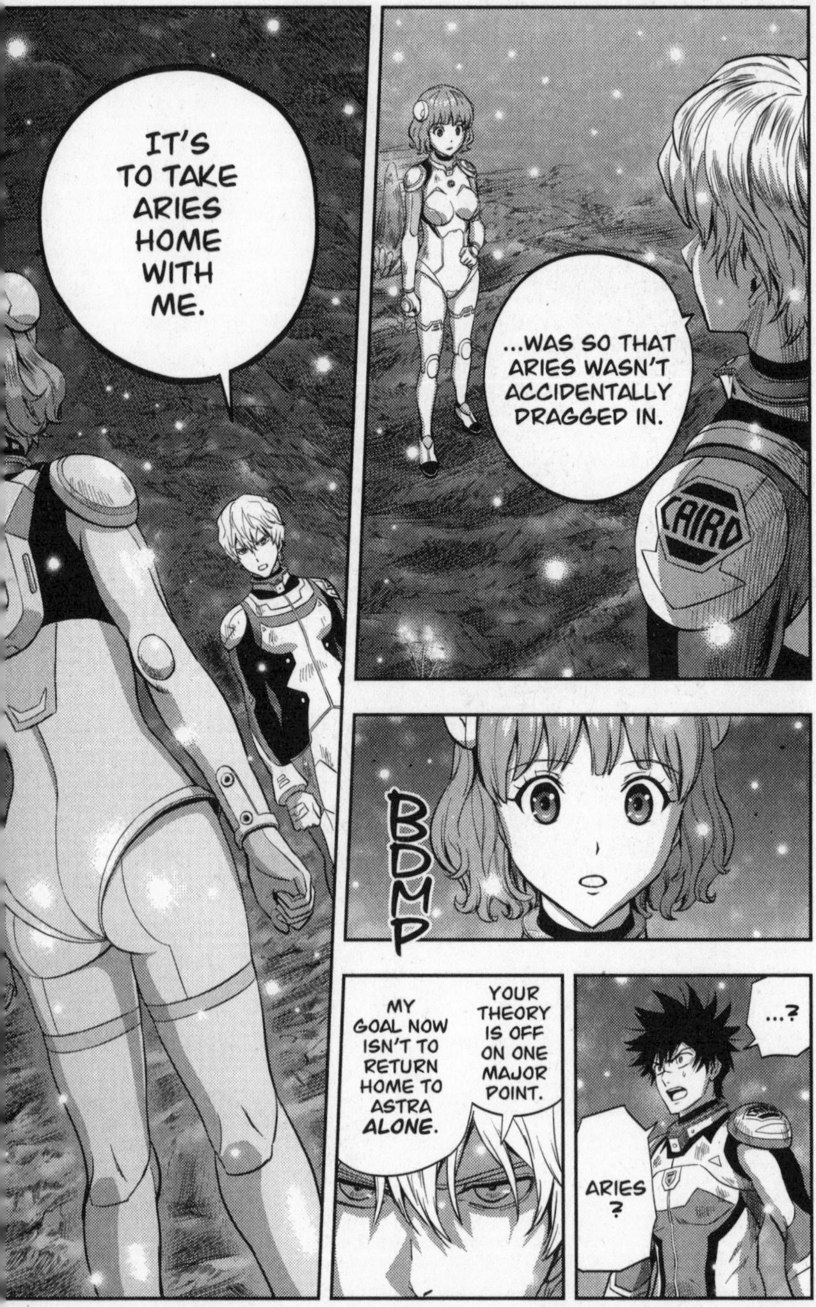
...WAS SO THAT ARIES WASN'T ACCIDENTALLY DRAGGED IN.
BDMP
...?
ARIES?
YOUR THEORY IS OFF ON ONE MAJOR POINT.
MY GOAL NOW ISN'T TO RETURN HOME TO ASTRA ALONE.
IT'S TO TAKE ARIES HOME WITH ME.

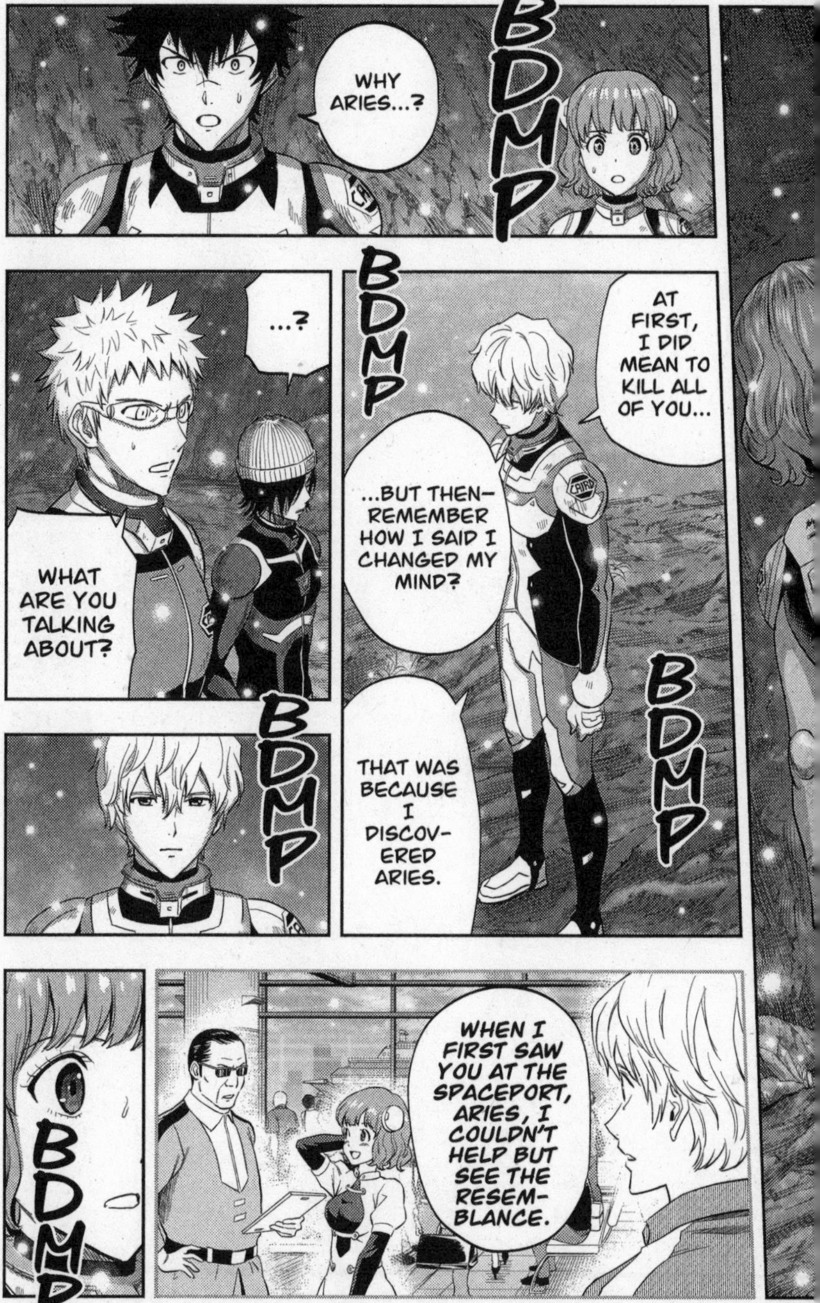
BDMP
WHY ARIES...?
BDMP
AT FIRST, I DID MEAN TO KILL ALL OF YOU...
...BUT THEN— REMEMBER HOW I SAID I CHANGED MY MIND?
BDMP
THAT WAS BECAUSE I DISCOV-ERED ARIES.
...?
WHAT ARE YOU TALKING ABOUT?
BDMP
WHEN I FIRST SAW YOU AT THE SPACEPORT, ARIES, I COULDN'T HELP BUT SEE THE RESEM-BLANCE.
BDMP

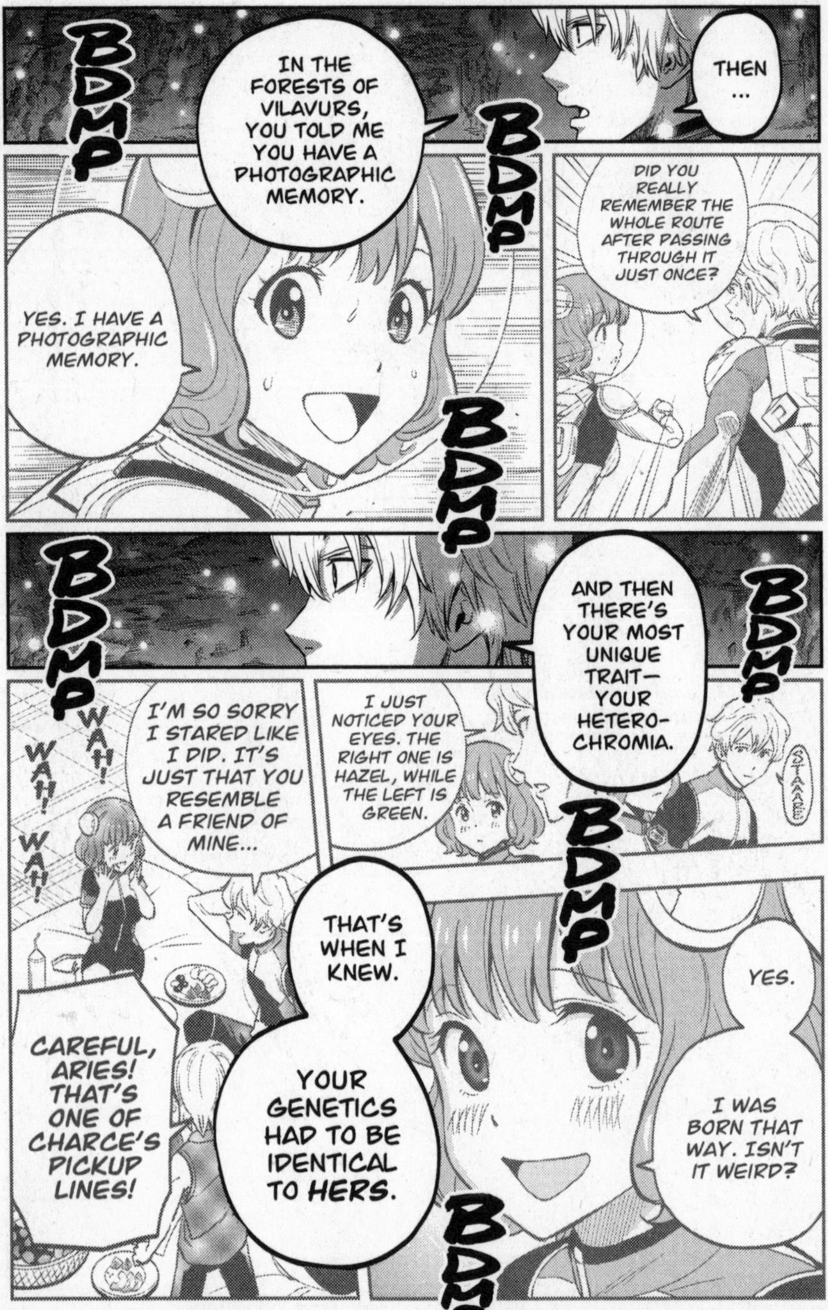
THEN ...
IN THE FORESTS OF VILAVURS, YOU TOLD ME YOU HAVE A PHOTOGRAPHIC MEMORY.
BDMP
BDMP
DID YOU REALLY REMEMBER THE WHOLE ROUTE AFTER PASSING THROUGH IT JUST ONCE?
YES. I HAVE A PHOTOGRAPHIC MEMORY.
BDMP
AND THEN THERE'S YOUR MOST UNIQUE TRAIT—YOUR HETERO-CHROMIA.
BDMP
BDMP
STAAARE
I JUST NOTICED YOUR EYES. THE RIGHT ONE IS HAZEL, WHILE THE LEFT IS GREEN.
BDMP
YES.
I WAS BORN THAT WAY. ISN'T IT WEIRD?
THAT'S WHEN I KNEW.
YOUR GENETICS HAD TO BE IDENTICAL TO HERS.
BDMP
I'M SO SORRY I STARED LIKE I DID. IT'S JUST THAT YOU RESEMBLE A FRIEND OF MINE...
WAH! WAH! WAH!
CAREFUL, ARIES! THAT'S ONE OF CHARCE'S PICKUP LINES!

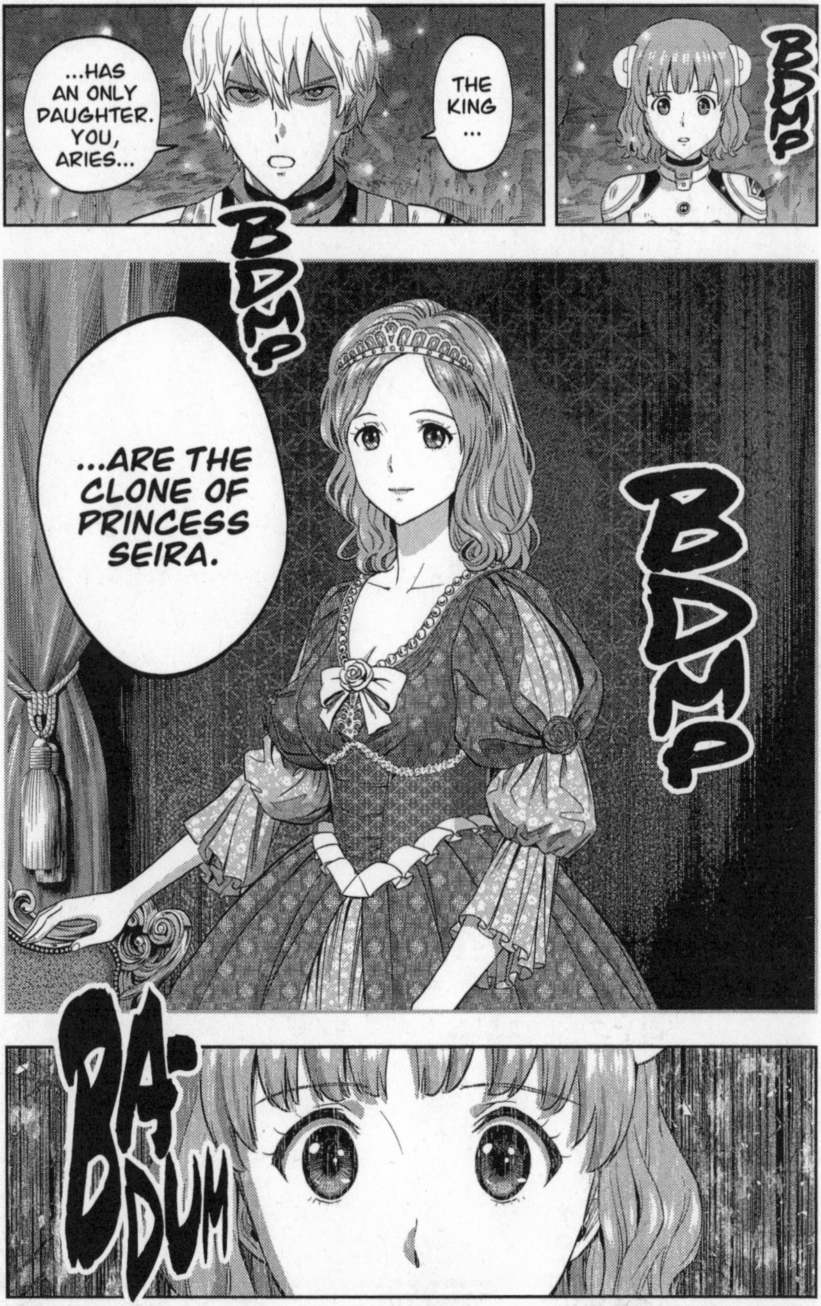
BDMP
THE KING...
...HAS AN ONLY DAUGHTER. YOU, ARIES...
BDMP
BDMP
...ARE THE CLONE OF PRINCESS SEIRA.
BA-DUM

Material Collection | Character Prototype Design

ULGAR

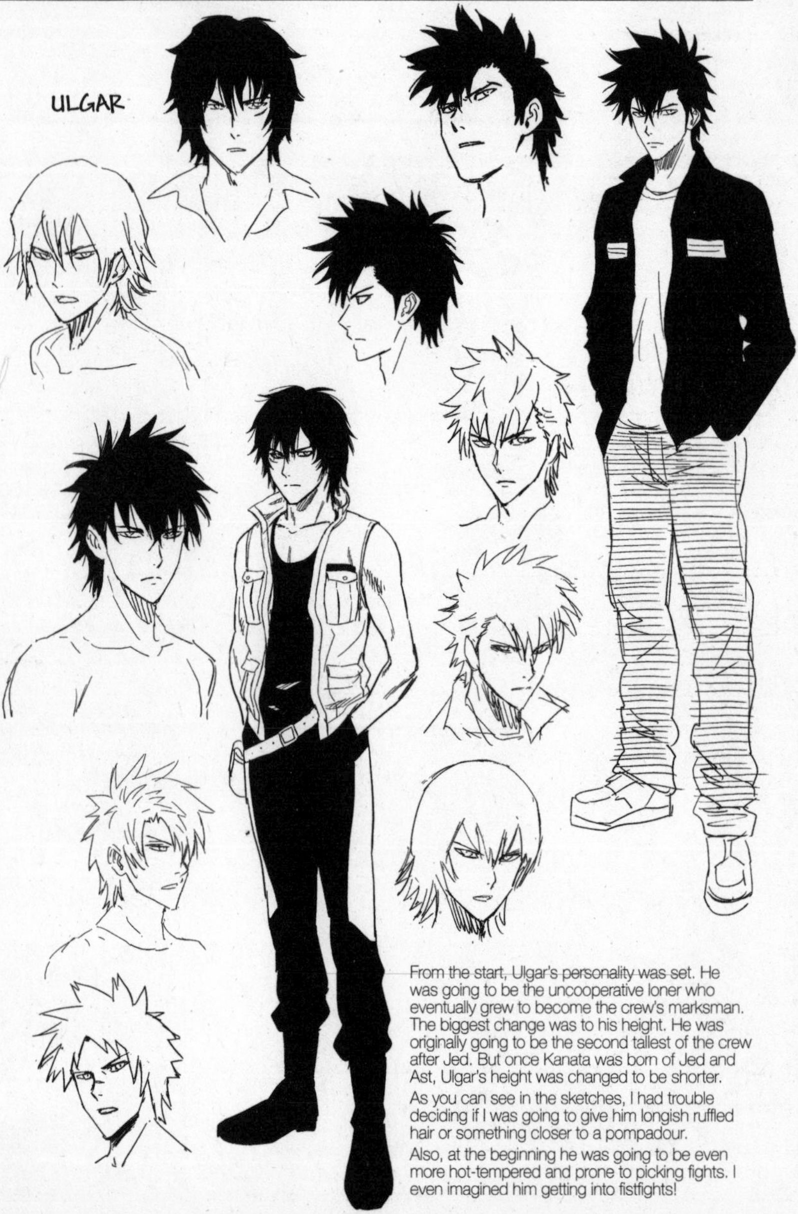
ULGAR

~~From the start, Ulgar's personality was set.~~ He was going to be the uncooperative loner who eventually grew to become the crew's marksman. The biggest change was to his height. He was originally going to be the second tallest of the crew after Jed. But once Kanata was born of Jed and Ast, Ulgar's height was changed to be shorter.

As you can see in the sketches, I had trouble deciding if I was going to give him longish ruffled hair or something closer to a pompadour.

Also, at the beginning he was going to be even more hot-tempered and prone to picking fights. I even imagined him getting into fistfights!

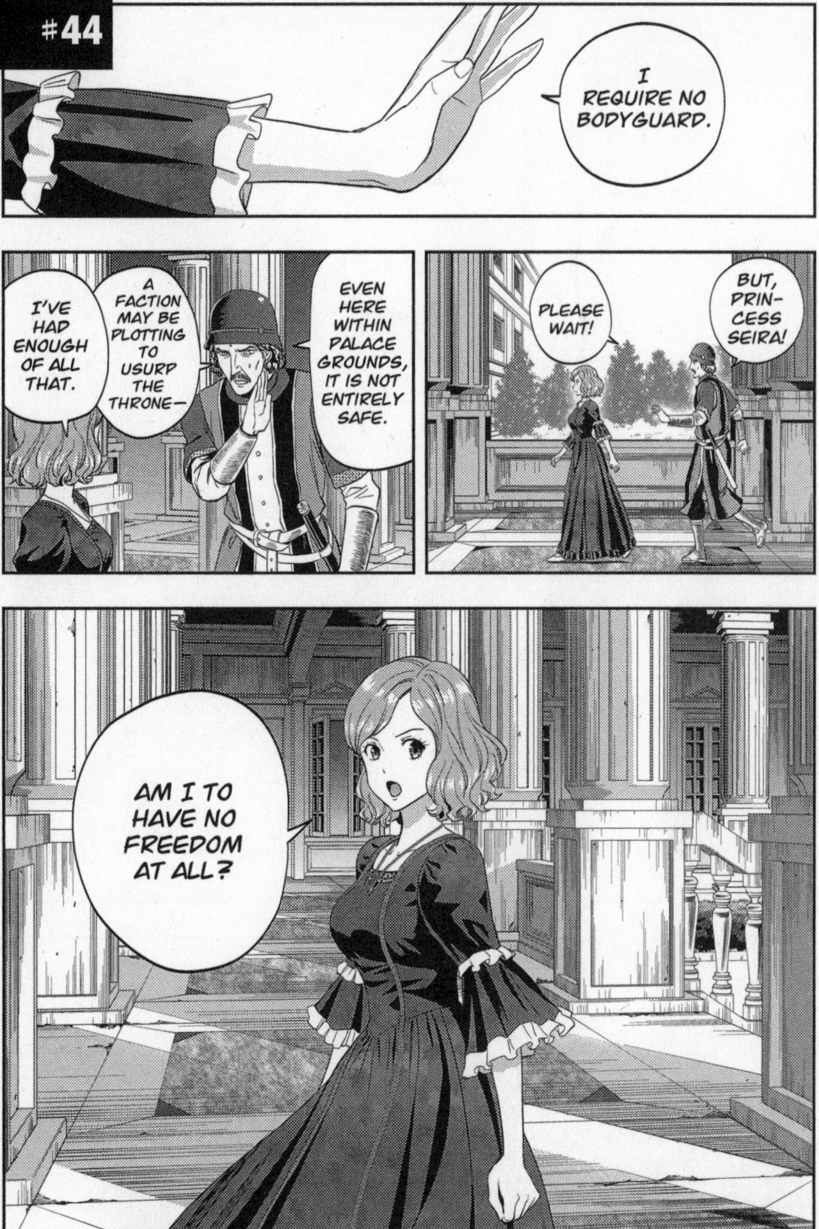
I REQUIRE NO BODYGUARD.
BUT, PRIN-CESS SEIRA!
PLEASE WAIT!
EVEN HERE WITHIN PALACE GROUNDS, IT IS NOT ENTIRELY SAFE.
A FACTION MAY BE PLOTTING TO USURP THE THRONE—
I'VE HAD ENOUGH OF ALL THAT.
AM I TO HAVE NO FREEDOM AT ALL?

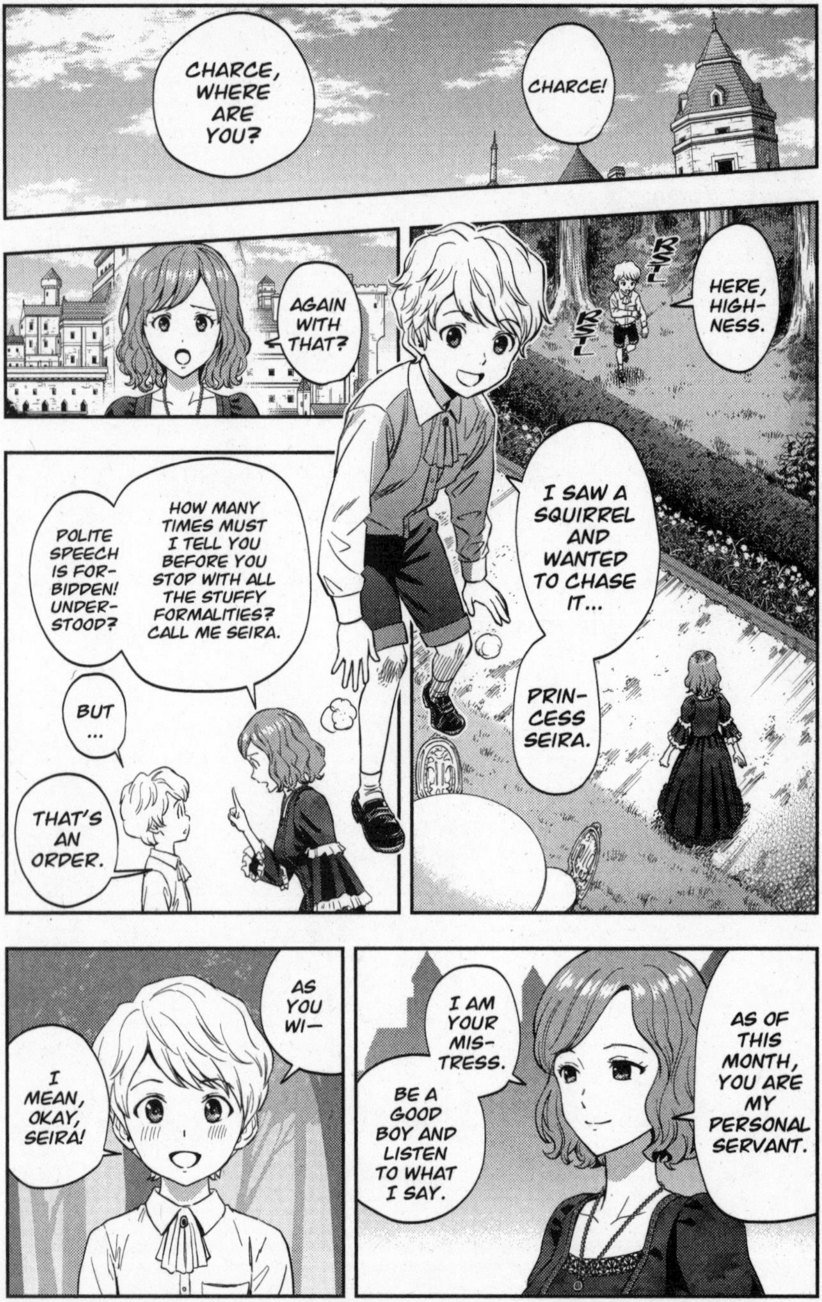
CHARCE!
CHARCE, WHERE ARE YOU?
HERE, HIGHNESS.
I SAW A SQUIRREL AND WANTED TO CHASE IT...
PRINCESS SEIRA.
AGAIN WITH THAT?
HOW MANY TIMES MUST I TELL YOU BEFORE YOU STOP WITH ALL THE STUFFY FORMALITIES? CALL ME SEIRA.
POLITE SPEECH IS FORBIDDEN! UNDERSTOOD?
BUT ...
THAT'S AN ORDER.
AS OF THIS MONTH, YOU ARE MY PERSONAL SERVANT.
I AM YOUR MISTRESS.
BE A GOOD BOY AND LISTEN TO WHAT I SAY.
AS YOU WI—
I MEAN, OKAY, SEIRA!

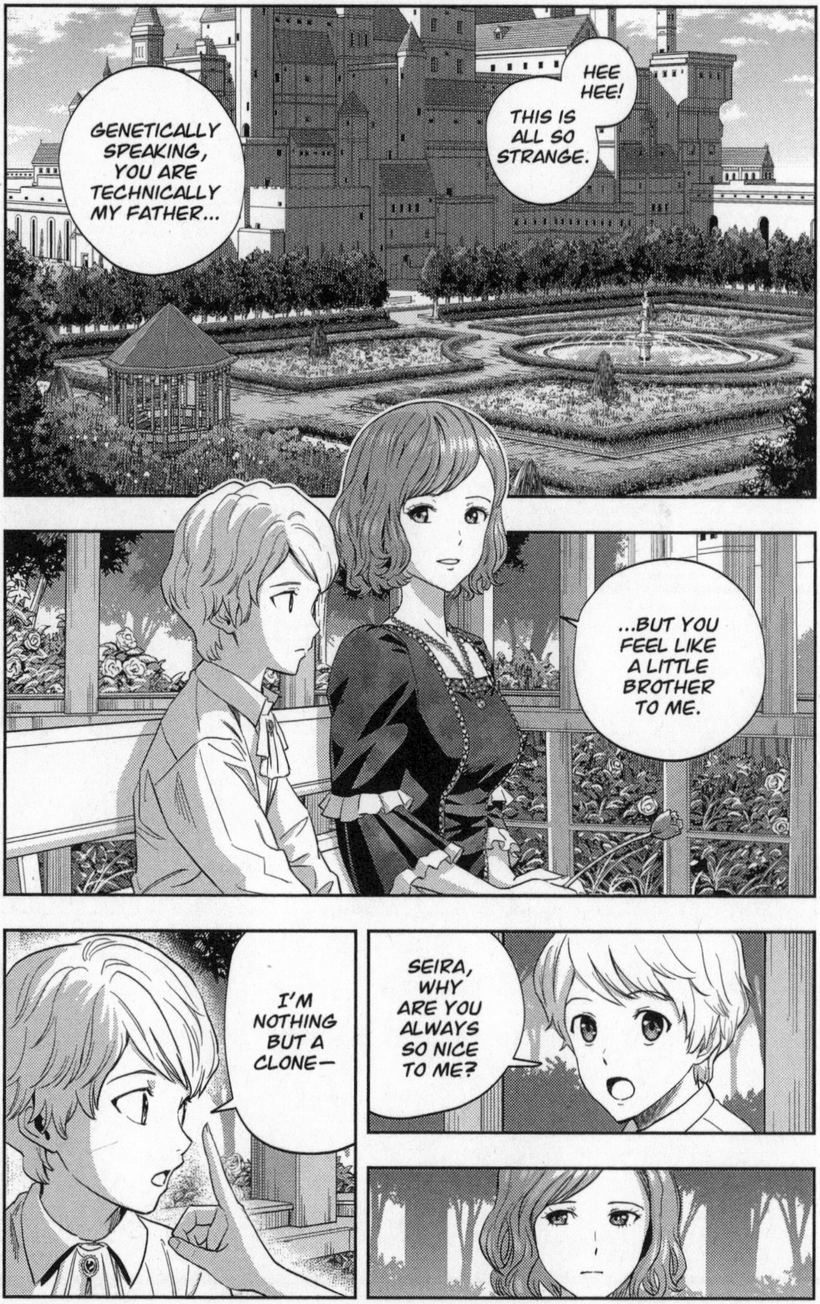
HEE HEE! THIS IS ALL SO STRANGE.
GENETICALLY SPEAKING, YOU ARE TECHNICALLY MY FATHER...
...BUT YOU FEEL LIKE A LITTLE BROTHER TO ME.
SEIRA, WHY ARE YOU ALWAYS SO NICE TO ME?
I'M NOTHING BUT A CLONE—

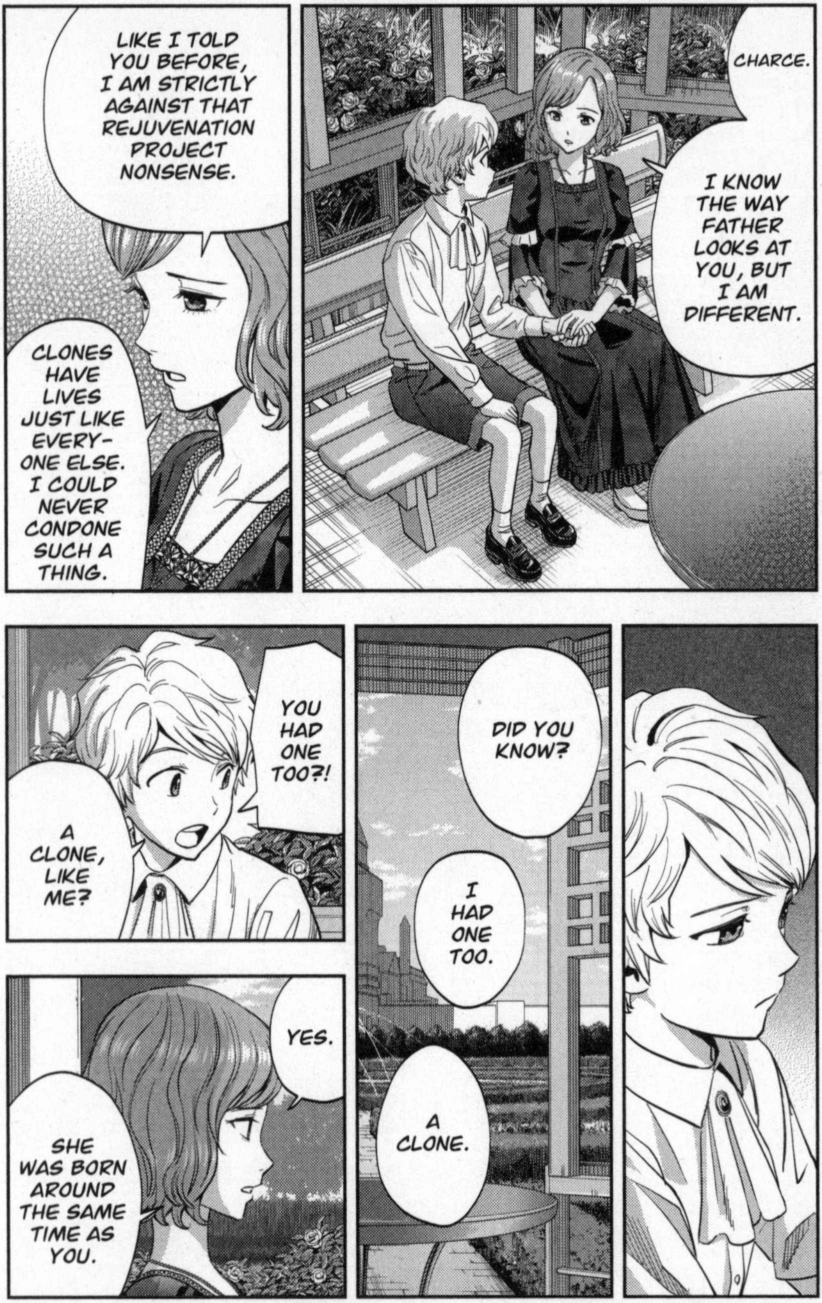
CHARCE.
I KNOW THE WAY FATHER LOOKS AT YOU, BUT I AM DIFFERENT.
LIKE I TOLD YOU BEFORE, I AM STRICTLY AGAINST THAT REJUVENATION PROJECT NONSENSE.
CLONES HAVE LIVES JUST LIKE EVERY-ONE ELSE. I COULD NEVER CONDONE SUCH A THING.
DID YOU KNOW?
I HAD ONE TOO.
A CLONE.
YOU HAD ONE TOO?!
A CLONE, LIKE ME?
YES.
SHE WAS BORN AROUND THE SAME TIME AS YOU.

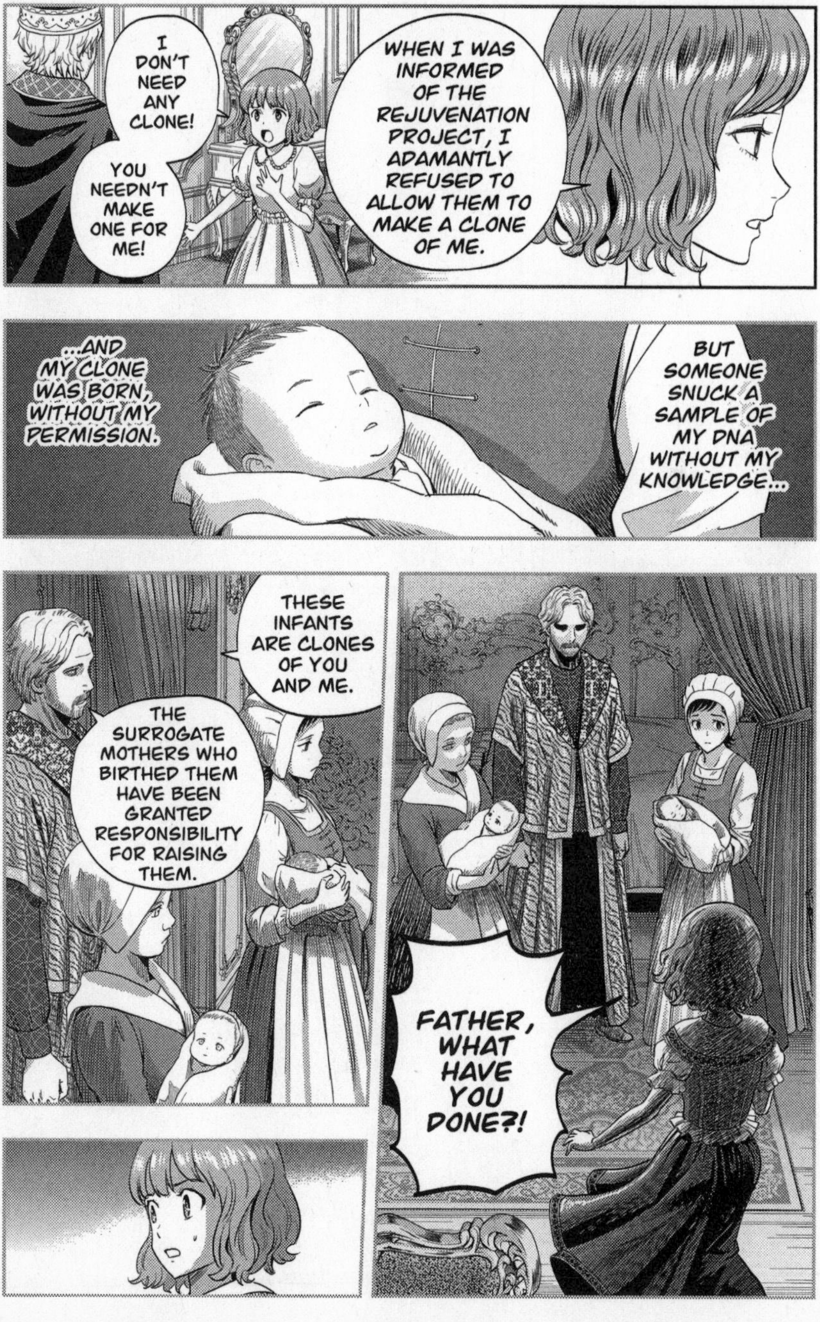
WHEN I WAS INFORMED OF THE REJUVENATION PROJECT, I ADAMANTLY REFUSED TO ALLOW THEM TO MAKE A CLONE OF ME.
I DON'T NEED ANY CLONE!
YOU NEEDN'T MAKE ONE FOR ME!
BUT SOMEONE SNUCK A SAMPLE OF MY DNA WITHOUT MY KNOWLEDGE...
...AND MY CLONE WAS BORN, WITHOUT MY PERMISSION.
FATHER, WHAT HAVE YOU DONE?!
THESE INFANTS ARE CLONES OF YOU AND ME.
THE SURROGATE MOTHERS WHO BIRTHED THEM HAVE BEEN GRANTED RESPONSIBILITY FOR RAISING THEM.

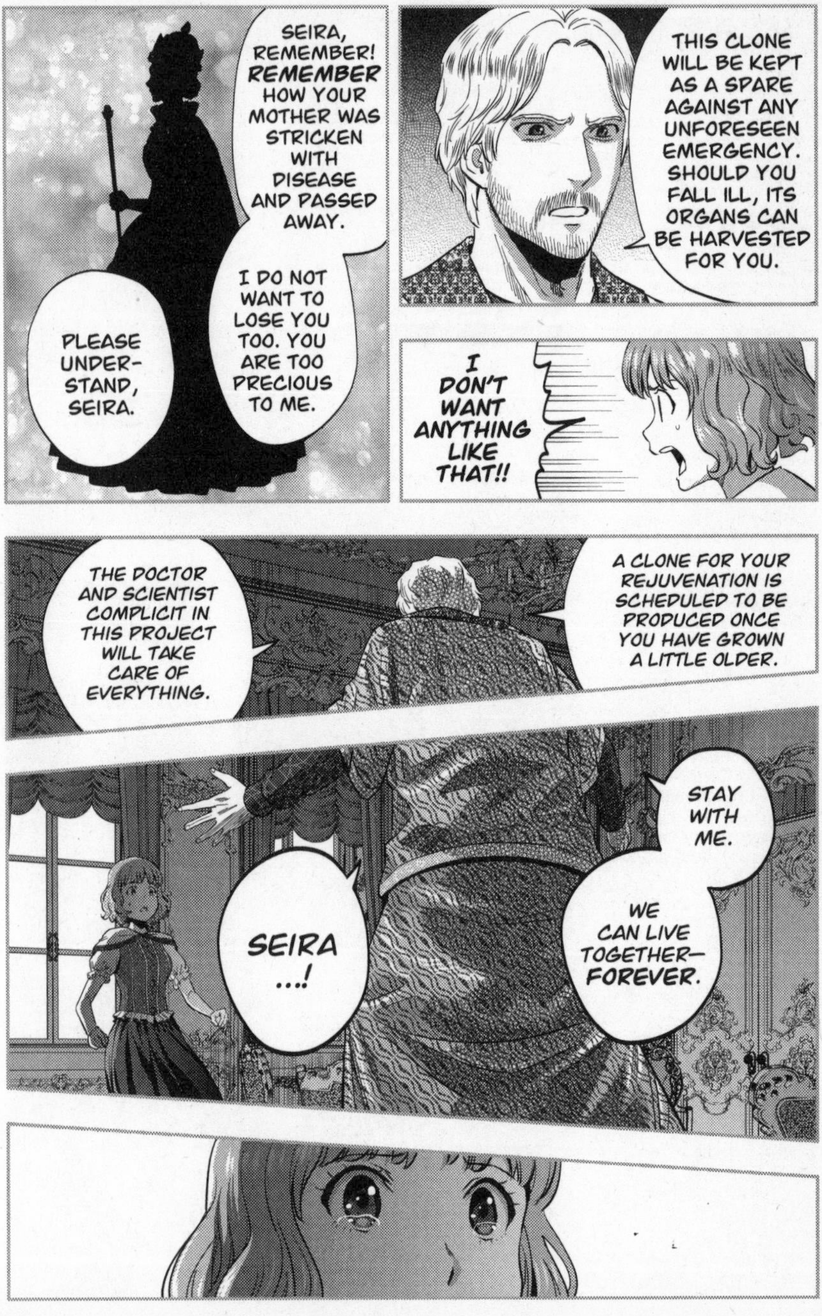
THIS CLONE WILL BE KEPT AS A SPARE AGAINST ANY UNFORESEEN EMERGENCY. SHOULD YOU FALL ILL, ITS ORGANS CAN BE HARVESTED FOR YOU.
I DON'T WANT ANYTHING LIKE THAT!!
SEIRA, REMEMBER! **REMEMBER** HOW YOUR MOTHER WAS STRICKEN WITH DISEASE AND PASSED AWAY.
I DO NOT WANT TO LOSE YOU TOO. YOU ARE TOO PRECIOUS TO ME.
PLEASE UNDER-STAND, SEIRA.
A CLONE FOR YOUR REJUVENATION IS SCHEDULED TO BE PRODUCED ONCE YOU HAVE GROWN A LITTLE OLDER.
THE DOCTOR AND SCIENTIST COMPLICIT IN THIS PROJECT WILL TAKE CARE OF EVERYTHING.
STAY WITH ME.
WE CAN LIVE TOGETHER— **FOREVER.**
SEIRA ...!

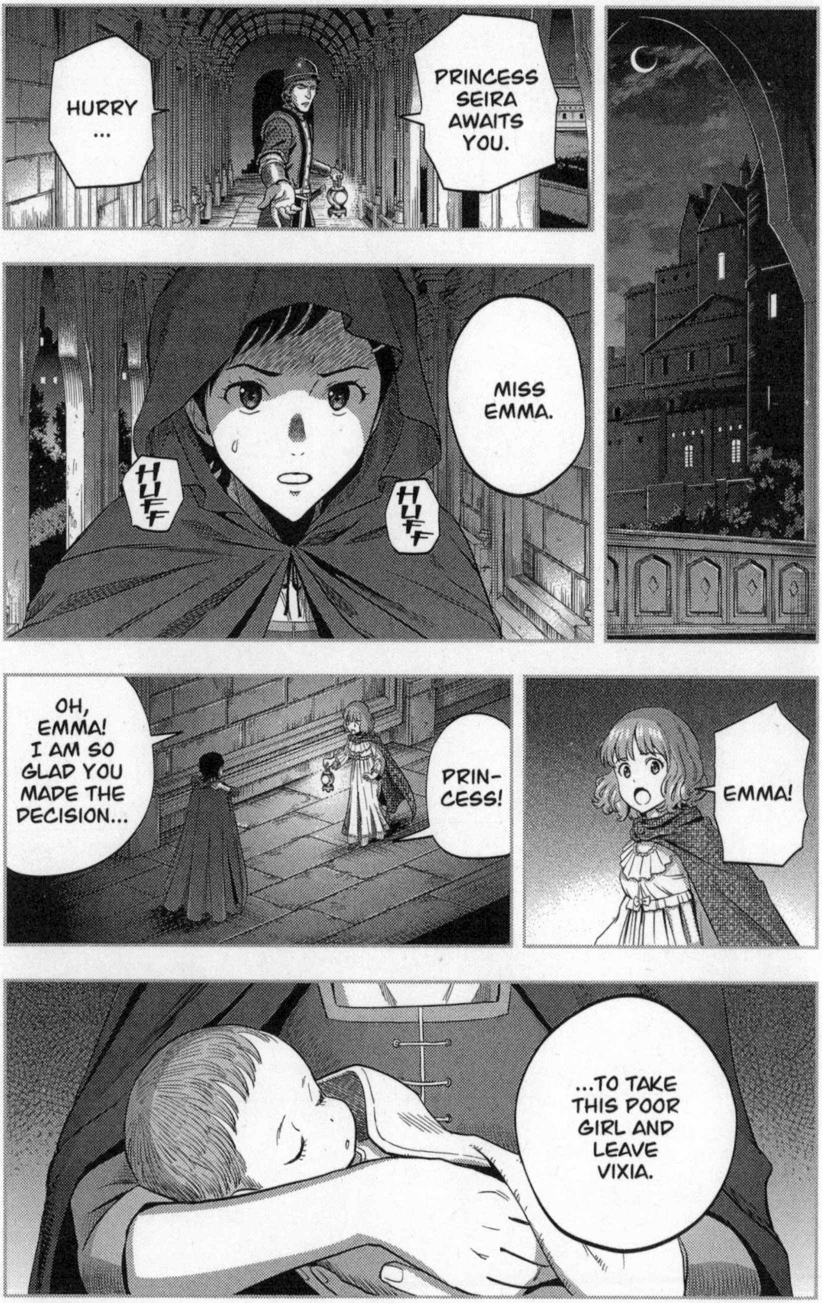
PRINCESS SEIRA AWAITS YOU.
HURRY ...
MISS EMMA.
HUFF
HUFF
EMMA!
PRIN-CESS!
OH, EMMA! I AM SO GLAD YOU MADE THE DECISION...
...TO TAKE THIS POOR GIRL AND LEAVE VIXIA.

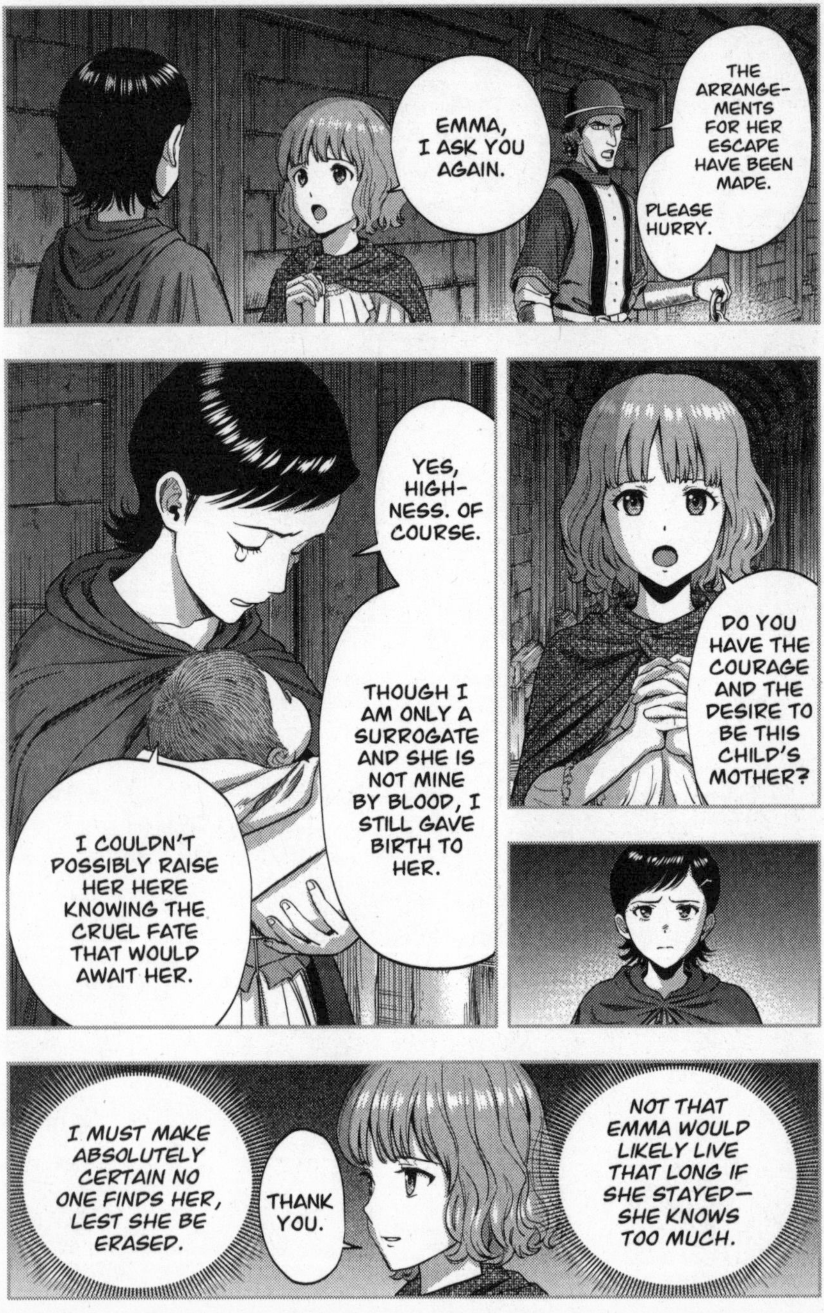
THE ARRANGEMENTS FOR HER ESCAPE HAVE BEEN MADE.
PLEASE HURRY.
EMMA, I ASK YOU AGAIN.
DO YOU HAVE THE COURAGE AND THE DESIRE TO BE THIS CHILD'S MOTHER?
YES, HIGHNESS. OF COURSE.
THOUGH I AM ONLY A SURROGATE AND SHE IS NOT MINE BY BLOOD, I STILL GAVE BIRTH TO HER.
I COULDN'T POSSIBLY RAISE HER HERE KNOWING THE CRUEL FATE THAT WOULD AWAIT HER.
NOT THAT EMMA WOULD LIKELY LIVE THAT LONG IF SHE STAYED—SHE KNOWS TOO MUCH.
THANK YOU.
I MUST MAKE ABSOLUTELY CERTAIN NO ONE FINDS HER, LEST SHE BE ERASED.

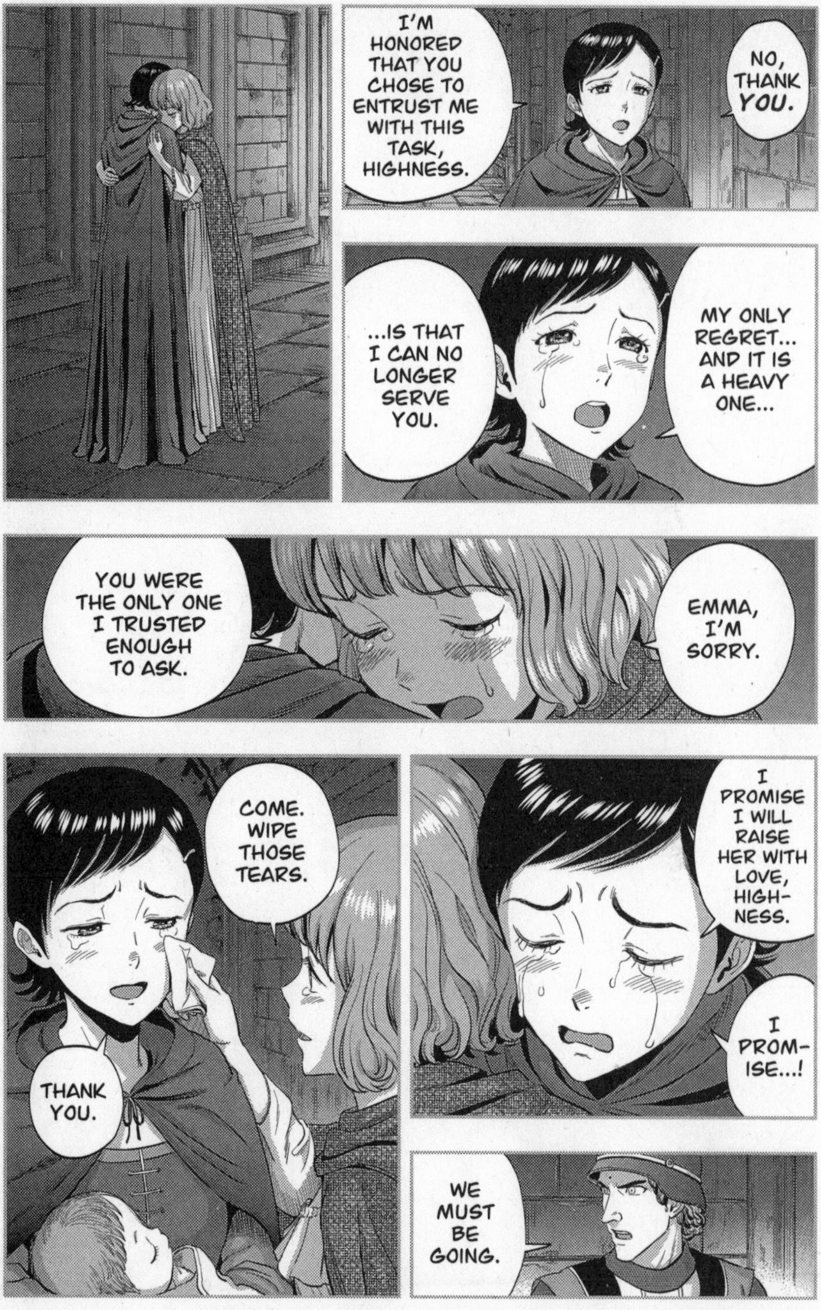
NO, THANK YOU.
I'M HONORED THAT YOU CHOSE TO ENTRUST ME WITH THIS TASK, HIGHNESS.
MY ONLY REGRET... AND IT IS A HEAVY ONE...
...IS THAT I CAN NO LONGER SERVE YOU.
EMMA, I'M SORRY.
YOU WERE THE ONLY ONE I TRUSTED ENOUGH TO ASK.
I PROMISE I WILL RAISE HER WITH LOVE, HIGHNESS.
I PROMISE...!
WE MUST BE GOING.
COME. WIPE THOSE TEARS.
THANK YOU.

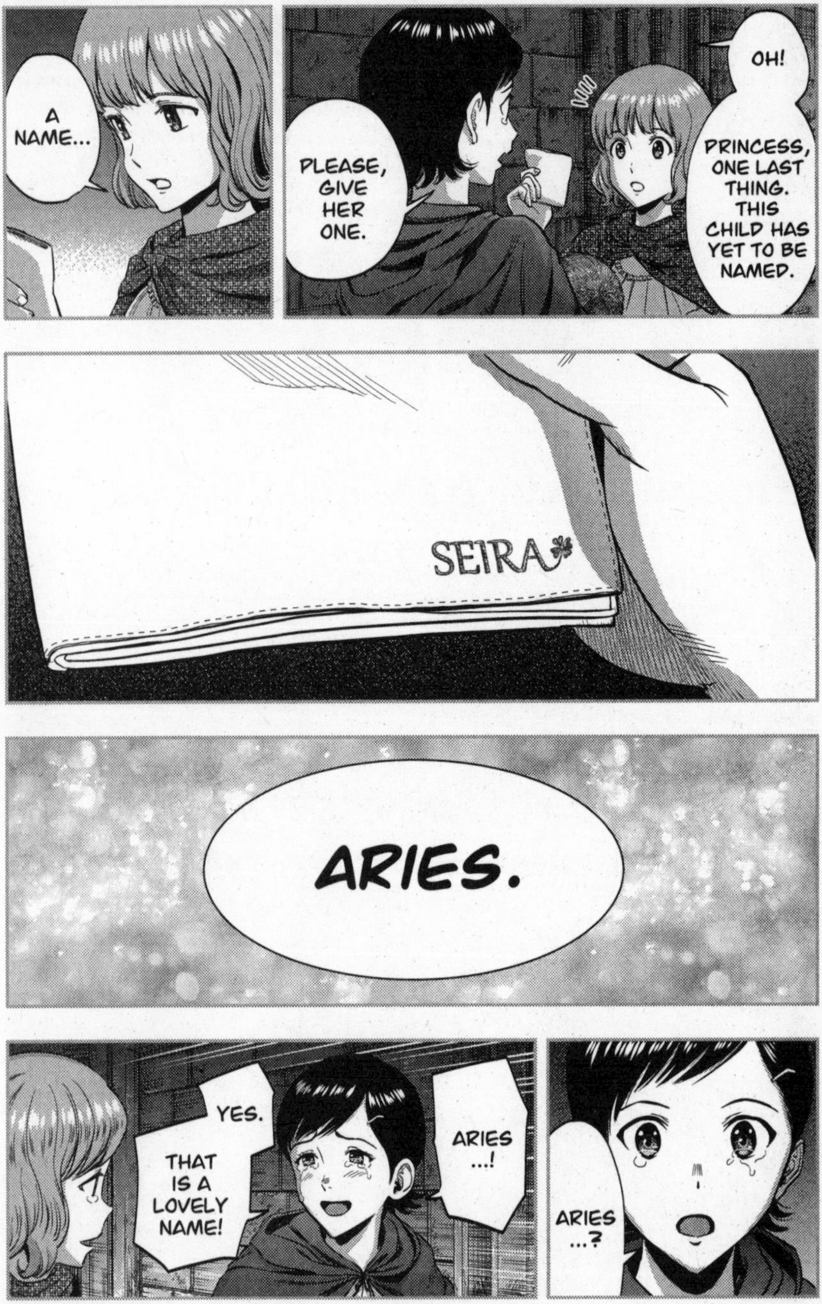
OH!
PRINCESS, ONE LAST THING. THIS CHILD HAS YET TO BE NAMED.
PLEASE, GIVE HER ONE.
A NAME...
SEIRA
ARIES.
ARIES ...?
ARIES ...!
YES.
THAT IS A LOVELY NAME!

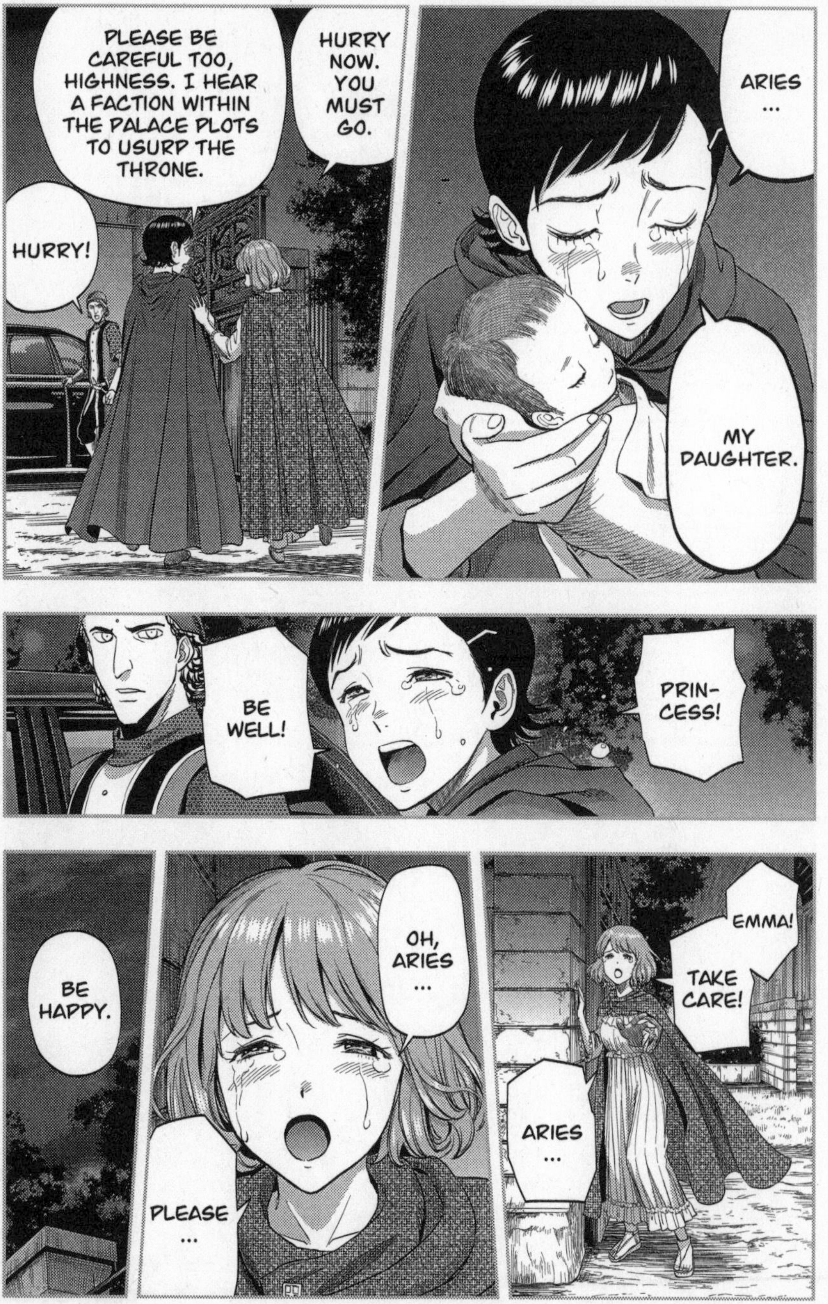
ARIES ...
MY DAUGHTER.
HURRY NOW. YOU MUST GO.
PLEASE BE CAREFUL TOO, HIGHNESS. I HEAR A FACTION WITHIN THE PALACE PLOTS TO USURP THE THRONE.
HURRY!
PRIN-CESS!
BE WELL!
EMMA!
TAKE CARE!
ARIES ...
OH, ARIES ...
PLEASE ...
BE HAPPY.

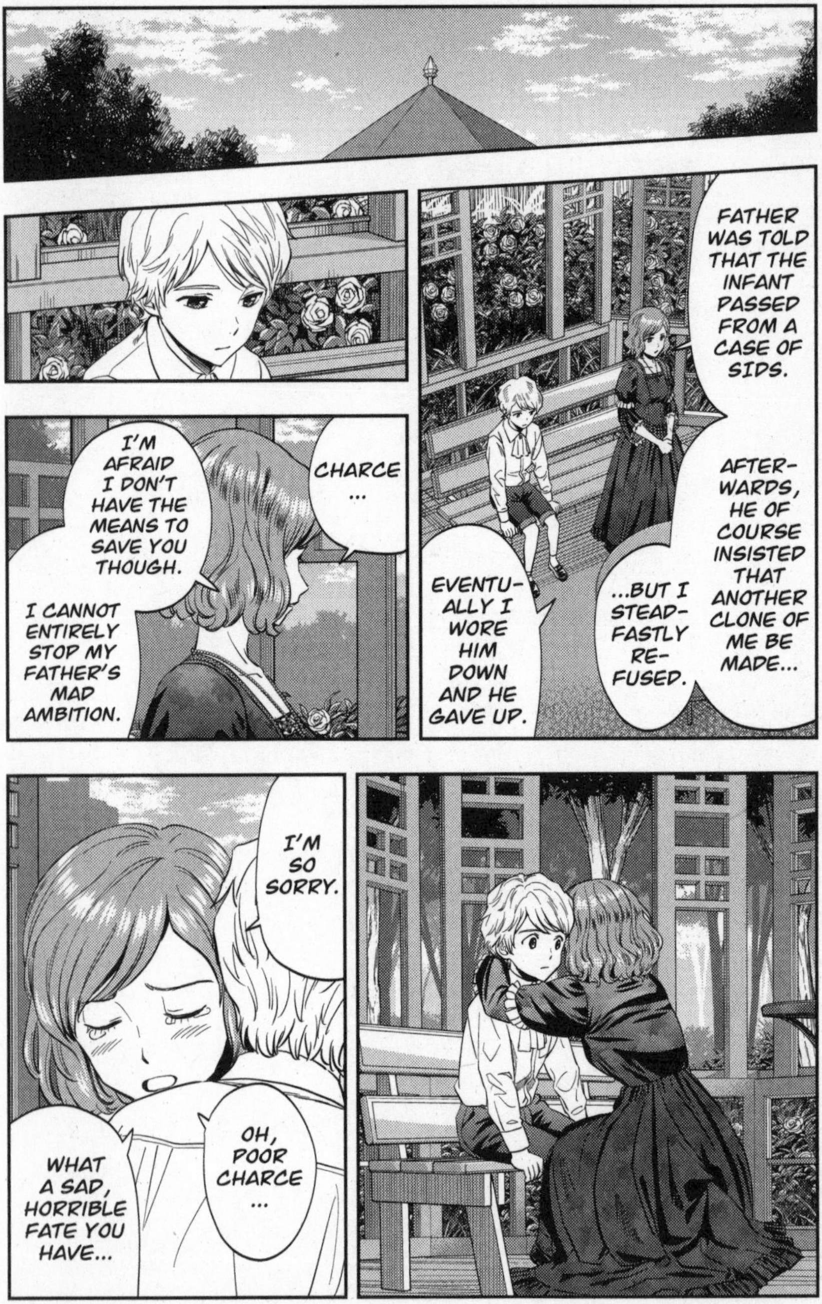
FATHER WAS TOLD THAT THE INFANT PASSED FROM A CASE OF SIDS.
AFTER-WARDS, HE OF COURSE INSISTED THAT ANOTHER CLONE OF ME BE MADE...
...BUT I STEAD-FASTLY RE-FUSED.
EVENTU-ALLY I WORE HIM DOWN AND HE GAVE UP.
CHARCE ...
I'M AFRAID I DON'T HAVE THE MEANS TO SAVE YOU THOUGH.
I CANNOT ENTIRELY STOP MY FATHER'S MAD AMBITION.
I'M SO SORRY.
OH, POOR CHARCE ...
WHAT A SAD, HORRIBLE FATE YOU HAVE...

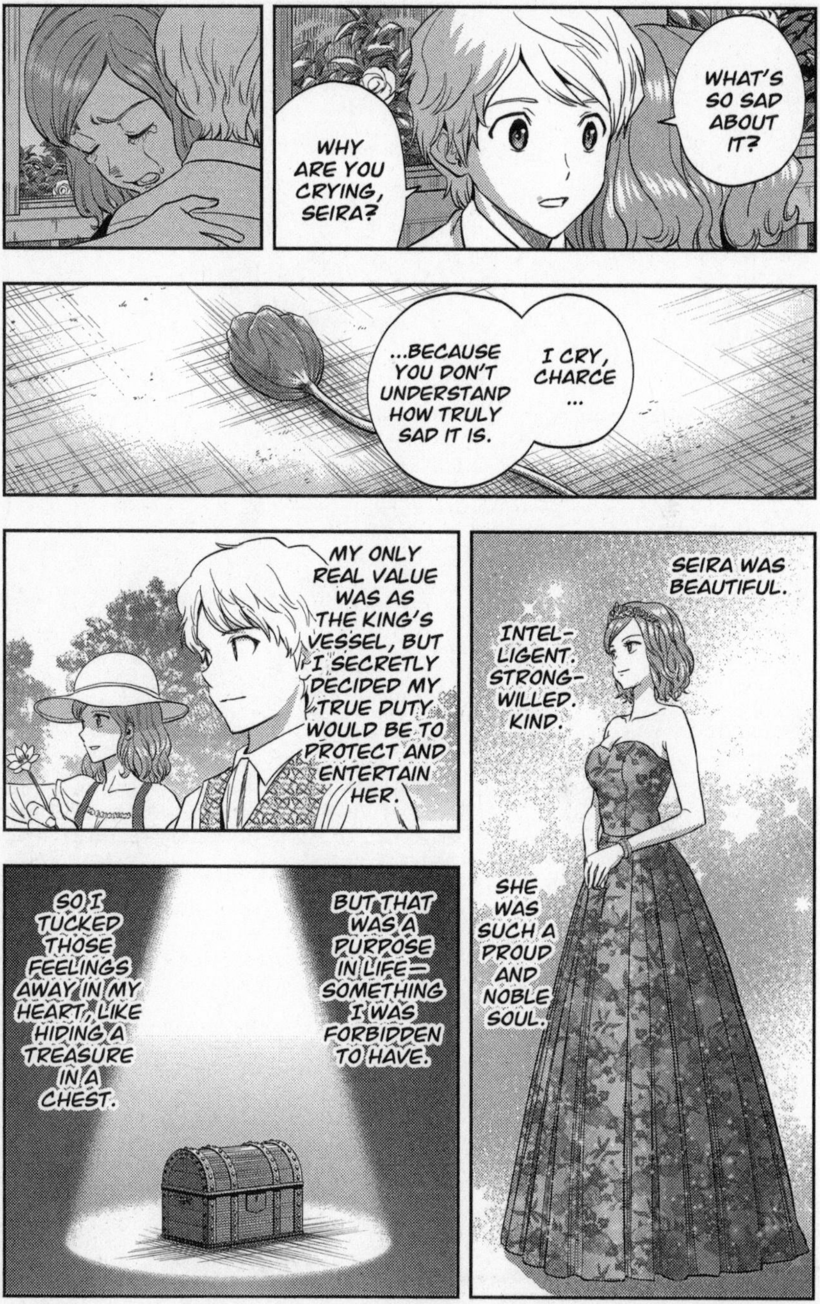
WHAT'S SO SAD ABOUT IT?
WHY ARE YOU CRYING, SEIRA?
I CRY, CHARCE ...
...BECAUSE YOU DON'T UNDERSTAND HOW TRULY SAD IT IS.
SEIRA WAS BEAUTIFUL.
INTEL-LIGENT. STRONG-WILLED. KIND.
SHE WAS SUCH A PROUD AND NOBLE SOUL.
MY ONLY REAL VALUE WAS AS THE KING'S VESSEL, BUT I SECRETLY DECIDED MY TRUE DUTY WOULD BE TO PROTECT AND ENTERTAIN HER.
BUT THAT WAS A PURPOSE IN LIFE— SOMETHING I WAS FORBIDDEN TO HAVE.
SO I TUCKED THOSE FEELINGS AWAY IN MY HEART, LIKE HIDING A TREASURE IN A CHEST.

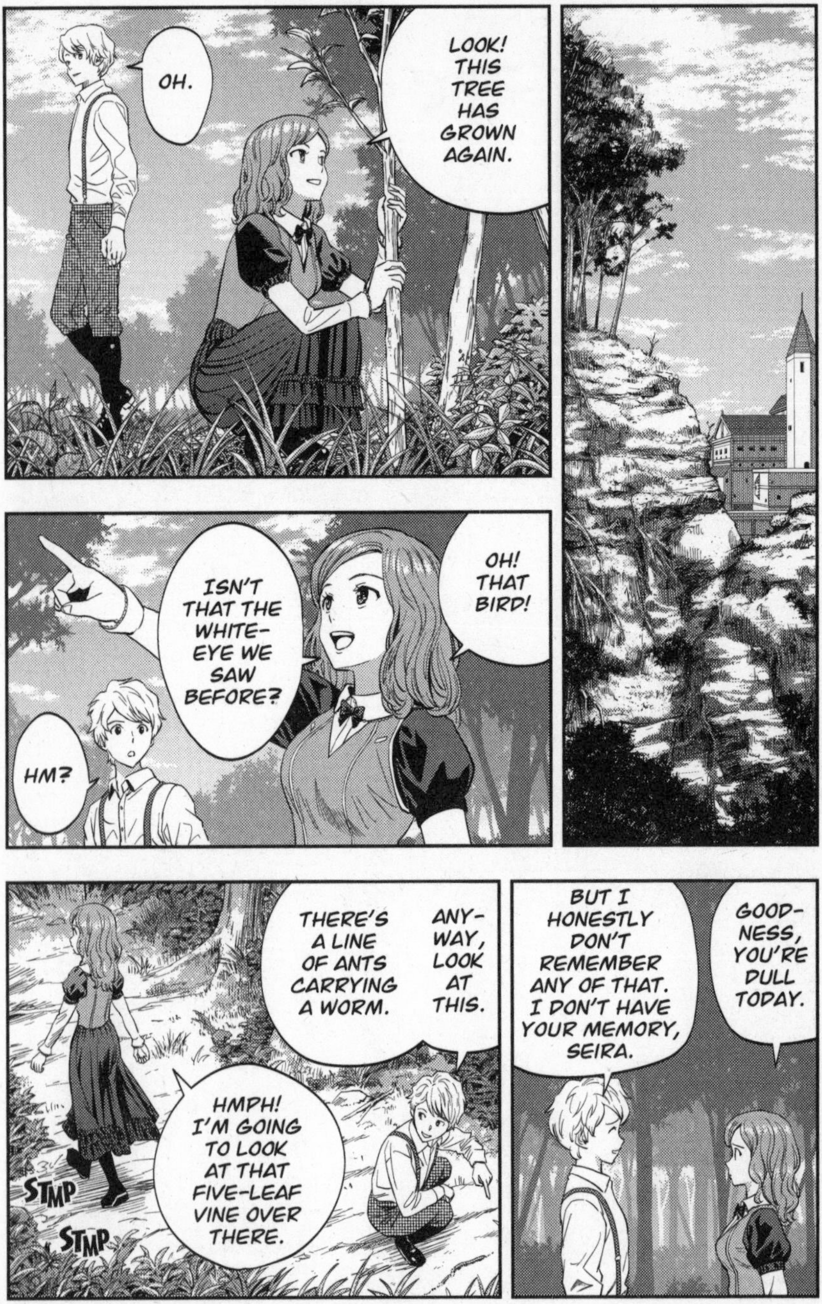
LOOK! THIS TREE HAS GROWN AGAIN.
OH.
OH! THAT BIRD!
ISN'T THAT THE WHITE-EYE WE SAW BEFORE?
HM?
GOODNESS, YOU'RE DULL TODAY.
BUT I HONESTLY DON'T REMEMBER ANY OF THAT. I DON'T HAVE YOUR MEMORY, SEIRA.
ANYWAY, LOOK AT THIS.
THERE'S A LINE OF ANTS CARRYING A WORM.
HMPH! I'M GOING TO LOOK AT THAT FIVE-LEAF VINE OVER THERE.
STMP
STMP

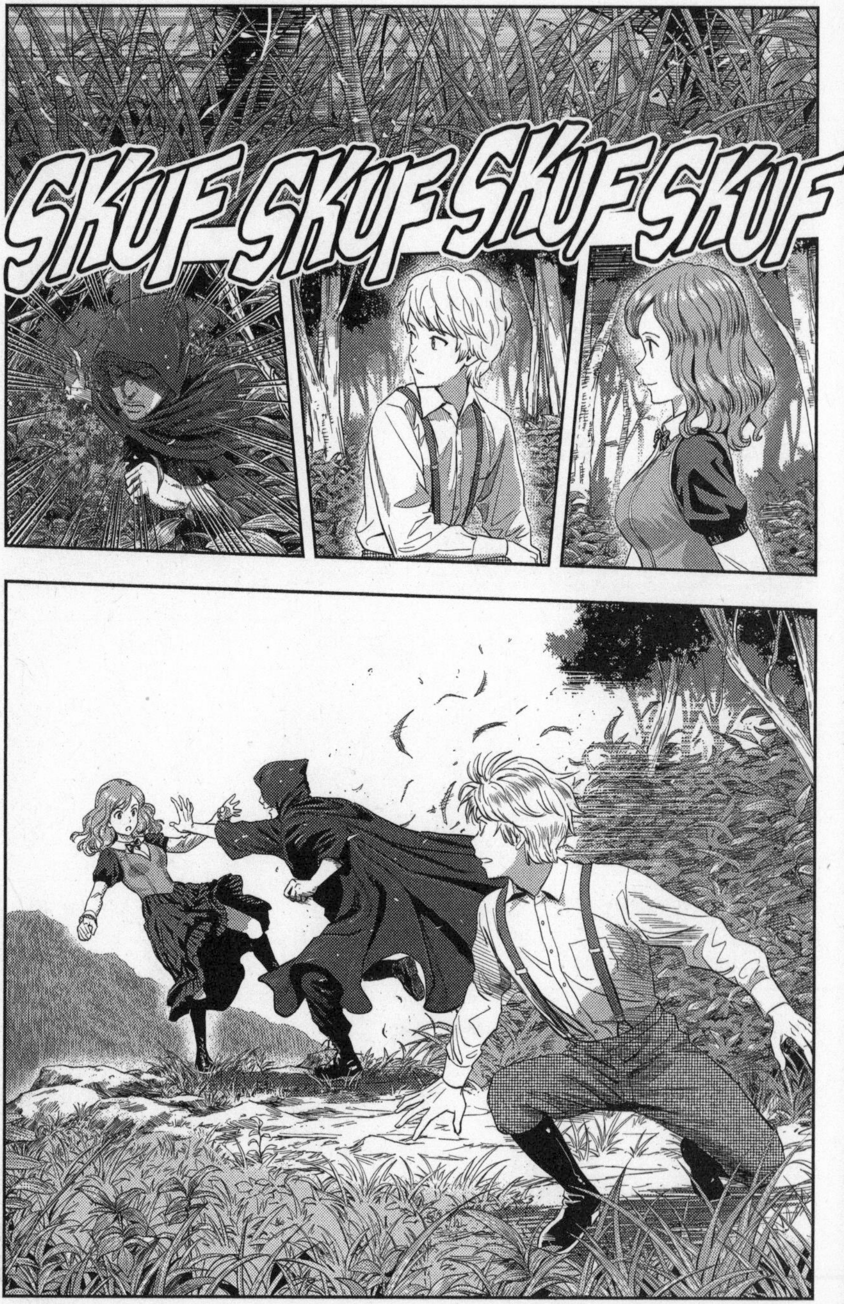
SKUF SKUF SKUF SKUF

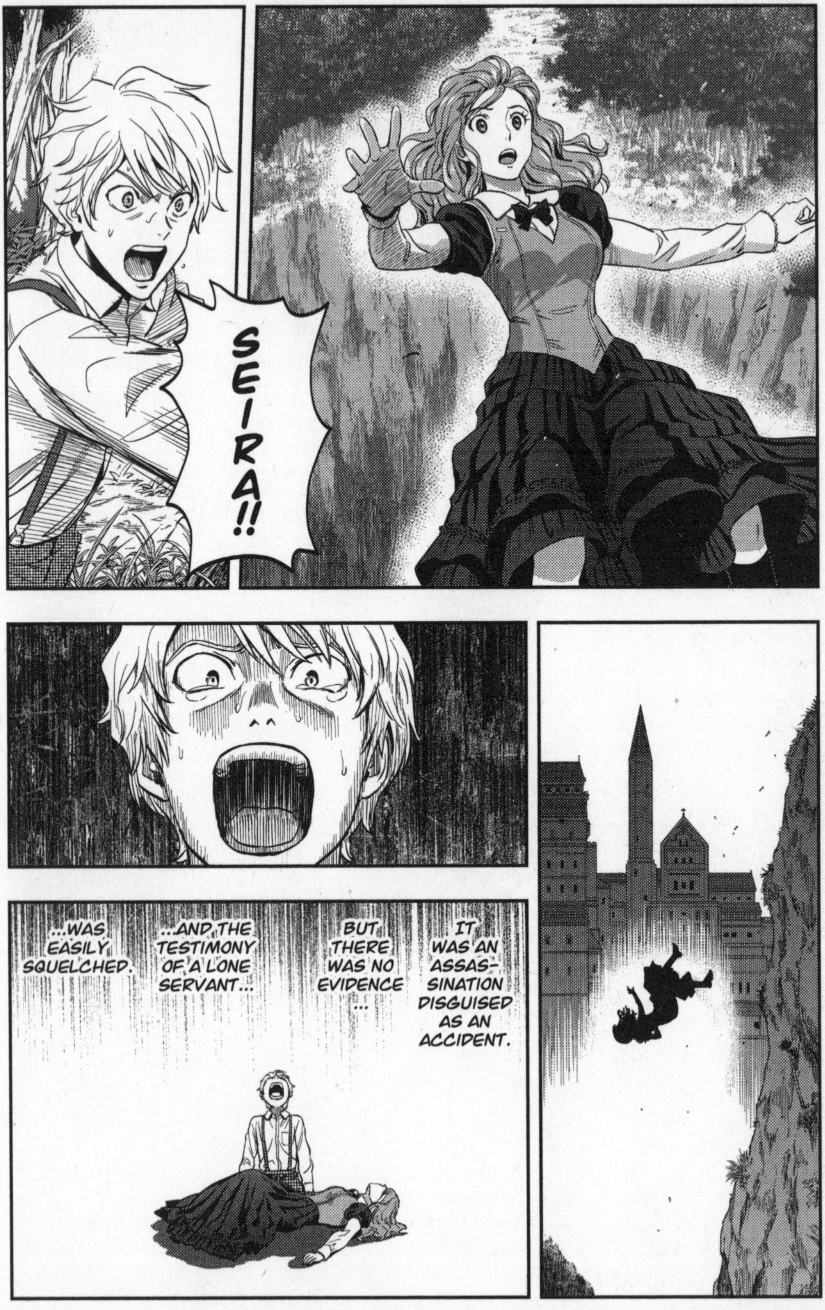
SEIRA!!
IT WAS AN ASSAS-SINATION DISGUISED AS AN ACCIDENT.
BUT THERE WAS NO EVIDENCE...
...AND THE TESTIMONY OF A LONE SERVANT...
...WAS EASILY SQUELCHED.

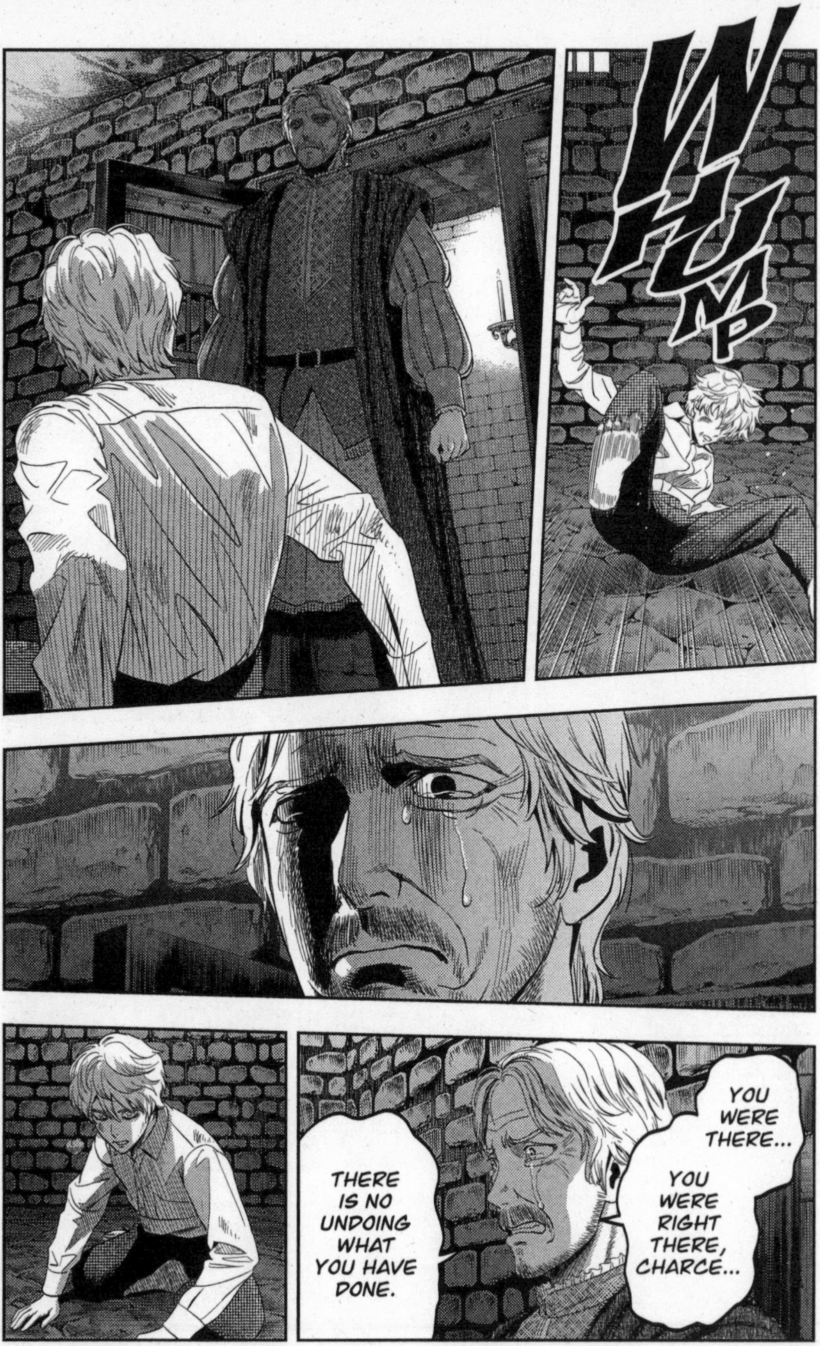
WHUMP
YOU WERE THERE...
YOU WERE RIGHT THERE, CHARCE...
THERE IS NO UNDOING WHAT YOU HAVE DONE.

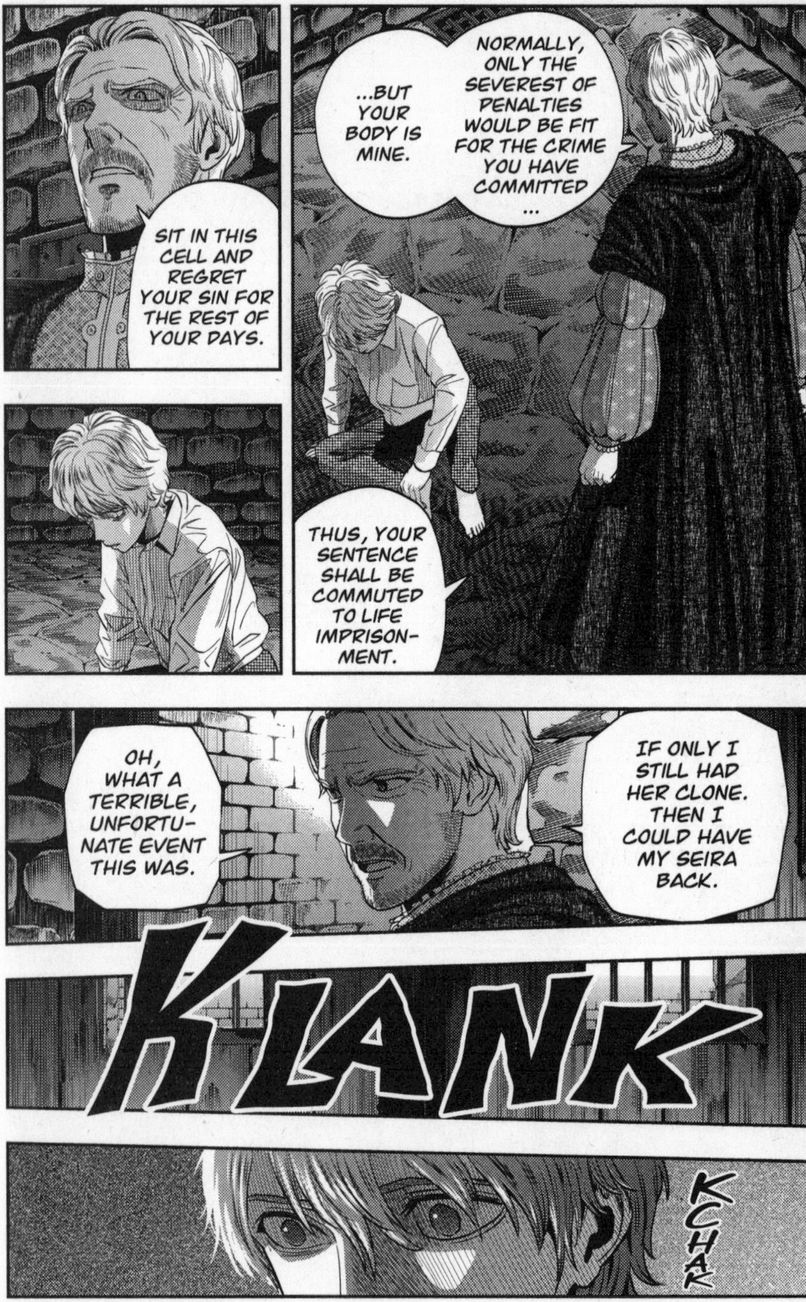
NORMALLY, ONLY THE SEVEREST OF PENALTIES WOULD BE FIT FOR THE CRIME YOU HAVE COMMITTED ...
...BUT YOUR BODY IS MINE.
THUS, YOUR SENTENCE SHALL BE COMMUTED TO LIFE IMPRISON-MENT.
SIT IN THIS CELL AND REGRET YOUR SIN FOR THE REST OF YOUR DAYS.
IF ONLY I STILL HAD HER CLONE. THEN I COULD HAVE MY SEIRA BACK.
OH, WHAT A TERRIBLE, UNFORTU-NATE EVENT THIS WAS.
KLANK
KCHAK

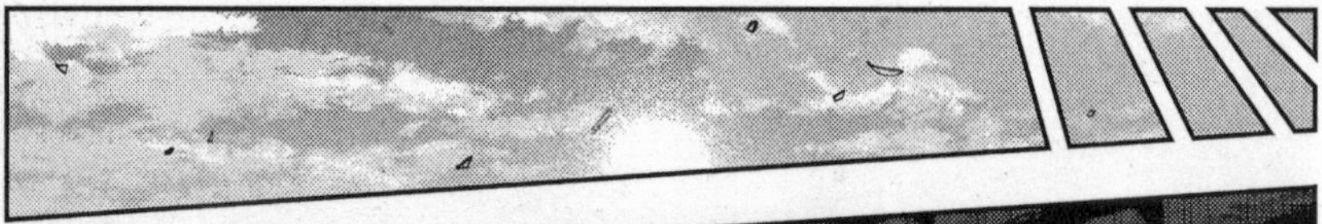

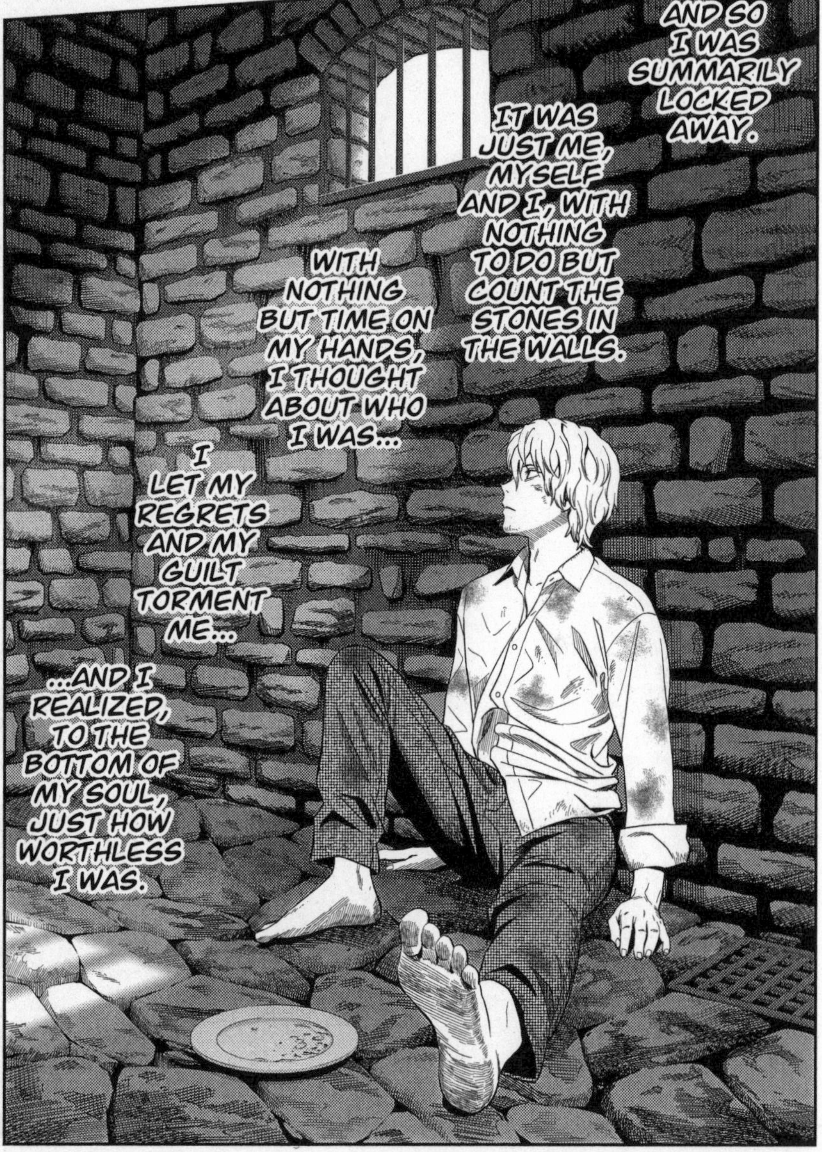
AND SO I WAS SUMMARILY LOCKED AWAY.
IT WAS JUST ME, MYSELF AND I, WITH NOTHING TO DO BUT COUNT THE STONES IN THE WALLS.
WITH NOTHING BUT TIME ON MY HANDS, I THOUGHT ABOUT WHO I WAS...
I LET MY REGRETS AND MY GUILT TORMENT ME...
...AND I REALIZED, TO THE BOTTOM OF MY SOUL, JUST HOW WORTHLESS I WAS.

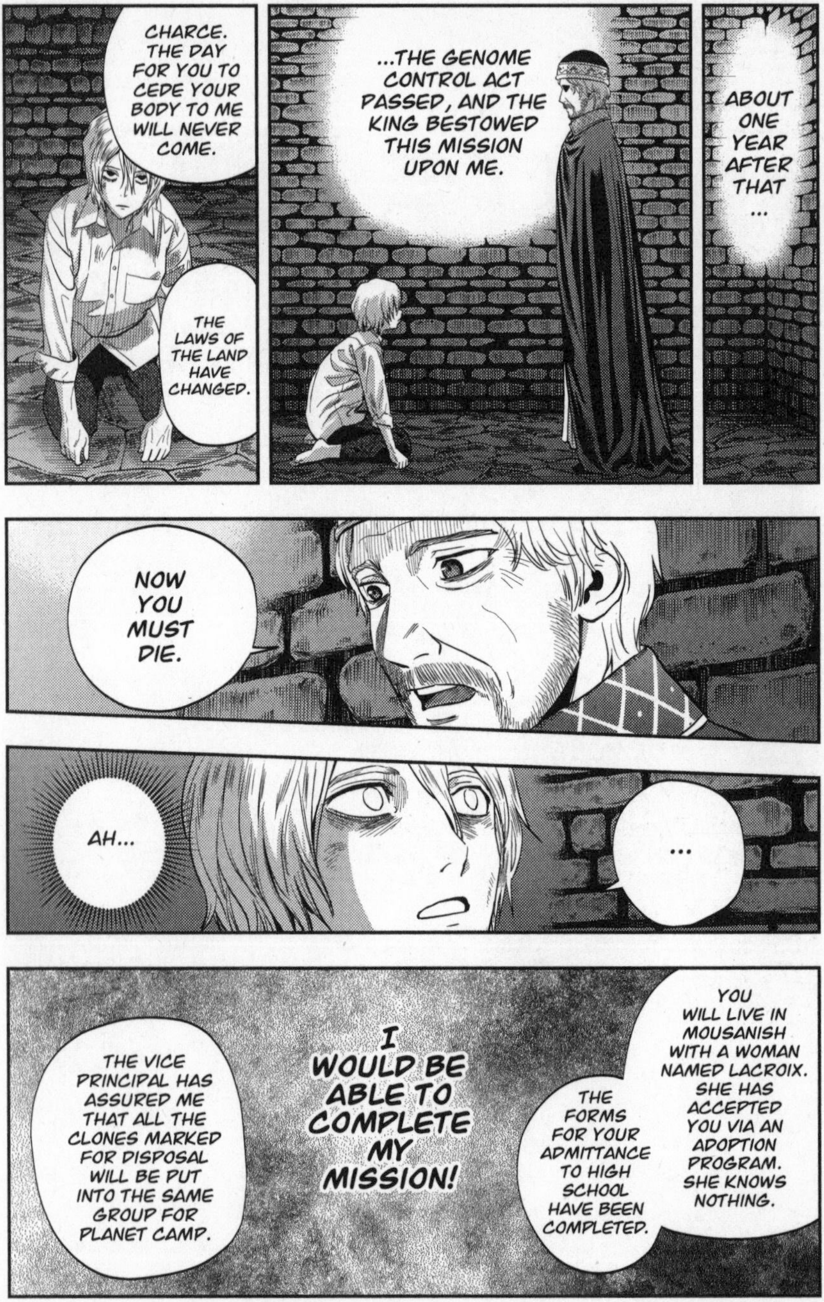
ABOUT ONE YEAR AFTER THAT ...
...THE GENOME CONTROL ACT PASSED, AND THE KING BESTOWED THIS MISSION UPON ME.
CHARCE. THE DAY FOR YOU TO CEDE YOUR BODY TO ME WILL NEVER COME.
THE LAWS OF THE LAND HAVE CHANGED.
NOW YOU MUST DIE.
...
AH...
YOU WILL LIVE IN MOUSANISH WITH A WOMAN NAMED LACROIX. SHE HAS ACCEPTED YOU VIA AN ADOPTION PROGRAM. SHE KNOWS NOTHING.
THE FORMS FOR YOUR ADMITTANCE TO HIGH SCHOOL HAVE BEEN COMPLETED.
I WOULD BE ABLE TO COMPLETE MY MISSION!
THE VICE PRINCIPAL HAS ASSURED ME THAT ALL THE CLONES MARKED FOR DISPOSAL WILL BE PUT INTO THE SAME GROUP FOR PLANET CAMP.

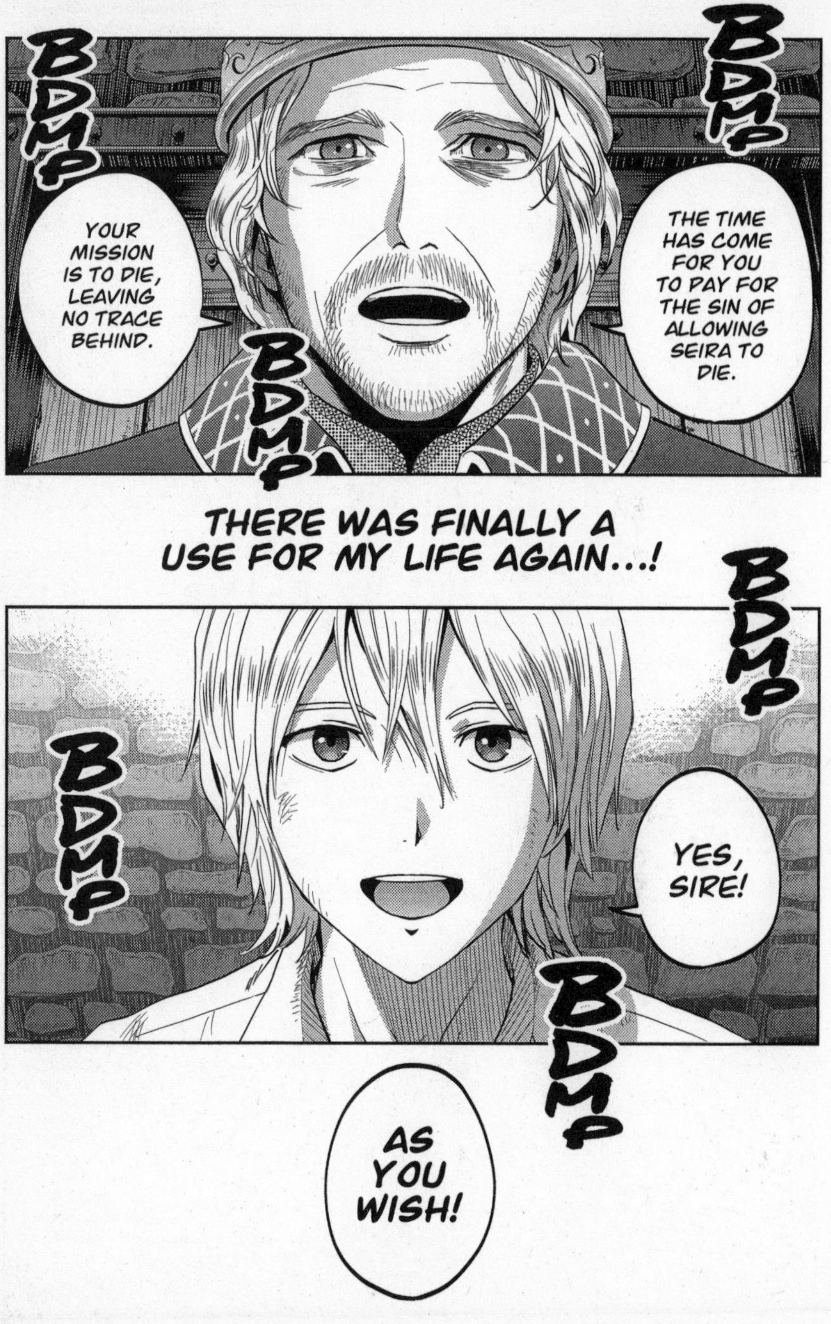
BDMP
THE TIME HAS COME FOR YOU TO PAY FOR THE SIN OF ALLOWING SEIRA TO DIE.
BDMP
YOUR MISSION IS TO DIE, LEAVING NO TRACE BEHIND.
BDMP
THERE WAS FINALLY A USE FOR MY LIFE AGAIN...!
BDMP
YES, SIRE!
BDMP
BDMP
AS YOU WISH!

Material Collection | Character Prototype Design

LUCA and FUNICIA

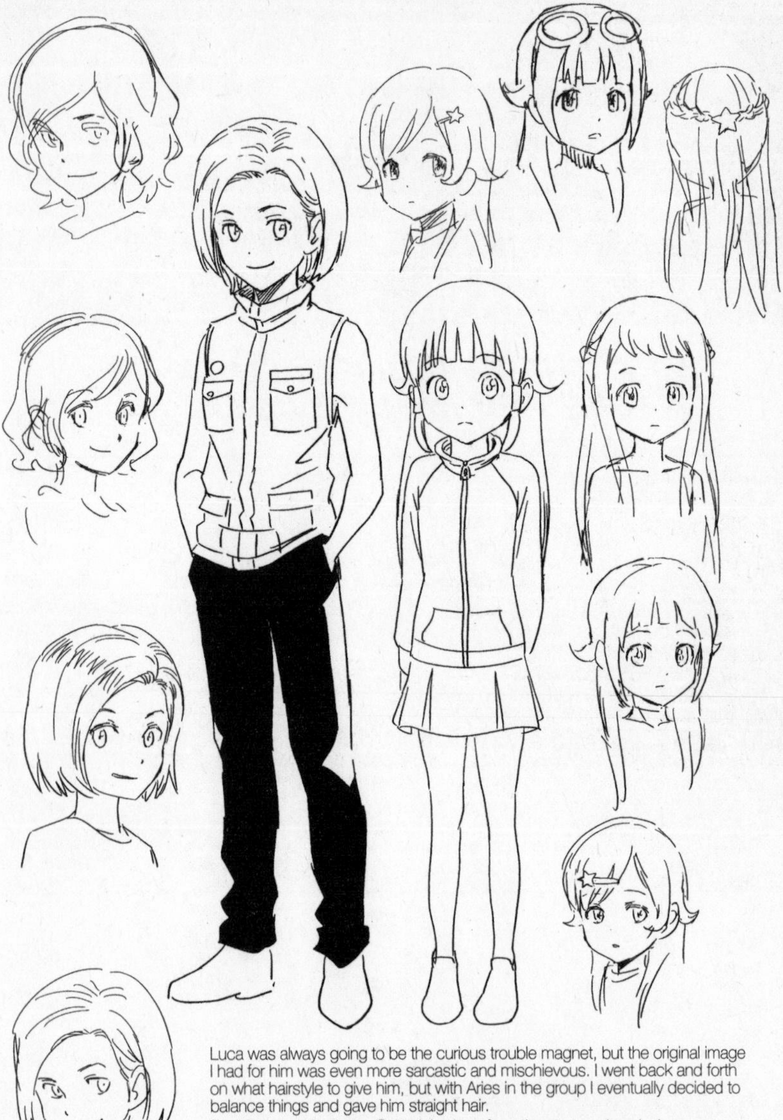

Luca was always going to be the curious trouble magnet, but the original image I had for him was even more sarcastic and mischievous. I went back and forth on what hairstyle to give him, but with Aries in the group I eventually decided to balance things and gave him straight hair.

Funicia was going to be Quitterie's clone from the start, so her design was left waiting until I decided on Quitterie's skin tone. At first she was going to be a bashful and quiet girl, but since that overlapped with Yun-hua's character, I switched her up to be the innocent and cheerful type.

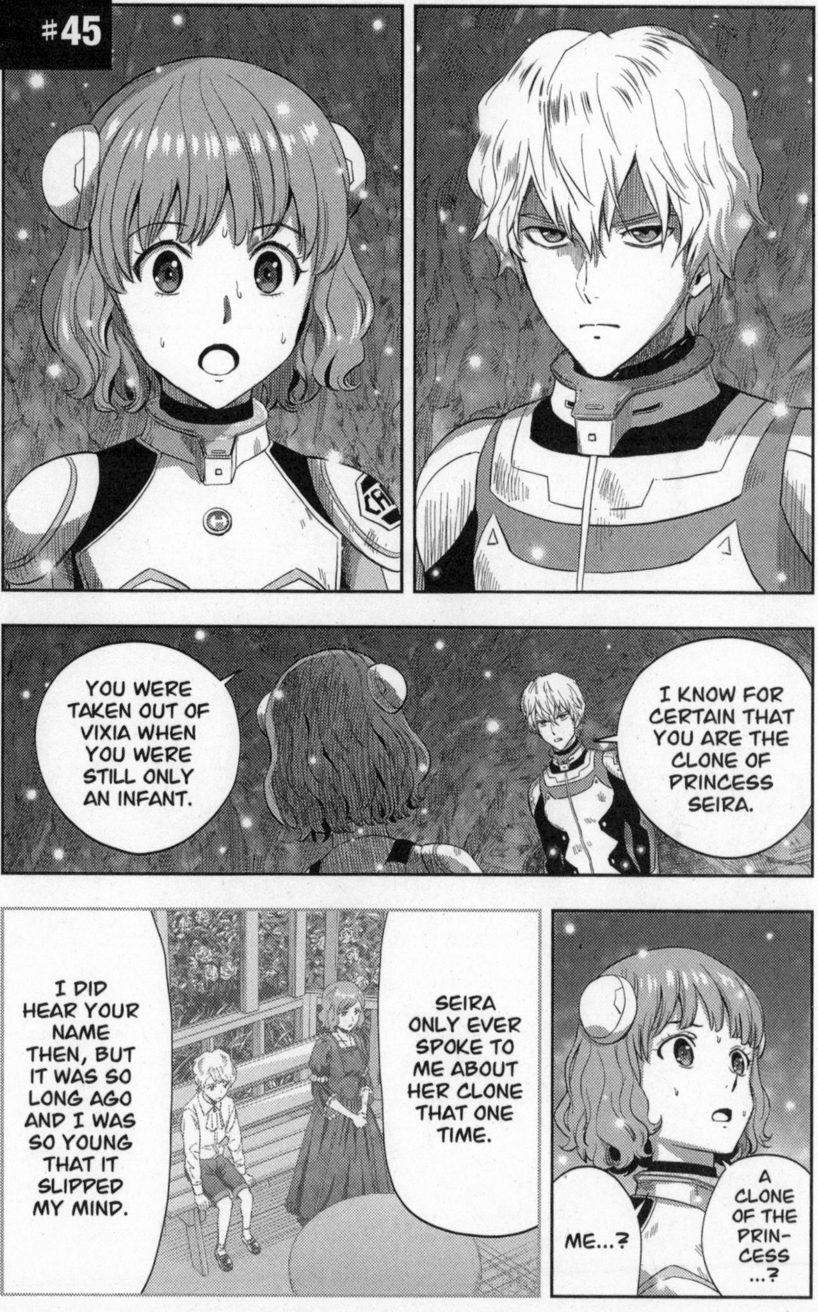
I KNOW FOR CERTAIN THAT YOU ARE THE CLONE OF PRINCESS SEIRA.
YOU WERE TAKEN OUT OF VIXIA WHEN YOU WERE STILL ONLY AN INFANT.
A CLONE OF THE PRIN-CESS ...?
ME...?
SEIRA ONLY EVER SPOKE TO ME ABOUT HER CLONE THAT ONE TIME.
I DID HEAR YOUR NAME THEN, BUT IT WAS SO LONG AGO AND I WAS SO YOUNG THAT IT SLIPPED MY MIND.

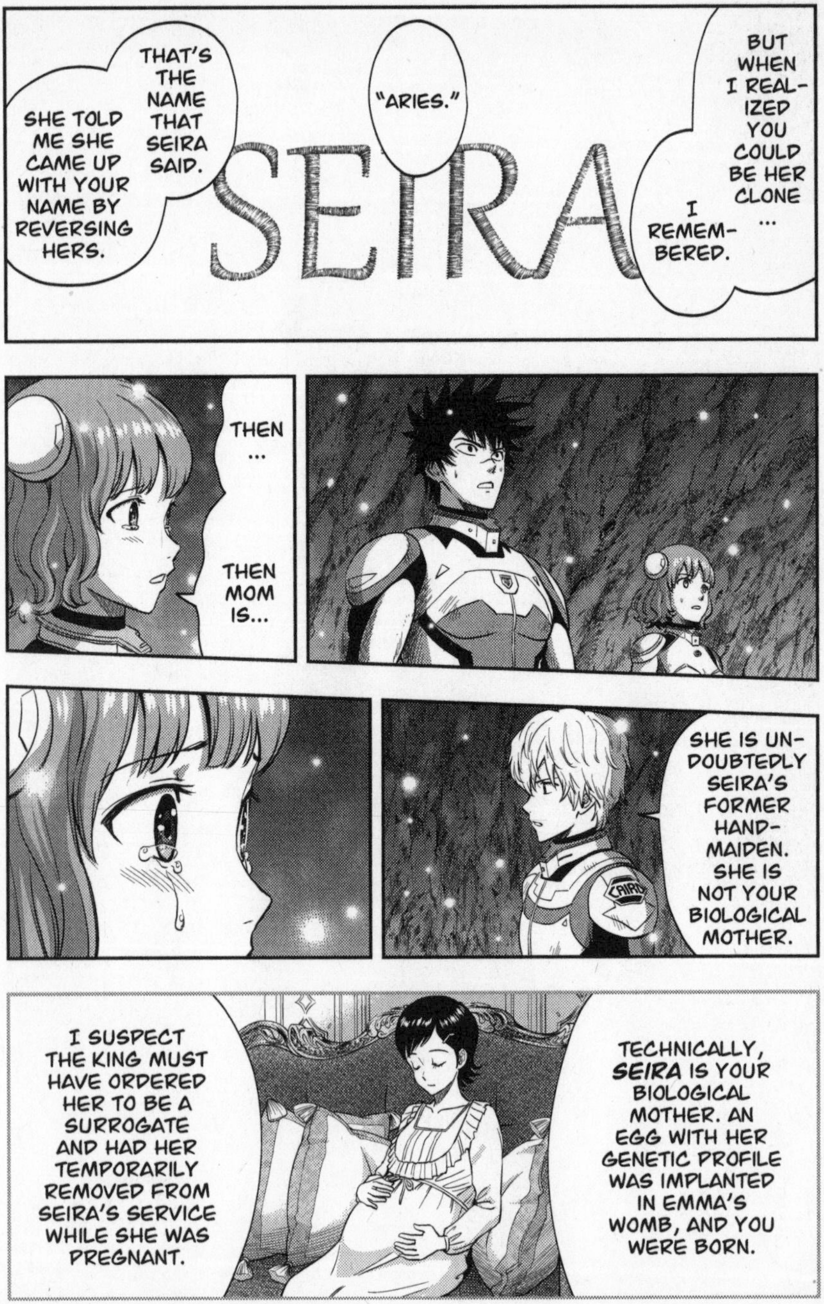
BUT WHEN I REAL- IZED YOU COULD BE HER CLONE ...
I REMEM- BERED.
"ARIES."
SEIRA
THAT'S THE NAME THAT SEIRA SAID.
SHE TOLD ME SHE CAME UP WITH YOUR NAME BY REVERSING HERS.
THEN ...
THEN MOM IS...
SHE IS UN- DOUBTEDLY SEIRA'S FORMER HAND- MAIDEN. SHE IS NOT YOUR BIOLOGICAL MOTHER.
TECHNICALLY, **SEIRA** IS YOUR BIOLOGICAL MOTHER. AN EGG WITH HER GENETIC PROFILE WAS IMPLANTED IN EMMA'S WOMB, AND YOU WERE BORN.
I SUSPECT THE KING MUST HAVE ORDERED HER TO BE A SURROGATE AND HAD HER TEMPORARILY REMOVED FROM SEIRA'S SERVICE WHILE SHE WAS PREGNANT.

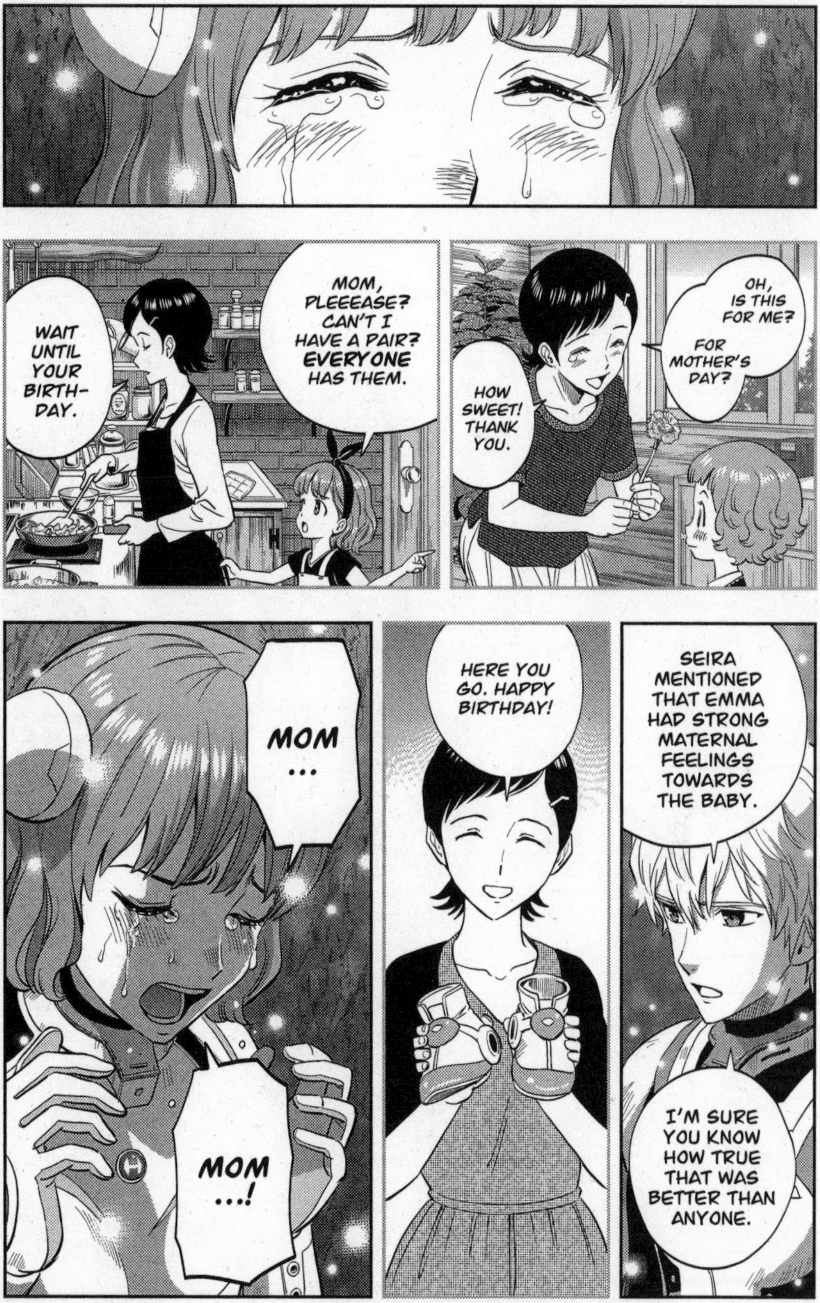

OH, IS THIS FOR ME?
FOR MOTHER'S DAY?
HOW SWEET! THANK YOU.
MOM, PLEEEASE? CAN'T I HAVE A PAIR? EVERYONE HAS THEM.
WAIT UNTIL YOUR BIRTH-DAY.
SEIRA MENTIONED THAT EMMA HAD STRONG MATERNAL FEELINGS TOWARDS THE BABY.
I'M SURE YOU KNOW HOW TRUE THAT WAS BETTER THAN ANYONE.
HERE YOU GO. HAPPY BIRTHDAY!
MOM ...
MOM ...!

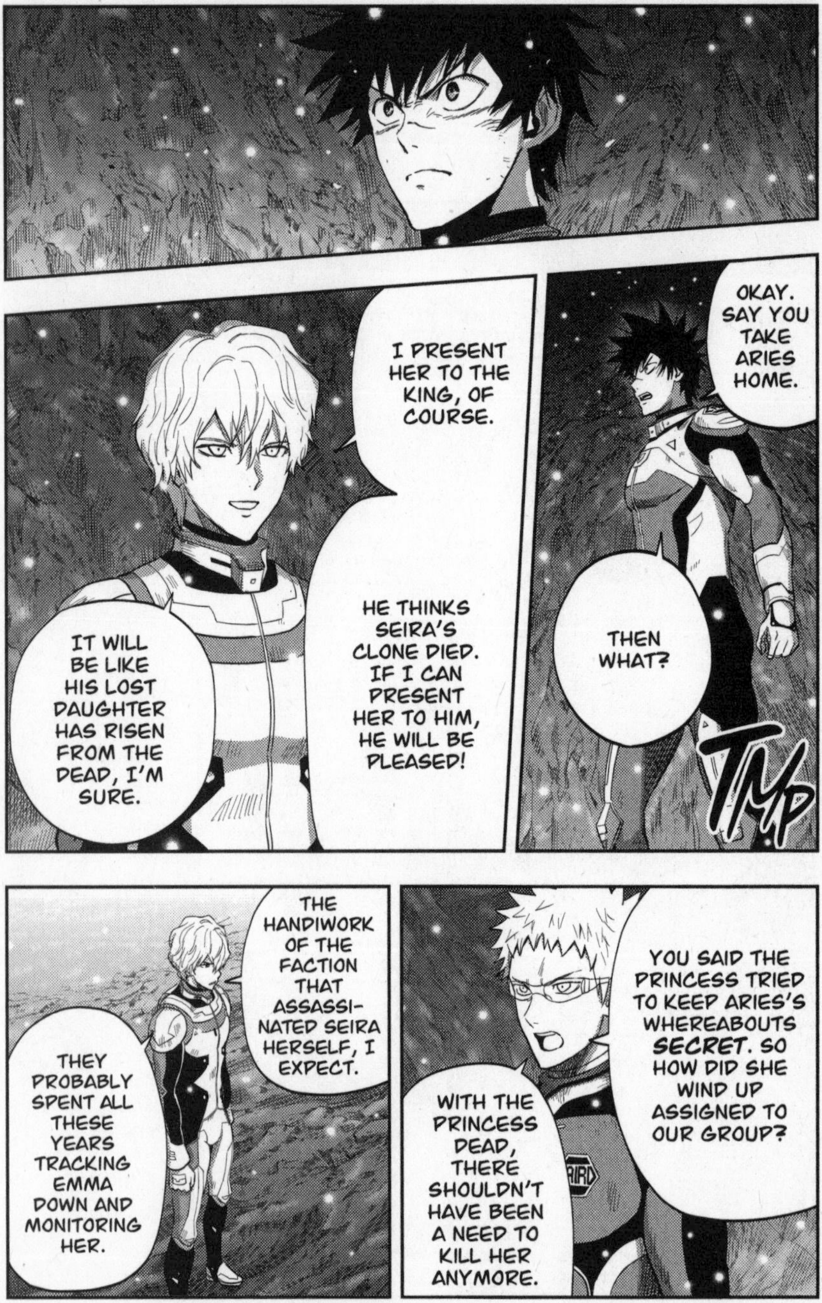
OKAY. SAY YOU TAKE ARIES HOME.
THEN WHAT?
TMP
I PRESENT HER TO THE KING, OF COURSE.
HE THINKS SEIRA'S CLONE DIED. IF I CAN PRESENT HER TO HIM, HE WILL BE PLEASED!
IT WILL BE LIKE HIS LOST DAUGHTER HAS RISEN FROM THE DEAD, I'M SURE.
YOU SAID THE PRINCESS TRIED TO KEEP ARIES'S WHEREABOUTS **SECRET**. SO HOW DID SHE WIND UP ASSIGNED TO OUR GROUP?
WITH THE PRINCESS DEAD, THERE SHOULDN'T HAVE BEEN A NEED TO KILL HER ANYMORE.
THE HANDIWORK OF THE FACTION THAT ASSASSI-NATED SEIRA HERSELF, I EXPECT.
THEY PROBABLY SPENT ALL THESE YEARS TRACKING EMMA DOWN AND MONITORING HER.

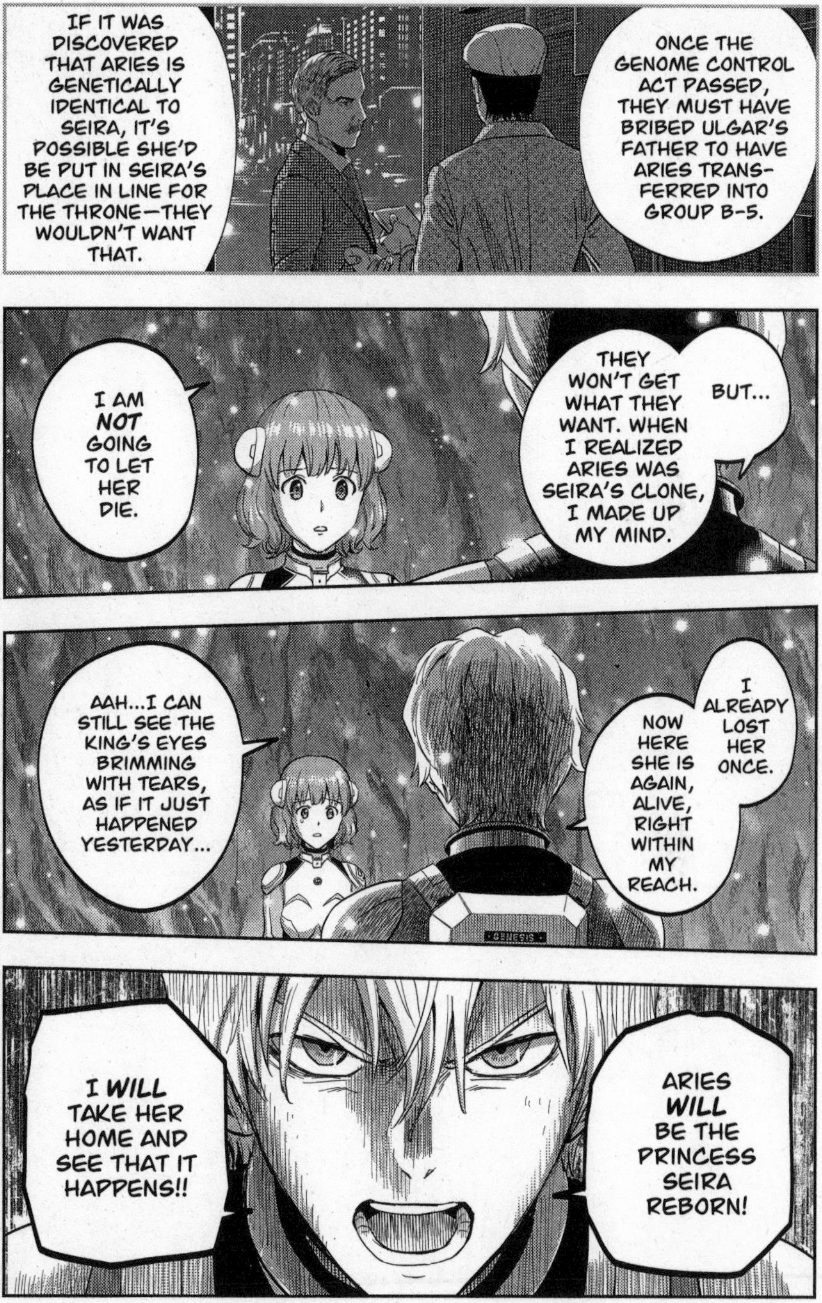
ONCE THE GENOME CONTROL ACT PASSED, THEY MUST HAVE BRIBED ULGAR'S FATHER TO HAVE ARIES TRANS-FERRED INTO GROUP B-5.
IF IT WAS DISCOVERED THAT ARIES IS GENETICALLY IDENTICAL TO SEIRA, IT'S POSSIBLE SHE'D BE PUT IN SEIRA'S PLACE IN LINE FOR THE THRONE—THEY WOULDN'T WANT THAT.
BUT...
THEY WON'T GET WHAT THEY WANT. WHEN I REALIZED ARIES WAS SEIRA'S CLONE, I MADE UP MY MIND.
I AM NOT GOING TO LET HER DIE.
I ALREADY LOST HER ONCE.
NOW HERE SHE IS AGAIN, ALIVE, RIGHT WITHIN MY REACH.
AAH...I CAN STILL SEE THE KING'S EYES BRIMMING WITH TEARS, AS IF IT JUST HAPPENED YESTERDAY...
GENESIS
ARIES WILL BE THE PRINCESS SEIRA REBORN!
I WILL TAKE HER HOME AND SEE THAT IT HAPPENS!!

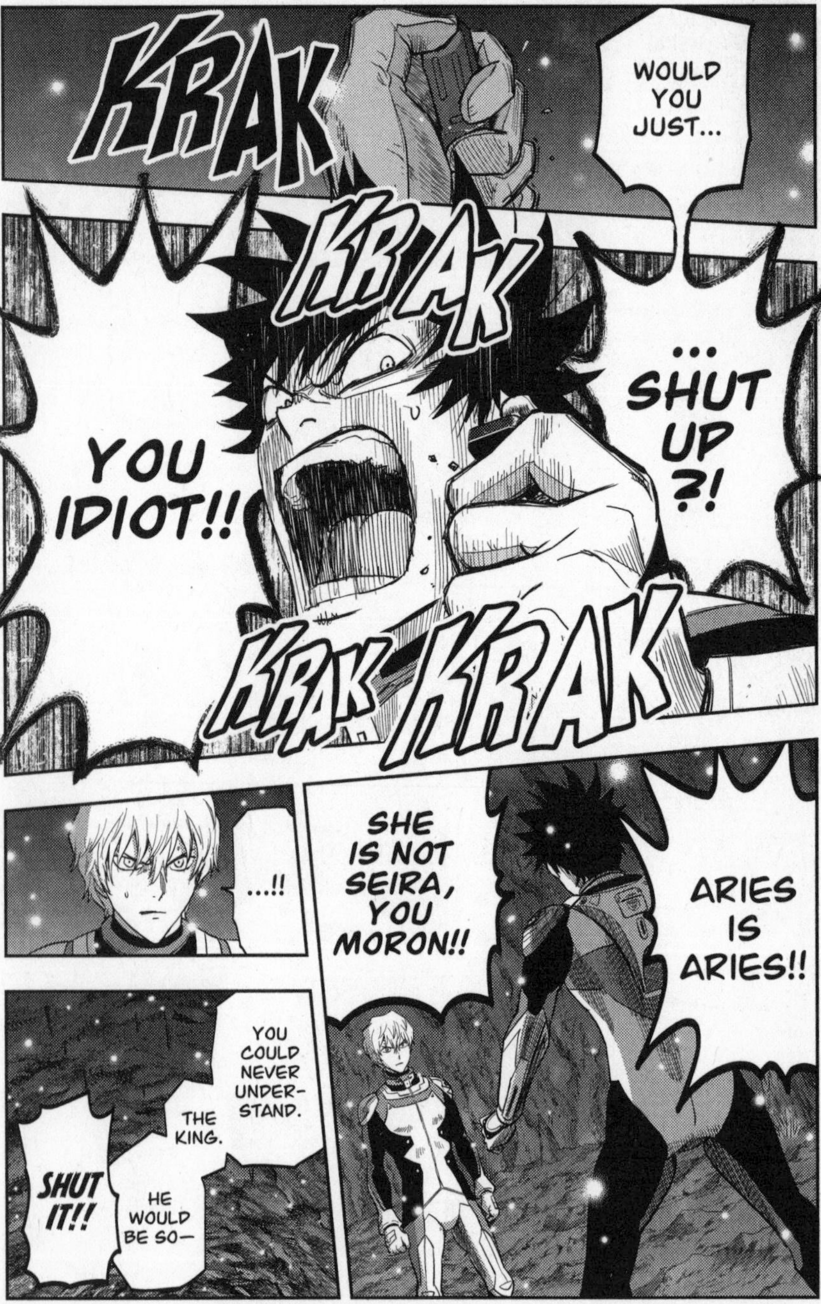
WOULD YOU JUST...
KRAK
KRAK
... SHUT UP ?!
YOU IDIOT!!
KRAK
KRAK
ARIES IS ARIES!!
SHE IS NOT SEIRA, YOU MORON!!
...!!
YOU COULD NEVER UNDER-STAND.
THE KING.
HE WOULD BE SO—
SHUT IT!!

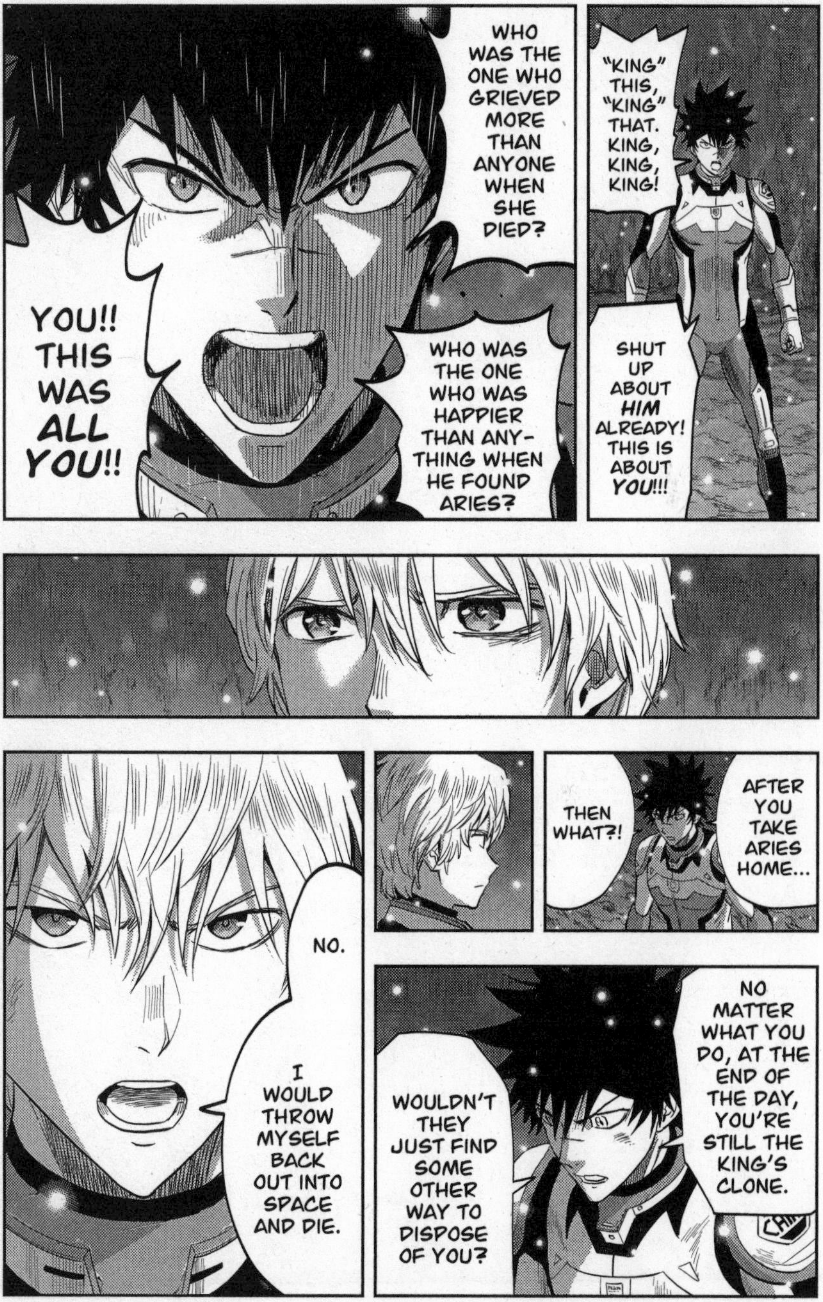
"KING" THIS, "KING" THAT. KING, KING, KING!
SHUT UP ABOUT HIM ALREADY! THIS IS ABOUT YOU!!!
WHO WAS THE ONE WHO GRIEVED MORE THAN ANYONE WHEN SHE DIED?
WHO WAS THE ONE WHO WAS HAPPIER THAN ANY-THING WHEN HE FOUND ARIES?
YOU!! THIS WAS ALL YOU!!
AFTER YOU TAKE ARIES HOME...
THEN WHAT?!
NO MATTER WHAT YOU DO, AT THE END OF THE DAY, YOU'RE STILL THE KING'S CLONE.
WOULDN'T THEY JUST FIND SOME OTHER WAY TO DISPOSE OF YOU?
NO.
I WOULD THROW MYSELF BACK OUT INTO SPACE AND DIE.

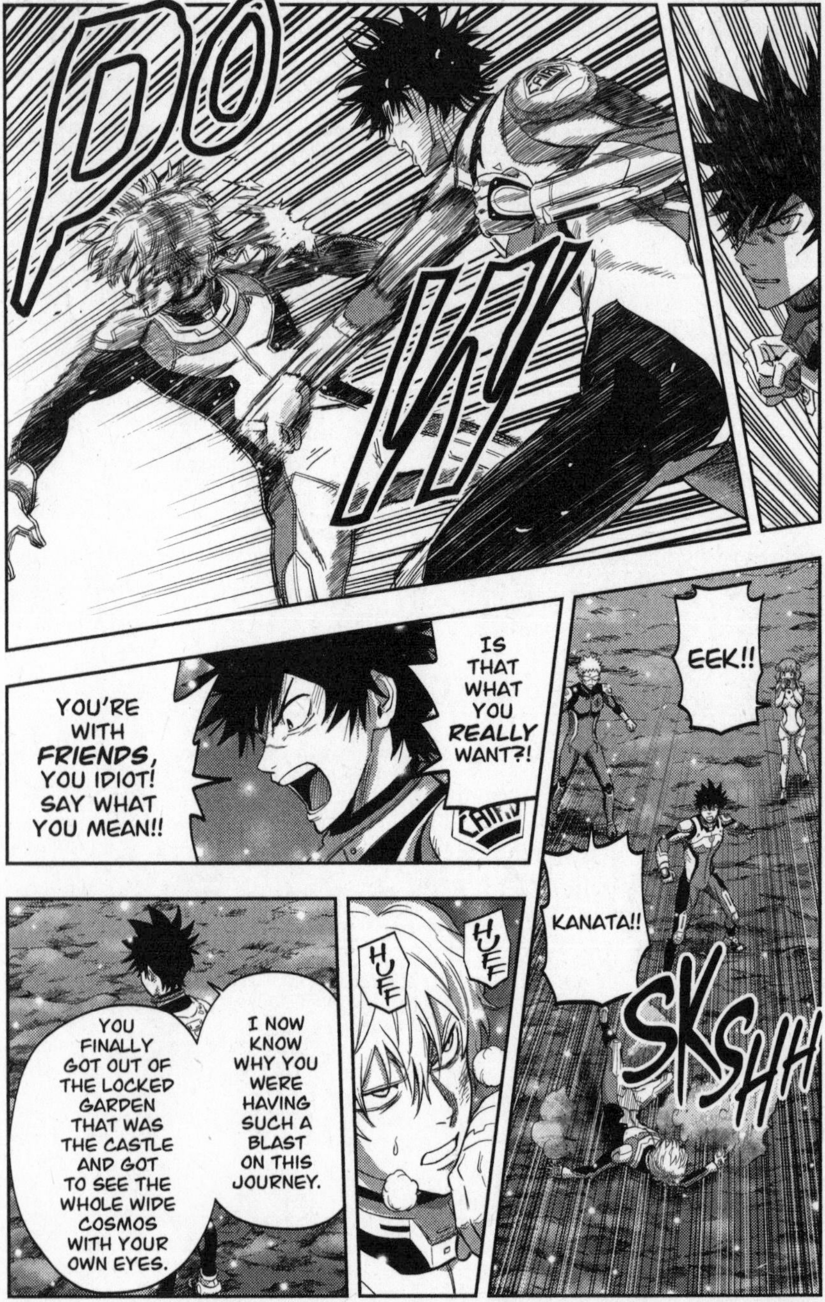
DOW
EEK!!
KANATA!!
SKSHH
IS THAT WHAT YOU REALLY WANT?!
YOU'RE WITH FRIENDS, YOU IDIOT! SAY WHAT YOU MEAN!!
HUFF
HUFF
I NOW KNOW WHY YOU WERE HAVING SUCH A BLAST ON THIS JOURNEY.
YOU FINALLY GOT OUT OF THE LOCKED GARDEN THAT WAS THE CASTLE AND GOT TO SEE THE WHOLE WIDE COSMOS WITH YOUR OWN EYES.

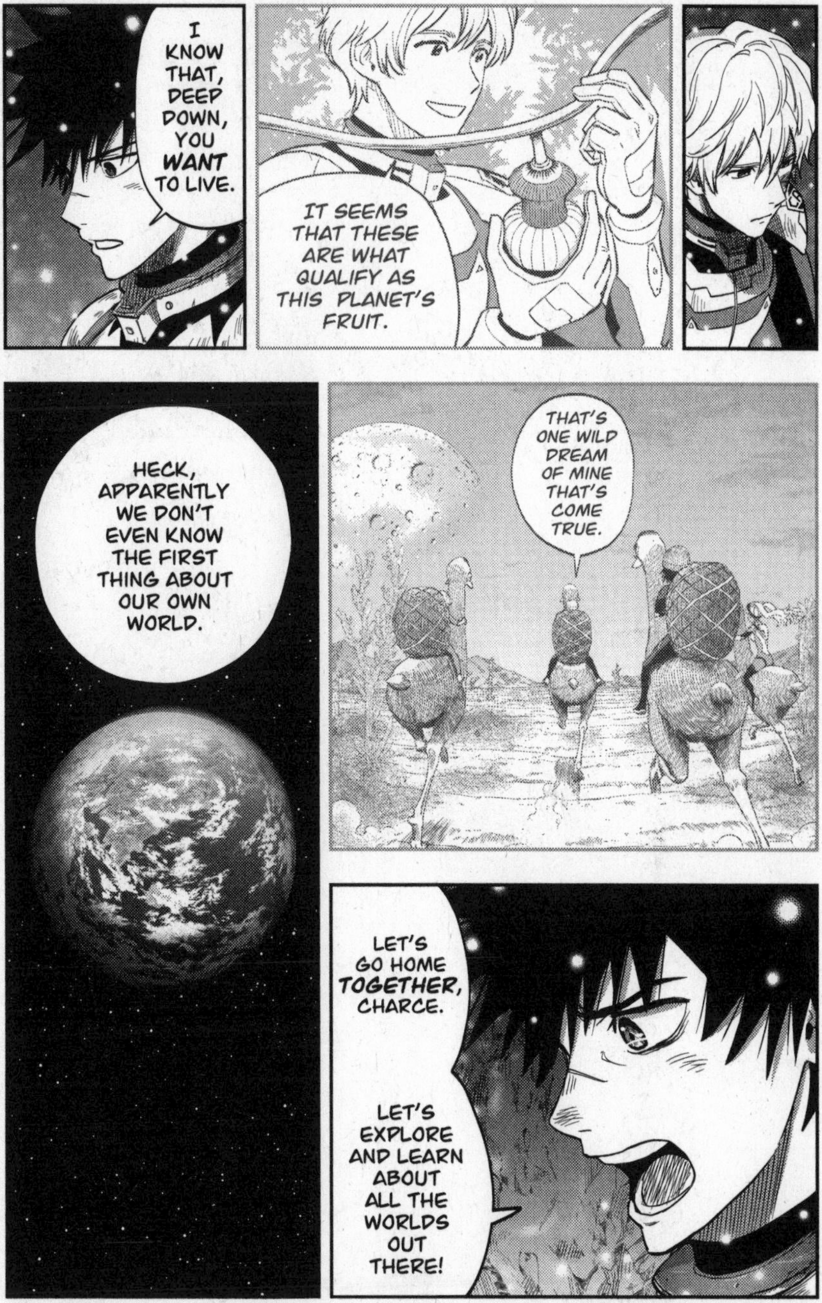
IT SEEMS THAT THESE ARE WHAT QUALIFY AS THIS PLANET'S FRUIT.
I KNOW THAT, DEEP DOWN, YOU WANT TO LIVE.
THAT'S ONE WILD DREAM OF MINE THAT'S COME TRUE.
LET'S GO HOME TOGETHER, CHARCE.
LET'S EXPLORE AND LEARN ABOUT ALL THE WORLDS OUT THERE!
HECK, APPARENTLY WE DON'T EVEN KNOW THE FIRST THING ABOUT OUR OWN WORLD.

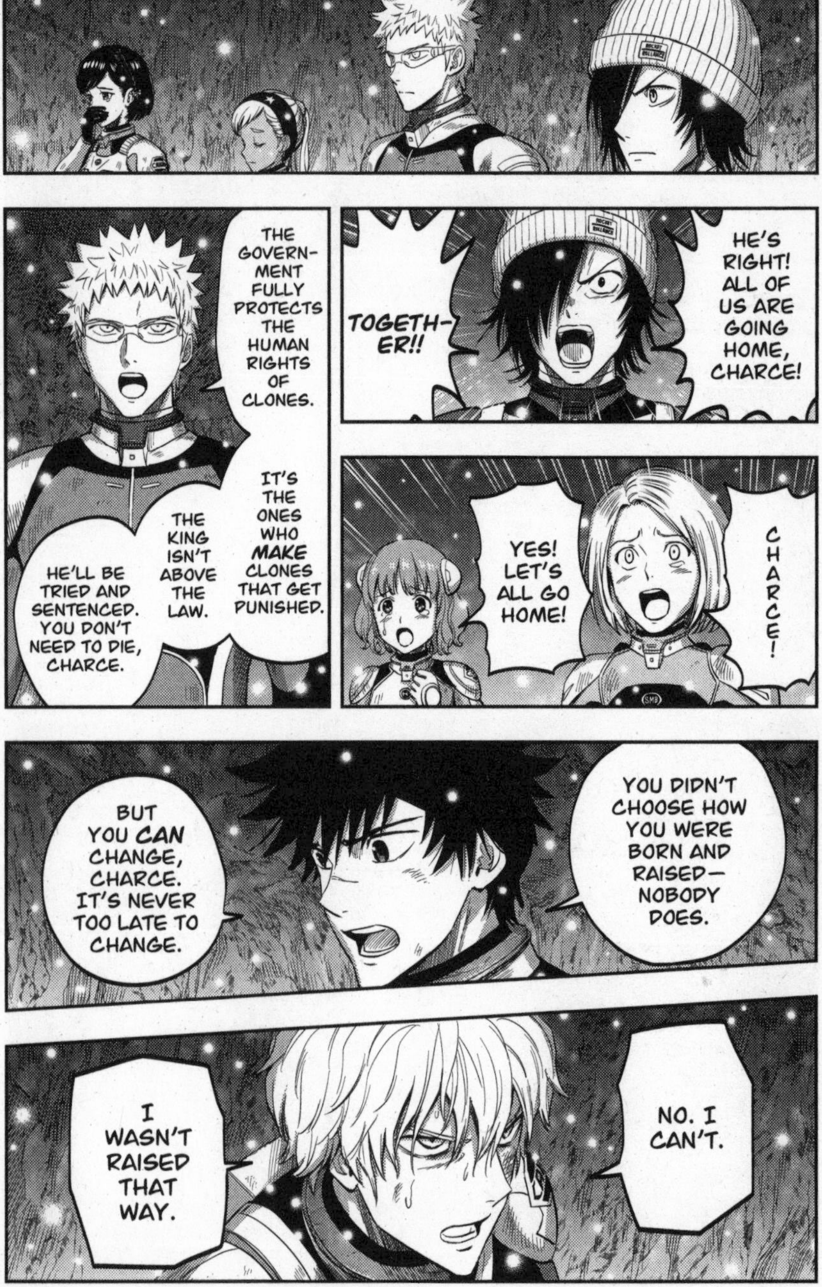
HE'S RIGHT! ALL OF US ARE GOING HOME, CHARCE!
TOGETHER!!
CHARCE!
YES! LET'S ALL GO HOME!
THE GOVERNMENT FULLY PROTECTS THE HUMAN RIGHTS OF CLONES.
IT'S THE ONES WHO **MAKE** CLONES THAT GET PUNISHED.
THE KING ISN'T ABOVE THE LAW.
HE'LL BE TRIED AND SENTENCED. YOU DON'T NEED TO DIE, CHARCE.
YOU DIDN'T CHOOSE HOW YOU WERE BORN AND RAISED—NOBODY DOES.
BUT YOU **CAN** CHANGE, CHARCE. IT'S NEVER TOO LATE TO CHANGE.
NO. I CAN'T.
I WASN'T RAISED THAT WAY.

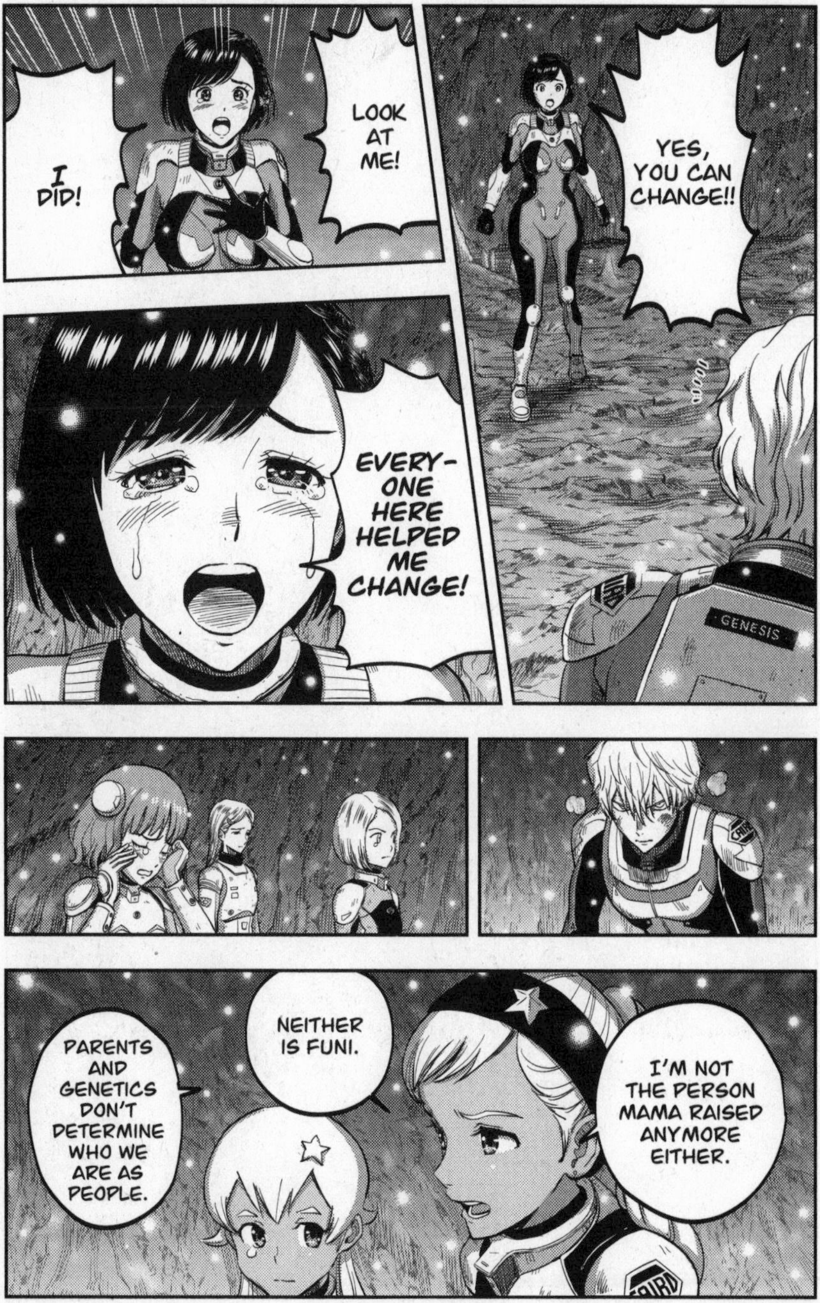
YES, YOU CAN CHANGE!!
LOOK AT ME!
I DID!
EVERY-ONE HERE HELPED ME CHANGE!
GENESIS
I'M NOT THE PERSON MAMA RAISED ANYMORE EITHER.
NEITHER IS FUNI.
PARENTS AND GENETICS DON'T DETERMINE WHO WE ARE AS PEOPLE.

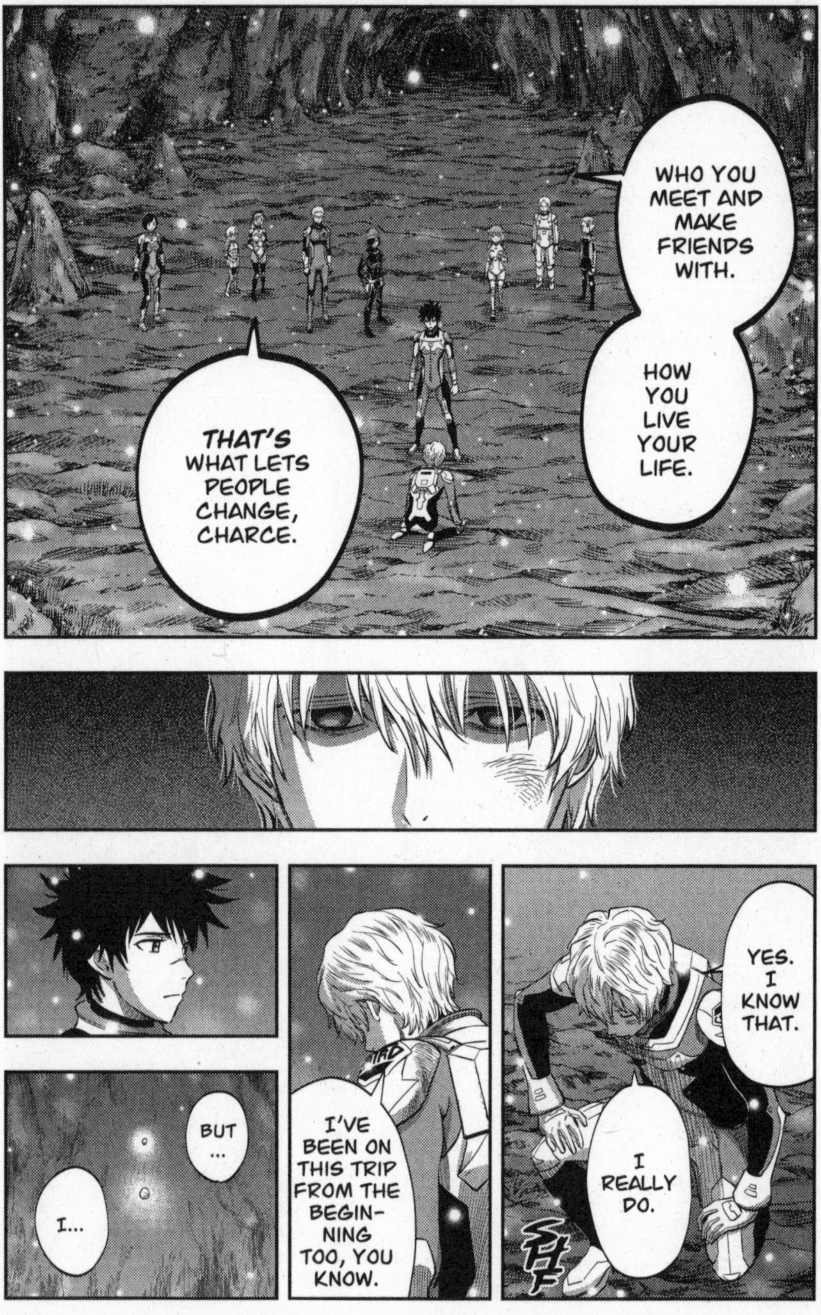
WHO YOU MEET AND MAKE FRIENDS WITH.
HOW YOU LIVE YOUR LIFE.
THAT'S WHAT LETS PEOPLE CHANGE, CHARCE.
YES. I KNOW THAT.
I REALLY DO.
SHF
I'VE BEEN ON THIS TRIP FROM THE BEGIN-NING TOO, YOU KNOW.
BUT ...
I...

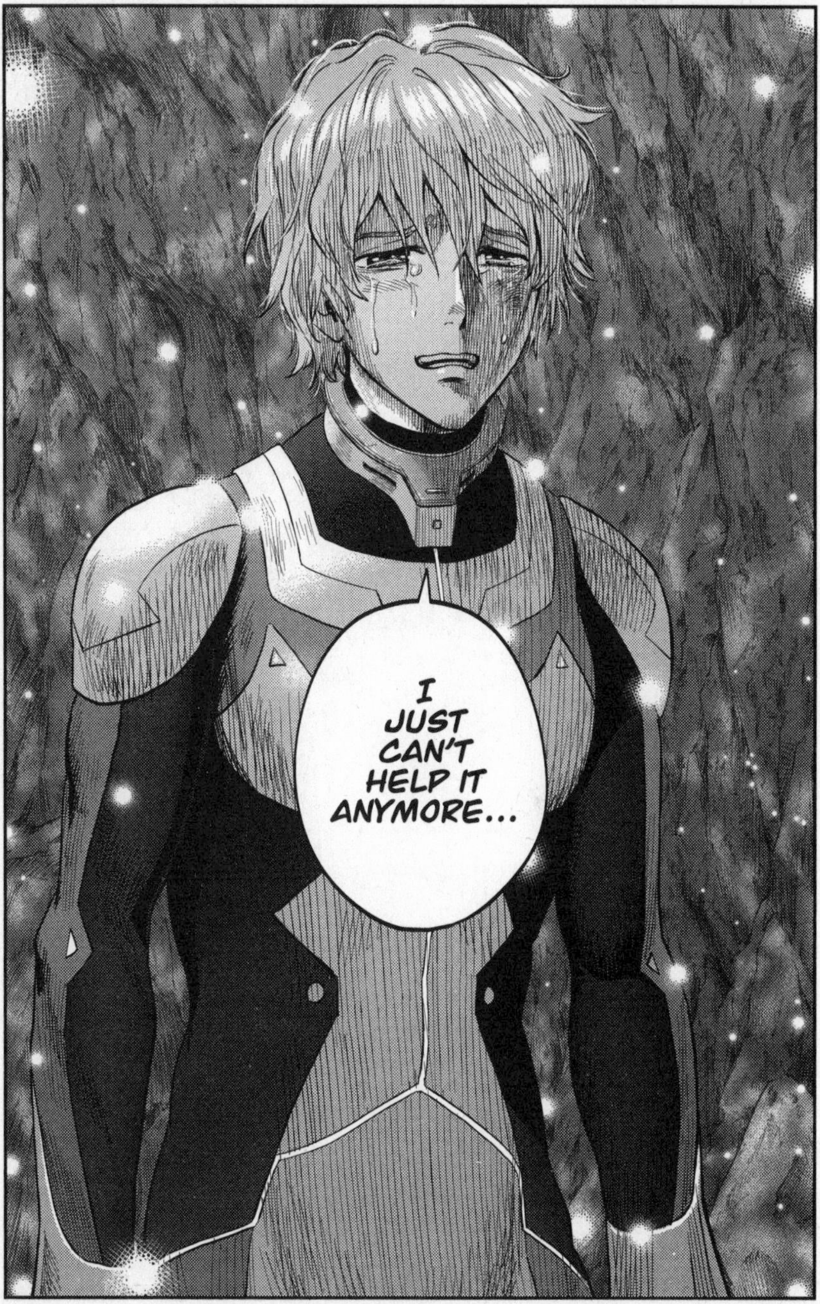
I JUST CAN'T HELP IT ANYMORE...

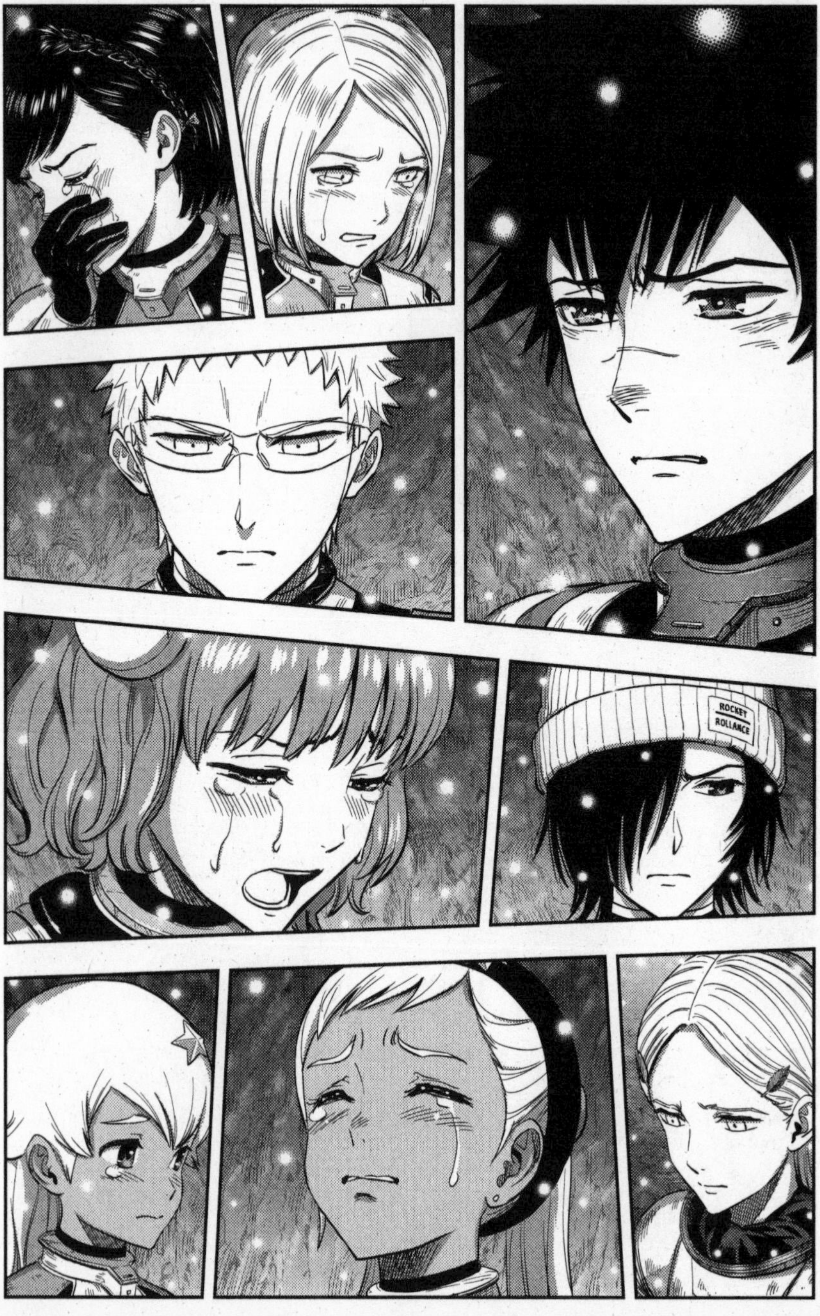
ROCKET
ROLLANCE

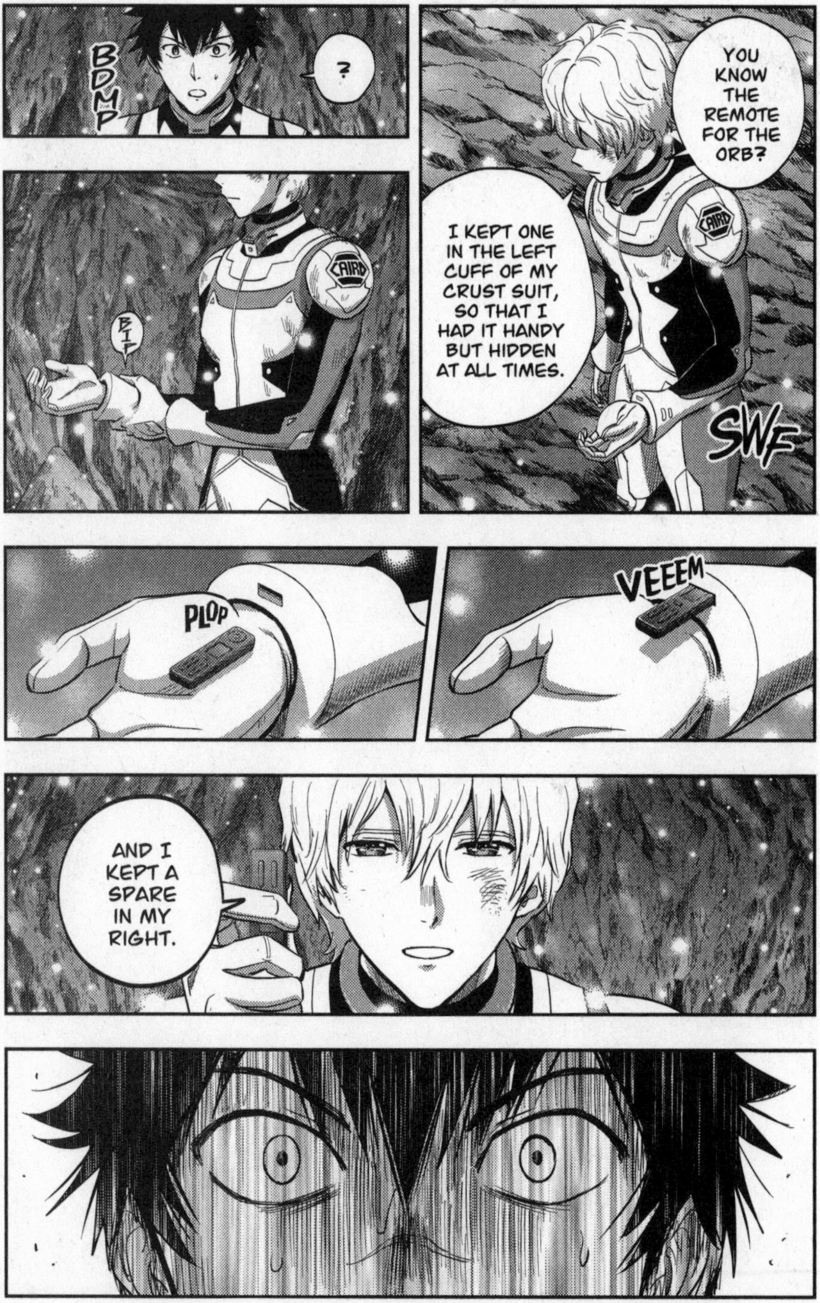
YOU KNOW THE REMOTE FOR THE ORB?
I KEPT ONE IN THE LEFT CUFF OF MY CRUST SUIT, SO THAT I HAD IT HANDY BUT HIDDEN AT ALL TIMES.
SWF
BDMP
?
BIP
VEEEM
PLOP
AND I KEPT A SPARE IN MY RIGHT.

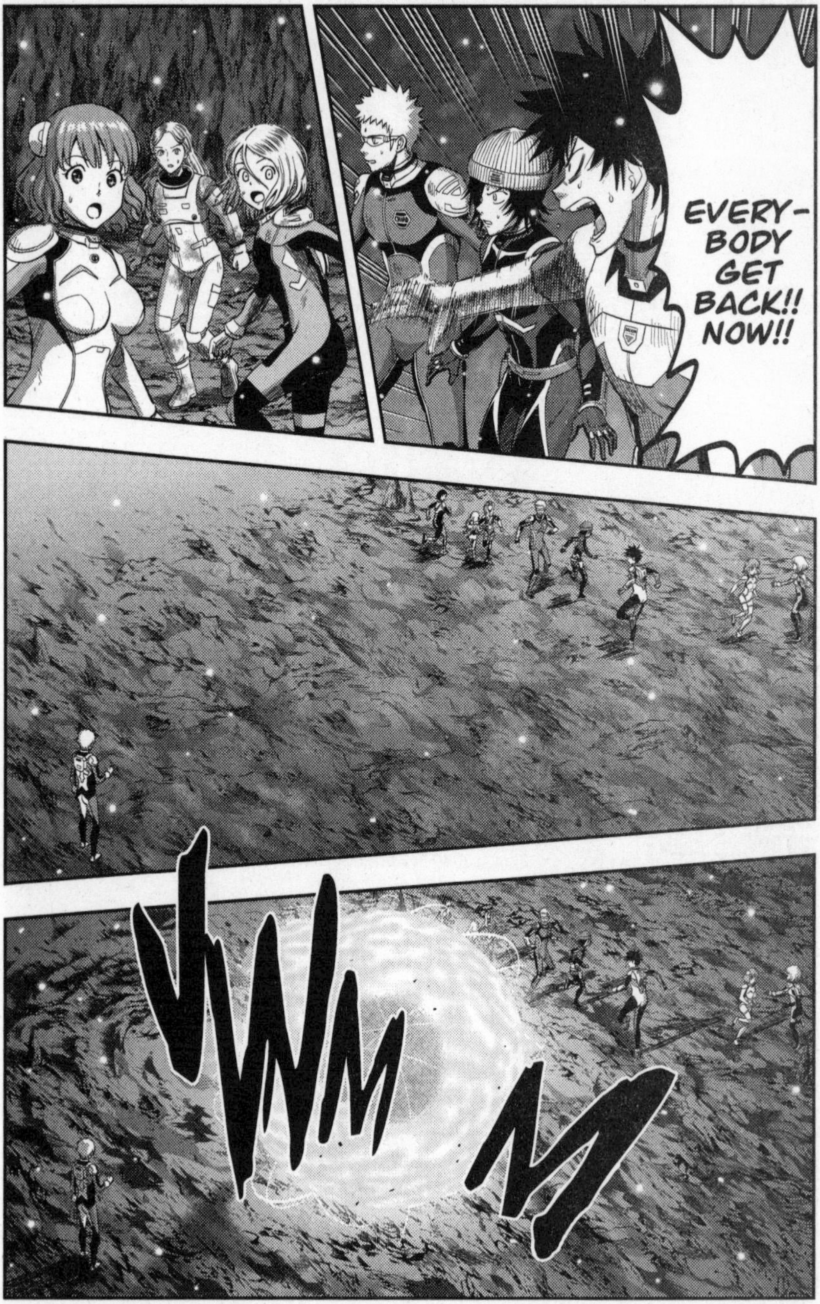
EVERY-BODY GET BACK!! NOW!!

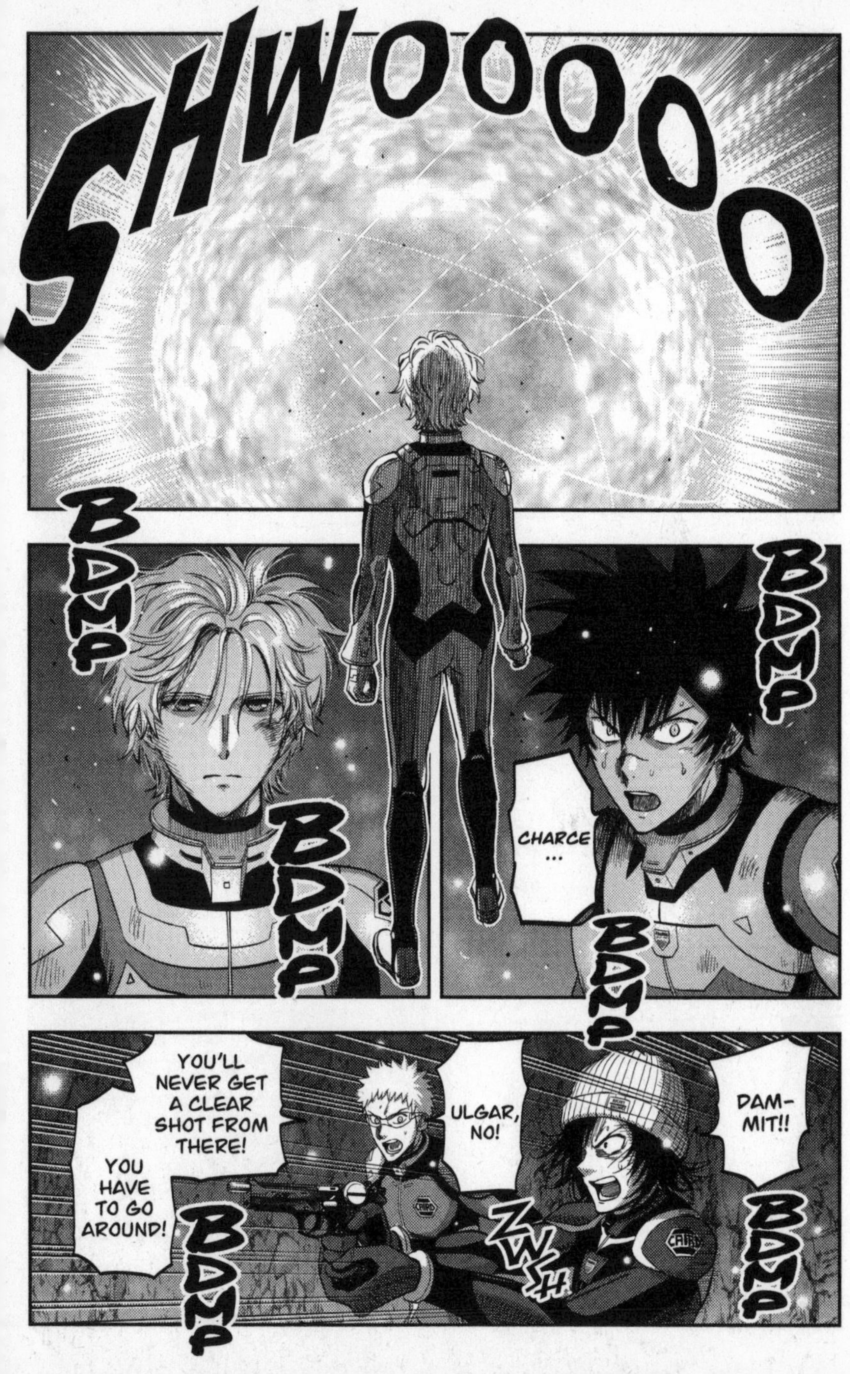
SHWOOOOOO
BDMP
CHARCE...
BDMP
BDMP
BDMP
DAM-MIT!!
BDMP
ZWSH
ULGAR, NO!
YOU'LL NEVER GET A CLEAR SHOT FROM THERE!
YOU HAVE TO GO AROUND!
BDMP

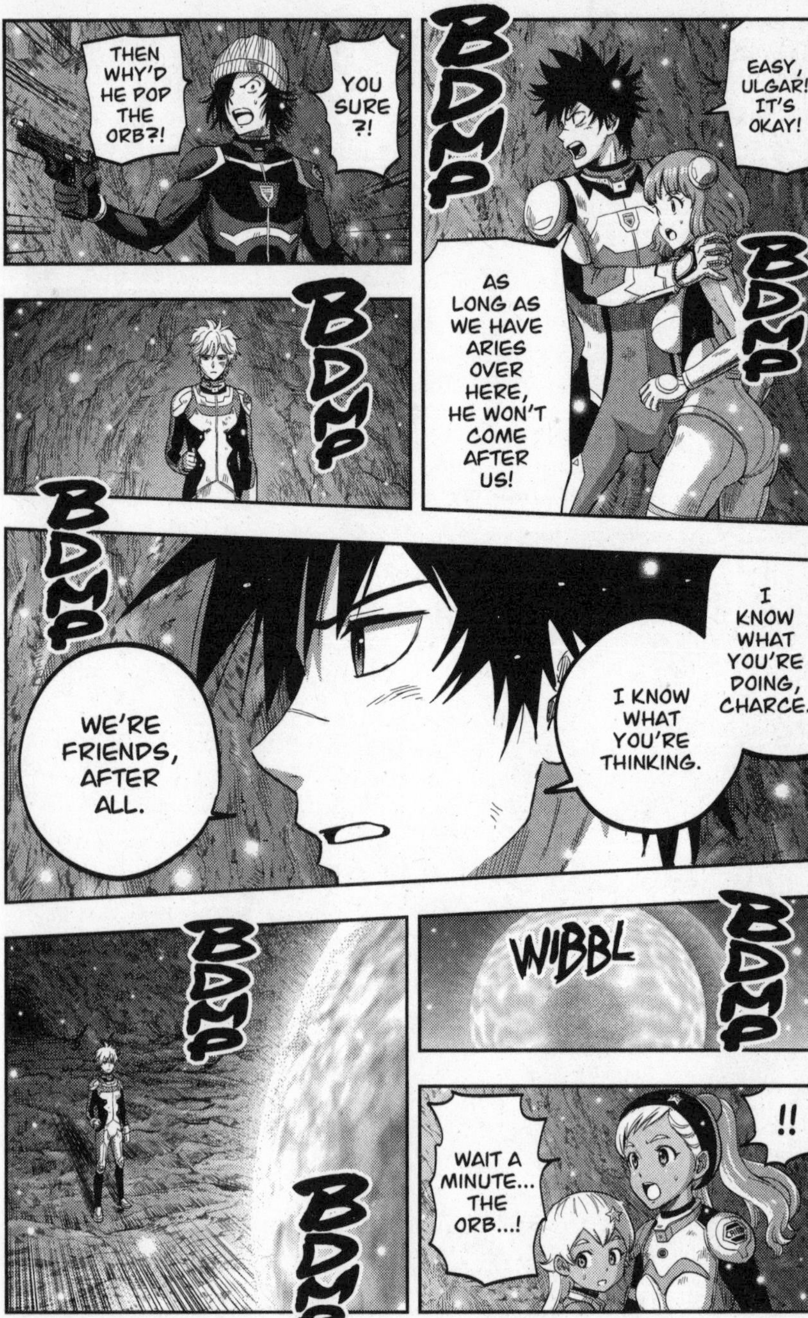
BDMP
EASY, ULGAR! IT'S OKAY!
BDMP
AS LONG AS WE HAVE ARIES OVER HERE, HE WON'T COME AFTER US!
YOU SURE?!
THEN WHY'D HE POP THE ORB?!
BDMP
BDMP
I KNOW WHAT YOU'RE DOING, CHARCE.
I KNOW WHAT YOU'RE THINKING.
WE'RE FRIENDS, AFTER ALL.
BDMP
WIBBL
!!
WAIT A MINUTE... THE ORB...!
BDMP
BDMP

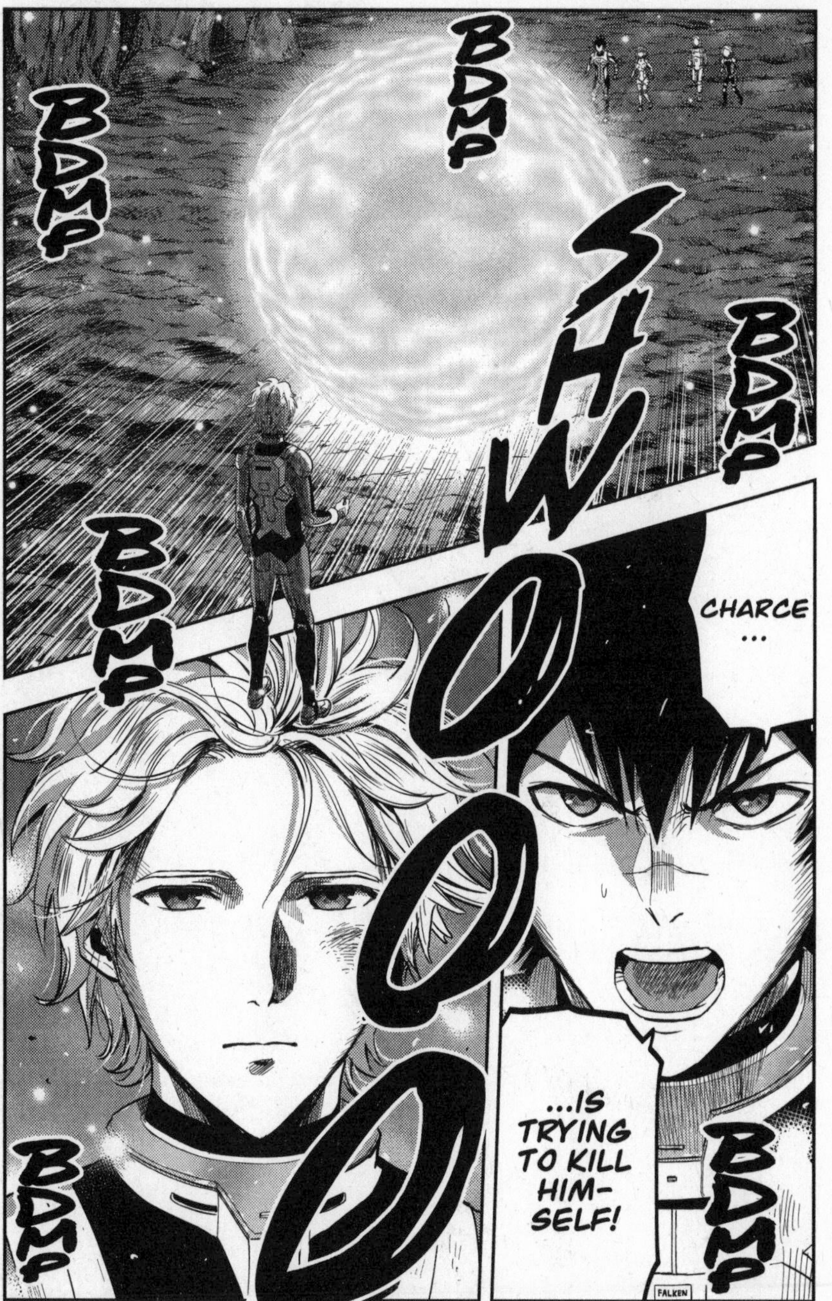
BDMP
BDMP
BDMP
BDMP
SHWOOOO
CHARCE ...
...IS TRYING TO KILL HIM-SELF!
BDMP
FALKEN
BDMP

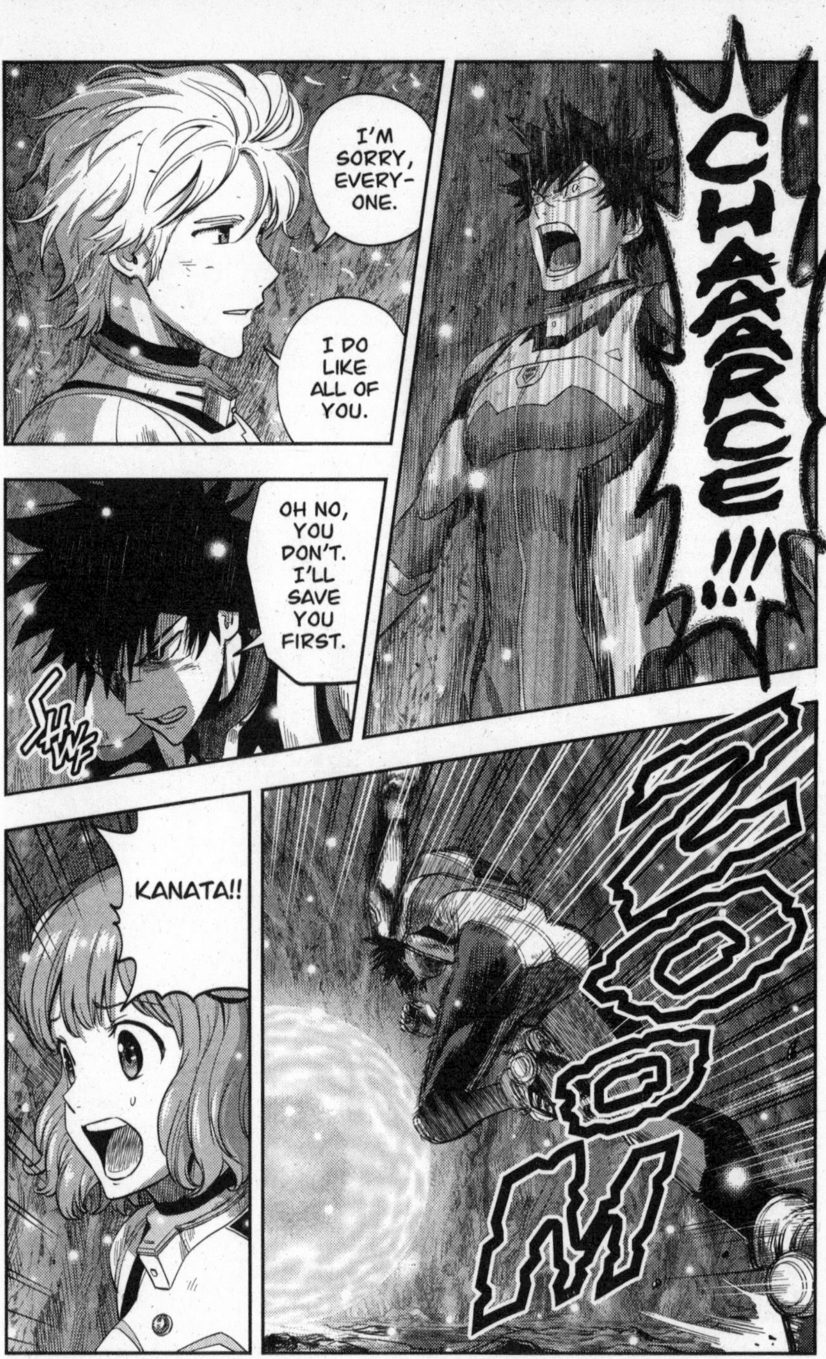
CHARGE!!!
I'M SORRY, EVERY-ONE.
I DO LIKE ALL OF YOU.
OH NO, YOU DON'T. I'LL SAVE YOU FIRST.
SHWF
KANATA!!

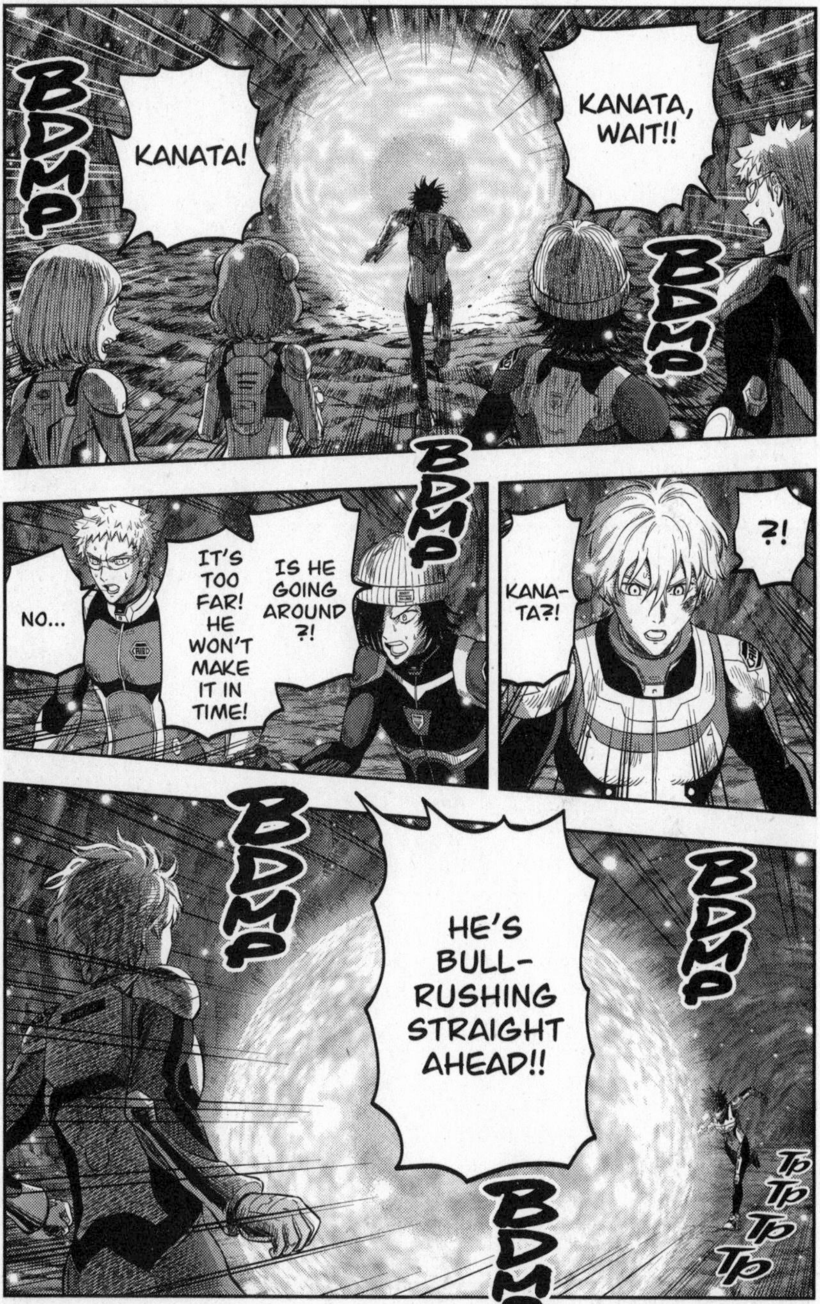
KANATA, WAIT!!
BDMP
KANATA!
BDMP
BDMP
?!
KANA-TA?!
IS HE GOING AROUND ?!
IT'S TOO FAR! HE WON'T MAKE IT IN TIME!
NO...
BDMP
HE'S BULL-RUSHING STRAIGHT AHEAD!!
BDMP
Tp Tp Tp Tp
BDMP

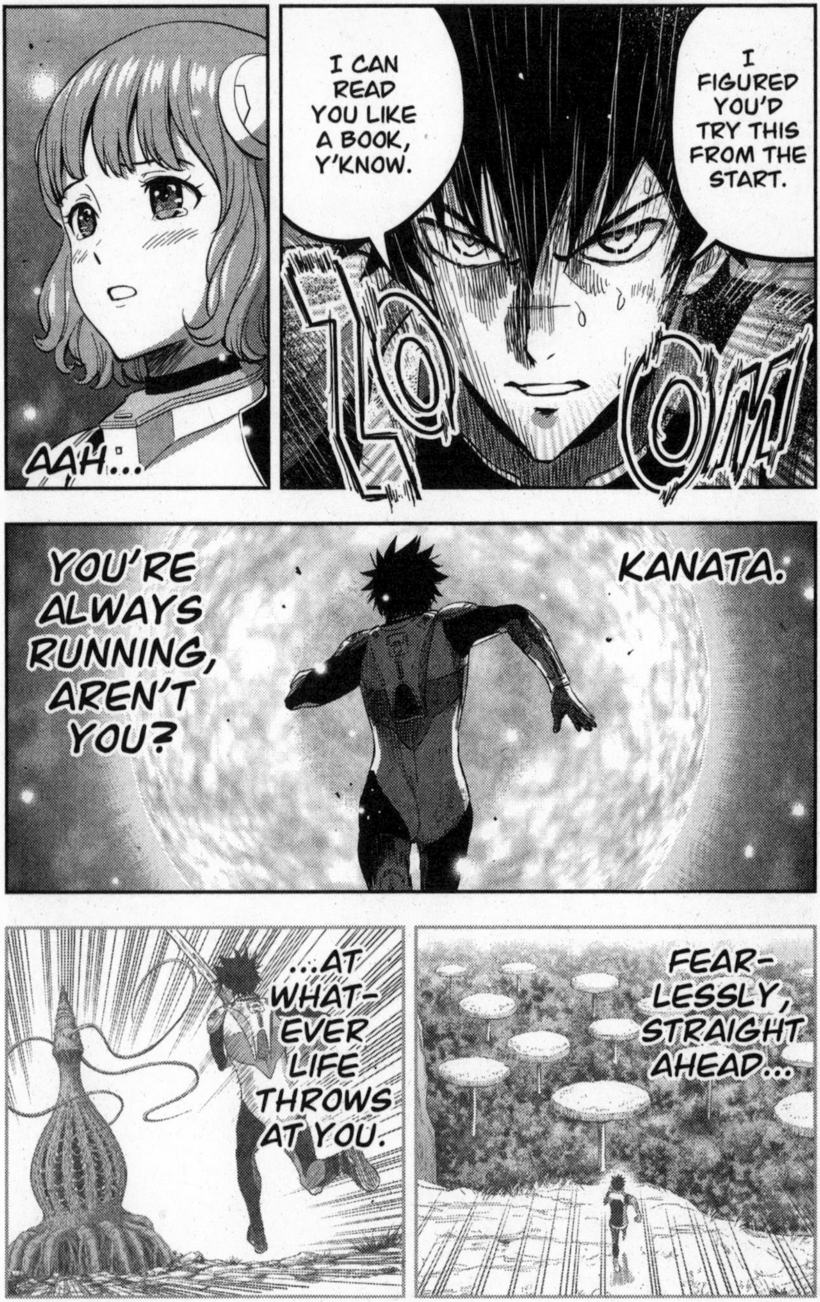
I FIGURED YOU'D TRY THIS FROM THE START.
I CAN READ YOU LIKE A BOOK, Y'KNOW.
ZOOM
AAH...
KANATA.
YOU'RE ALWAYS RUNNING, AREN'T YOU?
FEAR-LESSLY, STRAIGHT AHEAD...
...AT WHAT-EVER LIFE THROWS AT YOU.

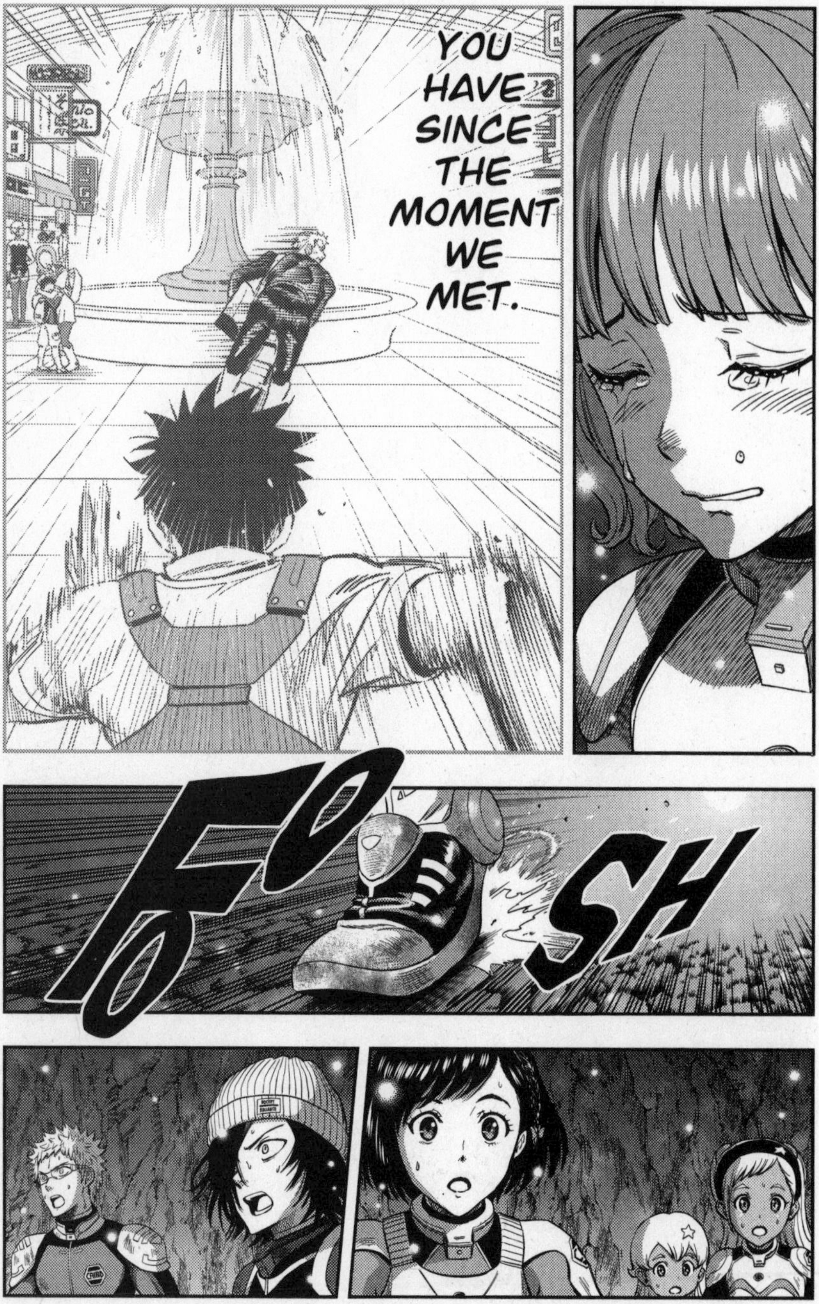
YOU HAVE SINCE THE MOMENT WE MET.
FOOOSH

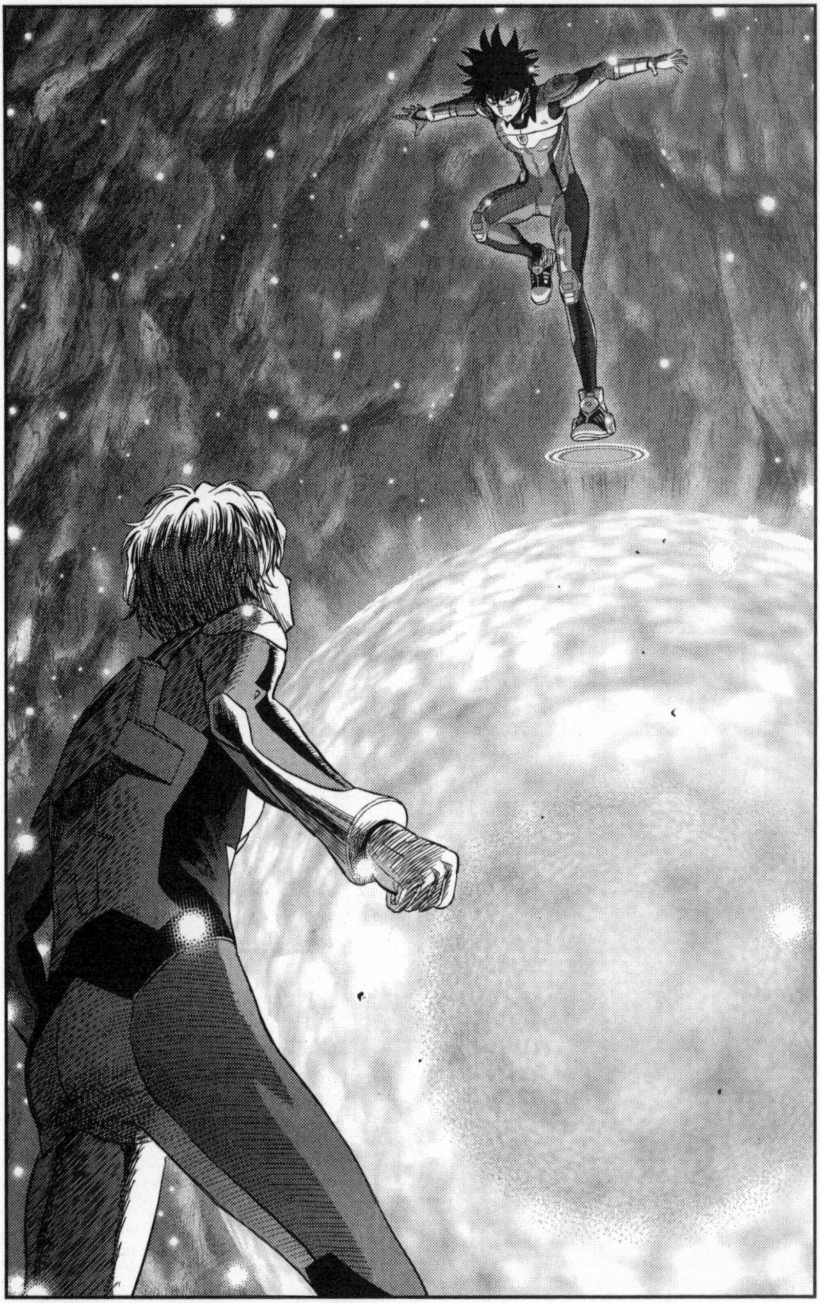

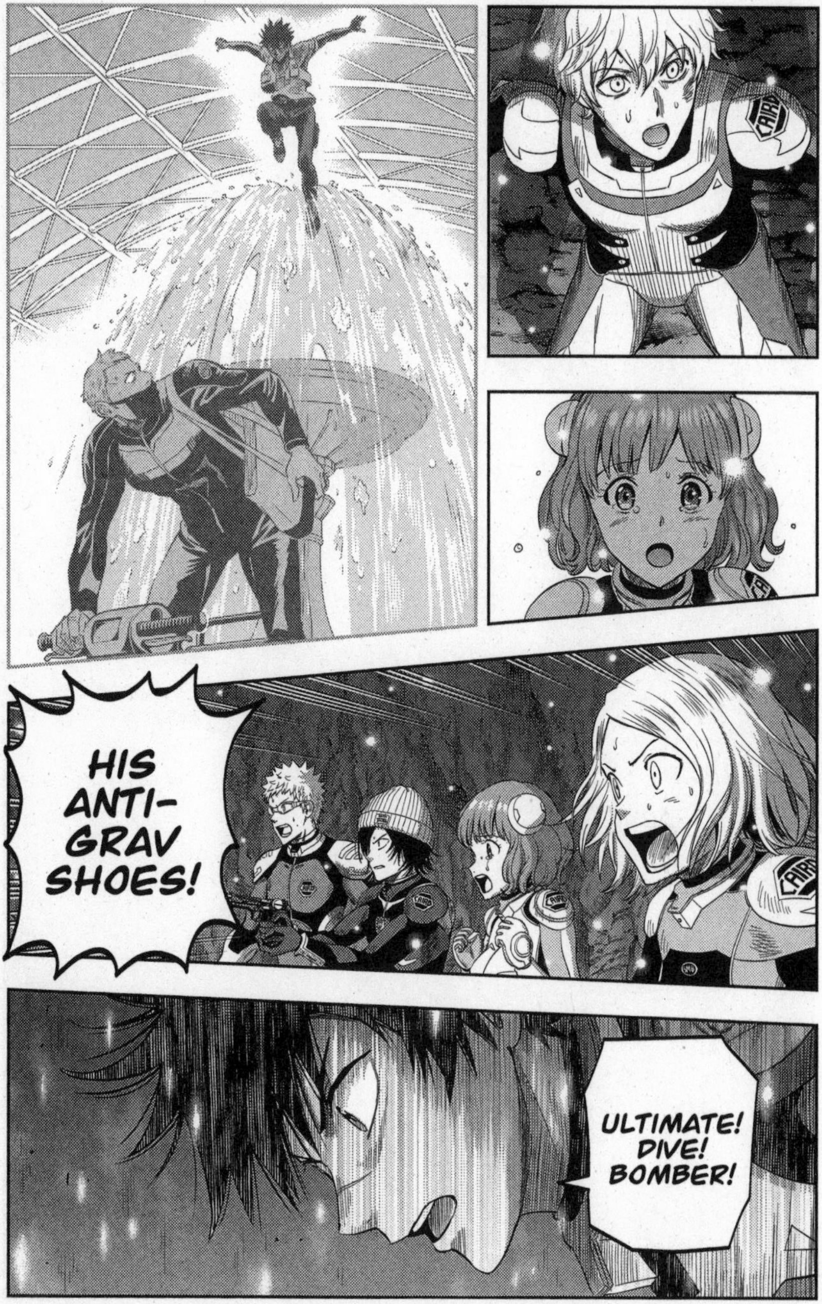
HIS ANTI-GRAV SHOES!
ULTIMATE! DIVE! BOMBER!

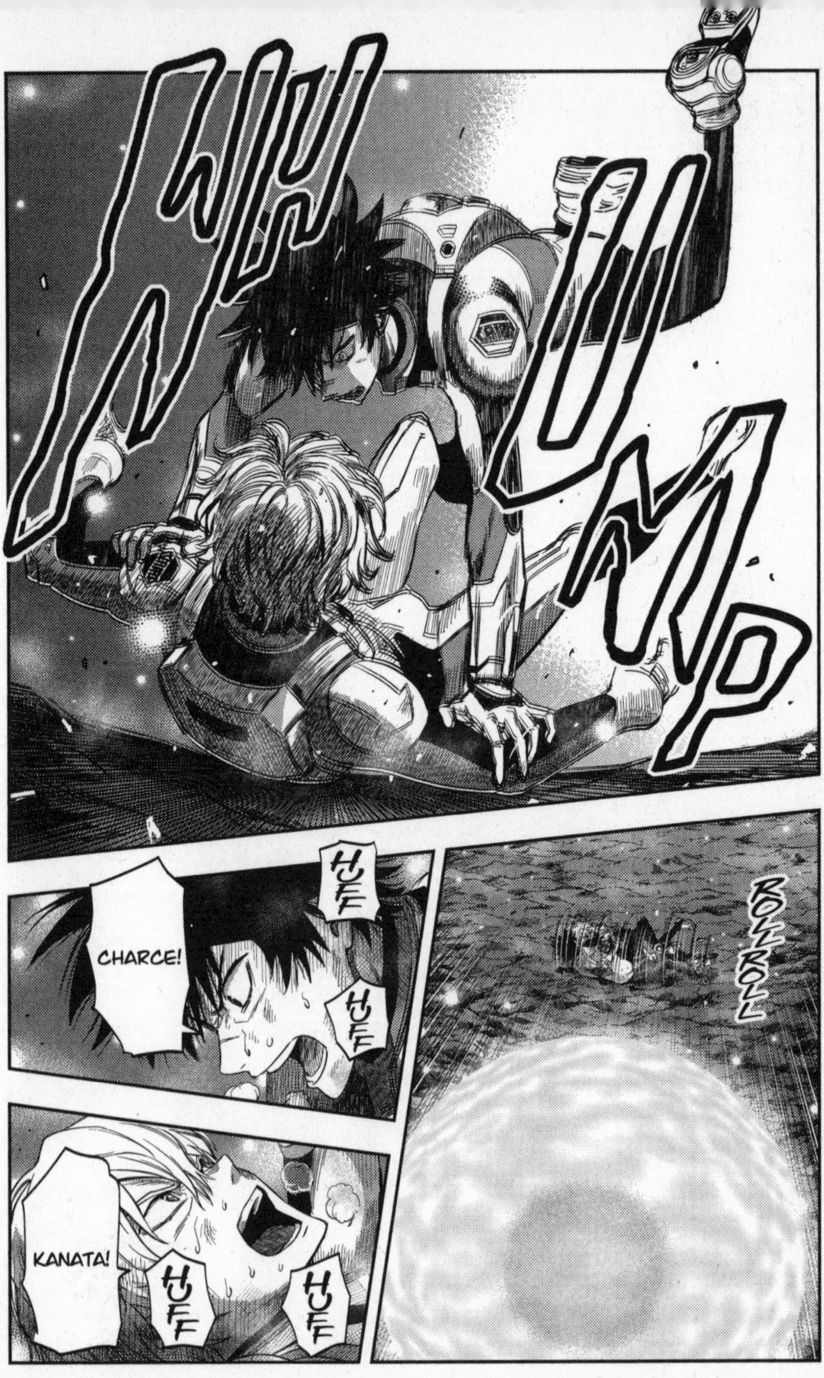
WHUMP
ROLL ROLL
HUFF
CHARCE!
HUFF
KANATA!
HUFF
HUFF

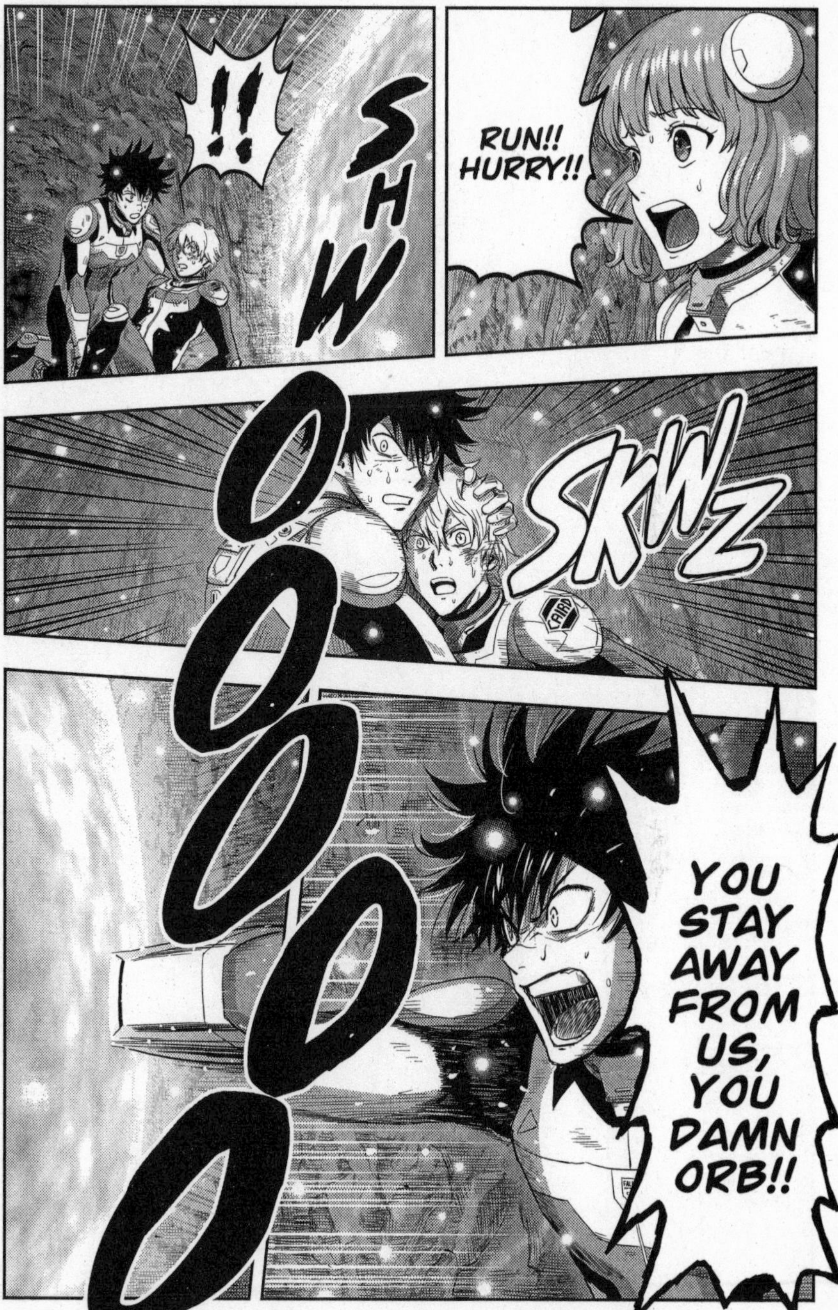
RUN!! HURRY!!
!!
SHW
OOOOOOO
SKWZ
YOU STAY AWAY FROM US, YOU DAMN ORB!!

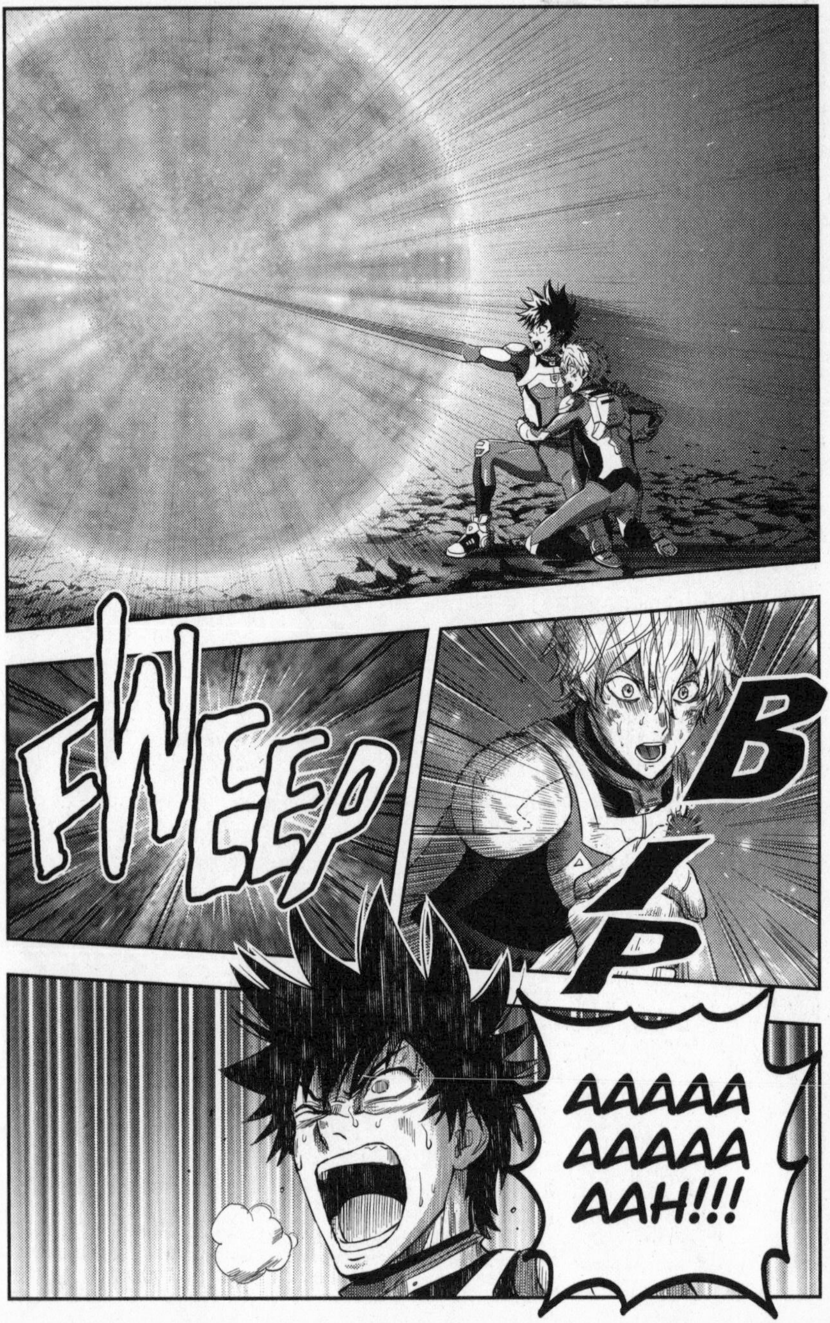
BIP
FWEEP
AAAAA
AAAAA
AAH!!!

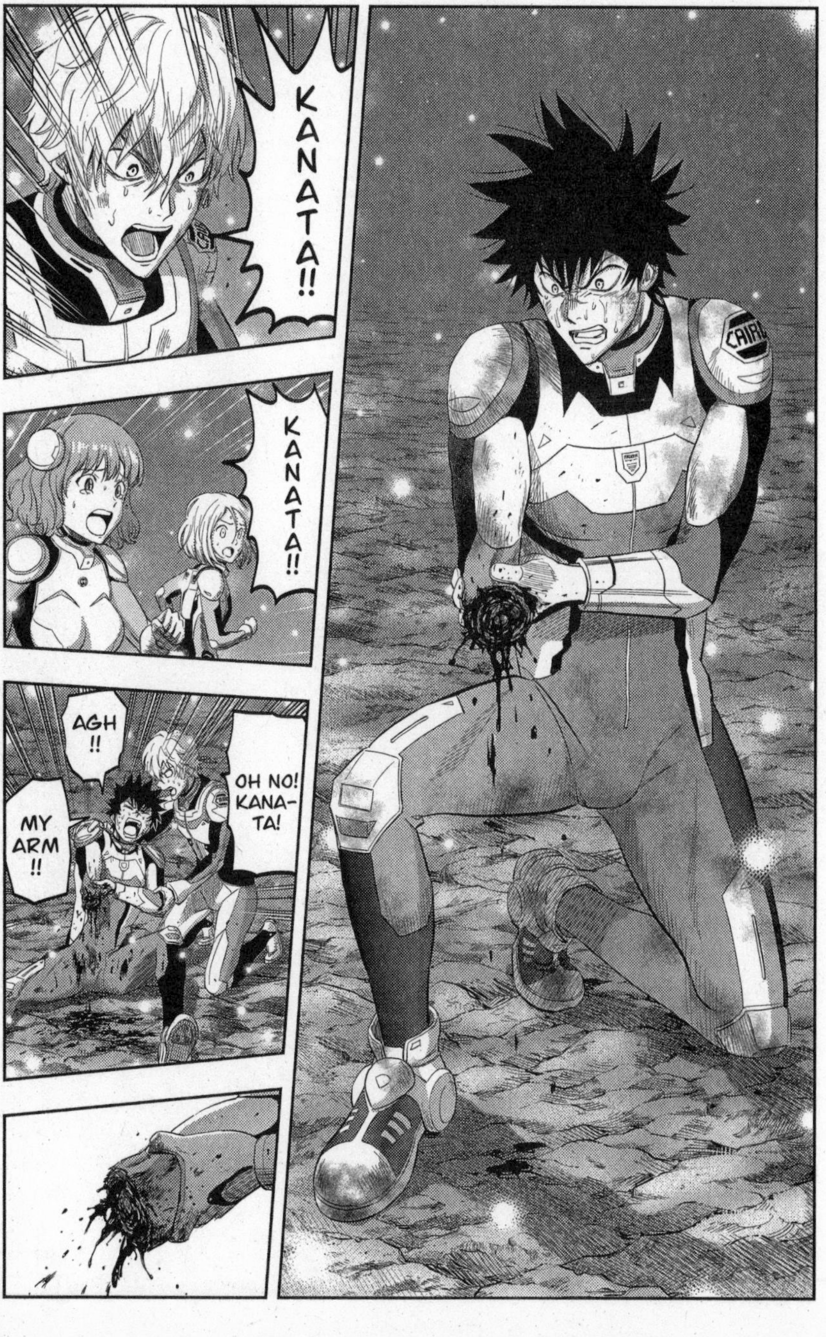
KANATA!!
KANATA!!
OH NO! KANATA!
AGH!!
MY ARM!!

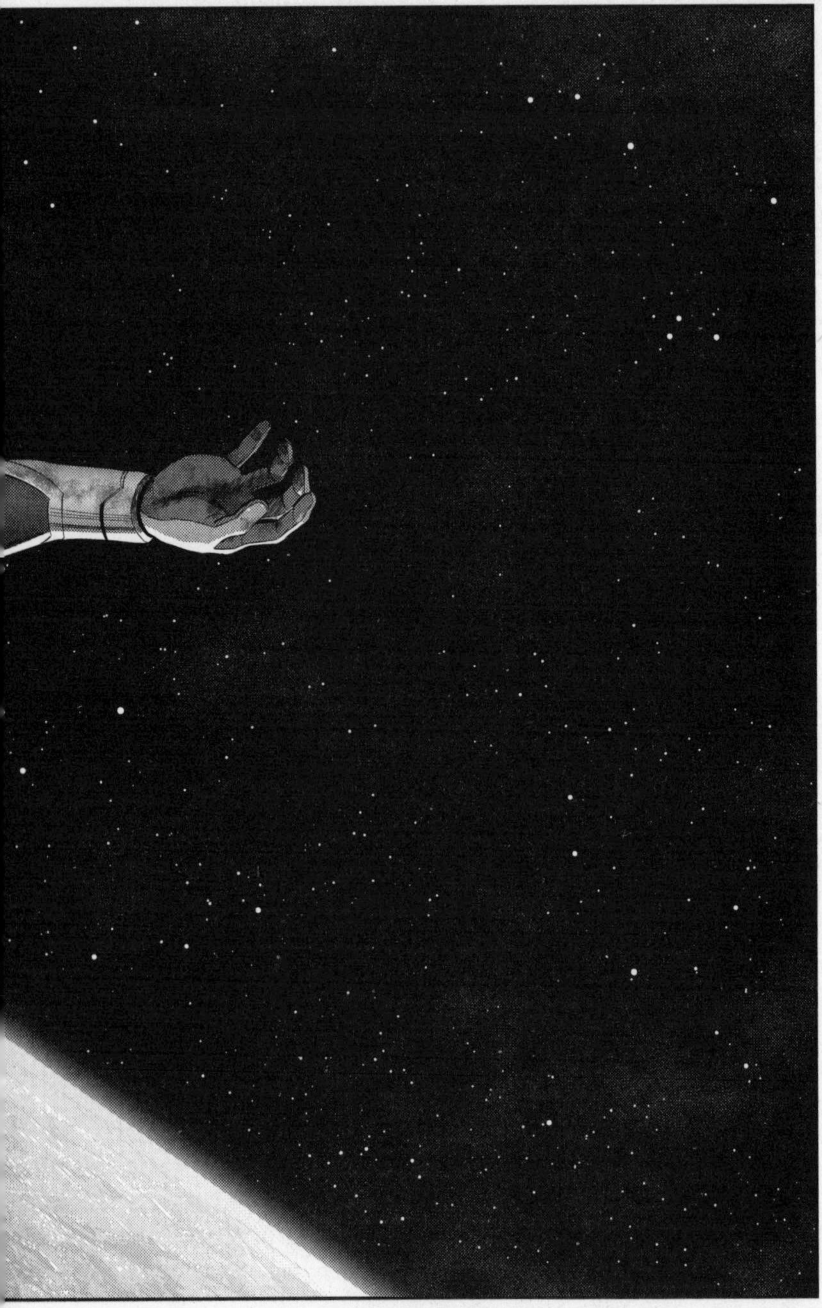

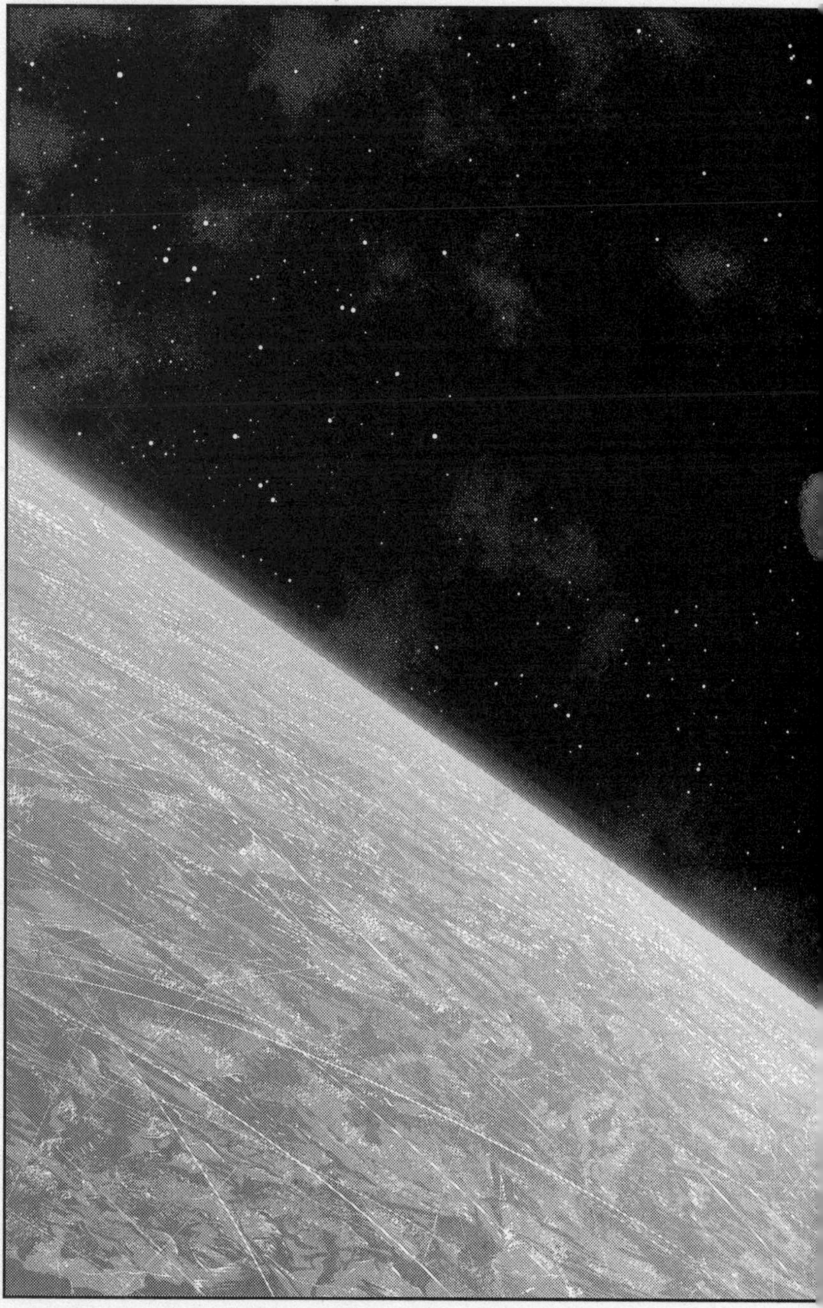

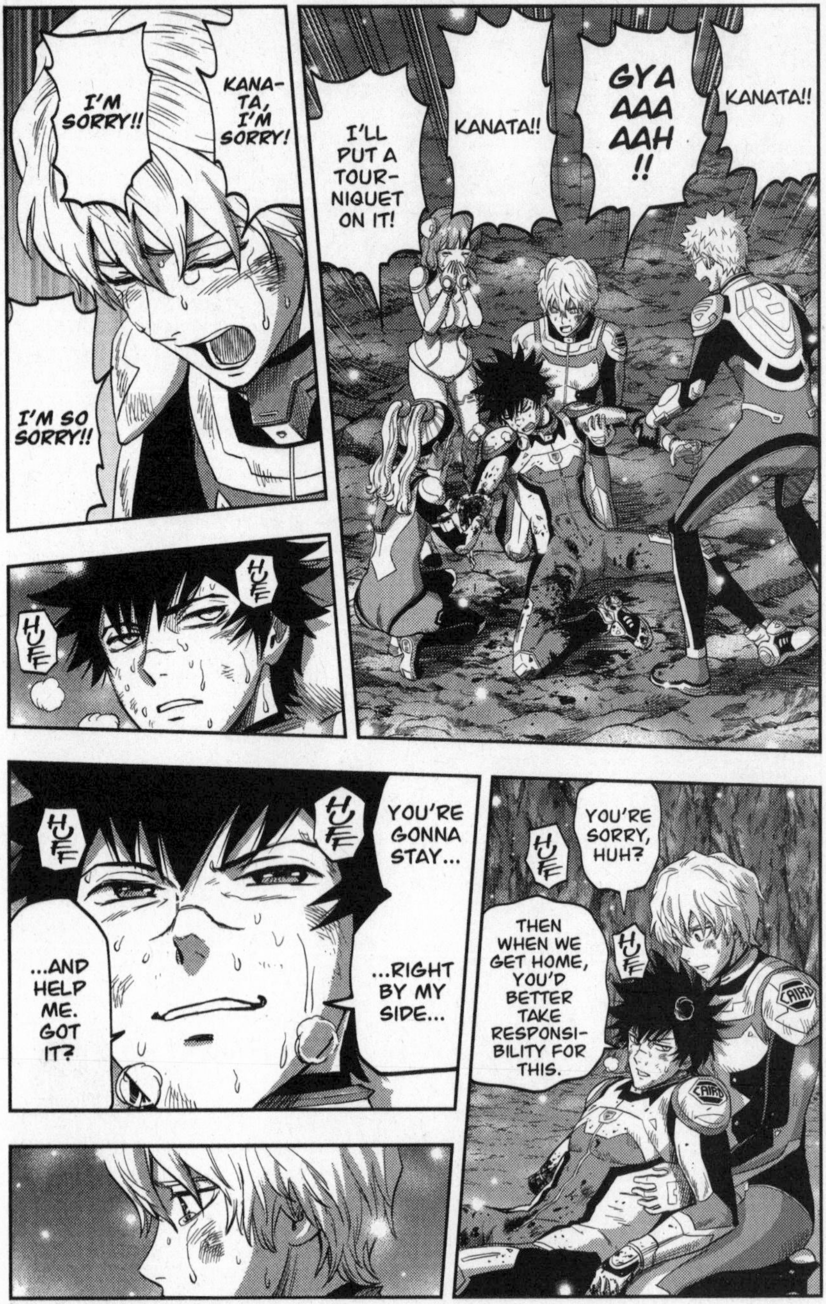
KANATA!!
GYA AAA AAH!!
KANATA!!
I'LL PUT A TOURNIQUET ON IT!
KANATA, I'M SORRY!
I'M SORRY!!
I'M SO SORRY!!
HUFF
HUFF
HUFF
YOU'RE SORRY, HUH?
HUFF
THEN WHEN WE GET HOME, YOU'D BETTER TAKE RESPONSIBILITY FOR THIS.
HUFF
YOU'RE GONNA STAY...
...RIGHT BY MY SIDE...
HUFF
...AND HELP ME. GOT IT?

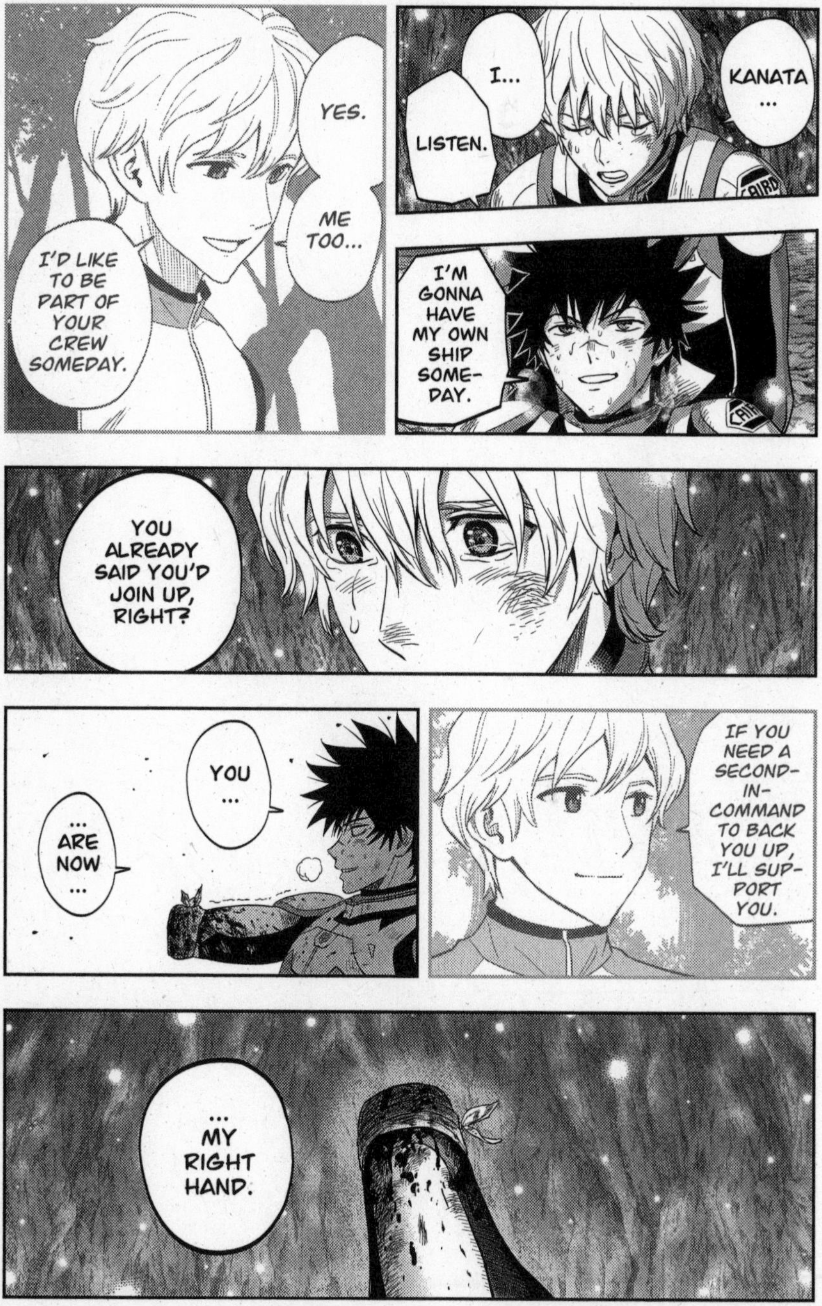
KANATA ...
I...
LISTEN.
I'M GONNA HAVE MY OWN SHIP SOME-DAY.
YES.
ME TOO...
I'D LIKE TO BE PART OF YOUR CREW SOMEDAY.
YOU ALREADY SAID YOU'D JOIN UP, RIGHT?
IF YOU NEED A SECOND-IN-COMMAND TO BACK YOU UP, I'LL SUP-PORT YOU.
YOU ...
... ARE NOW ...
... MY RIGHT HAND.

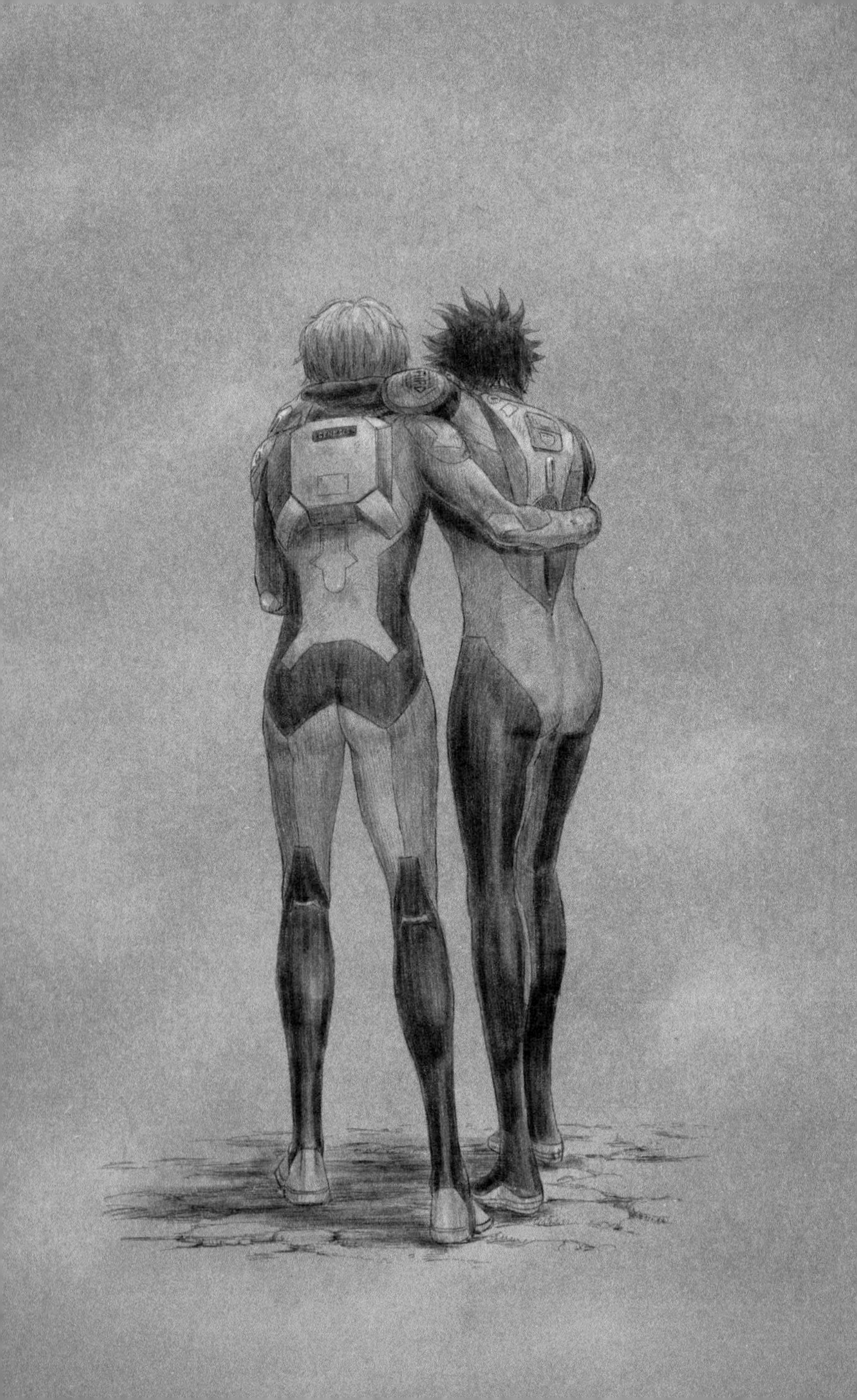

ASTRA LOST IN SPACE

#46

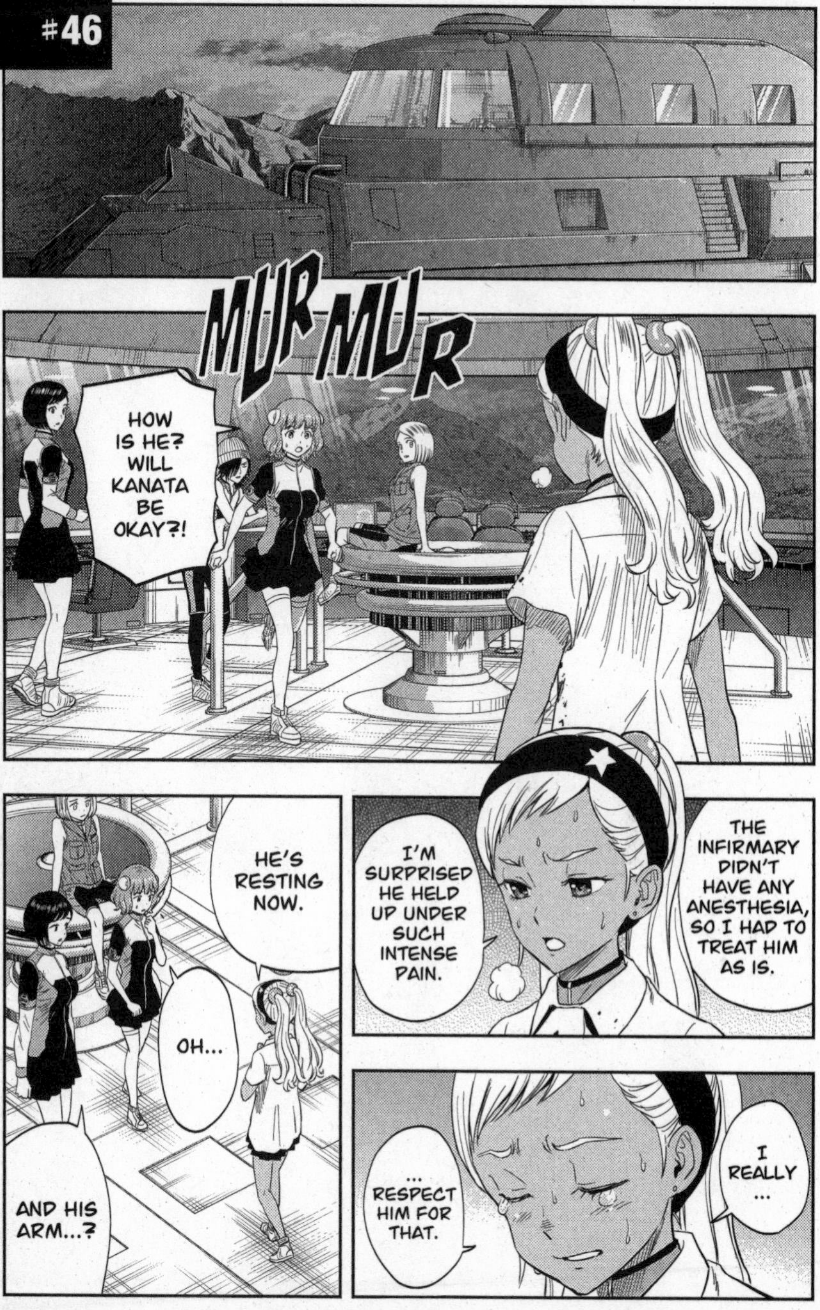
MUR MUR
HOW IS HE? WILL KANATA BE OKAY?!
THE INFIRMARY DIDN'T HAVE ANY ANESTHESIA, SO I HAD TO TREAT HIM AS IS.
I'M SURPRISED HE HELD UP UNDER SUCH INTENSE PAIN.
I REALLY ...
... RESPECT HIM FOR THAT.
HE'S RESTING NOW.
OH...
AND HIS ARM...?

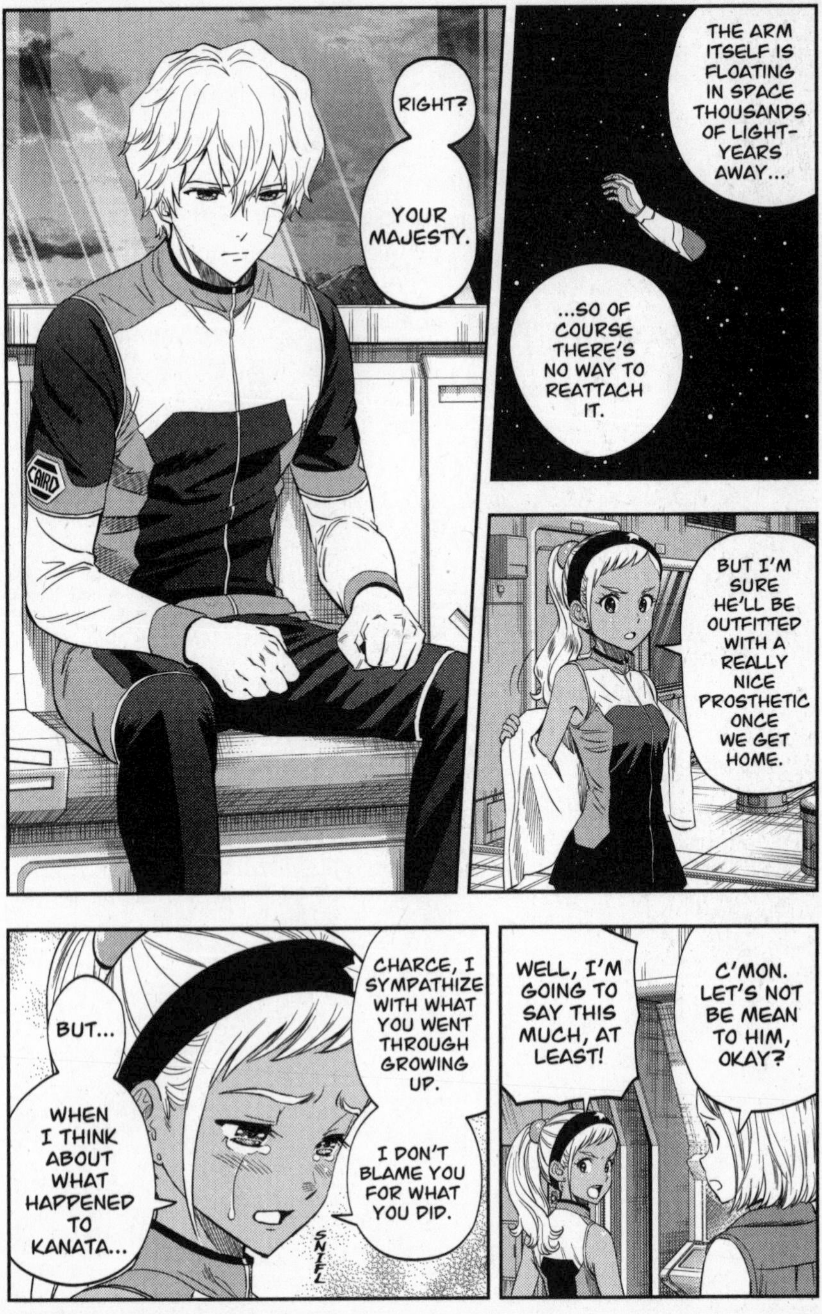
THE ARM ITSELF IS FLOATING IN SPACE THOUSANDS OF LIGHT-YEARS AWAY...
...SO OF COURSE THERE'S NO WAY TO REATTACH IT.
BUT I'M SURE HE'LL BE OUTFITTED WITH A REALLY NICE PROSTHETIC ONCE WE GET HOME.
RIGHT?
YOUR MAJESTY.
C'MON. LET'S NOT BE MEAN TO HIM, OKAY?
WELL, I'M GOING TO SAY THIS MUCH, AT LEAST!
CHARCE, I SYMPATHIZE WITH WHAT YOU WENT THROUGH GROWING UP.
BUT...
I DON'T BLAME YOU FOR WHAT YOU DID.
WHEN I THINK ABOUT WHAT HAPPENED TO KANATA...
SNIFL

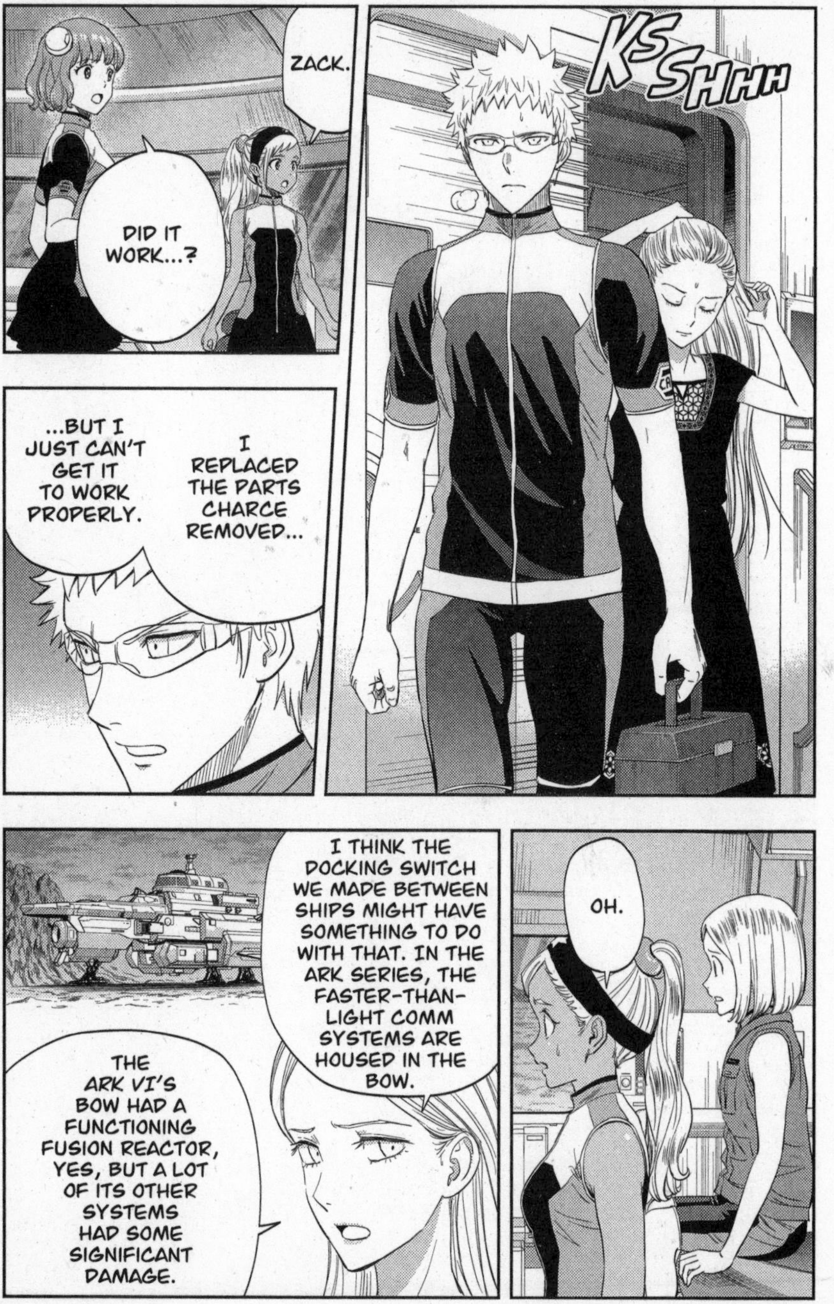
KSSHHH
ZACK.
DID IT WORK...?
I REPLACED THE PARTS CHARCE REMOVED...
...BUT I JUST CAN'T GET IT TO WORK PROPERLY.
OH.
I THINK THE DOCKING SWITCH WE MADE BETWEEN SHIPS MIGHT HAVE SOMETHING TO DO WITH THAT. IN THE ARK SERIES, THE FASTER-THAN-LIGHT COMM SYSTEMS ARE HOUSED IN THE BOW.
THE ARK VI'S BOW HAD A FUNCTIONING FUSION REACTOR, YES, BUT A LOT OF ITS OTHER SYSTEMS HAD SOME SIGNIFICANT DAMAGE.

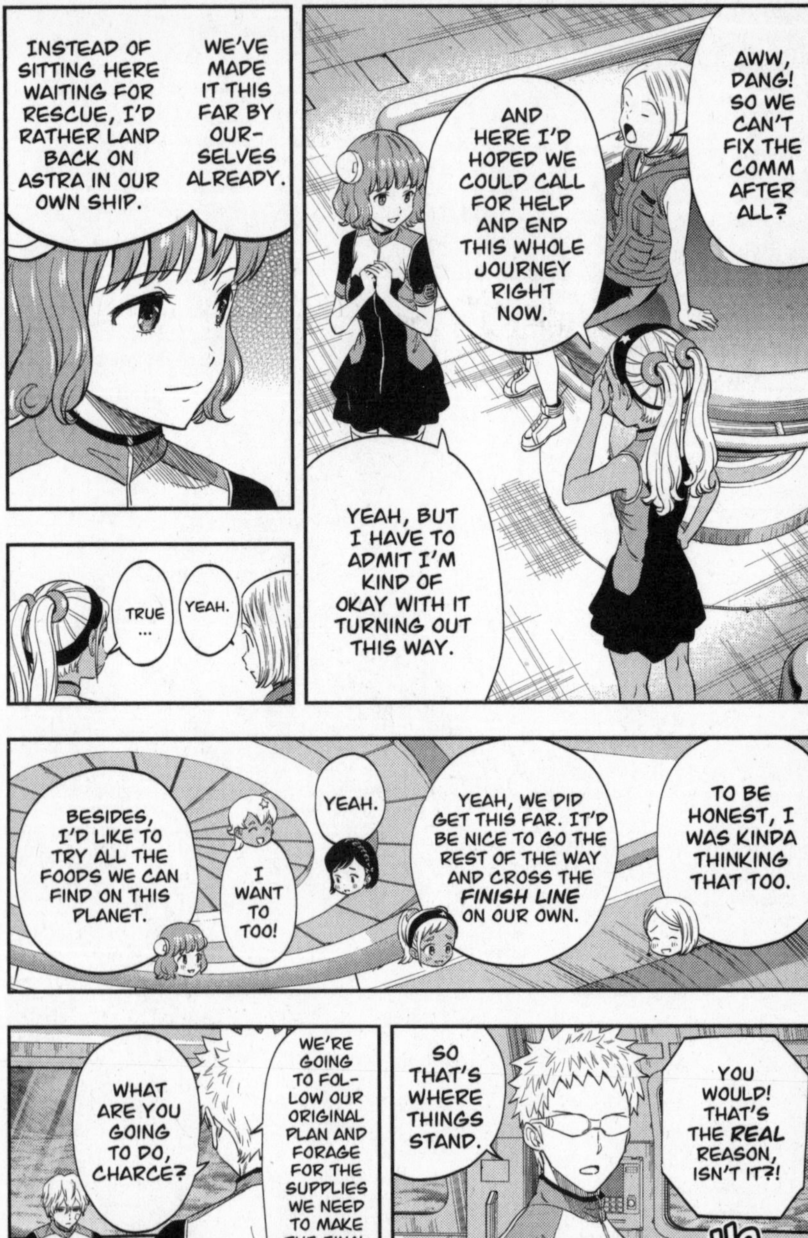
AWW, DANG! SO WE CAN'T FIX THE COMM AFTER ALL?
AND HERE I'D HOPED WE COULD CALL FOR HELP AND END THIS WHOLE JOURNEY RIGHT NOW.
YEAH, BUT I HAVE TO ADMIT I'M KIND OF OKAY WITH IT TURNING OUT THIS WAY.
WE'VE MADE IT THIS FAR BY OUR-SELVES ALREADY.
INSTEAD OF SITTING HERE WAITING FOR RESCUE, I'D RATHER LAND BACK ON ASTRA IN OUR OWN SHIP.
YEAH.
TRUE...
TO BE HONEST, I WAS KINDA THINKING THAT TOO.
YEAH, WE DID GET THIS FAR. IT'D BE NICE TO GO THE REST OF THE WAY AND CROSS THE ***FINISH LINE*** ON OUR OWN.
YEAH.
I WANT TO TOO!
BESIDES, I'D LIKE TO TRY ALL THE FOODS WE CAN FIND ON THIS PLANET.
YOU WOULD! THAT'S THE **REAL** REASON, ISN'T IT?!
HA HA
SO THAT'S WHERE THINGS STAND.
WE'RE GOING TO FOL-LOW OUR ORIGINAL PLAN AND FORAGE FOR THE SUPPLIES WE NEED TO MAKE THE FINAL LEG OF THE JOURNEY.
WHAT ARE YOU GOING TO DO, CHARCE?

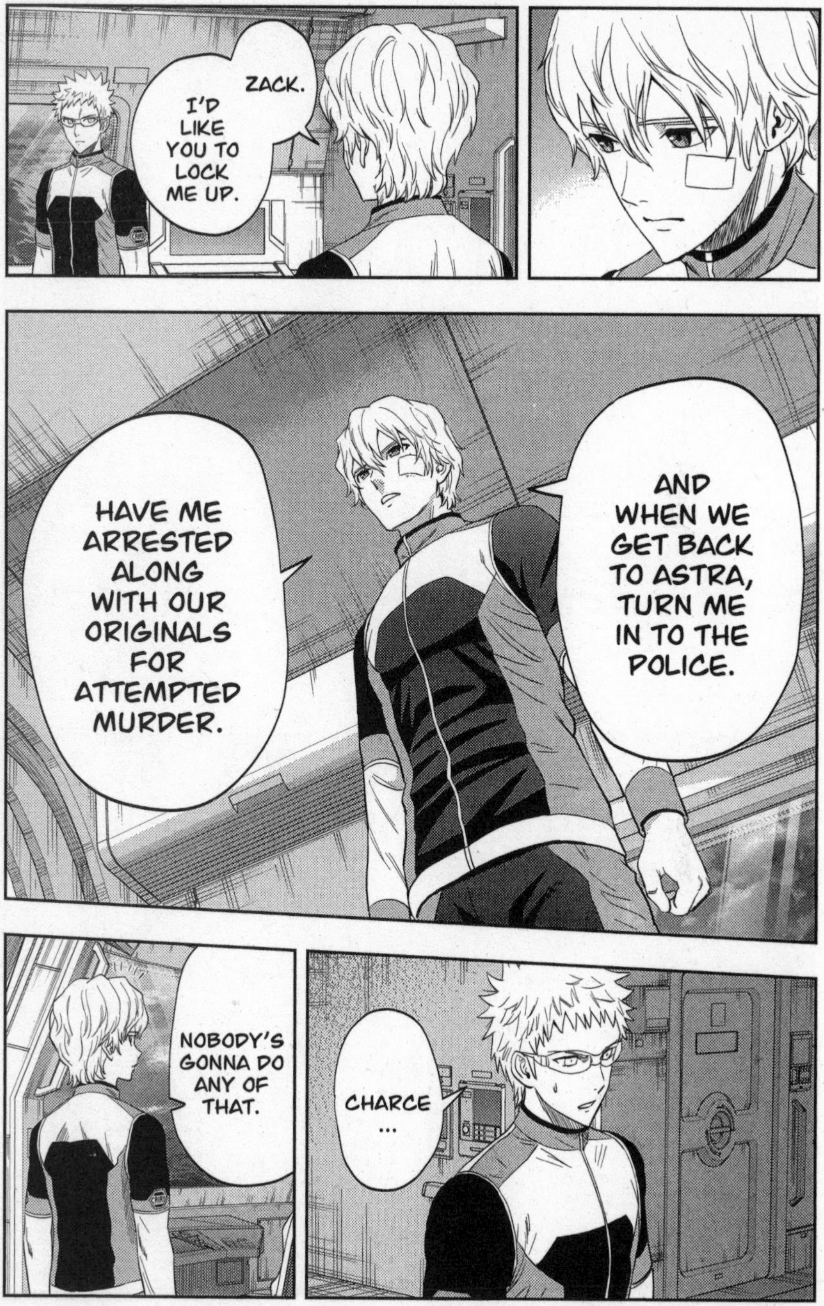
ZACK. I'D LIKE YOU TO LOCK ME UP.
AND WHEN WE GET BACK TO ASTRA, TURN ME IN TO THE POLICE.
HAVE ME ARRESTED ALONG WITH OUR ORIGINALS FOR ATTEMPTED MURDER.
CHARCE ...
NOBODY'S GONNA DO ANY OF THAT.

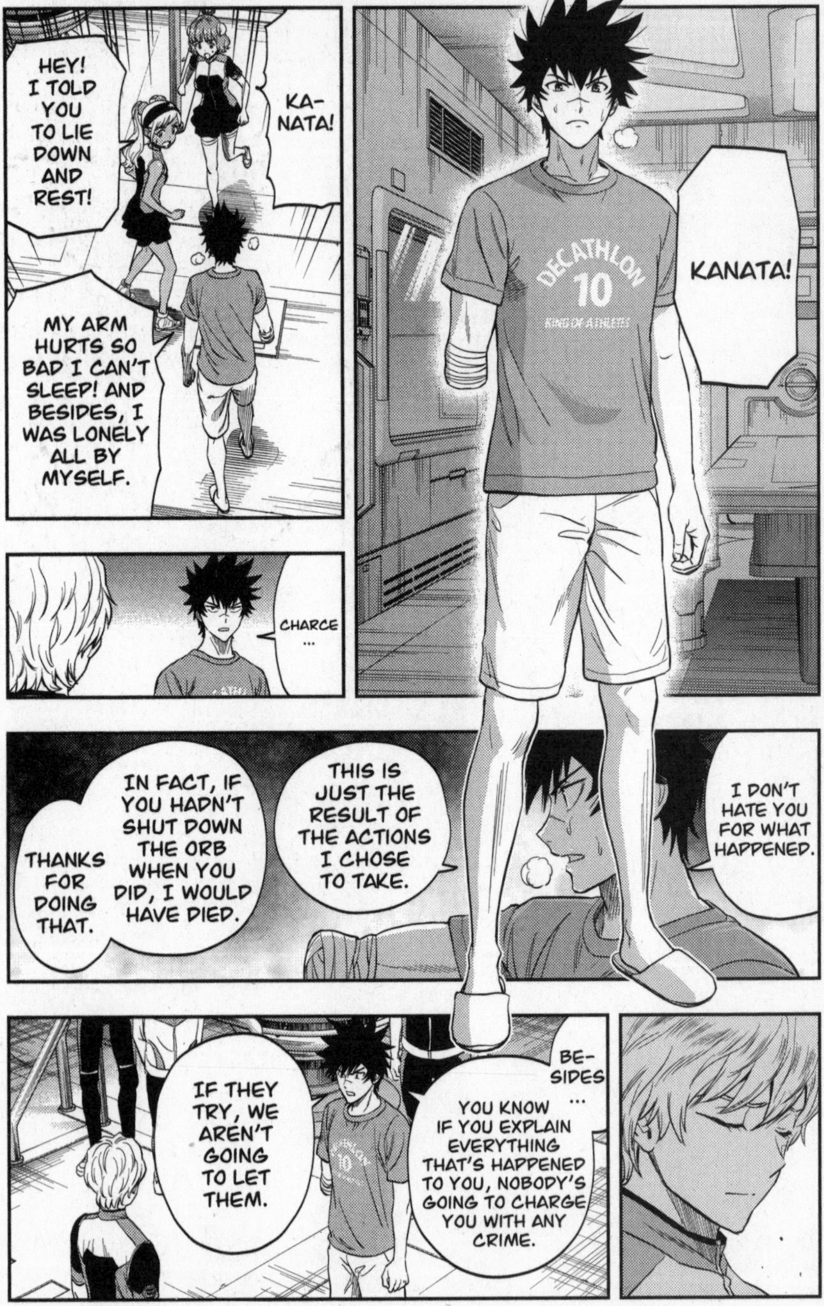
KANATA!
KA-NATA!
HEY! I TOLD YOU TO LIE DOWN AND REST!
MY ARM HURTS SO BAD I CAN'T SLEEP! AND BESIDES, I WAS LONELY ALL BY MYSELF.
CHARCE...
I DON'T HATE YOU FOR WHAT HAPPENED.
THIS IS JUST THE RESULT OF THE ACTIONS I CHOSE TO TAKE.
IN FACT, IF YOU HADN'T SHUT DOWN THE ORB WHEN YOU DID, I WOULD HAVE DIED.
THANKS FOR DOING THAT.
BE-SIDES...
YOU KNOW IF YOU EXPLAIN EVERYTHING THAT'S HAPPENED TO YOU, NOBODY'S GOING TO CHARGE YOU WITH ANY CRIME.
IF THEY TRY, WE AREN'T GOING TO LET THEM.

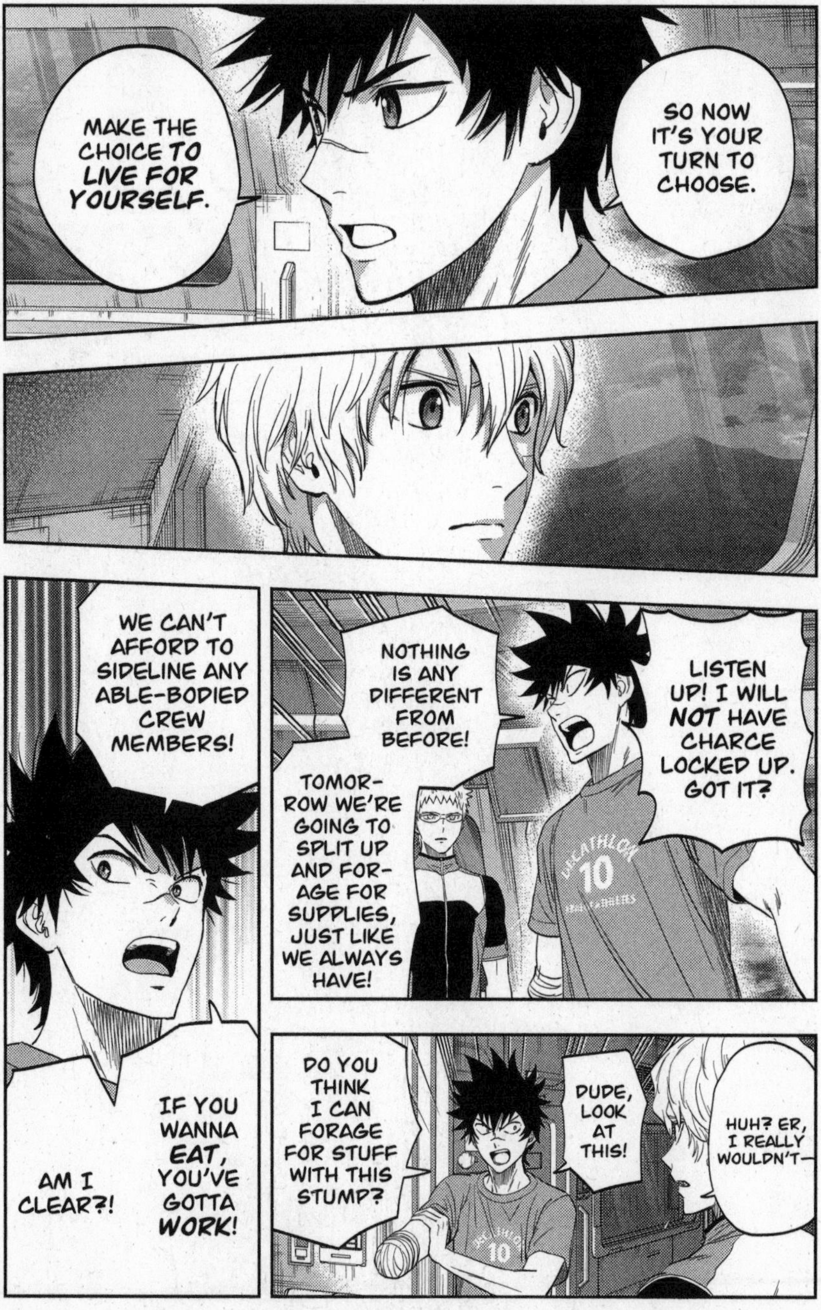
SO NOW IT'S YOUR TURN TO CHOOSE.
MAKE THE CHOICE TO LIVE FOR YOURSELF.
LISTEN UP! I WILL NOT HAVE CHARCE LOCKED UP. GOT IT?
NOTHING IS ANY DIFFERENT FROM BEFORE!
TOMOR-ROW WE'RE GOING TO SPLIT UP AND FOR-AGE FOR SUPPLIES, JUST LIKE WE ALWAYS HAVE!
HUH? ER, I REALLY WOULDN'T—
DUDE, LOOK AT THIS!
DO YOU THINK I CAN FORAGE FOR STUFF WITH THIS STUMP?
WE CAN'T AFFORD TO SIDELINE ANY ABLE-BODIED CREW MEMBERS!
IF YOU WANNA EAT, YOU'VE GOTTA WORK!
AM I CLEAR?!

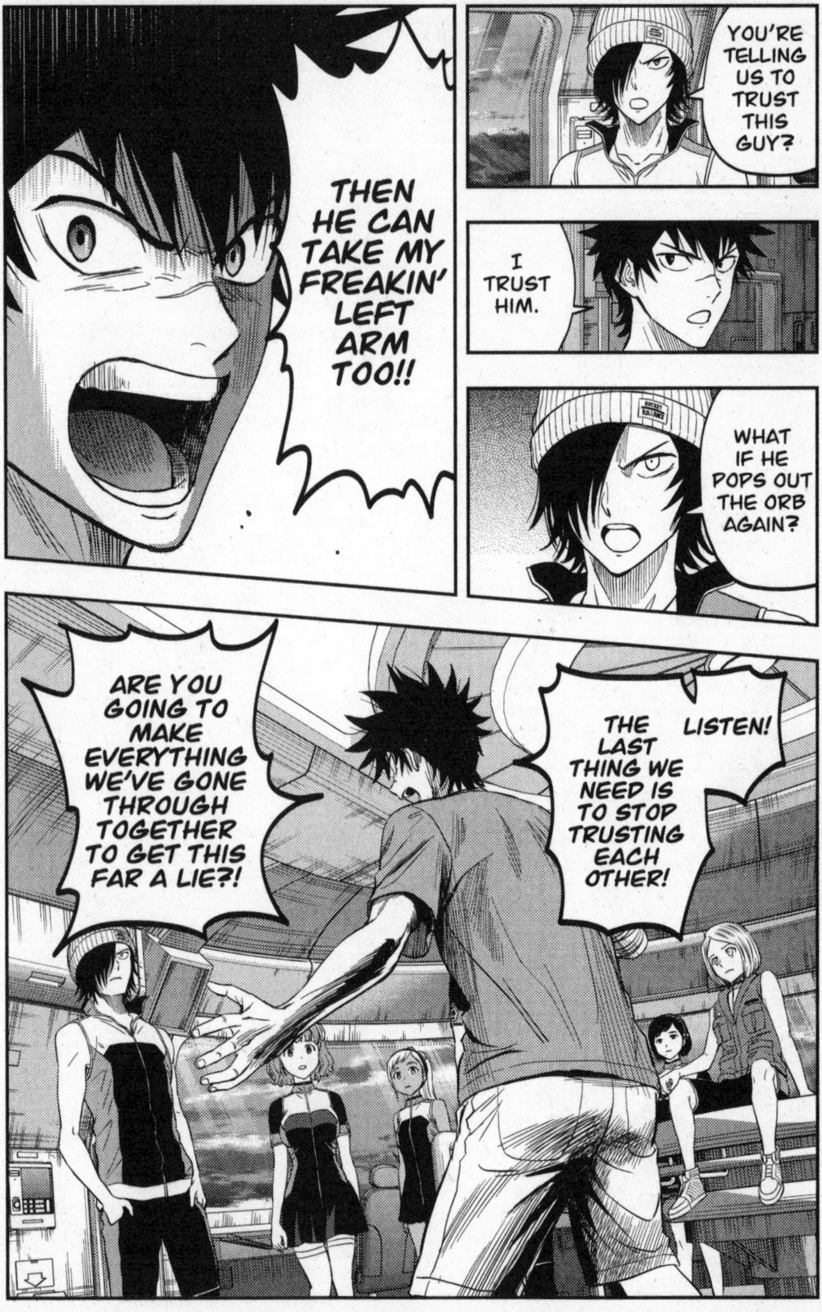
YOU'RE TELLING US TO TRUST THIS GUY?
I TRUST HIM.
WHAT IF HE POPS OUT THE ORB AGAIN?
THEN HE CAN TAKE MY FREAKIN' LEFT ARM TOO!!
LISTEN!
THE LAST THING WE NEED IS TO STOP TRUSTING EACH OTHER!
ARE YOU GOING TO MAKE EVERYTHING WE'VE GONE THROUGH TOGETHER TO GET THIS FAR A LIE?!

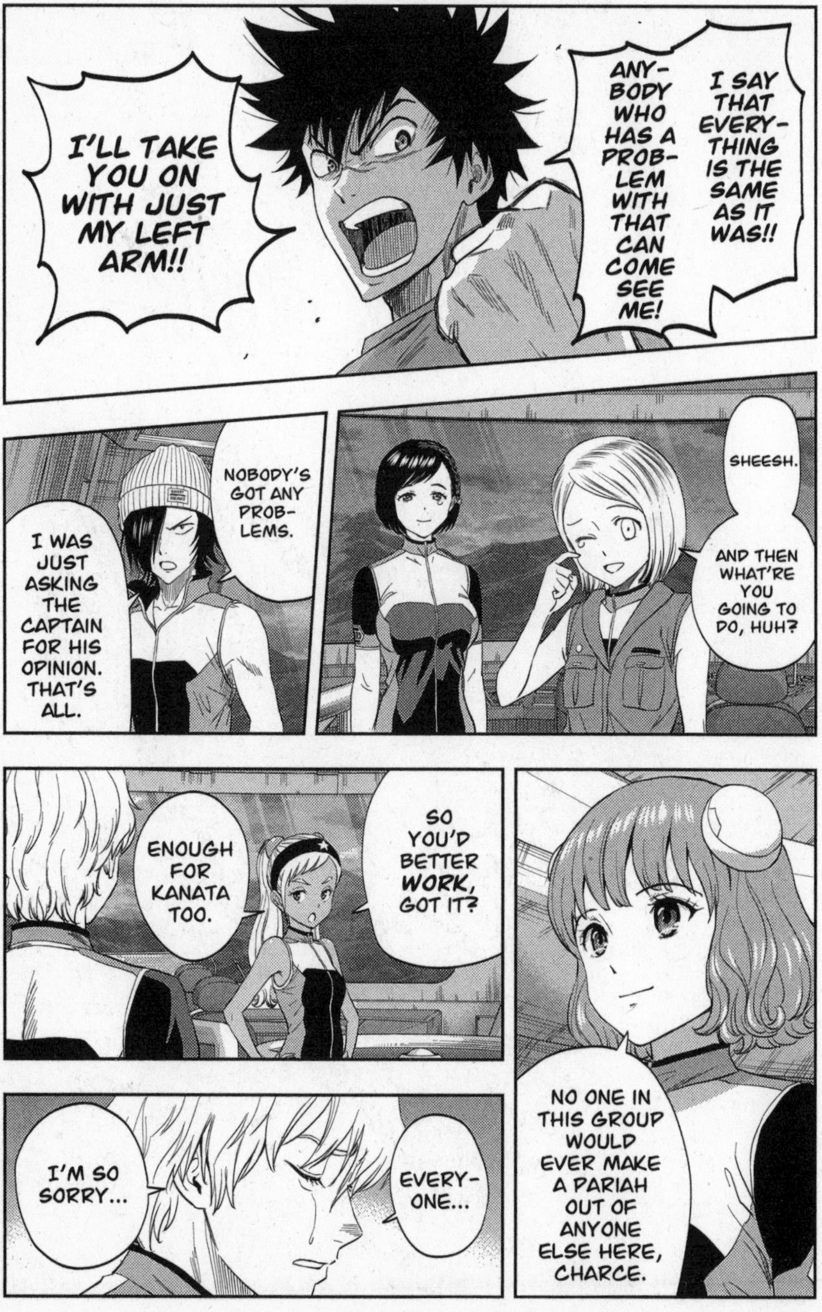
I SAY THAT EVERY-THING IS THE SAME AS IT WAS!!
ANY-BODY WHO HAS A PROB-LEM WITH THAT CAN COME SEE ME!
I'LL TAKE YOU ON WITH JUST MY LEFT ARM!!
SHEESH.
AND THEN WHAT'RE YOU GOING TO DO, HUH?
NOBODY'S GOT ANY PROB-LEMS.
I WAS JUST ASKING THE CAPTAIN FOR HIS OPINION. THAT'S ALL.
NO ONE IN THIS GROUP WOULD EVER MAKE A PARIAH OUT OF ANYONE ELSE HERE, CHARCE.
SO YOU'D BETTER WORK, GOT IT?
ENOUGH FOR KANATA TOO.
EVERY-ONE...
I'M SO SORRY...

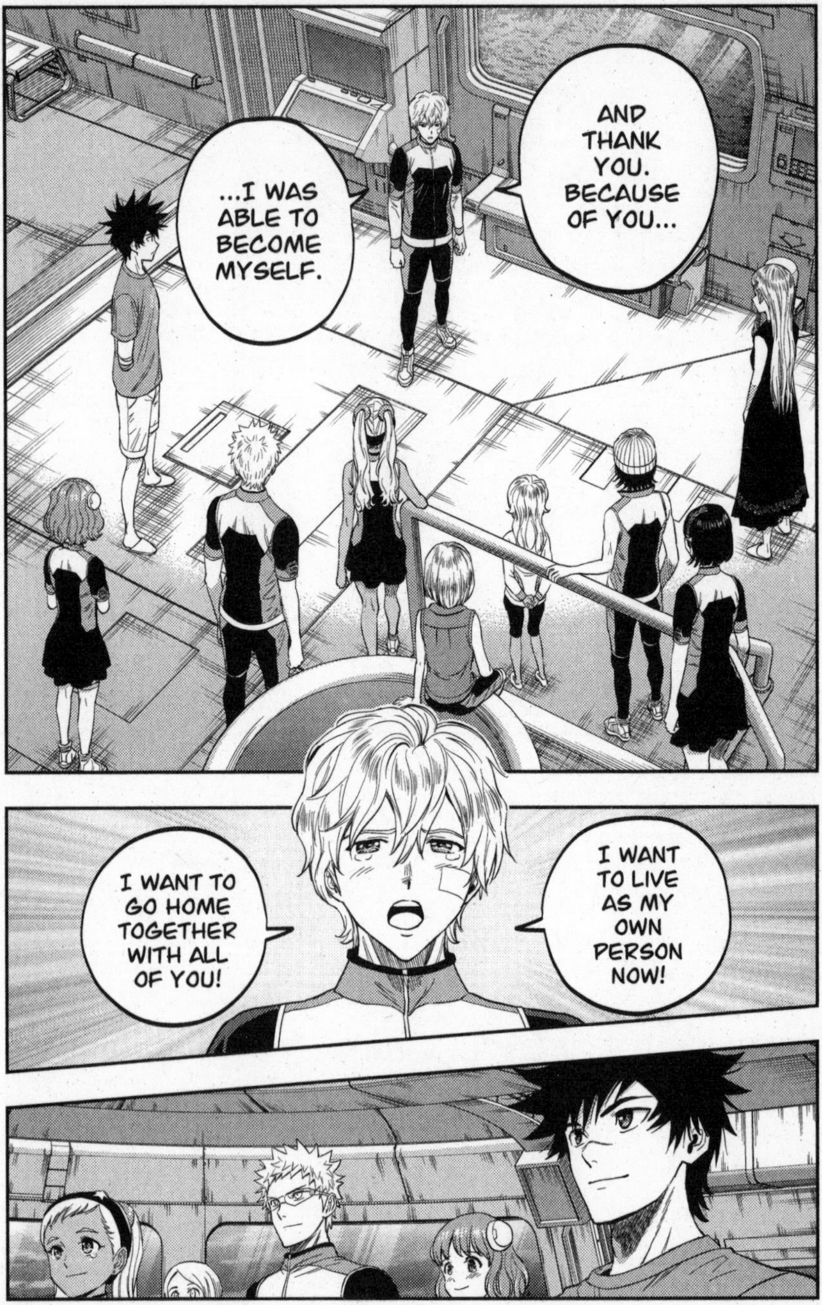
AND THANK YOU. BECAUSE OF YOU...
...I WAS ABLE TO BECOME MYSELF.
I WANT TO LIVE AS MY OWN PERSON NOW!
I WANT TO GO HOME TOGETHER WITH ALL OF YOU!

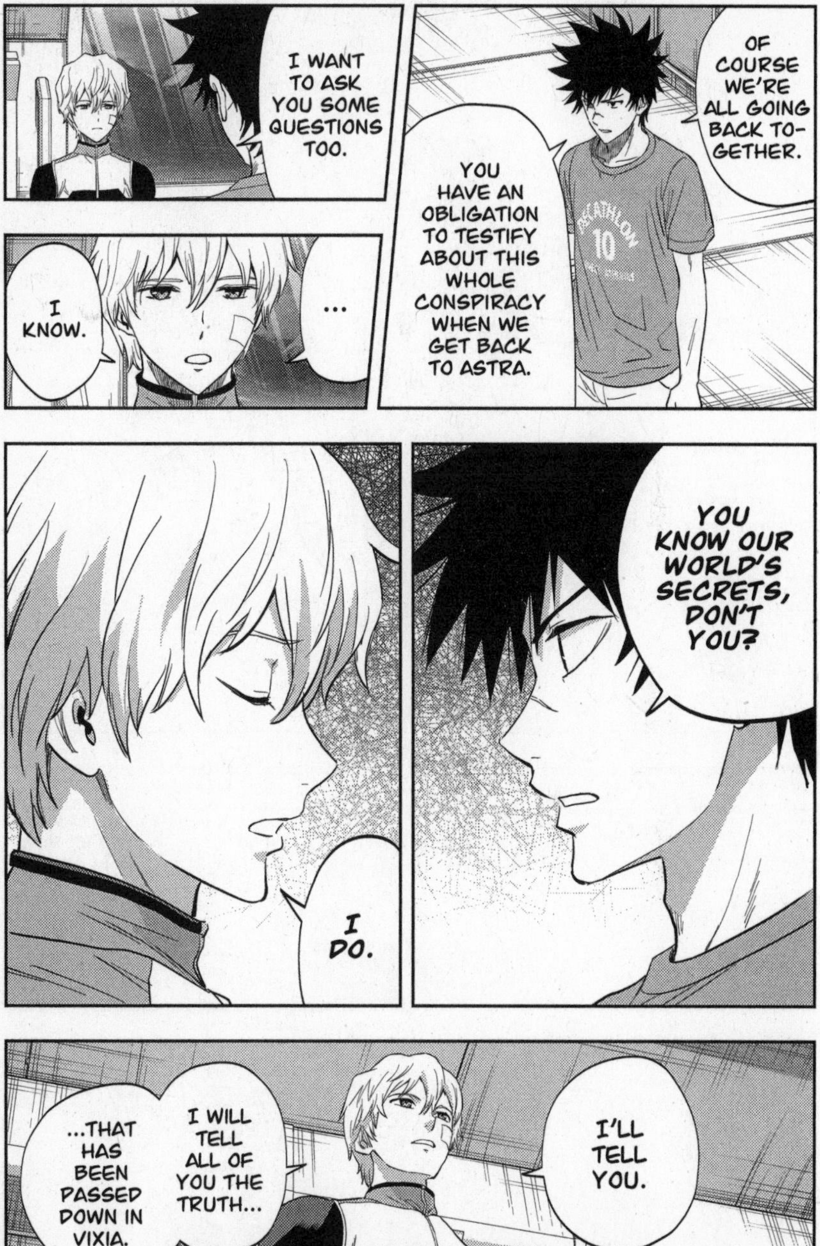
OF COURSE WE'RE ALL GOING BACK TO-GETHER.
YOU HAVE AN OBLIGATION TO TESTIFY ABOUT THIS WHOLE CONSPIRACY WHEN WE GET BACK TO ASTRA.
I WANT TO ASK YOU SOME QUESTIONS TOO.
...
I KNOW.
YOU KNOW OUR WORLD'S SECRETS, DON'T YOU?
I DO.
I'LL TELL YOU.
I WILL TELL ALL OF YOU THE TRUTH...
...THAT HAS BEEN PASSED DOWN IN VIXIA.

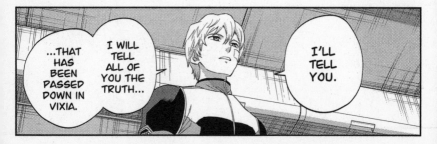

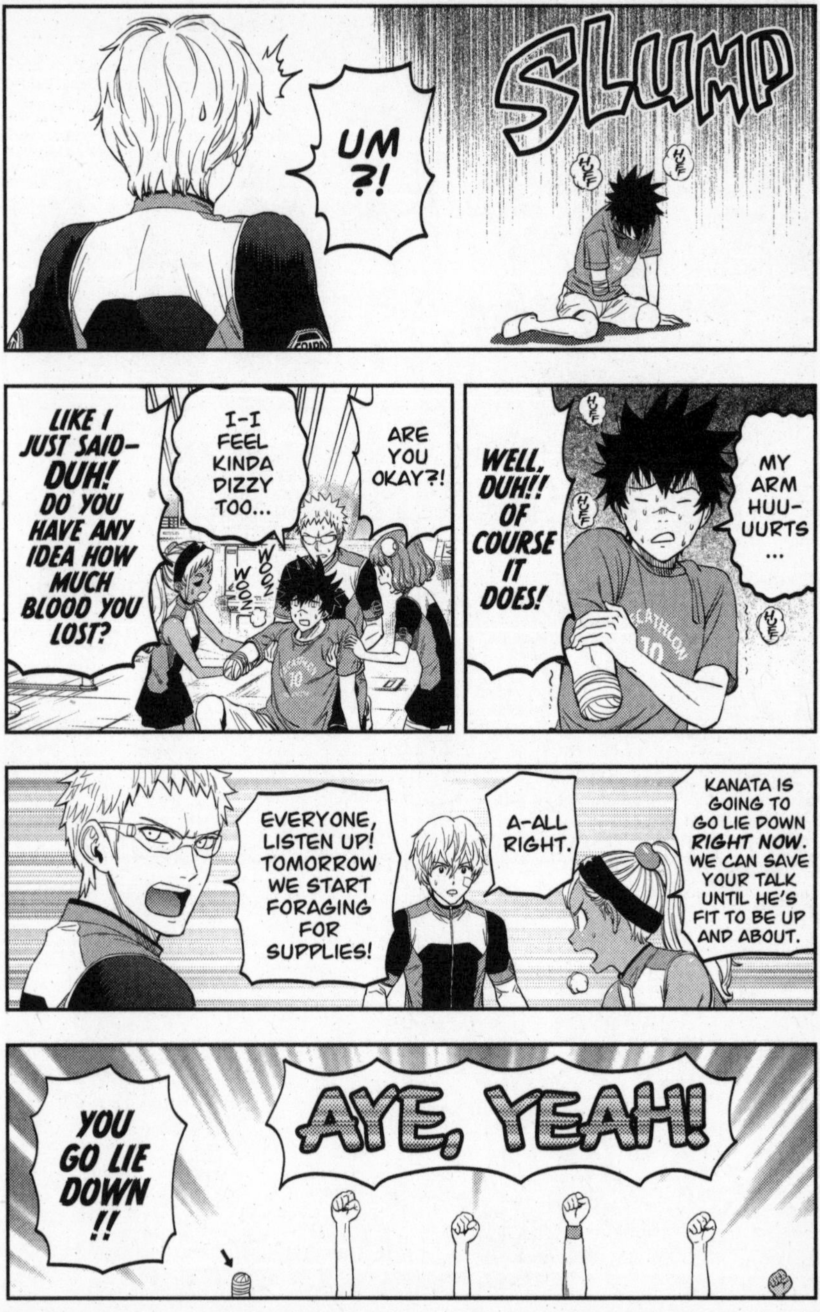
SLUMP
HUFF
HUFF
UM?!
HUFF
HUFF
MY ARM HUUU-UURTS...
WELL, DUH!! OF COURSE IT DOES!
HUFF
ARE YOU OKAY?!
I-I FEEL KINDA DIZZY TOO...
WOOZ
WOOZ
LIKE I JUST SAID— DUH! DO YOU HAVE ANY IDEA HOW MUCH BLOOD YOU LOST?
KANATA IS GOING TO GO LIE DOWN RIGHT NOW. WE CAN SAVE YOUR TALK UNTIL HE'S FIT TO BE UP AND ABOUT.
A-ALL RIGHT.
EVERYONE, LISTEN UP! TOMORROW WE START FORAGING FOR SUPPLIES!
AYE, YEAH!
YOU GO LIE DOWN!!

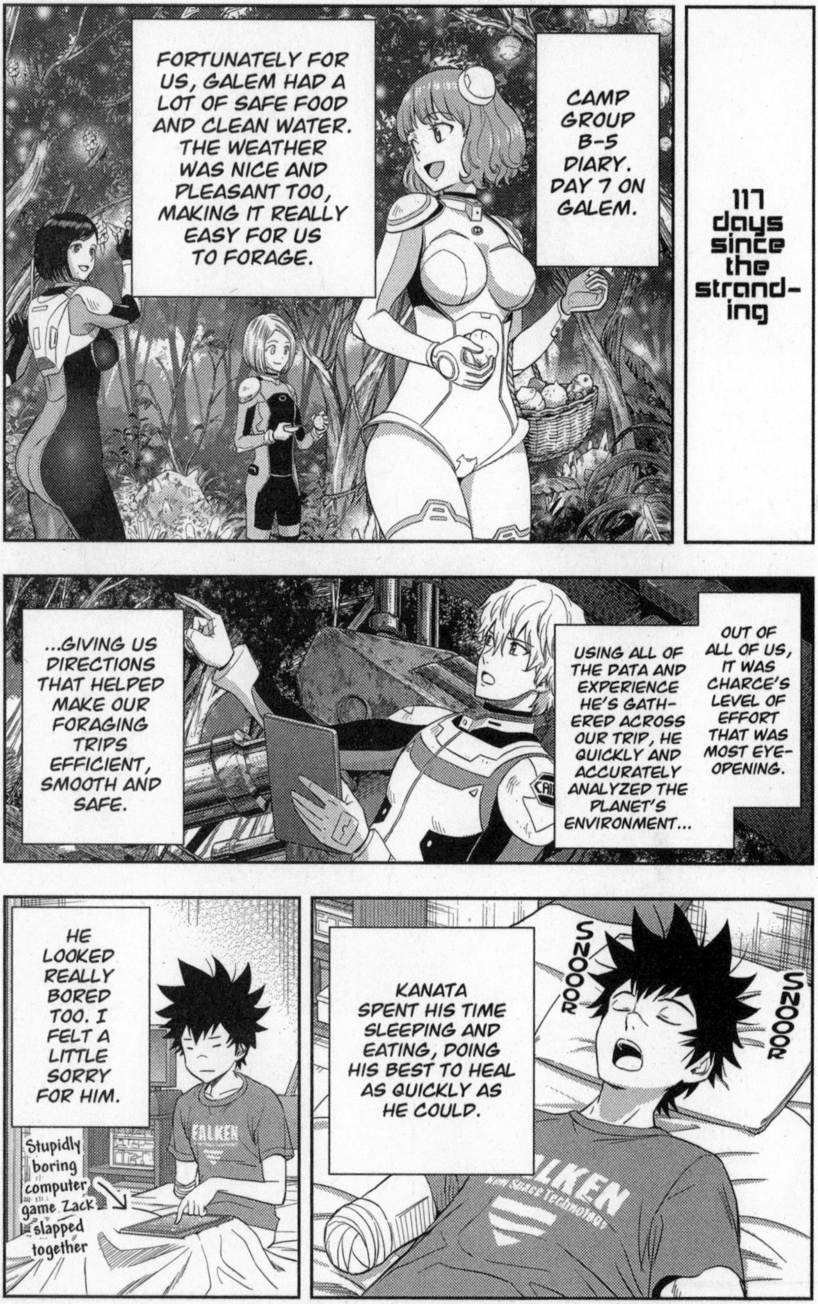
117 days since the strand-ing
CAMP GROUP B-5 DIARY. DAY 7 ON GALEM.
FORTUNATELY FOR US, GALEM HAD A LOT OF SAFE FOOD AND CLEAN WATER. THE WEATHER WAS NICE AND PLEASANT TOO, MAKING IT REALLY EASY FOR US TO FORAGE.
OUT OF ALL OF US, IT WAS CHARCE'S LEVEL OF EFFORT THAT WAS MOST EYE-OPENING.
USING ALL OF THE DATA AND EXPERIENCE HE'S GATH-ERED ACROSS OUR TRIP, HE QUICKLY AND ACCURATELY ANALYZED THE PLANET'S ENVIRONMENT...
...GIVING US DIRECTIONS THAT HELPED MAKE OUR FORAGING TRIPS EFFICIENT, SMOOTH AND SAFE.
SNOOOR
SNOOOR
KANATA SPENT HIS TIME SLEEPING AND EATING, DOING HIS BEST TO HEAL AS QUICKLY AS HE COULD.
HE LOOKED REALLY BORED TOO. I FELT A LITTLE SORRY FOR HIM.
Stupidly boring computer game Zack slapped together

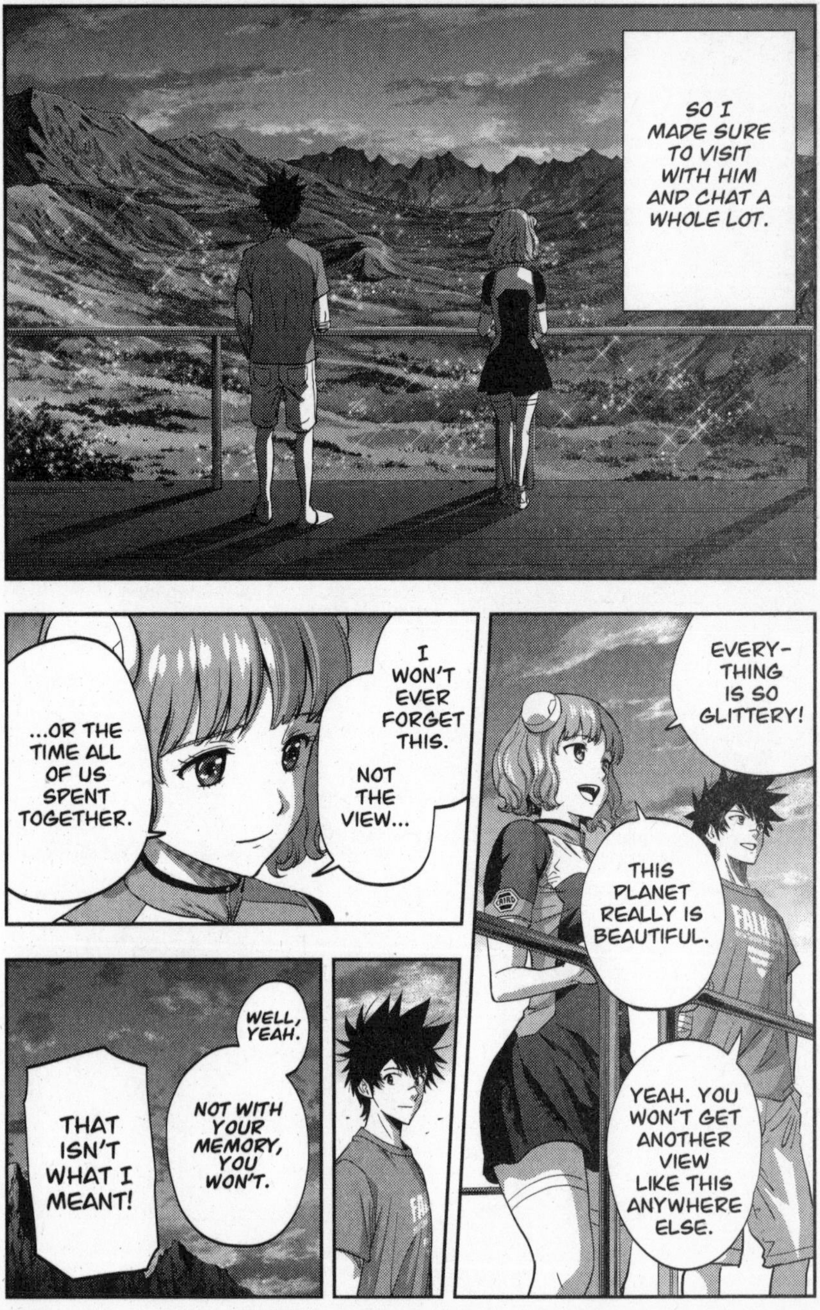
SO I MADE SURE TO VISIT WITH HIM AND CHAT A WHOLE LOT.
EVERY-THING IS SO GLITTERY!
THIS PLANET REALLY IS BEAUTIFUL.
YEAH. YOU WON'T GET ANOTHER VIEW LIKE THIS ANYWHERE ELSE.
I WON'T EVER FORGET THIS.
NOT THE VIEW...
...OR THE TIME ALL OF US SPENT TOGETHER.
WELL, YEAH.
NOT WITH YOUR MEMORY, YOU WON'T.
THAT ISN'T WHAT I MEANT!

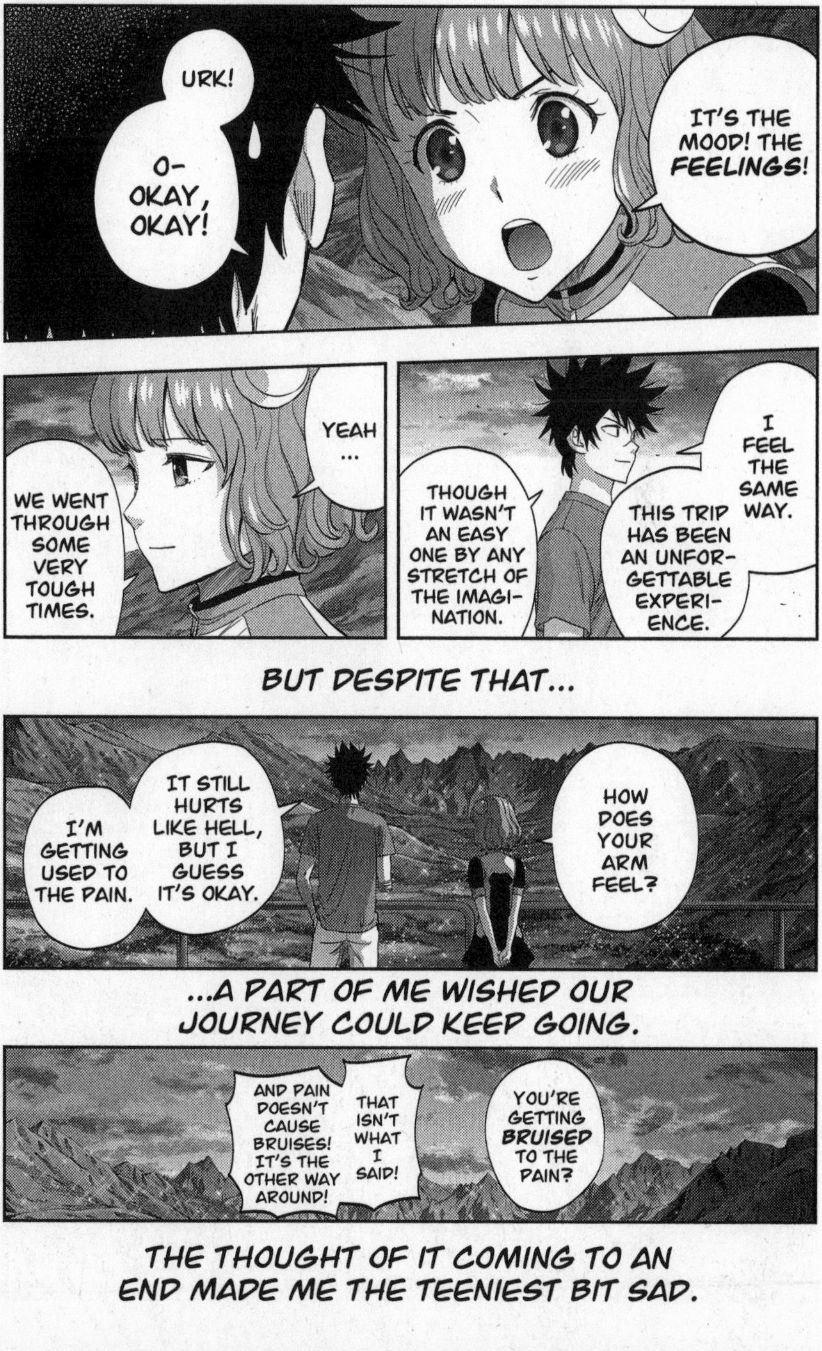
IT'S THE MOOD! THE FEELINGS!
URK!
O-OKAY, OKAY!
I FEEL THE SAME WAY.
THIS TRIP HAS BEEN AN UNFORGETTABLE EXPERIENCE.
THOUGH IT WASN'T AN EASY ONE BY ANY STRETCH OF THE IMAGINATION.
YEAH...
WE WENT THROUGH SOME VERY TOUGH TIMES.
BUT DESPITE THAT...
HOW DOES YOUR ARM FEEL?
IT STILL HURTS LIKE HELL, BUT I GUESS IT'S OKAY.
I'M GETTING USED TO THE PAIN.
...A PART OF ME WISHED OUR JOURNEY COULD KEEP GOING.
YOU'RE GETTING BRUISED TO THE PAIN?
THAT ISN'T WHAT I SAID!
AND PAIN DOESN'T CAUSE BRUISES! IT'S THE OTHER WAY AROUND!
THE THOUGHT OF IT COMING TO AN END MADE ME THE TEENIEST BIT SAD.

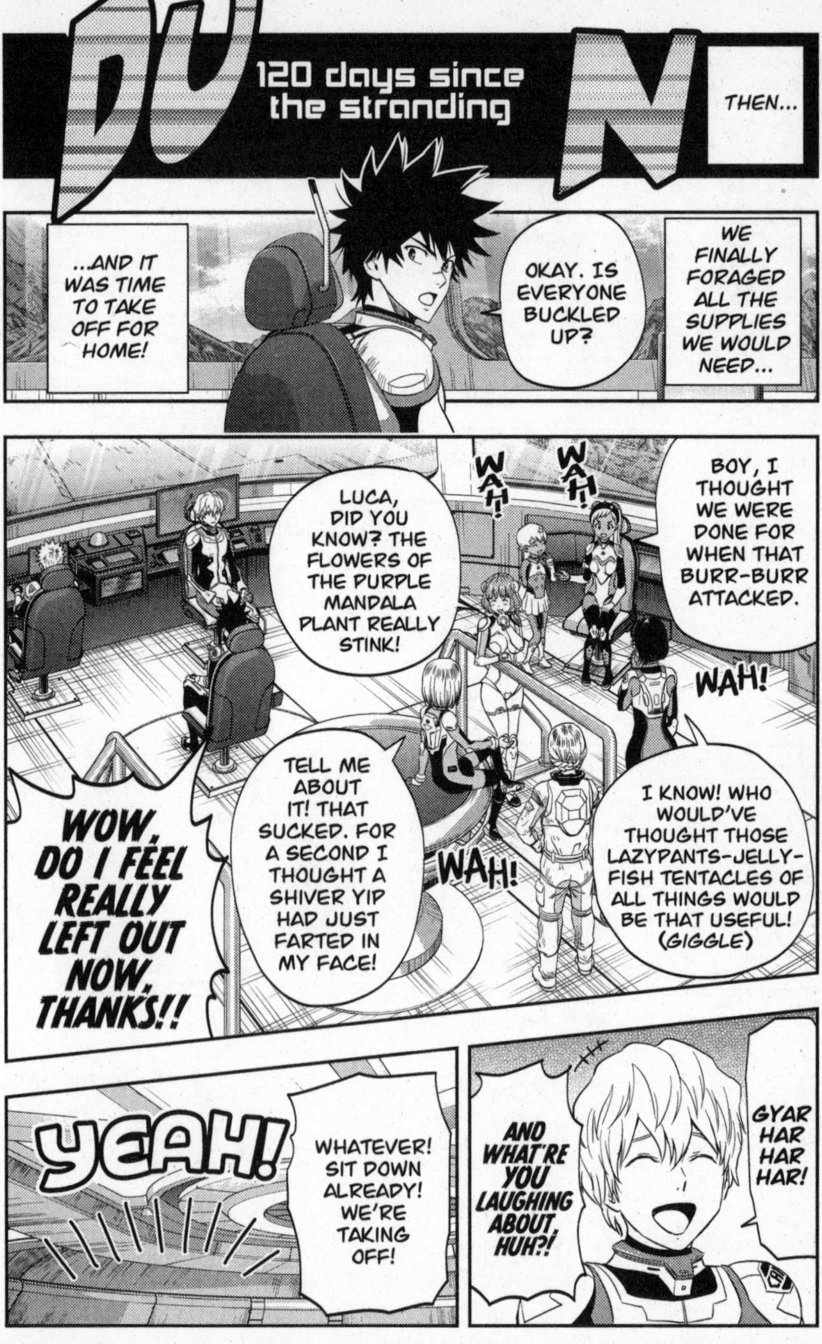
THEN...
120 days since the stranding
DUN
WE FINALLY FORAGED ALL THE SUPPLIES WE WOULD NEED...
OKAY. IS EVERYONE BUCKLED UP?
...AND IT WAS TIME TO TAKE OFF FOR HOME!
BOY, I THOUGHT WE WERE DONE FOR WHEN THAT BURR-BURR ATTACKED.
WAH!
WAH!
LUCA, DID YOU KNOW? THE FLOWERS OF THE PURPLE MANDALA PLANT REALLY STINK!
WAH!
I KNOW! WHO WOULD'VE THOUGHT THOSE LAZYPANTS-JELLY-FISH TENTACLES OF ALL THINGS WOULD BE THAT USEFUL! (GIGGLE)
WAH!
TELL ME ABOUT IT! THAT SUCKED. FOR A SECOND I THOUGHT A SHIVER YIP HAD JUST FARTED IN MY FACE!
WOW, DO I FEEL REALLY LEFT OUT NOW, THANKS!!
GYAR HAR HAR HAR!
AND WHAT'RE YOU LAUGHING ABOUT, HUH?!
WHATEVER! SIT DOWN ALREADY! WE'RE TAKING OFF!
YEAH!

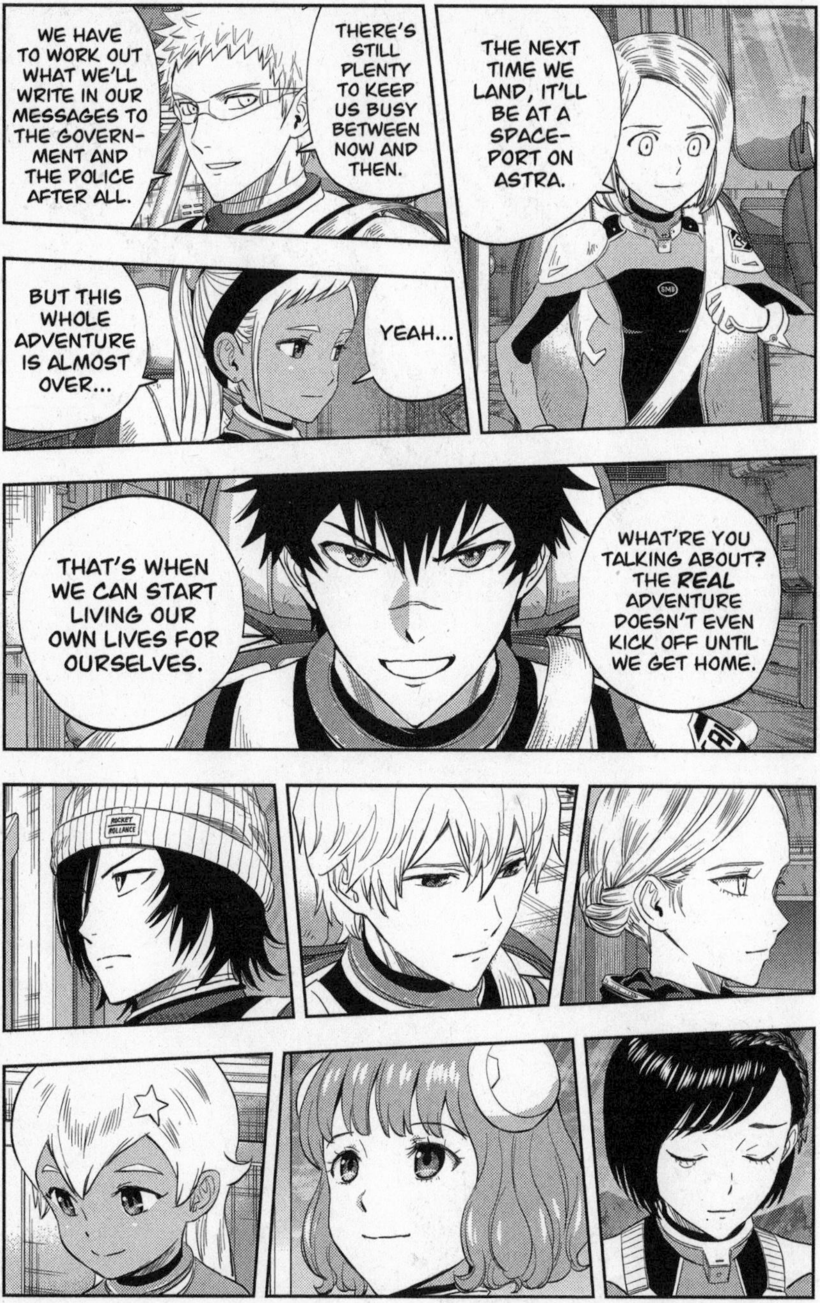
THE NEXT TIME WE LAND, IT'LL BE AT A SPACE-PORT ON ASTRA.
THERE'S STILL PLENTY TO KEEP US BUSY BETWEEN NOW AND THEN.
WE HAVE TO WORK OUT WHAT WE'LL WRITE IN OUR MESSAGES TO THE GOVERN-MENT AND THE POLICE AFTER ALL.
BUT THIS WHOLE ADVENTURE IS ALMOST OVER...
YEAH...
WHAT'RE YOU TALKING ABOUT? THE REAL ADVENTURE DOESN'T EVEN KICK OFF UNTIL WE GET HOME.
THAT'S WHEN WE CAN START LIVING OUR OWN LIVES FOR OURSELVES.

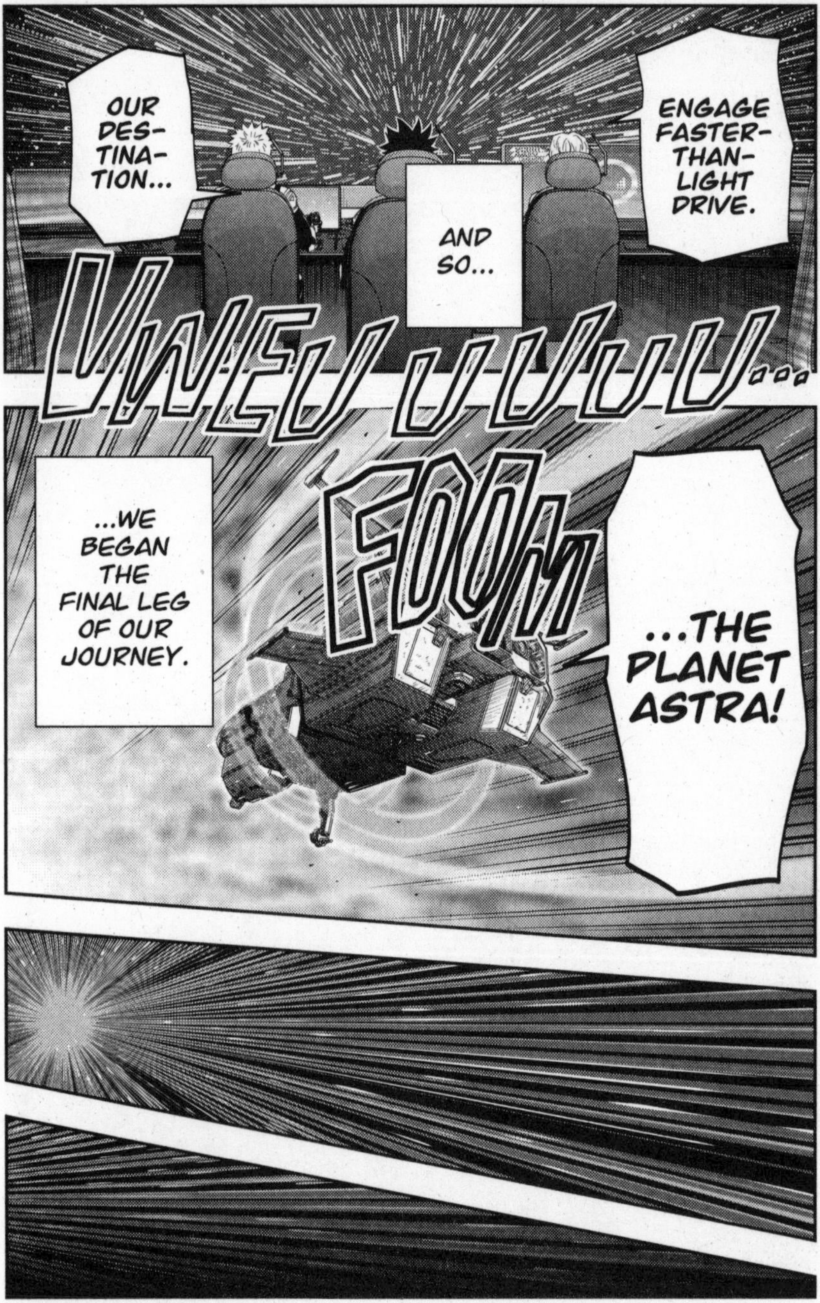
ENGAGE FASTER-THAN-LIGHT DRIVE.
AND SO...
OUR DESTINATION...
VWEUUUUU...
...THE PLANET ASTRA!
FOOM
...WE BEGAN THE FINAL LEG OF OUR JOURNEY.

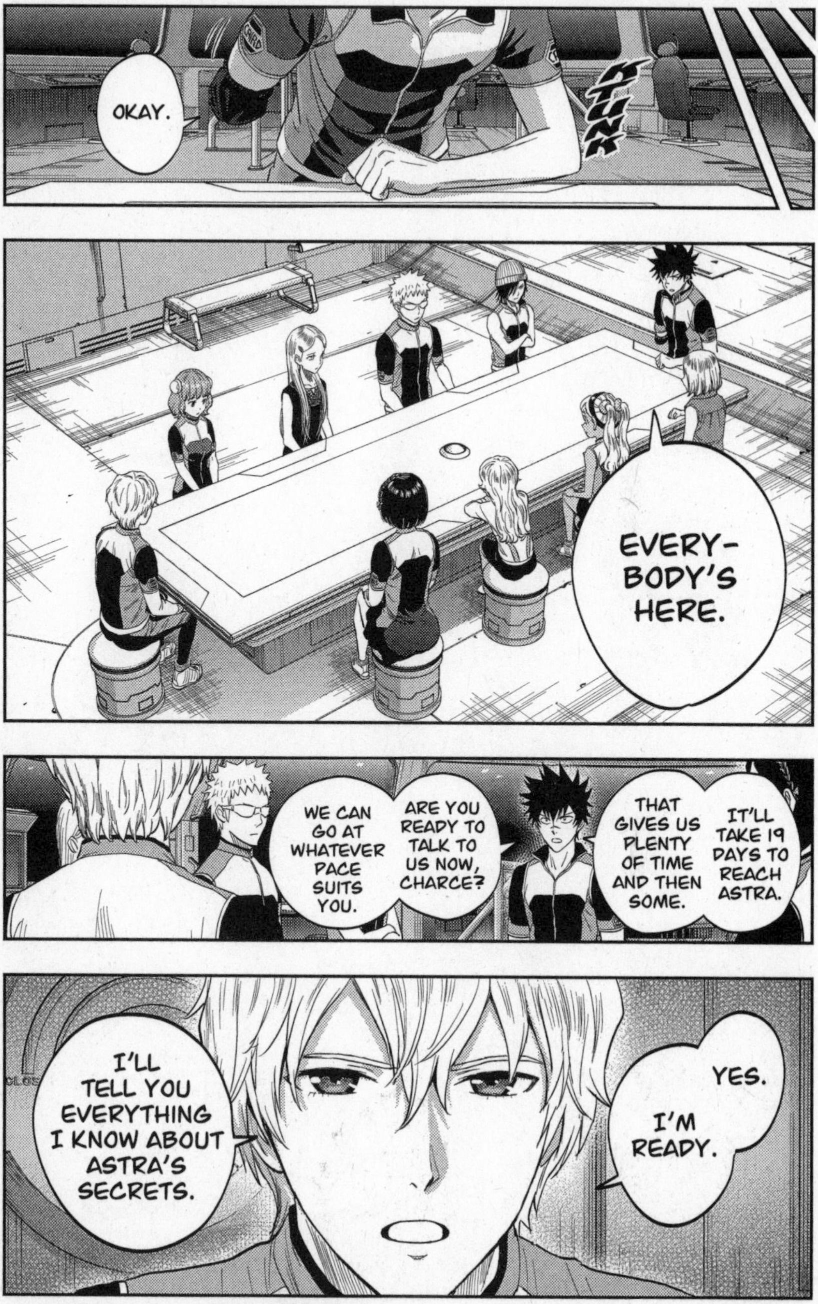
OKAY.
EVERY-BODY'S HERE.
IT'LL TAKE 19 DAYS TO REACH ASTRA.
THAT GIVES US PLENTY OF TIME AND THEN SOME.
ARE YOU READY TO TALK TO US NOW, CHARCE?
WE CAN GO AT WHATEVER PACE SUITS YOU.
YES.
I'M READY.
I'LL TELL YOU EVERYTHING I KNOW ABOUT ASTRA'S SECRETS.

Material Collection | Character Prototype Design

CUT CHARACTERS

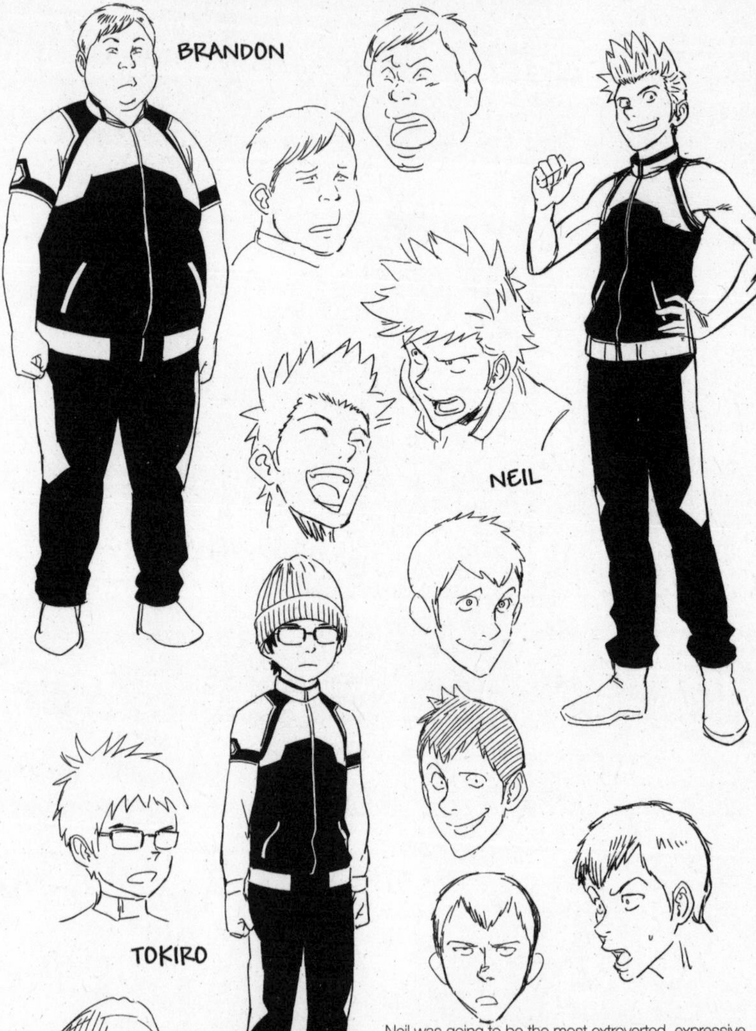
BRANDON
NEIL
TOKIRO

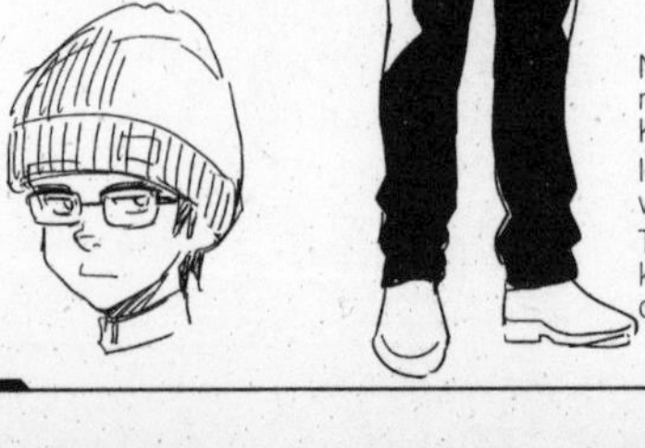

Neil was going to be the most extroverted, expressive member of the crew. Parts of his personality went to Kanata.

I deliberately gave up any hope of Brandon being popular with readers since he was meant to be the lazy complainer.

Tokiro was the too-serious intelligent one with encyclopedic knowledge. He was going to be the crew's planner, but he donated those traits to Zack. His cap went to Ulgar.

ASTRA
LOST IN SPACE
#47

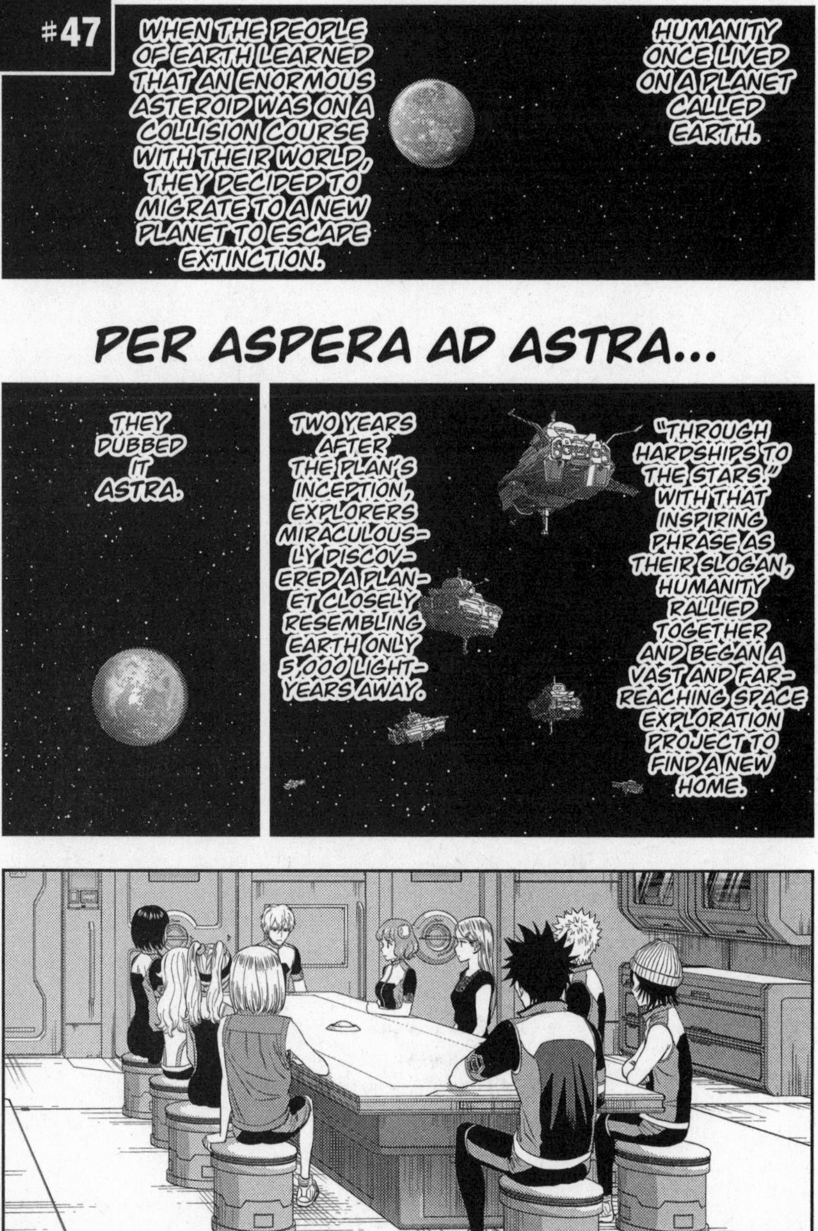
HUMANITY ONCE LIVED ON A PLANET CALLED EARTH.
WHEN THE PEOPLE OF EARTH LEARNED THAT AN ENORMOUS ASTEROID WAS ON A COLLISION COURSE WITH THEIR WORLD, THEY DECIDED TO MIGRATE TO A NEW PLANET TO ESCAPE EXTINCTION.
PER ASPERA AD ASTRA...
"THROUGH HARDSHIPS TO THE STARS." WITH THAT INSPIRING PHRASE AS THEIR SLOGAN, HUMANITY RALLIED TOGETHER AND BEGAN A VAST AND FAR-REACHING SPACE EXPLORATION PROJECT TO FIND A NEW HOME.
TWO YEARS AFTER THE PLAN'S INCEPTION, EXPLORERS MIRACULOUSLY DISCOVERED A PLANET CLOSELY RESEMBLING EARTH ONLY 5,000 LIGHT-YEARS AWAY.
THEY DUBBED IT ASTRA.

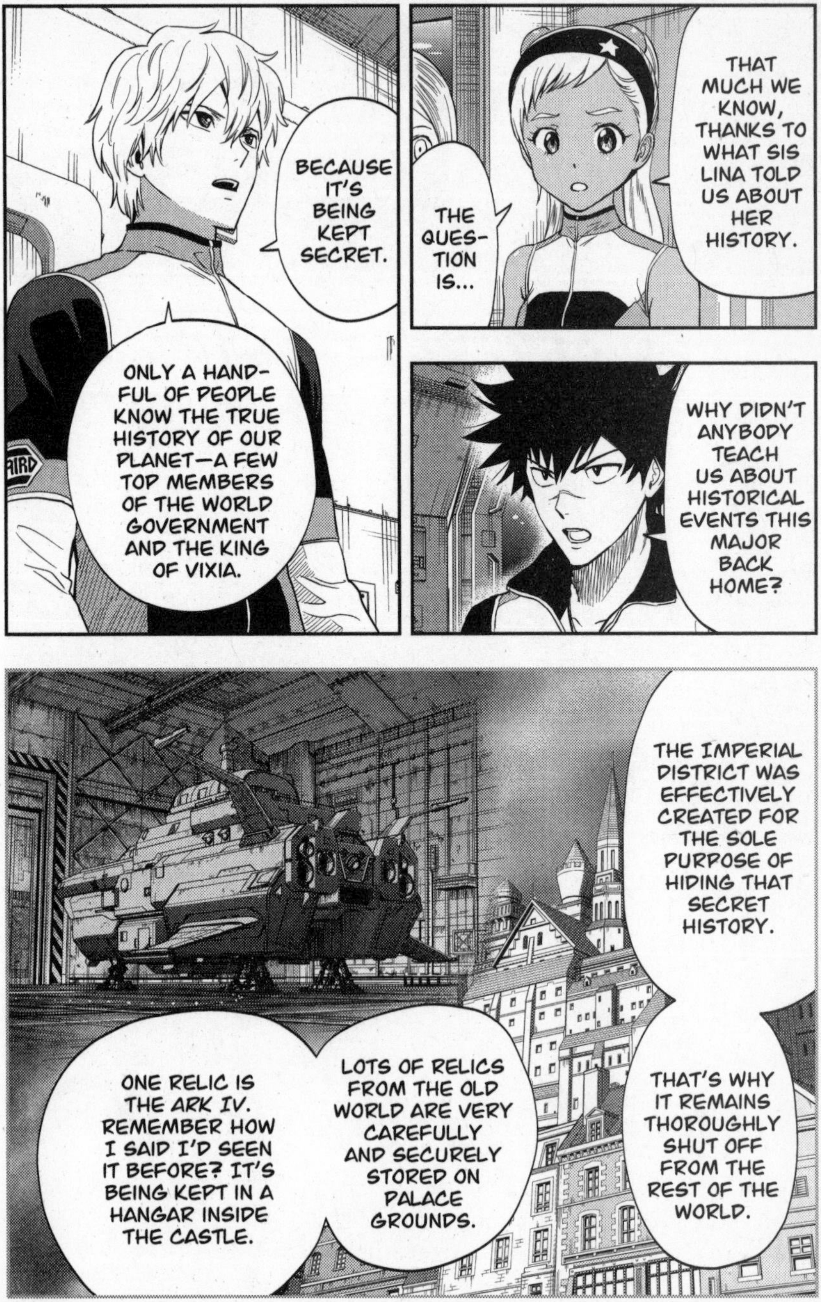
THAT MUCH WE KNOW, THANKS TO WHAT SIS LINA TOLD US ABOUT HER HISTORY.
THE QUESTION IS...
WHY DIDN'T ANYBODY TEACH US ABOUT HISTORICAL EVENTS THIS MAJOR BACK HOME?
BECAUSE IT'S BEING KEPT SECRET.
ONLY A HANDFUL OF PEOPLE KNOW THE TRUE HISTORY OF OUR PLANET—A FEW TOP MEMBERS OF THE WORLD GOVERNMENT AND THE KING OF VIXIA.
THE IMPERIAL DISTRICT WAS EFFECTIVELY CREATED FOR THE SOLE PURPOSE OF HIDING THAT SECRET HISTORY.
THAT'S WHY IT REMAINS THOROUGHLY SHUT OFF FROM THE REST OF THE WORLD.
LOTS OF RELICS FROM THE OLD WORLD ARE VERY CAREFULLY AND SECURELY STORED ON PALACE GROUNDS.
ONE RELIC IS THE ARK IV. REMEMBER HOW I SAID I'D SEEN IT BEFORE? IT'S BEING KEPT IN A HANGAR INSIDE THE CASTLE.

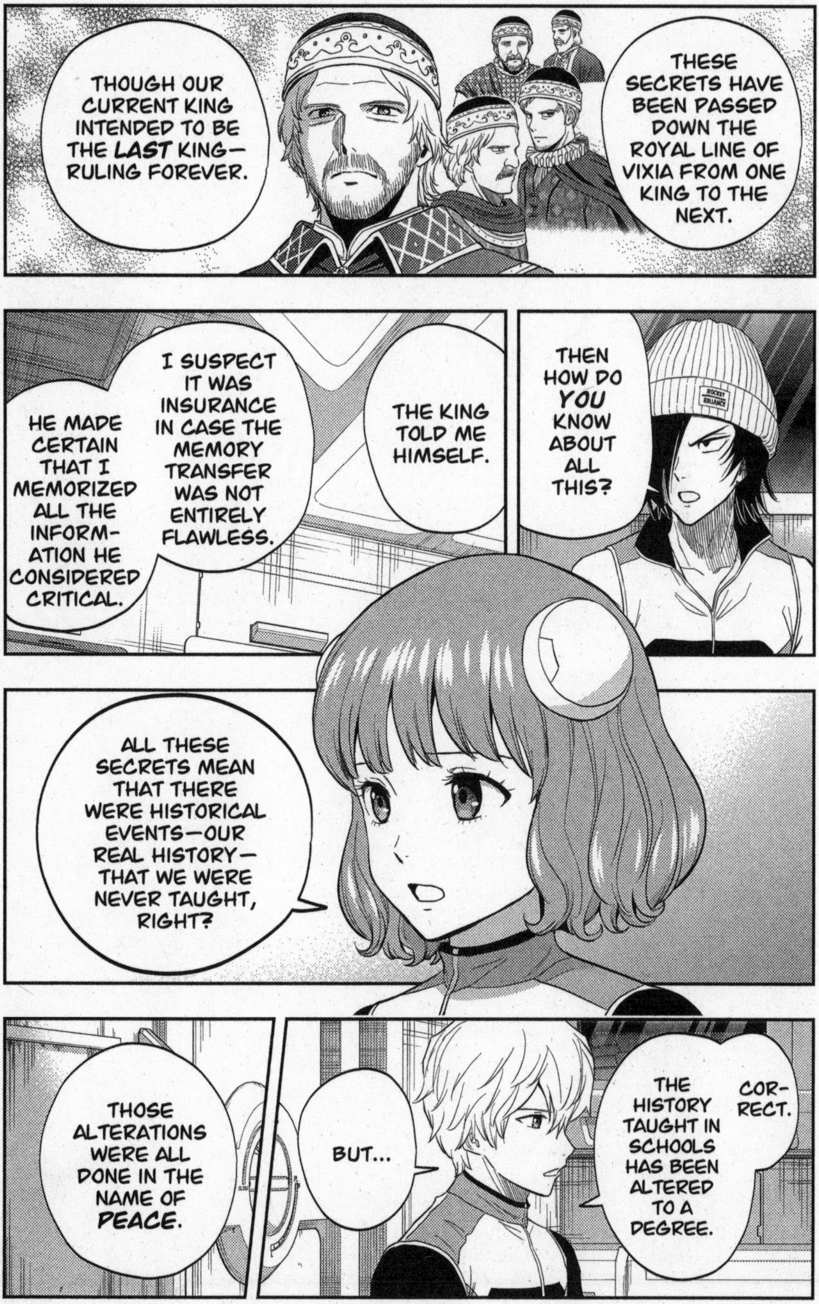
THESE SECRETS HAVE BEEN PASSED DOWN THE ROYAL LINE OF VIXIA FROM ONE KING TO THE NEXT.
THOUGH OUR CURRENT KING INTENDED TO BE THE LAST KING—RULING FOREVER.
THEN HOW DO YOU KNOW ABOUT ALL THIS?
THE KING TOLD ME HIMSELF.
I SUSPECT IT WAS INSURANCE IN CASE THE MEMORY TRANSFER WAS NOT ENTIRELY FLAWLESS.
HE MADE CERTAIN THAT I MEMORIZED ALL THE INFORMATION HE CONSIDERED CRITICAL.
ALL THESE SECRETS MEAN THAT THERE WERE HISTORICAL EVENTS—OUR REAL HISTORY—THAT WE WERE NEVER TAUGHT, RIGHT?
COR-RECT.
THE HISTORY TAUGHT IN SCHOOLS HAS BEEN ALTERED TO A DEGREE.
BUT...
THOSE ALTERATIONS WERE ALL DONE IN THE NAME OF PEACE.

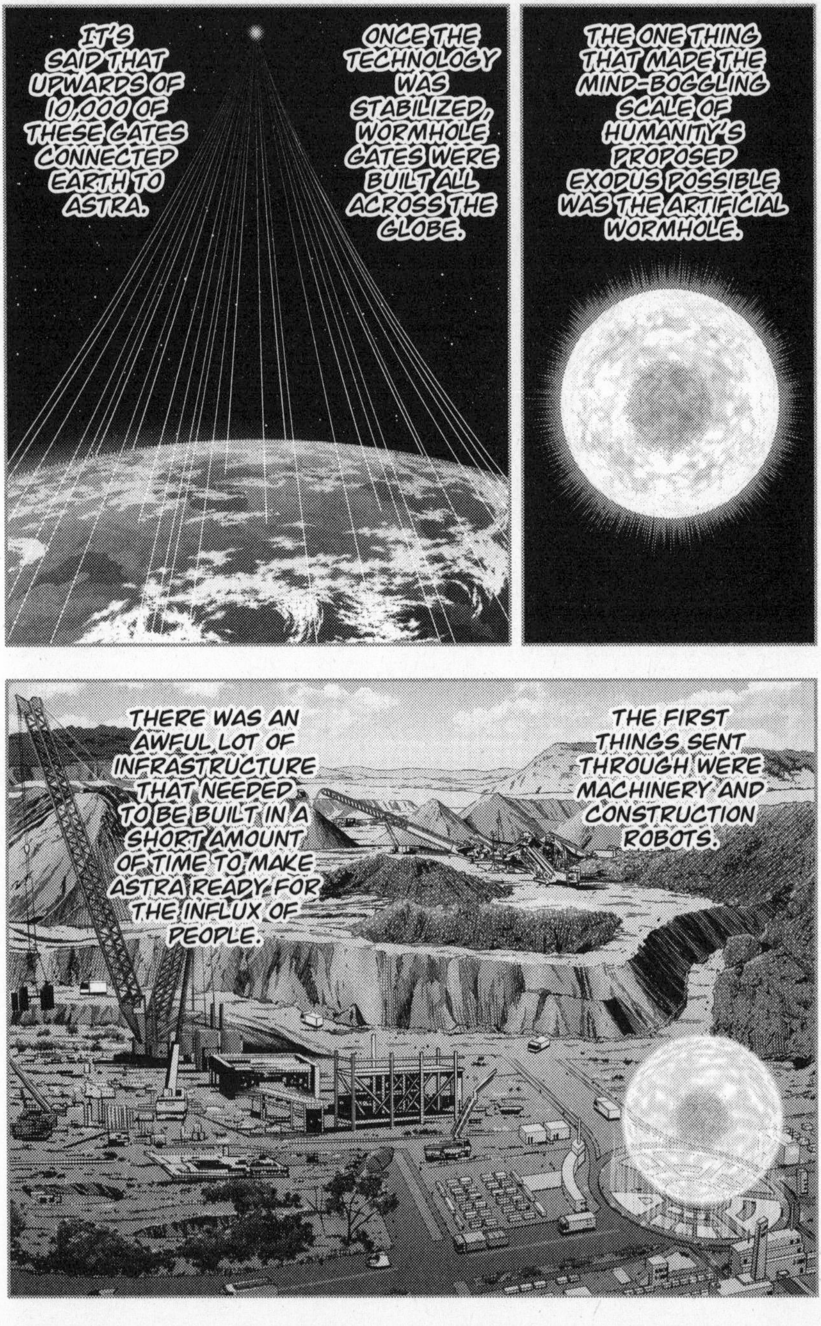
THE ONE THING THAT MADE THE MIND-BOGGLING SCALE OF HUMANITY'S PROPOSED EXODUS POSSIBLE WAS THE ARTIFICIAL WORMHOLE.
ONCE THE TECHNOLOGY WAS STABILIZED, WORMHOLE GATES WERE BUILT ALL ACROSS THE GLOBE.
IT'S SAID THAT UPWARDS OF 10,000 OF THESE GATES CONNECTED EARTH TO ASTRA.
THE FIRST THINGS SENT THROUGH WERE MACHINERY AND CONSTRUCTION ROBOTS.
THERE WAS AN AWFUL LOT OF INFRASTRUCTURE THAT NEEDED TO BE BUILT IN A SHORT AMOUNT OF TIME TO MAKE ASTRA READY FOR THE INFLUX OF PEOPLE.

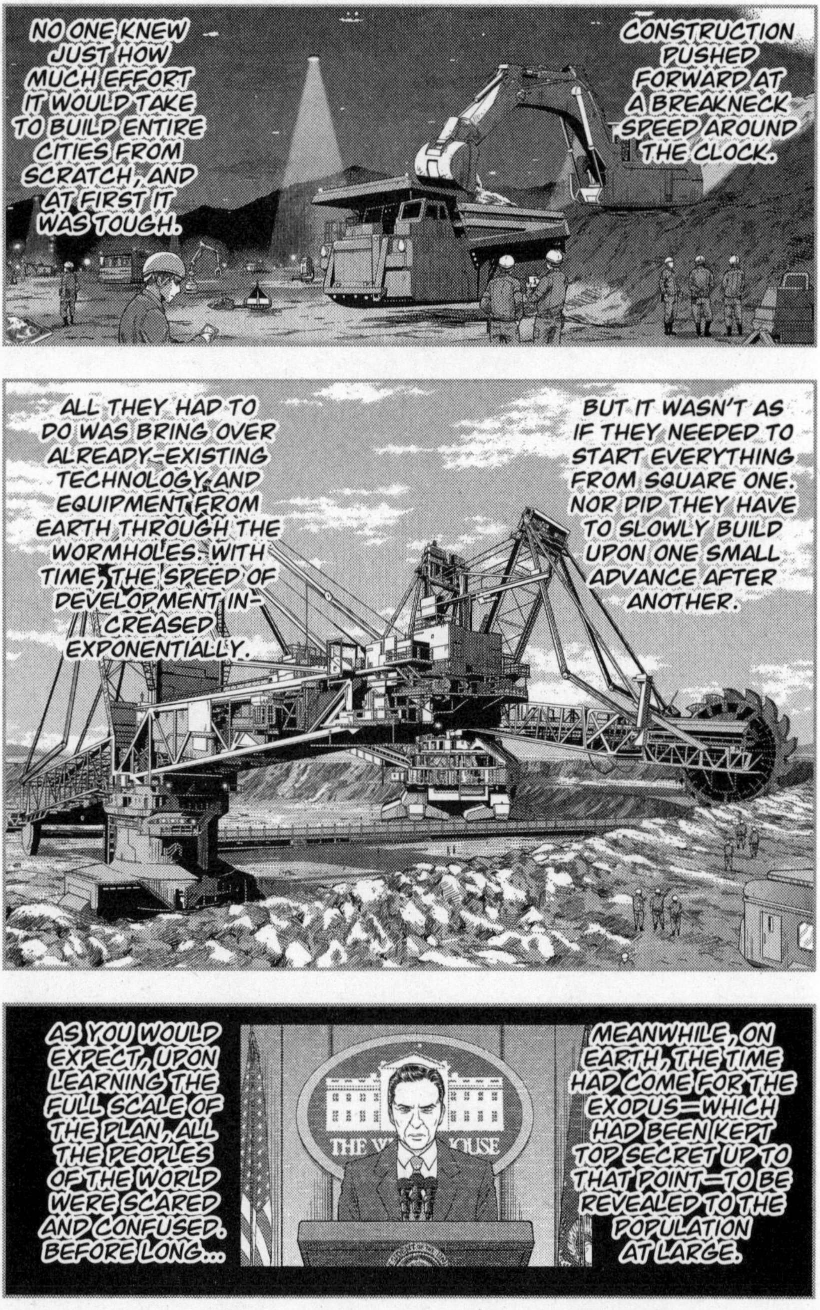
CONSTRUCTION PUSHED FORWARD AT A BREAKNECK SPEED AROUND THE CLOCK.
NO ONE KNEW JUST HOW MUCH EFFORT IT WOULD TAKE TO BUILD ENTIRE CITIES FROM SCRATCH, AND AT FIRST IT WAS TOUGH.
BUT IT WASN'T AS IF THEY NEEDED TO START EVERYTHING FROM SQUARE ONE. NOR DID THEY HAVE TO SLOWLY BUILD UPON ONE SMALL ADVANCE AFTER ANOTHER.
ALL THEY HAD TO DO WAS BRING OVER ALREADY-EXISTING TECHNOLOGY AND EQUIPMENT FROM EARTH THROUGH THE WORMHOLES. WITH TIME, THE SPEED OF DEVELOPMENT IN-CREASED EXPONENTIALLY.
MEANWHILE, ON EARTH, THE TIME HAD COME FOR THE EXODUS—WHICH HAD BEEN KEPT TOP SECRET UP TO THAT POINT—TO BE REVEALED TO THE POPULATION AT LARGE.
AS YOU WOULD EXPECT, UPON LEARNING THE FULL SCALE OF THE PLAN, ALL THE PEOPLES OF THE WORLD WERE SCARED AND CONFUSED. BEFORE LONG...

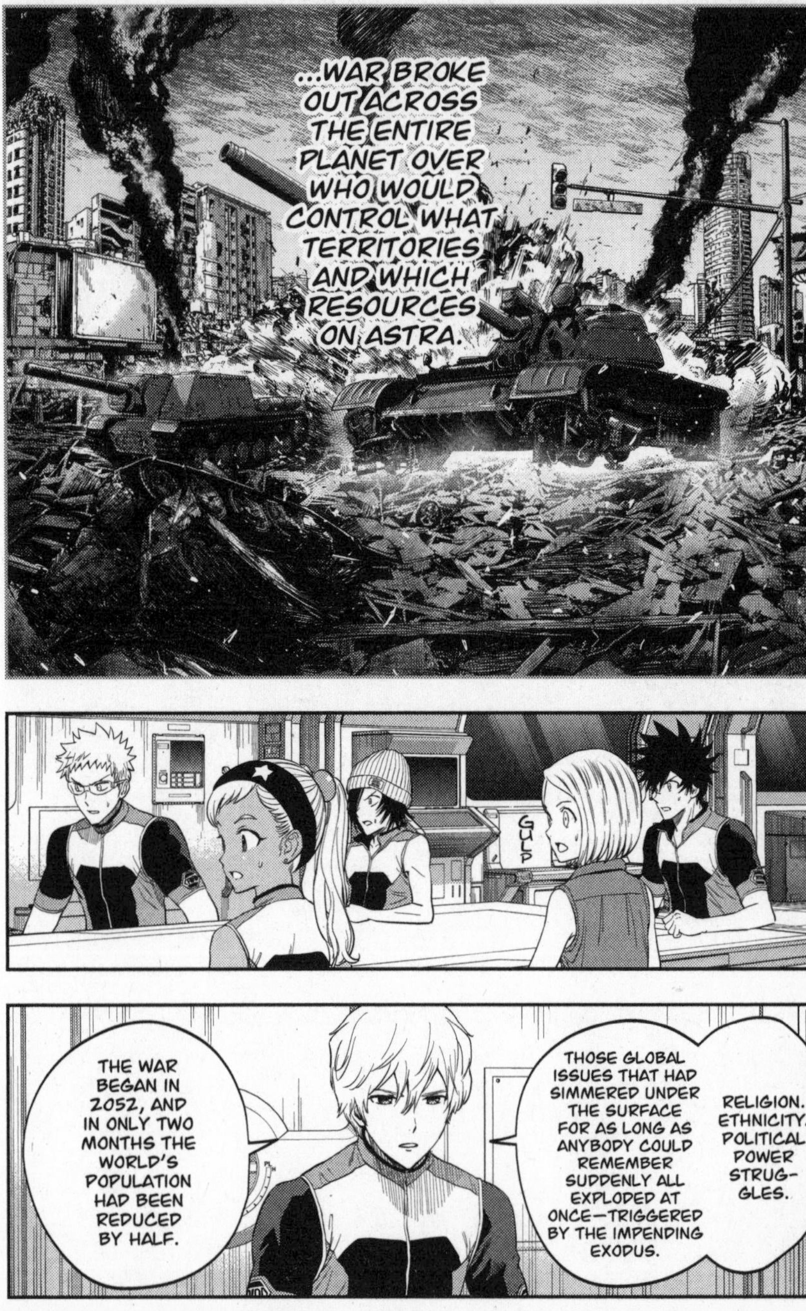
...WAR BROKE OUT ACROSS THE ENTIRE PLANET OVER WHO WOULD CONTROL WHAT TERRITORIES AND WHICH RESOURCES ON ASTRA.
GULP
RELIGION. ETHNICITY. POLITICAL POWER STRUG-GLES.
THOSE GLOBAL ISSUES THAT HAD SIMMERED UNDER THE SURFACE FOR AS LONG AS ANYBODY COULD REMEMBER SUDDENLY ALL EXPLODED AT ONCE—TRIGGERED BY THE IMPENDING EXODUS.
THE WAR BEGAN IN 2052, AND IN ONLY TWO MONTHS THE WORLD'S POPULATION HAD BEEN REDUCED BY HALF.

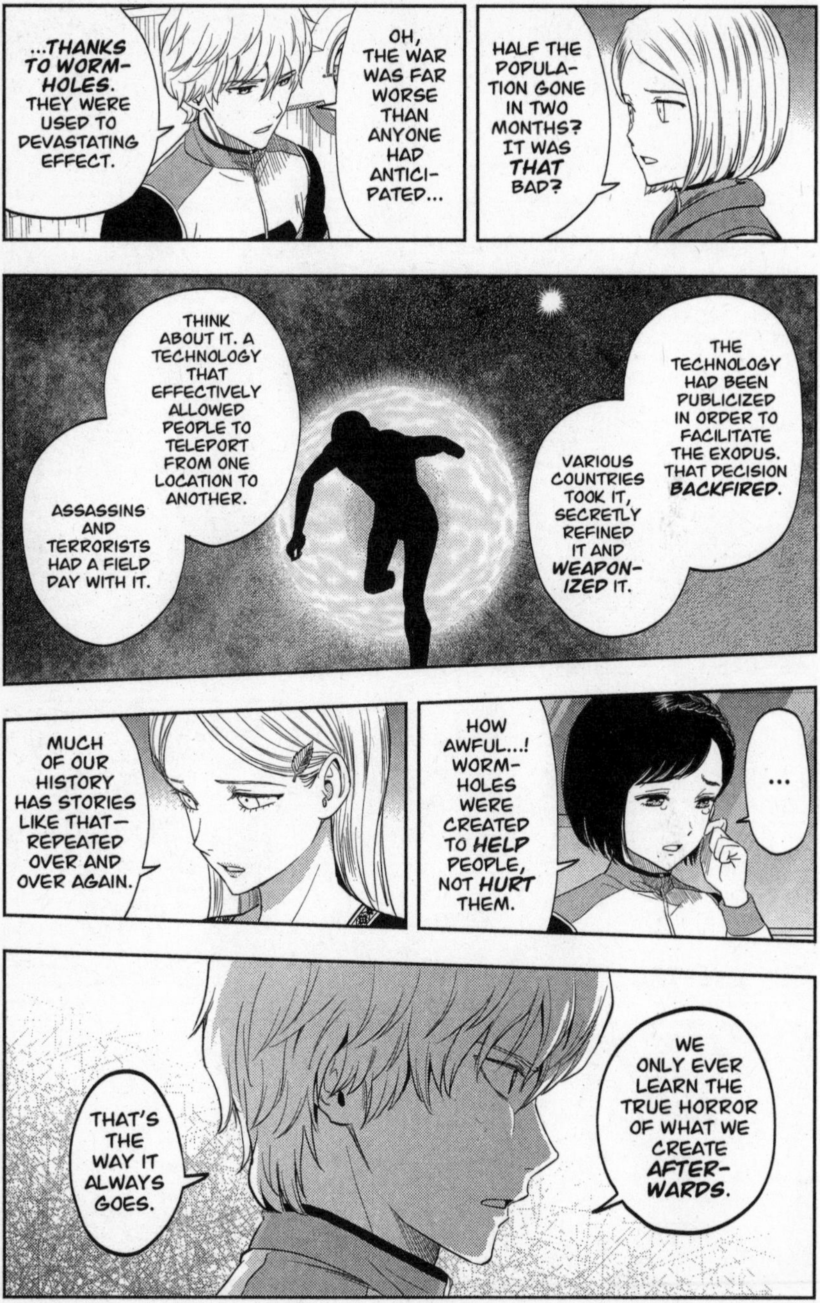
HALF THE POPULATION GONE IN TWO MONTHS? IT WAS **THAT** BAD?
OH, THE WAR WAS FAR WORSE THAN ANYONE HAD ANTICIPATED...
...**THANKS TO WORMHOLES.** THEY WERE USED TO DEVASTATING EFFECT.
THE TECHNOLOGY HAD BEEN PUBLICIZED IN ORDER TO FACILITATE THE EXODUS. THAT DECISION **BACKFIRED.**
VARIOUS COUNTRIES TOOK IT, SECRETLY REFINED IT AND **WEAPONIZED** IT.
THINK ABOUT IT. A TECHNOLOGY THAT EFFECTIVELY ALLOWED PEOPLE TO TELEPORT FROM ONE LOCATION TO ANOTHER.
ASSASSINS AND TERRORISTS HAD A FIELD DAY WITH IT.
...
HOW AWFUL...! WORMHOLES WERE CREATED TO **HELP** PEOPLE, NOT **HURT** THEM.
MUCH OF OUR HISTORY HAS STORIES LIKE THAT—REPEATED OVER AND OVER AGAIN.
WE ONLY EVER LEARN THE TRUE HORROR OF WHAT WE CREATE **AFTERWARDS.**
THAT'S THE WAY IT ALWAYS GOES.

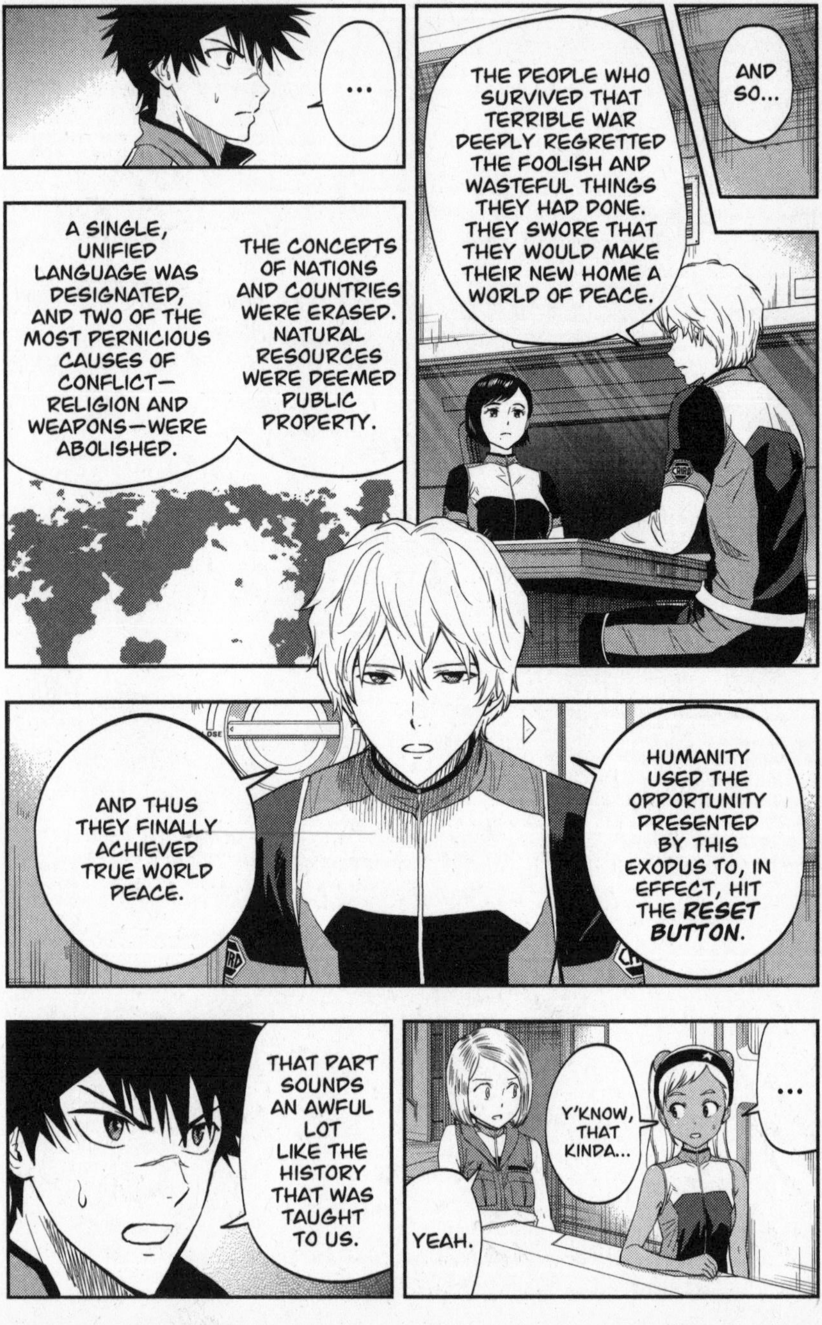
AND SO...
THE PEOPLE WHO SURVIVED THAT TERRIBLE WAR DEEPLY REGRETTED THE FOOLISH AND WASTEFUL THINGS THEY HAD DONE. THEY SWORE THAT THEY WOULD MAKE THEIR NEW HOME A WORLD OF PEACE.
...
THE CONCEPTS OF NATIONS AND COUNTRIES WERE ERASED. NATURAL RESOURCES WERE DEEMED PUBLIC PROPERTY.
A SINGLE, UNIFIED LANGUAGE WAS DESIGNATED, AND TWO OF THE MOST PERNICIOUS CAUSES OF CONFLICT—RELIGION AND WEAPONS—WERE ABOLISHED.
HUMANITY USED THE OPPORTUNITY PRESENTED BY THIS EXODUS TO, IN EFFECT, HIT THE **RESET BUTTON**.
AND THUS THEY FINALLY ACHIEVED TRUE WORLD PEACE.
...
Y'KNOW, THAT KINDA...
YEAH.
THAT PART SOUNDS AN AWFUL LOT LIKE THE HISTORY THAT WAS TAUGHT TO US.

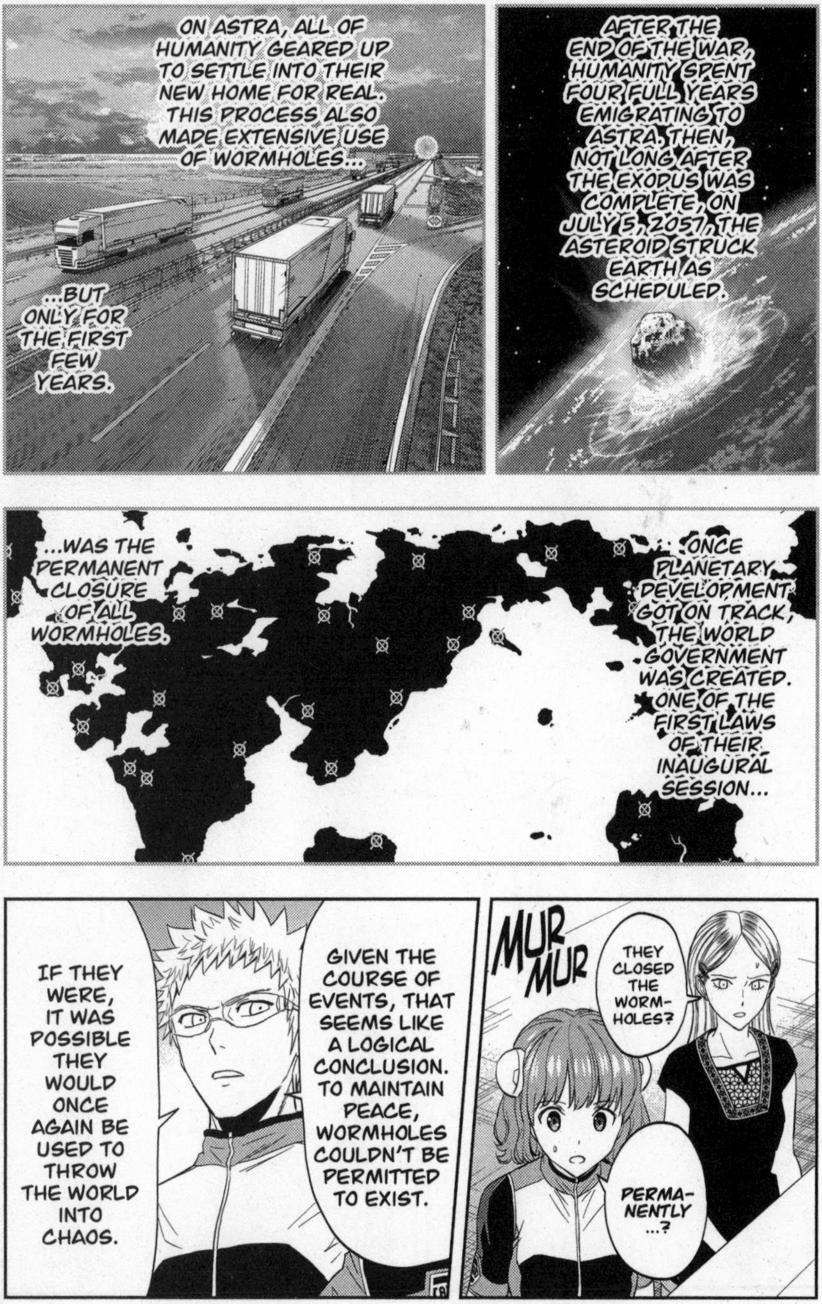
AFTER THE END OF THE WAR, HUMANITY SPENT FOUR FULL YEARS EMIGRATING TO ASTRA. THEN, NOT LONG AFTER THE EXODUS WAS COMPLETE, ON JULY 5, 2057, THE ASTEROID STRUCK EARTH AS SCHEDULED.
ON ASTRA, ALL OF HUMANITY GEARED UP TO SETTLE INTO THEIR NEW HOME FOR REAL. THIS PROCESS ALSO MADE EXTENSIVE USE OF WORMHOLES...
...BUT ONLY FOR THE FIRST FEW YEARS.
ONCE PLANETARY DEVELOPMENT GOT ON TRACK, THE WORLD GOVERNMENT WAS CREATED. ONE OF THE FIRST LAWS OF THEIR INAUGURAL SESSION...
...WAS THE PERMANENT CLOSURE OF ALL WORMHOLES.
MUR MUR
THEY CLOSED THE WORM-HOLES?
PERMA-NENTLY ...?
GIVEN THE COURSE OF EVENTS, THAT SEEMS LIKE A LOGICAL CONCLUSION. TO MAINTAIN PEACE, WORMHOLES COULDN'T BE PERMITTED TO EXIST.
IF THEY WERE, IT WAS POSSIBLE THEY WOULD ONCE AGAIN BE USED TO THROW THE WORLD INTO CHAOS.

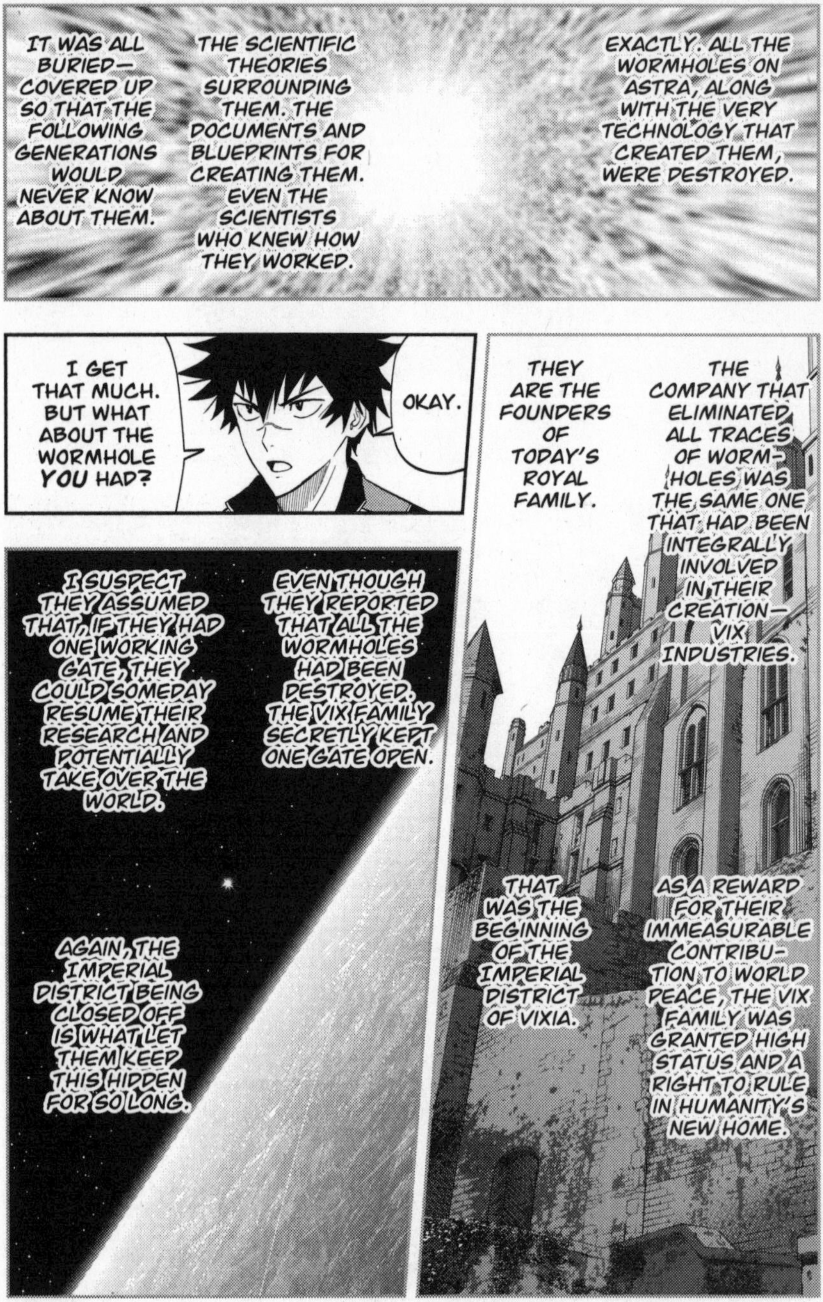
EXACTLY. ALL THE WORMHOLES ON ASTRA, ALONG WITH THE VERY TECHNOLOGY THAT CREATED THEM, WERE DESTROYED.
THE SCIENTIFIC THEORIES SURROUNDING THEM. THE DOCUMENTS AND BLUEPRINTS FOR CREATING THEM. EVEN THE SCIENTISTS WHO KNEW HOW THEY WORKED.
IT WAS ALL BURIED—COVERED UP SO THAT THE FOLLOWING GENERATIONS WOULD NEVER KNOW ABOUT THEM.
THE COMPANY THAT ELIMINATED ALL TRACES OF WORM-HOLES WAS THE SAME ONE THAT HAD BEEN INTEGRALLY INVOLVED IN THEIR CREATION—VIX INDUSTRIES.
THEY ARE THE FOUNDERS OF TODAY'S ROYAL FAMILY.
AS A REWARD FOR THEIR IMMEASURABLE CONTRIBU-TION TO WORLD PEACE, THE VIX FAMILY WAS GRANTED HIGH STATUS AND A RIGHT TO RULE IN HUMANITY'S NEW HOME.
THAT WAS THE BEGINNING OF THE IMPERIAL DISTRICT OF VIXIA.
OKAY.
I GET THAT MUCH. BUT WHAT ABOUT THE WORMHOLE **YOU** HAD?
EVEN THOUGH THEY REPORTED THAT ALL THE WORMHOLES HAD BEEN DESTROYED, THE VIX FAMILY SECRETLY KEPT ONE GATE OPEN.
I SUSPECT THEY ASSUMED THAT, IF THEY HAD ONE WORKING GATE, THEY COULD SOMEDAY RESUME THEIR RESEARCH AND POTENTIALLY TAKE OVER THE WORLD.
AGAIN, THE IMPERIAL DISTRICT BEING CLOSED OFF IS WHAT LET THEM KEEP THIS HIDDEN FOR SO LONG.

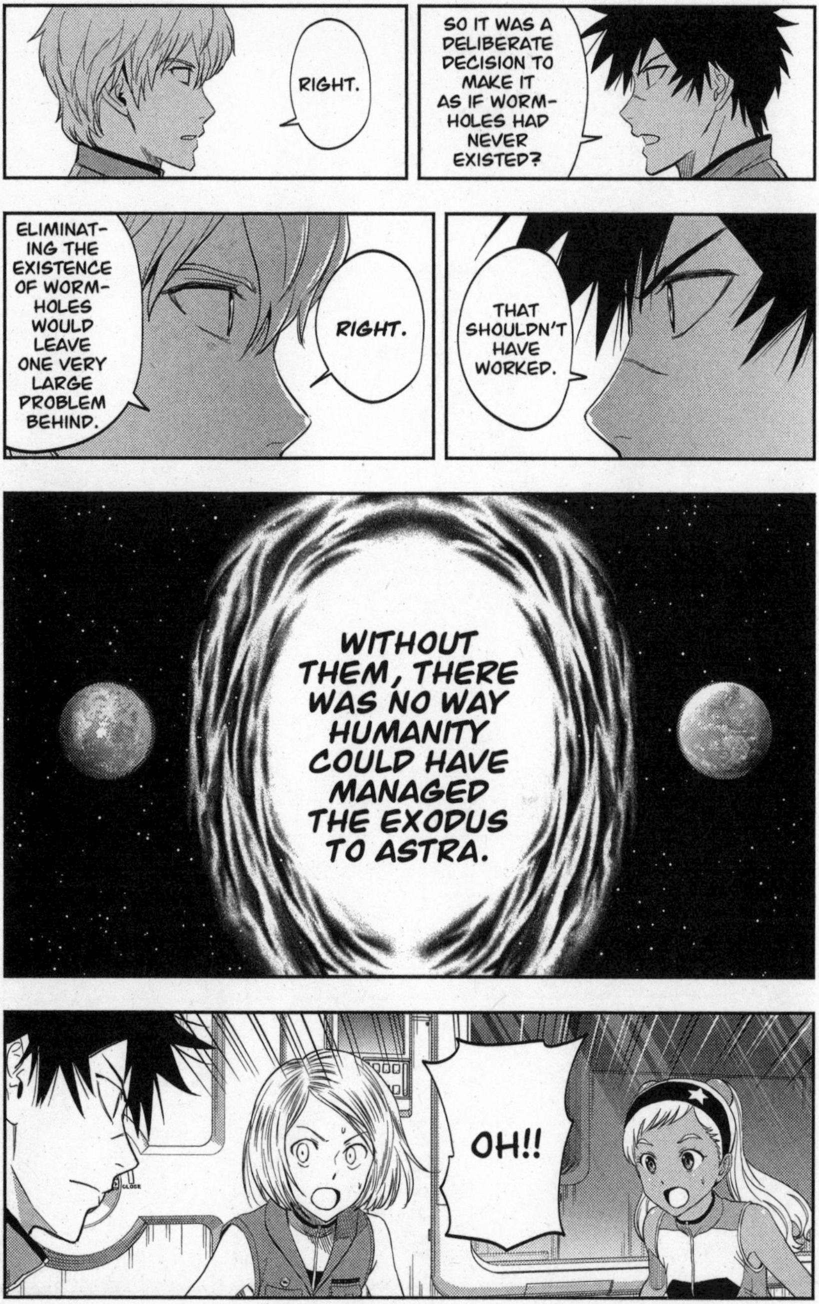
SO IT WAS A DELIBERATE DECISION TO MAKE IT AS IF WORMHOLES HAD NEVER EXISTED?
RIGHT.
THAT SHOULDN'T HAVE WORKED.
RIGHT.
ELIMINATING THE EXISTENCE OF WORMHOLES WOULD LEAVE ONE VERY LARGE PROBLEM BEHIND.
WITHOUT THEM, THERE WAS NO WAY HUMANITY COULD HAVE MANAGED THE EXODUS TO ASTRA.
OH!!

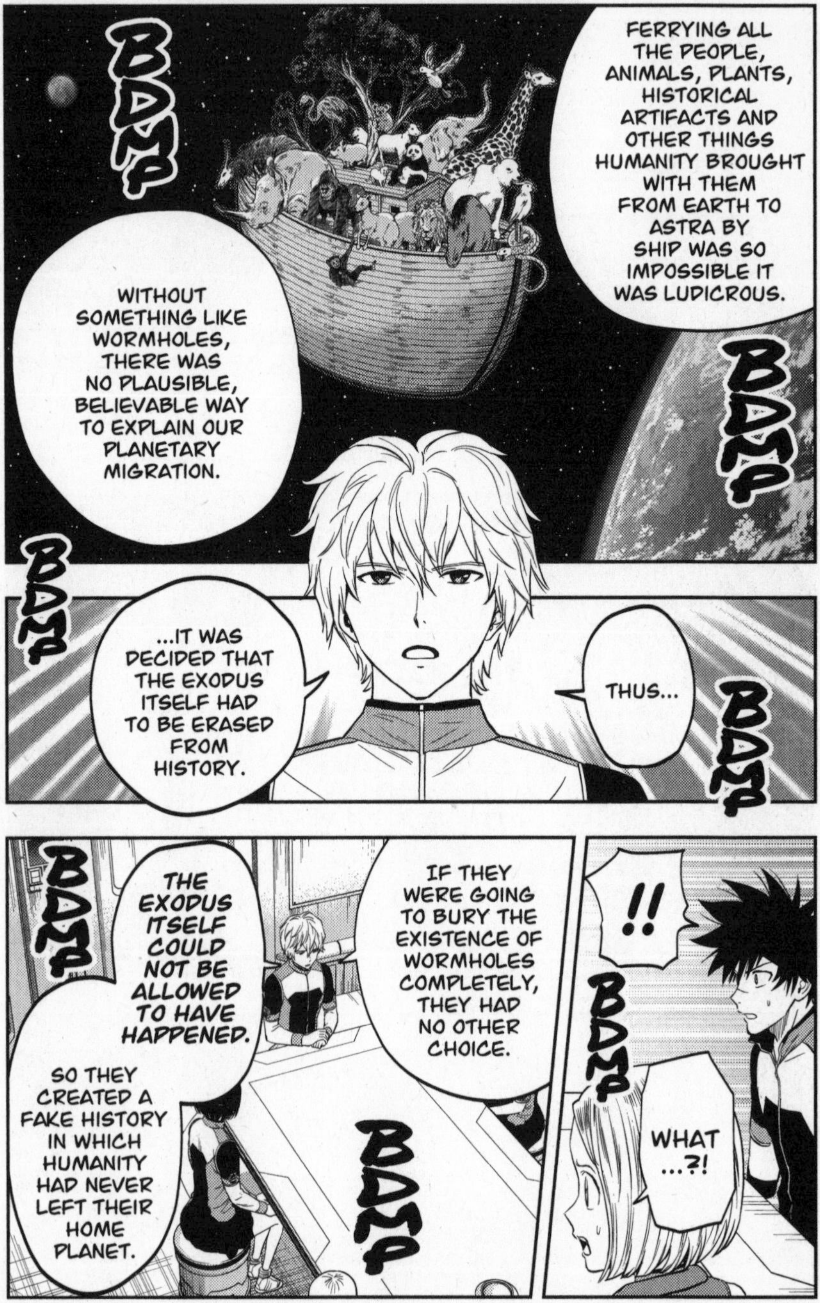

FERRYING ALL THE PEOPLE, ANIMALS, PLANTS, HISTORICAL ARTIFACTS AND OTHER THINGS HUMANITY BROUGHT WITH THEM FROM EARTH TO ASTRA BY SHIP WAS SO IMPOSSIBLE IT WAS LUDICROUS.
BDMP
BDMP
WITHOUT SOMETHING LIKE WORMHOLES, THERE WAS NO PLAUSIBLE, BELIEVABLE WAY TO EXPLAIN OUR PLANETARY MIGRATION.
BDMP
BDMP
THUS...
...IT WAS DECIDED THAT THE EXODUS ITSELF HAD TO BE ERASED FROM HISTORY.
!!
BDMP
WHAT ...?!
IF THEY WERE GOING TO BURY THE EXISTENCE OF WORMHOLES COMPLETELY, THEY HAD NO OTHER CHOICE.
BDMP
THE EXODUS ITSELF COULD NOT BE ALLOWED TO HAVE HAPPENED.
SO THEY CREATED A FAKE HISTORY IN WHICH HUMANITY HAD NEVER LEFT THEIR HOME PLANET.
BDMP

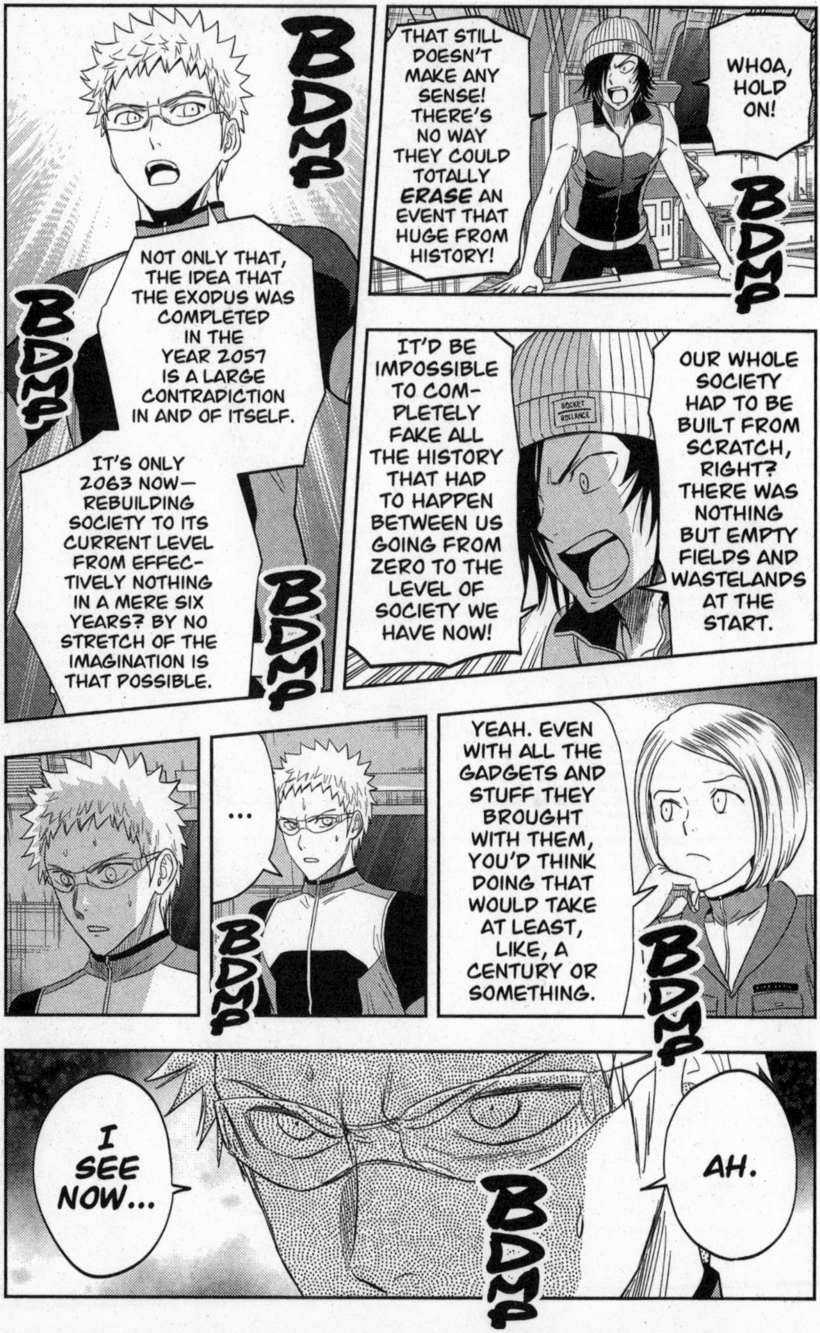
WHOA, HOLD ON!
THAT STILL DOESN'T MAKE ANY SENSE! THERE'S NO WAY THEY COULD TOTALLY ERASE AN EVENT THAT HUGE FROM HISTORY!
BDMP
OUR WHOLE SOCIETY HAD TO BE BUILT FROM SCRATCH, RIGHT? THERE WAS NOTHING BUT EMPTY FIELDS AND WASTELANDS AT THE START.
IT'D BE IMPOSSIBLE TO COM-PLETELY FAKE ALL THE HISTORY THAT HAD TO HAPPEN BETWEEN US GOING FROM ZERO TO THE LEVEL OF SOCIETY WE HAVE NOW!
BDMP
NOT ONLY THAT, THE IDEA THAT THE EXODUS WAS COMPLETED IN THE YEAR 2057 IS A LARGE CONTRADICTION IN AND OF ITSELF.
BDMP
IT'S ONLY 2063 NOW—REBUILDING SOCIETY TO ITS CURRENT LEVEL FROM EFFEC-TIVELY NOTHING IN A MERE SIX YEARS? BY NO STRETCH OF THE IMAGINATION IS THAT POSSIBLE.
BDMP
YEAH. EVEN WITH ALL THE GADGETS AND STUFF THEY BROUGHT WITH THEM, YOU'D THINK DOING THAT WOULD TAKE AT LEAST, LIKE, A CENTURY OR SOMETHING.
BDMP
...
BDMP
AH.
BDMP
I SEE NOW...

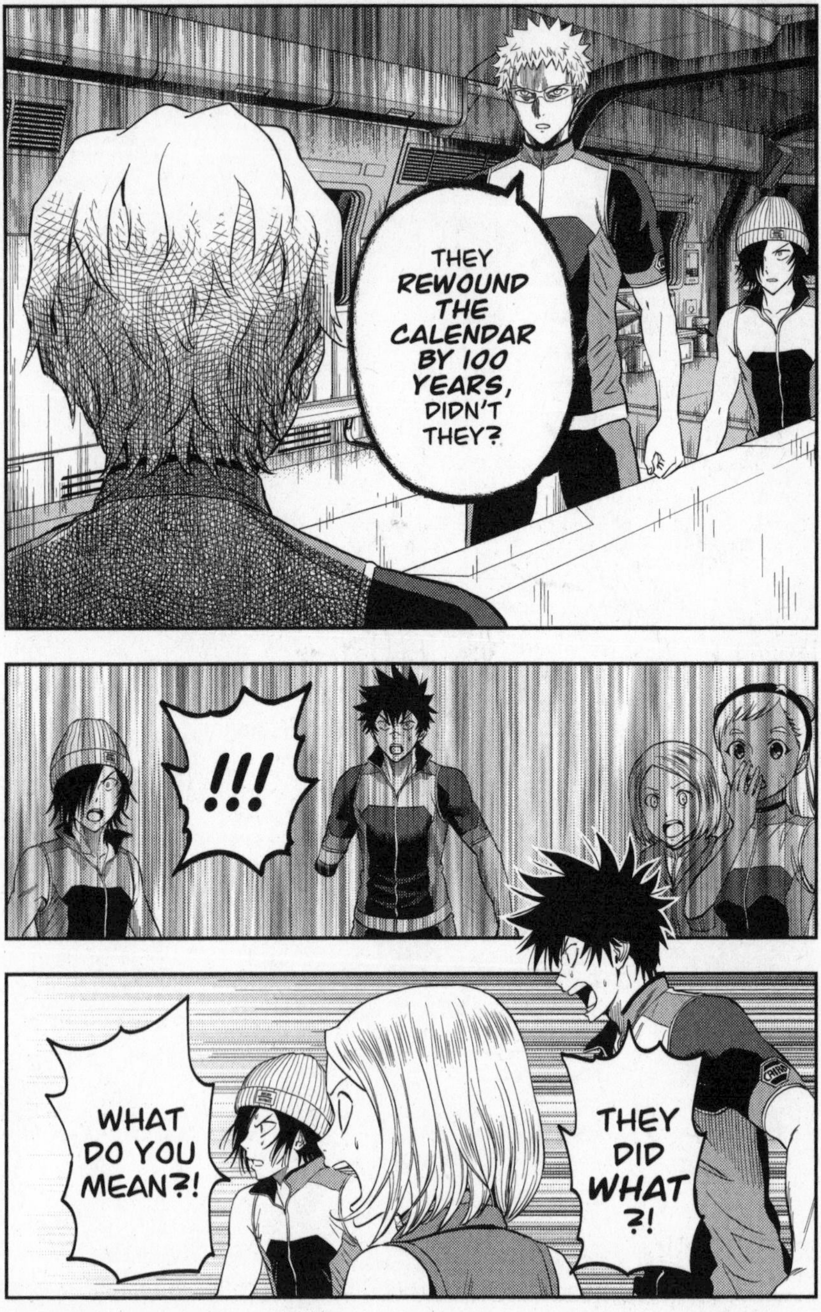
THEY REWOUND THE CALENDAR BY 100 YEARS, DIDN'T THEY?
!!!
THEY DID WHAT?!
WHAT DO YOU MEAN?!

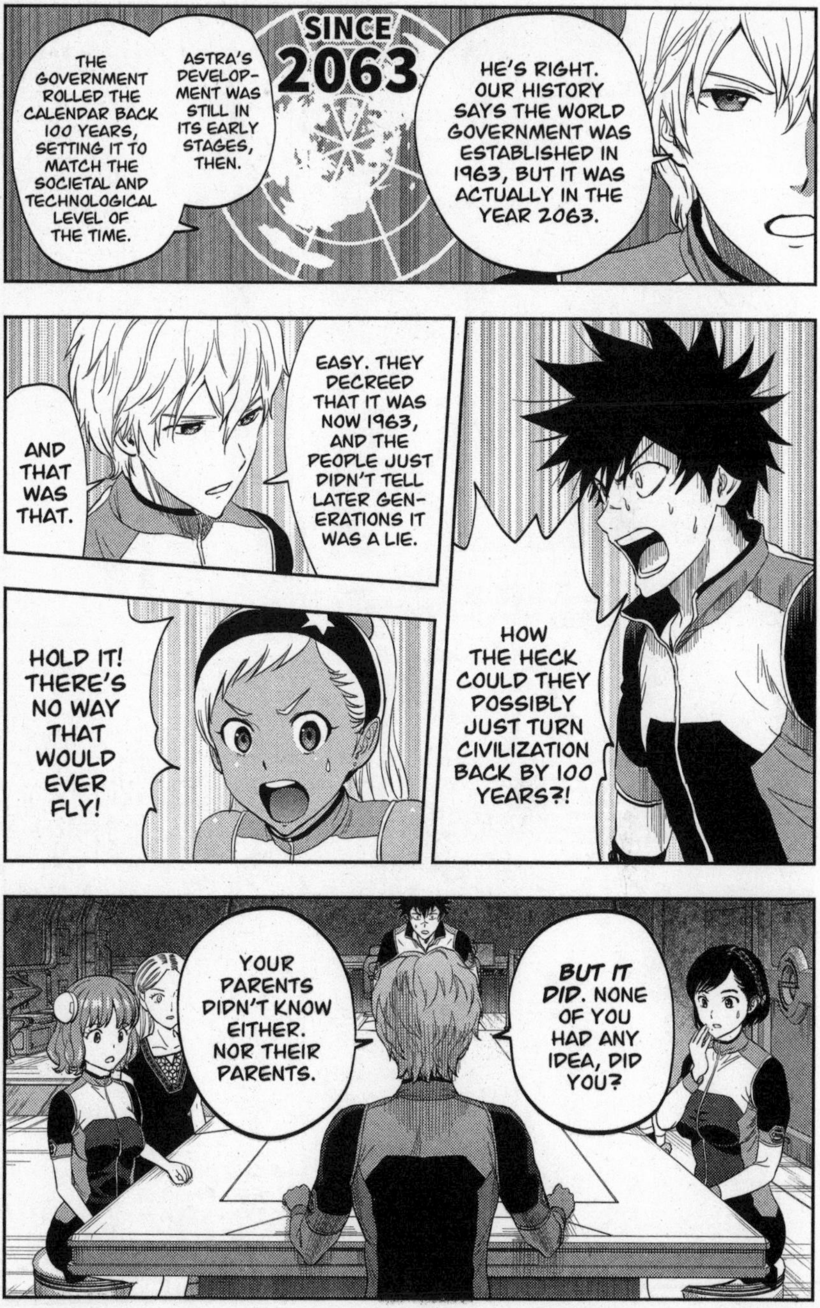
HE'S RIGHT. OUR HISTORY SAYS THE WORLD GOVERNMENT WAS ESTABLISHED IN 1963, BUT IT WAS ACTUALLY IN THE YEAR 2063.
SINCE 2063
ASTRA'S DEVELOP-MENT WAS STILL IN ITS EARLY STAGES, THEN.
THE GOVERNMENT ROLLED THE CALENDAR BACK 100 YEARS, SETTING IT TO MATCH THE SOCIETAL AND TECHNOLOGICAL LEVEL OF THE TIME.
HOW THE HECK COULD THEY POSSIBLY JUST TURN CIVILIZATION BACK BY 100 YEARS?!
EASY. THEY DECREED THAT IT WAS NOW 1963, AND THE PEOPLE JUST DIDN'T TELL LATER GEN-ERATIONS IT WAS A LIE.
AND THAT WAS THAT.
HOLD IT! THERE'S NO WAY THAT WOULD EVER FLY!
BUT IT DID. NONE OF YOU HAD ANY IDEA, DID YOU?
YOUR PARENTS DIDN'T KNOW EITHER. NOR THEIR PARENTS.

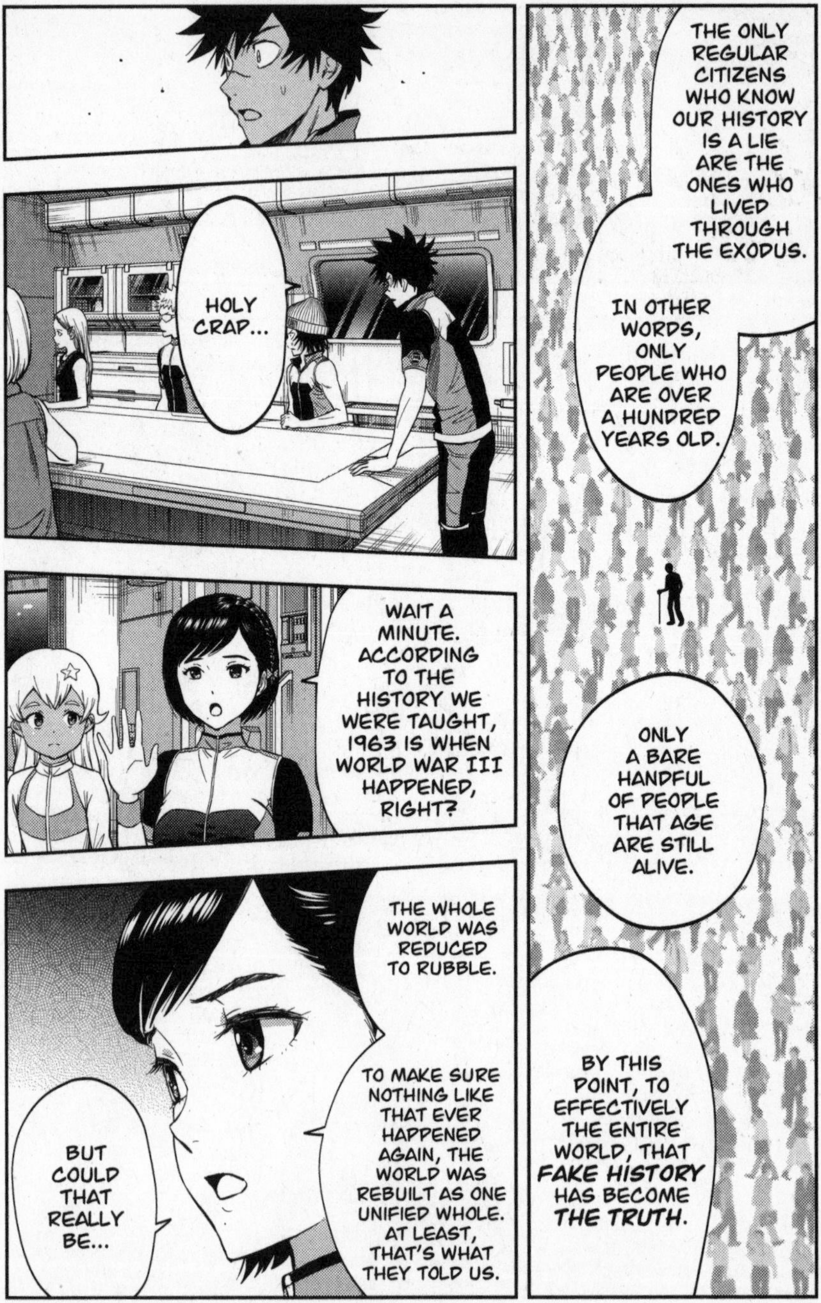
THE ONLY REGULAR CITIZENS WHO KNOW OUR HISTORY IS A LIE ARE THE ONES WHO LIVED THROUGH THE EXODUS.
IN OTHER WORDS, ONLY PEOPLE WHO ARE OVER A HUNDRED YEARS OLD.
ONLY A BARE HANDFUL OF PEOPLE THAT AGE ARE STILL ALIVE.
BY THIS POINT, TO EFFECTIVELY THE ENTIRE WORLD, THAT ***FAKE HISTORY*** HAS BECOME ***THE TRUTH***.
...
HOLY CRAP...
WAIT A MINUTE. ACCORDING TO THE HISTORY WE WERE TAUGHT, 1963 IS WHEN WORLD WAR III HAPPENED, RIGHT?
THE WHOLE WORLD WAS REDUCED TO RUBBLE.
TO MAKE SURE NOTHING LIKE THAT EVER HAPPENED AGAIN, THE WORLD WAS REBUILT AS ONE UNIFIED WHOLE. AT LEAST, THAT'S WHAT THEY TOLD US.
BUT COULD THAT REALLY BE...

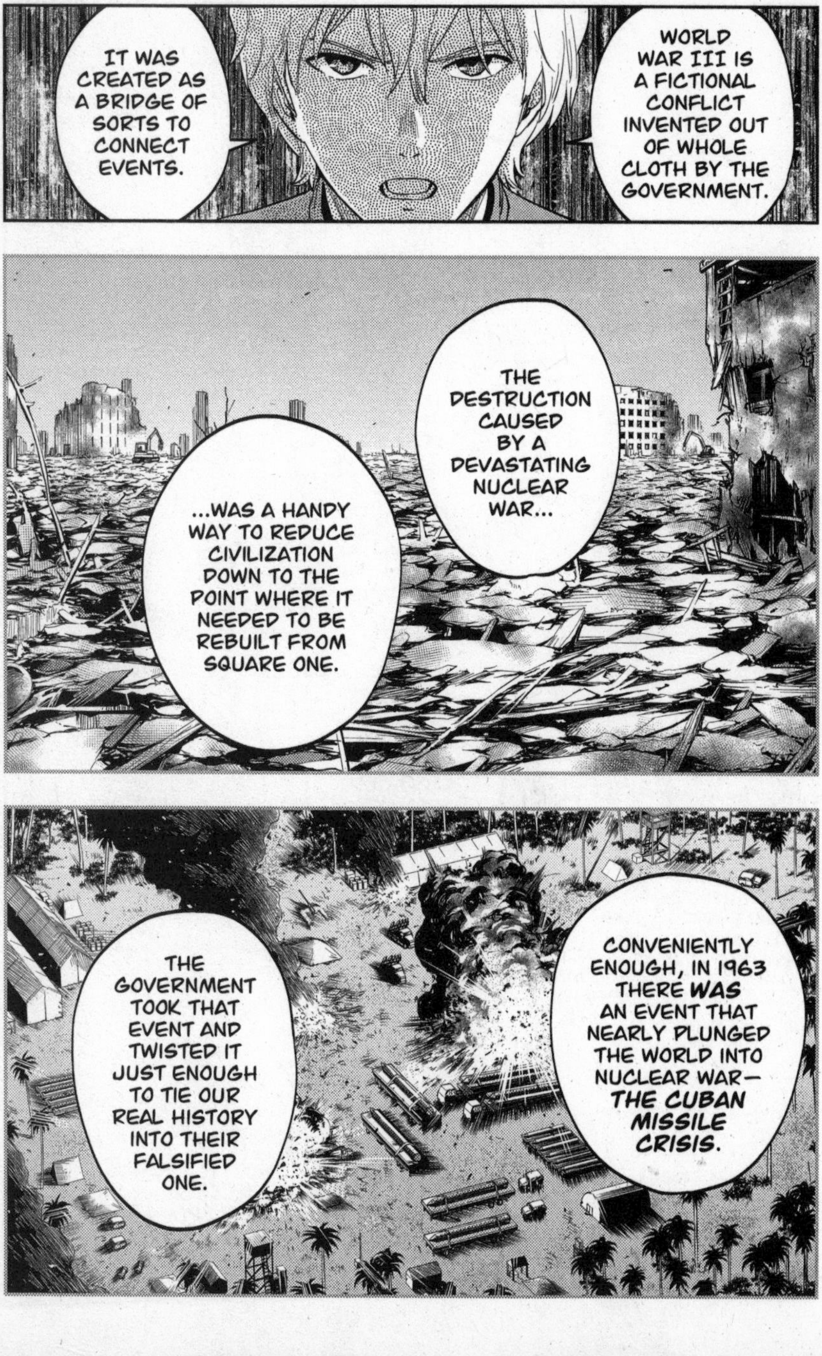
WORLD WAR III IS A FICTIONAL CONFLICT INVENTED OUT OF WHOLE CLOTH BY THE GOVERNMENT.
IT WAS CREATED AS A BRIDGE OF SORTS TO CONNECT EVENTS.
THE DESTRUCTION CAUSED BY A DEVASTATING NUCLEAR WAR...
...WAS A HANDY WAY TO REDUCE CIVILIZATION DOWN TO THE POINT WHERE IT NEEDED TO BE REBUILT FROM SQUARE ONE.
CONVENIENTLY ENOUGH, IN 1963 THERE WAS AN EVENT THAT NEARLY PLUNGED THE WORLD INTO NUCLEAR WAR—THE CUBAN MISSILE CRISIS.
THE GOVERNMENT TOOK THAT EVENT AND TWISTED IT JUST ENOUGH TO TIE OUR REAL HISTORY INTO THEIR FALSIFIED ONE.

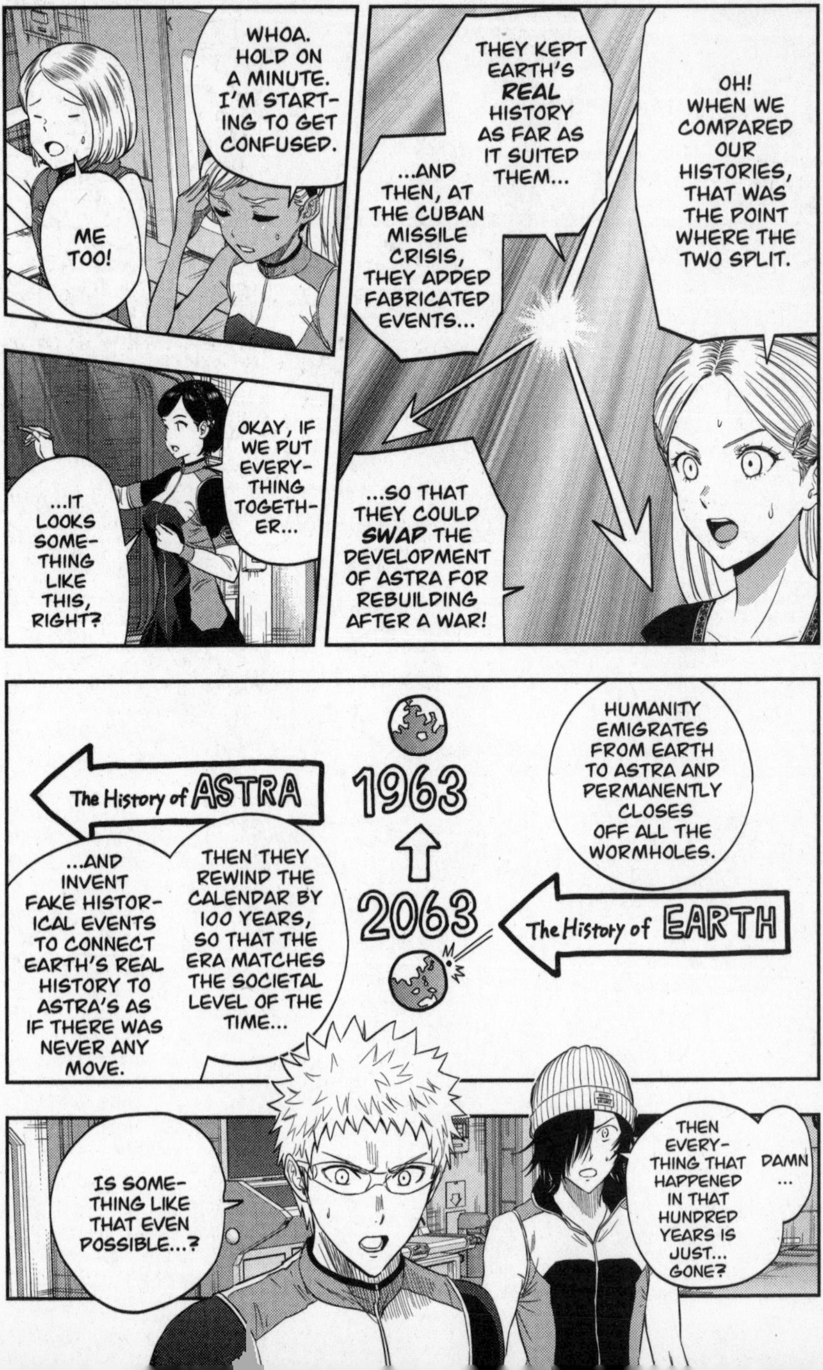
OH! WHEN WE COMPARED OUR HISTORIES, THAT WAS THE POINT WHERE THE TWO SPLIT.
THEY KEPT EARTH'S REAL HISTORY AS FAR AS IT SUITED THEM...
...AND THEN, AT THE CUBAN MISSILE CRISIS, THEY ADDED FABRICATED EVENTS...
...SO THAT THEY COULD SWAP THE DEVELOPMENT OF ASTRA FOR REBUILDING AFTER A WAR!
WHOA. HOLD ON A MINUTE. I'M STARTING TO GET CONFUSED.
ME TOO!
OKAY, IF WE PUT EVERYTHING TOGETHER...
...IT LOOKS SOMETHING LIKE THIS, RIGHT?
HUMANITY EMIGRATES FROM EARTH TO ASTRA AND PERMANENTLY CLOSES OFF ALL THE WORMHOLES.
1963
The History of ASTRA
2063
The History of EARTH
THEN THEY REWIND THE CALENDAR BY 100 YEARS, SO THAT THE ERA MATCHES THE SOCIETAL LEVEL OF THE TIME...
...AND INVENT FAKE HISTORICAL EVENTS TO CONNECT EARTH'S REAL HISTORY TO ASTRA'S AS IF THERE WAS NEVER ANY MOVE.
DAMN...
THEN EVERYTHING THAT HAPPENED IN THAT HUNDRED YEARS IS JUST... GONE?
IS SOMETHING LIKE THAT EVEN POSSIBLE...?

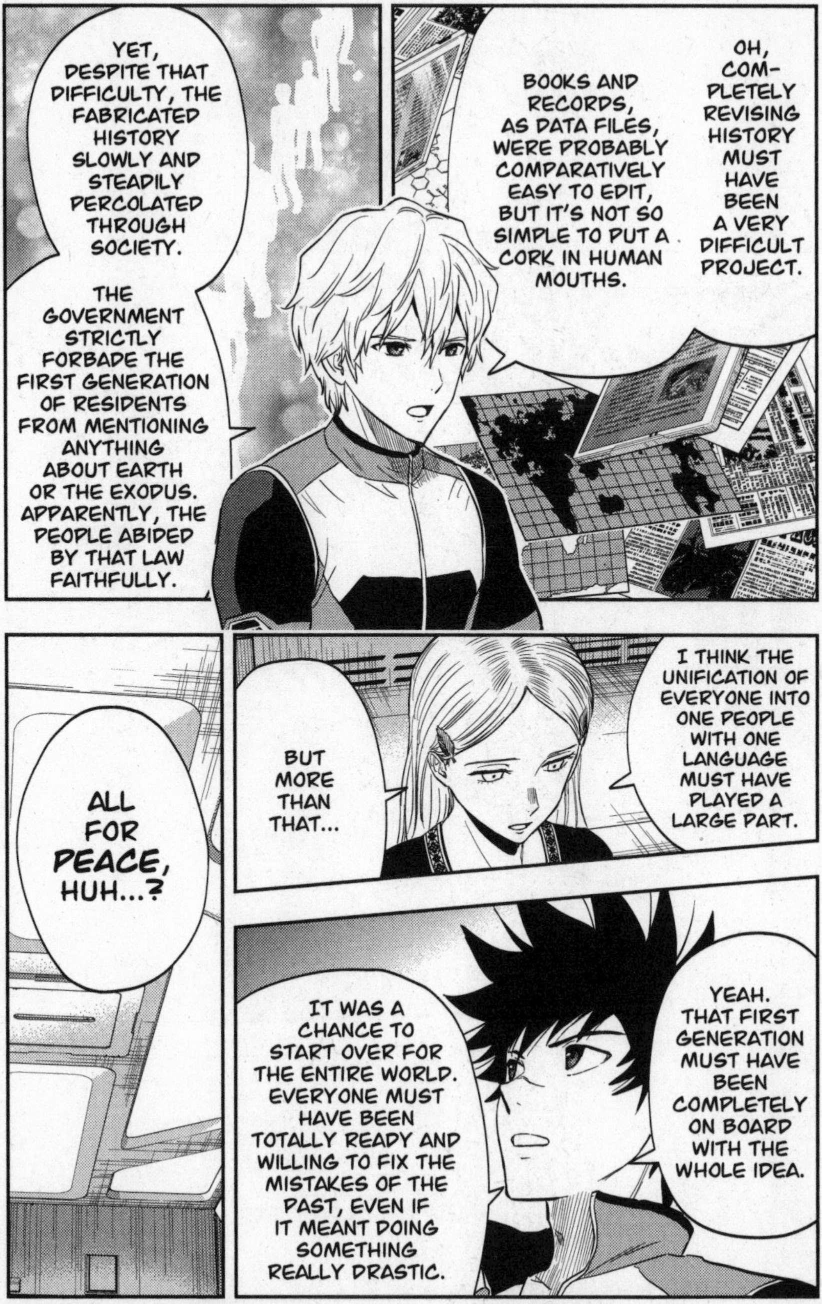
OH, COM- PLETELY REVISING HISTORY MUST HAVE BEEN A VERY DIFFICULT PROJECT.
BOOKS AND RECORDS, AS DATA FILES, WERE PROBABLY COMPARATIVELY EASY TO EDIT, BUT IT'S NOT SO SIMPLE TO PUT A CORK IN HUMAN MOUTHS.
YET, DESPITE THAT DIFFICULTY, THE FABRICATED HISTORY SLOWLY AND STEADILY PERCOLATED THROUGH SOCIETY.
THE GOVERNMENT STRICTLY FORBADE THE FIRST GENERATION OF RESIDENTS FROM MENTIONING ANYTHING ABOUT EARTH OR THE EXODUS. APPARENTLY, THE PEOPLE ABIDED BY THAT LAW FAITHFULLY.
I THINK THE UNIFICATION OF EVERYONE INTO ONE PEOPLE WITH ONE LANGUAGE MUST HAVE PLAYED A LARGE PART.
BUT MORE THAN THAT...
YEAH. THAT FIRST GENERATION MUST HAVE BEEN COMPLETELY ON BOARD WITH THE WHOLE IDEA.
IT WAS A CHANCE TO START OVER FOR THE ENTIRE WORLD. EVERYONE MUST HAVE BEEN TOTALLY READY AND WILLING TO FIX THE MISTAKES OF THE PAST, EVEN IF IT MEANT DOING SOMETHING REALLY DRASTIC.
ALL FOR PEACE, HUH...?

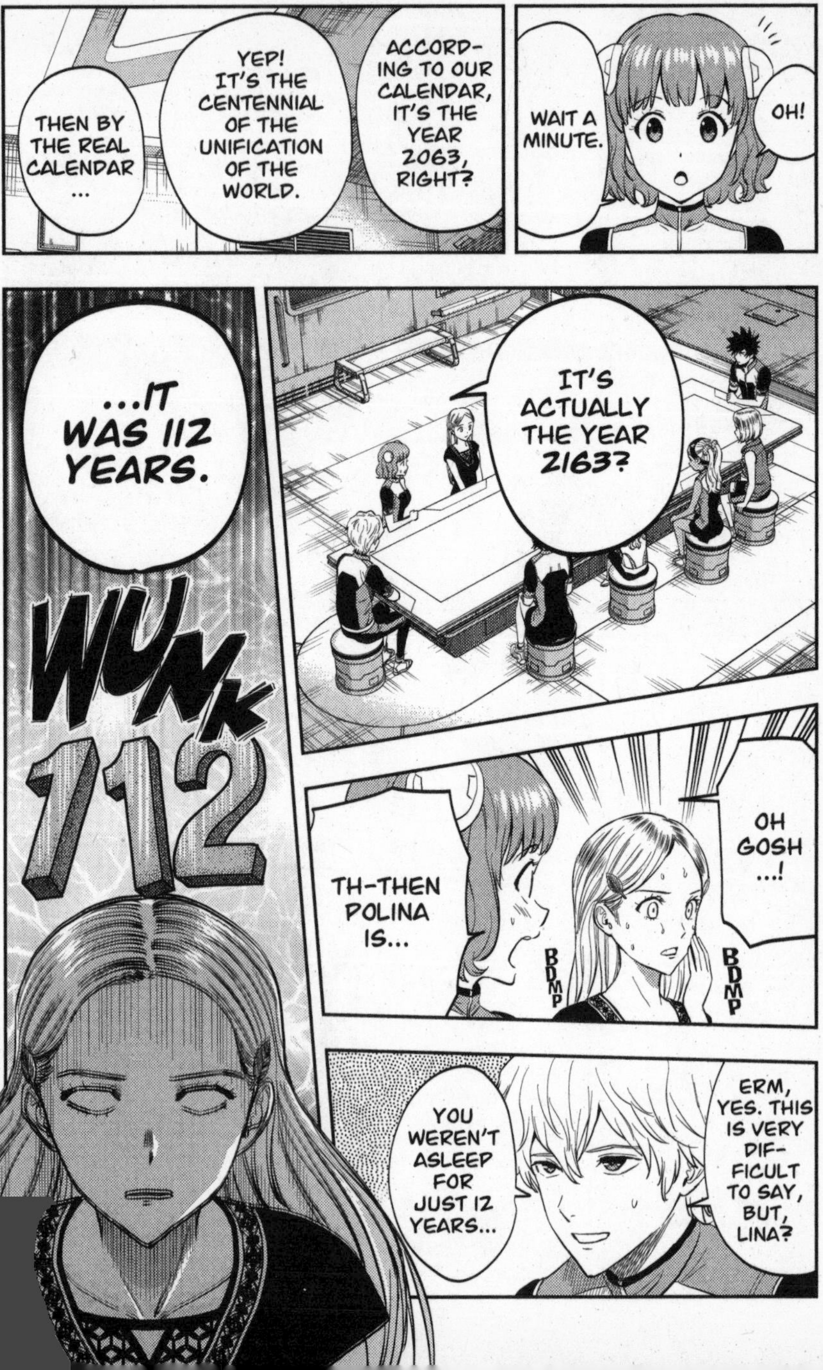
OH!
WAIT A MINUTE.
ACCORD-ING TO OUR CALENDAR, IT'S THE YEAR 2063, RIGHT?
YEP! IT'S THE CENTENNIAL OF THE UNIFICATION OF THE WORLD.
THEN BY THE REAL CALENDAR ...
IT'S ACTUALLY THE YEAR 2163?
OH GOSH ...!
TH-THEN POLINA IS...
BDMP
BDMP
ERM, YES. THIS IS VERY DIF-FICULT TO SAY, BUT, LINA?
YOU WEREN'T ASLEEP FOR JUST 12 YEARS...
...IT WAS 112 YEARS.
WUNK
112

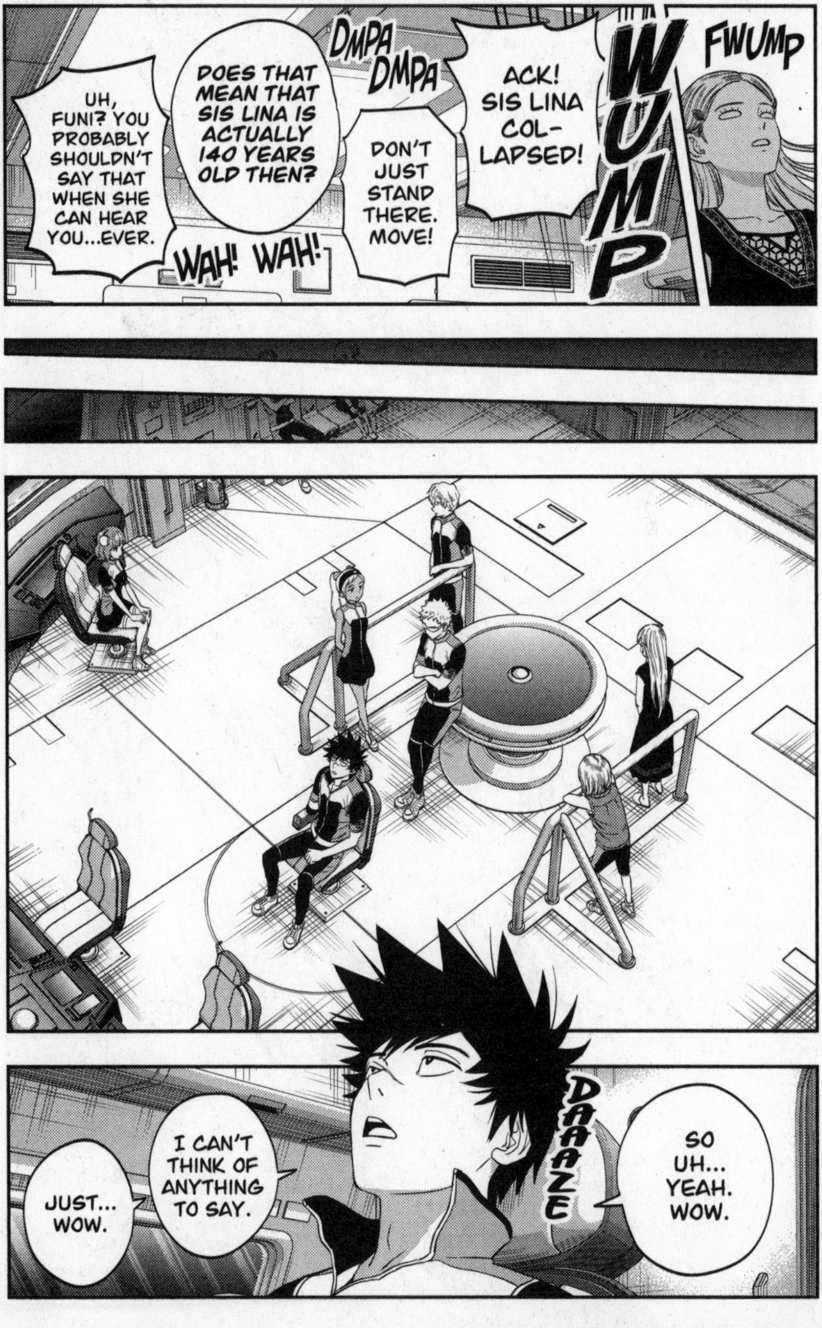
FWUMP
WUMP
ACK! SIS LINA COL-LAPSED!
DON'T JUST STAND THERE. MOVE!
DMPA DMPA
DOES THAT MEAN THAT SIS LINA IS ACTUALLY 140 YEARS OLD THEN?
WAH! WAH!
UH, FUNI? YOU PROBABLY SHOULDN'T SAY THAT WHEN SHE CAN HEAR YOU...EVER.
DAAAAZE
SO UH... YEAH. WOW.
I CAN'T THINK OF ANYTHING TO SAY.
JUST... WOW.

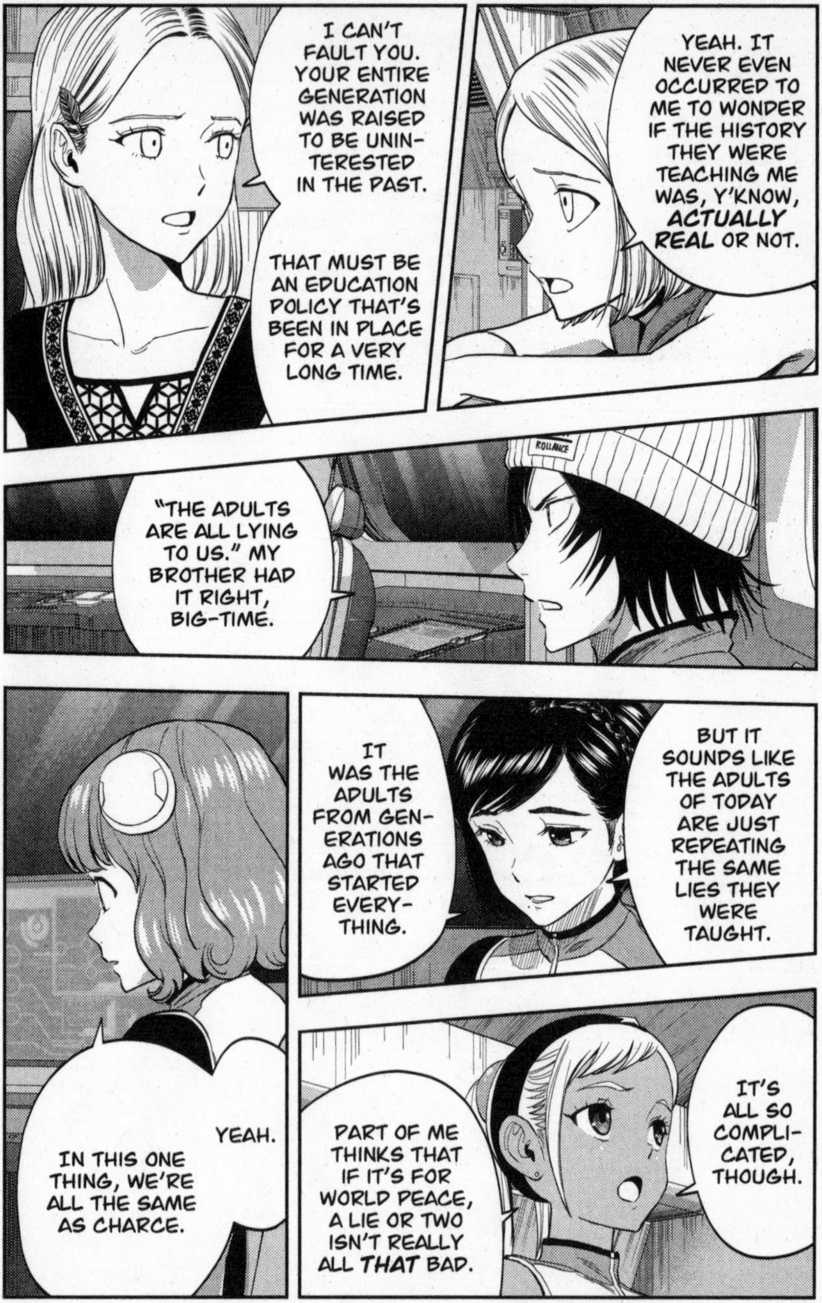
YEAH. IT NEVER EVEN OCCURRED TO ME TO WONDER IF THE HISTORY THEY WERE TEACHING ME WAS, Y'KNOW, **ACTUALLY REAL** OR NOT.
I CAN'T FAULT YOU. YOUR ENTIRE GENERATION WAS RAISED TO BE UNIN-TERESTED IN THE PAST.
THAT MUST BE AN EDUCATION POLICY THAT'S BEEN IN PLACE FOR A VERY LONG TIME.
ROLLANCE
"THE ADULTS ARE ALL LYING TO US." MY BROTHER HAD IT RIGHT, BIG-TIME.
IT WAS THE ADULTS FROM GEN-ERATIONS AGO THAT STARTED EVERY-THING.
BUT IT SOUNDS LIKE THE ADULTS OF TODAY ARE JUST REPEATING THE SAME LIES THEY WERE TAUGHT.
IT'S ALL SO COMPLI-CATED, THOUGH.
PART OF ME THINKS THAT IF IT'S FOR WORLD PEACE, A LIE OR TWO ISN'T REALLY ALL *THAT* BAD.
YEAH.
IN THIS ONE THING, WE'RE ALL THE SAME AS CHARCE.

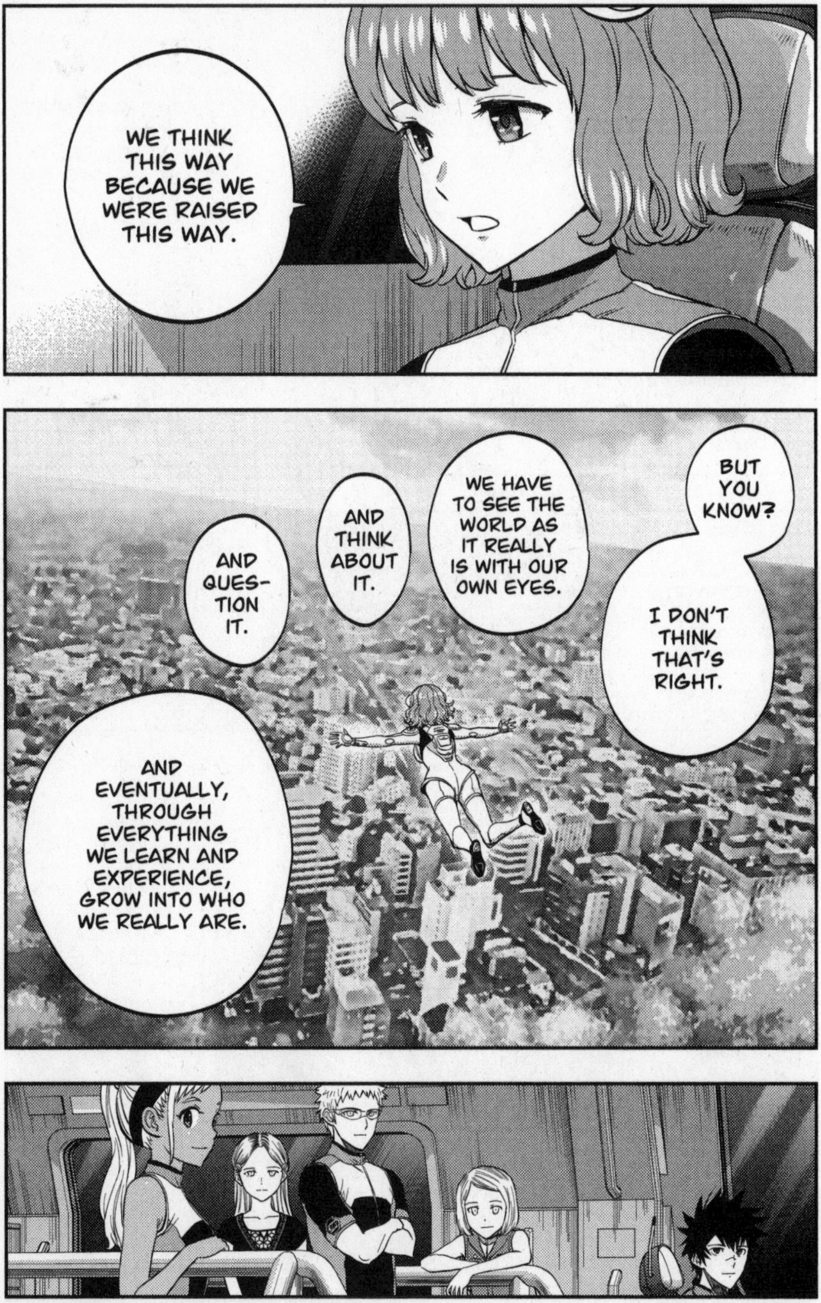
WE THINK THIS WAY BECAUSE WE WERE RAISED THIS WAY.
BUT YOU KNOW?
I DON'T THINK THAT'S RIGHT.
WE HAVE TO SEE THE WORLD AS IT REALLY IS WITH OUR OWN EYES.
AND THINK ABOUT IT.
AND QUES-TION IT.
AND EVENTUALLY, THROUGH EVERYTHING WE LEARN AND EXPERIENCE, GROW INTO WHO WE REALLY ARE.

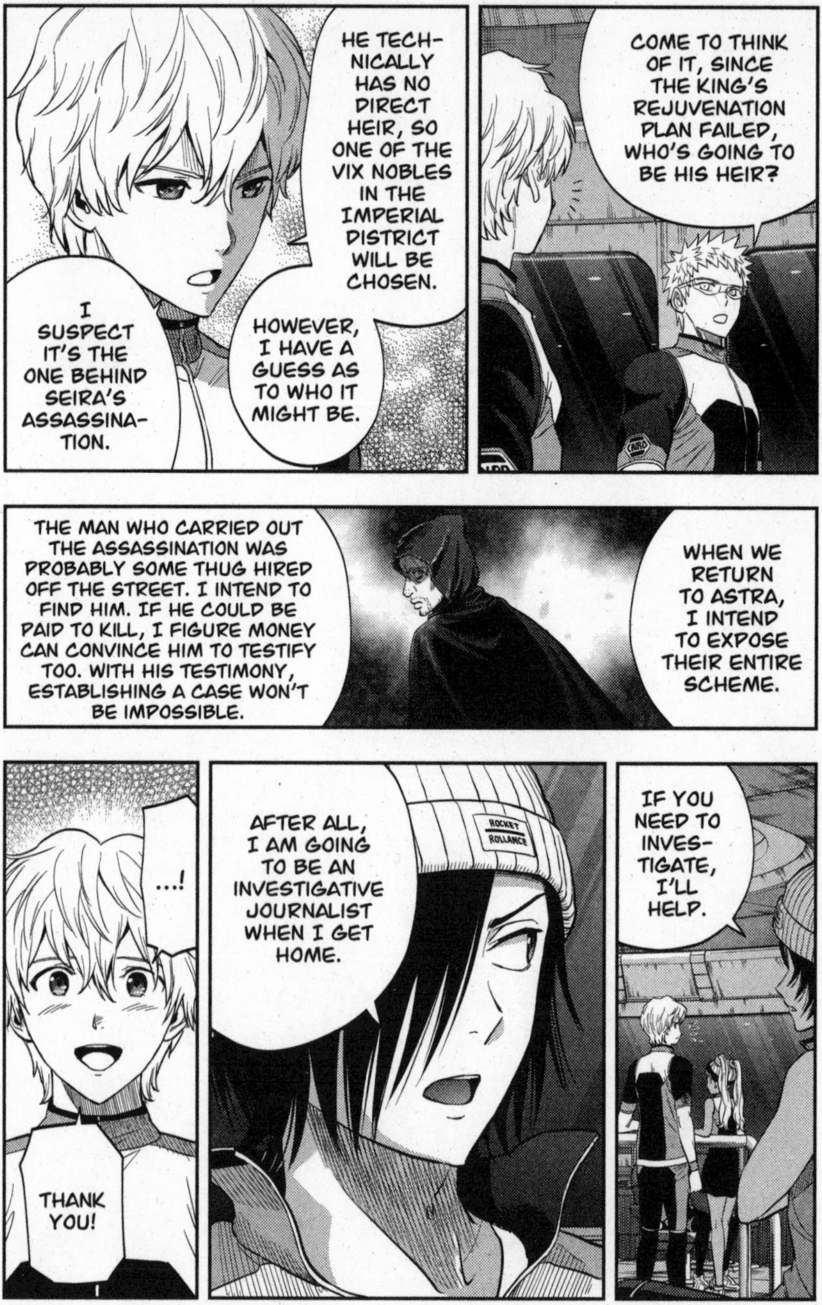
COME TO THINK OF IT, SINCE THE KING'S REJUVENATION PLAN FAILED, WHO'S GOING TO BE HIS HEIR?
HE TECHNICALLY HAS NO DIRECT HEIR, SO ONE OF THE VIX NOBLES IN THE IMPERIAL DISTRICT WILL BE CHOSEN.
HOWEVER, I HAVE A GUESS AS TO WHO IT MIGHT BE.
I SUSPECT IT'S THE ONE BEHIND SEIRA'S ASSASSINATION.
WHEN WE RETURN TO ASTRA, I INTEND TO EXPOSE THEIR ENTIRE SCHEME.
THE MAN WHO CARRIED OUT THE ASSASSINATION WAS PROBABLY SOME THUG HIRED OFF THE STREET. I INTEND TO FIND HIM. IF HE COULD BE PAID TO KILL, I FIGURE MONEY CAN CONVINCE HIM TO TESTIFY TOO. WITH HIS TESTIMONY, ESTABLISHING A CASE WON'T BE IMPOSSIBLE.
IF YOU NEED TO INVESTIGATE, I'LL HELP.
ROCKET ROLLANCE
AFTER ALL, I AM GOING TO BE AN INVESTIGATIVE JOURNALIST WHEN I GET HOME.
...!
THANK YOU!

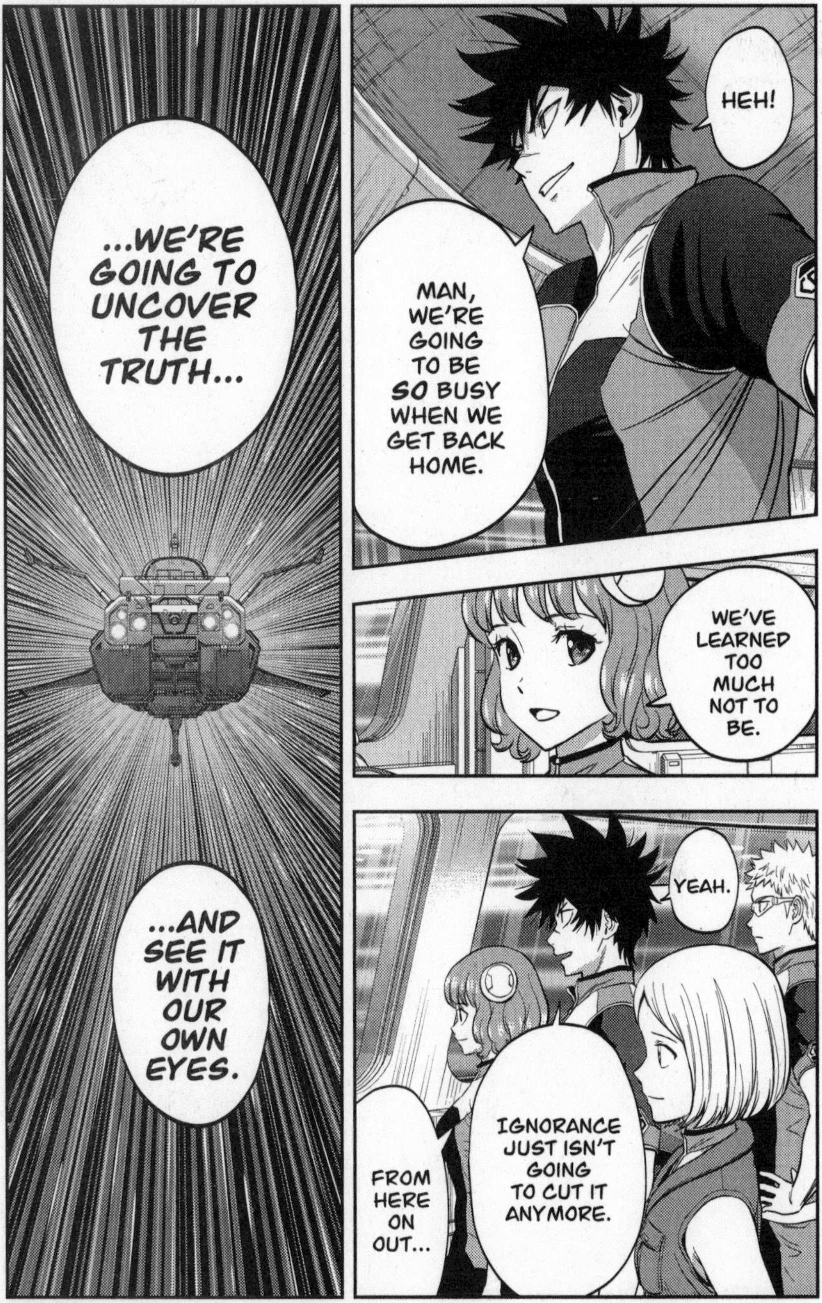
HEH!
MAN, WE'RE GOING TO BE SO BUSY WHEN WE GET BACK HOME.
WE'VE LEARNED TOO MUCH NOT TO BE.
YEAH.
IGNORANCE JUST ISN'T GOING TO CUT IT ANYMORE.
FROM HERE ON OUT...
...WE'RE GOING TO UNCOVER THE TRUTH...
...AND SEE IT WITH OUR OWN EYES.

TIME LINE

YEAR	EVENTS
2032	The mystery of gravity is solved / Technological revolution (materials creation time greatly reduced)
2045	Faster-than-light drives approved for practical use / Artificial wormhole invented
2049	Asteroid on collision course with Earth discovered / Exodus plan conceived / Unmanned exploration satellites launched to search for habitable worlds
2051	Ark Series planetary exploration spaceships completed / Manned exploration missions begin
	May – Polina and the *Ark VI* depart / Crash landing on Icriss
	July – Polina enters cryostasis
	August – Planet Astra discovered / Advance landing team departs
2052	Artificial wormhole gates set / Advance team begins construction of infrastructure / Exodus plan announced
	October – War breaks out (the Two-Month War) / Concludes by year-end
2053	Exodus begins
	(Exodus continues for 4 years)
2057	Exodus completed / Asteroid impacts Earth
	Astra development begins using wormholes (lasts 6 years)
1963←2063	Inauguration of the World Government
	Calendar rewound by 100 years / False history created
2016 (2116)	Founding of Caird High School
2063 (2163)	Centennial of the World Government / Group B-5 leaves for planet camp / Story begins

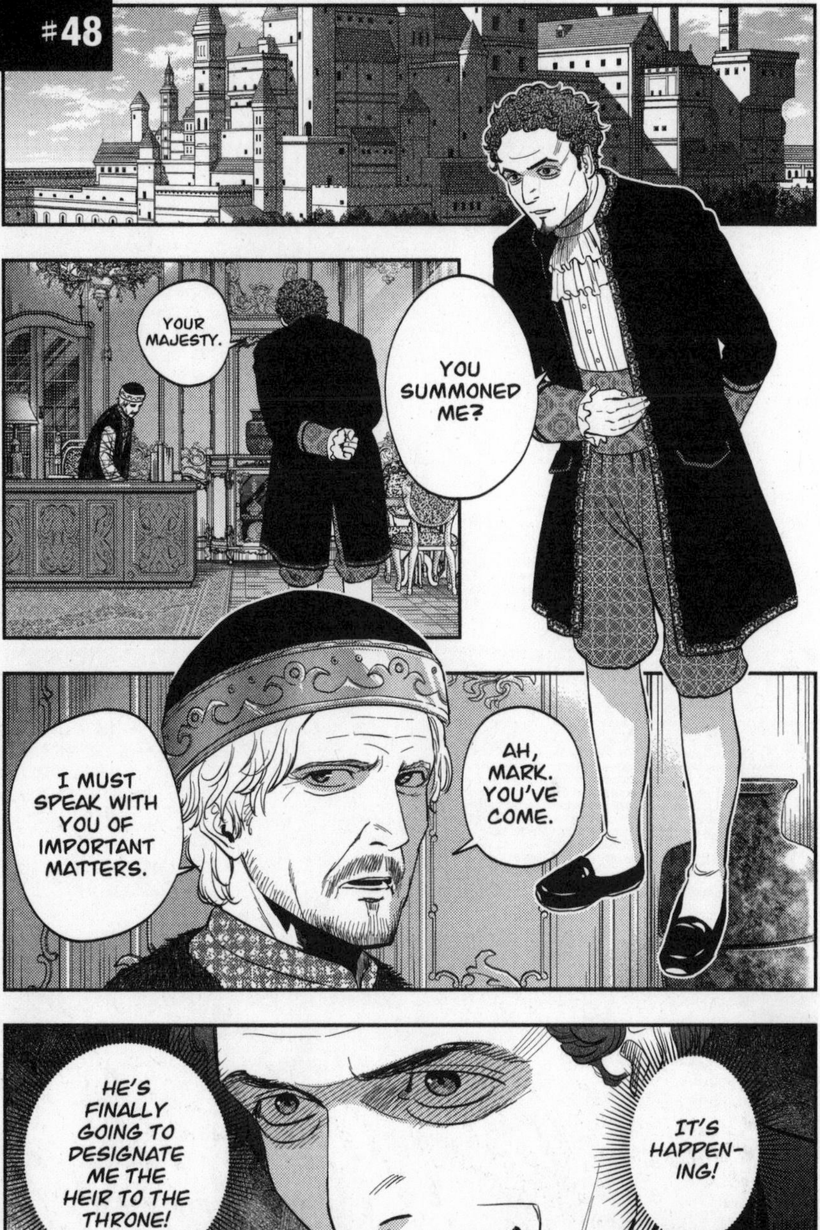
YOU SUMMONED ME?
YOUR MAJESTY.
AH, MARK. YOU'VE COME.
I MUST SPEAK WITH YOU OF IMPORTANT MATTERS.
IT'S HAPPENING!
HE'S FINALLY GOING TO DESIGNATE ME THE HEIR TO THE THRONE!

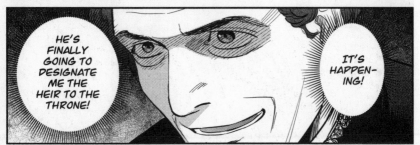

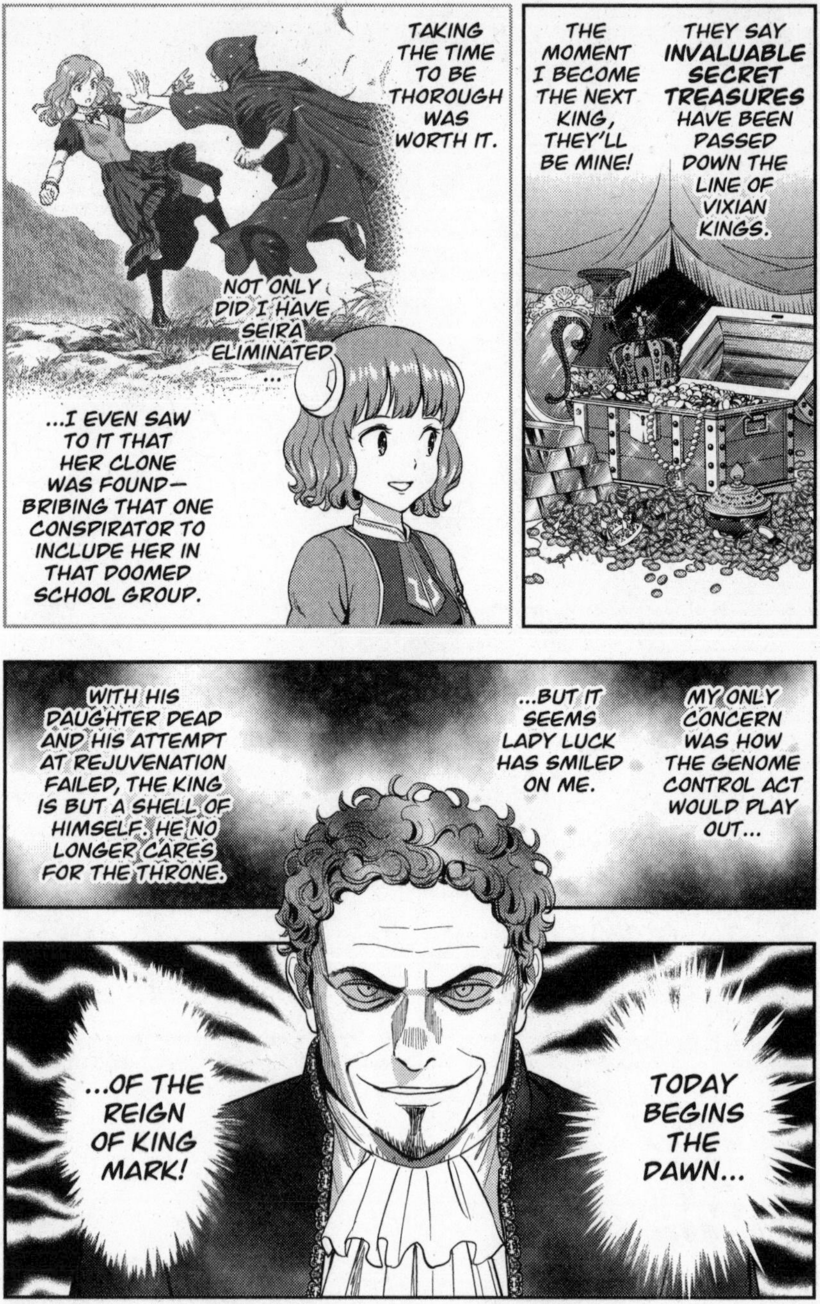
THEY SAY INVALUABLE SECRET TREASURES HAVE BEEN PASSED DOWN THE LINE OF VIXIAN KINGS.
THE MOMENT I BECOME THE NEXT KING, THEY'LL BE MINE!
TAKING THE TIME TO BE THOROUGH WAS WORTH IT.
NOT ONLY DID I HAVE SEIRA ELIMINATED...
...I EVEN SAW TO IT THAT HER CLONE WAS FOUND—BRIBING THAT ONE CONSPIRATOR TO INCLUDE HER IN THAT DOOMED SCHOOL GROUP.
MY ONLY CONCERN WAS HOW THE GENOME CONTROL ACT WOULD PLAY OUT...
...BUT IT SEEMS LADY LUCK HAS SMILED ON ME.
WITH HIS DAUGHTER DEAD AND HIS ATTEMPT AT REJUVENATION FAILED, THE KING IS BUT A SHELL OF HIMSELF. HE NO LONGER CARES FOR THE THRONE.
TODAY BEGINS THE DAWN...
...OF THE REIGN OF KING MARK!

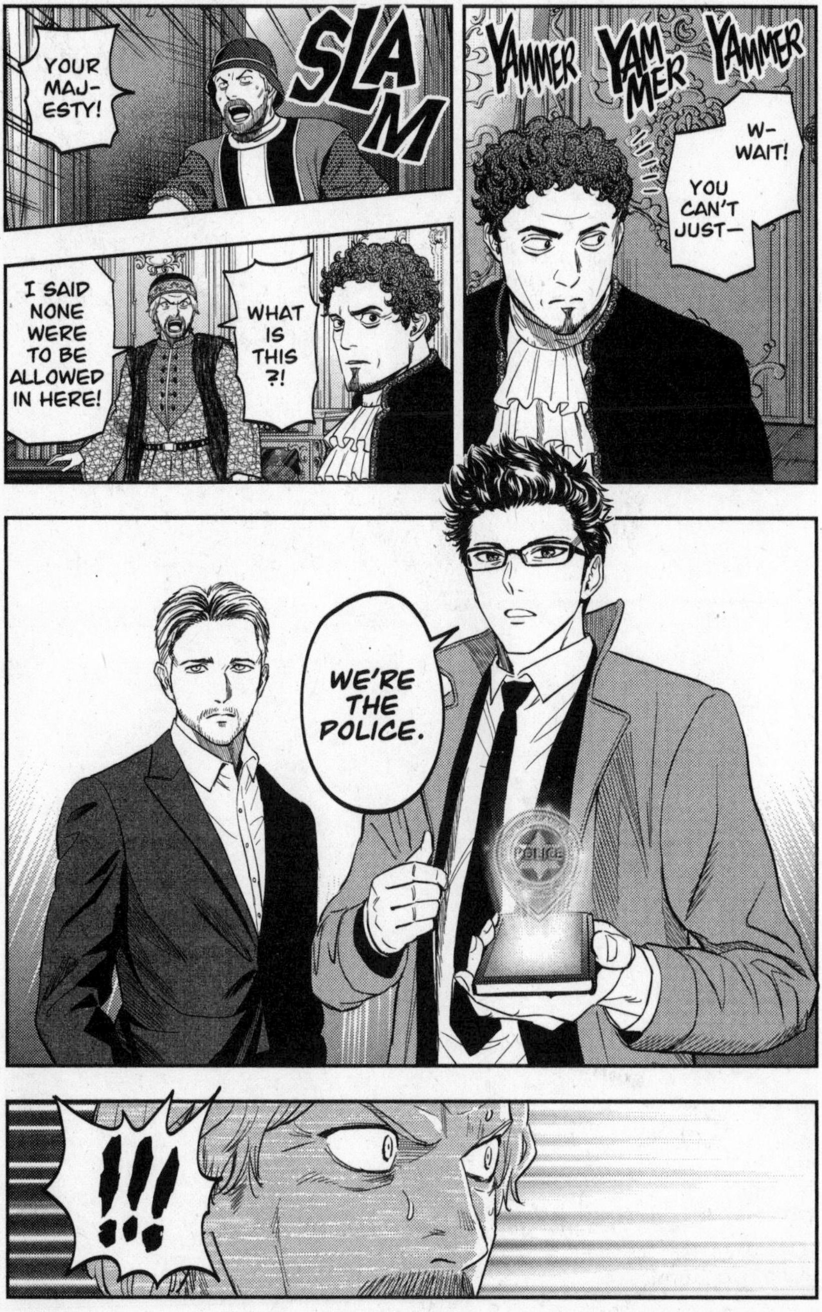
YAMMER YAMMER YAMMER
W-WAIT!
YOU CAN'T JUST—
SLAM
YOUR MAJESTY!
WHAT IS THIS?!
I SAID NONE WERE TO BE ALLOWED IN HERE!
WE'RE THE POLICE.
POLICE
!!!

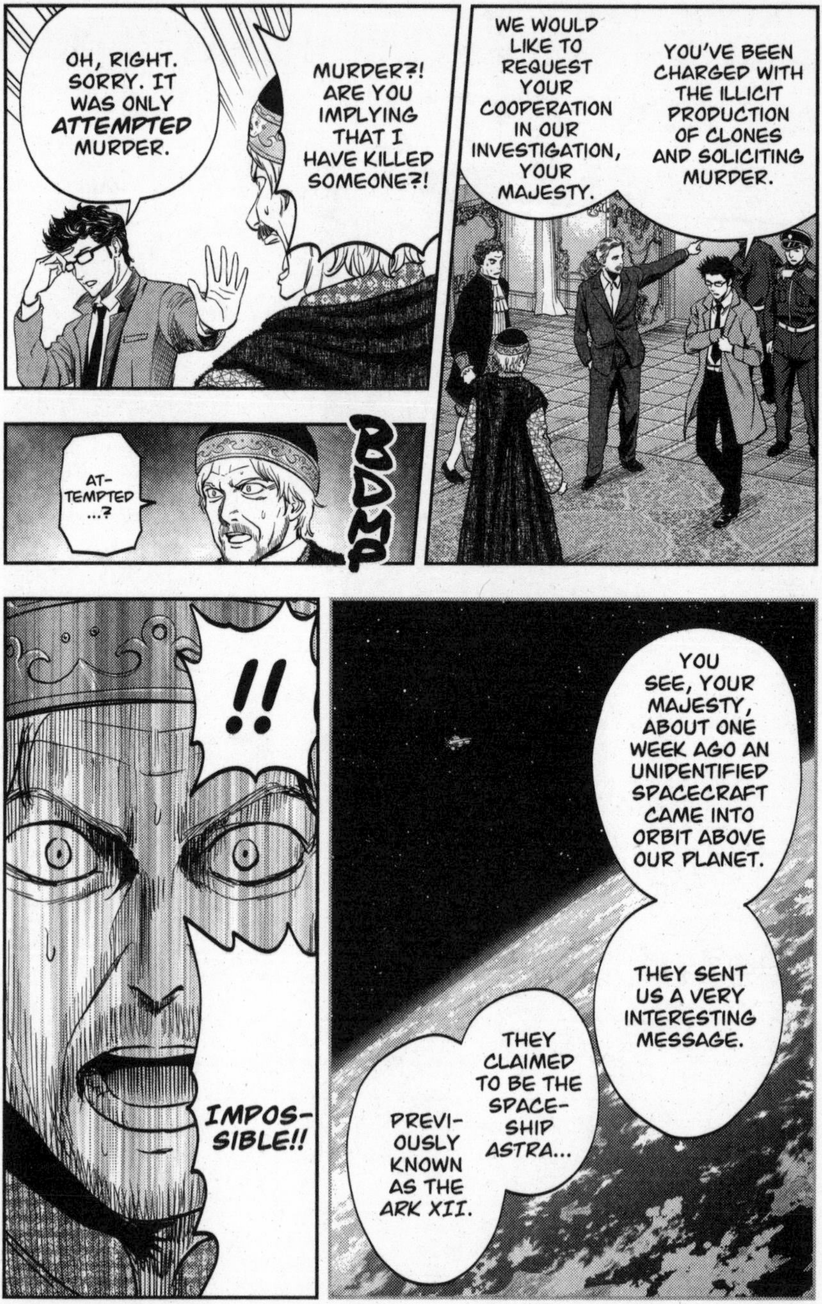
YOU'VE BEEN CHARGED WITH THE ILLICIT PRODUCTION OF CLONES AND SOLICITING MURDER.
WE WOULD LIKE TO REQUEST YOUR COOPERATION IN OUR INVESTIGATION, YOUR MAJESTY.
MURDER?! ARE YOU IMPLYING THAT I HAVE KILLED SOMEONE?!
OH, RIGHT. SORRY. IT WAS ONLY ATTEMPTED MURDER.
BDMP
AT-TEMPTED ...?
YOU SEE, YOUR MAJESTY, ABOUT ONE WEEK AGO AN UNIDENTIFIED SPACECRAFT CAME INTO ORBIT ABOVE OUR PLANET.
THEY SENT US A VERY INTERESTING MESSAGE.
THEY CLAIMED TO BE THE SPACE-SHIP ASTRA...
PREVI-OUSLY KNOWN AS THE ARK XII.
!!
IMPOS-SIBLE!!

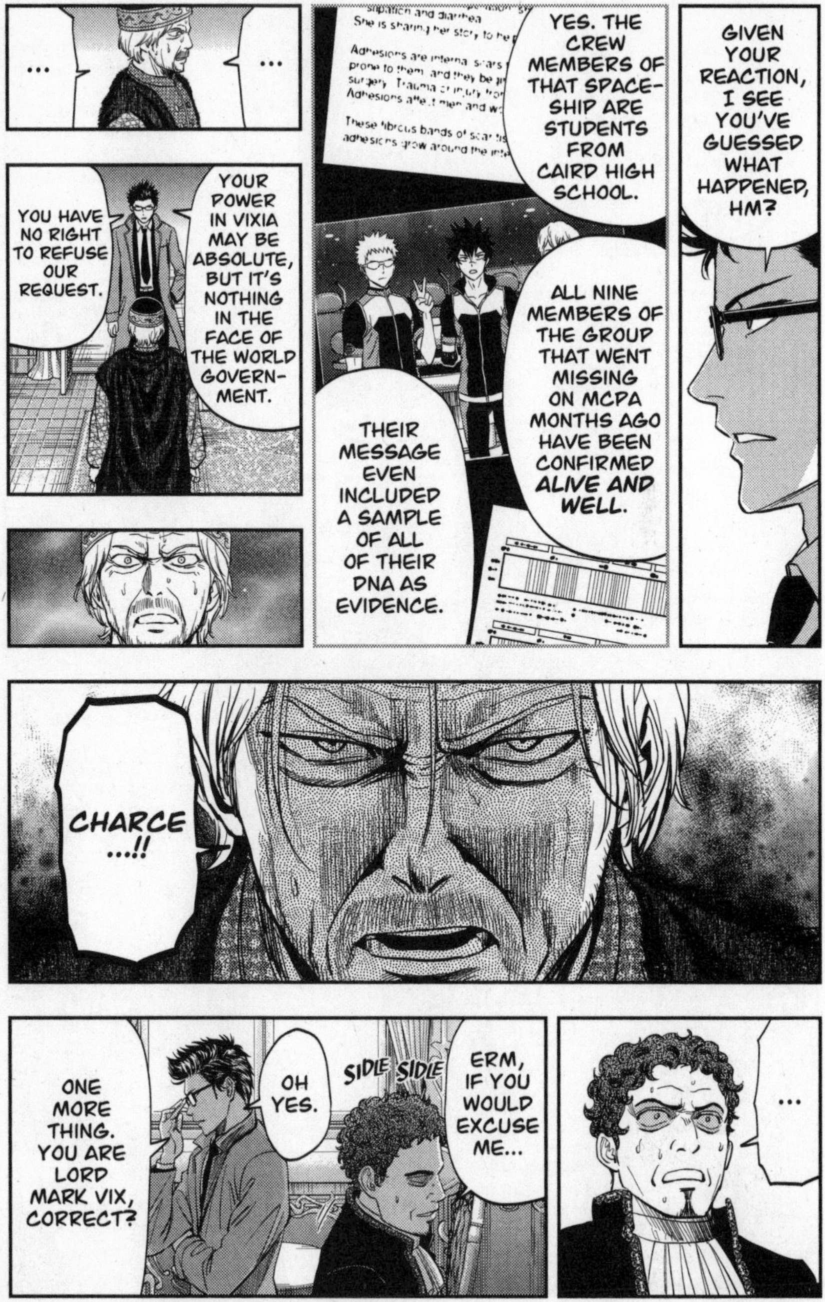

GIVEN YOUR REACTION, I SEE YOU'VE GUESSED WHAT HAPPENED, HM?
YES. THE CREW MEMBERS OF THAT SPACE-SHIP ARE STUDENTS FROM CAIRD HIGH SCHOOL.
ALL NINE MEMBERS OF THE GROUP THAT WENT MISSING ON MCPA MONTHS AGO HAVE BEEN CONFIRMED ALIVE AND WELL.
THEIR MESSAGE EVEN INCLUDED A SAMPLE OF ALL OF THEIR DNA AS EVIDENCE.
...
...
YOUR POWER IN VIXIA MAY BE ABSOLUTE, BUT IT'S NOTHING IN THE FACE OF THE WORLD GOVERN-MENT.
YOU HAVE NO RIGHT TO REFUSE OUR REQUEST.
CHARCE ...!!
...
ERM, IF YOU WOULD EXCUSE ME...
SIDLE SIDLE
OH YES.
ONE MORE THING. YOU ARE LORD MARK VIX, CORRECT?

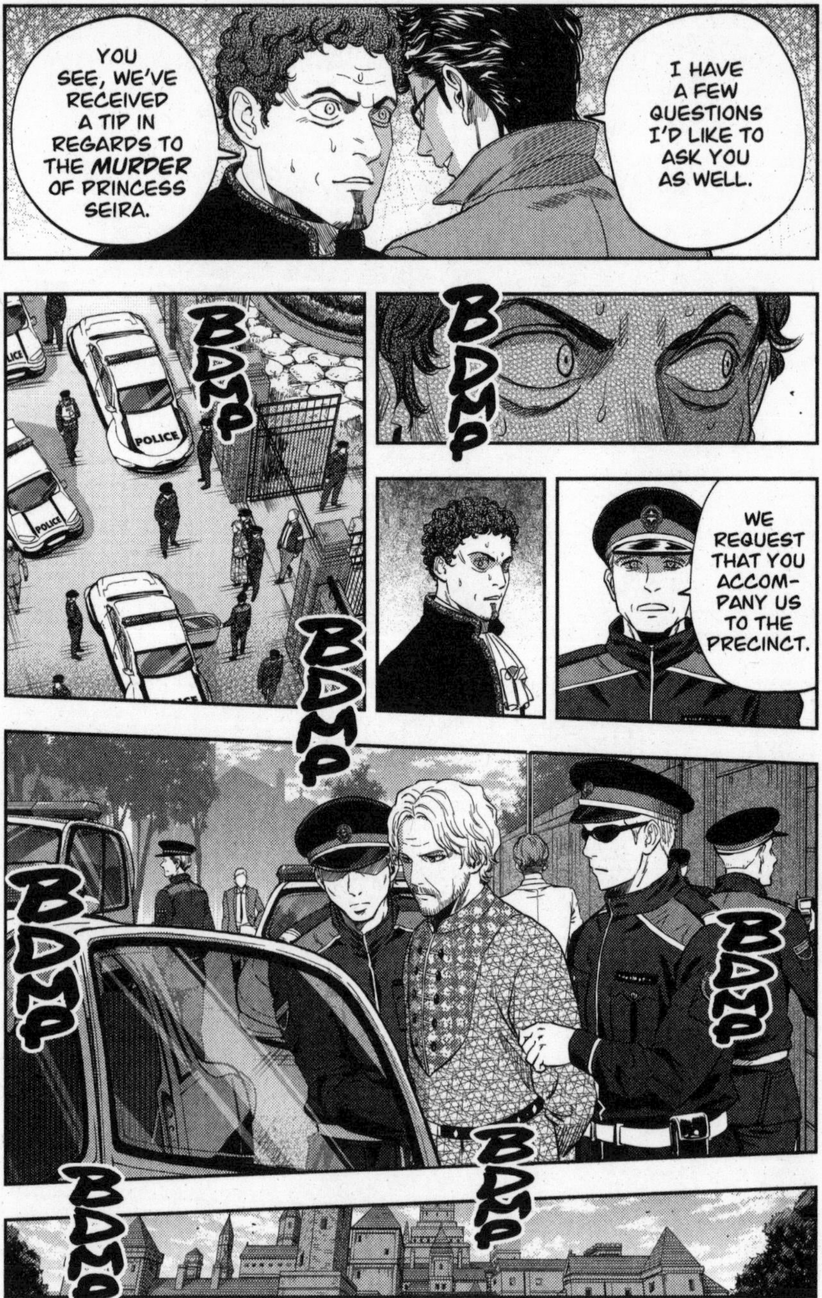
I HAVE A FEW QUESTIONS I'D LIKE TO ASK YOU AS WELL.
YOU SEE, WE'VE RECEIVED A TIP IN REGARDS TO THE MURDER OF PRINCESS SEIRA.
BDMP
WE REQUEST THAT YOU ACCOMPANY US TO THE PRECINCT.
BDMP
BDMP
BDMP
BDMP
BDMP
BDMP

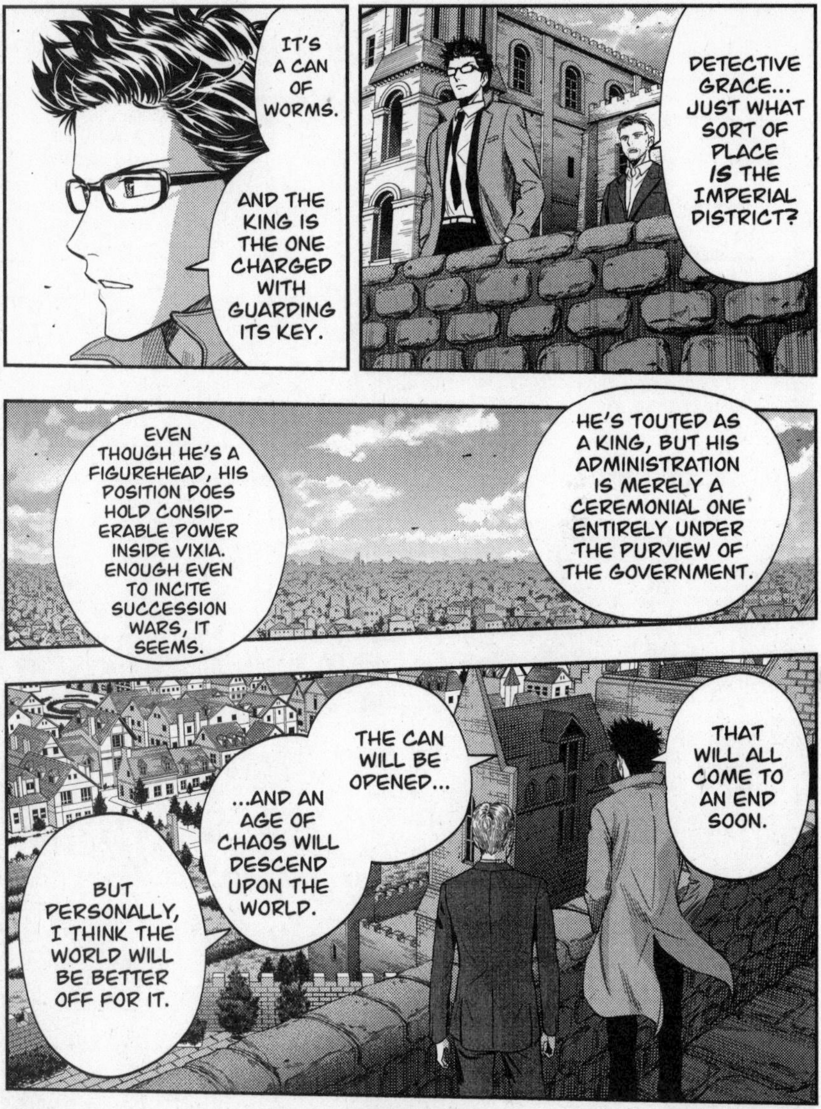
DETECTIVE GRACE... JUST WHAT SORT OF PLACE *IS* THE IMPERIAL DISTRICT?
IT'S A CAN OF WORMS.
AND THE KING IS THE ONE CHARGED WITH GUARDING ITS KEY.
HE'S TOUTED AS A KING, BUT HIS ADMINISTRATION IS MERELY A CEREMONIAL ONE ENTIRELY UNDER THE PURVIEW OF THE GOVERNMENT.
EVEN THOUGH HE'S A FIGUREHEAD, HIS POSITION DOES HOLD CONSID-ERABLE POWER INSIDE VIXIA. ENOUGH EVEN TO INCITE SUCCESSION WARS, IT SEEMS.
THAT WILL ALL COME TO AN END SOON.
THE CAN WILL BE OPENED...
...AND AN AGE OF CHAOS WILL DESCEND UPON THE WORLD.
BUT PERSONALLY, I THINK THE WORLD WILL BE BETTER OFF FOR IT.
ER, I'M SORRY, SIR, BUT I'M NOT CERTAIN I UNDERSTAND WHAT YOU MEAN...
DON'T WORRY. YOU'LL KNOW SOON ENOUGH.
THE WHOLE WORLD IS GOING TO BE ABUZZ WITH IT.

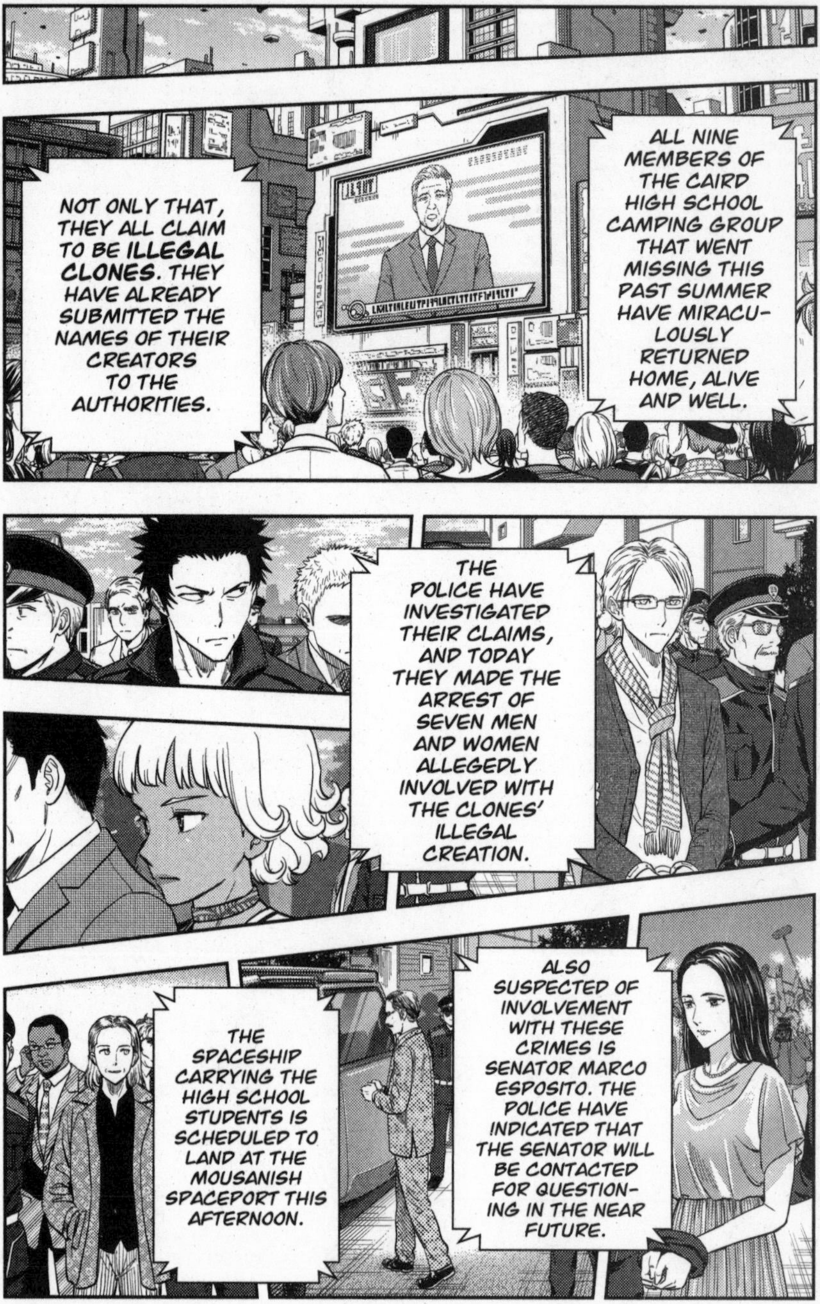
ALL NINE MEMBERS OF THE CAIRD HIGH SCHOOL CAMPING GROUP THAT WENT MISSING THIS PAST SUMMER HAVE MIRACU-LOUSLY RETURNED HOME, ALIVE AND WELL.
NOT ONLY THAT, THEY ALL CLAIM TO BE **ILLEGAL CLONES**. THEY HAVE ALREADY SUBMITTED THE NAMES OF THEIR CREATORS TO THE AUTHORITIES.
THE POLICE HAVE INVESTIGATED THEIR CLAIMS, AND TODAY THEY MADE THE ARREST OF SEVEN MEN AND WOMEN ALLEGEDLY INVOLVED WITH THE CLONES' ILLEGAL CREATION.
ALSO SUSPECTED OF INVOLVEMENT WITH THESE CRIMES IS SENATOR MARCO ESPOSITO. THE POLICE HAVE INDICATED THAT THE SENATOR WILL BE CONTACTED FOR QUESTION-ING IN THE NEAR FUTURE.
THE SPACESHIP CARRYING THE HIGH SCHOOL STUDENTS IS SCHEDULED TO LAND AT THE MOUSANISH SPACEPORT THIS AFTERNOON.

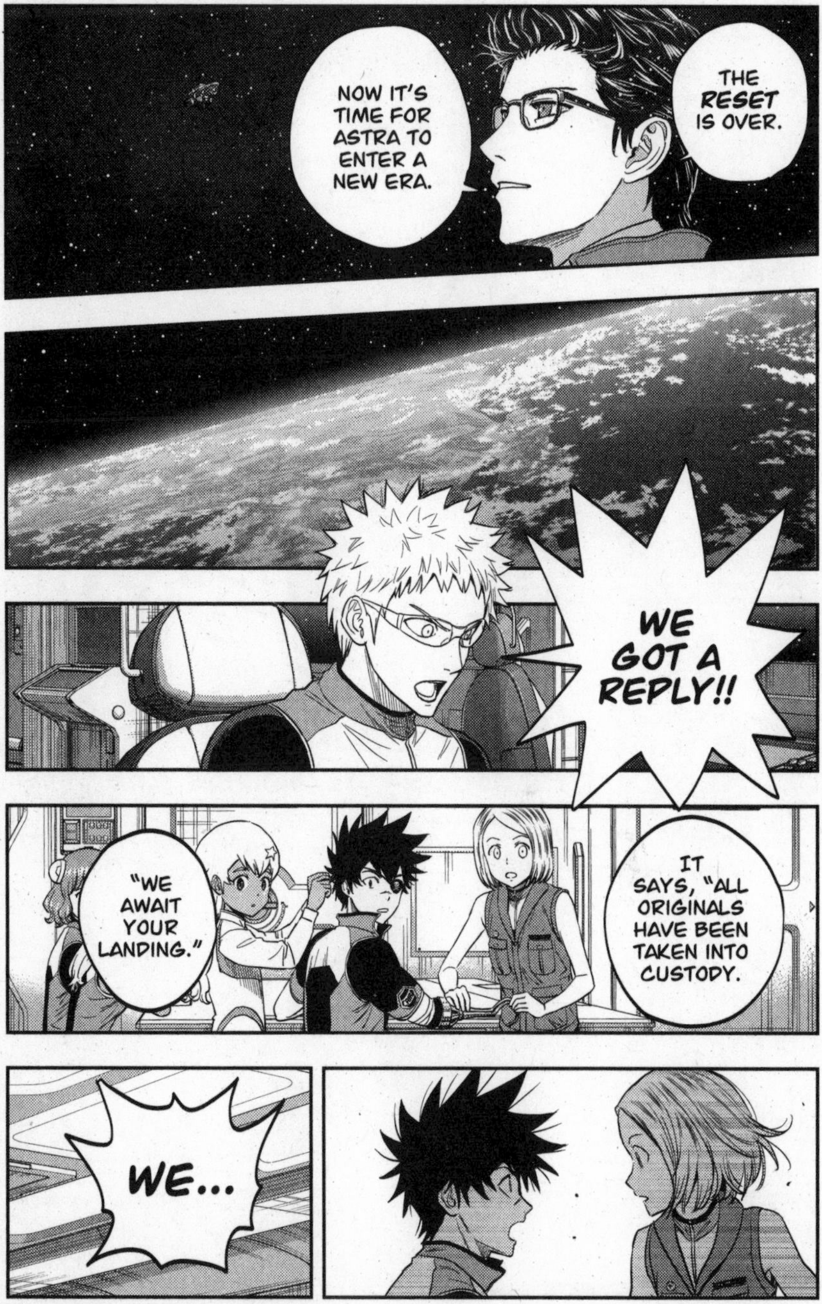
THE RESET IS OVER.
NOW IT'S TIME FOR ASTRA TO ENTER A NEW ERA.
WE GOT A REPLY!!
IT SAYS, "ALL ORIGINALS HAVE BEEN TAKEN INTO CUSTODY.
"WE AWAIT YOUR LANDING."
WE...

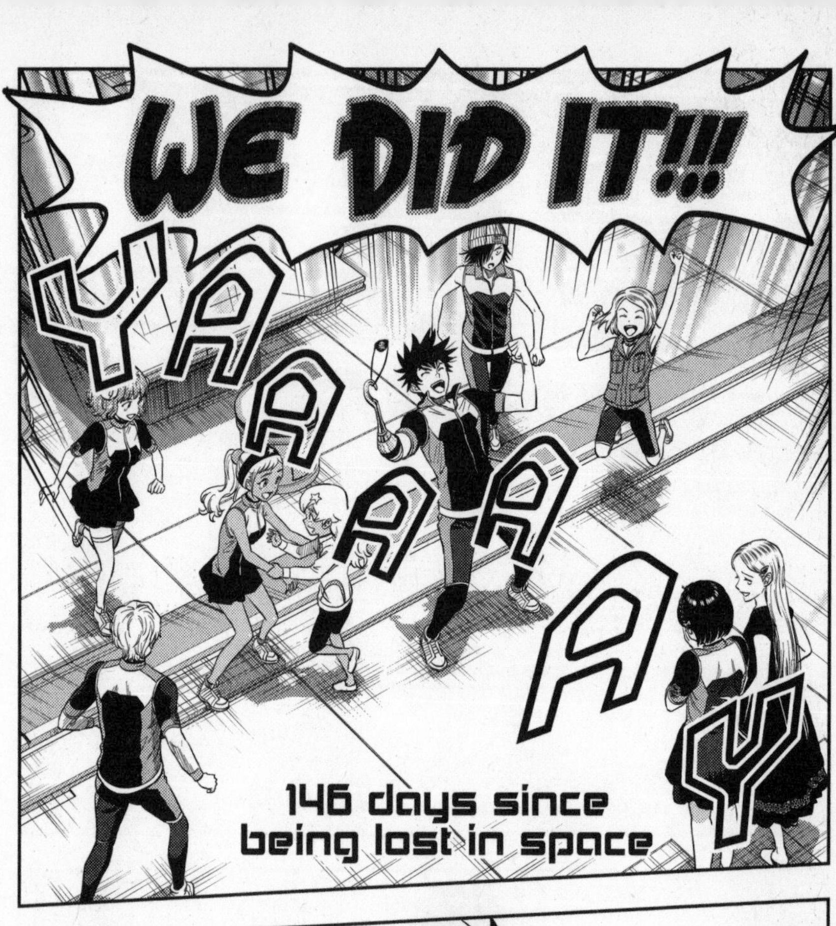
WE DID IT!!!
YAAAAAY
146 days since
being lost in space
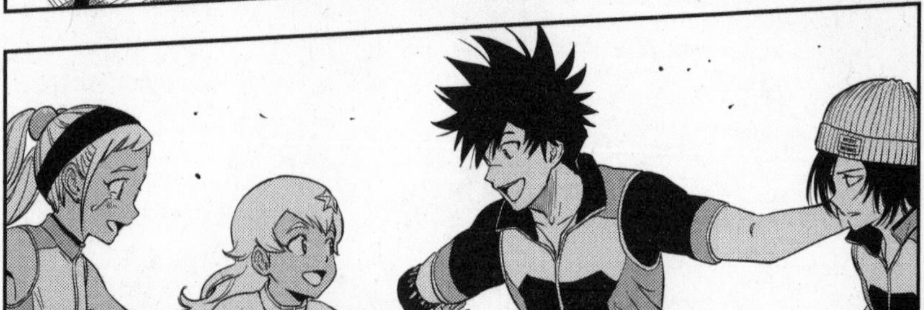
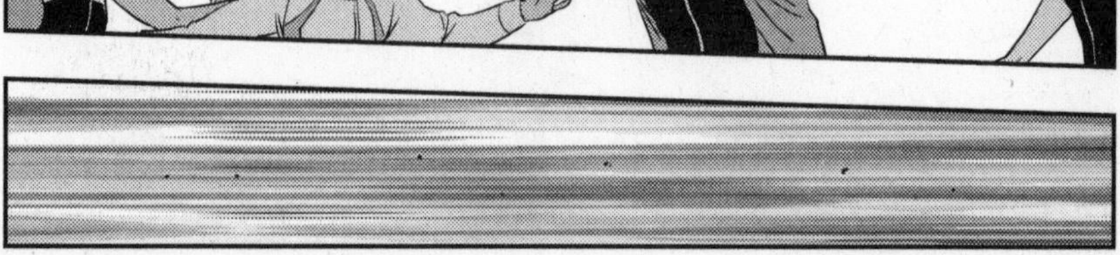

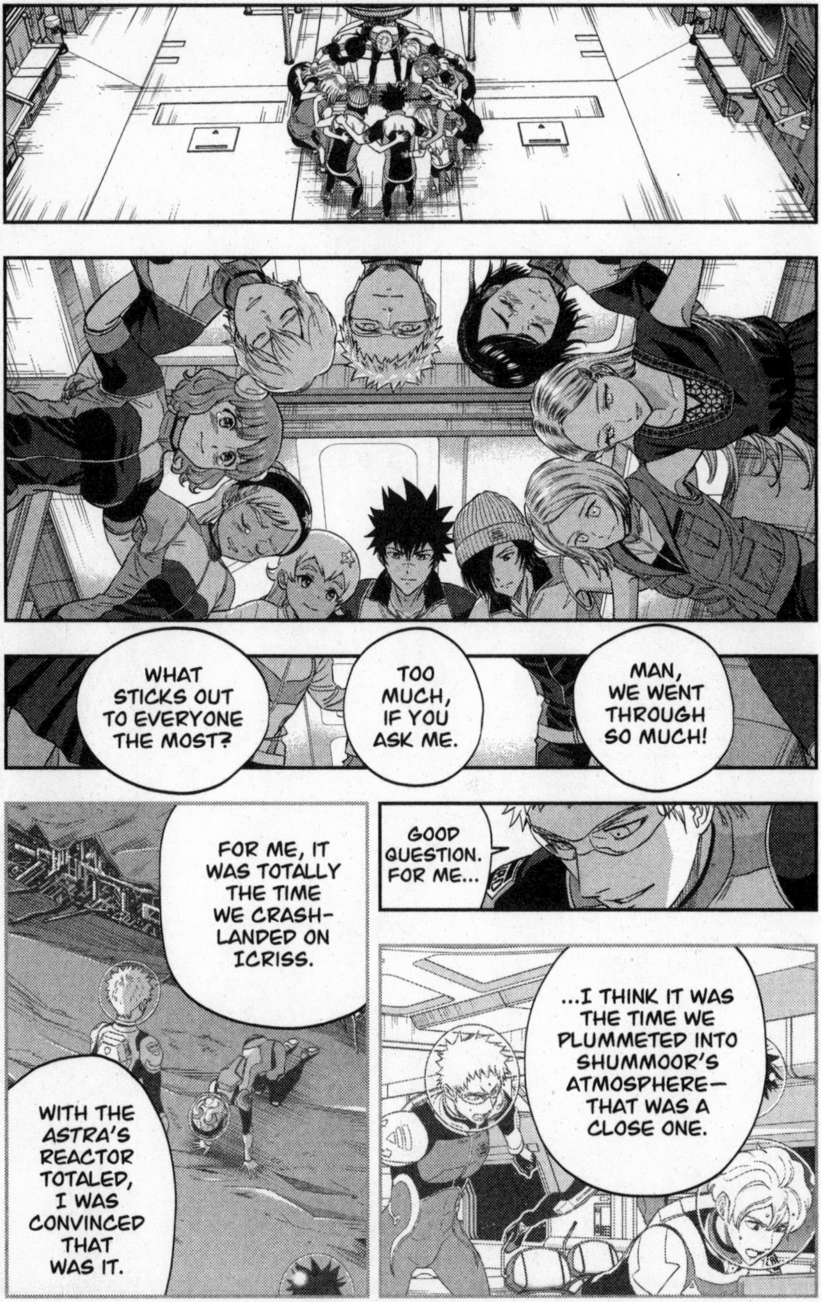
MAN, WE WENT THROUGH SO MUCH!
TOO MUCH, IF YOU ASK ME.
WHAT STICKS OUT TO EVERYONE THE MOST?
GOOD QUESTION. FOR ME...
...I THINK IT WAS THE TIME WE PLUMMETED INTO SHUMMOOR'S ATMOSPHERE—THAT WAS A CLOSE ONE.
FOR ME, IT WAS TOTALLY THE TIME WE CRASH-LANDED ON ICRISS.
WITH THE ASTRA'S REACTOR TOTALED, I WAS CONVINCED THAT WAS IT.

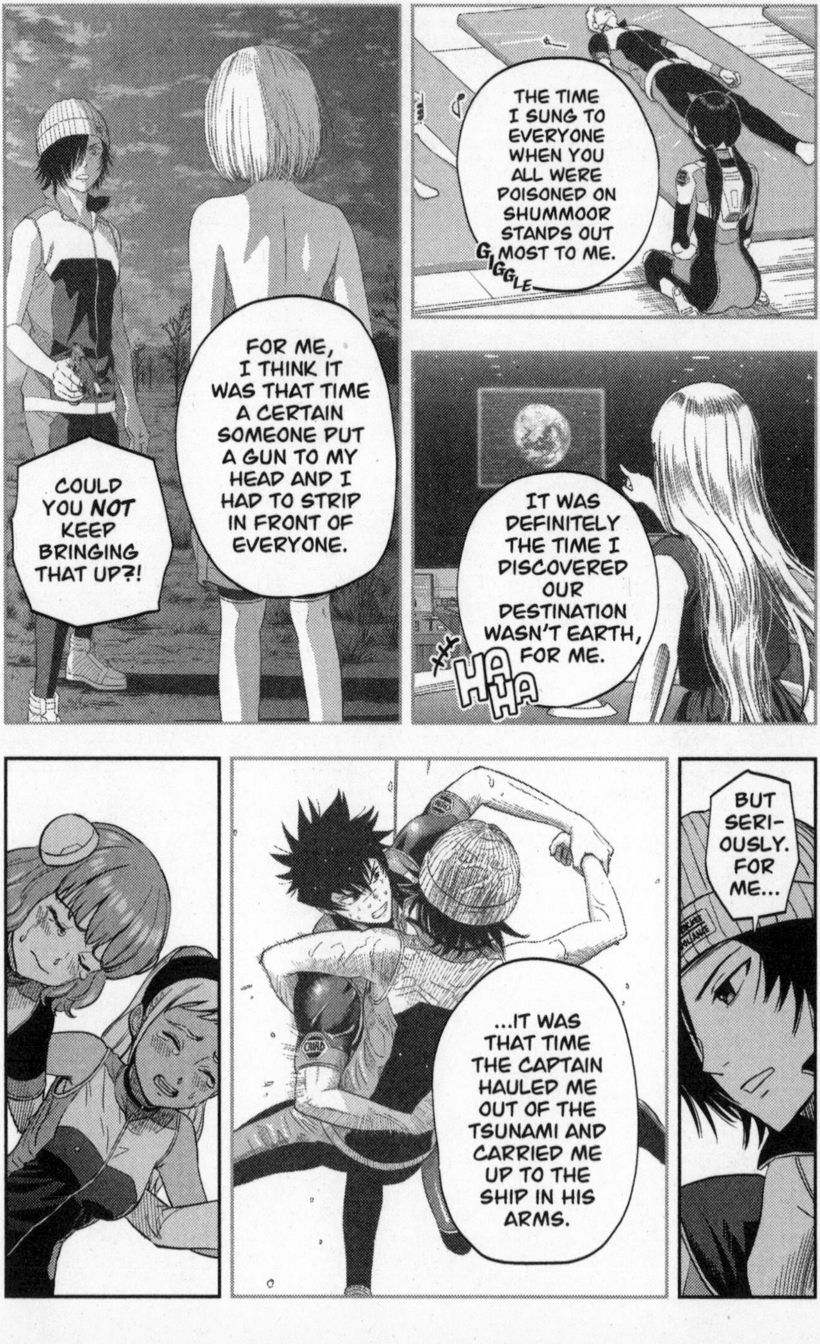
THE TIME I SUNG TO EVERYONE WHEN YOU ALL WERE POISONED ON SHUMMOOR STANDS OUT MOST TO ME.
GIGGLE
IT WAS DEFINITELY THE TIME I DISCOVERED OUR DESTINATION WASN'T EARTH, FOR ME.
HAHAHA
FOR ME, I THINK IT WAS THAT TIME A CERTAIN SOMEONE PUT A GUN TO MY HEAD AND I HAD TO STRIP IN FRONT OF EVERYONE.
COULD YOU **NOT** KEEP BRINGING THAT UP?!
BUT SERIOUSLY. FOR ME...
...IT WAS THAT TIME THE CAPTAIN HAULED ME OUT OF THE TSUNAMI AND CARRIED ME UP TO THE SHIP IN HIS ARMS.

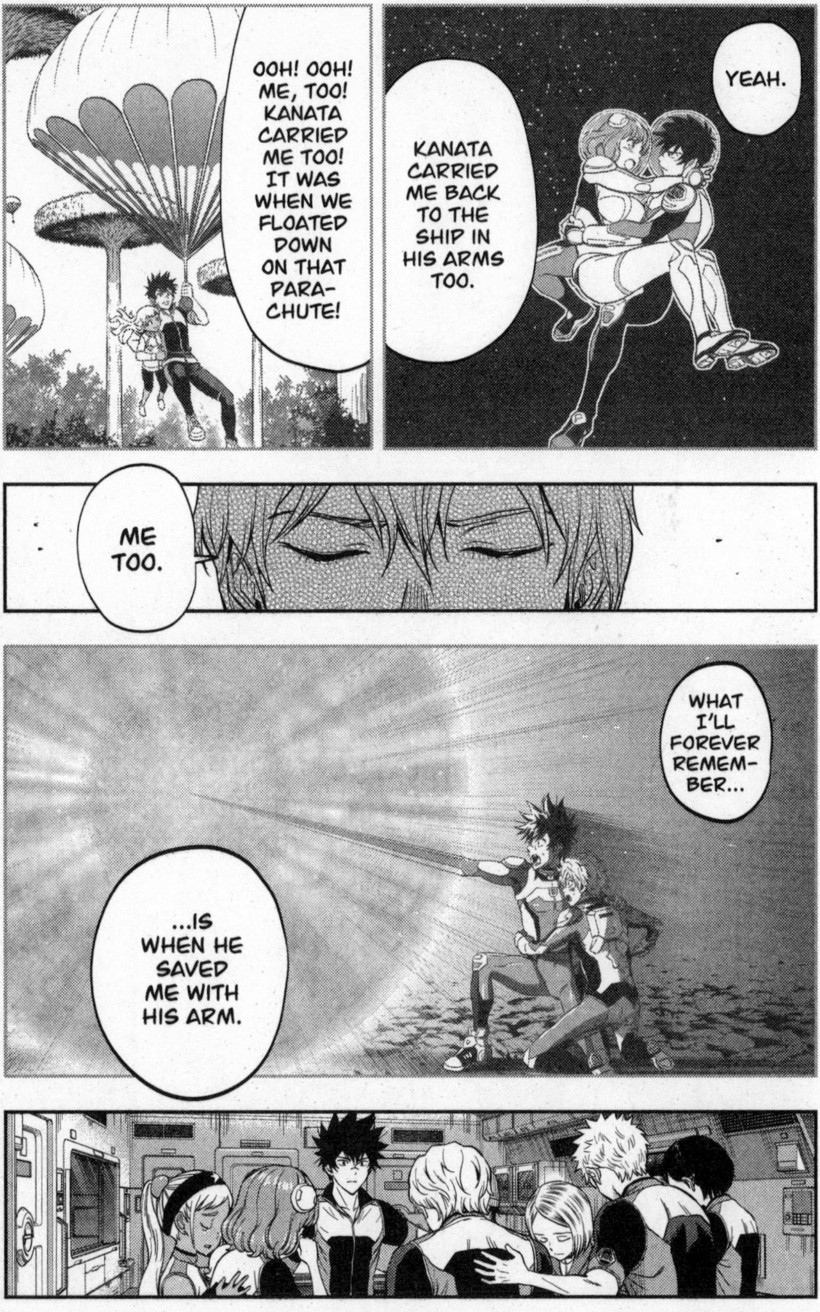
YEAH.
KANATA CARRIED ME BACK TO THE SHIP IN HIS ARMS TOO.
OOH! OOH! ME, TOO! KANATA CARRIED ME TOO! IT WAS WHEN WE FLOATED DOWN ON THAT PARA-CHUTE!
ME TOO.
WHAT I'LL FOREVER REMEM-BER...
...IS WHEN HE SAVED ME WITH HIS ARM.

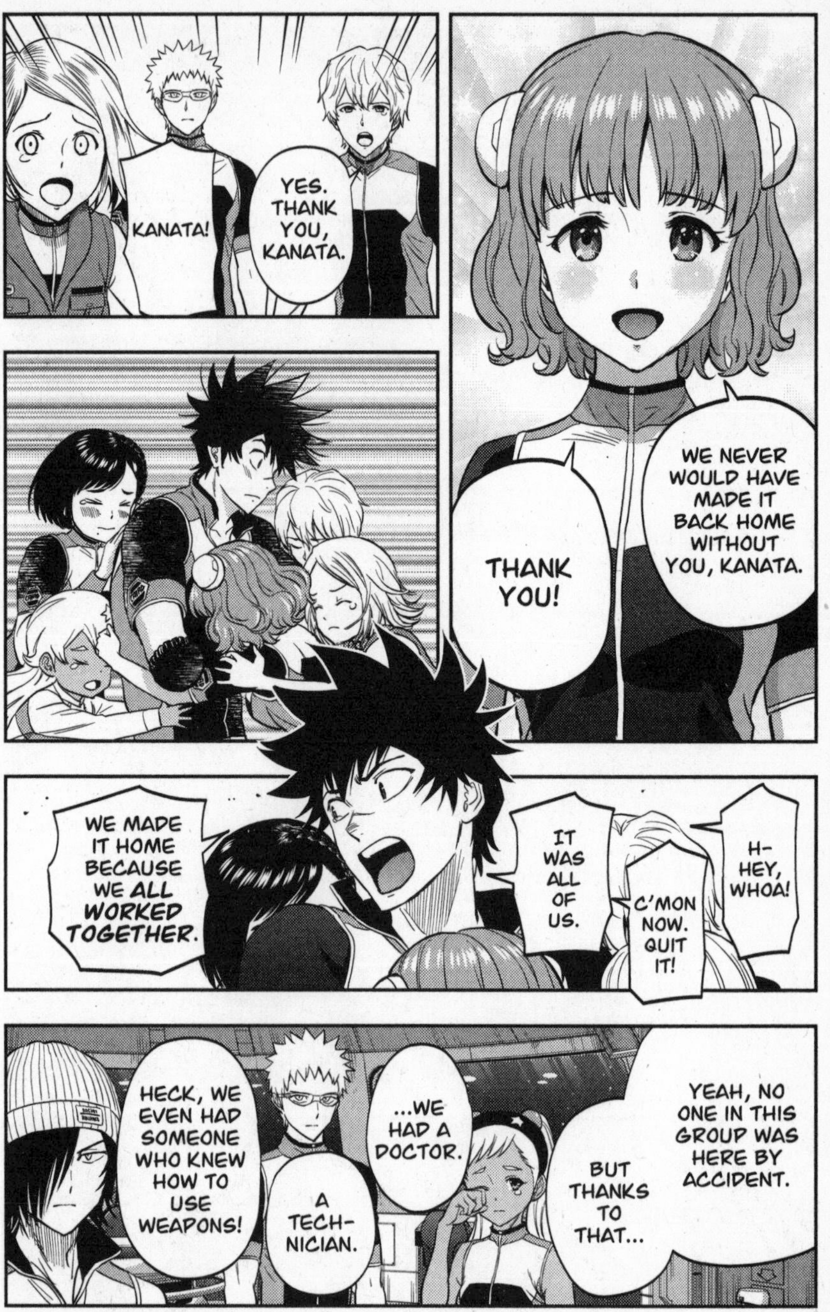
WE NEVER WOULD HAVE MADE IT BACK HOME WITHOUT YOU, KANATA.
THANK YOU!
YES. THANK YOU, KANATA.
KANATA!
H-HEY, WHOA!
C'MON NOW. QUIT IT!
IT WAS ALL OF US.
WE MADE IT HOME BECAUSE WE ALL WORKED TOGETHER.
YEAH, NO ONE IN THIS GROUP WAS HERE BY ACCIDENT.
BUT THANKS TO THAT...
...WE HAD A DOCTOR.
A TECHNICIAN.
HECK, WE EVEN HAD SOMEONE WHO KNEW HOW TO USE WEAPONS!

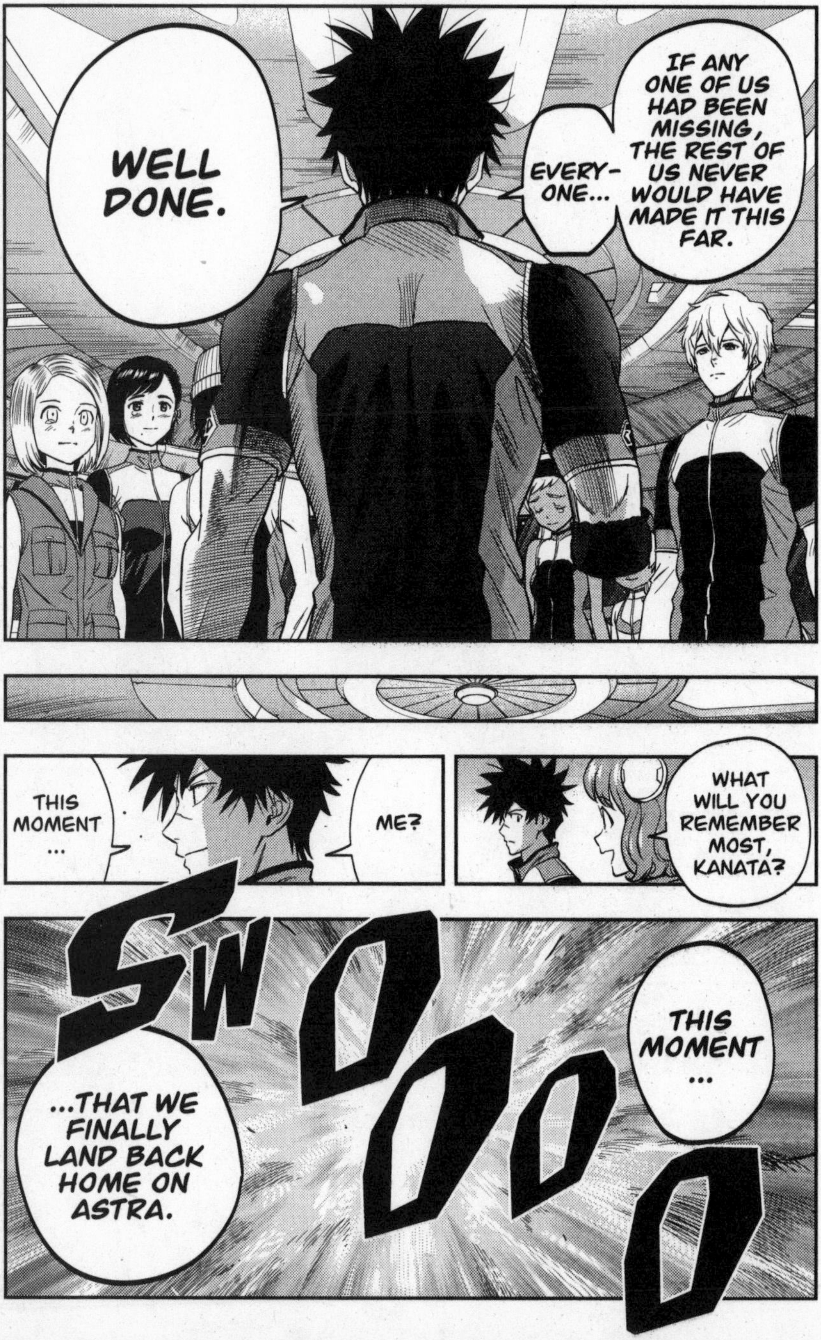
IF ANY ONE OF US HAD BEEN MISSING, THE REST OF US NEVER WOULD HAVE MADE IT THIS FAR.
EVERY-ONE...
WELL DONE.
WHAT WILL YOU REMEMBER MOST, KANATA?
ME?
THIS MOMENT ...
THIS MOMENT ...
SWOOOOO
...THAT WE FINALLY LAND BACK HOME ON ASTRA.

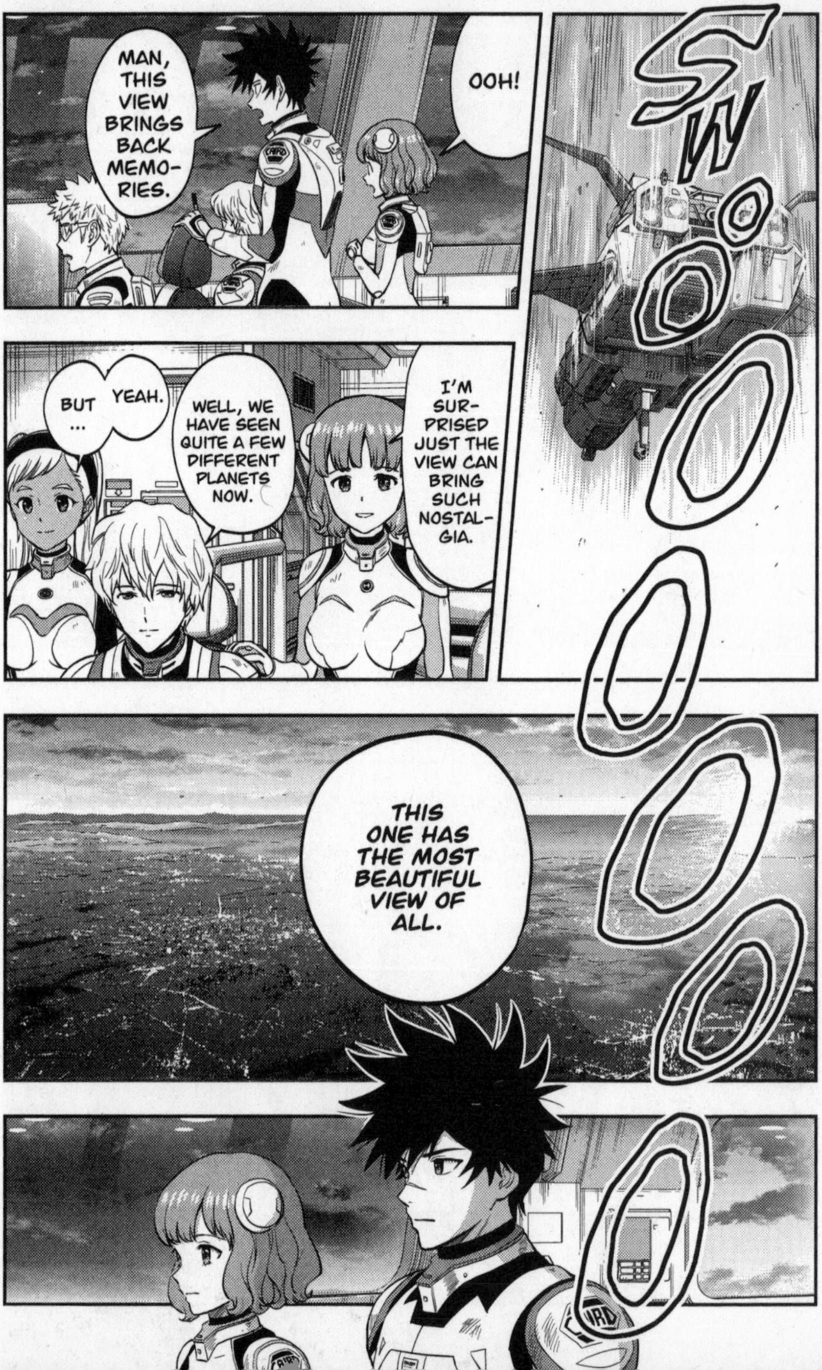
SWOOOOOOOO
OOH!
MAN, THIS VIEW BRINGS BACK MEMORIES.
I'M SURPRISED JUST THE VIEW CAN BRING SUCH NOSTALGIA.
WELL, WE HAVE SEEN QUITE A FEW DIFFERENT PLANETS NOW.
YEAH.
BUT ...
THIS ONE HAS THE MOST BEAUTIFUL VIEW OF ALL.

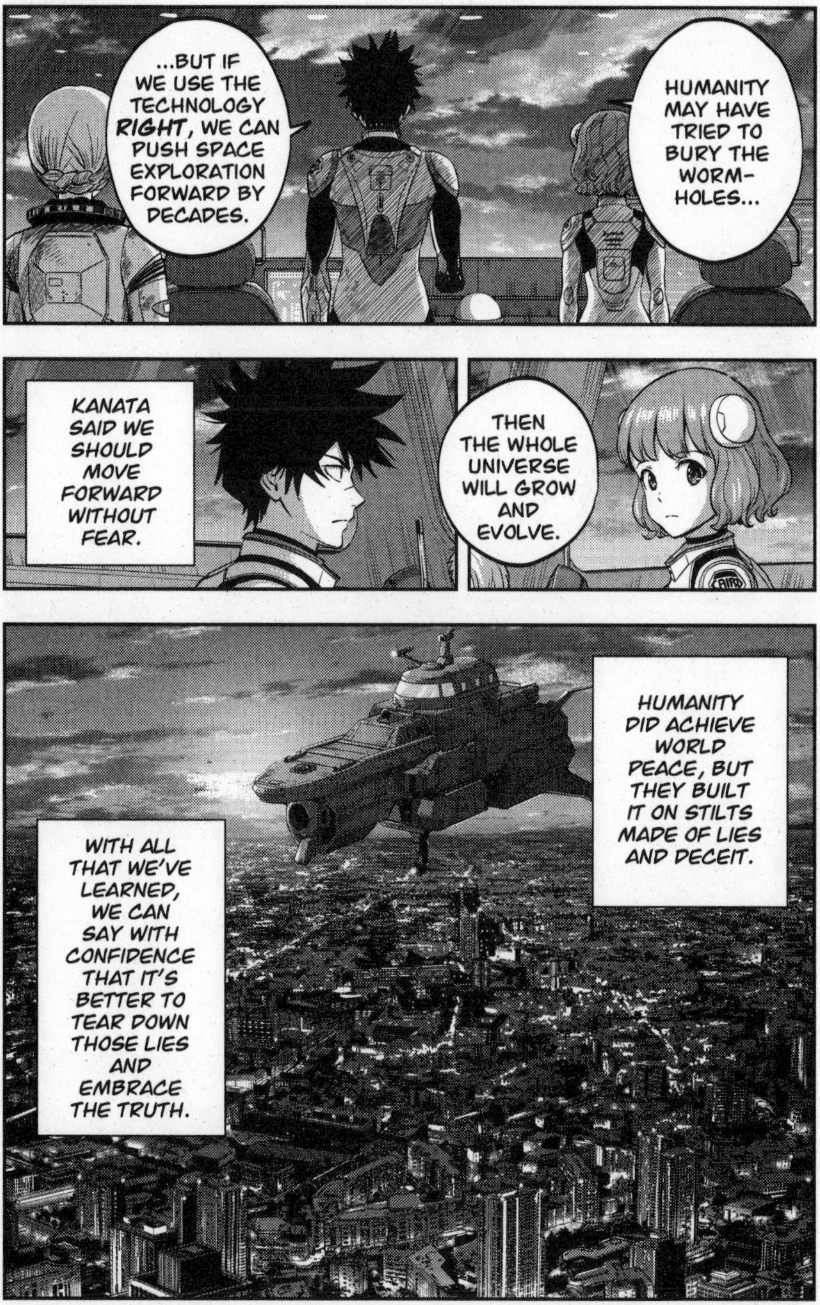
HUMANITY MAY HAVE TRIED TO BURY THE WORM-HOLES...
...BUT IF WE USE THE TECHNOLOGY RIGHT, WE CAN PUSH SPACE EXPLORATION FORWARD BY DECADES.
THEN THE WHOLE UNIVERSE WILL GROW AND EVOLVE.
KANATA SAID WE SHOULD MOVE FORWARD WITHOUT FEAR.
HUMANITY DID ACHIEVE WORLD PEACE, BUT THEY BUILT IT ON STILTS MADE OF LIES AND DECEIT.
WITH ALL THAT WE'VE LEARNED, WE CAN SAY WITH CONFIDENCE THAT IT'S BETTER TO TEAR DOWN THOSE LIES AND EMBRACE THE TRUTH.

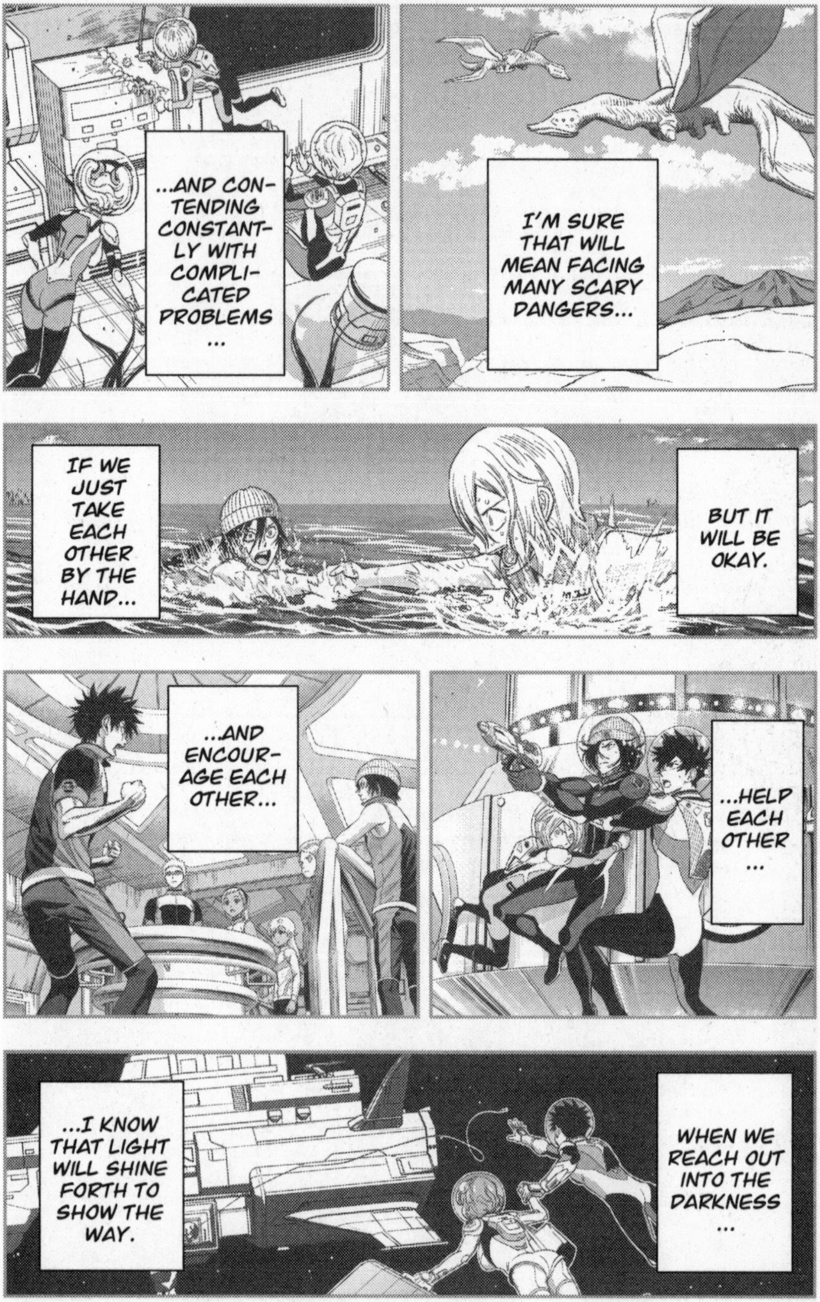
I'M SURE THAT WILL MEAN FACING MANY SCARY DANGERS...
...AND CONTENDING CONSTANTLY WITH COMPLICATED PROBLEMS ...
BUT IT WILL BE OKAY.
IF WE JUST TAKE EACH OTHER BY THE HAND...
...HELP EACH OTHER ...
...AND ENCOURAGE EACH OTHER...
WHEN WE REACH OUT INTO THE DARKNESS ...
...I KNOW THAT LIGHT WILL SHINE FORTH TO SHOW THE WAY.

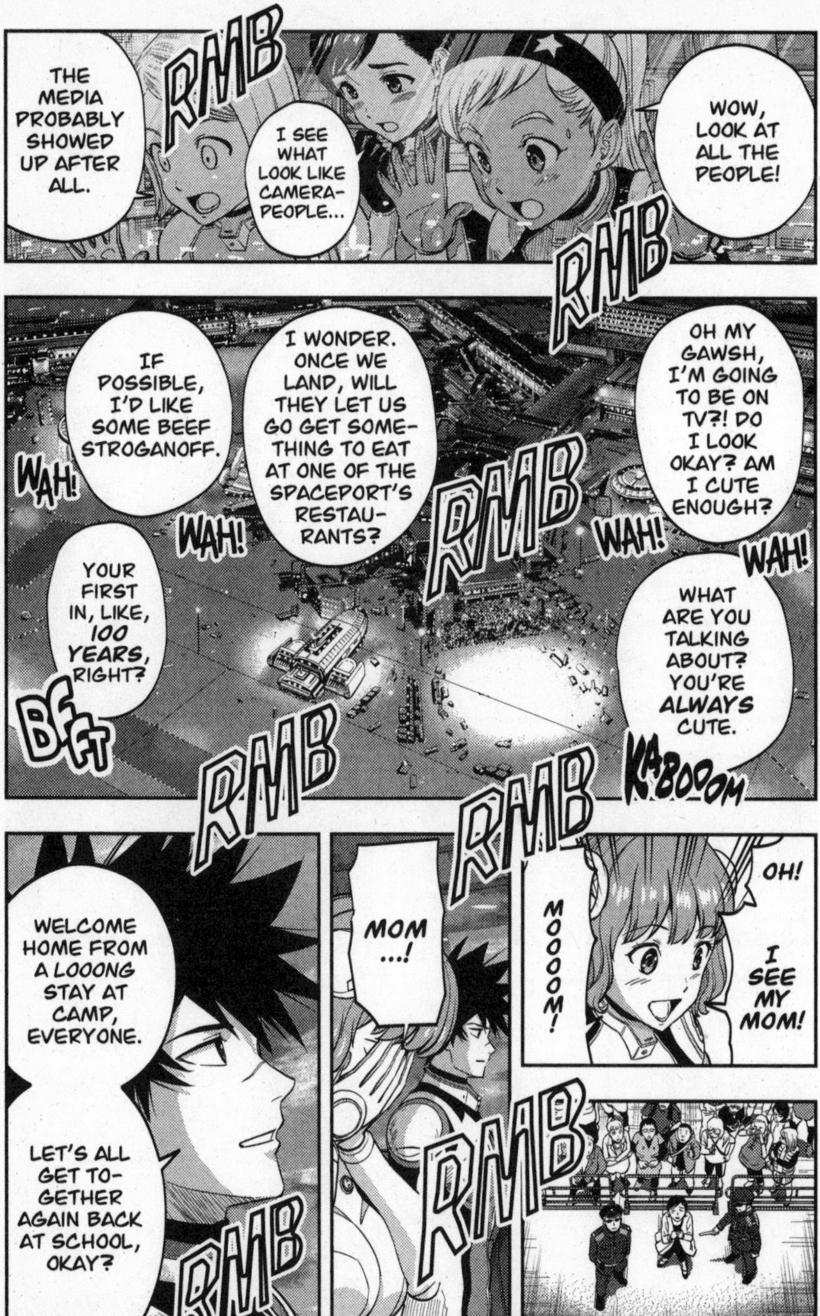
RMB
WOW, LOOK AT ALL THE PEOPLE!
I SEE WHAT LOOK LIKE CAMERA-PEOPLE...
THE MEDIA PROBABLY SHOWED UP AFTER ALL.
RMB
OH MY GAWSH, I'M GOING TO BE ON TV?! DO I LOOK OKAY? AM I CUTE ENOUGH?
WAH!
WAH!
I WONDER. ONCE WE LAND, WILL THEY LET US GO GET SOMETHING TO EAT AT ONE OF THE SPACEPORT'S RESTAURANTS?
RMB
IF POSSIBLE, I'D LIKE SOME BEEF STROGANOFF.
WAH!
WAH!
WHAT ARE YOU TALKING ABOUT? YOU'RE ALWAYS CUTE.
KABOOOM
YOUR FIRST IN, LIKE, 100 YEARS, RIGHT?
BFFT
RMB
RMB
OH!
I SEE MY MOM!
MOOOOOM!
RMB
MOM ...!
RMB
WELCOME HOME FROM A LOOONG STAY AT CAMP, EVERYONE.
LET'S ALL GET TOGETHER AGAIN BACK AT SCHOOL, OKAY?
RMB

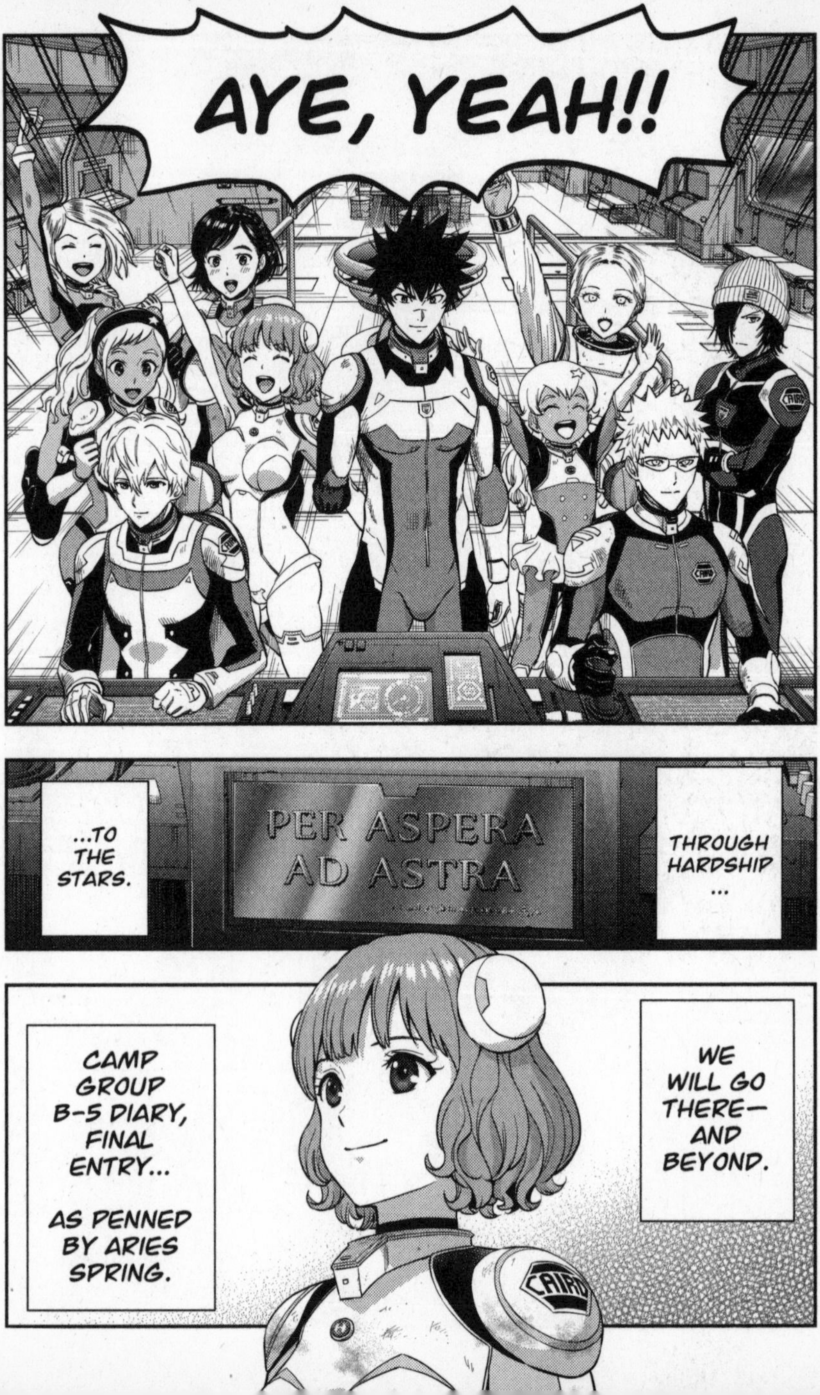
AYE, YEAH!!
THROUGH HARDSHIP ...
PER ASPERA AD ASTRA
...TO THE STARS.
WE WILL GO THERE— AND BEYOND.
CAMP GROUP B-5 DIARY, FINAL ENTRY...
AS PENNED BY ARIES SPRING.

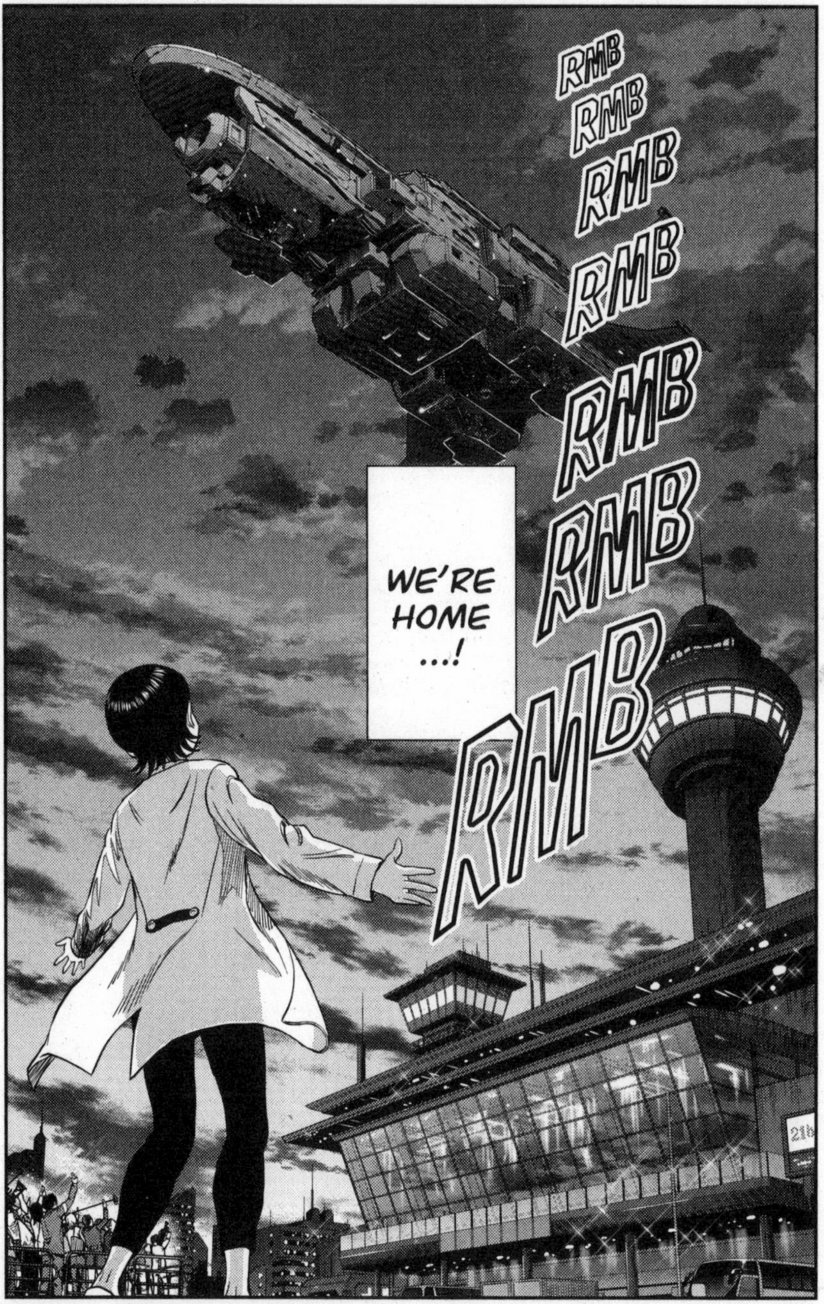
RMB RMB RMB RMB RMB RMB RMB
WE'RE HOME ...!

Material Collection

LOGBOOK

DAY	LOCATION	EVENTS	CH.#
1	McPa / Ship	Departure for Planet Camp / Swallowed by the orb	1~2
	Ship	3 days of faster-than-light (FTL) travel (first 3 days after stranding)	
4	Vilavurs Day 1	Arrival at Vilavurs / 1st foraging expedition / 2nd orb encounter / Crew introductions	3~4
5	Vilavurs Day 2	Kanata and Quitterie argue / Turgon encounter / Depart Vilavurs	5~7
	Ship	18 days of FTL travel (days 6~23 after stranding) / Kanata observes crew	8
24	Shummoor Day 1	Arrival at Shummoor / Existence of a killer suspected / Sudden plunge into atmosphere / Landing / 1st foraging expedition	9~13
25	Shummoor Day 2	Gloopies tamed / Investigation around pole tree	14
26	Shummoor Day 3	Yun-hua runs away / spore cloud poisoning / Antidote mushroom discovered	15~17
27	Shummoor Day 4	Crew recovers	18
28	Shummoor Day 5	Pole tree harvested / Subterranean lake found / Depart Shummoor	18
	Ship	16 days of FTL travel (days 29~44 after stranding) / Parents meet on Astra	19
45	Arispade Day 1	Arrival at Arispade	20
49	Arispade Day 5	"What's with all the peace?!" / Girls' talk	20
51	Arispade Day 7	Luca and Ulgar go fishing / Ulgar's attack / Tsunami / Depart Arispade	21~25
	Ship	23 days of FTL travel (days 52~74 after stranding)	
71	Ship	Charce opens up about his past	25~26
75	Icriss Day 1	Arrival at Icriss / Crash landing	27
76	Icriss Day 2	Zack's inspection results / Foraging expedition / Other Astra discovered / Polina found / Polina's story	28~30
77	Icriss Days 3~5	Astra & Ark VI's bow exchange / Charce's exploration	30
80	Icriss Day 6	Bow docking completed / Charce reports findings / Foraging expedition / Quitterie and Zack get engaged	31
81	Icriss Day 7	Funicia caught in blizzard / Funicia and Quitterie's DNA examined / Zack reports results to Kanata	32
82	Icriss Day 8	Crew discovers they're clones / Parents' secret meeting on Astra	33~34
84	Icriss Day 10	Kanata listens to the crew's stories / Zack and Quitterie announce engagement	35
87	Icriss Day 13	Foraging complete / Encounter with giant plant / Departure party	36~37
88	Ship	Depart Icriss / Crew and Polina compare histories	38
	Ship	23 days of FTL travel (days 88~110 after stranding)	
111	Galem Day 1	Arrival at Galem / 1st foraging expedition / Kanata's encounter with orb	39~40
112	Galem Day 2	Plan to capture killer enacted / Charce's story / Confrontation and peaceful conclusion	41~46
113	Galem Days 3~9	Foraging expeditions	46
120	Galem Day 10	Depart Galem / Secret history of Astra	46~47
		19 days of FTL travel (days 120~138 after stranding)	
139	Astra Day 1	Arrival at Astra / Messages sent / Awaiting response	
146	Astra Day 8	Originals arrested / Astra lands at the spaceport	48

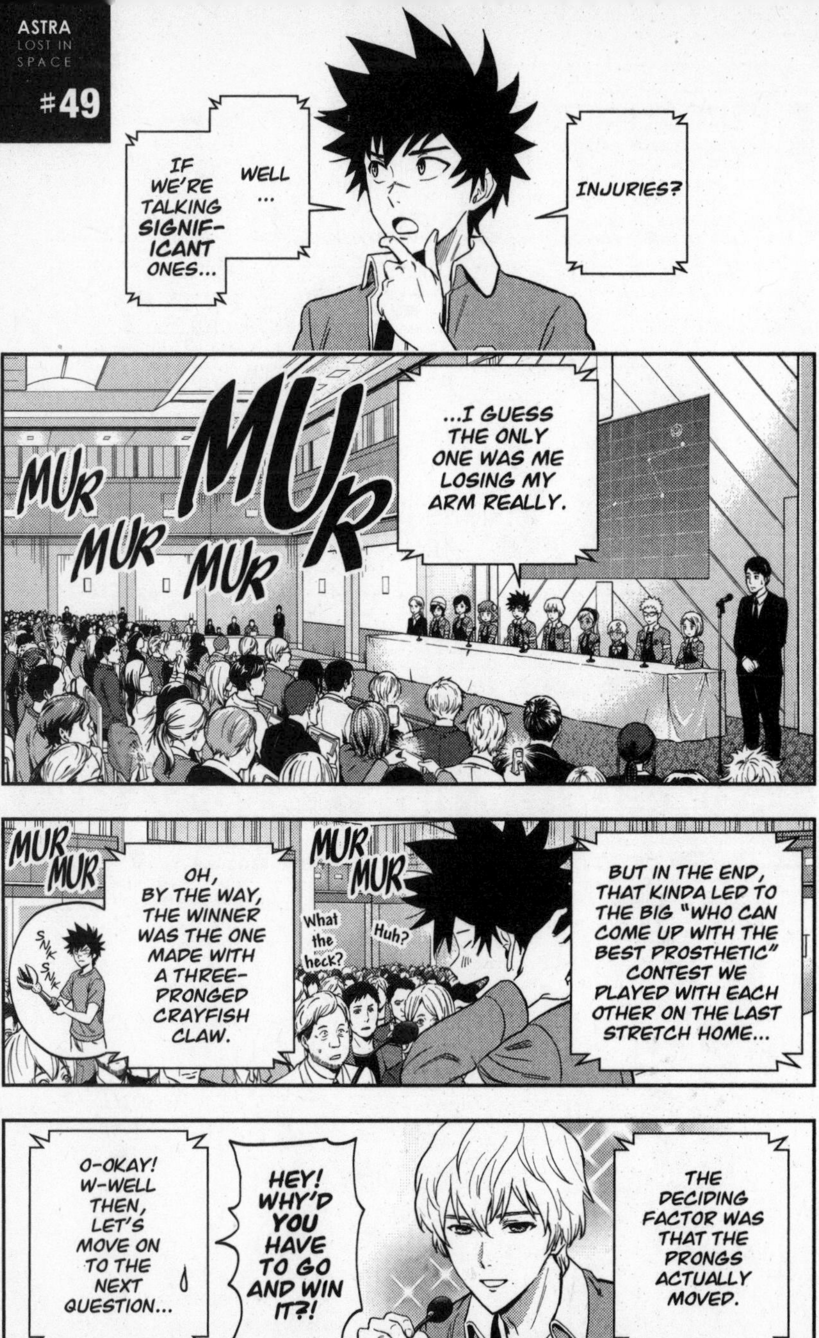
INJURIES?
WELL...
IF WE'RE TALKING SIGNIFICANT ONES...
...I GUESS THE ONLY ONE WAS ME LOSING MY ARM REALLY.
MUR
MUR
MUR
MUR
BUT IN THE END, THAT KINDA LED TO THE BIG "WHO CAN COME UP WITH THE BEST PROSTHETIC" CONTEST WE PLAYED WITH EACH OTHER ON THE LAST STRETCH HOME...
Huh?
What the heck?
MUR MUR
OH, BY THE WAY, THE WINNER WAS THE ONE MADE WITH A THREE-PRONGED CRAYFISH CLAW.
MUR MUR
SNIK SNIK
THE DECIDING FACTOR WAS THAT THE PRONGS ACTUALLY MOVED.
HEY! WHY'D YOU HAVE TO GO AND WIN IT?!
O-OKAY! W-WELL THEN, LET'S MOVE ON TO THE NEXT QUESTION...

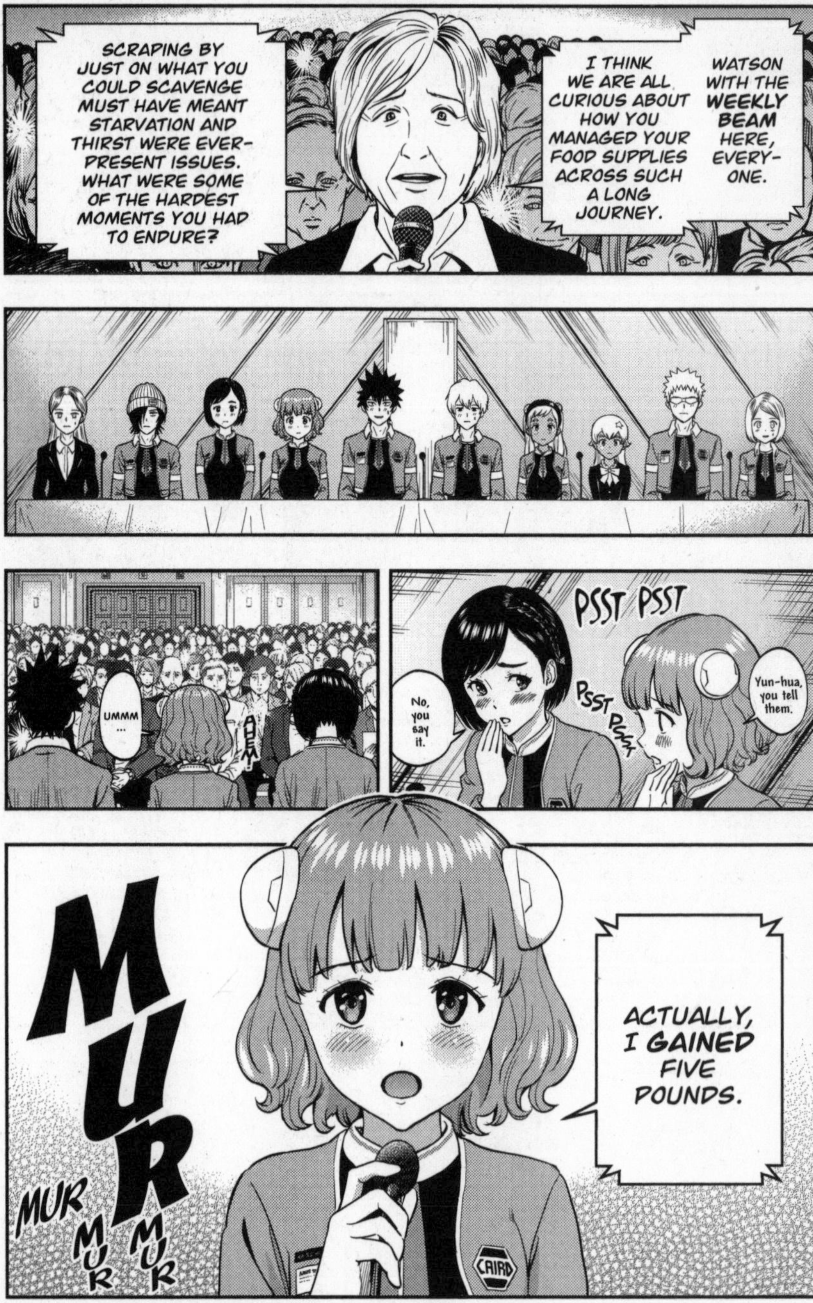
WATSON WITH THE WEEKLY BEAM HERE, EVERYONE.
I THINK WE ARE ALL CURIOUS ABOUT HOW YOU MANAGED YOUR FOOD SUPPLIES ACROSS SUCH A LONG JOURNEY.
SCRAPING BY JUST ON WHAT YOU COULD SCAVENGE MUST HAVE MEANT STARVATION AND THIRST WERE EVER-PRESENT ISSUES. WHAT WERE SOME OF THE HARDEST MOMENTS YOU HAD TO ENDURE?
PSST PSST
Yun-hua, you tell them.
PSST PSST
No, you say it.
AHEM!
UMMM ...
ACTUALLY, I GAINED FIVE POUNDS.
MUR MUR
MUR MUR
MUR MUR

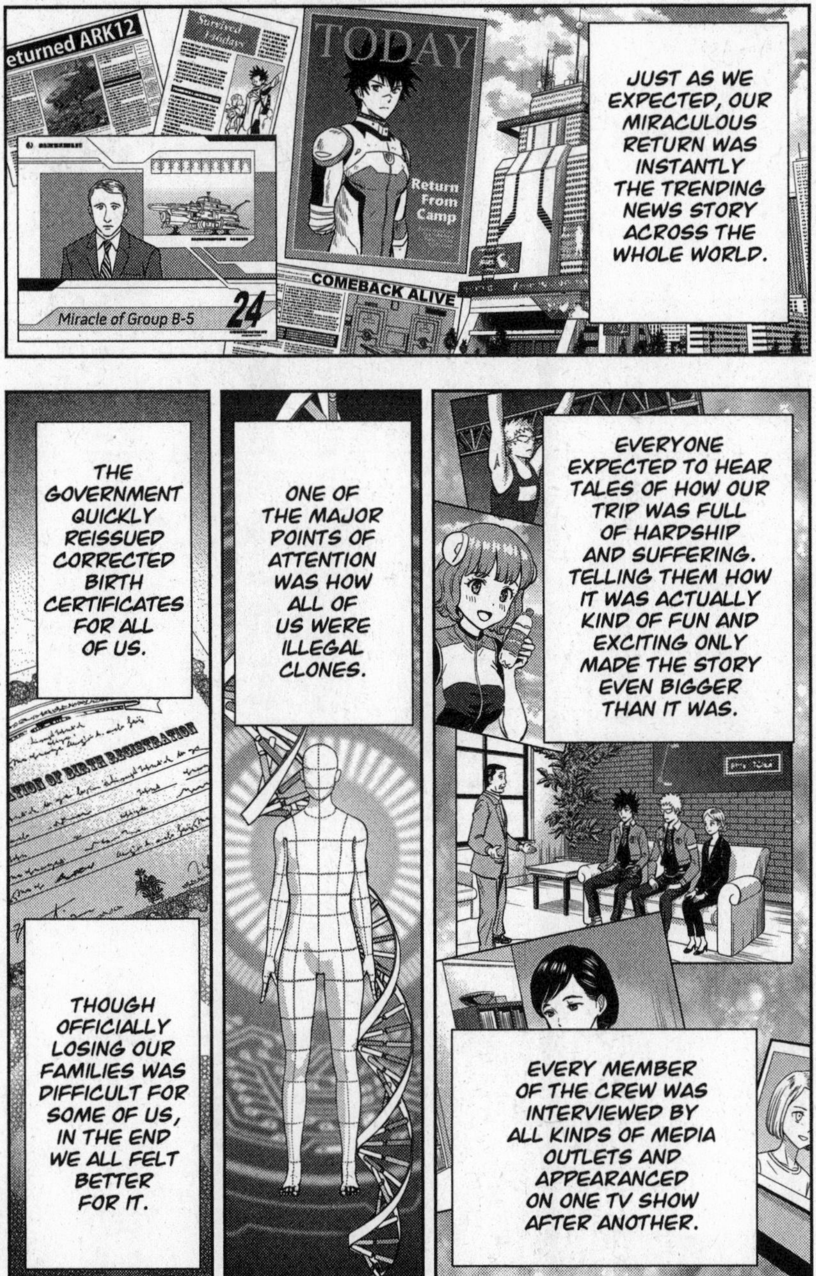
JUST AS WE EXPECTED, OUR MIRACULOUS RETURN WAS INSTANTLY THE TRENDING NEWS STORY ACROSS THE WHOLE WORLD.
TODAY
Return From Camp
eturned ARK12
COMEBACK ALIVE
Miracle of Group B-5
24
EVERYONE EXPECTED TO HEAR TALES OF HOW OUR TRIP WAS FULL OF HARDSHIP AND SUFFERING. TELLING THEM HOW IT WAS ACTUALLY KIND OF FUN AND EXCITING ONLY MADE THE STORY EVEN BIGGER THAN IT WAS.
EVERY MEMBER OF THE CREW WAS INTERVIEWED BY ALL KINDS OF MEDIA OUTLETS AND APPEARANCED ON ONE TV SHOW AFTER ANOTHER.
ONE OF THE MAJOR POINTS OF ATTENTION WAS HOW ALL OF US WERE ILLEGAL CLONES.
THE GOVERNMENT QUICKLY REISSUED CORRECTED BIRTH CERTIFICATES FOR ALL OF US.
THOUGH OFFICIALLY LOSING OUR FAMILIES WAS DIFFICULT FOR SOME OF US, IN THE END WE ALL FELT BETTER FOR IT.

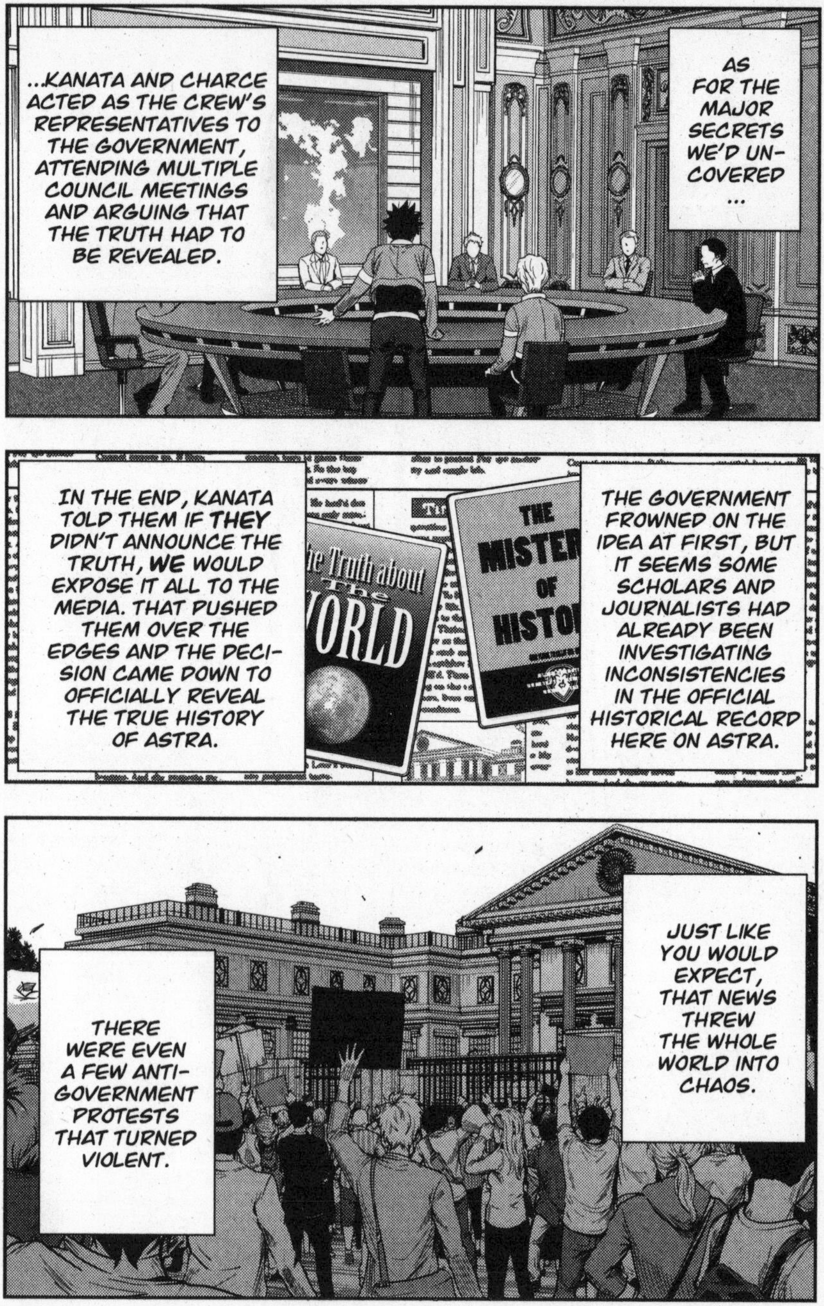
AS FOR THE MAJOR SECRETS WE'D UN-COVERED...
...KANATA AND CHARCE ACTED AS THE CREW'S REPRESENTATIVES TO THE GOVERNMENT, ATTENDING MULTIPLE COUNCIL MEETINGS AND ARGUING THAT THE TRUTH HAD TO BE REVEALED.
THE GOVERNMENT FROWNED ON THE IDEA AT FIRST, BUT IT SEEMS SOME SCHOLARS AND JOURNALISTS HAD ALREADY BEEN INVESTIGATING INCONSISTENCIES IN THE OFFICIAL HISTORICAL RECORD HERE ON ASTRA.
IN THE END, KANATA TOLD THEM IF **THEY** DIDN'T ANNOUNCE THE TRUTH, **WE** WOULD EXPOSE IT ALL TO THE MEDIA. THAT PUSHED THEM OVER THE EDGES AND THE DECI-SION CAME DOWN TO OFFICIALLY REVEAL THE TRUE HISTORY OF ASTRA.
JUST LIKE YOU WOULD EXPECT, THAT NEWS THREW THE WHOLE WORLD INTO CHAOS.
THERE WERE EVEN A FEW ANTI-GOVERNMENT PROTESTS THAT TURNED VIOLENT.

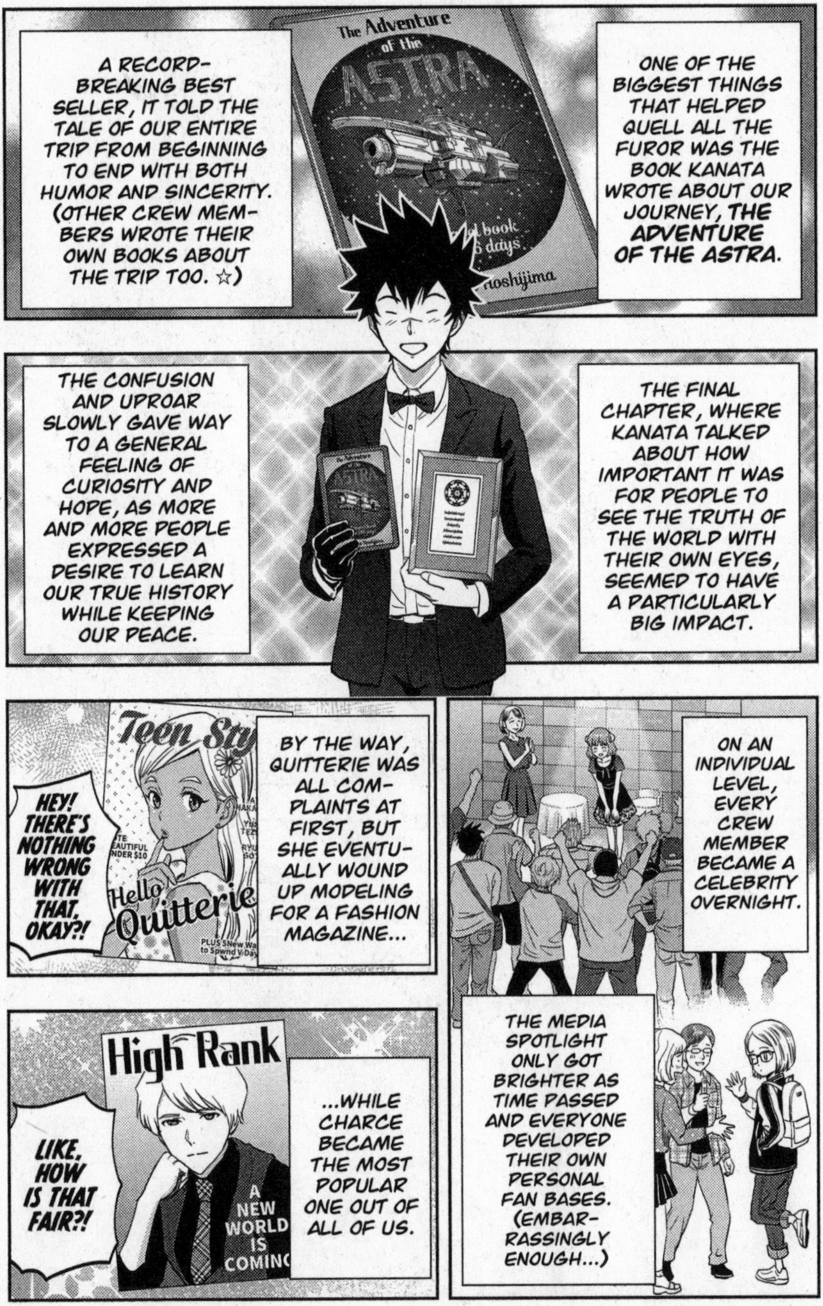
ONE OF THE BIGGEST THINGS THAT HELPED QUELL ALL THE FUROR WAS THE BOOK KANATA WROTE ABOUT OUR JOURNEY, THE ADVENTURE OF THE ASTRA.
The Adventure of the ASTRA
A RECORD-BREAKING BEST SELLER, IT TOLD THE TALE OF OUR ENTIRE TRIP FROM BEGINNING TO END WITH BOTH HUMOR AND SINCERITY. (OTHER CREW MEMBERS WROTE THEIR OWN BOOKS ABOUT THE TRIP TOO. ☆)
THE FINAL CHAPTER, WHERE KANATA TALKED ABOUT HOW IMPORTANT IT WAS FOR PEOPLE TO SEE THE TRUTH OF THE WORLD WITH THEIR OWN EYES, SEEMED TO HAVE A PARTICULARLY BIG IMPACT.
THE CONFUSION AND UPROAR SLOWLY GAVE WAY TO A GENERAL FEELING OF CURIOSITY AND HOPE, AS MORE AND MORE PEOPLE EXPRESSED A DESIRE TO LEARN OUR TRUE HISTORY WHILE KEEPING OUR PEACE.
ON AN INDIVIDUAL LEVEL, EVERY CREW MEMBER BECAME A CELEBRITY OVERNIGHT.
BY THE WAY, QUITTERIE WAS ALL COMPLAINTS AT FIRST, BUT SHE EVENTUALLY WOUND UP MODELING FOR A FASHION MAGAZINE...
Hello Quitterie
HEY! THERE'S NOTHING WRONG WITH THAT, OKAY?!
THE MEDIA SPOTLIGHT ONLY GOT BRIGHTER AS TIME PASSED AND EVERYONE DEVELOPED THEIR OWN PERSONAL FAN BASES. (EMBARRASSINGLY ENOUGH...)
High Rank
...WHILE CHARCE BECAME THE MOST POPULAR ONE OUT OF ALL OF US.
LIKE, HOW IS THAT FAIR?!

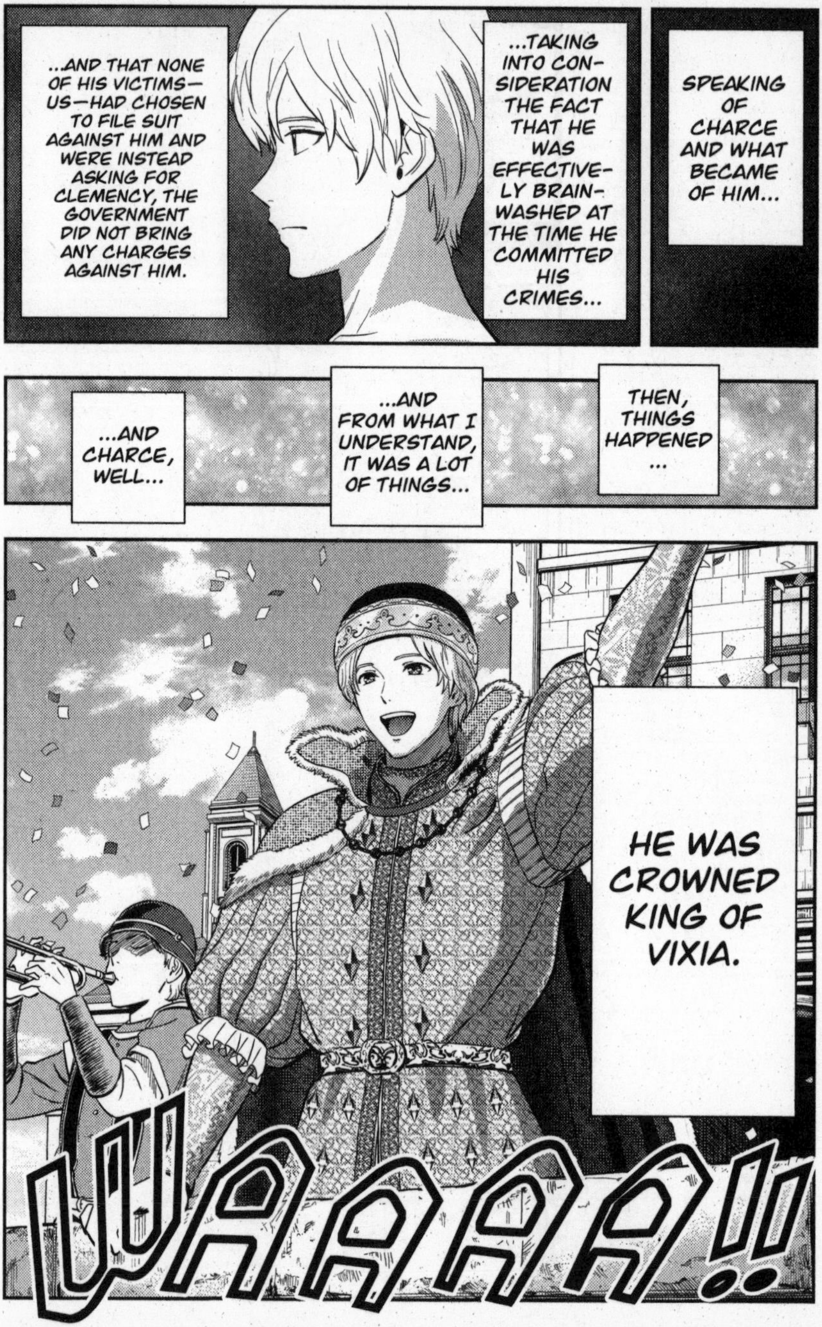
SPEAKING OF CHARCE AND WHAT BECAME OF HIM...
...TAKING INTO CONSIDERATION THE FACT THAT HE WAS EFFECTIVELY BRAINWASHED AT THE TIME HE COMMITTED HIS CRIMES...
...AND THAT NONE OF HIS VICTIMS—US—HAD CHOSEN TO FILE SUIT AGAINST HIM AND WERE INSTEAD ASKING FOR CLEMENCY, THE GOVERNMENT DID NOT BRING ANY CHARGES AGAINST HIM.
THEN, THINGS HAPPENED ...
...AND FROM WHAT I UNDERSTAND, IT WAS A LOT OF THINGS...
...AND CHARCE, WELL...
HE WAS CROWNED KING OF VIXIA.
VAAAAA!!

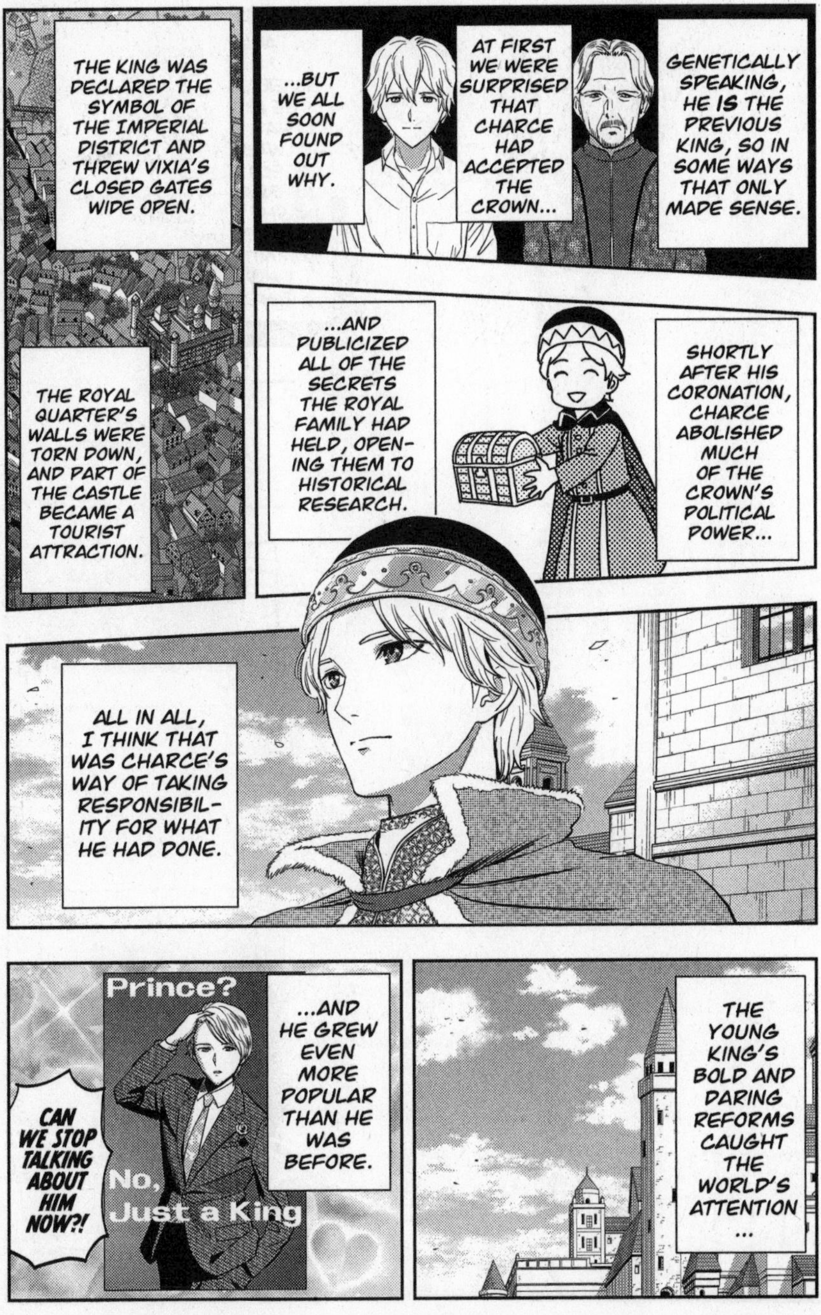
GENETICALLY SPEAKING, HE **IS** THE PREVIOUS KING, SO IN SOME WAYS THAT ONLY MADE SENSE.
AT FIRST WE WERE SURPRISED THAT CHARCE HAD ACCEPTED THE CROWN...
...BUT WE ALL SOON FOUND OUT WHY.
SHORTLY AFTER HIS CORONATION, CHARCE ABOLISHED MUCH OF THE CROWN'S POLITICAL POWER...
...AND PUBLICIZED ALL OF THE SECRETS THE ROYAL FAMILY HAD HELD, OPENING THEM TO HISTORICAL RESEARCH.
THE KING WAS DECLARED THE SYMBOL OF THE IMPERIAL DISTRICT AND THREW VIXIA'S CLOSED GATES WIDE OPEN.
THE ROYAL QUARTER'S WALLS WERE TORN DOWN, AND PART OF THE CASTLE BECAME A TOURIST ATTRACTION.
ALL IN ALL, I THINK THAT WAS CHARCE'S WAY OF TAKING RESPONSIBILITY FOR WHAT HE HAD DONE.
THE YOUNG KING'S BOLD AND DARING REFORMS CAUGHT THE WORLD'S ATTENTION...
...AND HE GREW EVEN MORE POPULAR THAN HE WAS BEFORE.
Prince?
CAN WE STOP TALKING ABOUT HIM NOW?!
No, Just a King

TIME PASSED IN A FLURRY OF ACTIVITY AND CHANGE...

...BUT WE ALL SLOWLY GOT MUCH OF OUR OLD, NORMAL LIVES BACK.

WE GRADUATED FROM CAIRD...

...AND THEN WE ALL SET OUT UPON THE LIFE PATHS WE HAD CHOSEN TO WALK.

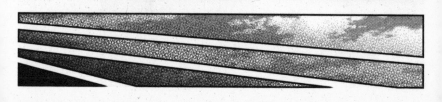

Seven Years Later

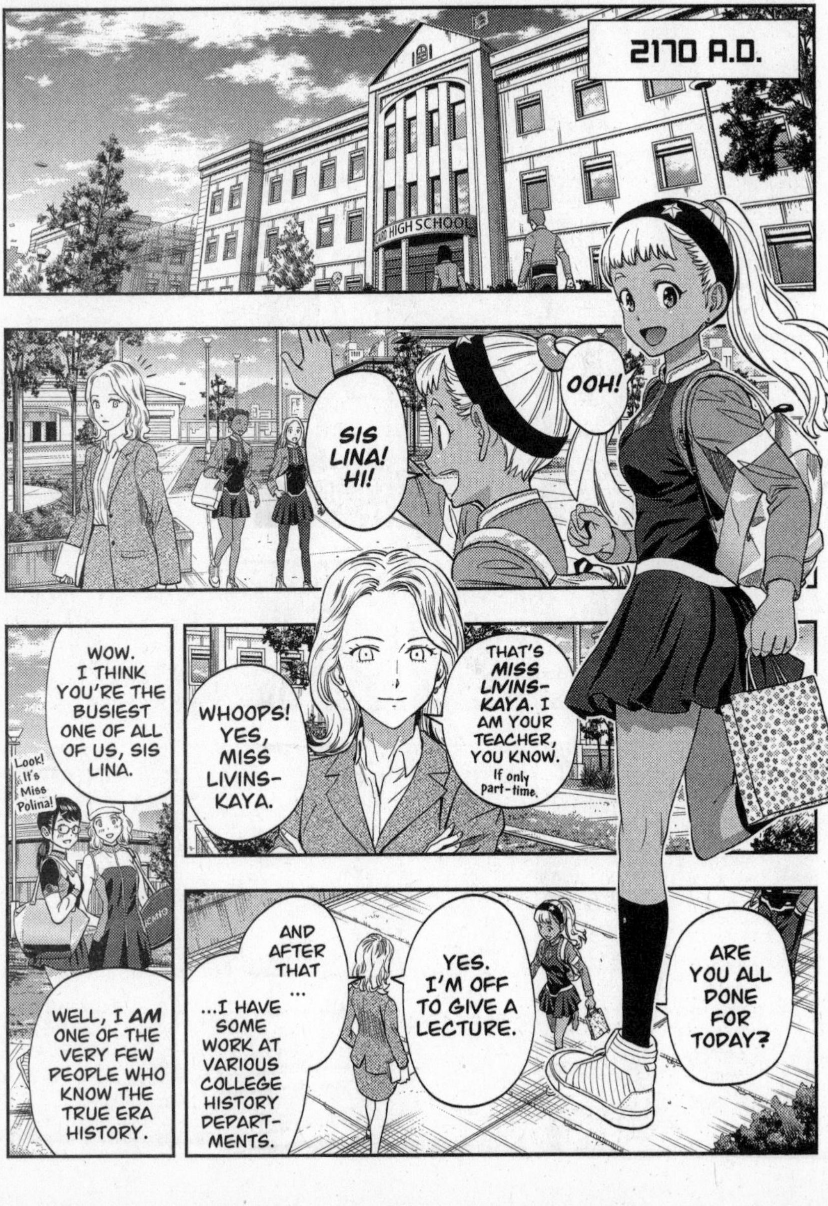
2170 A.D.
HIGH SCHOOL
OOH!
SIS LINA! HI!
THAT'S *MISS LIVINSKAYA*. I AM YOUR TEACHER, YOU KNOW.
If only part-time.
WHOOPS! YES, MISS LIVINSKAYA.
ARE YOU ALL DONE FOR TODAY?
YES. I'M OFF TO GIVE A LECTURE.
AND AFTER THAT ...
...I HAVE SOME WORK AT VARIOUS COLLEGE HISTORY DEPARTMENTS.
WOW. I THINK YOU'RE THE BUSIEST ONE OF ALL OF US, SIS LINA.
Look! It's Miss Polina!
WELL, I *AM* ONE OF THE VERY FEW PEOPLE WHO KNOW THE TRUE ERA HISTORY.

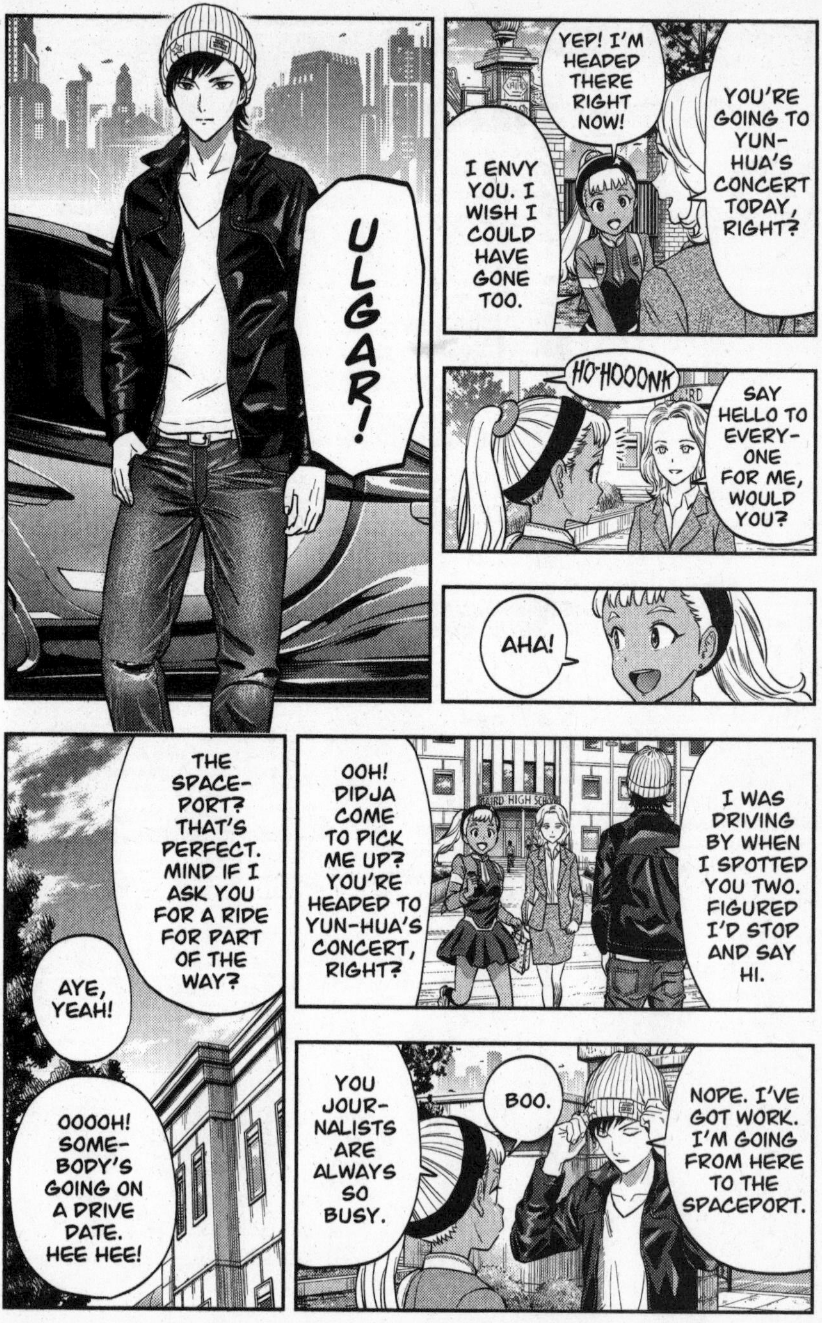
YOU'RE GOING TO YUN-HUA'S CONCERT TODAY, RIGHT?
YEP! I'M HEADED THERE RIGHT NOW!
I ENVY YOU. I WISH I COULD HAVE GONE TOO.
SAY HELLO TO EVERY-ONE FOR ME, WOULD YOU?
HO-HOOONK
AHA!
ULGAR!
I WAS DRIVING BY WHEN I SPOTTED YOU TWO. FIGURED I'D STOP AND SAY HI.
OOH! DIDJA COME TO PICK ME UP? YOU'RE HEADED TO YUN-HUA'S CONCERT, RIGHT?
NOPE. I'VE GOT WORK. I'M GOING FROM HERE TO THE SPACEPORT.
BOO.
YOU JOUR-NALISTS ARE ALWAYS SO BUSY.
THE SPACE-PORT? THAT'S PERFECT. MIND IF I ASK YOU FOR A RIDE FOR PART OF THE WAY?
AYE, YEAH!
OOOOH! SOME-BODY'S GOING ON A DRIVE DATE. HEE HEE!

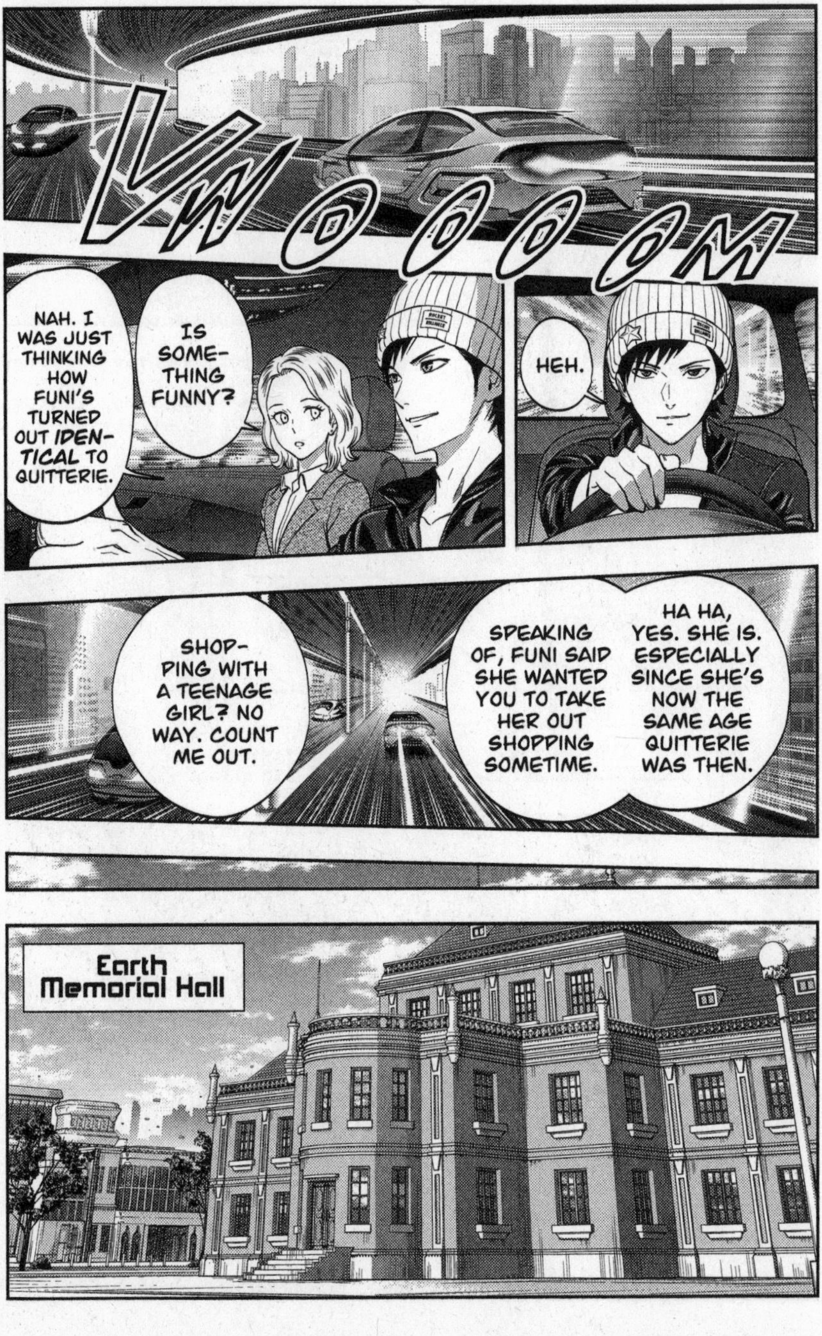
VWOOOOM
HEH.
IS SOME-THING FUNNY?
NAH. I WAS JUST THINKING HOW FUNI'S TURNED OUT IDEN-TICAL TO QUITTERIE.
HA HA, YES. SHE IS. ESPECIALLY SINCE SHE'S NOW THE SAME AGE QUITTERIE WAS THEN.
SPEAKING OF, FUNI SAID SHE WANTED YOU TO TAKE HER OUT SHOPPING SOMETIME.
SHOP-PING WITH A TEENAGE GIRL? NO WAY. COUNT ME OUT.
Earth Memorial Hall

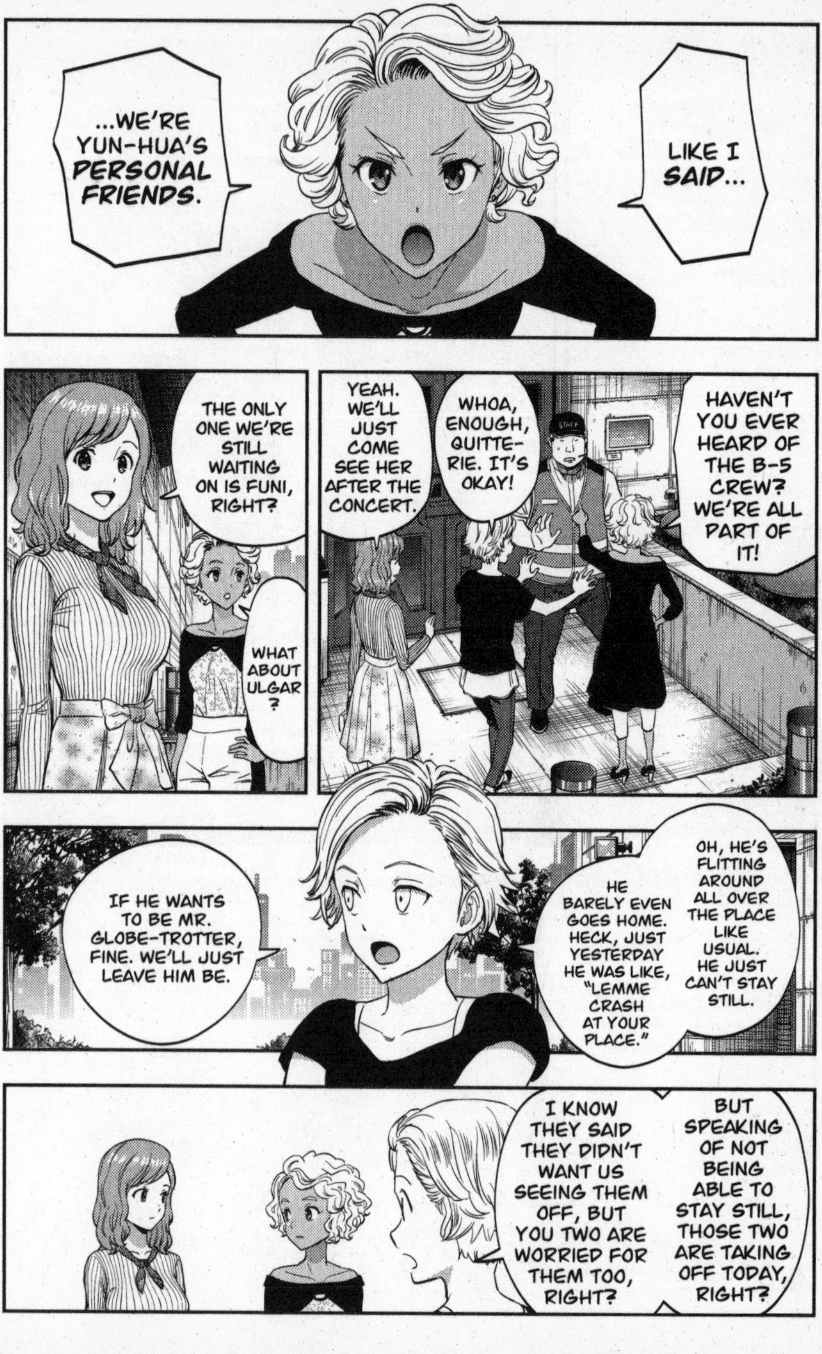
LIKE I SAID...
...WE'RE YUN-HUA'S PERSONAL FRIENDS.
HAVEN'T YOU EVER HEARD OF THE B-5 CREW? WE'RE ALL PART OF IT!
WHOA, ENOUGH, QUITTE-RIE. IT'S OKAY!
YEAH. WE'LL JUST COME SEE HER AFTER THE CONCERT.
THE ONLY ONE WE'RE STILL WAITING ON IS FUNI, RIGHT?
WHAT ABOUT ULGAR?
OH, HE'S FLITTING AROUND ALL OVER THE PLACE LIKE USUAL. HE JUST CAN'T STAY STILL.
HE BARELY EVEN GOES HOME. HECK, JUST YESTERDAY HE WAS LIKE, "LEMME CRASH AT YOUR PLACE."
IF HE WANTS TO BE MR. GLOBE-TROTTER, FINE. WE'LL JUST LEAVE HIM BE.
BUT SPEAKING OF NOT BEING ABLE TO STAY STILL, THOSE TWO ARE TAKING OFF TODAY, RIGHT?
I KNOW THEY SAID THEY DIDN'T WANT US SEEING THEM OFF, BUT YOU TWO ARE WORRIED FOR THEM TOO, RIGHT?

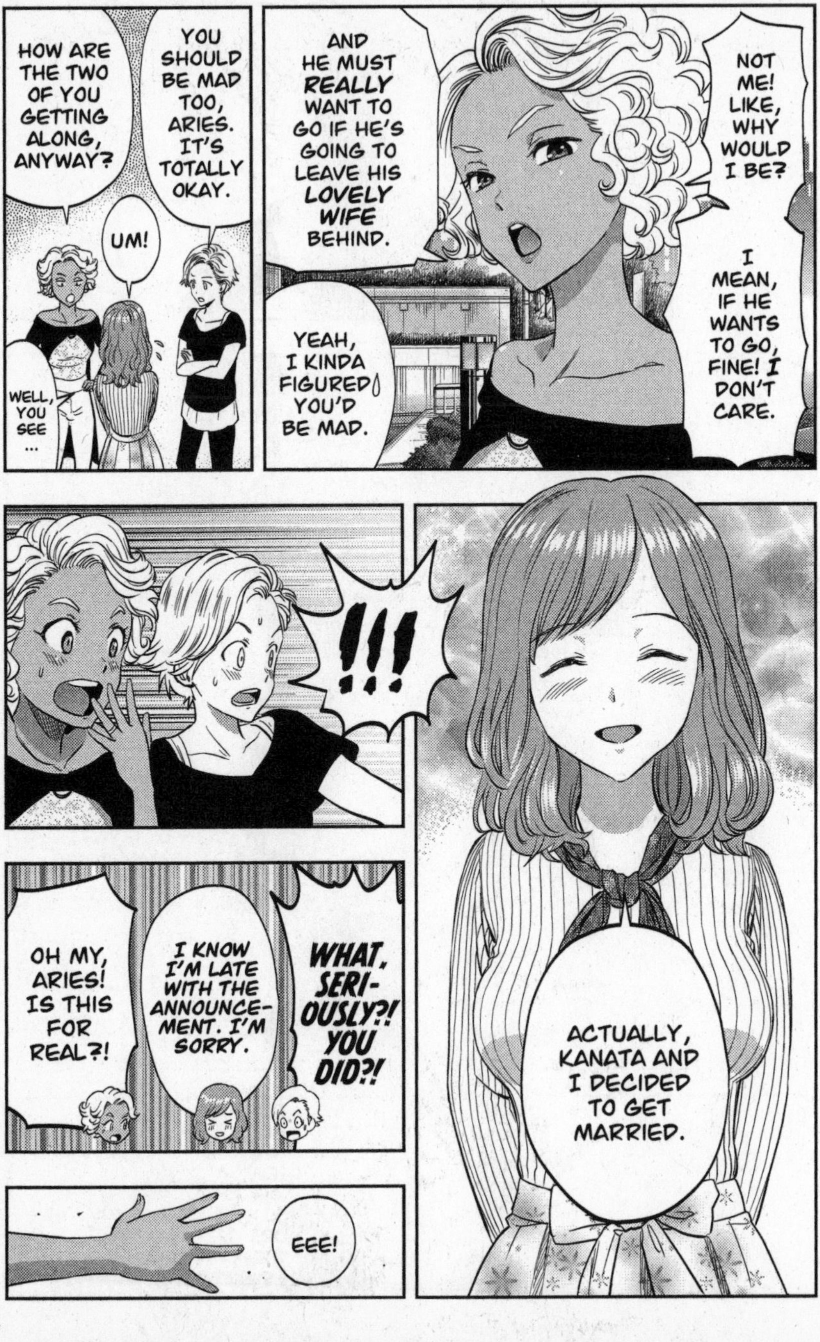
NOT ME! LIKE, WHY WOULD I BE?
I MEAN, IF HE WANTS TO GO, FINE! I DON'T CARE.
AND HE MUST REALLY WANT TO GO IF HE'S GOING TO LEAVE HIS LOVELY WIFE BEHIND.
YEAH, I KINDA FIGURED YOU'D BE MAD.
YOU SHOULD BE MAD TOO, ARIES. IT'S TOTALLY OKAY.
HOW ARE THE TWO OF YOU GETTING ALONG, ANYWAY?
UM!
WELL, YOU SEE ...
ACTUALLY, KANATA AND I DECIDED TO GET MARRIED.
!!!
WHAT, SERIOUSLY?! YOU DID?!
I KNOW I'M LATE WITH THE ANNOUNCEMENT. I'M SORRY.
OH MY, ARIES! IS THIS FOR REAL?!
EEE!

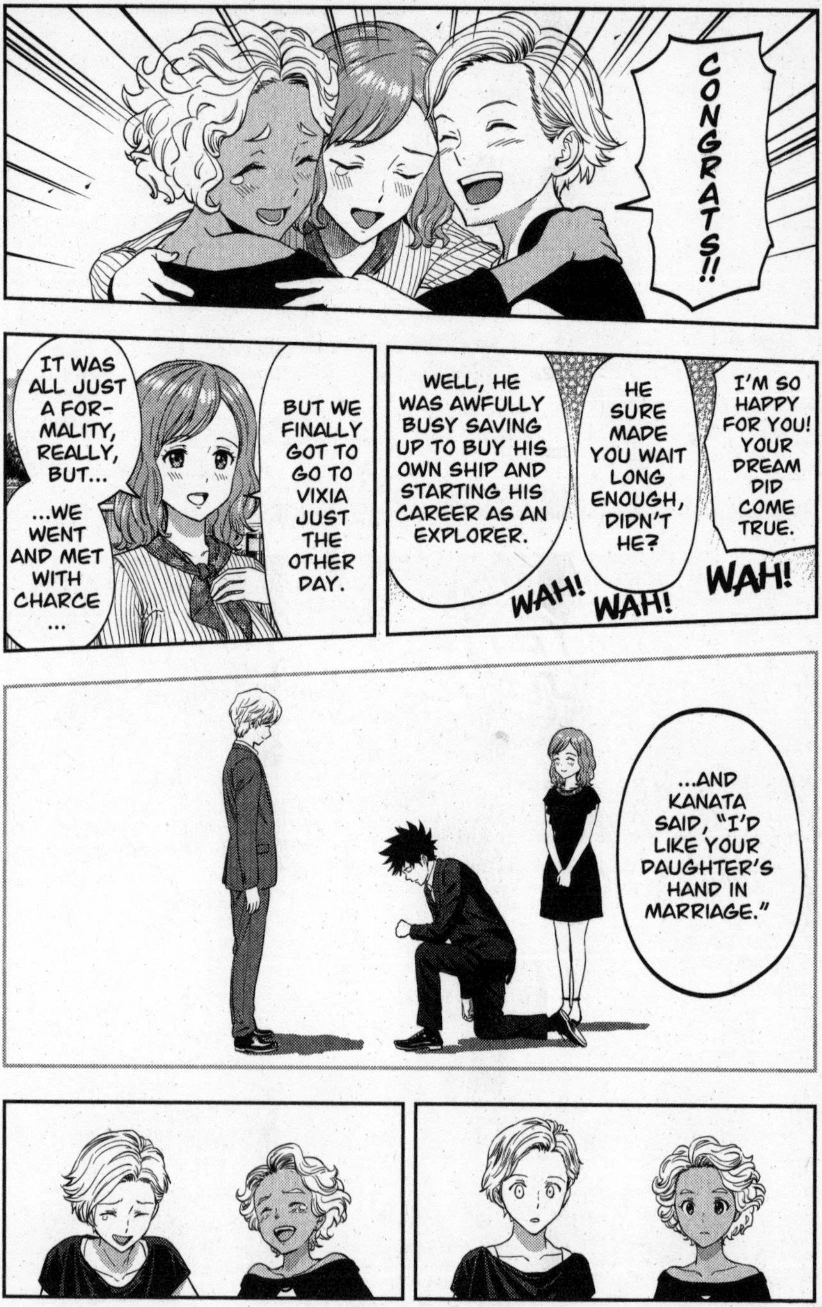
CONGRATS!!
I'M SO HAPPY FOR YOU! YOUR DREAM DID COME TRUE.
WAH!
HE SURE MADE YOU WAIT LONG ENOUGH, DIDN'T HE?
WAH!
WELL, HE WAS AWFULLY BUSY SAVING UP TO BUY HIS OWN SHIP AND STARTING HIS CAREER AS AN EXPLORER.
WAH!
BUT WE FINALLY GOT TO GO TO VIXIA JUST THE OTHER DAY.
IT WAS ALL JUST A FOR-MALITY, REALLY, BUT...
...WE WENT AND MET WITH CHARCE...
...AND KANATA SAID, "I'D LIKE YOUR DAUGHTER'S HAND IN MARRIAGE."

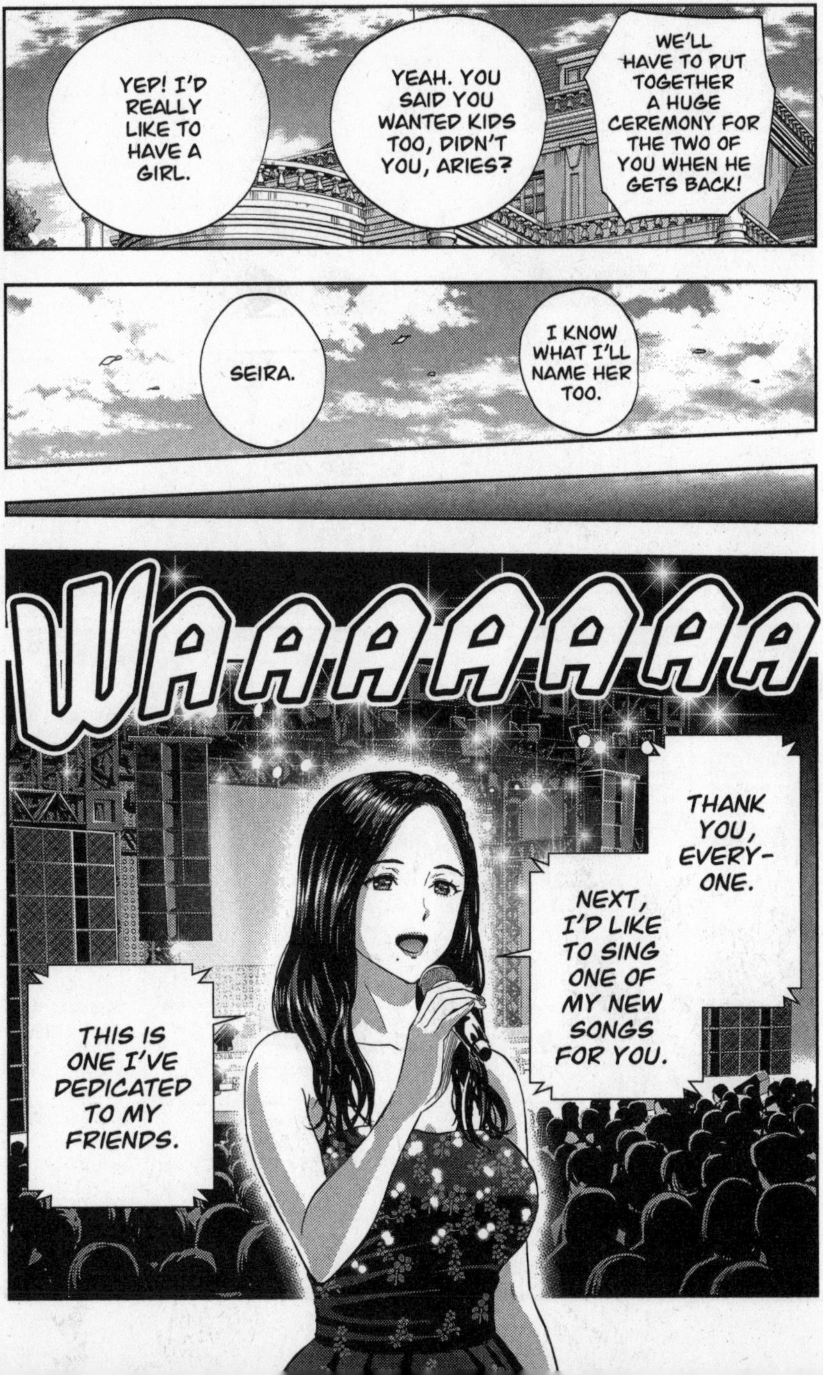
WE'LL HAVE TO PUT TOGETHER A HUGE CEREMONY FOR THE TWO OF YOU WHEN HE GETS BACK!
YEAH. YOU SAID YOU WANTED KIDS TOO, DIDN'T YOU, ARIES?
YEP! I'D REALLY LIKE TO HAVE A GIRL.
I KNOW WHAT I'LL NAME HER TOO.
SEIRA.
WAAAAAAA
THANK YOU, EVERY-ONE.
NEXT, I'D LIKE TO SING ONE OF MY NEW SONGS FOR YOU.
THIS IS ONE I'VE DEDICATED TO MY FRIENDS.

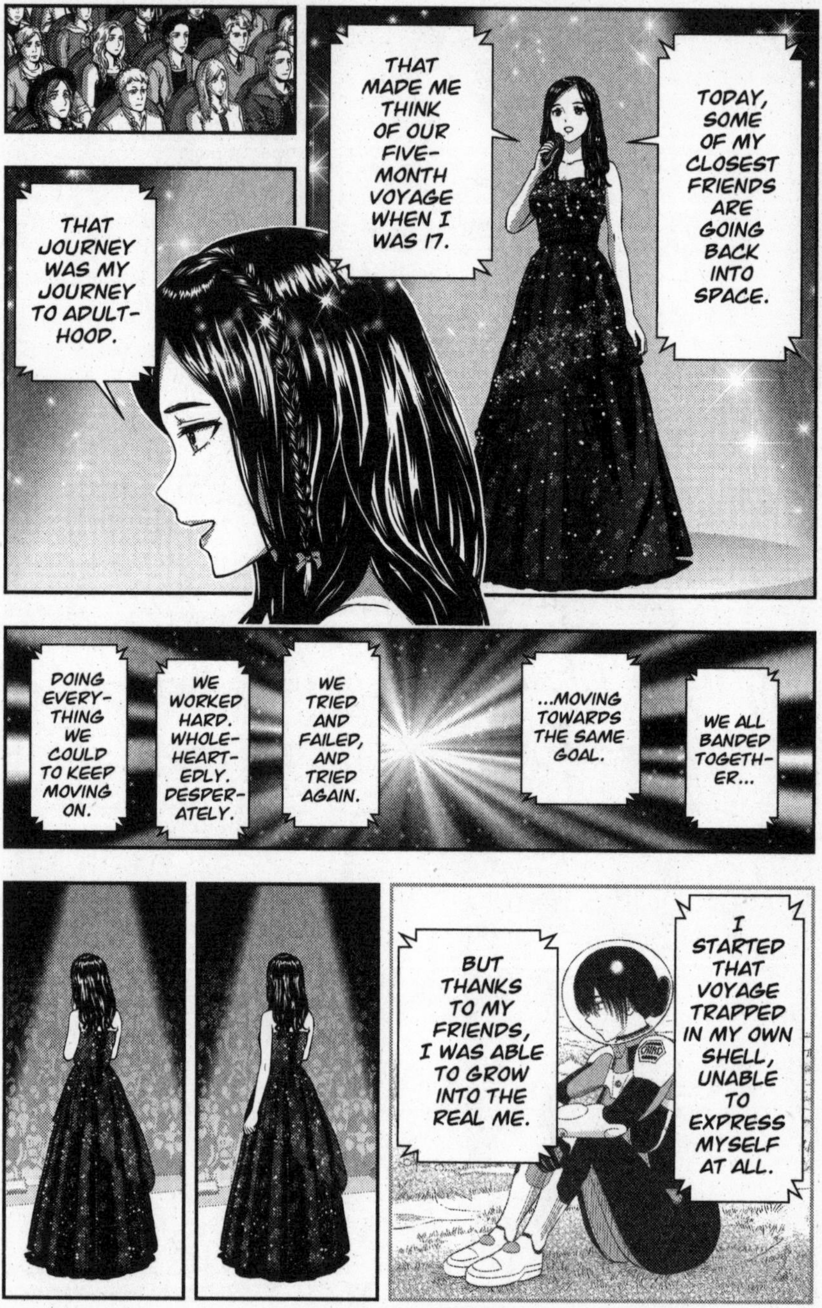
TODAY, SOME OF MY CLOSEST FRIENDS ARE GOING BACK INTO SPACE.
THAT MADE ME THINK OF OUR FIVE-MONTH VOYAGE WHEN I WAS 17.
THAT JOURNEY WAS MY JOURNEY TO ADULTHOOD.
WE ALL BANDED TOGETHER...
...MOVING TOWARDS THE SAME GOAL.
WE TRIED AND FAILED, AND TRIED AGAIN.
WE WORKED HARD. WHOLEHEARTEDLY. DESPERATELY.
DOING EVERYTHING WE COULD TO KEEP MOVING ON.
I STARTED THAT VOYAGE TRAPPED IN MY OWN SHELL, UNABLE TO EXPRESS MYSELF AT ALL.
BUT THANKS TO MY FRIENDS, I WAS ABLE TO GROW INTO THE REAL ME.

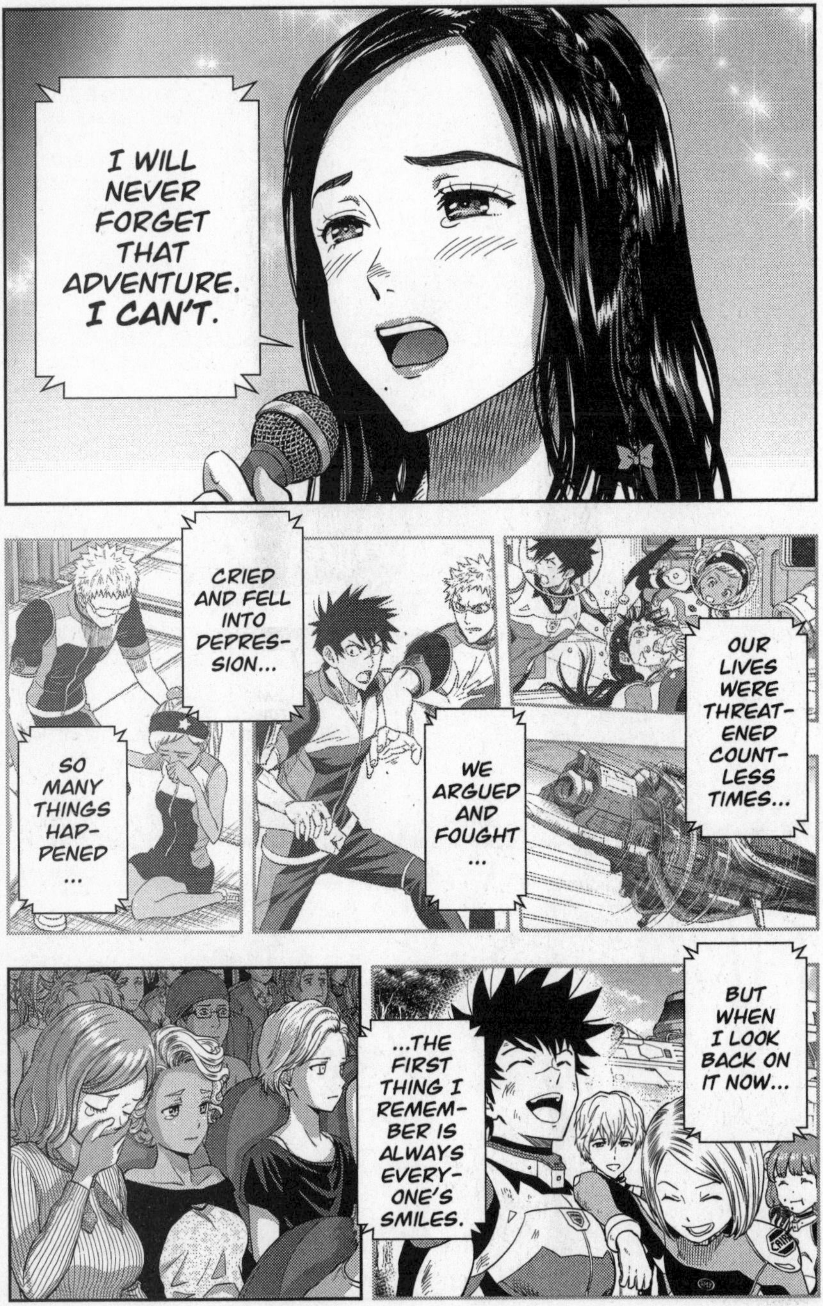
I WILL NEVER FORGET THAT ADVENTURE. I CAN'T.
OUR LIVES WERE THREATENED COUNTLESS TIMES...
WE ARGUED AND FOUGHT...
CRIED AND FELL INTO DEPRESSION...
SO MANY THINGS HAPPENED...
BUT WHEN I LOOK BACK ON IT NOW...
...THE FIRST THING I REMEMBER IS ALWAYS EVERYONE'S SMILES.

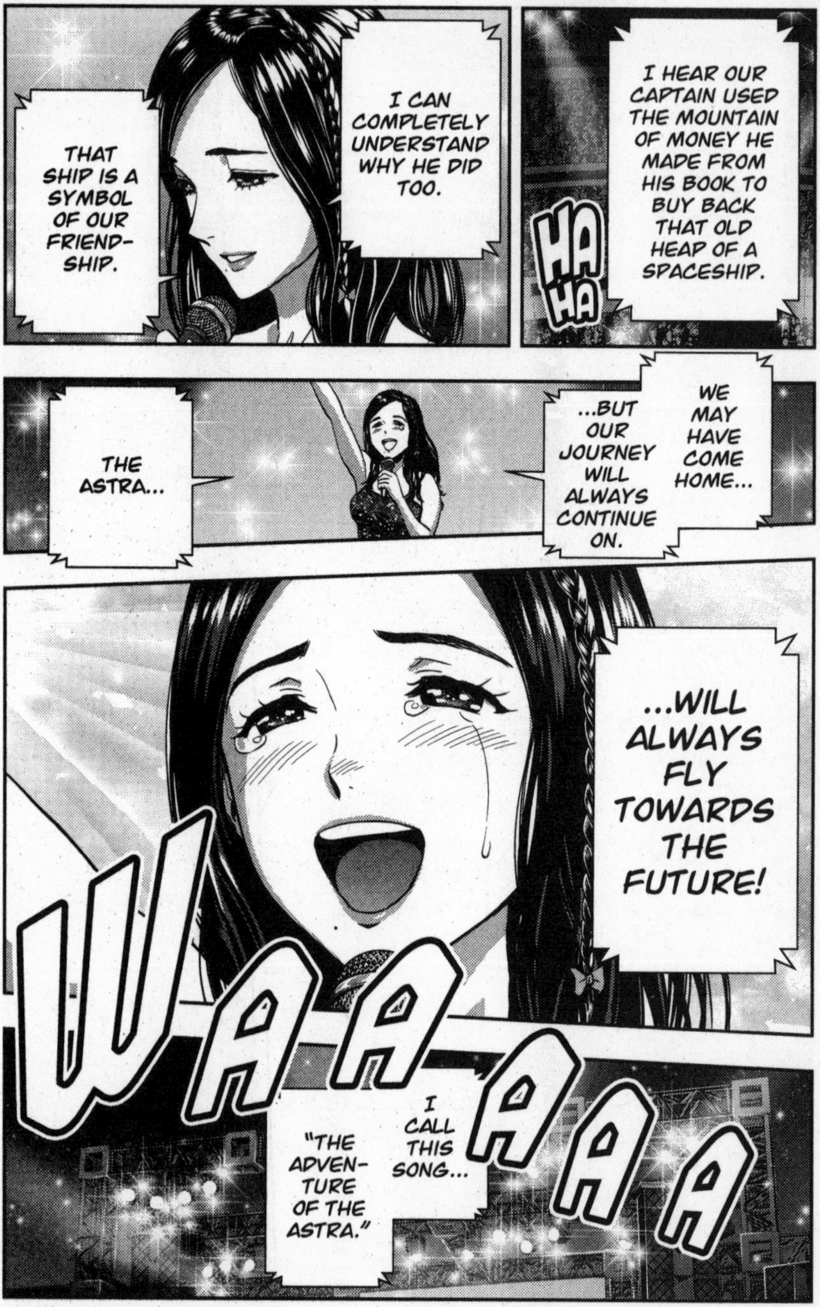
I HEAR OUR CAPTAIN USED THE MOUNTAIN OF MONEY HE MADE FROM HIS BOOK TO BUY BACK THAT OLD HEAP OF A SPACESHIP.
HA HA
I CAN COMPLETELY UNDERSTAND WHY HE DID TOO.
THAT SHIP IS A SYMBOL OF OUR FRIEND-SHIP.
WE MAY HAVE COME HOME...
...BUT OUR JOURNEY WILL ALWAYS CONTINUE ON.
THE ASTRA...
...WILL ALWAYS FLY TOWARDS THE FUTURE!
WAAAAAA
I CALL THIS SONG...
"THE ADVEN-TURE OF THE ASTRA."

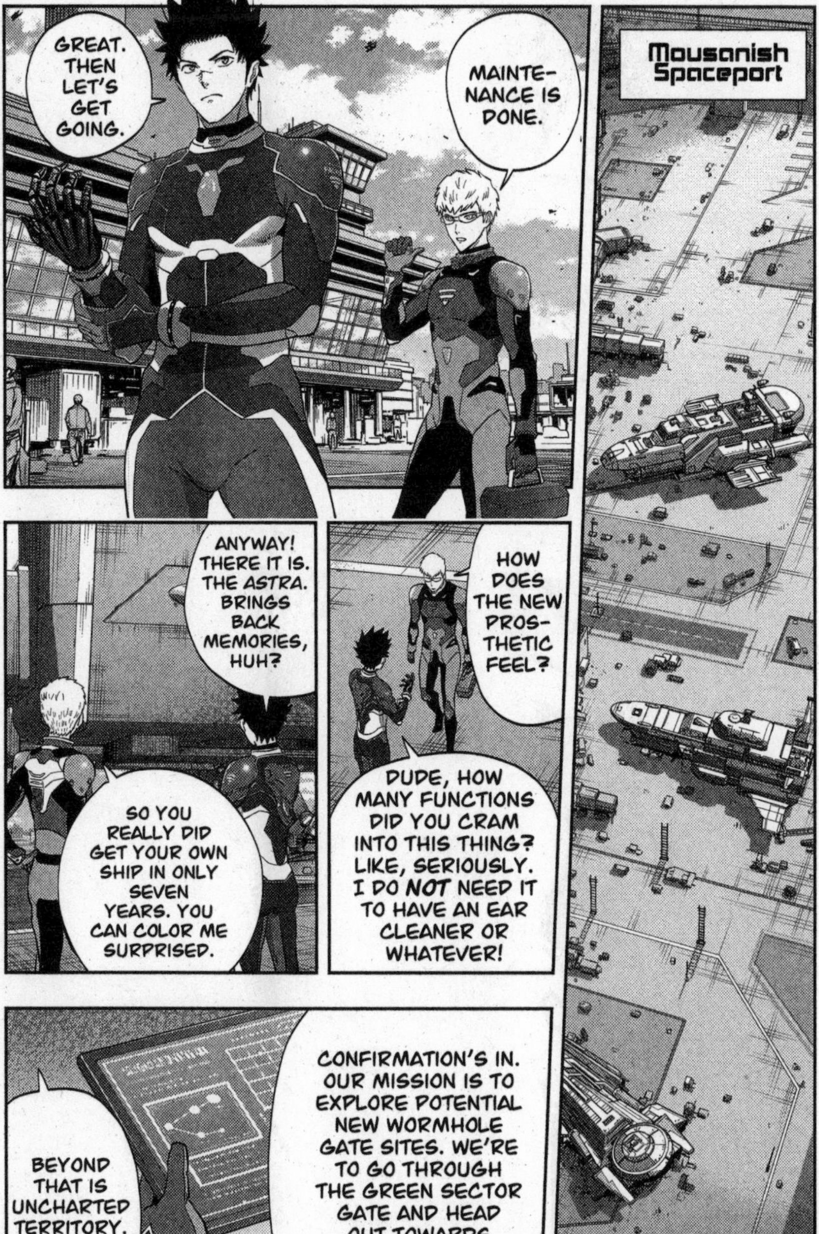
Mousanish Spaceport
MAINTENANCE IS DONE.
GREAT. THEN LET'S GET GOING.
HOW DOES THE NEW PROSTHETIC FEEL?
DUDE, HOW MANY FUNCTIONS DID YOU CRAM INTO THIS THING? LIKE, SERIOUSLY. I DO *NOT* NEED IT TO HAVE AN EAR CLEANER OR WHATEVER!
ANYWAY! THERE IT IS. THE ASTRA. BRINGS BACK MEMORIES, HUH?
SO YOU REALLY DID GET YOUR OWN SHIP IN ONLY SEVEN YEARS. YOU CAN COLOR ME SURPRISED.
CONFIRMATION'S IN. OUR MISSION IS TO EXPLORE POTENTIAL NEW WORMHOLE GATE SITES. WE'RE TO GO THROUGH THE GREEN SECTOR GATE AND HEAD OUT TOWARDS GAZENETT.
BEYOND THAT IS UNCHARTED TERRITORY. PERFECT.

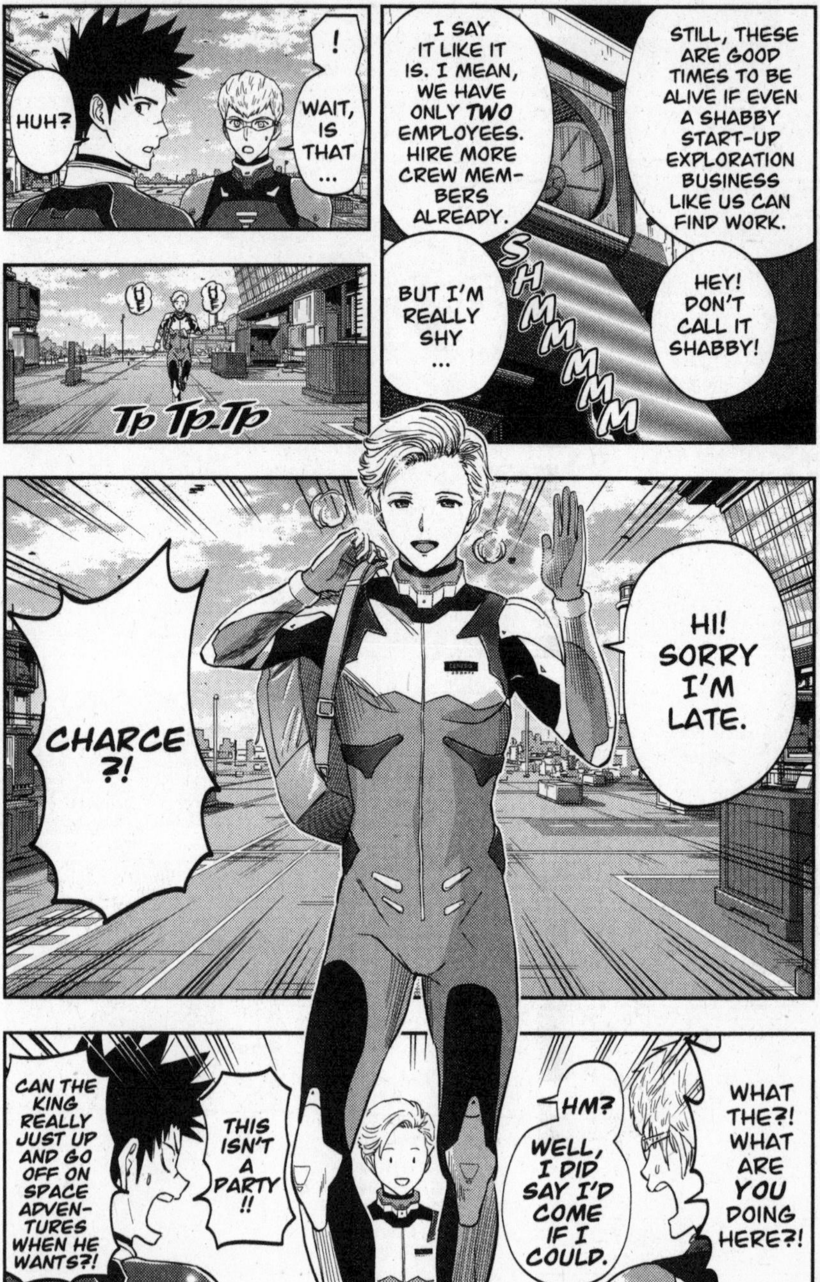

STILL, THESE ARE GOOD TIMES TO BE ALIVE IF EVEN A SHABBY START-UP EXPLORATION BUSINESS LIKE US CAN FIND WORK.
I SAY IT LIKE IT IS. I MEAN, WE HAVE ONLY TWO EMPLOYEES. HIRE MORE CREW MEMBERS ALREADY.
HEY! DON'T CALL IT SHABBY!
BUT I'M REALLY SHY...
SHMMMMM
!
WAIT, IS THAT...
HUH?
Tp Tp Tp
HI! SORRY I'M LATE.
CHARCE?!
WHAT THE?! WHAT ARE YOU DOING HERE?!
HM?
WELL, I DID SAY I'D COME IF I COULD.
THIS ISN'T A PARTY!!
CAN THE KING REALLY JUST UP AND GO OFF ON SPACE ADVENTURES WHEN HE WANTS?!

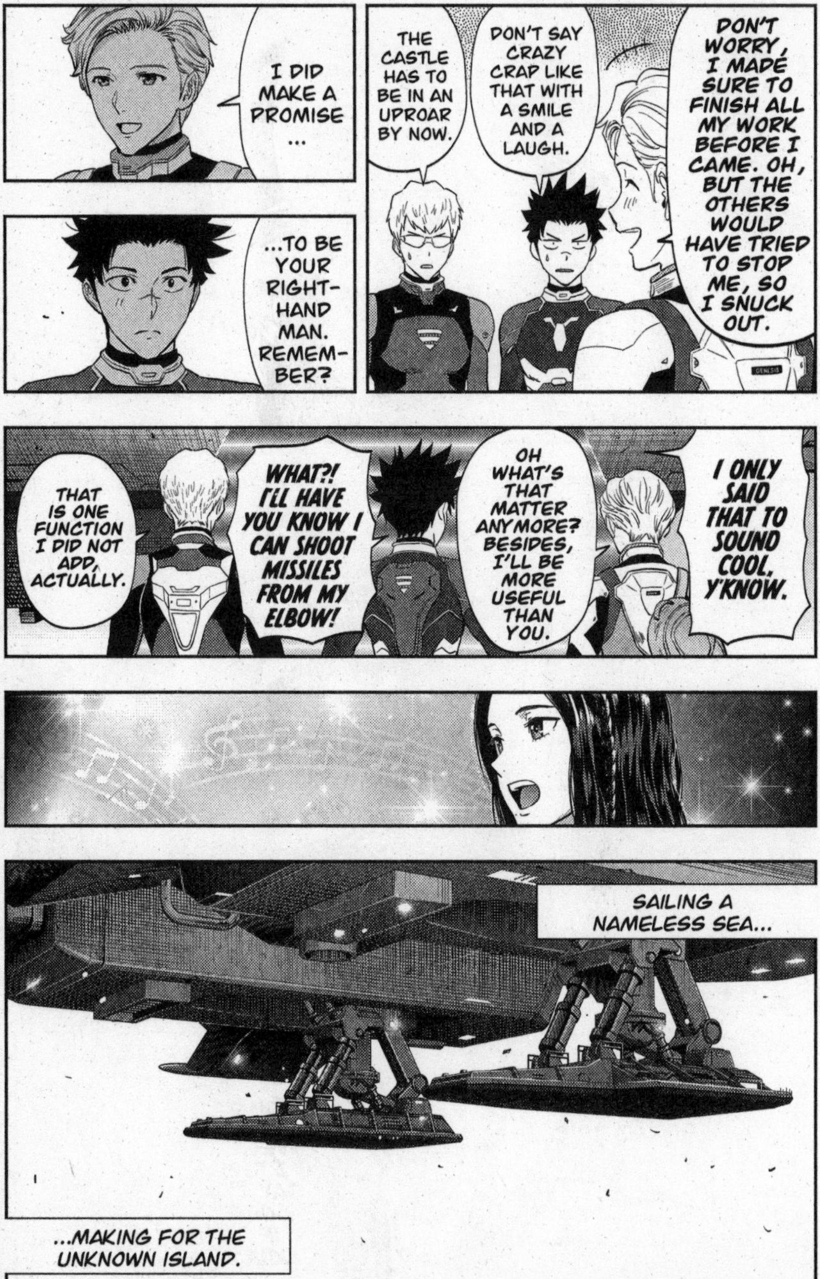
DON'T WORRY, I MADE SURE TO FINISH ALL MY WORK BEFORE I CAME. OH, BUT THE OTHERS WOULD HAVE TRIED TO STOP ME, SO I SNUCK OUT.
DON'T SAY CRAZY CRAP LIKE THAT WITH A SMILE AND A LAUGH.
THE CASTLE HAS TO BE IN AN UPROAR BY NOW.
I DID MAKE A PROMISE...
...TO BE YOUR RIGHT-HAND MAN. REMEMBER?
I ONLY SAID THAT TO SOUND COOL, Y'KNOW.
OH WHAT'S THAT MATTER ANYMORE? BESIDES, I'LL BE MORE USEFUL THAN YOU.
WHAT?! I'LL HAVE YOU KNOW I CAN SHOOT MISSILES FROM MY ELBOW!
THAT IS ONE FUNCTION I DID NOT ADD, ACTUALLY.
SAILING A NAMELESS SEA...
...MAKING FOR THE UNKNOWN ISLAND.

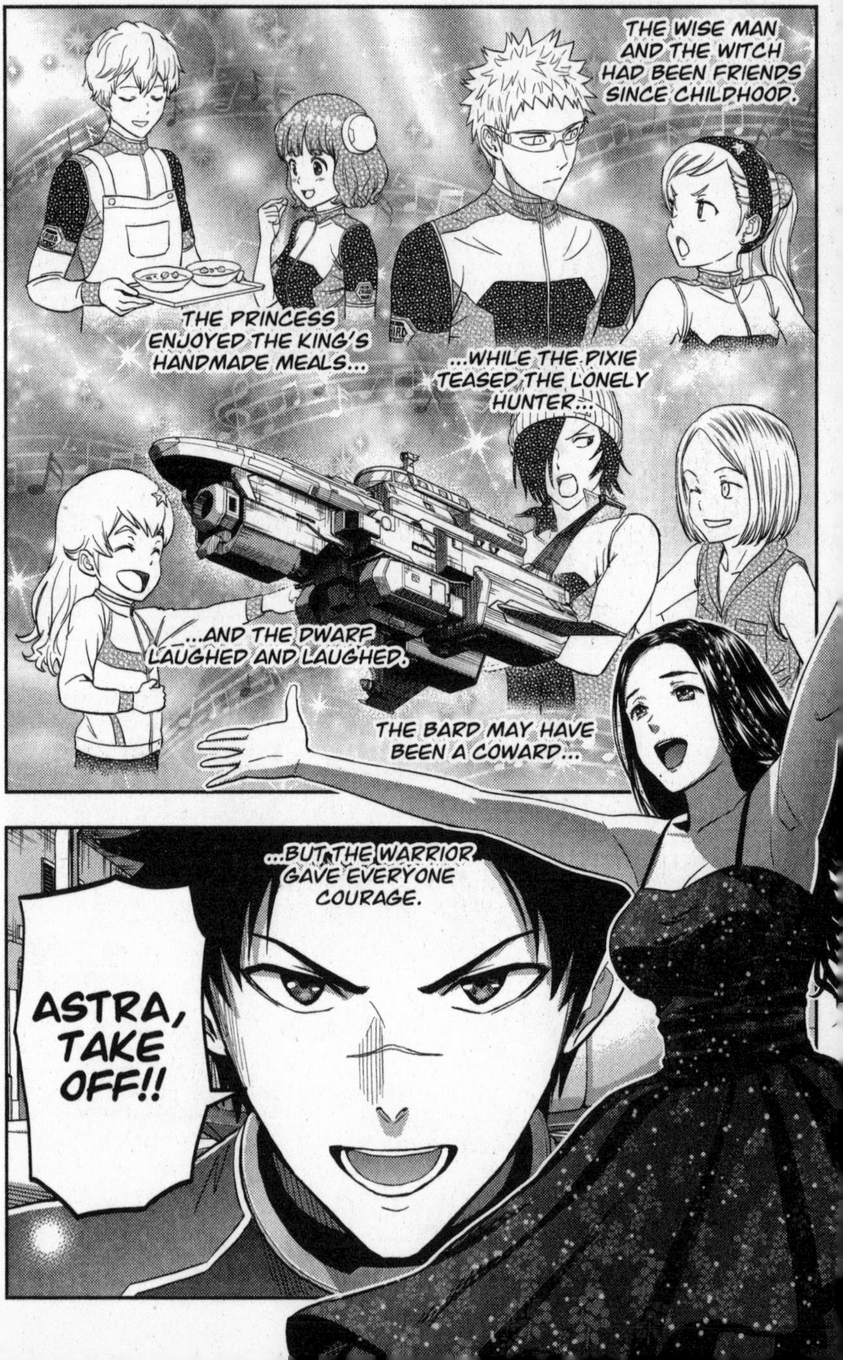
THE WISE MAN AND THE WITCH HAD BEEN FRIENDS SINCE CHILDHOOD.
THE PRINCESS ENJOYED THE KING'S HANDMADE MEALS...
...WHILE THE PIXIE TEASED THE LONELY HUNTER...
...AND THE DWARF LAUGHED AND LAUGHED.
THE BARD MAY HAVE BEEN A COWARD...
...BUT THE WARRIOR GAVE EVERYONE COURAGE.
ASTRA, TAKE OFF!!

OUR SHIP SAILS EVER ON...

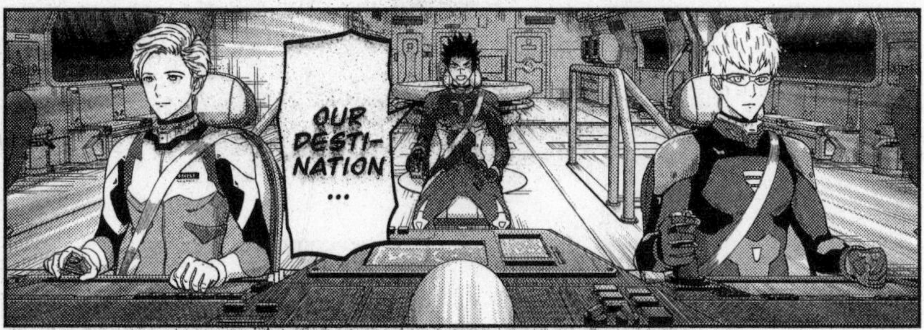
OUR DESTI- NATION ...

...FOLLOWING THE TRACKLESS PATH.

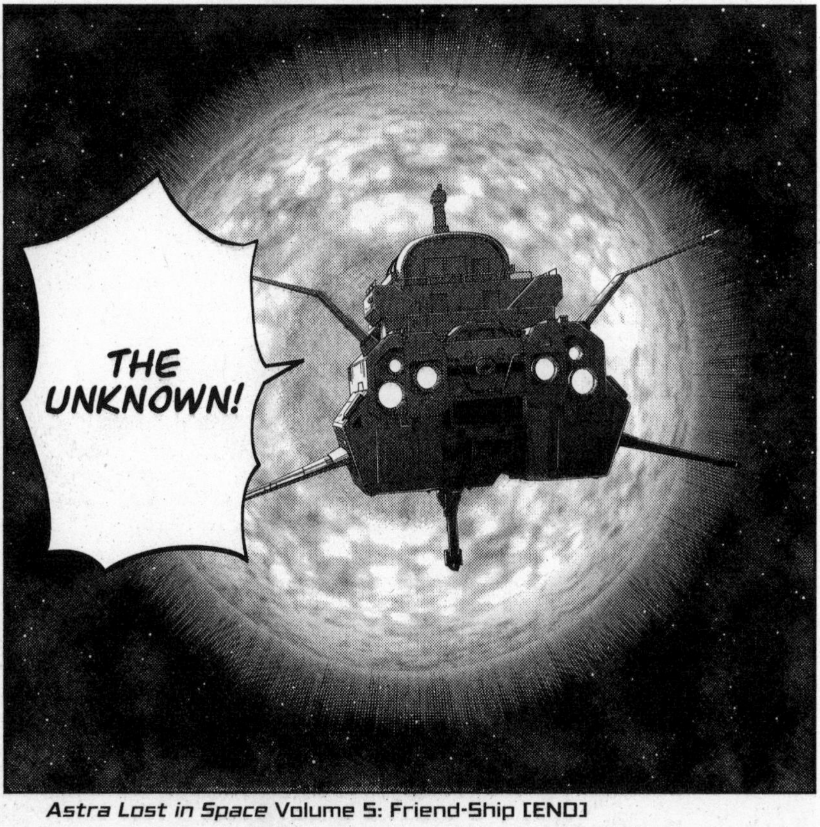
THE UNKNOWN!

Astra Lost in Space Volume 5: Friend-Ship [END]

ASTRA
LOST IN SPACE

[THE END]

Afterword

After I finished my previous work, *Sket Dance*, I spent a while in limbo wondering what I wanted to do next. Even when I had the inklings of an idea, I wound up taking the long way around getting an official outline solidified. Not only was it going to be considerably different from my previous series, it was also going to be hard sci-fi, which is a relatively unpopular genre for manga. I did get some pushback from my editors. Heck, I'm not even that knowledgeable about science fiction myself. I knew I was setting up a rough road for myself, so why did I feel like this had to be the next story I wrote? Well, precisely *because* it was so different. At the time, I had told myself that I was going to—I needed to—step outside my comfort zone and challenge myself with a story utterly different from what I'd done before. Not only that, I was going to draw the entire thing digitally, a big change from my previous methods.

So I started work on a completely new story in a genre I didn't know using methods I wasn't familiar with. It felt like I, too, had been tossed into the depths of space and had to fight my way towards my goal, overcoming hardships and trials along the way.

I think this work was a necessary challenge I had to overcome for the betterment of my career as a manga creator. Now that I've completed it, it feels like I've earned the right to go wherever I want next. I'm thankful to my editors for giving me the chance to do this, to my supervisors for supporting me and to my assistants for doing such amazing work. And last but not least, I am very grateful to everyone who chose to read this series. I hope that our paths will cross again in my next work.

Kenta Shinohara

Book Rankings

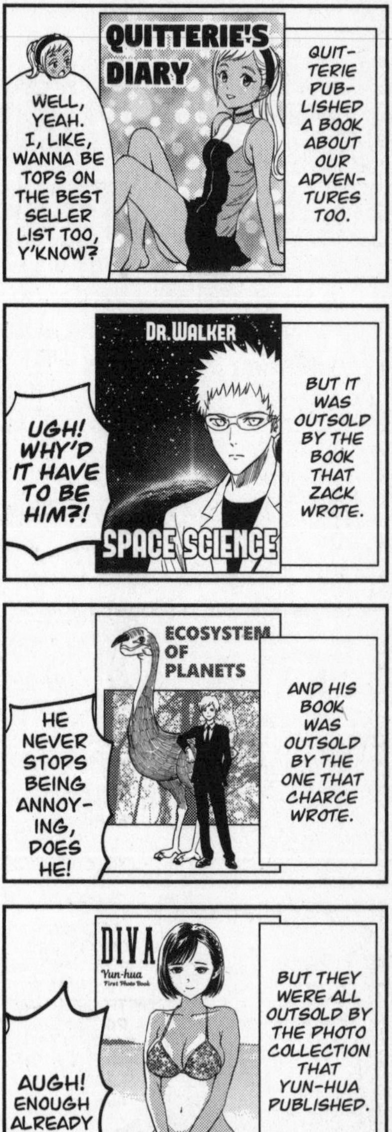
QUITTERIE PUBLISHED A BOOK ABOUT OUR ADVENTURES TOO.
QUITTERIE'S DIARY
WELL, YEAH. I, LIKE, WANNA BE TOPS ON THE BEST SELLER LIST TOO, Y'KNOW?
BUT IT WAS OUTSOLD BY THE BOOK THAT ZACK WROTE.
DR. WALKER
SPACE SCIENCE
UGH! WHY'D IT HAVE TO BE HIM?!
AND HIS BOOK WAS OUTSOLD BY THE ONE THAT CHARCE WROTE.
ECOSYSTEM OF PLANETS
HE NEVER STOPS BEING ANNOYING, DOES HE!
BUT THEY WERE ALL OUTSOLD BY THE PHOTO COLLECTION THAT YUN-HUA PUBLISHED.
DIVA
Yun-hua
First Photo Book
AUGH! ENOUGH ALREADY!!

28 + 112 + 7

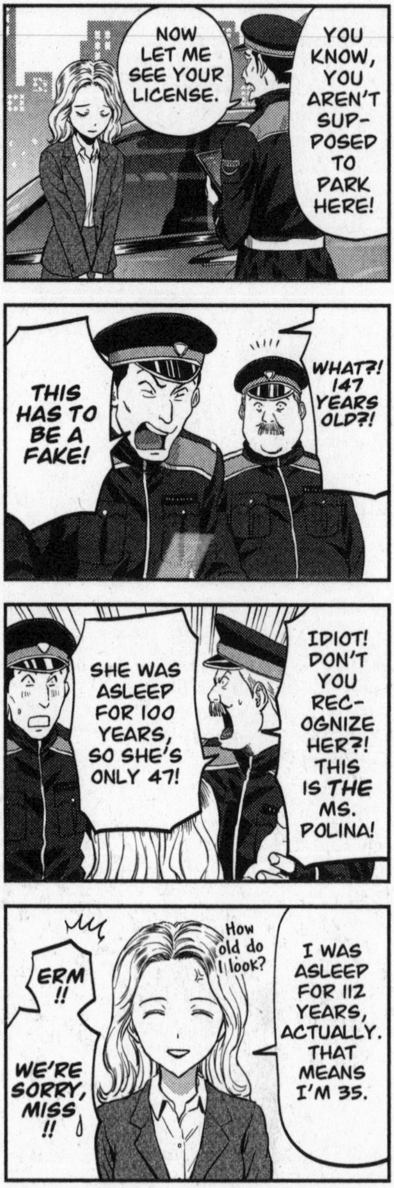
YOU KNOW, YOU AREN'T SUPPOSED TO PARK HERE!
NOW LET ME SEE YOUR LICENSE.
WHAT?! 147 YEARS OLD?!
THIS HAS TO BE A FAKE!
IDIOT! DON'T YOU RECOGNIZE HER?! THIS IS THE MS. POLINA!
SHE WAS ASLEEP FOR 100 YEARS, SO SHE'S ONLY 47!
I WAS ASLEEP FOR 112 YEARS, ACTUALLY. THAT MEANS I'M 35.
How old do I look?
ERM!!
WE'RE SORRY, MISS!!

Hanging Out with Ulgar

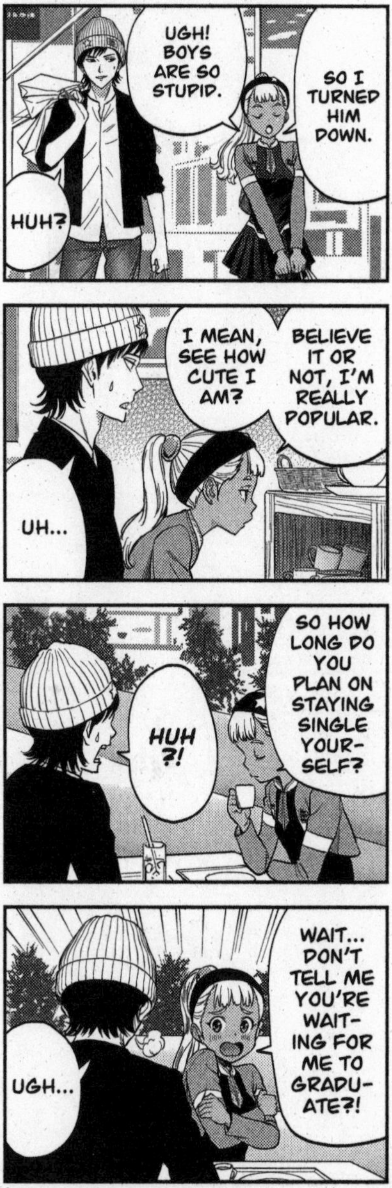
SO I TURNED HIM DOWN.
UGH! BOYS ARE SO STUPID.
HUH?
BELIEVE IT OR NOT, I'M REALLY POPULAR.
I MEAN, SEE HOW CUTE I AM?
UH...
SO HOW LONG DO YOU PLAN ON STAYING SINGLE YOURSELF?
HUH ?!
WAIT... DON'T TELL ME YOU'RE WAITING FOR ME TO GRADUATE?!
UGH...

The Eve of the Ceremony

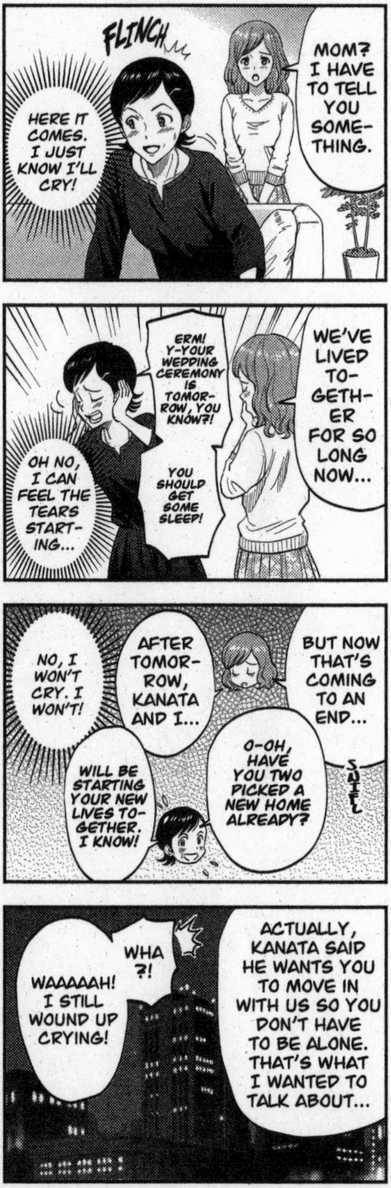
MOM? I HAVE TO TELL YOU SOMETHING.
FLINCH
HERE IT COMES. I JUST KNOW I'LL CRY!
WE'VE LIVED TOGETHER FOR SO LONG NOW...
ERM! Y-YOUR WEDDING CEREMONY IS TOMORROW, YOU KNOW?!
YOU SHOULD GET SOME SLEEP!
OH NO, I CAN FEEL THE TEARS STARTING...
BUT NOW THAT'S COMING TO AN END...
SNIFF
AFTER TOMORROW, KANATA AND I...
NO, I WON'T CRY. I WON'T!
O-OH, HAVE YOU TWO PICKED A NEW HOME ALREADY?
WILL BE STARTING YOUR NEW LIVES TOGETHER. I KNOW!
ACTUALLY, KANATA SAID HE WANTS YOU TO MOVE IN WITH US SO YOU DON'T HAVE TO BE ALONE. THAT'S WHAT I WANTED TO TALK ABOUT...
WHA ?!
WAAAAAH! I STILL WOUND UP CRYING!

KENTA SHINOHARA started his manga career as an assistant to the legendary creator Hideaki Sorachi of **Gin Tama**. In 2006, he wrote and published a one-shot, **Sket Dance**, that began serialization in 2007 in **Weekly Shonen Jump** in Japan. **Sket Dance** went on to win the 55th Shogakukan Manga Award in the shonen manga category and inspired an anime in 2011. Shinohara began writing **Astra Lost in Space** in 2016 for **Jump+**.

ASTRA LOST IN SPACE 5

SHONEN JUMP MANGA EDITION

STORY AND ART BY KENTA SHINOHARA

Translation/Adrienne Beck
Touch-Up Art & Lettering/Annaliese Christman
Design/Julian [JR] Robinson
Editor/Marlene First

NEXT PLANET

Printed in the U.S.A.

Published by VIZ Media, LLC
P.O. Box 77010
San Francisco, CA 94107

10 9 8 7 6 5 4 3 2 1
First printing, December 2018

VIZ MEDIA
viz.com

SHONEN JUMP
shonenjump.com

RATED T TEEN ratings.viz.com

PARENTAL ADVISORY
ASTRA LOST IN SPACE is rated T for Teen and is recommended for ages 13 and up. Contains mild language and fantasy violence.

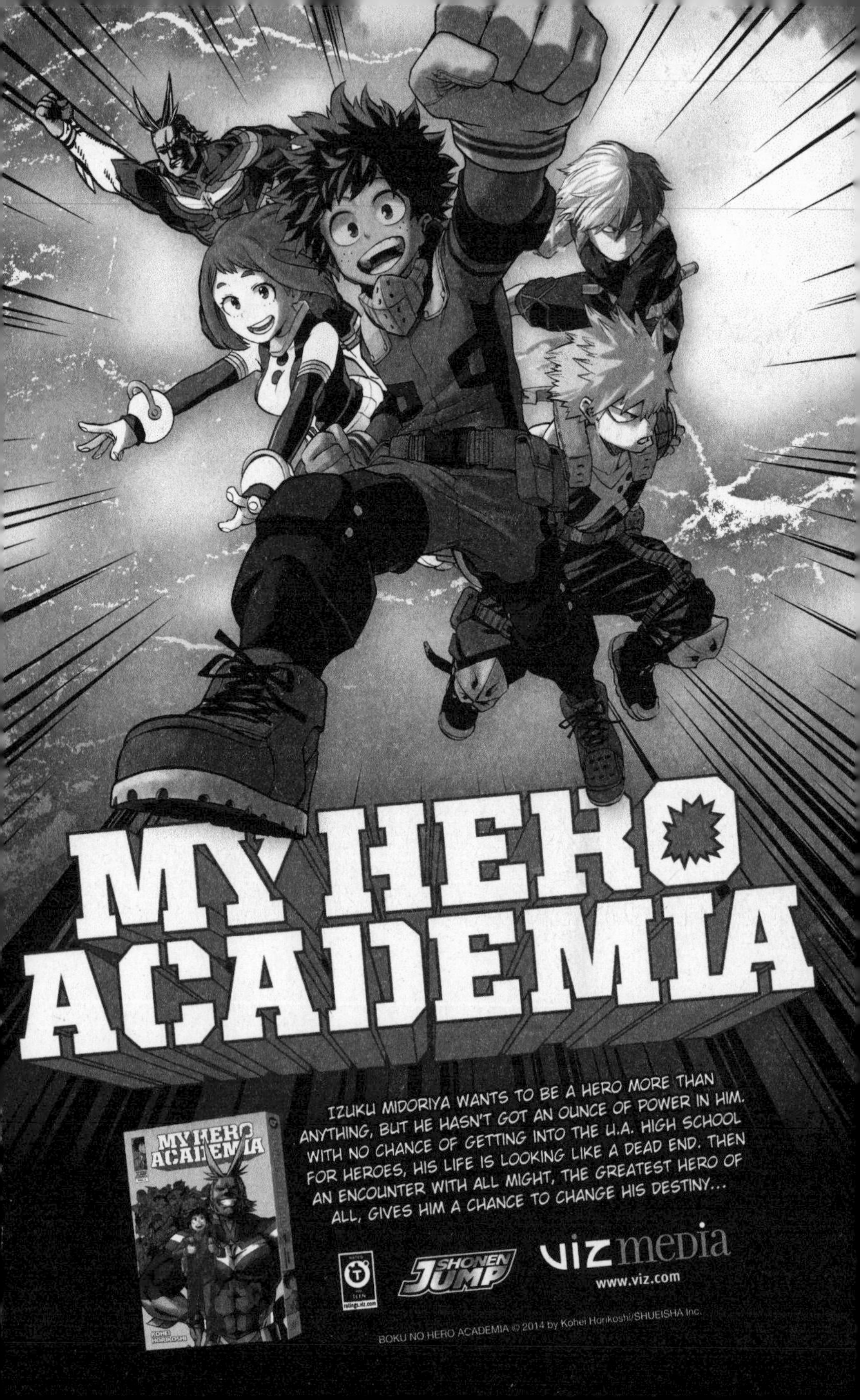
MY HERO ACADEMIA
IZUKU MIDORIYA WANTS TO BE A HERO MORE THAN ANYTHING, BUT HE HASN'T GOT AN OUNCE OF POWER IN HIM. WITH NO CHANCE OF GETTING INTO THE U.A. HIGH SCHOOL FOR HEROES, HIS LIFE IS LOOKING LIKE A DEAD END. THEN AN ENCOUNTER WITH ALL MIGHT, THE GREATEST HERO OF ALL, GIVES HIM A CHANCE TO CHANGE HIS DESTINY...
MY HERO ACADEMIA
KOHEI HORIKOSHI
TEEN
ratings.viz.com
SHONEN JUMP
viz media
www.viz.com
BOKU NO HERO ACADEMIA © 2014 by Kohei Horikoshi/SHUEISHA Inc.

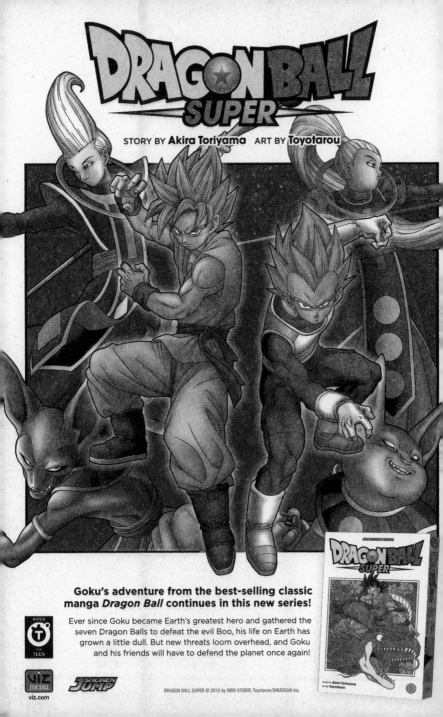

Black ✤ Clover

STORY & ART BY YŪKI TABATA

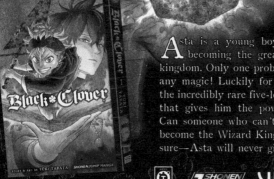

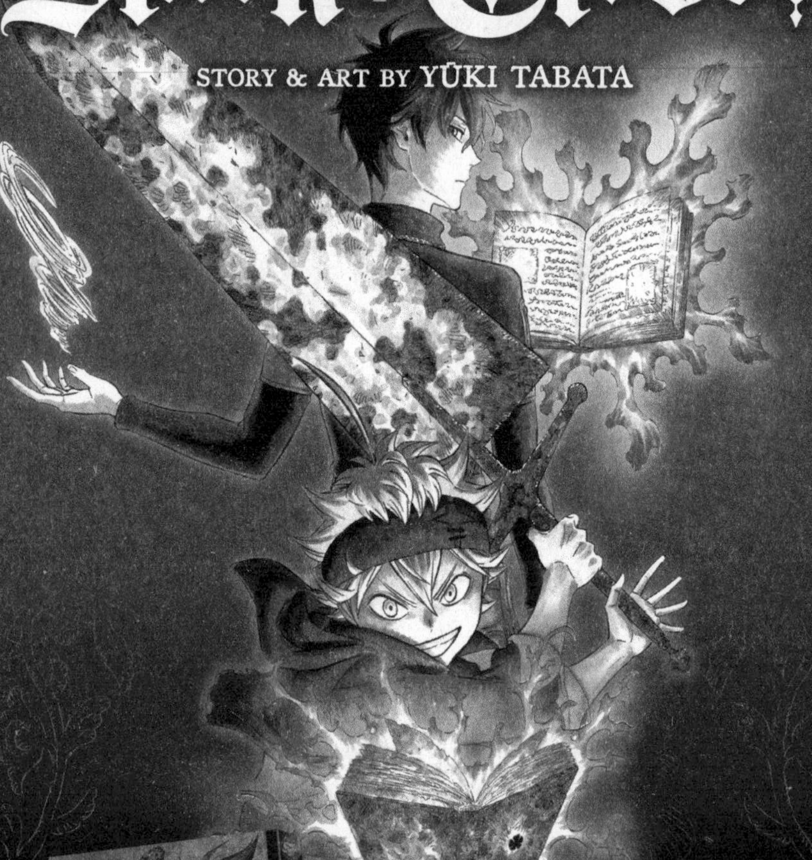

Asta is a young boy who dreams of becoming the greatest mage in the kingdom. Only one problem—he can't use any magic! Luckily for Asta, he receives the incredibly rare five-leaf clover grimoire that gives him the power of anti-magic. Can someone who can't use magic really become the Wizard King? One thing's for sure—Asta will never give up!

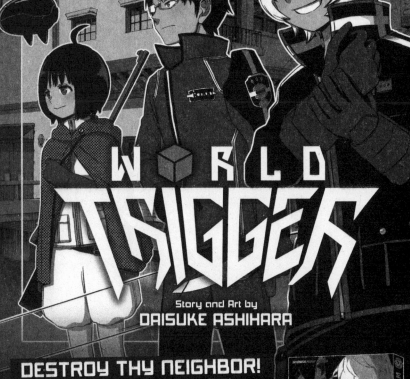

WORLD TRIGGER

Story and Art by
DAISUKE ASHIHARA

DESTROY THY NEIGHBOR!

A gate to another dimension has burst open, and invincible monsters called Neighbors invade Earth. Osamu Mikumo may not be the best among the elite warriors who co-opt other-dimensional technology to fight back, but along with his Neighbor friend Yuma, he'll do whatever it takes to defend life on Earth as we know it.

YOU'RE READING THE WRONG WAY!

Astra Lost in Space reads from right to left, starting in the upper-right corner. Japanese is read from right to left, meaning that action, sound effects and word-balloon order are completely reversed from English order.

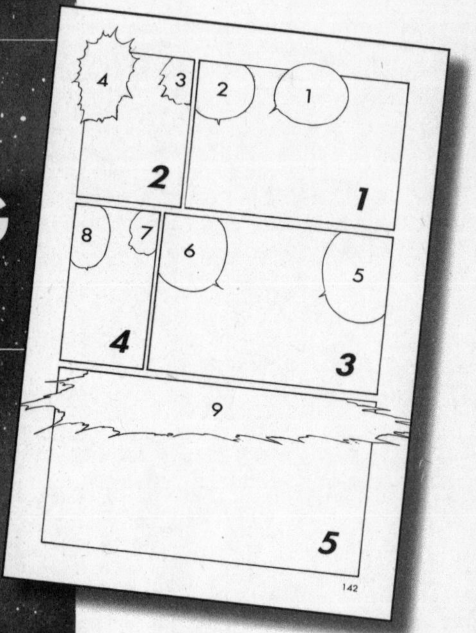
1
2
3
4
5
142

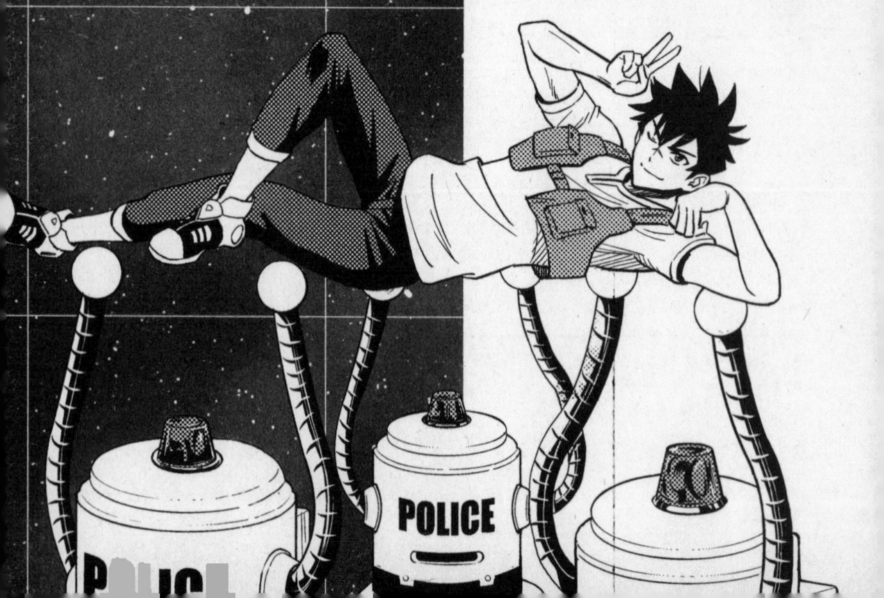
POLICE